Economic Growth and Income Distribution in the Development of China's Dual Economy

Since the start of the process of economic reform in 1978, China has maintained the structure of a dual economy, with concurrent development of the agricultural and industrial sectors. This book explores the key issues of China's economic growth and income distribution in this context.

Pivoting on analysis of China's real GDP and growth rate, the first part of the book analyzes the evolution of economic growth and characteristics of economic structural changes across a period of forty years, scrutinizing the different determinants that contribute to growth. Then, chapters in the second part of the volume study the relationship between China's economic growth and economic development, elucidating the mechanism of interaction between the former and key factors of the latter, including investment, housing, education, and healthcare. The final chapters center on the development and current landscape of income distribution, providing explanation for sharpening income inequalities and advancing suggestions and feasible solutions to the income gap problem.

This book is targeted at scholars, students, and policymakers interested in China's economy, income distribution, and economic growth.

Wang Dihai is a Professor of Economics and Deputy Director in the School of Economics at Fudan University, China. His main research fields include macroeconomics, income inequality, health economics, economic restructuring, and economic growth.

China Perspectives

The *China Perspectives* series focuses on translating and publishing works by leading Chinese scholars, writing about both global topics and China-related themes. It covers Humanities & Social Sciences, Education, Media and Psychology, as well as many interdisciplinary themes.

This is the first time any of these books have been published in English for international readers. The series aims to put forward a Chinese perspective, give insights into cutting-edge academic thinking in China, and inspire researchers globally.

To submit a book proposal, please contact the Taylor & Francis Publisher for the China Publishing Programme, Lian Sun (Lian.Sun@informa.com)

Titles in economics include:

China's New Normal, Supply-side, and Structural Reform
Cai Fang

The Dual-Entity of Market Competition
Establishment and Development of Mezzoeconomics
Yunxian Chen

A Study of Labor Mobility in China
Sun Wenkai

Economic Growth and Income Distribution in the Development of China's Dual Economy
Wang Dihai

Fintech
Frontier and Beyond
Zhong Xu and Chuanwei Zou

For more information, please visit https://www.routledge.com/China-Perspectives/book-series/CPH

Economic Growth and Income Distribution in the Development of China's Dual Economy

Wang Dihai

Routledge
Taylor & Francis Group
LONDON AND NEW YORK

The Publication of this book is sponsored by the Shanghai Institute of International Economics and Finance.

First published in English 2023
by Routledge
2 Park Square, Milton Park, Abingdon, Oxon OX14 4RN

and by Routledge
605 Third Avenue, New York, NY 10158

Routledge is an imprint of the Taylor & Francis Group, an informa business

Translated by Zhang Yuliang

British Library Cataloguing-in-Publication Data
A catalogue record for this book is available from the British Library

Library of Congress Cataloging-in-Publication Data
Names: Wang, Dihai, 1972– author.
Title: Economic growth and income distribution in the development of China's dual economy / Wang Dihai.
Other titles: Zhongguo er yuan jing ji fa zhan zhong de jing ji zeng zhang he shou ru fen pei. English
Description: Abingdon, Oxon; New York, NY: Routledge, 2022. |
Series: China perspectives |
Includes bibliographical references and index. |
Identifiers: LCCN 2021044966 (print) | LCCN 2021044967 (ebook) |
ISBN 9781032199610 (hardback) | ISBN 9781032199627 (paperback) |
ISBN 9781003261629 (ebook)
Subjects: LCSH: Dual economy—China. | China—Economic conditions—1976–2000. | China—Economic conditions—2000–
Classification: LCC HC427.92 .W34716513 2019 (print) |
LCC HC427.92 (ebook) | DDC 330.951—dc23
LC record available at https://lccn.loc.gov/2021044966
LC ebook record available at https://lccn.loc.gov/2021044967

ISBN: 978-1-032-19961-0 (hbk)
ISBN: 978-1-032-19962-7 (pbk)
ISBN: 978-1-003-26162-9 (ebk)

DOI: 10.4324/9781003261629

Typeset in Times New Roman
by codeMantra

Contents

Figures

Tables

Introduction

Section 1 China's economic development since the reform and opening-up: achievements and changes

1.1 The great achievements of China's economic development since the reform and opening-up

Since 1978, China's economy has been maintaining rapid growth, with total economic output and comprehensive national power improved significantly, and people's living standards raised remarkably. According to the data of the National Bureau of Statistics of China, Mainland China's nominal gross domestic product (hereinafter referred to as "GDP") was 0.37 trillion yuan in 1978 and about 99.09 trillion yuan in 2019,[1] which amounted to approximately 14.45 trillion yuan at 1978 prices with an average annual real GDP growth of 9.36%. China's GDP per capita was about 385 yuan in 1978, and 70,900 yuan in 2019, which amounted to approximately 10,349 yuan at 1978 prices, and the average annual real GDP growth was 8.36%. China's consumption per capita was 183 yuan in 1978 and 21,600 yuan in 2019, which was approximately 3,150 yuan at 1978 prices, with an average annual real GDP growth of 7.19%. The increased labor productivity since the reform and opening-up constitutes the main contributor to China's rapid economic growth. China's GDP per labor force was 916 yuan in 1978 and 115,000 yuan in 2019, amounting to about 16,700 yuan at 1978 prices, with an average annual growth of 7.35%.

Over the past 40 years, the share and ranking of China's economic output in the world have risen rapidly. According to World Bank data, China's GDP accounted for about 1.8% of the world in 1978 by the market exchange rate of the year, ranking about 11th in the world; the share rose to 4.8% in 2005, ranking fifth in the world; in 2006, it exceeded the UK, ranking fourth; and then Germany, ranking third in 2007; in 2010, it exceeded Japan, ranking second in the world. In 2019, China's GDP was approximately USD14.34 trillion, accounting for 16.34% of the global GDP. China has been exerting an increasing influence on the global economy. During the Southeast Asian Financial Crisis in 1998, China, with its strong economic strength and massive foreign exchange reserves, successfully fought against

DOI: 10.4324/9781003261629-1

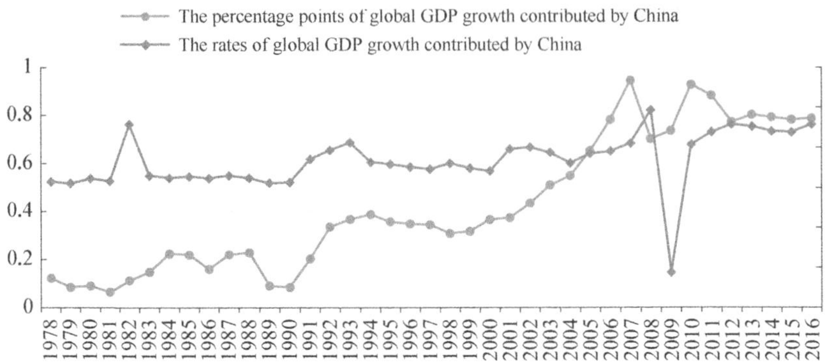

Figure 0.1 Annual growth points and contribution rates of the world economy driven by China: 1978–2016.

the attack of the world's financial barons against Hong Kong dollar and curbed the spread of the crisis. In 2008, China successfully avoided the adverse effects of the global financial crisis started in the United States. Through timely adjustment of various policies, China stopped the decline of economic growth at the end of 2008, successfully got rid of the impact of the global financial crisis in 2009, and became the first to come out of the shadow of the global economic crisis, thus paving the way for global economic recovery (Barry Norton, 2010). Since 1978, the percentage points and rates of global GDP growth contributed by China have been climbing. As shown in Figure 0.1, China stimulated the global GDP to grow by about 0.12 percentage points in 1978, contributing 3.05% to the global economic growth in the year; the contribution was about 0.78 percentage points and 31.52%, respectively, in 2016.

Since the reform and opening-up, the health and education level of Chinese residents has been improved significantly. According to the data of the National Bureau of Statistics, the number of medical beds, medical practitioners, and health technicians per thousand people in China were 2.12, 1.07, and 2.56, respectively, in 1978, which increased to 6.02, 2.59, and 6.83, respectively, in 2018; during this period, the mortality rates of infants, adult males, and adult females dropped from 5.30%, 17.74%, and 14.40% to 0.85%, 9.21%, and 6.71%, respectively. According to the data of the *World Development Indicators*, China's average life expectancy was 65.9 years in 1978, 64.5 years for men and 67.3 years for women. By 2017, China's average life expectancy had increased to 76.4 years, 75.0 years for men and 78.0 years for women. According to the data of the *China Public Health and Birth Control Statistical Yearbooks*, the rates of incidence and mortality of notifiable Class A and B infectious diseases in China were 2.37% and 4.86 per hundred thousand, respectively, in 1978, dropping to 0.21% and 1.31 per hundred thousand, respectively, by 2016. In terms of education, according to the data of *World Development Indicators*, in 1978, the proportions of students in schools at all levels against the population at school age in China were as follows: 8.72% for early childhood education, 110.10% for primary education, 60.03% for middle school education, and 7.72% for college education. In 2015, the proportions were changed to 83.62% for early childhood education, 104.13% for primary education, 94.30% for middle school education, and 43.39% for college education.[2]In 1978, the student-teacher ratios of kindergartens, primary schools, and middle schools in China were 26.8, 28.0, and 20.9, respectively, while the ratios dropped to 19.1, 16.5, and 13.5, respectively, in 2016. China's years of education per capita has been boosted significantly. According to the data of the *China Statistical Yearbooks*, the years of education per capita in China was about 5.27 in 1982, which rose to 9.07 in 2016; among the 15-year-old school-agers, those with a junior college degree or above accounted for 1.62% in 1989, which rose to 12.94% by 2016.

With 40 years' rapid economic development, people's living standards have been generally improved, and now China has shifted its main goal from solving the problem of food and clothing shortage to pursuing a higher quality of life. According to the data of the *China Statistical Yearbooks*, the Engel coefficients of rural and urban residents in China have dropped from 67.7% and 57.5% in 1978 to 32.2% and 29.3%, respectively, in 2016. According to the standard of the Food and Agriculture Organization of the United Nations (FAO) on Engel coefficients, the living standard of Chinese residents was basically categorized at the "impoverished" level at the early stage of the reform and opening-up. And in 2016, it had already reached the "relatively wealthy" level and was about to join the ranks of rich countries. The consumption structures, food, and durable goods of urban and rural residents in China have also been significantly improved. In 1985, the basic living expenses for food, clothing, household equipment, and services accounted for as much as 76% of the total consumption expenditure of urban residents and 73% of rural residents; however, the sum of the three basic living expenses only made up 44% of the total consumption expenditure in 2016. In 1985, China's urban residents mainly consumed grain (135 kg per capita per year) and vegetables (144 kg per capita per year), while the consumption proportion of meat (18.7 kg per capita per year), poultry (3.2 kg per capita per year), and aquatic products (7.1 kg per capita per year) was very small; in 2018, meats became the main consumption food of urban residents, and the consumption of meat (31.2 kg per capita per year), fish and shrimp (14.3 kg per capita per year), poultry (9.8 kg per capita per year), eggs (10.8 kg per capita per year), and dairy products (16.5 kg per capita per year) increased significantly; by comparison, the consumption of grain and vegetables decreased remarkably, and they were no longer the main foods. In 1978, grain (248 kg per capita per year) and vegetables (142 kg per capita per year) were the main foods of rural residents in China, while little meat (5.8 kg per capita per year) was consumed. In 2018, the consumption of grain (148.5 kg per capita per year) and vegetables (87.5 kg per capita per year) had fallen considerably, though they were still very important food for rural residents; meats (27.5 kg per capita per year), fish, and shrimp (7.8 kg per capita per year), poultry (8.0 kg per capita per year), milk (6.9 kg per capita per year), eggs (8.4 kg per capita per year), and the relevant products have been commonly seen on the dinner table of rural households. At the early stage of reform and opening-up, the main consumer durables of urban residents in China were basic necessities like sewing machines, bicycles, electric fans, large wardrobes, and sofas. The main consumer durables of rural residents were bicycles, sewing machines, clocks, radios, and other simple mechanical goods, which were owned by less than 30% families. At present, the main durable consumer goods of urban residents in China have been upgraded to high-end household goods such as air conditioners, color TVs, refrigerators, washing machines, mobile phones, home computers, water heaters, and cars; mobile phones and color TVs have been popularized in rural households. Washing machines and refrigerators are owned by most families, and air conditioners and home computers are also more common than before. Moreover, China's housing area per capita increased from 10 square meters in 1985 to 36.6 square meters in 2016. At present, most Chinese urban and rural households have been moving towards the living condition that has been equipped with automated travel, electrical appliances, wireless communication, and online entertainment.

1.2 The structural changes in China's economic development since the reform and opening-up

Over the past 40 years, China's economic structure has also undergone great changes, manifested mainly in demand structure, industrial structure, population structure, graduation structure, and residents' income structure. In the demand structure, the investment-GDP ratio is increasing, while the consumption-GDP ratio is decreasing. According to the data of the National Bureau of Statistics, the shares of household consumption, total investment, government consumption, and net export in GDP in 1978 were 48.4%, 38.9%, 13.0%, and −0.3%, respectively. By comparison, the shares were 38.8%, 43.1%, 16.6%, and 1.5%, respectively, in 2019. In terms of industrial structure, according to the data of the CEIC database, there was not much gap among the ratio of China's three industries in the economy in 1978. In fact, 47.7% of the total GDP was taken by the secondary industry, of which industrial output value accounted for 92.4%, the primary industry output value accounted for 27.7%, and the tertiary industry accounted for 24.6%. Of the tertiary industry, transportation, warehousing, and postal-industry accounted for 21.1% and the wholesale and retail industry accounted for 26.8% of the output value. Other industries such as real estate and finance accounted for 8.5% and 8.8%, respectively. In 2019, the share of China's primary and secondary industries in GDP dropped to 7.1% and 39.0%, respectively, and the proportion of industry in the output value of the secondary industries declined to 82.1%; the proportion of the tertiary industry in GDP increased to 53.9%, of which the proportion of transportation, warehousing, and postal industry and wholesale and retail industry decreased to 8.1% and 17.9%, respectively, and the proportion of real estate and finance increased to 13.0% and 14.4%, respectively. In the past 40 years, the tertiary and the secondary industries have become dominant in China's industrial structure. In particular, the tertiary industry has become the largest one. Comparatively, the primary industry's percentage over GDP is even smaller than the percentage of some major segments of the tertiary industry over GDP.

The employment structure of China's labor force has also undergone significant changes in the process of economic growth. Employment in the primary industry (agriculture) and its share in total employed population of the three industries (hereinafter referred to as the employment ratio) decreased significantly, while employment in the secondary industry (industry in a narrow sense) and the tertiary industry (service industry) increased significantly. At the beginning of the reform and opening-up, the vast majority of China's labor force was engaged in the primary industry, mainly in agriculture, while a smaller proportion was employed in the secondary and tertiary industries. In 1978, 70.5% of the employed population was engaged in the primary industry, 17.3% in the secondary industry, and 12.2% in the tertiary industry. In 2018, the proportion of employed population in the primary industry decreased to 26.1%, while that in secondary industry and tertiary industry increased to 27.6% and 46.3%, respectively. At present, China's employed population structure is basically divided equally by the three major industries, but the employment ratio in the tertiary industry is slightly larger. An interesting phenomenon worth noting is that the sum of the output value of China's secondary and tertiary industries accounts for more than 90% of the total output value of the three industries, but the proportion of the primary industry is less than 10%. Seemingly China has already become an industrialized country. However, from the perspective of employed population structure and urban-rural population structure, China is still an agricultural country, as the employed population in agriculture and the rural population still account for a vast majority of the total Chinese population, showing obvious characteristics of a dual economic structure. This phenomenon reflects the incompleteness and lagging characteristics of labor market reform in the process of China's gradual reform.

Over the past 40 years, China's population structure has also undergone significant changes, mainly reflected in two aspects: First, the urban-rural population structure has greatly changed. The proportion of urban population has been growing. According to the data of National Bureau of Statistics, the urban population made up 27.9% of China's population in 1978, while the proportion climbed to 60.6% in 2019, exceeding the rural population, and the urban registered population accounted for 44.38%. Second, is change in age structure. The ratio of children aged 0–14 in the total population (referred to as the population ratio) continues to decline. The population ratio of the elderly over 65 continues to climb, and the ratio of the working-age population aged 15–64 has gone through a process of first rising and then falling. According to the data of *World Development Indicators*, China's population aged 0–14, 15–64, and over 65 accounted for 37.6%, 57.9%, and 4.46%, respectively, in 1978; in 2018, the ratio of population aged 0–14 decreased to 16.83%, while the ratio of population aged over 65 increased to 11.94%; the population percentage of people who aged 15–64 rose before 2010, and then declined to 71.2% in 2018.

Since the reform and opening-up, with the transformation of China's income distribution mode from "distribution according to performance" to "the integration of distribution based on both performance and factors of production," and then to "distribution according to the contribution of production factors," factor market began to determine rewards arising from production factors, and the income structure of Chinese residents has undergone significant changes. In the early stage of the reform and opening-up, farmers in China mainly yielded income from crops, while urban residents mainly from wages. By comparison, the income structure of China's urban and rural residents is obviously diversified at present. According to the data of the *China Statistical Yearbooks*, in 1985, the wage of Chinese urban workers accounted for 83.1% of disposable income, which decreased to 71% in 2000 and 61% in 2016. In 1985, the sum of operational income and property income of urban residents in China accounted for 1.9% of disposable income. However, the sum of the two parts increased to 5.9% in 2000, and the operational income made up 11.2% and property income made up 9.7% in 2016. In 1978, the labor income of Chinese farmers from collective-owned units made up 66.1% of their net income, and the family business income accounted for 26.8% of their net income, of which the income from agriculture, forestry, animal husbandry, and fishery accounted for 21.4%; when the reform of the household contract responsibility system was completed in 1985, the labor income of Chinese farmers accounted for 18.0% of their net income, and the family business income accounted for 74.4%, of which the income from agriculture, forestry, animal husbandry, and sidelines accounted for 61.8%; in 2000, the wage income of Chinese farmers accounted for 31.2% of the net income, and the family business income accounted for 63.3%, of which the income from agriculture, forestry, animal husbandry, and fishery accounted for 48.4%; by 2012, the wage income accounted for 43.5% of the net income, and the family business income accounted for 44.6%, of which the income from agriculture, forestry, animal husbandry, and fishery accounted for 34.4%. In 2016, wage income, operating income, property income, and transfer income made up 40.6%, 38.3%, 2.2%, and 18.8%, respectively, of the disposable income of Chinese rural residents.

Section 2 China‘s economic growth: main features, stylized facts, and challenges

In the course of its economic development over the past 40 years, China has exhibited many unique features and stylized facts with Chinese characteristics. Some of the features and facts are drawn from China's successful economic development, and some are the results of policy compromise and the compromise of stakeholders when developing economy under China's unique system. These kind of compromises, that were harmless to economy and may possibly promote economic growth during the early period of economic development, may become the obstacle hampering China's further growth and development along with the further economic development.

2.1 Continuous improvement of the incomplete Chinese market economy system under the gradual reform

China's reform and opening-up shows a process of gradual reform from the planned economy system to the socialist market economy system, and also a process of transformation from planned economy to market economy. Under the original planned economy system, neither commodities nor markets were available, and there was a lack of market entities and mechanisms. All economic activities were carried out in accordance with the command plans of the government. Due to the problems of unclear property rights and information asymmetry, this planned economy system provided no effective incentives for economic entities and was insufficient in economic efficiency. China started to shift towards a market economy after the reform. All conditions necessary for the operation of a market economy, including market transaction entities (or product property right holders), product pricing mechanism, market price system, laws and regulations governing market transactions, etc., must start from scratch. Unlike Eastern European and CIS countries, which adopted the "shock therapy" type radical market economy reforms, China experienced a gradual economic reform that featured "wading across the stream by feeling the way." The establishment of all market factors, entities, mechanisms, laws, and regulations required by a market economy is a process of gradual formation and improvement. The implementation of specific reform measures is a phased process that starts from local trials and then proceeds to nationwide promotion. It is certain that there must be many aspects yet to be improved during this process. Moreover, in every step of advancement towards a market economy, each improvement of the market system contributes to the rapid growth of the economy. Meanwhile, the gradual advancement has not caused as much great social impacts and shocks as the "shock therapy" in East European countries and other countries has done which brought hindrance to economic growth.

China's economic system reform started with the rural household contract responsibility system adopted in the late 1970s and early 1980s. This system clarifies the boundaries between residual control and claim rights of production for production parties, and directly links the output of workers with their remunerations. By doing so, the system has greatly increased the enthusiasm of farmers towards production and lowered the supervision cost brought by private information (Zhang, 1998, p.13). According to the data of the *China Statistical Yearbook* (1995), thanks to the widespread promotion of the household contract responsibility system in China, the country's total grain output had an average annual growth of 4.95%, with cotton output 19.3%, edible oil output 14.7%, and sugar output 12.3% during the years 1978–1984. According to Prof. Lin (1994, p. 95), during this period, China's rural reforms contributed 48.6% to the output growth in rural areas, with the contribution rate of the household contract responsibility system being 46.89%. The increase in rural productivity brought about by the system unleashed a large amount of surplus labor productivity. Additionally, China's reform in this period relaxed the state's monopoly on the sales and purchase of agricultural products. In this context, the agricultural products that were originally produced and sold by commune- and brigade-run enterprises only were allowed to enter the broader rural market nationwide, releasing a large number of product markets for rural enterprises in the country.[3] Both factors enabled the rapid growth of rural enterprises in China. According to relevant data, during the years from 1980 to 1990, the added value of China's rural enterprises increased from 28.53 billion to 250.43 billion yuan, with an average annual growth of 24.3%; the number of employees from 30 million to 92.6 million, with an average annual growth of 11.9%; and the share of added value of rural enterprises to GDP increased from less than 6% in 1978 to 26% in 1996 (Wu, 2016, p. 120). As one of the major drivers for China's growth, the reforms launched during this period opened up the domestic product market to rural enterprises. However, China adopted the dual-track economy that contained both planned economy and market economy, including the dual-track system adopted in state-owned and private sectors, in the systems concerning distribution and prices of production material, and in national bank loan interest rates and market interest rates. The labor market where labor forces in China's urban and rural areas could not be established; the market-related pricing system and mechanism were not fully formed; and the confirmation of market transaction entities and definition of corporate property rights remained unclear either.

After Deng Xiaoping made south tour speeches in 1992, China's reforms accelerated, contributing to the further development of China's economy. At the 14th National Congress of the Communist Party of China (CPC) held in 1992, the reform goal of establishing a socialist economy system was put in place. And at the Third Plenary Session of the Fourteenth Central Committee of the CPC in 1993, it was proposed that a socialist market economy system be initially established in the late 20th century. In 1994, the State

Council embarked on the reform of state-owned enterprises, and established the guiding principle of "restructuring major enterprises and relaxing control over small ones." Afterwards, large- and medium-sized state-owned enterprises restructured themselves by following the three steps: separating the functions of the government from those of enterprises, breaking monopoly and promoting competition, and enabling corporate reorganization and listing (Wu, 2016, p. 159). At the 15th National Congress of the CPC held in 1997, the principle of public ownership playing a dominant role and different economic sectors developing side by side was identified as the basic economic system and the non-public sector as a key component of the socialist market economy. The reform of China's state-owned economic system and political recognition of the non-public sector ensured the identification of production and transaction entities in China's market economy, and promoted the rapid growth of Chinese private enterprises in the late 1990s, playing a vital role in China's economic growth and employment. According to the data of the *China Statistical Yearbooks*, during the years from 1997 to 2002, the proportion of annual fixed asset investment in China's private enterprises rose from 32% to 43%, and that of urban employment in private enterprises from 33% to 67%. Undoubtedly, the reform of state-owned enterprises and the layoffs of state-owned enterprise workers during this period also caused a significant decline in economic growth. Nevertheless, the improvement of the market mechanism laid a solid foundation for the next stage of economic growth.

After 2001, with the ending of the reform of state-owned enterprises and the improvement of the modern enterprise system, the modern Chinese enterprises with clear property rights, as market entities, greatly increased their enthusiasm and motivation to discover the market and effectively produce the products that met market demand. Along with the huge world market brought by China's accession to the WTO, the increased production capacity and efficiency of Chinese enterprises brought by the improved market economy system became a strong driver for the country's further economic growth, and allowed China to usher in a new round of rapid economic growth. The annual real GDP growth rates of China from 2002 to 2011 were maintained above 9%. According to World Bank data, the share of China's net exports in China's GDP jumped from −0.54% to 2.62% from 1978 to 2001 and the proportion of dependence on foreign trade (percentage of imports plus exports over GDP) increased from 9.65% to 39.0% in the same period. Following China's accession to the WTO in 2001, the country's share of net exports in its GDP rose rapidly from 2.62% in 2001 to 9.23% in 2007, began to decline after the global financial crisis in 2008, and dropped to 2.23% in 2016. China's dependence on foreign trade rose to 43.1% in 2002, reached a peak of 65.6% in 2006, and then started to drop, to 37.1% in 2016. According to the calculations based on World Bank data, during the years 2002 to 2007, exports contributed to an average annual growth of China's GDP by 6.2%, with an average annual contribution of 56.2% to China's economic growth; and net exports enabled an average annual growth of China's GDP by −17.7%, with an average annual contribution of −14.8% to the same. The strong demand for housing due to the rise in the income level of Chinese residents and the housing system reform represented one of the main drivers for China's economic growth after 2001 as well. In particular, the development of the real estate sector brought about by the housing system reform became a main driver for the country's growth after the 2008 global financial crisis and the decline in China's exports.

Since the reform and opening-up, despite China continuing to reform and improve the market economic system, China's market conditions are not completely satisfied in general. These incomplete market economic conditions are the most important obstacle to the further growth of China's economy. For example, the barriers to rural-urban labor mobility and regional labor mobility caused by the household registration system have seriously hindered the free flow of labor forces and resulted in an incomplete labor market in China. Due to the imperfect financial system and government monopoly in China, huge differences exist between China's state-owned enterprises and private ones in terms of financing cost. Discrimination by state-owned enterprises against different ownership systems makes private enterprises assume high borrowing cost, and even fail in applying for loans sometimes. State-owned monopolies and administrative monopolies in many markets have severely hindered technological progress and increase in production efficiency of these industries. For example, due to state-owned monopolies, telecommunications, banking, petrochemical, railway, hydropower, and other industries or sectors often obtain monopoly profits by increasing prices or reducing quality, and have long-standing problems including shortage of product supply, technological stagnation, and enterprises' lack of innovation resources. Additionally, state-owned monopolies and administrative monopolies have widened the gaps in industry incomes, and led to worsened income inequality. The incomplete market economy system has constituted a serious obstacle to the further growth of China's economy. So, determining how to further deepen reforms and continuously improve the socialist market economy is one of the biggest challenges facing China's economic growth today.

2.2 Promoting institutional reform and economic development through sustained opening-up

The 40 years of reform and opening-up is a process during which China has gradually shifted from a closed economy to a competitive, open economy and from a domestically oriented economy to an internationally oriented economy. Just like in the early stages of the reform, China regarded opening-up as an important part and immediate goal of its reform. The opening-up to the outside world for 40 years has become an important driver for China's institutional reform and economic growth all the time. In the 1980s, China first carried out its regional pilot reform and opening-up establishing special economic zones, attracting a large number of foreign investments and developing foreign trade. By doing so, China promoted the development of domestic-funded enterprises and regional economic growth, drew market economy-related experience from developed countries, and explored a new system of economic reform and opening-up. In the 1990s, China gradually promoted, in different regions, the successful experience and measures drawn from its successful practice of the reform and opening-up in special economic zones to accelerate the opening pace of the inland economy in accordance with the "four-along" strategies, namely along the basin of Yangtze River, the riverside areas, the lakeside areas, and the coastal areas. A new model of focused, all-round, wide-ranging, and multi-layered opening-up was formed then. Since the early 21st century, by taking the opportunity of accession to the World Trade Organization (WTO), China has comprehensively lifted the level of opening-up nationwide, become deeply integrated into the macro environment of economic globalization, competition, and development, and participated in the international cooperation, competition, and development in a larger scope, in wider fields, and at higher levels. Under the guidance of this policy and the favorable situation of China's accession to the WTO, China ushered in another period of rapid growth that lasted more than ten years. China also started to attract foreign investments by issuing more favorable policies for western China according to the strategy of "Great Western Development," and encouraged foreign businessmen and enterprises in eastern China to move to the central and western parts of the country, and guided the enterprises in central and western China to become engaged in foreign trade and export of labor services. After 2013, China proposed the new opening-up strategy, titled "Belt and Road Initiative" (BRI).

Through the export-oriented economic development strategy and the strategy of opening to the outside world in stages and at different levels with coastal areas as strategic focus, opening-up has promoted China's economic growth at least in terms of supply and demand. Firstly, on the supply side, due to the backward outmoded technology, equipment, and management of China before the reform, the capital necessary for developing economy was rather insufficient as well. Thus, among the four major factors required in the production process, namely labor, capital, technology, and organizational management, the other three except labor were seriously inadequate and relatively backward in terms of production. During the process of opening to the outside world, a lot of foreign capital and foreign-funded enterprises were introduced based on such favorable policies as special zone economy and Pudong development. The advanced productive and technological capacity was improved through the import of advanced foreign technologies and equipment. And the capital accumulation needed in production was rapidly obtained through the introduction of foreign capital. Moreover, advanced technologies and management experience were learnt by China from abroad through the foreign-funded enterprises the country introduced. Just as Comrade Deng Xiaoping pointed out in 1984, the special economic zones are a window of opening to the outside world. They are a window through which sophisticated technologies, advanced managerial expertise, and up-to-date know-how can be brought in from abroad. They are also a window through which China's foreign policies are disseminated. During the opening-up from 1978 to 2016, China's foreign investment continued to grow. According to the data of the Ministry of Commerce, the foreign investment used by China in total was US$ 916 million in 1983, with the share in GDP of the year (hereinafter referred to as the "share in GDP") being 0.3%; US$ 33.667 billion in 1994, with the share in GDP being 6.0%; and US$ 40.715 billion in 2001, before China's accession to the WTO, with the share in GDP being 3.4% (Wu, 2016, p. 331). According to the data released by the National Bureau of Statistics of China in August 2018, China used a total of foreign direct investment valued at US$ 2 trillion in aggregate, with nearly 540,000 registered foreign-funded enterprises. In 2017, China actually used foreign capital of US$ 136.3 billion, accounting for 10.7% of the total GDP. Since then, China has become the world's second largest country of foreign capital inflow. In 2017, the amount of foreign capital used in China was 60 times more than that of 1983, with an average annual growth of 12.8%. In terms of technology and equipment introduction, the Chinese government invested US$ 16.6 billion to introduce technologies for factories, and US$ 30.2 billion to introduce new capital construction projects in the 1980s. In the early 1980s, China introduced more than 100 color TV production lines (Barry Norton, 2010, p. 320). After 2000, with respect to China's technology import, the direct import of hardware was shifted to the import of the right to license soft technologies. In 2003 alone, China signed a technology import contract valued at US$ 13.45 billion, of which US$ 9.5 billion was used for importing the intellectual property purchased (Barry Norton, 2010, p. 320). Opening to the outside world also plays a huge role in driving the development of Chinese enterprises. On the one hand, the policy has promoted the continuous improvement of China's market economy conditions, and created a better business environment for domestic enterprises. In order to attract foreign investments, governments at all levels of China have continuously improved their administration and management; maintained and improved a fair, open, and regulated market; strengthened infrastructure construction and supporting policy reform; delegated the administrative monopoly power to lower-level governments; and expanded the domestic and foreign markets of enterprises. On the other hand, the policy has also increased the awareness of domestic enterprises towards competition, and urging and encouraging these enterprises to improve their technologies, product quality, and competitiveness. Also, domestic labor forces have acquired technology and management knowledge through "learning in practice," increased the flow of human capital between foreign-funded and domestic enterprises, and improved the technologies and management of domestic enterprises and their production capacity and competitiveness.

Secondly, on the demand side, opening-up has brought a huge goods market space for China. Under the planned economy system before the reform and opening-up, all the ownership, management, and operation rights in relation to China's foreign trade were monopolized by the state, and foreign trade could only be monopolized solely by the Foreign Trade Corporation under the Ministry of Foreign Trade and Economic Cooperation of China. After the reform and opening-up, the first movc was to break the state-owned monopoly system for foreign trade, and grant enterprises of varying ownership systems the right to import and export independently, which directly widened the market scope of many domestic enterprises. Additionally, China has gradually lowered import and export tariffs, abolished import quotas and licensing system, and reformed the foreign exchange management system, enabling the free convertibility of RMB under the current account. This reform has greatly reduced the transaction costs of domestic products in the international market, and increased their international competitiveness. With the in-depth reform of China's opening-up, its total imports and exports have continuously increased, the dependence of economic development on foreign trade is being lifted day by day, and China is becoming more and more closely integrated with the world's economic development and participation in global competition. According to the data of the *China Statistical Yearbooks*, China's total imports and exports reached 35.5 billion yuan in 1978, of which exports were 16.76 billion yuan and imports 18.74 billion yuan. In 2001, before China's accession to the WTO, the total imports and exports amounted to 4,218.36 billion yuan, of which exports were 2,202.44 billion yuan and imports 2,015.92 billion yuan. In the case of exclusion of the influence of inflation by the GDP fluctuation index, at the constant prices of 1978, the figures were 1,133.19 billion yuan, 2,202.44 billion yuan, and 2,015.92 billion yuan, respectively. During the years 1978–2001, the total imports and exports, single imports and single exports had an average annual growth of 5.1%, 16.8%, and 15.7% respectively. In 2016, the total imports and exports arrived at 24,338.65 billion yuan, of which exports were 13,841.93 billion yuan and imports 10,496.72 billion yuan. At the constant prices of 1978, these figures were 3,820.33 billion yuan, 2,172.65 billion yuan, and 1,647.58 billion yuan, respectively. During the years 2001–2016, the total imports and exports, single imports and single exports had an average annual growth of 8.4%, 9.1%, and 7.7%, respectively. According to World Bank data shown in Figure 0.2, China's imports and exports accounted for less than 5% of its GDP, the dependence on foreign trade was basically lower than 10%, and the proportion of net exports over GDP was basically maintained at 1% or so. After the reform and opening-up in 1978, the share of imports and exports in GDP rose from 5.1% and 4.5% in 1978 to 20.1% and 23.0% in 2001. After China's accession to the WTO, the figures continued to rise until the peaks of 28.4% and 37.2% in 2006, and declined after the occurrence of the global financial crisis in 2008. Moreover, both proportions were still as high as 17.4% and 19.6%, respectively, in 2016.

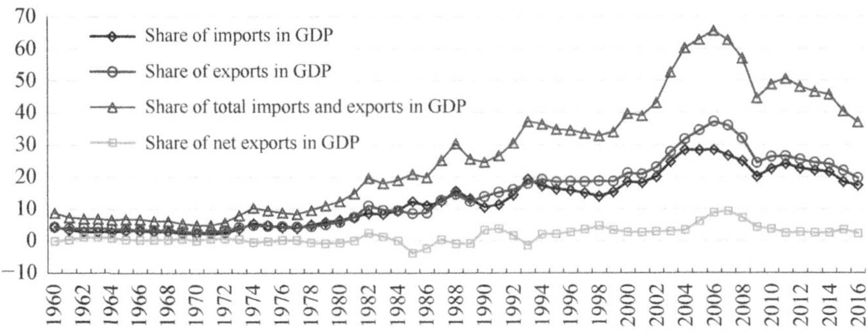

Figure 0.2 Changes in the proportions of China's imports, exports, total imports and exports, and share of net exports in GDP: 1960–2016.

China's dependence on foreign trade increased from 9.7% in 1978 to 39.1% in 2001, to 65.7% in 2006 and then 37.1% in 2016. According to the statistical data released by the China customs authorities in August 2018, China had a total imports and exports of goods trade of 27.79 trillion yuan in 2017, and has ranked first in the world for years. According to WTO data, in 2017, the total global imports and exports amounted to US$ 347.7 billion, of which exports were US$ 1.7198 billion and imports were US$ 1.7572 billion. And in the same year, China's total imports and exports reached US$ 4.1 trillion, with a share of 11.8% in the total global imports and exports, among which exports and imports was US$ 226 million and USD 184 million, with a share of 13.14% and 10.47%, respectively, in the global exports and imports. China's dependence on foreign trade was 33.50%. China's economic development can no longer be separated from the world market, and its economic growth has been integrated with global growth.

What should be pointed out is that opening to the outside world has brought about great vitality and opportunities to China's economic development in the past, promoted the rapid growth of China's economy, deepened the integration of China's economy into the world economy, and meanwhile deepened the dependence of the country's economic growth, especially the dependence of its market demand on the world. However, in recent years, there has been a trend of toward anti-globalization in the world, which could greatly affect the demand for China's exports. So, the questions are as follows: How do we increase the domestic demand and lower the impact of foreign market on the effective demand of China? How do we pursue independent technological innovation and reduce China's dependence on foreign technologies? And how do we reduce China's dependence on foreign countries and reduce the impact of uncertain factors that exist in world economy, such as global economic fluctuations? All these are difficulties and challenges facing China's current economic development.

2.3 Typical urban-rural dual economic development model

Since the adoption of reform and opening-up in 1978, China has shown obvious dual economy characteristics. In people's impressions, China was apparently a major agricultural country then. Related data reveal that, in 1978, the rural population accounted for 82% of the total population, and the employed workers in the primary industry more than 70% of the total employees. However, in terms of the industrial structure of the GDP, the total output value of China's secondary industry contributed 48% to the GDP in 1978, among which the industrial segment accounted for 44% of the GDP, and while that of primary industry only contributed 27.8% to the GDP then. This shows that industry played an important role in China's economy; and the status of agriculture in the entire economy was high as expected. Through 40 years of economic development after the reform and opening-up, despite great changes in China's economic structure and significant increase in the rates of industrialization and urbanization, farmers, rural areas, and agriculture remain important parts of China's society and economy. In fact, in 2016, although the share of the output value of the primary industry in the total GDP dropped to around 9%, rural areas were still an important area in terms of the employment and living conditions of Chinese residents. China's rural population still accounted for up to 42.7% of the total population and the proportion of the primary industry workers over the total employees reached 27.8%. Therefore, since 1978, China's economy has undergone a dual economic development process in which agriculture and industry develop together, and urban economy and rural economy have grown simultaneously.

This dual economic development in China over the past 40 years is a modernization process in which China's economy has continuously pursued industrialization, an employment transition process in which employees have gradually moved from the primary industry to the secondary and tertiary industries, and also an urbanization process where the rural population has moved to urban areas. From 1978 to 2016, the proportion of China's industrial output value did not witness an increase but a drop of 4 percentage points; and the proportion of workers in the secondary industry only increased from the previous 14.8% to 28.8%. In 2016, the share of secondary industry workers in the total employees of China was not less than 1/3 of the total employed population. Moreover, the productivity per labor force for China's secondary industry has greatly improved. If by the constant prices of secondary industry products, the real output value of secondary industry per labor force was up 14.3 times and grew at an average annual growth of 7.2%, basically at the same level with the real GDP growth rate per labor force (7.66%) in the same period. The abundance of material products of a country represents the material basis for the improvement of its residents' income level and living standards. Due to the improvement of the industrial productivity per labor force that China's industrial development has brought about a large number of labor forces for the development of its service industry, also provided a great support for the supply of industrial material products and an increase in people's income. Over 40 years of economic development since the reform, the tertiary industry, which is also called the service industry, has developed the fastest in China. During the period 1978–2016, the real output value of China's tertiary industry was up 75.5 times, with an average annual growth of 11.8%, 2.2 percentage points higher than the average annual growth rate (9.6%) of the real GDP in the same period. The proportion of the output value of the tertiary industry over the total GDP increased from 25% to 52%, and the share of tertiary industry employees over total employees increased from 12.2% to 43.5%. The rapid development of the tertiary industry should be attributed to the increase in the productivity of the secondary industry, which in turn provides material products, labor productivity, and the demand for service consumption for the development of tertiary industry. And the development of the tertiary industry represents the foundation of and the key to the transformation of China's employment structure and urbanization. The huge demand for labor forces of the tertiary industry enables rural populations to get jobs in urban areas; the growth in the value of real output of the tertiary industry provides income guarantee for rural populations to flow to urban areas, and further drives the demand for secondary industry products.

China's dual economic development model has also caused major challenges in the further development of China's economy. As mentioned above, the output value of China's primary industry only accounted for around 8% of the total GDP compared to over 90% jointly contributed by the secondary and tertiary industries. So, China is not at a low level in industrialization compared to other countries. Nevertheless, China has a low urbanization level. Among the total population, the rural population has a share of up to 42.7%, and industrial workers account for nearly 1/3. Farmers and rural areas still account for a very large share in China's economy, and a large number of populations rely on agriculture and rural areas for a living. Additionally, China's agriculture and rural areas are still outmoded. In terms of agriculture, traditional production methods involving human and livestock power as main power are still adopted, with low productivity, output per capita, and income per capita. If the outdated modes of production that constrain the development of farmers and rural areas cannot be completely solved, there is no way for China's economy to achieve long-term sustainable growth and income per capita to reach the level of developed countries. Thus, the urbanization of rural areas in China is necessary so that a large number of farmers can turn into urban residents. It is also essential to enable large-scale mechanized operation of agriculture and develop modern agriculture. However, how can the problem of land ownership and management rights in China's rural areas be solved in order to promote the urbanization of rural areas and the expansion of agriculture? How do we boost China's rural land system reform? How do we solve the problem of rural land transfer? How do we solve the problems of livelihood security and employment after farmers leave their lands? How do we absorb the farmers who leave their lands with sufficient job opportunities to develop China's non-agricultural economy? How do we safeguard the rights of farmers during the process of land system reform and land transfer? How do we avoid the new aggravated income inequality and widening income gap during China's rural urbanization and land system reform in the future? These are the biggest challenges in China's current development. The way-out of farmers, rural areas, and agriculture is also one of the biggest dilemmas China's economic development is facing.

2.4 Economic growth pattern of high savings and high investments

The consistent and rapid economic growth for nearly 40 years has never been seen in any other country in the world in any period of time, and China's growth can be called a miracle. Moreover, China's extremely high growth is closely associated with its economic growth pattern of high savings and high investments. The research in Chapter 6 of this book shows that high savings and high investments are not only prerequisites for China's rapid economic growth, but also an inevitable result of China's growth. That is because, under the declining marginal consumption of residents, the product supply brought about by rapid economic growth cannot be supported by the growth of residents' consumption demand, the insufficiency of which should be inevitably and necessarily covered by the growing investment demand. Actually, since 1953, the growth pattern of high savings and high investments has remained a typical feature of China's economic development. According to the data of the *China Statistical Yearbooks*, from 1953 to 2016, the average annual growth rate of China's investments reached 11.1%, among which that of fixed asset investment was 12.7%. The investment growth before the reform and opening-up was higher than that of after the reform and opening-up. During the period 1953–1978, the average annual growth rate of China's investments arrived at 11.8%, among which that of fixed asset investment was 13.8%. During the years 1978–2016, the average annual growth rate of China's investments arrived at 10.6%, among which that of fixed asset investment was 11.1%.

However, the reasons and characteristics of China's high savings and high investment growth pattern are different before and after the reform and opening-up. Before the reform, China gave priority to the development of heavy industry in order to rapidly develop its heavy industry and military industry and achieve the goal of making the country powerful in military strength (Lin, 2012, pp. 76–77). Heavy industry is generally capital intensive, with a long construction cycle, large capital input, and import of key technologies and equipment. Before the reform, China was still a backward developing country dominated by agriculture, with little capital and lack of foreign exchange. The foreign exchange price was high then. In order to prioritize the heavy industry, the Chinese government has to adopt a distorted price system to lower the prices of agricultural products and consumer demand to support investments. Such heavy industry investment through mandated reduced consumption would be restricted by the lower limit of consumer demand, so the investment was extremely unstable. That is because investments cannot be increased and high investment growth be sustained once reduced consumption fails to guarantee the minimum demand of people for food in order to maintain basic living conditions. For this reason, the growth rate of investment in China before the reform showed a trend of big ups and downs. Different from the pre-reform planned economy, which aimed at increasing investments through reduced consumption, after the reform, the Chinese government mainly adopted various policies and measures to guide economy, reduce consumption, and increase savings and investments under the market economy system in order to achieve its ultimate goal of increasing residents' income. Guided by the goal of promoting economic growth and increasing residents' income, China mainly focused on infrastructure investment after the reform, including in railways, highways, airports, bridges, water conservancy works, and other infrastructure projects. This kind of investment would guide economic entities to make choices through market price systems and policies rather than directly compel residents to reduce their consumption. Therefore, the investment growth after the reform was more sustainable and less volatile than that before the reform.

The growth pattern of high savings and high investments has produced profound impacts on China's economic growth from two aspects: Firstly, high investments directly affect the economic growth pattern of China. On the one hand, investment growth produces a multiplier effect on output. As one of the parts for effective demand, investment growth can directly stimulate effective demand, thus increasing output. Also, it can indirectly drive consumption demand by increasing income. In fact, it is precisely due to China's extremely high investment growth that China maintained relatively high growth rates before and after the opening-up. According to Chapter 3, the average annual real GDP growth directly driven by China's total investment growth in the period 1953–2016 reached 3.48%, and its direct contribution to GDP growth was 41.3%, among which that from 1953 to 1977 was 2.54%, with a direct contribution rate of 39.2%, and that from 1978–2016 was 4.01%, with a direct contribution rate of 43.4%. On the other hand, due to highly fluctuated investments, under the impact of the investment multiplier, the dependence of China's growth on investments has also caused huge fluctuations in China's economic growth rates, which was particularly prominent in the pre-reform economic growth. According to the data of the *China Statistical Yearbooks*, the standard deviation and coefficient of variation of China's investment growth rates from 1953 to 2006 were 18.1% and 1.64, 4.16 times and 2.78 times more than those of household consumption growth rates and 2.60 times and 1.98 times more than those of GDP growth rates, respectively, among which those from 1953 to 1977 were 27.5% and

2.34, respectively, 5.11 and 2.23 times more than those of household consumption growth rates and 2.62 times and 1.44 times more than those of GDP growth rates; those from 1978 to 2016 were 8.17% and 0.77, 2.98 times and 2.48 times more than those of household consumption growth rates and 3.03 times and 2.75 times more than those of GDP growth rates. Secondly, the growth pattern of China featuring high savings and high investments has also changed the demand structure of China's economy, enabling an increasingly larger proportion of investments in the total demand structure of GDP and lower consumption percentage. According to the data of the *China Statistical Yearbooks*, during the years 1953 to 2016, the average annual growth rate of investment in China was about 3.4 percentage points higher than that of household consumption. This figure was 11.76% before the reform, 6.5 percentage points higher than that of household consumption and 10.59% after the reform, 1.73 percentage points higher than that of household consumption. As the growth rates of investments have always been higher than those of household consumption, the share of investments in China's GDP jumped from 22% (1953) to 39% (1978), and then to 44% after the reform (2016); while the share of household consumption in GDP dropped from 65% (1953) to 48% (1978), and then to 39% (2016). Currently, China is one of the countries with the smallest share of household consumption in the world.

China's long-term economic growth pattern of high savings and high investments has led to an increasing proportion of investment in China's GDP and a drop in the proportion of residents' consumption demand. As a result, this growth pattern has also brought major challenges against China's long-term economic development. According to the multiplier-acceleration model, a larger proportion of investments means higher investment growth in the case of the same economic growth rate; investment is an increase in production capacity, and more investments will enable faster growth of production capacity, which requires higher effective demand growth to maintain the productivity. In the long run, the increase in investment demand cannot keep pace with the increase in the output brought about by economic growth. Therefore, the effective demand required by long-term economic growth must be pulled by the growth of consumer demand. However, this growth pattern resulted in the declined proportion of household consumption over GDP and obviously insufficient consumer demand growth. Thus, how China improves its residents' effective demand and transforms its economic growth driven by high investments to that driven by household consumption represents a major challenge against the economic development of China in the new era.

2.5 Changes in income distribution patterns and continued expansion of income gaps among residents

During the past 40 years of reform, China has witnessed great changes in its income distribution pattern. Since 1978, China's social income gaps have continued to widen and income distribution inequality has significantly worsened. The country has evolved from one of the countries with the most equal global income distribution to a country with wide income gaps. For example, according to World Bank data, the Gini coefficient of China's income distribution was 0.29 in 1981, 0.39 in 1995, and 0.45 in 2005, breaking the international alert line. According to the data of the National Bureau of Statistics, the Gini coefficients of all Chinese residents' income reached 0.479 in 2003, rose to 0.491 in 2008, started to drop in 2009, to 0.462 in 2015, to 0.465 in 2016, and continued to rise to 0.467 in 2017. According to the estimates of other research institutes and scholars, the inequality was even higher (Li, 2003).[4] However, approximately starting from 2010, China's income gaps have been narrowed a little as the growth of China's economy has decelerated. It is generally believed by academic circles that the overall Gini coefficient of China's income distribution has been close to 0.5.

Since the reform and opening-up, China has experienced all-around income gap widening, as reflected in many aspects of economic development, such as between urban and rural areas, among regions, among urban areas or rural areas, among industries and in factor distribution, etc. In terms of urban-rural income gap, the absolute difference between the annual per capita disposable income of Chinese urban residents and the annual per capita net income of rural residents in 1978 was 109.8 yuan, and the income of urban residents was 2.57 times more than that of rural residents. In 2000, the absolute urban-rural income gap rose to 4,027 yuan, and the ratio of urban-rural income rose to 2.79 times. In 2010, the absolute urban-rural income gap reached 13,190 yuan, and the ratio of urban-rural income widened to 3.23 times. In 2017, the absolute urban-rural income gap expanded to 22,964 yuan but the urban-rural income ratio fell to 2.71, which was slightly narrowed. From the perspective of the income gap of Chinese residents in different provinces, although the gap between regions was narrowed in the initial stage of the reform, it continued to widen after 1982, and then it was not until 2006 that the income gap between regions was narrowed again. According to the calculations based on the data of the *China Statistical Yearbooks*, the coefficient of variation (CV) for the average annual income of urban residents in the provinces of China was 0.179 in 1978, with the ratio of the maximum to the minimum being 1.87, and rose to 0.275 in 2000, with the ratio above being 2.31. The CV decreased after 2006, and the ratio started to drop around 2013. In 2015, the CV dropped to 0.260, and the ratio continued to rise to 2.41. In 2016, the CV was 0.252 and the ratio was 2.25. The income gap among rural residents in China's provinces has also undergone similar changes. In 1978, the CV for the average annual income of rural residents in different provinces of China was 0.2868, with the ratio of the maximum to the minimum being 2.784. Both figures reached the peak around 2006, with the CV jumping to 0.462 and the ratio to 4.40. Afterwards, both figures started to decline, and reached 0.358 and 3.38, respectively, in 2016. The income gap between Chinese urban and rural residents is also widening. Through estimation, a lot of scholars believe that the Gini coefficient of rural areas in China was probably 0.21 to 0.25 in 1978, which rose to around 0.35 in 2000, and basically stayed at 0.35 to 0.37 after 2010. Currently, the Gini coefficient of rural areas in China is approximately 0.36, almost at the same level as that of developed countries around 2010, lower than the international alert line of 0.4. The Gini coefficient of urban areas in China was approximately 0.16, rose to 0.25–0.35 in 2000, and basically stayed at 0.30–0.35. However, according to estimates of different scholars, the Gini coefficient of urban areas in China should exceed 0.30, but be lower than the international alert line of 0.4. During the period 1978–2016, the income gap of different industries in China showed a trend of wave-shaped expansion. According to the data from the National Bureau of Statistics, the ratio of China's highest industry wages to lowest industry wages has been declining compared to that before 1990. It gradually increased after 1991, slightly narrowed after 2008, but rose again in 2016; the ratios of highest industry wages to the national average wages and of lowest industry wages to the same have shown the same trend; the CV for industry wages kept declining from the early age of the reform until 1989, gradually expanded after 1990, reached the pre-reform level in 1994, but showed a trend of slight narrowing after 2008. In terms of factor income gap, according to the data of labor compensation as a percentage of GDP, the proportion of labor income in China dropped from a peak of 52.0% in 1987 to 39.7% in 2007. In 2007, this proportion began to rise, to 50.9% in 2016, but dropped a lot from the beginning of the reform.

There are many complex reasons behind widened income gaps in China. It is generally believed that China's market economy reform may be the initial cause of the country's widening income gap. That is because, without market economy reform, it would be impossible and not allowable to have excessive income gaps in the conditions of the public ownership economy and the system of distribution according to work. In that conditions, production and living materials can almost only be equally distributed among the public due to their shortage; otherwise, someone may be unable to maintain basic living standards. Something has changed since the adoption of the market economy reform. On the one hand, the abundant material products brought about by the increase in productivity made it possible for people to obtain non-equal distribution. In order to stimulate the enthusiasm of producers and promote the effective use of production materials, it is necessary to implement the non-equal distribution based on the marginal return of production factors. On the other hand, since the market-oriented reform, the principle of income distribution has gradually shifted from distribution based on work to that based on a combination of work and factors, and further changed to distribute according to the marginal contributions of production factors in the action of the market mechanism. The income arising from capital, land, management, knowledge, technology, and other factors is accounting for an increasingly large proportion over individual income. The shifting from the distribution purely based on work to that based on the marginal contributions of production factors is actually equivalent to expanding the impact of inequality of personal work capacity on income gaps, which will inevitably widen individual income gaps. Moreover, since wealth is also a production factor, the time accumulation effect of wealth inequality may further widen individual income gaps. However, the incomplete market economy system brought about by the gradual reform under the dual economy is the major cause for the sustained widening of China's income gaps. For example, existing research indicates that dual economic development, household system, and urban-rural labor market division are the causes for the continuous expansion of China's urban-rural income gaps and drop in the percentage of income arising from work; regional unbalanced economic growth, household system, and regional labor market division are the root causes for widened regional income gaps in China. Meanwhile, education, administrative monopolies, rent seeking, and other incomplete market mechanisms have further deepened the widening of income gaps.

Since the adoption of reform and opening-up, China has faced aggravated inequality of distribution and significantly widened income gaps among residents. Although China has seen a trend of gap narrowing in recent years, it is uncertain whether it is just a short-term phenomenon under the declining economic growth of China in recent years. An excessively larger income gap does not only go against the reform goal of "shared prosperity" and cause social inequality, but also reduces the overall consumption demand of residents, thus leading to insufficient effective demand of economy and hampering economic growth. It may also cause social instability or disturbances and increase the risks and uncertainties of the economy, thus affecting the enthusiasm of investors for investment and production. Therefore, how to improve China's income distribution pattern and narrow income gaps among residents is also one of the challenges facing China's economic development.

2.6 Other features and problems

China's rapid economic growth also has other typical characteristics and challenges. For example, the housing demand unleashed by the housing reform that began in 2000, as well as some policy measures adopted by the Chinese government to improve the living conditions of residents, have enabled the rapid growth of China's real estate sector, which has become a major driver for the country's rapid growth in the past ten years. However, at the same time, sustained high housing prices have followed. As a result, the balance between other real sectors in China and the real estate sector in price structure and profit structure has been seriously broken, resulting in high dependence of China's economic growth on the real estate sector. And how to get rid of the high dependence of China on real estate is also one of the challenges facing China's economy. Take one more example. Despite its rapid economic growth, China still has a low GDP per capita. This has constrained the development of China's medical and educational undertakings and the education and medical health level per capita. According to the new growth theory, the improvement of a country's human capital in health and education constitutes one of the most important driving forces for its growth in the long run. How China promotes sustainable economic development by improving the human capital of education and health may also be a problem to be solved in China's current economic growth. Additionally, as Chapter 5 of this book suggests, while pursuing growth in the past, China has relied on the growth of its labor productivity and employment structure adjustments among industries to a large extent. The demographic dividend represents one of the main drivers for China's rapid growth in the past 40 years. However, under the impact of the family planning policy, China entered the stage of demographic transition ahead of schedule when the income per capita did not reach the level of developed countries. China has started to show a trend of aging population, with a relatively declining labor supply. With the deepening of China's aging population in the future, how to decelerate the decline in labor supply and the increase in the dependency ratio of labor forces will become one of the major challenges against the long-term economic growth of China. Whether China can solve these challenges successfully and properly may directly affect its future economic growth.

Section 3 Research contents and structure of the book

This book will focus on the economic growth and income distribution issues during China's dual economic development. In addition to this introduction, this book consists of three parts, totaling 16 chapters.

Part 1 mainly looks at the general law and structural change characteristics of China's economic growth. By adopting China's real GDP and growth rate as the indicators for measuring economic growth, this part analyzes the overall evolution law and structural transition characteristics for China's economic growth. This part is comprised of Chapters 1–5. Chapter 1 mainly combs the history of China's economic growth during the period 1960–2016, analyzes the variation in China's GDP and share of global GDP, and compares the phased differences of China's economic growth in different periods, as well as differences of countries in economic growth in the same period. Chapter 2 studies the changes in the income level of Chinese residents since the reform and opening-up. Chapter 3 analyzes the reasons for China's economic growth during the period 1953–2016 from the demand side, investigates the structural change characteristics of China's economic growth before and after the reform, and analyzes the contribution of different demand types to China's economy based on the breakdown of demand factors for the GDP growth rate. Chapters 4 and 5 analyze the impact of industrial structure changes during the period 1952–2016 on China's economic growth on the supply side. By proposing a new decomposition formula that can decompose the impact of price structure changes over the real GDP growth rate, Chapter 4 decomposes China's real GDP growth rate by industrial factors, and examines the contribution of the growth of tertiary industry and price structure changes to China's real GDP growth. Chapter 5 mainly studies the causes for the improvement in the productivity per labor force in China. This chapter first proposes the growth rate decomposition formula to break down the impact of dual structure changes on the growth of GDP per labor force, then decomposes the growth rate of China's real GDP per labor force by industry, and analyzes the impacts of tertiary industry growth, employment structure changes, and price structure changes on the GDP growth per labor force.

Part 2 mainly discusses the changes and characteristics of investment, housing, health, and education during China's economic growth, as well as their interactions with the growth. This part consists of Chapters 6–11. Chapter 6 mainly studies the relationship between investment and China's economic growth. This chapter first theoretically studies the determining mechanism of saving rate and investment rate in the process of economic growth, then analyzes the causes for China's high saving rates, and discusses the impact of China's growth pattern of high savings and high investments on the future economy. Chapter 7 analyzes the mutual relationship between real estate development and China's economic growth. This chapter first probes into the interactions among land and housing supply, economic growth, and housing prices, then uses China's inter-provincial panel data to analyze the impacts of China's housing supply on the economic growth and housing price growth in different provinces, and finally discusses the reasons for the sustained rise in China's housing prices and the challenges facing the government's regulation. Chapter 8 analyzes the development of education during China's economic growth, and interprets in detail the characteristics and differences in the education development of China before and after the reform. Chapter 9 studies the role of China's education development on economic growth, and re-estimates the contribution of China's education improvement to the economy. Chapter 10 examines in detail the changes in the development of medical health conditions for Chinese residents since the founding of the People's Republic of China, including total health expenditure and its structure, national medical health facility conditions, as well as the health of Chinese residents. Chapter 11 looks at the roles of China's health human capital and health investment in economic growth, analyzes the influence mechanism and long-term effect of health factors on economic growth, and empirically discovers the effect of China's health human capital on economic growth.

Part 3 looks at the evolution of income distribution in the development of China's dual economy, including evolution and current status of income distribution pattern, reasons and mechanisms for widened income gaps, as well as possible future countermeasures and strategies. Part 3 covers Chapters 12–16. Chapter 12 focuses on the evolution and current status of China's income distribution pattern and analyzes and discusses the evolution and changes of income gaps among Chinese residents. Chapter 13 looks at the impact of incomplete labor market on regional income gaps. Chapter 14 studies the impact of labor market monopoly and minimum wage restrictions on income gaps and economic development. Chapter 15 analyzes the reasons for continuously widened income gaps, and proposes policy suggestions and ideas on how to improve China's current income distribution and narrow the country's income gaps.

Notes

1 Unless otherwise specified, the data and analysis in this book cover Taiwan, Hong Kong, and Macao.

2 The proportion of students in schools in the population at school age is equal to the percentage of students in schools in primary school-age population. The proportion of primary school students in the population at school age is larger than 100%, maybe because some children who have not reached the admission age enter primary school, and the children over school age in backward areas are still at primary school.

3 Before the end of the Cultural Revolution, China adopted a household registration system to control urban household registration, and "rural-to-non-rural household conversion" (that is, the conversion of rural household to non-rural household registration) was strictly controlled. At the same time, rural development of community and brigade enterprises (later rural enterprises) must also follow the principle of "three-local" principle (namely local materials, local processing, and local sales) (Wu, 2016, p. 120). Therefore, the market for products of community and brigade run enterprises was greatly restricted. In 1984, the state implemented a new policy stipulation, "No matter what is appropriate, processing agricultural products in rural areas is economically rational, so rural enterprises should gradually take over the processing industry" (National Institutional Reform Commission, 1984, pp. 97–104). This policy has liberated the product market of rural enterprises.

4 For more details on the Gini coefficient and China's income gaps, please refer to Chapter 12 of this book. All income gap data here are also sourced from Chapter 12.

References

[1] Li, S. (2003). Review and Prospect of research on individual income distribution in China. *China Economic Quarterly*, 2(2).

[2] Lin, Y. F. (1994).*Institution, technology and agricultural development in China.* Shanghai: Shanghai Joint Publishing Press.

[3] Wu, J. L. (2016). *Understanding and interpreting China's economic reform*. Shanghai: Shanghai Far East Publishers.

[4] Zhang, J. (1998). *Double-track economics: Economic reform in China (1978–1992).* Shanghai: Shanghai Joint Publishing Press.

Part 1

1 China's economic growth

1960–2016

Since 1978, China has maintained a rapid, sustained economic growth, and both its GDP and global GDP ranking have steadily risen. Now China is the second-largest economy in the world today, and its status and influence in global economy have significantly improved. So, how has China gradually moved from a backward state to the world's second largest economy? How has China's economy evolved since the launch of the reform and opening-up? How did the pre-reform economic development impact China's overall economic growth? What are the significant differences in China's economic growth before and after the reform? What are the specific differences? And how does China differ from other countries in the same period in terms of economic development before and after the reform? All the above issues will be explored in this chapter. Here, we will analyze and discuss in detail China's economic growth from 1978 to 2016. For comparative analysis, we will also probe into the country's pre-reform economic growth in this chapter if data permits.

This chapter is organized as follows. Section 1 describes the change of China's total GDP and its global SHARE of GDP from 1960 to 2016, using the official exchange rate of that year as the conversion standard. In the second section, a comparative analysis is made on both real GDP growth rates and growth rates of per capita of China and other major economies at constant prices during the period 1960–2016. The third section describes the growth of China's real GDP and real GDP per capita from 1978 to 2016 at constant prices. In the fourth section, the growth of China's GDP per capita and the gap between China and developed countries in this respect are analyzed using the official exchange rate of each year as the conversion criterion.

Section 1 China's GDP and variation in the share of global GDP

China has witnessed a significant increase in total economic output and improvement of its status in the global economy. Both are the most striking achievements of China since the reform and opening-up 40 years ago.

DOI: 10.4324/9781003261629-3

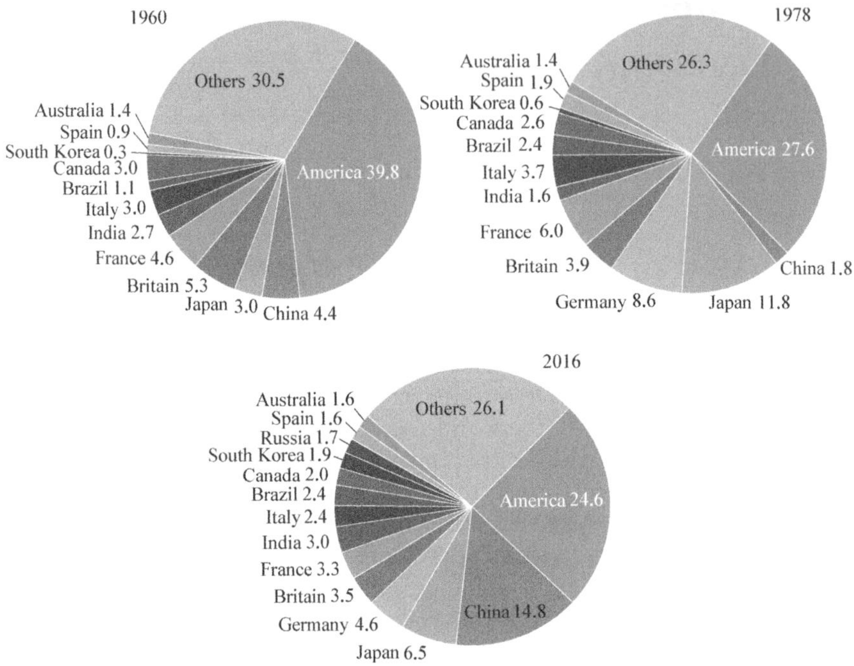

Figure 1.1 Share of major economies in global GDP in 1960, 1978, and 2016.

Figure 1.1 shows the shares of major economies in global GDP in 1960, 1978, and 2016, and Figure 1.2 shows the variations in the shares of major countries in global GDP from 1960 to 2016. According to both figures, during the period from the 1950s to the 1970s, a golden age for the rapid economic development of western countries, China's economy obviously lagged behind that of other countries in the world before 1978. Due to a lack of data for the 1950s, Figures 1.1 and 1.2 only show the data for the period following 1960. According to Figure 1.2a, in 1960, the global GDP was US$ 1.366 trillion in current U.S. dollars, among which China contributed US$ 0.597 trillion, with a share of 4.4% in contrast to a share of roughly 40% for America. China probably ranked 4th among the existing countries in 1960 in terms of GDP in the world if the disintegrated Soviet Union and Germany, which had not been unified then, are not taken into account and 6th if West Germany and the Soviet Union are included.

From the 1960s to the 1970s, China's economy barely grew as compared with the rest countries in the world. According to the official exchange rates at that time (as shown in the upper part of Figure 1.2), in terms of total economic output, France and Japan surpassed China in 1961, Italy surpassed China in 1962, Canada surpassed China in 1974, Brazil surpassed China in 1977, and Spain surpassed China in 1978. By 1978, the global GDP had reached US$

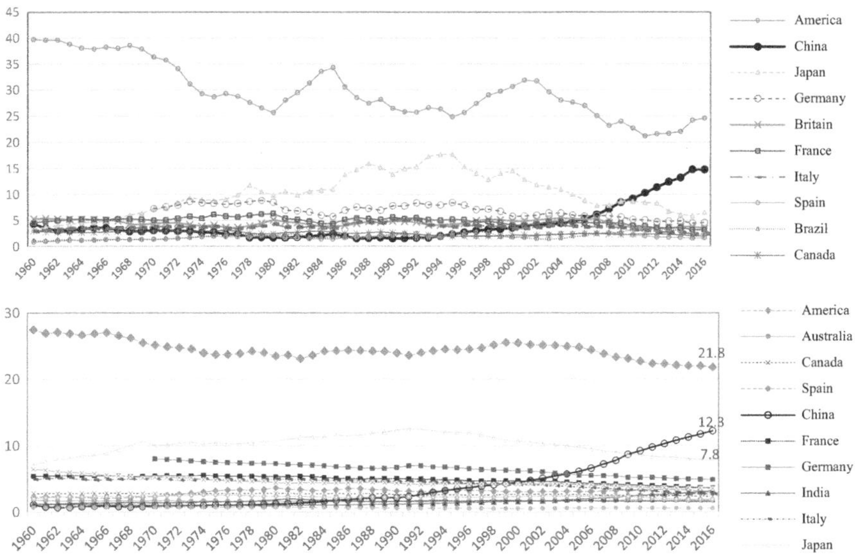

Figure 1.2 Variation in the share of major economies in global GDP: 1960–2016.

8.538 trillion, up 5.2 times over 1960, with an average annual growth of 9.6%.[1] In 1978, China had a GDP of approximately US$ 1.495 trillion, up 1.50 times over 1960, with an average annual growth of 2.5%.[2] In the same year, China contributed 1.8% to the global GDP, America 27.6%, Japan 11.8%, and Germany 8.6% (as shown in Figure 1.1b). Of course, at the official exchange rates of different countries in 2010 (as shown in Figure 1.2), China ranked even lower in 1960, and surpassed India in the period 1960–1978. In 1978, China fell behind America, Japan, Germany, France, Italy, Britain, Brazil, Canada, Spain, and Australia, and ranked 11th if the Soviet Union is excluded.

Since 1978, China's economy has accelerated significantly relative to that of other countries. However, at the official exchange rates of each year, when compared to other countries, China's economic growth remained relatively volatile in the early stages of reform due to the impact of exchange rate fluctuations. As shown in Figure 1.2, China's share in global GDP first increased and then decreased from 1978 to 1990. From 1978 to 1985, the country's share in global GDP saw a significant rise. In terms of GDP, China exceeded Spain in 1982 and Brazil in 1983. In 1985, China contributed 2.44% to the global GDP. However, the GDP growth of the country continued to decline after 1985 and reached the new minimum of 1.6% in 1991. After 1991, China's economy grew even faster than other countries in the world. In terms of total economic output, China surpassed Brazil in 1992, Spain in 1994, and Canada in 1995, making it 6th in the world. In 2001 when China was about to join the World Trade Organization (hereinafter referred to as "accession to WTO"), the global GDP was about US$ 33.34 trillion, in which China's GDP was about US$1.34 trillion, with a share of 4.0%. That year, America had a share of 31.9%, Japan 12.9%, Germany 5.9%, Britain 4.8%, and France 4.1%. In 2001, China ranked 6th in terms of global GDP ranking, returning to its position for the year 1960. Since 2001, China's economy has grown even faster. In 2005, China had a share of 4.8% in global GDP, ranking 5th in the world by surpassing France. The country ranked 4th by surpassing Britain in 2006; 3rd by surpassing Germany in 2007; and 2nd by surpassing Japan in 2010. If the influence of exchange rate change is not taken into account, China would show even more significant growth since 1978. As shown in Figure 1.2, at the official exchange rates in 2010, China surpassed Australia in 1984, Mexico in 1986, Spain in 1992, and Canada in 1993. In 1995, China contributed 3.5% to the global GDP, ranking 7th by surpassing Brazil. From 1995 to 2004, China's GDP had a share of 5.73% in global GDP, ranking 3rd by surpassing Italy, Britain, France, and Germany in succession. China surpassed Japan in terms of GDP in 2009 and has remained second since then.

According to the latest data released by the World Bank on October 1, 2020, the global GDP in 2019 was US$ 87.75 trillion at the official exchange rates of different countries in 2017. Among them, America's GDP was US$ 21.42 trillion, with a share of 24.42% in global GDP; China's GDP was US$ 14.34 trillion, with a share of 16.34%. The GDP and share in global GDP for ten major economies in the world are as follows: Japan, US$ 5.08 trillion, 5.79%; Germany, US$ 3.85 trillion, 4.38%; India, US$ 2.87 trillion, 3.28%; Britain, US$ 2.83 trillion, 3.22%; France, US$ 2.72 trillion, 3.10%; Italy, US$ 2.00 trillion, 2.28%; Brazil, US$ 1.84 trillion, 2.10%; and Canada, US$ 1.74 trillion, 1.98%. Currently, China still has a low GDP per capita. According to the data released by the World Monetary Fund, in 2017, the world had a GDP per capita of US$ 10,728 and China US$ 8,643, ranking 71st in the world.

Section 2 Real GDP growth rate and real GDP per capita growth rate: 1960–2016

Due to the influence of short-term factors such as supply and demand in the foreign exchange market over the exchange rates of the current year, the share of global GDP converted at the exchange rates of the year cannot fully and truly reflect the actual economic growth of different countries, although it can comprehensively reflect the economic strength of a country and its status in the world. In light of this, Figures 1.3a, 1.3b and Table 1.1 show the economic growth of major economies in the world in constant local currency. This data also show China grew slower than other countries from 1960 to 1977 and obviously faster than some from 1978 to 2016. China's actual economic growth before and after the reform are reviewed in detail through international comparative analysis in the subsequent sections.

2.1 Economic growth before the reform: 1960–1977

It can be seen from Figure 1.3 that China's economy showed dramatic, volatile growth and significant stagnation relative to the global economy during the period 1960–1977. Table 1.1 shows that the world's real GDP was up 1.25 times from 1960 to 1977, with an average annual growth rate of 4.9%; China's was up 1.06 times, with an average annual growth rate of 4.3%, around 0.6 percentage points lower than the world's annual average. From 1960 to 1977, the average annual real GDP of Japan and South Korea grew by 7.2% and 10%, respectively, with the total economic output being up 2.27 and 4.05 times; Brazil, almost at the same level as China in total economic output, had an average annual growth rate of 7.5%, and its total economic output was up 2.40 times. In fact, except for a few countries such as India, Germany, Britain, and Australia, most developed economies in the world had

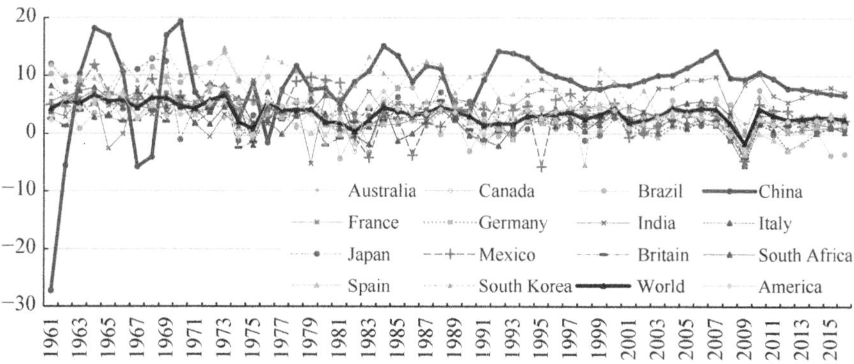

Figure 1.3a Real GDP growth rates of different countries.

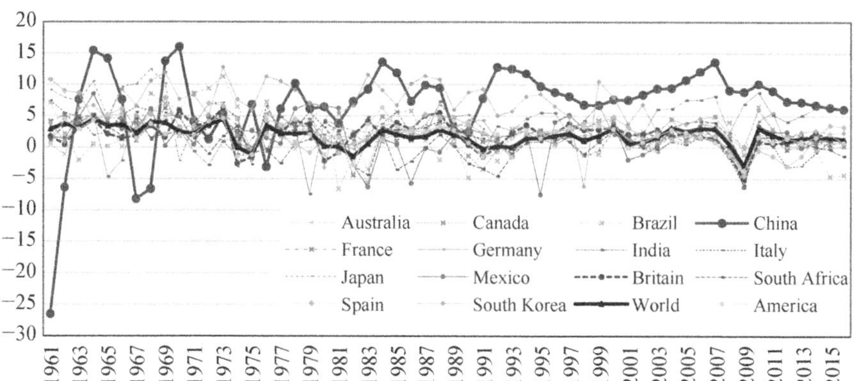

Figure 1.3b Real GDP per capita growth rates of different countries.

Table 1.1 The GDP growth rates of major countries in the world

Variable	*Average annual real GDP per capita growth rate (%)*			*Average Annual real GDP growth rate (%)*		
Period	**61–77**	**78–01**	**02–16**	**61–77**	**78–01**	**02–16**
America	2.83	2.13	1.01	4.03	3.23	1.86
Japan	6.01	2.60	0.82	7.23	3.08	0.82
Germany	2.93[a]	2.01	1.17	2.91[b]	2.23	1.20
Britain	2.42	2.39	0.98	2.85	2.61	1.68
France	3.92	1.89	0.51	4.87	2.38	1.09
Italy	4.21	2.22	−0.43	4.85	2.29	−0.02
Canada	3.13	1.66	0.90	4.86	2.80	1.95
Spain	5.18	2.24	0.52	6.31	2.72	1.39
Australia	2.34	1.89	1.51	4.28	3.23	2.99
South Korea	7.63	6.82	3.30	9.99	8.00	3.85
Mexico	3.09	1.42	0.92	6.27	3.43	2.36
South Africa	1.90	−0.09	1.46	4.57	2.08	2.89
India	1.53	2.99	5.94	3.71	5.16	7.44
Brazil	4.74	0.75	1.46	7.46	2.67	2.52
China	2.24	8.37	8.97	4.34	9.73	9.56
Global average	2.90	1.34	1.60	4.89	2.98	2.85

Source: Source of raw data: the World Bank.

[a,b] The data of Germany are the average annual growth rates from 1971 to 1977, and the data of West Germany and East Germany are consolidated into the pre-reunification data.

higher real economic growth rates than China during this period. In terms of real GDP per capita growth, the GDP per capita of the world grew by 62% from 1961 to 1977, with an average annual growth rate of 2.9%; that of China was 46%, with an average annual growth rate of 2.24%, still significantly lower than the average global level. Additionally, among the world's major economies listed in Table 1.1, the real GDP per capita growth rates of other countries except for a very few ones including India and South Africa were significantly higher than China. As China's GDP per capita growth rates were significantly lower than those of other major economies then, China's living standard of the common people in 1977 was much lower than that of other major economies.

From 1960 to 1977, China also showed significantly larger economic fluctuations than other major economies, showing a trend of dramatic ups and downs in economic growth. Figures 1.3a and 1.3b show the real GDP growth rates and real GDP per capita growth rates of the world's major economies at the constant prices of each country. It can be seen from Figure 1.2 that China's economic growth during this period has an obvious zigzag, with fluctuations being greater than that of other major economies. During this period, China's real GDP growth rates were higher than 10% for six years and exhibited a five-year negative growth rate (at around −5% for four years). In 1970, when China's economy grew fastest, its real GDP growth rate and real GDP per capita growth rate reached 19.3% and 16%, respectively, followed by the year 1964, with both aforementioned rates being 18.2% and 15.5%, respectively. The two figures were −27.3% and −26.5% in 1961, when China had the lowest GDP growth, and reached −5.8% and −8.2% in 1967 when the second economic recession started. During this period, China's economy experienced ups and downs, just like a roller coaster. In the same period, the annual growth rates of other countries in the world basically held steady between 0% and 5% (except Brazil, Japan, and South Korea, as the annual economic growth rates of these three countries were higher than 7%).

Tables 1.2a and 1.2b show the coefficients of variation (CVs) and standard deviations (STDEVs) for the real GDP growth rates and real GDP per capita growth rates of major economies. As seen in both tables, from 1960 to 1977, the STDEVs for the real GDP growth rate and real GDP per capita growth rate of the world were 1.56 and 1.49, respectively; and the CVs[3] for both rates above were 0.32 and 0.52, respectively. In the same period, the STDEVs for the real GDP growth rates and real GDP per capita growth rates of major economies except China fluctuated from 1.6 to 4.5 and from 1.5 to 4.5; the CVs for the real GDP growth rates and GDP per capita growth rates of such economies were from 0.3 to 0.9 and 0.4 to 2.2. However, only India and South Africa are exceptions, with the CVs for real GDP per capita growth rates exceeding 1. For China, the STDEVs for the real GDP growth rates and real GDP per capita growth rates were up to 11.6 and 10.8, respectively; and the CVs for the real GDP growth rates and GDP per capita growth rates were up to 2.23 and 3.84.

Table 1.2a Fluctuations of average annual real GDP growth rates of major economies

Variable	*Coefficient of variation (CV)*			*Standard deviation (STDEV)*		
Period	**61–77**	**78–01**	**02–16**	**61–77**	**78–01**	**02–16**
America	0.53	0.61	0.86	2.12	1.98	1.60
Japan	0.61	0.72	2.58	4.46	2.21	2.10
Germany	0.74[a]	0.68	1.99	2.17[b]	1.51	2.38
Britain	0.82	0.75	1.10	2.33	1.95	1.86
France	0.37	0.53	1.26	1.80	1.25	1.37
Italy	0.53	0.62	−86.15	2.58	1.43	2.01
Canada	0.33	0.79	0.80	1.63	2.21	1.56
Spain	0.46	0.66	1.88	2.90	1.78	2.61
Australia	0.47	0.58	0.24	2.02	1.87	0.71
South Korea	0.30	0.53	0.45	2.99	4.22	1.75
Mexico	0.36	1.21	1.03	2.28	4.16	2.43
South Africa	0.49	1.16	0.68	2.22	2.42	1.96
India	0.88	0.56	0.26	3.32	2.89	1.96
Brazil	0.51	1.34	1.30	3.80	3.58	3.28
China	**2.32**	**0.31**	**0.22**	**11.62**	**3.03**	**2.13**
Global average	0.32	0.37	0.54	1.56	1.11	1.53

Source: Source of raw data: the World Bank.

[a,b] For Germany, the data for 1971–1977 are given here, and the data of West Germany and East Germany are consolidated into the pre-reunification data.

Table 1.2b Variation in average annual real GDP per capita growth rates of major economies

Variable	*Coefficient of variation (CV)*			*Standard deviation (STDEV)*		
Period	**61–77**	**78–01**	**02–16**	**61–77**	**78–01**	**02–16**
America	0.73	0.93	1.58	2.06	1.98	1.59
Japan	0.74	0.80	2.55	4.47	2.08	2.10
Germany	0.71[a]	0.72	2.18	2.07[b]	1.44	2.56
Britain	0.93	0.81	1.93	2.26	1.94	1.89
France	0.43	0.64	2.62	1.66	1.21	1.33
Italy	0.60	0.63	−4.91	2.54	1.40	2.12
Canada	0.51	1.39	1.75	1.58	2.30	1.58
Spain	0.57	0.85	4.38	2.93	1.91	2.29
Australia	0.87	0.98	0.60	2.03	1.85	0.91
South Korea	0.42	0.61	0.53	3.18	4.16	1.75
Mexico	0.70	2.80	2.61	2.17	3.98	2.41
South Africa	1.13	−26.94	1.38	2.14	2.47	2.02
India	2.13	0.96	0.33	3.26	2.88	1.93
Brazil	0.81	4.67	2.18	3.83	3.49	3.18
China	**3.84**	**0.36**	**0.24**	**10.79**	**2.99**	**2.11**
Global average	0.52	0.83	0.94	1.49	1.10	1.51

Source: Source of raw data: the World Bank.

[a,b] For Germany, the data for 1971–1977 are given here and the data of West Germany and East Germany are consolidated into the pre-reunification data.

As Italy has a negative economic growth in the period 2002–2016, its CV is also negative.

2.2 China's economic growth since the reform till the accession to the WTO

According to Figure 1.3, China's economy showed rapid growth from 1978 to 2001. During this period, China's economic fluctuations were large in absolute range but the relative magnitude decreased significantly. It can be seen from Table 1.1 that, from 1978 to 2001, the world's real GDP was up 1.02 times, with an average annual growth rate of 2.9%; China's real GDP was up about 8.2 times, with an average annual growth rate of 9.7%, almost three times higher than the global average. During this period, only South Korea and India were able to maintain high growth, with an average annual real GDP growth rate of 8% and 5.7%, respectively. The average annual real GDP growth rates of other major economies in the world during the same period were between 2% and 3%, almost the same as the global average. In the same period, the real GDP per capita of the world and China was up 34% and 5.8 times, respectively, with an average annual growth rate of about 1.34% and 8.7%, respectively; that of South Korea was up 3.8 times, with an average annual growth rate of 6.7% compared to 2% to 3% for other major economies in the world. Thus, China's real GDP per capita growth rate was obviously higher than that of other countries and the global average. Overall, the growth of China's economy in these 24 years was not only significantly higher than its growth before the reform but also higher than that of any other country in the world.

In terms of economic growth fluctuations, despite the large absolute range of China's economic fluctuations from 1978 to 2001, China's economy did not fluctuate much in relative terms in consideration of its high economic growth during this period. According to the data from the World Bank and *China Statistical Yearbooks*, in 1984, China's real GDP grew fastest at a rate of 15% and average annual real GDP of 13.6% compared to the previous year. From 1992 to 1995, both China's real GDP growth rate and real GDP per capita growth rate almost exceed 10%. In 1989 and 1990, when China had the lowest economic growth, both rates above were roughly 3%. During this period, the range of economic fluctuations was more than 10%, exceeding that of any other country in the world. In fact, in terms of absolute fluctuation range, the STDEVs for the fluctuation range of China's real GDP and real GDP per capita growth rates were 3.3 and 2.9, respectively, and those for the fluctuation range of the real global GDP and real global GDP per capita growth rates were 1.11 and 1.10, respectively. For major economies in the world, their STDEVs for GDP growth rate fluctuation range were all no more than 2, with the exceptions of South Korea, India, Brazil, Mexico, and other emerging developing countries whose STDEVs for GDP growth rate fluctuation range being 3 to 4. The relatively high fluctuations of China's GDP growth rates are correlated with the country's high average growth rates. If the impact of the high economic growth rate is excluded, the relative volatility of China's economic growth during this period was not too great. It can be seen from Table 1.2a and 1.2b that the CVs for China's real GDP growth rates and real GDP per capita growth rates during the period 1978–2001 were 0.31 and 0.36, respectively; and those for both real GDP growth rates and real GDP per capita growth rates of the world during the same period were 0.37 and 0.83, respectively. For major economies in the world, the CVs for both real GDP growth rates and real GDP per capita growth rates were above 0.5. Thus, in terms of relative range, China did not experience large economic fluctuations during this period.

2.3 China's economic growth since its accession to the WTO: 2002–2016

China maintained rapid, steady economic growth from 2002 to 2016. As seen in Figure 1.3, compared with other countries, China did not only have higher economic growth rates but smaller fluctuations in such rates. During this period, the average annual real GDP of the world grew by 2.85% and that of China by 9.3%. In the same period, India, second to China, had an average annual real GDP growth rate of 7.4%, followed by South Korea (3.85%). All the economic growth rates of other major economies in the world were less than 3%. In terms of per capita growth, during this period, the average annual real GDP per capita of the world grew by 1.6% and that of China by 9%. The same data was 3.3% for South Korea, 5.9% for India, and below 1.5% for other major economies in the world. Thus, the real GDP per capita growth rates of China were significantly higher than the rest of the world and the world average.

Regardless of comparison with what it was like previously or with what other major economies were like, China's economic growth fluctuated the least from 2002 to 2016. According to Table 1.2, the STDEV for the fluctuation range of China's real GDP growth rates was 2.13 and the country's range of fluctuations witnessed a significant drop compared with the previous periods 1960–1978 (STDEV: 11.63) and 1978–2001 (STDEV: 3.03) when the economic growth did not drop. Of course, in contrast to global average and other major economies, the fluctuation range of China's growth rates was lower than the intermediate level, higher than that of the global average (STDEV: 1.51) but lower than that of Germany (STDEV: 2.38), Spain (STDEV: 2.61), Mexico (STDEV: 2.43), Brazil (STDEV: 2.38), and almost the same as Japan (STDEV: 2.10), which had a growth rate of 0.82. If the effect of the average GDP growth rate is not considered, during the period from 2002–2016, the CV for the real GDP growth rates of China was 0.22, lower than that from 1960 to 1977 (2.32) and 1978–2001 (0.31). In the same period, the CV for the global average was 0.94. All the CVs for other major economies in the world except India (0.26), Australia (0.24), and South Korea (0.45), with CVs being lower than 0.5, were above 0.5. When population growth is stripped out, the data also show that China has maintained the smoothest growth in terms of fluctuations in the growth rate of real GDP per capita. Table 1.2b shows that, during the period 2002–2016, the STDEV for China's real GDP per capita growth rate was 2.11, smaller than 10.79 before the reform and 2.99 after the reform till the accession to the WTO, at the intermediate level compared with other economies in the same period. The CV for real GDP per capita growth rates were 0.24, smaller than 3.83 for the period 1960–1977 and 0.333 for the period 1978–2001.

Section 3 Overview of China's economic growth: 1960–2016

Tables 1.3a and 1.3b show the growth of real GDP and real GDP per capita of China and other major economies in 2016 relative to those of 1960, 1977, and 2001. As can be seen, from 1960 to 2016, the real GDP growth of the world, China, America, and the Organization for Economic Co-operation and Development ((OECD) was up 5.92 times, 73.29 times, and around 4.5 times respectively; that of other countries was up 2 to 10 times (e.g., 54.24 times for South Korea and 17.03 times for India). During this period, the real GDP per capita of the world was up 1.82 times on average; that of other countries except South Korea (up 25.96 times), Japan (up 5.12 times), India (up 4.53 times), and China (up 34.94 times) was up one to three times. Regardless of real GDP or real GDP per capita, China was the fastest growing country during this period.

In fact, the economic development of China after the reform and opening-up played a key role in China becoming a major economy. Tables 1.3a and 1.3b show that, during the pre-reform period of 1960–1977, the country's real GDP was up 1.06 times, with an average annual growth rate of 1.25%. Except for America, Britain, Australia, and India, all the other major

Table 1.3a Real GDP growth multiples of major economies in the world during different periods

Period	*1960–1977*	*1977–2001*	*2001–2016*	*1960–2016*	*1977–2016*
America	0.95	1.13	0.32	4.49	1.81
OECD	1.18	0.99	0.28	4.53	1.54
Japan	2.27	1.05	0.13	6.60	1.32
Germany	0.22[a]	0.70	0.19	1.47[a]	1.02
Britain	0.60	0.85	0.28	2.80	1.37
France	1.24	0.76	0.17	3.62	1.06
Italy	1.24	0.73	−0.01	2.82	0.71
Canada	1.24	0.93	0.33	4.76	1.57
Spain	1.81	0.89	0.23	5.53	1.32
Australia	1.04	1.13	0.56	5.77	2.32
South Korea	4.05	5.22	0.76	54.24	9.94
Mexico	1.82	1.21	0.41	7.80	2.12
South Africa	1.13	0.63	0.53	4.31	1.49
India	0.86	2.31	1.93	17.03	8.70
Brazil	2.40	0.86	0.44	8.09	1.68
China	**1.06**	**8.20**	**2.92**	**73.29**	**35.06**
Global average	1.25	1.02	0.52	5.92	2.07
China/World	0.85	8.04	5.62	12.38	16.94

Source: Calculations based on raw data from the World Bank.
The real GDP of each country is calculated at the constant prices of its local currency.
[a] The growth of Germany is relative to its growth in 1970, and the data of West Germany and East Germany are consolidated into the pre-reunification data.

Table 1.3b Real GDP per capita growth multiples of major economies in the world during different periods

Period	*1960–1977*	*1977–2001*	*2001–2016*	*1960–2016*	*1977–2016*
America	0.60	0.66	0.16	2.07	0.92
OECD	0.79	0.64	0.15	2.38	0.89
Japan	1.66	0.84	0.13	4.53	1.08
Germany	0.22[a]	0.61	0.19	1.33[a]	0.91
Britain	0.50	0.77	0.15	2.03	1.03
France	0.92	0.56	0.08	2.23	0.69
Italy	1.01	0.70	−0.07	2.16	0.58
Canada	0.69	0.48	0.14	1.84	0.69
Spain	1.35	0.69	0.08	3.28	0.83
Australia	0.48	0.56	0.25	1.88	0.95
South Korea	2.47	3.80	0.62	25.96	6.77
Mexico	0.67	0.38	0.14	1.63	0.57
South Africa	0.37	−0.03	0.24	0.65	0.20
India	0.28	1.01	1.37	5.12	3.77
Brazil	1.17	0.18	0.23	2.16	0.45
China	**0.46**	5.82	**2.62**	**34.94**	**23.68**
Global average	0.62	0.37	0.27	1.82	0.74
China/World	0.74	15.72	9.70	19.20	32.00

Source: Calculations based on raw data from the World Bank.
The real GDP of each country is calculated at the constant prices of its local currency.
[a] The growth of Germany is relative to its growth in 1970, and the data of West Germany and East Germany are consolidated into the pre-reunification data.

economies grew faster than China. During this period, China's share of global GDP dropped from 5% to 2%, and the country's global GDP ranking dropped from 6th to 11th in the world. In the same period, the real GDP per capita of the world grew by 62% while that of China by only 46%. Except for India and South Africa, the real GDP per capita growth rates of all the other major economies were higher than those of China. During the post-reform period of 1977–2016, the real GDP growth of China was up more than 35 times while that of the world was up 2.07 times. The GDP growth of all the other major economies in the world except India (8.70 times) and South Korea (9.94 times) was up less than 2.5 times. During this period, the real GDP per capita growth of China was up 23.68 times; that of the world 74% on average; and that of the other economies except India (3.77 times) and South Korea (6.77 times) was up two times at most. In the years 1977 and 2016, China's real GDP and real GDP per capita growth was 17 and 32 times more than the global average. It can be seen that, since the reform and opening-up, China's economy has grown at a speed and rate never before seen. China's status as a major economy is mainly attributed to its rapid economic growth since the reform and opening-up (Tables 1.4a and 1.4b).

Table 1.4a Nominal GDP growth multiples of major economies in the world in different periods

Period	*1960–1977*	*1977–2001*	*2001–2016*	*1960–2016*	*1977–2016*
America	2.84	4.09	0.75	33.28	7.93
OECD	4.31	3.76	0.75	43.25	7.32
Japan	15.20	5.00	0.15	110.50	5.88
Germany	1.78[a]	2.26	0.78	15.17[a]	4.81
Britain	2.64	5.16	0.63	35.61	9.07
France	5.57	2.36	0.78	38.35	4.99
Italy	5.36	3.53	0.60	45.03	6.24
Canada	4.15	2.48	1.08	36.23	6.23
Spain	9.94	3.74	0.98	101.49	8.37
Australia	4.93	2.44	2.18	63.79	9.92
South Korea	8.67	12.93	1.65	355.57	35.88
Mexico	5.27	7.86	0.44	79.19	11.79
Russia		−0.39[b]	3.19		1.54[b]
South Africa	4.37	1.99	1.43	38.00	6.27
India	2.28	3.00	3.73	60.96	17.89
Brazil	10.62	2.18	2.21	117.44	9.20
China	1.93	6.66	7.36	186.54	63.02
Global average	4.31	3.60	1.27	54.50	9.45
China/World	0.45	1.85	5.78	3.42	6.67

Source: Calculations based on raw data from the World Bank.
Nominal GDP is calculated at the US dollars converted based on the official exchange rate of the year.

a The growth of Germany is relative to its growth in 1970, and the data of West Germany and East Germany are consolidated into the pre-reunification data.

b The growth of Russia is relative to that of 1989.

Table 1.4b Nominal GDP growth multiples of major economies in the world in different periods

Period	*1960–1977*	*1977–2001*	*2001–2016*	*1960–2016*	*1977–2016*
America	2.15	2.94	0.54	18.11	5.07
OECD	3.36	2.93	0.58	26.05	5.21
Japan	12.16	4.37	0.15	80.20	5.17
Germany	1.78[a]	2.09	0.77	14.25[a]	4.48
Britain	2.39	4.83	0.46	27.91	7.52
France	4.61	2.00	0.64	26.54	3.91
Italy	4.70	3.45	0.50	36.95	5.65
Canada	2.88	1.66	0.78	17.37	3.74
Spain	8.13	3.24	0.74	66.21	6.36
Australia	3.29	1.51	1.56	26.59	5.43
South Korea	5.64	9.71	1.45	173.04	25.21
The Netherlands	7.47	1.94	0.70	41.38	4.01
Mexico	2.72	4.53	0.17	22.98	5.45
Russia		−0.39[b]	3.17		1.55[b]
South Africa	2.46	0.78	0.97	11.11	2.50
India	1.27	1.43	2.82	20.03	8.28
Brazil	6.43	1.02	1.75	40.18	4.54
China	1.07	4.68	6.71	89.74	42.81
Global average	2.82	2.12	0.89	21.54	4.89
China/World	0.38	2.20	7.57	4.17	8.75

Source: Calculations based on raw data from the World Bank.

Nominal GDP is calculated at the US dollars converted based on the official exchange rate of the year.

[a] The growth of Germany is relative to its growth in 1970, and the data of West Germany and East Germany are consolidated into the pre-reunification data.

[b] The growth of Russia is relative to that of 1989.

Section 4 Low GDP per capita: China remains to be a developing country

Despite its 40-year rapid economic growth, China still has a small GDP per capita. In terms of GDP per capita, China is still a typical developing country. Figure 1.4 shows the variation in GDP per capita of major economies during the period 1960–2016. As can be seen, first, despite China's ever-growing GDP, the growth curve of China's GDP per capita has always been classified being in the low-income country group and lower than the GDP per capita of the world. Second, although China's GDP per capita has grown fast, the absolute growth of China's GDP per capita remains extremely low if compared to developed countries in Europe and America due to China's low GDP per capita (only US$ 90 in 1960).

Figure 1.5 shows the GDP per capita at the exchange rates of the major economies in 1960, 1977, 2001, and 2016. As can be seen, in 1960, China had a GDP per capita of US$ 90 only, about 1/33 of that of America and 1/5 of the global average. Among the BRICS countries, China ranked nearly last, only higher than India, in terms of GDP per capita. Since China's economic

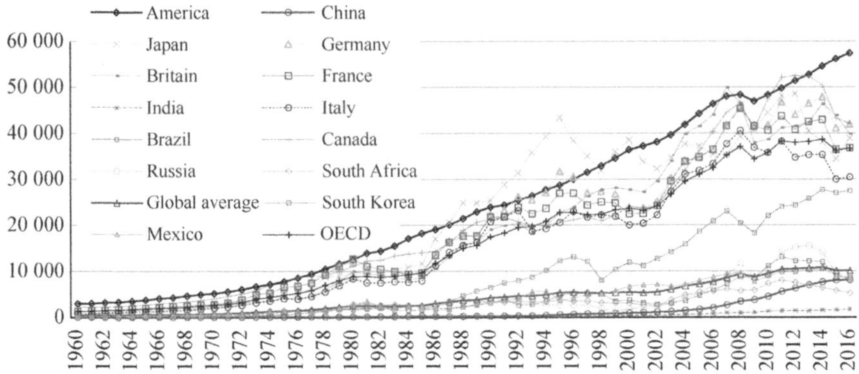

Figure 1.4 Variation in the nominal GDP per capita of major countries in the world: 1960–2016.

growth lagged behind that of other countries in the world during the period 1960–1977, its GDP per capita growth rates were lower than those of any country in Figure 1.5, with an increase of only US$ 95 in these 17 years. In 1977, China's GDP per capita was US$ 185, with only a difference of US$ 1 from India. This figure was less than 1/50 of that of America, representing 1/10 of the global average and roughly 1/8 of that of Brazil or South Africa. China's GDP per capita in US dollars had increased significantly by 2001 due to the fact that China had even higher GDP per capita growth rates than other countries in the world after its reform and opening-up in 1978. During the 24 years from 1977 to 2001, China's GDP per capita increased from the previous US$ 151 to 1,053, with an increase of more than US$ 900. In 2001, the GDP per capita of China was over twice as large as that of India, with the relative gap from Brazil and South Africa narrowed to about 1/3 of what

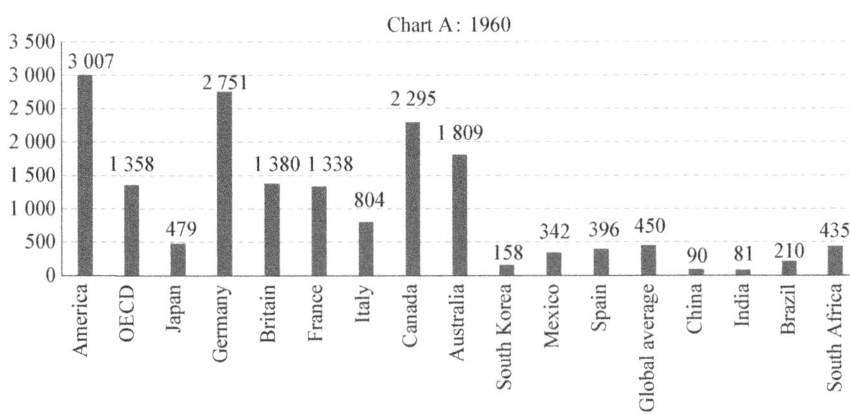

Figure 1.5 GDP per capita of major economies in the world in 1960, 1977, 2001, and 2016.

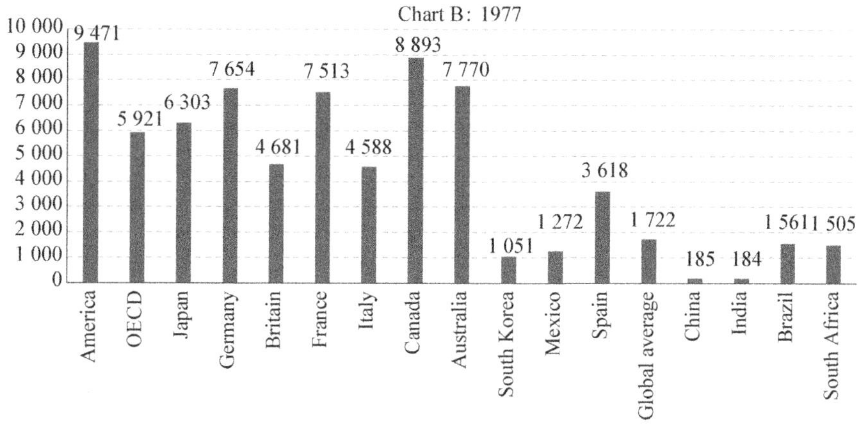

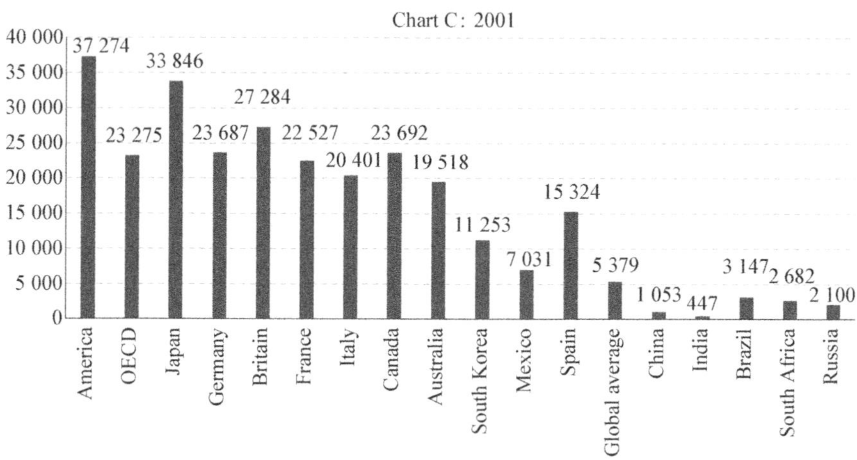

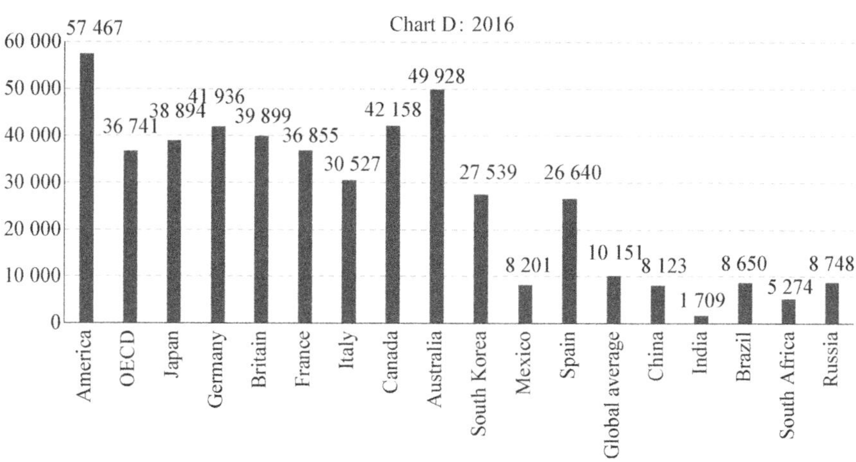

Figure 1.5 (Continued).

it was previously. However, since China had not yet joined the WTO, the degree of the country's openness was affected, thus resulting in low exchange rates. At that time, China lagged far behind from Brazil, South Africa, Russia and other BRICS countries, as well as European and American developed countries. In 2001, China's GDP per capita was about 1/35 of that of America and 1/5 of the global average. In 2016, 15 years after the country's accession to the WTO, under the dual impacts of high growth and sustained appreciation of RMB, China's GDP per capita reached US$ 8,000, making it 3rd in BRICS countries. That year, China's GDP per capita was about 1/10 of that of Brazil and Russia, respectively, which was also higher than that of India and South Africa and almost the same as the global average of US$ 10,000. However, China lagged far behind from developed countries. In 2016, China's GDP per capita was approximately 1/7 of that of America, 1/5 of that of Japan, and 1/3 of that of South Korea. Also, according to the data released by the World Bank in 2020, China had a GDP per capita of US$ 10,144 in 2019, making it 72nd in the rankings of 187 countries. According to the global GDP per capita for 2020 released by the World Monetary Fund (in US dollars then), in 2019, the global average GDP per capita was US$ 11,395 and the GDP per capita of China US$ 10,098, making the country 65th in the world.

Apparently, there is no absolute range of GDP per capita used to determine whether a country is a developing country or not. There is also no international organization that has explicitly proposed the concept of developing countries and identified them in laws. The UN has clearly identified the 50 least developed countries, but not given a precise definition of developing countries. According to the *World Development Indicators* released by the World Bank, all countries in the world are classified into three categories: high-income countries, middle-income countries, and low-income countries. Table 1.5 compares the average per capita GDP of countries in different income groups and that of China for the years 1960, 1977, 2001,

Table 1.5 The average GDP per capita of China and of the countries classified into different income groups (unit: US$)

	Least developed countries	*Low-income countries*	*Middle-income countries*			*Low & middle income countries*	*High-income countries*	*China*
			Lower-middle-income countries	*Middle-income countries*	*Upper-middle-income countries*			
1960	–	–	–	146.1	185.7	141.6	1,405	89.5
1977	–	–	314.5	521.4	698.3	500.9	7,552	185.4
2001	287.6	234.2	566.4	1,263.6	1,983.6	1,170.9	2,5341	1,053.1
2016	960.1	615.1	2,075.1	4,781.4	7,937.3	4,334.0	4,0678	8,123.2
2019	1070.1	689.7	2354.6	5481.4	9572.9	4999.7	45453.0	10143.8

Source: Source of raw data: the World Bank.

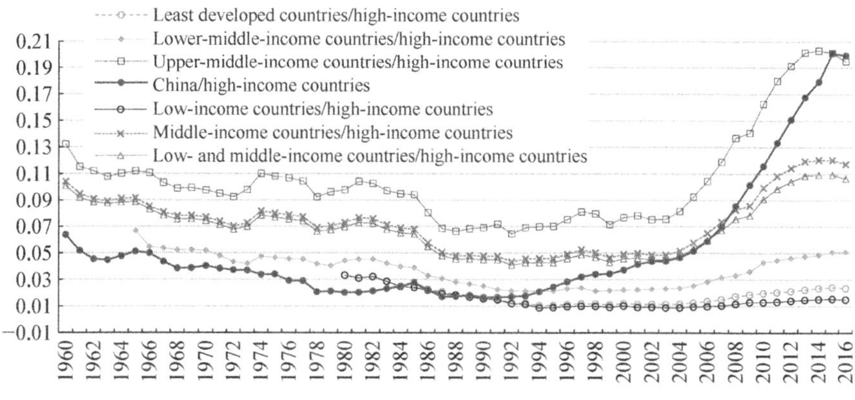

Figure 1.6 Variation in the ratios of average GDP per capita of different income groups to those of highest income groups: 1960–2016.

and 2016 according to the classification by the UN and the World Bank. Figure 1.6 shows the variation in the ratios of average GDP per capita for the countries classified into other income groups and that for the countries classified into the highest income group, as well as the variations in the ratios of average GDP per capita for China and those for the countries classified into the highest income group. As can be seen in Figure 1.6, China's GDP per capita had not reached the average level of low-income countries and least-developed countries till 1984. China's per capita was lower than this average during the period 1984–1991, exceeded this average starting from 1992, surpassed the average of lower-middle-income countries in 1995, reached the average of lower-middle-income countries in 2001, and exceeded the average of middle-income countries around 2008. Currently, China's GDP per capita is roughly equivalent to 20% of the average of high-income countries, at the average of upper-middle-income countries but within the middle-income group, and is still within the middle-income countries classified according to the criteria of the World Bank. According to the above analysis, through 40 years of development, China has jumped from a least developed low-income country to a country with high income per capita in the middle-income group. However, China still lags behind developed countries in terms of GDP per capita and remains a developing country.

The nominal GDP per capita for countries in each group is calculated based on the exchange rates of the year.

Notes

1 Note: The global economic growth rates calculated in US dollars overestimate the real global economic growth. There are two reasons for this. First, America itself accounts for a large share of global GDP, and the US dollar itself has inflations, thus making the global GDP denominated in US dollars show inflations.

Second, the economy of other countries grew faster than that of America, and their currencies appreciated relative to the US dollar, thus likely overestimating their GDP growth priced in US dollars.

2 Note: The price in US dollars may underestimate China's real economic growth rates during this period. That is because, during this period, Western countries adopted the blockage policy against China, which separated China's economy from the global economy and led to the continuous depreciation of the RMB in the international market. Therefore the RMB depreciation factor has been taken into account when calculating China's real growth rate denominated in US dollars, thus underestimating China's economic growth. The data in this chapter show that the real GDP growth rates calculated at the constant prices in China would be significantly higher than those priced in US dollars. Similarly, due to the sustained appreciation of the RMB against the US dollar since 2000, China's economic growth rate was overestimated when priced in US dollars. However, due to the fact that the substantial appreciation or depreciation of the RMB is also a manifestation of China's rise and fall in the world economy, the variation in GDP growth rates may fully reflect the variation of a country's comprehensive strength in the world.

3 CV refers to the standard deviation (or the square root of the variance) divided by the mean value of the variable. Affected by the mean value of the variable and the measuring unit of the variable, both variance and standard deviation measure the absolute fluctuation range of the variable. Mean value, especially the impact of the measuring unit for the variable, is not taken into account in the calculation of CV. As a dimensionless unit, CV measures the fluctuation range of the variable relative to the mean value. However, when the average of the CVs is very small, a large CV value may result in the case of a minor fluctuation range of the variable.

2 China's economic growth and people's livelihood after the reform

This chapter analyzes the changes in Chinese residents' living standards since 1978, and is organized as follows: The first section describes the overall changes in the disposable income per capita and consumption per capita of Chinese residents as well as in the Engel coefficients of Chinese residents; the second section discusses the changes in the living standards of Chinese urban residents since the reform and opening-up; and the third section analyzes the changes in the living standards of Chinese rural residents.

Section 1 Overview of the changes in Chinese residents' living standards

During the 40 years of reform and opening-up, the income and consumption levels of Chinese residents significantly improved, and the living standards per capita generally rose. According to the data of *China Statistical Yearbooks*, during the period 1978–2016, the nominal disposable income per capita of China's urban areas increased from 343 yuan to 33,616 yuan or about 5,060 yuan at the constant prices of 1978, up 13.75 times and with an average annual growth of 7.4%; that of the country's rural areas increased from 134 yuan to 12,363 yuan or about 2,149 yuan at the constant prices of 1978, up 15.03 times and with an average annual growth of 7.7%. The national consumption level per capita increased from 184 yuan to 21,228 yuan or about 3,383 yuan at the constant prices of 1978, up 17.39 times and with an average annual growth of 8.0%. In order to make the changes in Chinese residents' living standards clearer, Figures 2.1 and 2.2 show the changes in China's income and consumption levels per capita and their growth rates, respectively, since the adoption of reform and opening-up in 1978.

The consumption structure of residents in China has also improved. Take the Engel coefficients as an example. According to data from the *China Statistical Yearbooks*, the Engel coefficients of Chinese rural and urban residents in 1978 were 67.7% and 57.5%, respectively. During the 40 years of reform and opening-up, the Engel coefficients of the urban and rural

DOI: 10.4324/9781003261629-4

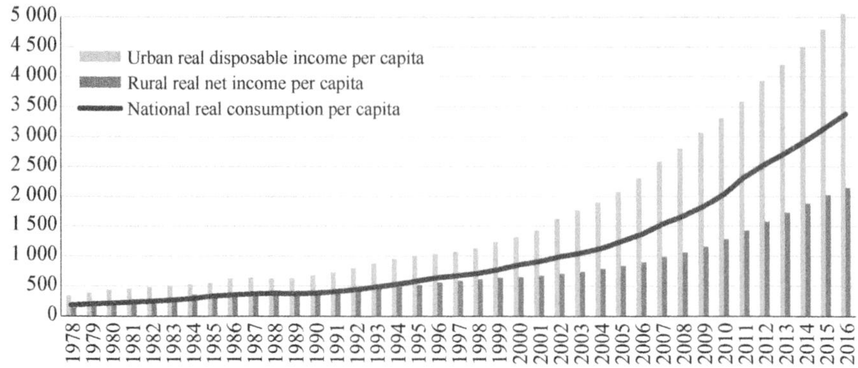

Figure 2.1 Disposable income per capita of urban residents, net income per capita of rural residents, and real consumption per capita in China: 1978–2016.

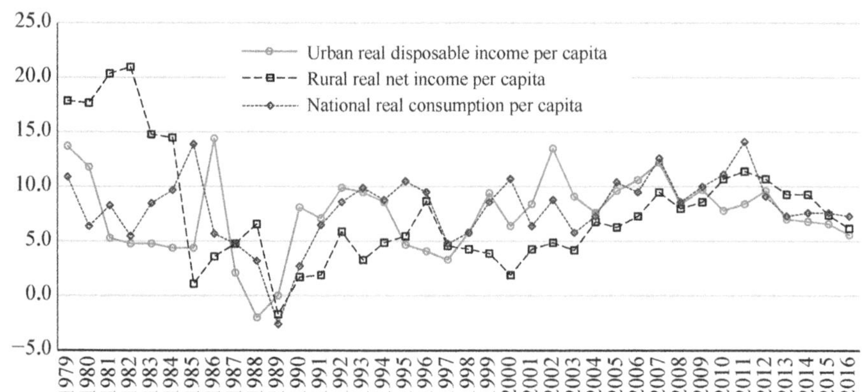

Figure 2.2 The growth rates of China's real income per capita and of consumption per capita: 1979–2016.

residents kept declining, as shown in Figure 2.3. In 2016, the Engel coefficients of urban and rural residents in China dropped to 32.2% and 29.3%, respectively. According to the standard of the Food and Agriculture Organization of the United Nations (FAO) on Engel coefficients, in terms of living standards, China basically ranked among the list of poor countries in the early period of the reform, entered the ranks of relatively rich countries in 2016, and is about to enter the ranks of rich countries. According to the data on economic research from the United States Department of Agriculture (USDA), China's Engel coefficient was even lower, only about 22.5%, as shown in Figure 2.4. Nevertheless, it should be pointed out that China still has low consumption per capita since it remains a developing country.

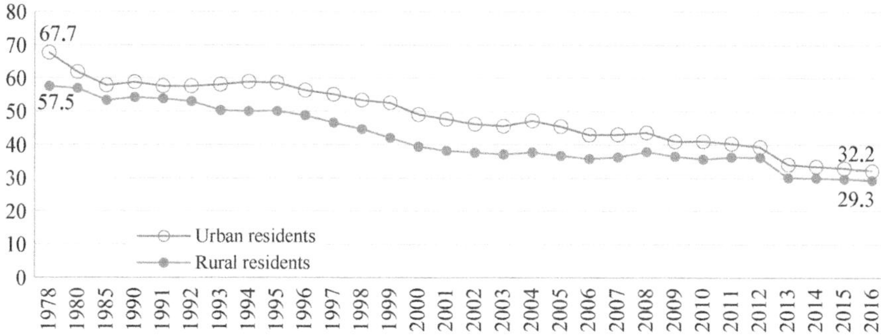

Figure 2.3 Income per capita and Engel coefficients of Chinese urban and rural residents: 1978–2016.

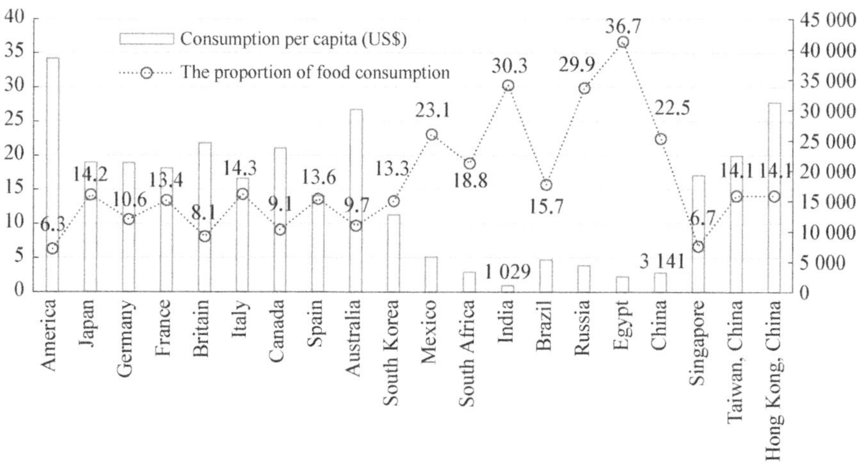

Figure 2.4 Consumption per capita and the proportion of food consumption for major economies and the Four Asian Tigers in 2016.

As can be seen in Figure 2.4, China's consumption per capita was only around US$ 3,000, far less than that of developed countries. The figure was even less than that of BRICS countries such as Mexico, Brazil, and Russia, and almost the same as that of South Africa and Egypt, but US$ 2,000 more than that of India. Since China adopts the typical dual urban-rural economy, there has long been a deep gap between the living standards of urban residents and those of rural residents in the country. The average living standards discussed, if China is regarded as a whole, may be quite different from those of Chinese urban and rural residents. The changes in the living standards of Chinese urban and rural residents are discussed below separately.

Section 2 Urban life changes in China

2.1 Changes in the overall income and consumption levels of Chinese urban residents

Figure 2.5 shows the changes in Chinese urban residents' real disposable income per capita, real consumption per capita, and the percentage of their consumption over disposable income during the period 1985–2016. As can be seen in this figure, during the above period, the disposable income per capita of Chinese urban residents was up 13.75 times, with an average annual growth of 7.34%. The real expenditure per capita of Chinese urban residents increased from 673 yuan in 1985 to 4,577 yuan in 2016, with an average annual growth of 6.38%. The ratio of consumption per capita to real disposable income (or average propensity to consume, abbreviated as "APC") dropped from 91% in 1985 to 69% in 2016. That is to say, more than 90% of the disposable income of Chinese urban residents in 1985 was used for the consumption of the current year, and most residents almost had no savings. In 2016, more than 30% of the annual disposable income of Chinese urban residents was saved. Thus, the income of Chinese residents has significantly increased relative to their consumption.

2.2 Changes in the consumption of Chinese urban residents

The consumption structure of Chinese urban residents has also continued to improve along with increases in consumption expenditure. Table 2.1 shows the changes in the total consumption per capita in each type of consumption in China's urban areas during the period 1985–2016. As seen from Table 2.1, the nominal consumption per capita in urban areas grew from 673 yuan to 23,079 yuan during the same period. At the constant prices of 1985,

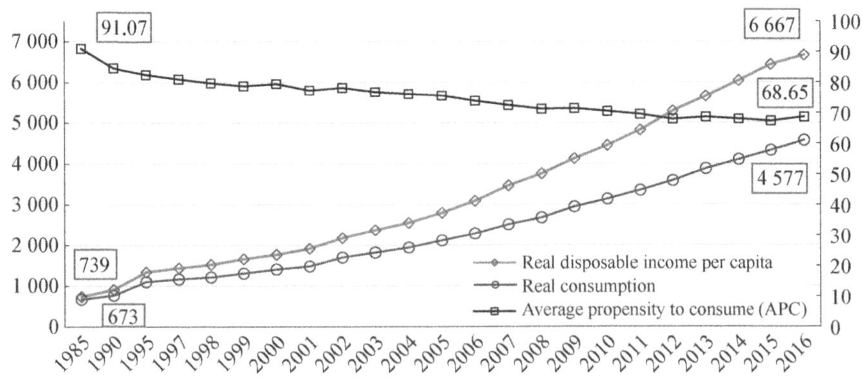

Figure 2.5 Changes in real disposable income per capita and real consumption per capita of Chinese urban residents: 1985–2016.

Table 2.1 Structure of consumption expenditures per capita of urban residents: 1985–2016 (unit: yuan)

Year	*Nominal consumption expenditure*	*Real consumption expenditure*	*Food*	*Clothing*	*Household goods & services*	*Health care & medical services*	*Transportation & communication*	*Culture, education & recreation*	*Housing*	*Other expenditures*
1985	673	673	352	98	58	17	14	55	32	47
1990	1,279	773	694	171	108	26	41	112	61	67
1995	3,538	1,105	1,772	479	263	110	183	331	284	115
1997	4,186	1,166	1,943	521	317	180	233	448	359	186
1998	4,332	1,214	1,927	481	357	205	257	499	408	197
1999	4,616	1,310	1,932	482	395	246	311	567	454	229
2000	4,998	1,407	1,971	500	374	318	427	670	565	172
2001	5,309	1,485	2,028	534	376	343	494	737	611	187
2002	6,030	1,703	2,272	591	389	430	626	902	624	196
2003	6,511	1,823	2,417	638	410	476	721	934	699	215
2004	7,182	1,946	2,710	687	407	528	844	1,033	734	240
2005	7,943	2,119	2,914	801	447	601	997	1,097	809	278
2006	8,697	2,286	3,112	902	498	621	1,147	1,203	904	309
2007	9,997	2,514	3,628	1,042	602	699	1,357	1,329	982	358
2008	11,243	2,678	4,260	1,166	692	786	1,417	1,358	1,145	418
2009	12,265	2,948	4,479	1,284	787	856	1,683	1,473	1,229	474
2010	13,471	3,137	4,805	1,444	908	872	1,984	1,628	1,332	499
2011	15,161	3,353	5,506	1,675	1,023	969	2,150	1,852	1,405	581
2012	16,674	3,590	6,041	1,823	1,116	1,064	2,456	2,034	1,484	657
2013	18,488	3,880	5,571	1,554	1,129	1,136	2,318	1,988	4,301	490
2014	19,968	4,104	6,000	1,627	1,233	1,306	2,637	2,142	4,490	533
2015	21,392	4,332	6,360	1,707	1,307	1,443	2,895	2,383	4,726	572
2016	23,079	4,577	6,762	1,739	1,427	1,631	3,174	2,638	5,114	595
Growth multiple	33.3	5.8	18.2	16.7	23.6	94.9	225.7	47.0	158.8	11.7

Source: Source for raw data: *China Statistical Yearbooks*;
Real consumption expenditure per capita is calculated on the basis of the constant prices of 1985 and is the nominal consumption expenditure per capita divided by the urban consumer price index. The consumption expenditure per capita for each category is a nominal value and is the product of the nominal consumption expenditure of the year multiplied by the share of the corresponding category given in *China Statistical Yearbooks*.

the real consumption per capita for urban areas in 2016 was 4,577 yuan, up six times relative to that of 1985, with an average annual growth of 6.38%. The consumption of various categories for urban households also increased. As the level of people's consumption demand would be lifted along with the increase in their income and consumption levels, the growth rates of urban residents' consumption by category are different. According to Table 2.1, the changes in the consumption of urban residents conform to the law of development from low to high levels in relation to food, clothing, housing, and transportation. During the years 1985–2016, food and clothing expenditures were up 16.7 times and 18.2 times, respectively, whose growth was slower than the total consumption growth, as well as was the household goods and services growth. Both housing expenditures and transportation & communication expenditures were up 155.8 times and 225.7 times, far exceeding the total consumption growth. The other two categories whose growth exceeded the growth of total consumption were health care & medical services and culture, education & recreation, up 94.9 times and 47 times, respectively.

In the case of constant supply, goods prices change along with demand. Thus, the increased consumption of residents would affect the total expenditure of different consumption categories through two factors, namely demand and price. Since the price factor has been included in nominal consumption, the changes in consumption structure will be exaggerated only if the nominal growth rates of various expenditures are compared. In order to further analyze the changes in the consumption structure of urban residents, the changes in the proportions of various categories of consumption in the total consumption will be further analyzed below. Figures 2.6 and 2.7 give the consumption structure charts of Chinese urban residents in the years 1985, 2001, and 2016 and the changes in the proportions of cash expenditure of Chinese urban residents during the period 1985–2016. As indicated in Figure 2.6, in 1985, most of the consumption of Chinese urban residents was spent on food, clothing, and other necessities of life. To the total expenditure, food contributed 52%, clothing 15%, and household goods & services 9%, with a total share of 76%; health care & medical services and transportation & communication contributed only 2% each, and culture, education & recreation only 8%. This is a typical subsistence type consumption structure. In 2001, among the consumption of urban residents, the contributions of food and clothing dropped to 38% and 10%, respectively, with a total share of less than 50%; the contribution of household goods & services dropped to 7%; the contributions of health care & medical services, transportation & communication, culture, education & recreation increased to 6%, 9% and 14%, respectively; and the contribution of housing increased from 5% in 1985 to 12% in the year. It can be said that, by 2001, among the consumption of Chinese urban residents, expenditures in pursuit of life quality, such as health care & medical services, transportation & communication, and culture, education & recreation, had increased to a large extent. Residents had transitioned from the pursuit of food and

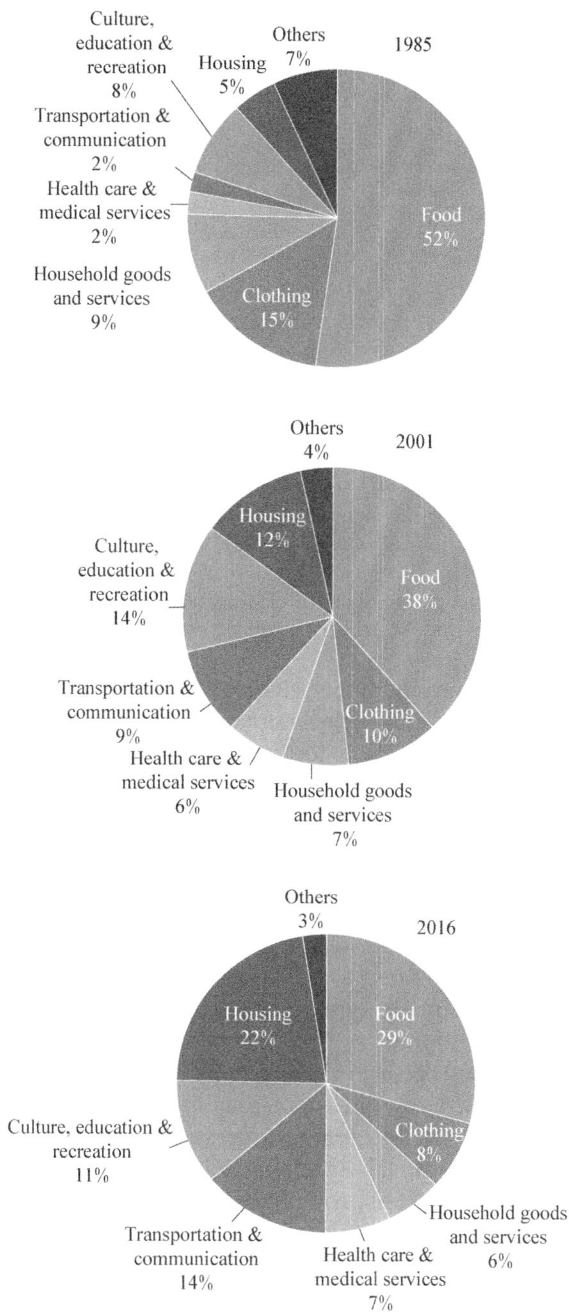

Figure 2.6 The structure of total consumption expenditure per capita of Chinese urban residents: 1985–2016.

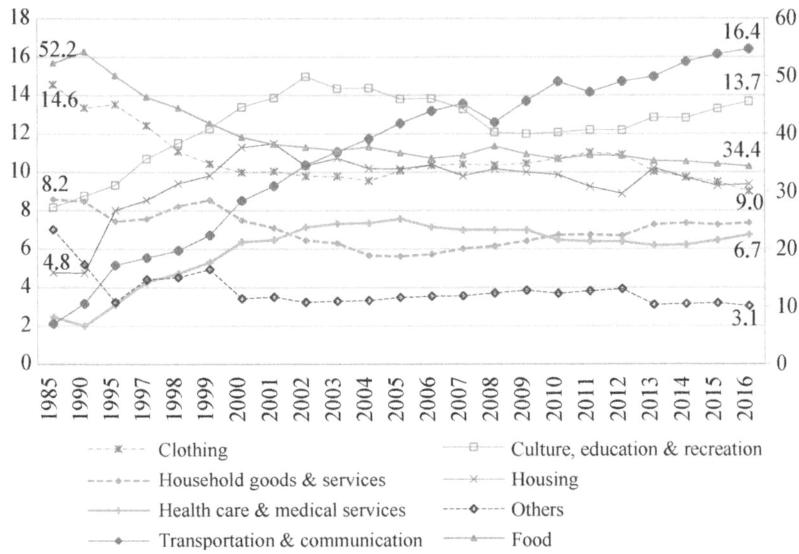

Figure 2.7 Changes in the proportions of cash expenditures over the total cash expenditure of Chinese urban residents: 1985–2016.

clothing adequacy to the enjoyment-centric stage of life in pursuit of interpersonal communication and social recreation. In 2016, the proportions of urban residents' expenditures on food, clothing, and household goods & services continued to drop to 29%, 8%, and 6%, respectively, with a total share of about 44%; those of health care & medical services and transportation & communication rose to 7% and 14%, respectively; and the proportion of housing expenditure witnessed a significant rise, to 22%, becoming second to food expenditure in urban residents' consumption; but that of expenditure on culture, education & recreation dropped to 11%. Thus, Chinese urban residents graduated to the stage of living and working in peace and contentment in terms of living consumption, and mainly focused on housing and transportation.

As can be seen in the structure of consumption per capita of Chinese urban residents shown in Figure 2.7, the proportion of food expenditure kept declining during the period 1985–2016, reaching the fastest speed in the 1990s, along with that of food expenditure. The proportion of transportation & communication expenditure had been growing fast almost all the time, except the year 2008. The proportions of expenditures on culture, education & recreation and health care & medical services first increased and then decreased, which may be primarily related to China's education system reform and medical system reform. The popularization of government-funded compulsory education may be the cause for the drop in the education expenditure for the years following 2000. Subsequently, the expansion and popularization of higher education may be the main reason for the increase in the proportion of education expenditure for the years after 2010. Likewise, the changes in the proportion of health care & medical services expenditures may be subject to the influence of medical insurance system, although the increase in income had also attracted a wider attention of residents towards health care & medical services. After 1985, the health and medical expenses for urban residents increased significantly due to the gradual transformation of government-funded to self-funded medical treatment for urban residents and the restrictions imposed on residents through the medical insurance system reform. However, with the continuous improvement of the medical insurance system, the proportion of urban residents' health care & medical services expenditure declined again. Similarly, housing expenditures were affected by the housing system reform. Before and in the early period of the reform and opening-up, the houses of urban residents were provided by their employers, with a few rents if any. Subsequently, following the commercialization and privatization of houses, as well as the increases in housing prices and rents, the proportion of housing expenditure rose fast. Certainly, as the data in Figure 2.7 show the proportion of cash expenditure on housing increased rather than decreased after 2001 due to the increase in the share of self-owned houses following the housing reform. However, the rightmost chart for 2016, as shown in Figure 2.6, indicates that housing consumption was already been very high in terms of its proportion of the total consumption.

2.3 Structural changes in the food and consumer durable expenditures of Chinese urban residents

The abovementioned changes in people's livelihoods show that the living conditions of Chinese urban residents have greatly improved since the adoption of reform and opening-up. However, the analysis of the above figures may be comparatively abstract. Also, the impact of price changes may lead to deviations between monetary amounts and actual living standards. The improvement of the living standards of Chinese urban residents are analyzed in more detail through the physical quantity of consumer goods.

Figure 2.8 shows the changes in the number of major goods purchased by a Chinese urban resident on average throughout the years 1985–2016. As can be seen from Figure 2.8, among the food consumed by Chinese urban residents in 1985, grain and vegetables were the main one. On average, each urban resident consumed 134.8 kg of grain and 144.4 kg of vegetables every year but only 18.7 kg of meat every year or about 50 g every day; and 7.1 kg of aquatic products, 5.8 kg of edible oil, and 3.2 kg of poultry every year. Fresh eggs, fruits, and fresh milk are not included in the statistical scope of the *China Statistical Yearbook* that year. In 1990, the annual consumption of fresh eggs, melons & fruits, and dairy products per capita for urban residents was only 9.74 kg (this data for the year 1995 were sourced), 41.1 kg, and 4.6 kg. It can be said that in 1985, Chinese urban residents still adopted

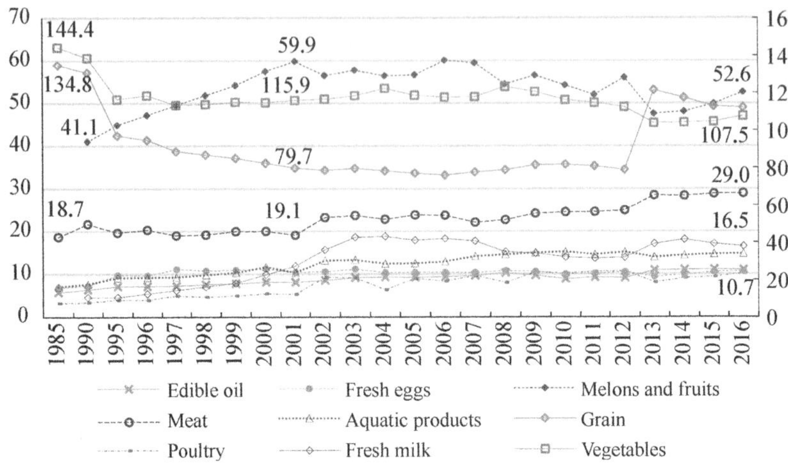

Figure 2.8 Amount of main goods purchased by every urban resident in China on average: 1978–2016.

a subsistence type lifestyle, with grain, vegetables, and other vegetarian food as their main food and aimed at alleviating hunger. During the period 1985–2001, the consumption of grain and vegetables of Chinese urban residents witnessed a rapid drop; that of edible oil, melons & fruits, fresh milk, poultry, and aquatic products increased significantly; while that of meat and fresh eggs stayed almost the same. In 2001, the annual consumption of food and vegetables per capita of Chinese urban residents was 79.7 kg and 115.9 kg, respectively; that of edible oil, melons & fruits, fresh milk, poultry, and aquatic products was 8.1 kg, 59.9 kg, 11.9 kg, 5.3 kg, and 10.3 kg; and that of meat and fresh eggs was 19.1 kg and 10.1 kg. In that year, the food consumed by Chinese urban residents tended to be diversified; grain consumption was cut in half compared to that of 1985; melons, fruits, and meat accounted for a certain proportion over people's nutrition, but grain and vegetables were still the major food. During the period 2001–2016, meat consumption among Chinese urban residents changed the most. In 2016, the annual consumption of meat per capita was 29 kg, representing an increase of more than 50% compared to that of 2001. Meat was followed by poultry and aquatic products, whose consumption grew from 5.3 kg in 2001 to 10.2 kg in 2016, about a two-fold increase. The consumption of aquatic products grew from 10.3 kg to 14.8 kg, with an increase of approximately 40%. Milk consumption first rose and then declined. This figure was 16.56 kg in 2016, an increase of about 40% in contrast to that of the year 2001. There was not much change for fresh eggs and edible oil. The consumption of grain, vegetables, and fruits showed a downward trend. As can be seen, Chinese urban residents changed their food consumption mode to meat-based in 2016.

Table 2.2 Housing area per capita of urban residents and average amount of consumer durables owned by every 100 urban households

Year	*1985*	*1990*	*1995*	*2000*	*2005*	*2010*	*2015*
Sewing machine (set)	70.82	70.14	63.67	51.46	–	–	–
Wool coat (piece)	116.2	169.98	204.15	169.63	–	–	–
Blanket (piece)	86.79	123.82	139.75	143.27	–	–	–
Large wardrobe (piece)	102.08	99.85	88.3	83.45	–	–	–
Sofa (piece)	131.49	157.3	210.12	198.82	–	–	–
Writing desk (piece)	80.06	87.23	88.14	83.44	–	–	–
Bicycle/electric bicycle (unit)	152.3	188.6	194.3	162.7	–	–	45.8[a]
Motorcycle (unit)	–	1.9	6.3	18.8	24.8	22.5	22.7
Private car (unit)	–	–	–	0.5	3.4	13.1	30
Electric fan (set)	73.9	135.5	167.4	167.9	–	–	–
Air conditioner (set)	–	0.3	8.1	30.8	80.7	112.1	114.6
Washing machine (set)	48.3	78.4	89	90.5	95.9	96.9	92.3
Refrigerator (set)	6.6	42.3	66.2	80.1	90.2	96.6	94
Color TV (set)	17.2	59	89.8	116.6	133.4	137.4	122.3
Camera (set)	8.5	19.2	30.6	38.4	46.9	43.5	33
Mobile phone (unit)	–	–	–	19.5	137	188.9	223
Home computer (set)	–	–	–	9.7	41.5	71.2	78.5
Water heater (set)	–	–	30.1	49.1	72.7	84.8	85.6
Housing area per capita (square meter)	10	13.7	16.3	20.3	27.8	32.7	36.6[b]

Source: *China Statistical Yearbooks*. Since no bicycle data is included in the *China Statistical Yearbooks* for the years after 2001, no data before 2013 is available.

[a] Data for electric bicycles; there is no data of housing area per capita of Chinese urban residents after 2012;

[b] The data of 2016 published by the National Bureau of Statistics of China in 2017.

Table 2.2 shows the housing area per capita of Chinese urban residents and the amount of consumer durables owned by per 100 households at year-enduring the period 1985–2016. According to Table 2.2, in 1985, the consumer durables with a penetration rate exceeding 50% mainly included bicycles (152.3 units per 100 households), electric fans (73.9 sets per 100 households), sewing machines (70.82 sets per 100 households) and wool coats (116.2 pieces per 100 households), blankets (86.79 pieces per 100 households), large wardrobes (102.08 pieces per 100 households), sofas (131.49 pieces per 100 households), and writing desks (80.06 pieces per 100 households). Other consumer durables at a slightly higher end were quite low in ownership rate, including washing machines (48.3 sets per 100 households), refrigerators (6.6 sets per 100 households), and color TVs (17.2 sets per 100 households) and cameras (8.5 sets per 100 households). These products may have been luxury goods at that time and may have only been owned by rich households. The housing area per capita then was only 10 square meters. By 2000, bicycles, sewing machines, large wardrobes, writing desks, and other items had been gradually replaced or eliminated, and wool coats, blankets, sofas, and electric fans had been basically popularized. These durables were excluded in the *China Statistical Yearbooks* for the years following 2001. In 2000, major consumer durables in the homes of Chinese urban residents were changed to washing machines (90.5 sets per 100 households), refrigerators (80.1 sets per 100 households), and color TVs (116.6 sets per 100 households); the ownership rate of air conditioners (30.8 sets per 100 households), cameras (38.4 sets per 100 households), and water heaters (49.1 sets per 100 households) exceeded 30% each; middle- and high-income households started to buy motorcycles (0.5 unit per 100 households), mobile phones (19.5 units per 100 households), home computers (9.7 sets per 100 households), and private cars (18.8 units per 100 households) started to be included in the goods consumed by urban residents. In that year, the housing area per capita reached 16.3 square meters, an increase of over 60% compared to that of the year 1985. By 2016, in the homes of Chinese urban residents, mobile phones (223 units per 100 households), air conditioners (114.6 sets per 100 households), refrigerators (94 sets per 100 households), water heaters (85.6 sets per 100 households), washing machines (96.2 sets per 100 households), and color TVs (122.3 sets per 100 households) had been basically popularized; in terms of travel, the original mode of human-powered travel, such as on foot and by bicycle, had been upgraded to automated travel, such as electric bicycle (45.8 units per 100 households), motorcycle (22.7 units per 100 households), and private car (30 units per 100 households); the popularization rate of home computers arrived at 78.5 sets per 100 households; and the housing area per capita increased to 36.6 square meters. Thus, it can be seen that Chinese urban households have now reached the state of automated travel, electrical appliances, wireless communication, and online entertainment.

Section 3 Changes in the life of Chinese rural residents

3.1 Changes in the overall income and consumption levels of rural residents

Figure 2.9 shows the changes in the net income per capita, real consumption per capita, and average propensity to consume (APC) of Chinese rural residents during the period 1978–2016. As can be seen in the figure, in 1978, Chinese rural residents only had a net income per capita of 134 yuan and consumption per capita of 116 yuan, with an APC of 86.6%. During this period, both net income per capita and consumption per capita of Chinese rural residents kept rising. In 2016, the real net income per capita in China's rural areas increased to 2,149 yuan, up 15.0 times over 1978, with an average annual growth of 7.58%. The real consumption per capita in rural areas reached 1,649 yuan, up 13.2 times over 1978, with an average annual growth of 7.23%. The APC of rural residents showed a weak trend of fluctuations. In 2016, the APC of Chinese rural residents was 85.7%, basically the same as that of 1978, with only a decrease of 0.9 percentage point.

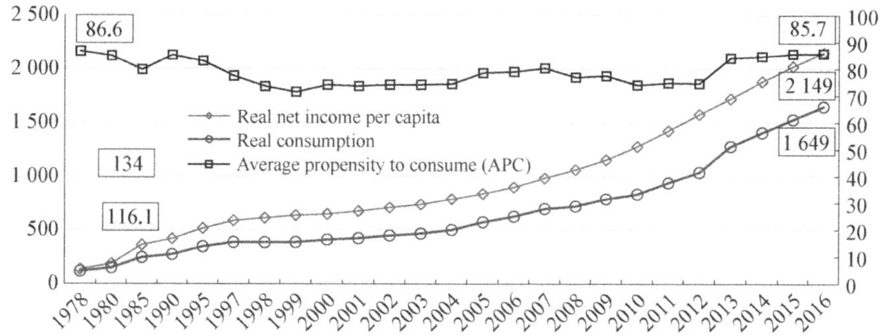

Figure 2.9 Real net income per capita and consumption expenditure per capita in China's rural areas: 1978–2016.

3.2 Structural changes in the consumption of Chinese rural residents

Table 2.3 shows the changes in the consumption per capita of Chinese rural residents and its structure during the period 1978–2016. According to the table, during this period, the nominal consumption per capita of Chinese rural residents grew from 116.1 yuan to 10,130 yuan or 1,649 yuan at the constant prices of 1978, up over 13.2 times, with an average annual growth of 7.23%. The increase in income had been followed by the increase in rural residents' consumption level, just like that of urban residents. As seen in Table 2.3, rural residents' expenditures on housing and on transportation & communication were up 178 times and 125 times over those of 1978; those on culture, education & recreation and health care & medical services were up 85 times and 120 times, with both growth rates higher than the growth multiple of total consumption. However, the growth rates of food, clothing, and household goods expenditures were all much lower than the growth multiple of the total consumption (up 41 times, 38 times and 36 times, respectively, less than half of the total consumption growth multiple).

Since the nominal consumption involves the price factor, both absolute price increase and relative price changes will affect the analysis of the changes in the consumption structure based on nominal expenditure. Thus, it is not enough to analyze the real changes in the consumption structure by comparing the nominal growth rates of different expenditure categories. In order to analyze the changes in the consumption structure of Chinese rural residents, the changes in the proportions of various consumption categories over the total consumption are further analyzed below. Figures 2.10 and 2.11 give the consumption charts of Chinese rural residents in 1985, 2001, and 2016, as well as the changes in the proportions of Chinese rural residents' consumption by cash during the period 1978–2016.

As known from Figure 2.10, among the income of Chinese rural residents in 1985, most were spent on food, clothing, and other daily necessities. Among

Table 2.3 The structure of consumption expenditures per capita of rural residents: 1978–2016 (unit: yuan)

Year	*Nominal consumption expenditure*	*Real consumption expenditure*	*Food*	*Clothing*	*Housing*	*Household goods & services*	*Transportation & communication*	*Culture, education & recreation*	*Health care & medical services*	*Other expenditures*
1978	116.1	116.1	78.6	14.7	12.0	–	10.8	–	–	–
1980	162.2	147.9	100.2	20.0	22.5	–	19.6	–	–	–
1985	317.4	244.3	183.4	30.9	57.9	16.3	5.5	12.5	7.7	3.4
1990	584.6	272.8	343.8	45.4	101.4	30.9	8.4	31.4	19.0	4.3
1995	1,310	346.2	768.2	89.8	182.2	68.5	33.8	102.4	42.5	23.1
1997	1,617	386.4	890.3	109.4	233.2	85.4	53.9	148.2	62.5	34.3
1998	1,590	383.8	849.6	98.1	239.6	81.9	60.7	159.4	68.1	32.9
1999	1,577	386.4	829.0	92.0	232.7	82.3	68.7	168.3	70.0	34.3
2000	1,670	409.6	820.5	95.9	258.3	75.4	93.1	186.7	87.6	52.4
2001	1,741	423.6	830.7	98.7	279.1	77.0	110.0	192.6	96.6	56.4
2002	1,834	448.0	848.4	105.0	300.2	80.4	128.5	210.4	103.9	57.7
2003	1,943	467.1	886.0	110.3	308.4	81.7	162.5	235.7	115.8	43.0
2004	2,185	501.1	1,032	120.2	324.2	89.1	192.7	247.5	130.6	48.3
2005	2,555	573.4	1,162	148.6	370.2	111.4	245.0	295.5	168.1	54.5
2006	2,829	625.5	1,217	168.0	469.0	126.6	288.8	305.1	191.5	63.1
2007	3,324	697.3	1,432	199.5	591.6	153.8	338.6	315.1	216.8	76.5
2008	3,661	721.1	1,599	212.0	678.7	173.9	360.2	314.5	246.0	76.5
2009	3,994	789.0	1,636	232.4	805.1	204.9	402.9	340.6	287.5	84.3

2010	4,382	835.6	1,801	264.0	835.2	234.1	461.1	366.7	326.0	94.0
2011	5,221	941.1	2,109	339.4	960.7	308.0	548.2	396.8	438.6	120.1
2012	5,908	1,039	2,322	395.8	1,087	342.7	649.9	443.1	514.0	147.7
2013[a]	6,626	1,133	2,496	438.3	1,234	387.1	796.0	486.0	614.2	174.9
2013[b]	7,485	1,280	2,554	453.8	1,580	455.1	874.9	754.6	668.2	144.3
2014	8,383	1,409	2,814	510.4	1,763	506.5	1,013	859.5	753.9	163.0
2015	9,223	1,530	3,048	550.5	1,926	545.6	1,163	969.3	846.0	173.9
2016	10,130	1,649	3,266	575.4	2,147	595.7	1,360	1,070	929.2	186.1
Growth multiple	86.25	13.20	40.55	38.14	177.9	35.55[c]	124.9	84.60[c]	119.7[c]	53.74[c]

Source: Source for raw data: *China Statistical Yearbooks*;

[a] Real consumption expenditure per capita is calculated on the basis of the constant prices of 1978 and is the nominal consumption expenditure per capita divided by the rural consumer price index. The consumption expenditure for each category is a nominal value, which is obtained by multiplying the nominal consumption expenditure of the year by the proportion of each category given in the corresponding *China Statistical Yearbooks*.

[b] The *China Statistical Yearbooks* for 2014 and previous years show the survey results of rural residents given by the National Bureau of Statistics of China, while the data of rural consumption expenditure per capita in *China Statistical Yearbook 2015* give the results of survey made by the bureau on the income, expenditure and living conditions of urban-rural integration households, with the data starting from 2013. Therefore, there are two data items in *China Statistical Yearbook 2013*. For facilitation of comparisons, both are listed in the table.

[c] Row a is the data from *China Statistical Yearbook 2014*; b is the data from *China Statistical Yearbook 2015*.
These four items are all growth multiples relative to those of 1985.

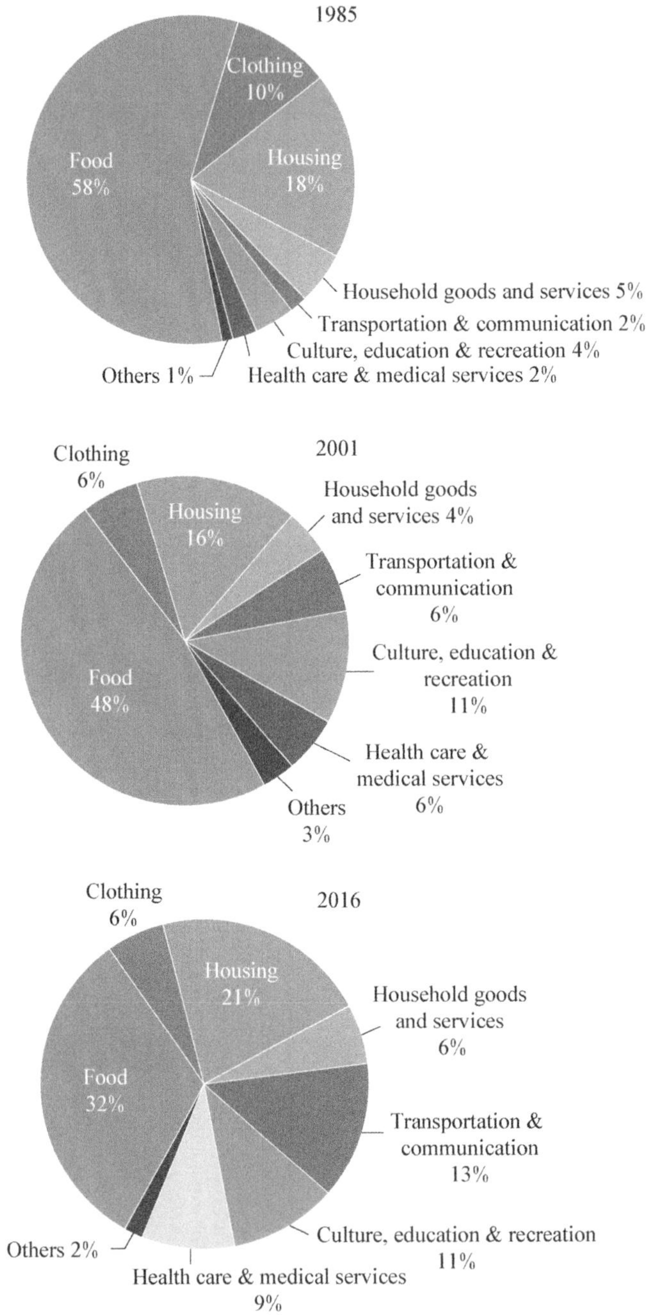

Figure 2.10 Structure of consumption expenditures per capita of Chinese rural residents: 1985–2016.

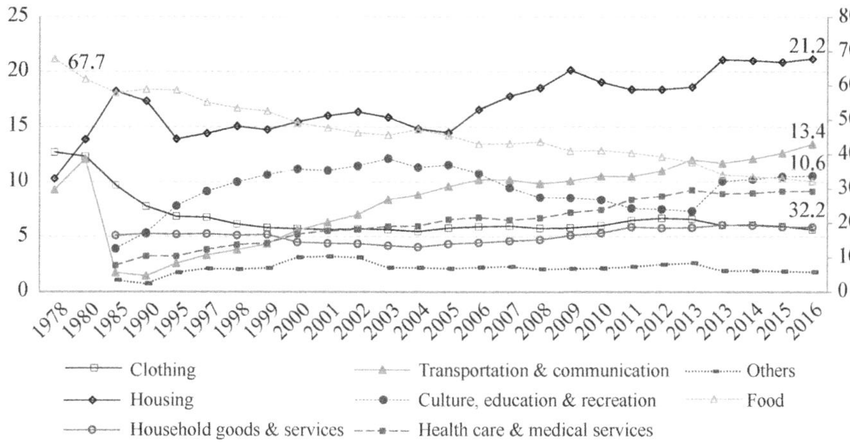

Figure 2.11 Changes in the proportions of various expenditure categories of Chinese rural residents over the total expenditure: 1978–2016.

them, food contributed 58%, clothing 10%, and household goods & services 5%, with a total contribution of 73% to the total consumption. Health care & medical services and transportation & communication contributed only 2% of the total consumption each, and culture, education & recreation only 4% of the total. This consumption structure, quite similar to that of Chinese urban residents during the same period, is a typical subsistence type consumption structure. In contrast, the housing expenditure of Chinese rural residents during this period had a share of 18% of the total consumption, higher than that of urban residents in the same period, but had a smaller proportion of clothing, household goods & service. In 2001, in the total consumption of Chinese rural residents, the proportions of food and clothing expenditures dropped to 48% and 6%, respectively, with an aggregate share of 54% over the total consumption; the proportion of household goods & services expenditure dropped to 4%; that of health care & medical services, transportation & communication, culture, education & recreation increased to 6%, 6%, and 11%, respectively; and that of housing expenditure dropped from 18% in 1985 to 16% in the year. Expenditures on culture, education & entertainment, transportation & communication, health care & medical services, which focus on quality of life, greatly increased in rural areas, similar to those of Chinese urban residents. And rural residents had started to graduate to a different stage of life, from the phase of food and clothing adequacy to the well-off stage where the quality of life such as interpersonal communication and social recreation had been improved. In 2016, the proportions of food, clothing, household goods& services of Chinese rural residents of the total consumption dropped to 32%, 6%, and 6%, respectively, with a total share of approximately 44% over the three necessities. The proportions of expenditures on health care & medical services and transportation & communication increased by 9% and 13%, respectively; the proportion of housing expenditure increased significantly to 21%, becoming second to food expenditure in residents' consumption; and the proportion of culture, education & recreation remained unchanged at 11%. Thus, basically similar to the consumption structure of Chinese urban residents, the living consumption of Chinese rural residents developed into a stage of living and working in peace and contentment, with a focus on housing and travel.

Also, as can be seen from Figure 2.11, firstly, in the structure of consumption per capita of Chinese rural residents, the proportion of food expenditure kept declining from 58% in 1978 to 32% in 2016, except for the years 1985–1995, although the decline rate varied from period to period. The decrease in the proportion of clothing expenditure continued over this period but reached the fastest speed during 1978–2000 and became insignificant following 2001. It can be seen that the proportions of food and clothing expenditures declined with the increase in rural residents' income, which is in line with the general consumption law.

Secondly, the proportion of household goods & services expenditure had a tendency to fluctuate. This figure first declined (1985–2003), then rose (2003–2013), and then declined again (2013–2016). However, the fluctuation range during the period 1978–2016 was not large and had a difference between the peak and bottom values of only 1.1 percentage points. In addition, the proportion of rural residents' expenditure on household goods & services in 2016 increased by 0.9 percentage point compared with that in 1978. In contrast to the fluctuations in the proportion of household goods & services, the proportion of expenditure on culture, education & recreation first rose (1985–2003), then declined (2004–2013) and then rose again (2014–2016) and fluctuated most, with the difference between the peak value of 12.1% in 2003 and the bottom value of 7.3% in 2013 being nearly 5 percentage points. The dramatic fluctuations in the proportion of expenditure on culture, education & recreation may be correlated with China's education system reform, just like those of urban residents. In the early stage of reform and opening-up, on the one hand, as China's primary education costs came to be borne by rural residents themselves, the primary education type was gradually shifted from government funding to semi self-funding and self-funding, and the increase of prices following the price system reform caused tuitions to rise; on the other hand, the increase in income also raised the education needs of rural residents. Both factors contributed to the increase in the education expenditure of rural residents. Since 2003, due to the popularization of national compulsory education and then the free access to compulsory education, education expenditure has been reduced from the supply side. Additionally, the decreasing enthusiasm of rural residents toward receiving higher education due to the ending of job assignment upon their graduation from college and the lowered demand for primary education followed by the decrease in the number of rural children have also reduced the education expenditure of rural residents on the demand side. Both factors, supply and demand, jointly contributed to a rapid decline in the proportion of rural residents' education expenditure. Once the two drivers reached equilibrium, the increase in residents' income would lead to an increase in education and recreation demand and also a slow rise in the proportion of expenditure on culture, education & recreation.

Thirdly, the trend for proportions of expenditures on transportation & communication, health care & medical services, and housing showed a significant increase. Among the three, the proportion of transportation & communication expenditure grew at the fastest speed. During the period 1985–2016, the proportion of this expenditure almost rose at a constant rate, except for during the years 1980–1985 and 2008. In 1985, the transportation & communication expenditure of Chinese rural residents accounted for only 1.7%, an almost insignificant part of the total consumption. In 2016, the figure rose to 13.4% and became a very important aspect of the consumption of rural residents. During the nearly 40 years since the reform, the proportion of transportation & communication expenditure has increased by nearly 12 percentage points. During the period 1978–2016, the proportion of rural residents' housing expenditure also increased significantly, from 10.3% to 21.2%, representing an increase of 10 percentage points. However, unlike the changing proportion of transportation & communication expenditure, the proportion of housing expenditure showed substantial fluctuations. It first rose rapidly from 10.3% in 1978 to 18% in 1985; then dropped in the following ten consecutive years to 14% in 1995; then gradually rose in the following seven years to 16.4% in 2002; then dropped to 14.5% in 2005, rose to 20.2% in 2009, and then dropped slightly to 18.6% in 2013 and finally jumped to 21.2% in 2016. Although the expenditure on health care & medical services of rural residents was on the rise during the period 1978–2016, the increase was much smaller than the former two. Additionally, with the improvement of the rural medical insurance system in recent years, the proportion of rural residents' expenditure on health care & medical services has tended to drop. Specifically, the proportion of rural residents' expenditure on health care & medical services was about 2.4% in 1985, reached the peak in 2013 (about 9.27%), and slightly dropped in the following three years, arriving at 9.17% in 2016. For Chinese rural residents, such expenditure has approximately increased by 7 percentage points over the past 30 years.

3.3 Changes in the food and durable consumption structure of Chinese rural residents

As mentioned earlier, the above analysis regarding changes in residents' lifestyles, as measured by the monetary amount, may be comparatively abstract and vulnerable to the changes in prices. The following will be a further analysis of the changes in the life of Chinese rural residents through the physical quantity of consumer goods.

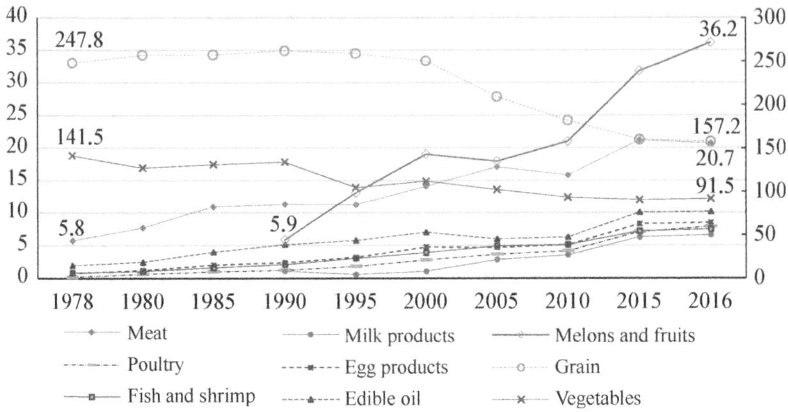

Figure 2.12 Annual consumption of major consumer goods per capita in Chinese rural households: 1978–2016.

Figure 2.12 shows the changes in the amount of major food purchased by each person in China's rural households on average during the period 1978–2016. As can be seen from Figure 2.12, among the food consumed by Chinese rural residents in 1978, grain and vegetables were the most important. The average annual consumption of grain and vegetables per capita was 247.8 kg and 141.5 kg, respectively; the average annual consumption of meat per capita was only 5.8 kg, equivalent to the average monthly consumption per capita of less than 0.5 kg; the average annual consumption of edible oil per capita was only 2 kg; and the average annual consumption of poultry, eggs, fish, shrimp, and dairy products, etc., per capita was less than 1 kg each. The consumption of melons and fruits is excluded from the scope of statistics, and may be mainly based on the mode of self-production and self-distribution featuring self-planting or collection of natural products. It can be seen that the Chinese rural residents in 1978 were basically "vegetarians" whose main goal was to fill their stomachs.

During the period 1978–1990, grain and vegetables remained the most important food for rural residents. Among the total consumption, food consumption kept rising, from 247.8 kg per capita in 1978 to 261.2 kg per capita in 1990; vegetable consumption per capita dropped significantly during the same period, with a slightly upward trend in the years 1980–1990. The consumption of meat, poultry, dairy products, egg products, fish, shrimp, and other goods also decreased during this period. In 1990, the consumption of grain and vegetables by Chinese rural residents reached its peak, with annual consumption per capita of 261.2 kg and 134.0 kg, respectively; the annual meat consumption per capita increased to 11.3 kg, approximately 1 kg per capita per month. The annual consumption of other consumer goods per capita was as follows: 5.2 kg for edible oil, 2.4 kg for egg products, 2.1

kg for fish and shrimp, 1.1 kg for dairy products, and 5.9 kg for melons and fruits. This shows that, by 1990, the problem of food and clothing shortage for Chinese rural residents had been basically solved. It can be said that rural residents had struggled with the problem of food and clothing shortage before they consumed more.

During the years 1990–2000, the consumption of fruits and vegetables by Chinese rural residents started to decline, and the consumption of other food except for dairy products showed an upward trend. This indicates that rural residents had started to pursue food quality. In 2000, the annual consumption of grain and vegetables by rural residents per capita reached 250.2 kg and 112.0 kg; the annual consumption of meat by rural residents per capita was 14.1 kg, equivalent to daily consumption of 39 g per capita, and the annual consumption of other consumer goods per capita was as follows: 7.1 kg for edible oil, 4.8 kg for egg products, 3.9 kg for fish and shrimp, 2.8 kg for poultry, 1.06 kg for dairy products, and 19.05 kg for melons and fruits. The annual consumption of egg products, fish and shrimp, poultry, melons and fruits per capita by Chinese rural residents almost doubled in 2000 compared to that of 1990.

During the period 2000–2016, among the food consumption of Chinese rural residents, the consumption of grain and vegetables kept declining. Among them, the consumption of grain dropped sharply while that of other food rose significantly. In 2016, for rural residents, the annual grain consumption per capita was 157.2 kg, with a decrease of about 40% compared with that of 2000; the annual vegetable consumption per capita was 91.5 kg, representing a decrease of approximately 20% compared to that of the same year; the annual per capita consumption of meat was 20.7 kg, equivalent to daily consumption per capita of 57 g, with an increase of 50%, and the annual consumption per capita of other consumable goods was as follows: 10.2 kg for edible oil, 8.5 kg for egg products, 7.5 kg for fish and shrimp, 7.9 kg for poultry, 6.6 kg for dairy products, and 36.2 kg for melons and fruits. The consumption of other items except for edible oil more than doubled compared to that in 2000.

Table 2.4 shows the housing area per capita of rural residents and the amount of consumer durables owned by every 100 households in China at the end of each year during the period 1978–2016. According to the data of *China Statistical Yearbooks* (see Table 2.4), the most expensive consumer durables in China's rural households in 1978 were basically household necessities, such as bicycles (30.73 units per 100 households), sewing machines (19.8 sets per 100 households), clocks (24.33 pieces per 100 households), watches (27.43 pieces per 100 households), and radios (17.44 sets per 100 households). These durables were not much popular, with ownership rates being generally lower than 30%. In 1980, the ownership rates of these durables reached 30% or so, and the housing area per capita was only 4.06 square meters.

Following five years of economic reform of the household responsibility contract system, in 1985, watches (126.3 units per 100 households) and

Table 2.4 Housing area per capita and the amount of consumer durables owned by every 100 households in China in the end of each year

Year	*1980*	*1985*	*1990*	*1995*	*2000*	*2005*	*2010*	*2015*
Sewing machine (set)	23.31	43.21	55.19	65.74	67.06[a]	–	–	–
Watch (piece)	37.58	126.3	172.2	169.1	152.7[a]	–	–	–
Clock (piece)	30.95	37.32	49.01	67.95	81.45[a]	–	–	–
Large wardrobe (piece)	–	53.37	75.67	84.88	86.47[a]	–	–	–
Sofa (piece)	–	13.7	36.98	65.41	84.24[a]	–	–	–
Writing desk (piece)	–	38.21	56.08	79	84.52	–	–	–
Bicycle/electric bicycle (unit)	30.7	80.6	118.8	147.0	120.5	98.4	96.0	50.1[b]
Motorcycle (unit)	–	–	0.89	4.91	21.94	40.7	59.0	67.5
Private car (unit)	–	–	–	–	–	–	9.9[c]	13.3
Electric fan (set)	–	9.66	41.36	88.96	122.6	146.4	–	–
Air conditioner (set)	–	–	–	0.18	1.32	6.40	16	38.8
Washing machine (set)	–	1.9	9.12	16.9	28.6	40.2	57.3	78.8
Refrigerator (set)	–	0.06	1.22	5.15	12.31	20.1	45.2	82.6
Black-and-white TV (set)	–	10.94	39.72	63.81	52.97	21.77	6.38	1.66[d]
Color TV (set)	0.39	0.8	4.72	16.9	48.7	84.0	111.8	116.9
Camera (set)	–	–	0.7	1.42	3.12	4.05	5.17	4.10
Mobile phone (unit)	–	–	–	–	4.30	50.24	136.5	226.1
Home computer (set)	–	–	–	–	0.47	2.10	10.37	25.7
Housing area per capita (square meter)	4.06	5.11	17.83	21.01	24.82	29.68	34.08	45.8[e]

Source: *China Statistical Yearbooks.*

As no bicycle data is included in the *China Statistical Yearbooks* for the years following 2001 and there is no electric vehicle data for the years before 2013.

a Indicates the data of 1999; as such data following 1999 are not included

b Indicates electric bicycle data;

c Indicates the data of 2013, with no statistical data for this item;

d Indicates the data of 2011, with no statistical data in the subsequent years; and

e The data released by the National Bureau of Statistics of China in 2016.

bicycles (80.6 units per 100 households) were commonly used daily by Chinese rural households. Large wardrobes (53.37 pieces per 100 households), writing desks (38.21 pieces per 100 households), and sewing machines (43.21 sets per 100 households) started to enter the homes of ordinary farmers. Some rich families had already purchased sofas (13.7 pieces per 100 households), electric fans (9.66 sets per 100 households), washing machines (1.9 sets per 100 households), black-and-white TVs (10.4 sets per 100 households), and other enjoyment-centric consumer durables. Color TVs (0.8 set per 100 household), refrigerators (0.06 set per 100 household), and other high-end consumer durables were also more commonly purchased by rural residents. The housing area per capita in rural areas increased to 5.11 square meters, an increase of about 15% compared to that of 1980.

By 2000, the living standards of China's rural areas had further improved. Bicycles (120.5 units per 100 households), sewing machines (67.6 sets per 100 households), large wardrobes (86.47 pieces per 100 households), writing desks (84.52 pieces per 100 households), sofas (84.24 pieces per 100 households), and electric fans (122.6 sets per 100 households) were quite popular in rural areas, and these durables were owned by nearly all rural ordinary households. After 2001, these consumer durables were not included in the *China Statistical Yearbooks*. Washing machines (28.6 sets per 100 households), refrigerators (12.31 sets per 100 households), color TVs (48.7 sets per 100 households), air conditioncrs (12.3 sets per 100 households), and motorcycles (21.94 units per 100 households) had become common in the top 10% of the richest rural households. Owning these durables had become a symbol of the wealthy rural families. The ownership rates of mobile phones (4.3 units per 100 households), cameras (3.12 sets per 100 households), and air conditioners (1.3 sets per 100 households) had also exceeded 1% each, becoming the key goods pursued by wealthy families. Computers (0.47 set per 100 households) had also started to be purchased by the richest households. The housing area per capita reached 24.82 square meters at that time.

According to the *China Statistical Yearboo*k *2017*, by 2015, mobile phones (226.1 units per 100 households) and color TVs (126.9 sets per 100 households) had been basically popularized in rural households of China; washing machines (78.8 sets per 100 households) and refrigerators (82.6 sets per 100 households) were owned by most rural households; and air conditioners (38.8 sets per 100 households) and home computers (25.7 sets per 100 households) had become quite common, with about one set in every four families. The mode of travel basically changed from a human-powered mode, such as on foot and by bicycle, to fuel- or electricity-powered modes such as electric bicycles (50.1 units per 100 households), motorcycles (67.5 units per 100 households), and even private cars (13.3 units per 100 households), whose total ownership rates of three transportation means exceeded 100%. As can be seen rural families in China are moving toward automated travel, electrical appliances, wireless communication, and online entertainment.

3 Changes in GDP expenditure structure and breakdown of demand factors in GDP growth

This chapter focuses on the characteristics of the changes in China's economic structure from the demand side, decomposes the real GDP growth rate by using the expenditure method and according to different expenditure categories, and studies the contribution of different demand categories to China's real economic growth rate. It is organized as follows: The first section analyzes the changes in the four major expenditures (household consumption, government consumption, total investment, and net exports) in the composition of China's GDP expenditure along with GDP growth; the second section provides a theoretical basis for the decomposition of GDP growth demand factors, and on this basis, analyzes the contributions of the four major expenditures to China's GDP growth during the period 1953–2016.

Section 1 Growth and fluctuations in GDP and its four expenditure categories

1.1 Data sources

The sources for the data used in this chapter are as follows: Firstly, China's real GDP growth rate for the period 1953–2016 is available from *China Statistical Yearbooks* and the *Collection of Statistical Data for New China during the 50 Years of Its Founding.* China's real GDP for the period 1952–2016 can be calculated at the constant prices of 1952 according to the country's real GDP in 1952 and the real GDP growth rate of 1953–2016, as shown in Figure 3.1. Secondly, China's nominal GDP for the period 1952–2016 and its four major expenditure categories that are divided by using the expenditure method, namely household consumption, government consumption, inventory investment and net exports, can be obtained from the database of China Entrepreneur Investment Club (hereinafter referred to as the "CEIC database"). The proportions of different components of China's GDP for the period 1952–2016, as shown in Figure 3.3, can be calculated on the basis of the above data. Finally, the actual value of each component of GDP for the period 1952–2016, including household consumption, government

DOI: 10.4324/9781003261629-5

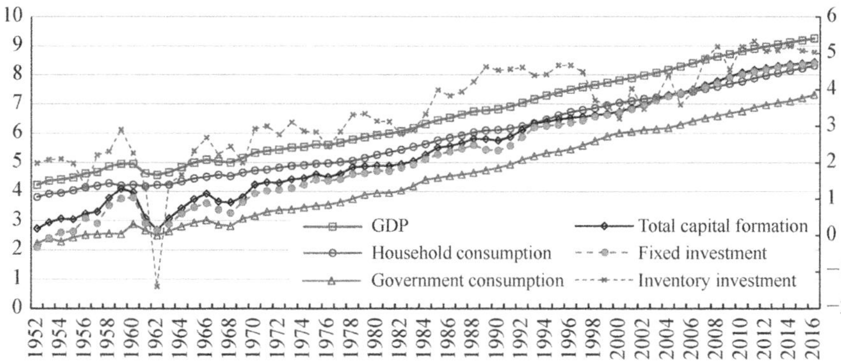

Figure 3.1 Changes in the logarithms of China's real GDP and components in different categories: 1952–2016.

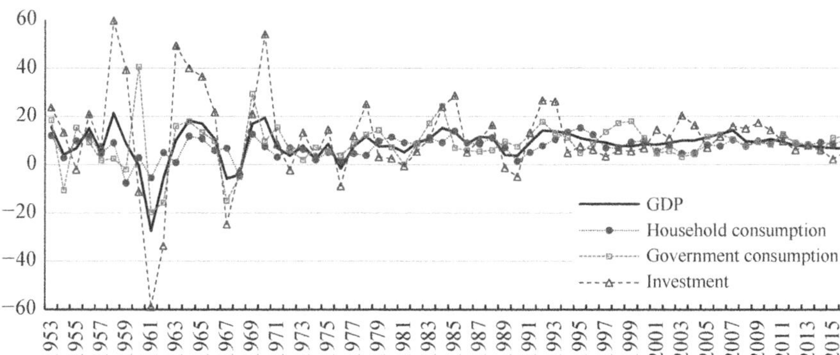

Figure 3.2 Real growth rates of China's household consumption, government consumption, and investment: 1952–2016.

consumption, inventory investment, and net exports, as shown in Figure 3.1, can be calculated by using the proportion of each component of GDP and the real GDP. Therefore, the real growth rate of each component, including household consumption, government consumption, total investment, fixed asset investment, inventory investment, and net exports, as shown in Figure 3.2, can be obtained.

1.2 The growth and fluctuations in GDP and its components: visual graphical analysis

Based on the data obtained by using the above calculation method and at the constant prices of 1952, Figure 3.1 shows the changes in China's GDP and variables such as total consumption, household consumption, government consumption, total investment, fixed asset investment, and inventory investment. The ordinate in Figure 3.1 indicates the logarithms of GDP and its components, measured in billion yuan and at the prices of 1952. Thus, the slope of each curve in the figure can represent the growth rate of the corresponding variable. As can be seen from Figure 3.1, except for inventory investment, expenditures increased along a straight line in most of the years, with some exceptions during the period 1958–1970. At the constant prices of 1952, China had a total GDP of 10.5 trillion yuan relative to 69.2 billion yuan in 1952, approximately up 151 times. Among the GDP, household consumption increased from 45.3 billion yuan to 4.13 trillion yuan, approximately up 90 times; government consumption from 9.3 billion yuan to 1.52 trillion yuan, approximately up 162 times; and the total investment (or total capital formation) from 15.4 billion yuan to 4.65 trillion yuan, approximately up 302 times. In the total investment, fixed asset formation grew from 8.1 billion yuan to 4.50 trillion yuan, approximately up 556.2 times; inventory investment from 7.3 billion yuan to 15 trillion yuan, approximately up 20 times, with a smaller change in relative terms. Additionally, the positions of different curves for most of the years are basically arranged as follows:

> GDP> household expenditure>total investment>fixed asset investment>government consumption>inventory investment

As can be seen from Figure 3.2, China's economic growth for the period 1952–2016 has the following characteristics: Firstly, the investment growth rate had been fluctuating dramatically, with the largest range and frequency in terms of fluctuations; the government consumption growth rate ranked second in terms of fluctuations, with larger fluctuation range and frequency than the GDP growth rate; and the household consumption growth rate had the smallest fluctuations, which were even smaller than those of GDP growth rate. Secondly, in most of these years, the household consumption growth rate was lower than the GDP growth rate; and the years with higher GDP growth rates were normally those when the GDP growth rate declined. Thirdly, except for a few years (such as 1996–1999), the changes in the government consumption growth rate were generally consistent with the GDP growth rate. Finally, both frequency and range of changes in net exports were extremely large, far beyond the range of changes in the growth rates of the above four items. To avoid the impact on the overall view of the changes in GDP, household consumption, investment, and government consumption growth rates, Figure 3.2 excludes the graph showing the changes in the net export growth rate.

Figure 3.3 shows the changes in the proportion of China's GDP during the period 1952–2016. Firstly, the proportion of government consumption

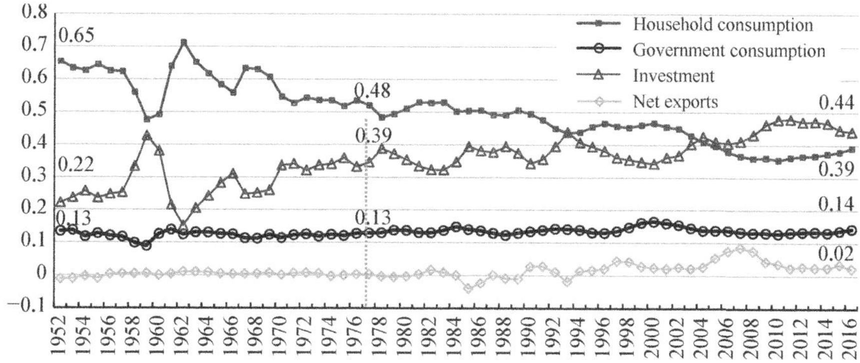

Figure 3.3 Changes in the proportions of four expenditure categories over China's GDP calculated by using the expenditure method: 1952–2016.

over GDP was basically stable, without significant fluctuations and changes. This figure was generally maintained at 11% to 16% during the same period (except the years 1958–1959, less than 10%), with an average value of 13.2%. Secondly, the proportion of net exports over GDP had always been small, generally between −2% and 3%, with an average value of 1.3% during the period; the curve showed a horizontal trend on the whole, without significant fluctuations. However, there were obvious differences in the fluctuations before and after 1982, which were mainly due to China's low degree of opening to the outside world before the year, when net exports were generally around 0, with few fluctuations. Thirdly, there almost existed the relationship of mirror symmetry between the proportion of household consumption and that of investment. Specifically, the proportion of household consumption showed a downward trend, with significant fluctuations, and that of investment showed an upward trend, also with significant fluctuations; and the stage when the proportion of household consumption fell corresponded to the stage when the proportion of investment rose. The trough for the proportion of household consumption corresponded to the peak for the proportion of investment. However, the fluctuation range of the proportion of investment over GDP was larger than that of the proportion of household consumption over GDP. Fourthly, the proportion of household consumption over GDP dropped from 65% to 39% during the period 1952–2016, representing a decrease of 26 percentage points; the proportion of investment over GDP rose from 22% to 44%, representing an increase of 22 percentage points. It can be seen that the increase in the proportion of China's investment over GDP is generally replaced by the decline in the proportion of household consumption over GDP. Although the proportion of household consumption over GDP has been higher than that of investment over GDP for a long time during this period, the proportion of household consumption over GDP has been smaller than that of investment over GDP since the year 2005.

1.3 Changes in GDP and its components: data-based statistical analysis

In order to reflect in a more accurate way the economic growth and fluctuations in different periods, Tables 3.1 and 3.2 show the real growth rates of China's consumption, investment, and net exports by stages in different periods. Statistical indicators here include the total growth multiple, average annual growth, standard deviation (STDEV), and coefficient of variation (CV) for each period.

1.3.1 Overall characteristics of economic growth: 1952–2016

According to the first column of Table 3.1, during the period 1952–2016, China's real GDP was approximately up 151 times, with an average annual GDP growth of about 8.17%, the STDEV and CV for GDP growth of 6.98% and 0.83 respectively. In the composition of GDP, real investment grew fastest, approximately up 301 times, with an average annual growth of 9.34%. Investment growth was mainly reflected in fixed asset investment. Fixed assets were approximately up 556 times, with an average annual growth of 10.38%; inventory investment was up 20 times, with an average annual growth of 4.86%; household consumption was about up 90 times, with an average annual growth of 7.3%; and government consumption was about up 161 times, with an average annual growth of 8.28%.

Table 3.2 gives the following data in terms of fluctuation range. Firstly, either in terms of STDEV or CV, the growth rate of household consumption had the smallest fluctuations. The STDEV for the annual growth rates of household consumption was 62.5% of that of GDP, and the CV for the former was 71% of that of the latter. Secondly, net exports fluctuated most in terms of growth rate. The STDEV for the net export growth rate was 478 times more than that for the GDP growth rate, and that for the former was 9.9 times more than that of the latter. Thirdly, the investment growth rate also fluctuated significantly; STDEV was about 2.6 times more than that of GDP growth rate and CV was about 1.98 times more than that of GDP growth rate. Fourthly, the government consumption growth rate fluctuated more than the GDP growth rate; its STDEV was about 1.34 times more than that of GDP growth rate and CV about 1.3 times more than that of GDP growth rate. The fluctuations in the growth rates of GDP and its components are consistent with the general law of economic growth (i.e., the fluctuations of investment growth rate should be generally larger than those of GDP growth and the fluctuations of household consumption growth rate generally should be less than those of GDP growth).

Table 3.1 The growth of China's real GDP and its components calculated by using the expenditure method: 1952–2016

	Total growth multiple (in times)				
Period	*1952–2016*	*1952–1977*	*1977–2016*	*1977–2001*	*2001–2016*
GDP	**151.01**	**3.22**	**35.00**	**8.18**	**2.92**
Total consumption	**102.28**	**2.48**	**28.70**	**7.71**	**2.41**
Household consumption	90.09	2.36	26.13	7.04	2.37
Government consumption	161.47	3.06	39.05	10.37	2.52
Total investment	**301.46**	**5.60**	**44.86**	**8.61**	**3.77**
Fixed asset investment	556.16	9.42	52.46	9.92	3.90
Inventory investment	19.89	1.36	7.83	2.24	1.73
Net exports	***(297.66)***[a]	***(2.20)***[a]	**247.17**	**59.16**	**3.13**

	Geometric average annual growth rate (in %)				
Period	*1953–2016*	*1953–1977*	*1978–2016*	*1978–2001*	*2002–2016*
GDP	**8.17**	**5.93**	**9.62**	**9.68**	**9.53**
Total consumption	**7.51**	**5.11**	**9.08**	**9.44**	**8.52**
Household consumption	7.30	4.96	8.83	9.08	8.44
Government consumption	8.28	5.76	9.92	10.66	8.76
Total investment	**9.34**	**7.84**	**10.31**	**9.89**	**10.98**
Fixed asset investment	10.38	9.83	10.74	10.47	11.17
Inventory investment	4.86	3.50	5.74	5.01	6.92
Net exports	–	–	**15.19**	**18.61**	**9.91**

	Arithmetic average annual growth rate (in %)				
Period	*1953–2016*	*1953–1977*	*1978–2016*	*1978–2001*	*2002–2016*
GDP	**8.42**	**6.48**	**9.66**	**9.72**	**9.55**
Total consumption	**7.61**	**5.28**	**9.11**	**9.47**	**8.54**
Household consumption	7.39	5.10	8.86	9.12	8.46
Government consumption	8.69	6.61	10.02	10.79	8.79
Total investment	**11.05**	**11.76**	**10.59**	**10.28**	**11.10**
Fixed asset investment	12.17	13.84	11.10	10.98	11.28
Inventory investment	37.67	73.80	14.50	11.47	19.35
Net exports	**−407.38**	**103.96**	**−735.16**	**−1204.9**	**16.42**

Source: Source for raw data: *China Statistical Yearbooks*. The data are calculated by the author based on the data from *China Statistical Yearbooks*.

[a] This is the value calculated according to the definition. As China's net exports were negative in 1952 and positive in 2016, the value calculated according to the definition was negative. Generally, a negative growth rate indicates negative growth, and the negative value here indicates the change of net exports from a deficit to a surplus. Thus, it is marked in bold italic font as its meaning is different from the general meaning.

Table 3.2 Fluctuations in the growth rates of China's real GDP and its components calculated by using the expenditure method: 1952–2016

	STDEV for annual growth rates (in %)				
Period	*1953–2016*	*1953–1977*	*1978–2016*	*1978–2001*	*2002–2016*
GDP	**6.98**	**10.48**	**2.70**	**3.05**	**2.12**
Total consumption	**4.52**	**5.92**	**2.43**	**2.64**	**1.99**
Household consumption	4.36	5.38	2.74	3.20	1.83
Government consumption	9.37	13.67	4.79	5.54	3.02
Total investment	**18.12**	**27.49**	**8.17**	**9.65**	**5.27**
Fixed asset investment	19.21	28.86	9.10	10.97	5.17
Inventory investment	201.53	317.53	47.39	41.21	57.14
Net exports	**3,343**	**329**	**4,263**	**5,425**	**42.76**

	CV for annual growth rates				
Period	*1953–2016*	*1953–1977*	*1978–2016*	*1978–2001*	*2002–2016*
GDP	**0.83**	**1.62**	**0.28**	**0.31**	**0.22**
Total consumption	**0.59**	**1.12**	**0.27**	**0.28**	**0.23**
Household consumption	0.59	1.05	0.31	0.35	0.22
Government consumption	1.08	2.07	0.48	0.51	0.34
Total investment	1.64	2.34	0.77	0.94	0.48
Fixed asset investment	1.58	2.08	0.82	1.00	0.46
Inventory investment	5.35	4.30	3.27	3.59	2.95
Net exports	**−8.21**	**3.16**	**−5.80**	**−4.50**	**2.60**

Source: Obtained by the author according to the data from *China Statistical Yearbooks*

1.3.2 Differences in economic growth during the periods before and after 1978

As can be seen from Tables 3.1 and 3.2, firstly, the gap in China's economic growth before and after the reform is reflected in the huge gap in GDP growth rates for the two periods. During the period 1952–1977, before the reform, China's real GDP was up 3.22 times, with an average annual growth of 5.93%. And during the years 1978–2016, the real GDP was up 35.00 times, with an average annual growth of 9.62%. Despite the relatively high economic growth before the reform, the economic growth after the reform was obviously higher, 1.62 times higher than the average annual growth rate before the reform. Secondly, there was a huge gap between the two periods in terms of economic growth structure. During the period 1952–1977, the average annual growth of China's household consumption was 4.96%; that of government consumption was 5.76% and that of total investment was 7.84%. And net exports changed from a deficit of 780 million yuan to a surplus of 930 million yuan. Among the total investment, fixed asset investment had an average annual growth of 9.83%; and inventory investment had an average annual growth of 3.50%. The growth rates of household consumption, government consumption, and total investment were 83%, 97%, and 1.32 times more than the GDP growth rate, respectively. While during the period 1978–2016, the average annual growth of China's household consumption was 8.83%, that of government consumption was 9.92%, and that of total investment was 10.31%. Net exports had increased from a surplus of 930 million yuan to 231.39 billion yuan, up 247 times and with an average annual growth of 15.19%. Among the total investment, fixed asset investment had an average annual growth of 10.74% and inventory investment had an average annual growth of 5.74%. The growth rates of household consumption, government consumption, total investment, and net exports were 92%, 1.03 times, 1.07 times, and 1.57 times, respectively, more than the GDP growth rate. By comparing these figures it can be seen that, during China's post-reform economic development, the growth rate of each component for GDP was much higher than that before the reform, and the growth rates of household consumption, government consumption, total investment, and inventory investment were 62.3%, 77.9%, 72.2%, 35.5%, and 9.3%, respectively, higher than those before the reform. Thus, despite the faster growth of investment compared to the GDP growth either before or after the reform, the growth of each component of GDP after the reform was more balanced. In particular, the average annual growth gap between consumption and investment after the reform (geometric average difference: 1.48%, arithmetic average difference: 1.73%) was much smaller than that before the reform (geometric average difference: 1.48%, arithmetic average difference: 1.73%). This indicates that the economic growth after the reform produced a more significant effect on the improvement of residents' living standards than that before the reform did.

Secondly, in terms of economic growth fluctuations, as seen from Table 3.2, all net exports were larger than total investment, government investment, GDP, and household consumption by sequence either in terms of absolute or relative fluctuations of the growth rates during the period 1952–1977. The STDEVs for the growth rates of net exports, total investment, government consumption, and household consumption were 31.4 times, 2.62 times, 1.30 times, and 51%, respectively, larger than those of GDP growth rates, and the CVs for the growth rates of the four components were 1.96 times, 1.44 times, 1.28 times, and 65%, respectively, larger than those of GDP growth rates. There are three differences between the period 1978–2016 and the period before the reform. First, the fluctuations in the growth rates of GDP and its components, except net exports, dropped significantly compared to those before the reform. The STDEVs for the growth rates of GDP, household consumption, government consumption, total investment, fixed asset investment, and inventory investment during this period were only 26%, 51%, 35%, 30%, 32%, and 15%, respectively, of those before the reform. The CVs for the growth rates of these economic indicators were only 17%, 29%, 23%, 33%, 36%, and 76% of the CVs for the same before the reform. The CV of net exports growth rate had an increase of 83%, which was mainly due to China's opening up to the outside world. Second, as for the ranks of various growth rates in terms of fluctuations, the fluctuations of the others except the household consumption growth rate after the reform were the same. When sorted in terms of fluctuations measured by CV and STDEV, net export fluctuations were larger than total investment fluctuations, government consumption fluctuations, household consumption fluctuations, and GDP fluctuations by sequence. Third, the fluctuations in the growth rate of each component of GDP were larger than those in GDP growth rate. The STDEVs for the growth rates of net exports, total investment, government consumption, and household consumption were 1,579 times, 3.03 times, 1.77 times, and 1.02 times, respectively, larger than those of the GDP growth rate, and the CVs for the growth rates of the four components were 20.74 times, 1.71 times, 2.76 times, and 1.11 times larger than those of the GDP growth rate. Such changes are also related to the fourth point below. Fourth, the correlation between the components of GDP after the reform was much smaller than that before the reform. Table 3.3 shows the mutual CVs among household consumption, government consumption, and investment and GDP growth rate in different pairs during two periods before and after the reform. Before the reform, there was a mutual significant correlation among household consumption, government consumption, and investment in pairs, with CVs being 0.3 to 0.5. And the CVs of household consumption with government consumption and investment were less than 0.1 and the CV of total investment with government consumption was only 0.19% and not significant. Figure 3.4 shows the scatter plots among the growth rates of household consumption, government consumption, and total investment before and after the reform. As can be seen from the figure, there was a significantly positive correlation among the growth rates of household consumption, government consumption, and total investment before the reform. After the reform, the trend curve among the three was almost flat. The changes in the correlation among the growth rates of household consumption, government consumption, and investment may be correlated with different economic systems adopted before and after the reform. The planned economy system was adopted before the reform. Household consumption, government consumption, and investment were all set by the state according to the overall economic growth. It's evident that there were correlations among them. Since the reform, household consumption, government consumption, and investment have been set by different economic entities based on their own conditions. So, there is no correlation among them.

Table 3.3 CVs among the growth rates of GDP and its components

1953–1977				*1978–2016*			
	Household consumption	*Government consumption*	*Total investment*		*Household consumption*	*Government consumption*	*Total investment*
Government consumption	0.447^{**} (0.025)	1		Government consumption	0.039 (0.816)	1	
Total investment	0.342^{*} (0.094)	0.431^{****} (0.032)	1	Total investment	0.026 (0.876)	0.193 (0.238)	1
GDP	0.648^{*} (0.077)	0.570 (0.190)	0.913^{****} (0.009)	GDP	0.333^{*} (0.059)	0.0335 (0.510)	0.780^{***} (0.018)

Source: Obtained by the author according to the data from *China Statistical Yearbooks*; the values in parentheses indicate p values; "*", "**" and "***" indicate significance at the levels of 10%, 5% and 1% respectively.

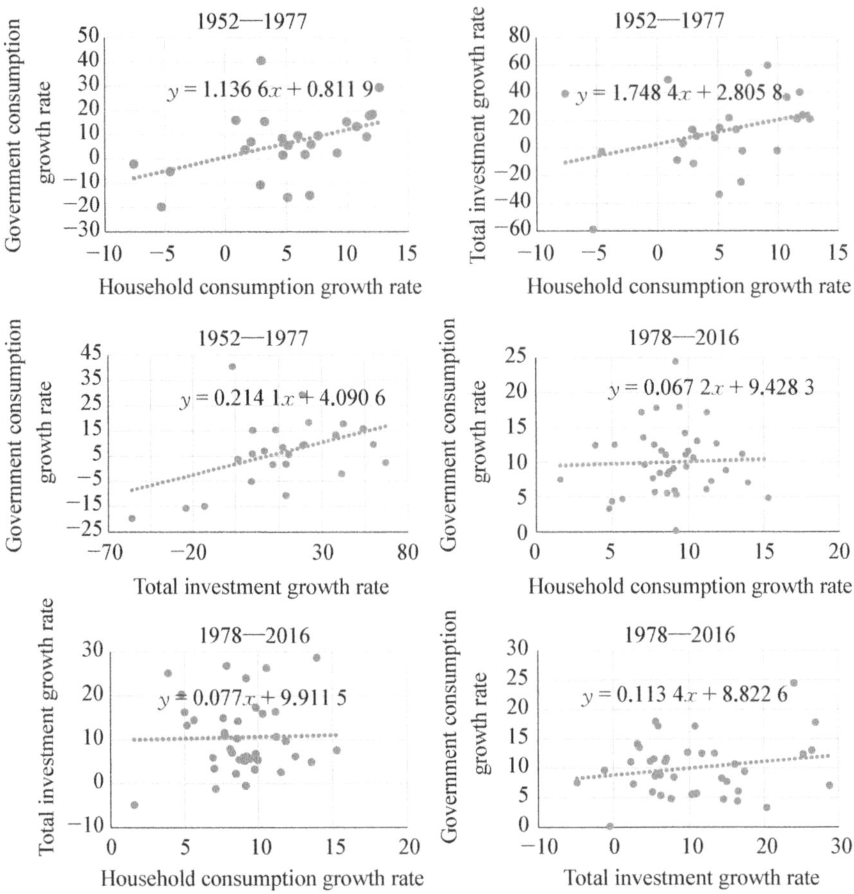

Figure 3.4 Scatter plot among growth rates of household consumption, government consumption, and total investment.

Section 2 GDP Growth rate and its structural breakdown in demand

2.1 Theoretical basis for structural breakdown of demand factors in GDP

Let Y denote a country's GDP, C denote consumption, I denote investment, G denote government purchases, and NX denote imports and exports. According to the national income calculation formula, we can get:

$$Y_t = C_t + I_t + G_t + NX_t$$

Thus, for any period t:

$$\frac{Y_t}{Y_{t-1}} = \frac{C_t}{C_{t-1}}\frac{C_{t-1}}{Y_{t-1}} + \frac{I_t}{I_{t-1}}\frac{I_{t-1}}{Y_{t-1}} + \frac{G_t}{G_{t-1}}\frac{G_{t-1}}{Y_{t-1}} + \frac{NX_t}{NX_{t-1}}\frac{NX_{t-1}}{Y_{t-1}} \tag{3.1}$$

Let α^C, α^I, α^G, and α^{NX} denote the proportions of C, $I|$, G, and NX over GDP, g^Y, g^C, g^I, g^G, and g^{NX} denote the growth rates of Y, C, $I|$, G, and NX. Since $\alpha^C+\alpha^I+\alpha^G+\alpha^{NX}=1$, the following formula can be obtained according to Formula (3.1):

$$g_t^Y = \alpha_{t-1}^C g_t^C + \alpha_{t-1}^I g_t^I + \alpha_{t-1}^G g_t^G + \alpha_{t-1}^{NX} g_t^{NX} \tag{3.2}$$

As can be known from Formula (3.2), the GDP growth arising from the growth of C, $I|$, G, and NX and their contributions to GDP growth can be expressed, respectively, as follows:

$$g_t^{jY} = \alpha_{t-1}^j g_t^j = (j_t - j_{t\text{-}1})/Y_{t-1}, \quad \text{where } j = C, I, G, NX \tag{3.3}$$

$$R_t^j = g_t^{jY} / g_t^Y = \alpha_{t-1}^j g_t^j / g_t^Y, \quad \text{where } j = C, I, G, NX \tag{3.4}$$

where g_t^{jY} (j= C, I, G, and NX) indicates the GDP growth arising from Type j expenditure and R_t^j (J= C, I, G, and NX) indicates the contribution of Type j expenditure to GDP growth.

2.2 Factor breakdown of China's real GDP growth rate according to the expenditure method

2.2.1 Breakdown of GDP growth rate: 1953–2016

By applying Formulas (3.3) and (3.4) and the data introduced in the first section of this chapter, China's real GDP growth rate can be decomposed from the perspective of demand, in terms of household consumption, investment, government consumption, and net exports. Thus, their contributions can be calculated. Specifically, their real growth rates (i.e., the data of g^Y, g^C, g^I, g^G, and g^{NX}, as shown in Figure 3.2) are calculated according to the data of China's real household consumption, investment, government consumption, and net exports during the period 1952–2016. Then, the real GDP growth arising from the four factors above, as shown in Figure 3.5, is calculated using Formula (3.3) based on their proportions over GDP (i.e., the data of α^C, α^I, α^G, and α^{NX}, as shown in Figure 3.3). Finally, their contributions to the GDP growth rates are calculated using Equation (3.4), as shown in Figure 3.6. According to such breakdown data, Table 3.4 shows the growth arising from the four factors above to China's GDP growth rates in different periods and their contributions.

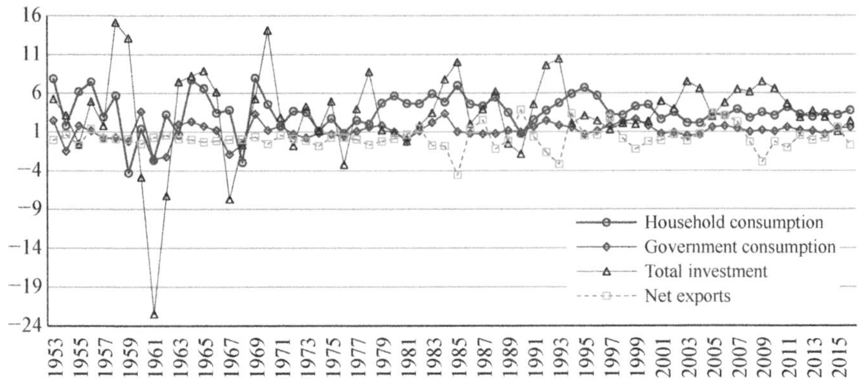

Figure 3.5 Annual GDP growth arising from four expenditure categories as calculated using the expenditure method: 1953–2016.

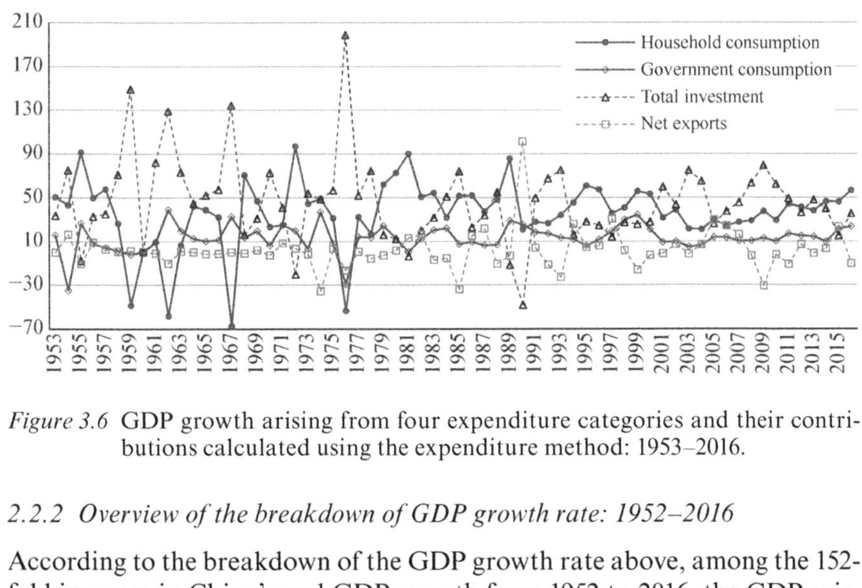

Figure 3.6 GDP growth arising from four expenditure categories and their contributions calculated using the expenditure method: 1953–2016.

2.2.2 Overview of the breakdown of GDP growth rate: 1952–2016

According to the breakdown of the GDP growth rate above, among the 152-fold increase in China's real GDP growth from 1952 to 2016, the GDP arising from household consumption was up 59.96 times, with a contribution of 39.04% to GDP growth; the GDP arising from government consumption was up 21.76 times, with a contribution of 14.41%; the GDP arising from total investment was up 66.94 times, in which the GDP arising from fixed asset investment was up 64.82 times and from inventory investment was up 2.10 times, with a total contribution of 44.33%; and the GDP arising from net exports was up 3.35 times, with a contribution of 2.22%. It can be seen that, during China's nearly-64-year economic growth, the main force driving GDP growth was household consumption and total investment, with the contribution of total investment to GDP growth being close to 83.37%. The contributions of household consumption and total investment to GDP growth were almost the same, basically around 40%, with the contribution of the investment about 5 percentage points higher than that of the household consumption. Moreover, the contribution of government consumption to GDP growth was only about 14%, and that of net exports to GDP growth was less than 3%.

It can be known from the GDP decomposition formulas (3.3) to (3.4) that only the impact of overall structural changes in GDP at the beginning and end of the period on the growth structure is taken into account by reference to the method of total growth multiple decomposition within the GDP interval; and no impact of the intermediate growth process on the growth of GDP driven by decomposition factors and on their contributions to GDP growth are considered. In fact, by observing Figures 3.5 and 3.6, we can see both growths driven by household consumption to China's annual GDP growth rate and the household consumption's contribution rate were more stable than the investment's. In particular, the GDP growth driven by annual investment growth has been negative in many of the years, with large absolute values. The method of calculating the growth multiple within the total interval cannot reflect the impact of the fluctuation differences of household consumption and investment over the breakdown of GDP growth rates. In order to illustrate the negative impact of the volatility of various factors on GDP growth during the process of increase, the breakdown of average annual GDP growth rates is further calculated using the annual arithmetic average method below.

According to Table 3.4, the GDP for the period 1952–2016 had an average annual growth of 8.43% where the GDP arising from household consumption had an average annual growth of 3.63%, with a contribution of 43.04%; the GDP arising from government consumption had an average annual growth of 1.13%, with a contribution of 13.41%; the GDP arising from total investment had an average annual growth of 3.48%, in which the GDP arising from fixed asset investment had an average annual growth of 3.16% and that from inventory investment 0.32%, with the contribution of total investment to the average annual growth of GDP being 41.27%; and the GDP arising from net exports had an average annual growth of 0.19%, with a contribution of 2.28%. Since the growth rates of investment and government consumption fluctuate more than the growth rate of consumption, according to this decomposition method, the contributions of investment and government consumption to GDP growth decreased by 3 percentage points and 1 percentage point; the contribution of household consumption to the same rose by 4 percentage points; and the contribution of net exports decreased by 0.02 percentage point. According to the method of calculating the average annual growth rate, the total contributions of household consumption and the total investment to GDP growth reached 84.31% but the contribution of household consumption to GDP growth was about 1.8 percentage points greater than that of total investment to the same.

Table 3.4 GDP Growth arising from four expenditure categories and their contributions calculated using the expenditure method

The GDP growth multiples arising from the growth of different expenditure categories (in times)

	1952–2016	*1952–1977*	*1977–2016*	*1977–2001*	*2001–2016*
Total consumption	80.72	1.96	18.65	5.01	1.49
Household consumption	58.96	1.54	13.60	3.67	1.08
Government consumption	21.76	0.41	5.06	1.34	0.40
Total investment	66.94	1.24	15.56	2.99	1.37
Fixed asset investment	64.84	1.10	15.10	2.85	1.33
Inventory investment	2.10	0.14	0.46	0.13	0.04
Net exports	3.35	0.02	0.79	0.19	0.07
Total GDP	151.01	3.22	35.00	8.18	2.92

The annual arithmetic average of GDP growth arising from the growth of different expenditure categories (in %)

	1953–2016	*1953–1977*	*1978–2016*	*1978–2001*	*2002–2016*
Total consumption	4.76	3.86	5.33	5.89	4.44
Household consumption	3.63	3.12	3.96	4.40	3.24
Government consumption	1.13	0.75	1.38	1.49	1.20
Total investment	3.48	2.54	4.08	3.70	4.69
Fixed asset investment	3.16	2.21	3.77	3.28	4.55
Inventory investment	0.32	0.33	0.32	0.43	0.14
Net exports	0.19	0.08	0.27	0.13	0.48
Total GDP	8.43	6.48	9.41	9.59	9.13

Contributions of different expenditure categories to GDP growth multiples (in %)

	1952–2016	*1952–1977*	*1977–2016*	*1977–2001*	*2001–2016*
Total consumption	53.45	60.68	53.30	61.20	50.88
Household consumption	39.04	47.89	38.85	44.79	37.03
Government consumption	14.41	12.79	14.45	16.41	13.85
Total investment	44.33	38.56	44.45	36.49	46.88
Fixed asset investment	42.94	34.09	43.13	34.88	45.65
Inventory investment	1.39	4.47	1.32	1.61	1.23
Net exports	2.22	0.77	2.25	2.31	2.24
Total GDP	100	100	100	100	100

Contributions of different expenditure categories to the average annual GDP growth rates (in %)

	1952–2016	*1952–1977*	*1977–2016*	*1977–2001*	*2001–2016*
Total consumption	56.45	59.63	56.64	61.39	48.65
Household consumption	43.04	48.12	42.02	45.90	35.49
Government consumption	13.41	11.52	14.62	15.49	13.16
Total investment	41.27	39.19	43.36	38.61	51.35
Fixed asset investment	37.44	34.04	40.00	34.16	49.81
Inventory investment	3.83	5.15	3.36	4.44	1.54
Net exports	2.28	1.17	2.83	1.37	5.29
Total GDP	100	100	100	100	100

Source: Source for raw data: *China Statistical Yearbooks*; the data here are calculated by the author according to the data from *China Statistical Yearbooks*.

2.2.3 Comparisons on the periods before and after the reform: 1953–1977 vs. 1978–2016

As can be seen from Table 3.4, during the period 1952–1977 before the reform, China's real GDP was up 3.22 times, in which the GDP arising from household consumption was up 1.96 times, with a contribution of 47.89%; and that arising from total investment was up 1.24 times, with a contribution of 38.56%. If calculated based on the average annual growth rate, China's real GDP had an average annual growth of 6.48%, in which the GDP growth driven by added household consumption was 3.12%, with a contribution of 48.12%, and that from investment was 2.54%, with a contribution of 34.04%. It can be seen that although the average annual growth rate of household consumption (5.28%) was far lower than that of total investment (11.76%), the contribution of household consumption to GDP growth was larger than that of total investment as consumption occupied a large proportion over GDP. During this period, the GDP growth driven by the growth of government consumption was 41%, representing an average annual GDP growth of 0.75% and a contribution to GDP growth of approximately 11.52% to 12.79%; the GDP growth driven by added net exports was around 2%, representing an average annual growth of 0.08% and a contribution to GDP growth of approximately 0.77% to 1.17%.

During the period 1978–2016 after the reform, China's real GDP was up 35.00 times, in which the GDP arising from household consumption was up 13.60 times, with a contribution of 38.85%, and that from investment was up 15.56 times, with a contribution of 44.45%. The contribution of consumption to GDP growth after the reform dropped by almost 10 percentage points, and that of investment rose by nearly 6 percentage points compared with those before the reform. If calculated based on the average annual growth rate, China's real GDP had an average annual growth of 9.41%, in which the GDP growth driven by added household consumption was 3.96%, with a contribution of 42.02%. The average annual growth of GDP driven by household consumption did not differ much compared with that before the reform, with a difference of only 0.84 percentage points and a decrease in its contribution to GDP growth of 6 percentage points. After the reform, the GDP growth driven by investment was 4.08%, with a contribution of 43.36%. The annual growth of GDP driven by the growth of investment rose by 1.54 percentage points but the contribution to the average annual growth rate of GDP rose by 4.17 percentage points compared to those before the reform. The GDP growth driven by added government consumption was up 5.06 times, representing an average annual growth of 1.38% and a contribution of approximately 14.5%. The GDP growth driven by net exports was 79%, representing an average annual growth of 0.27% and a contribution of approximately 2.25% to 2.83%.

It can be found by comparing the data before and after the reform that the biggest difference in China's GDP growth structure lies in the changes in the contributions of household consumption and total investment to GDP growth. The contribution of household consumption to GDP growth dropped by 6 to 10 percentage points and that of total investment to the same rose by 4 to 6 percentage points after the reform compared with those before the reform. However, the gap between the average annual growth rates of investment and household consumption after the reform did not change much compared with that before the reform. Instead, such gap after the reform (1.48%) was narrowed by 1.4 percentage points compared with that before the reform (2.88%). So, this change is mainly due to the great change in the proportions of household consumption and total investment over GDP after the reform relative to those before the reform. After the reform, the proportion of household consumption continued to decline but the proportion of total investment continued to rise. Take the beginning of the two periods as an example. During the period 1952–1977, the proportion of China's household consumption dropped from 65% to 48% and then to 39% in 2016. During the same period, the proportion of investment rose from 22% to 39% and continued to rise to 44% in 2016. Another change in GDP growth structure after the reform lies in the significant increase in the contributions of government investment and net exports to GDP growth relative to that before the reform. Where, the contribution of government investment increased by 1.6 to 2 percentage points and that of net exports by approximately 1.5 percentage points. The increase in the contributions of the two is due to the higher GDP growth rate after the reform, with the growth of government investment and next exports being up 0.3 percentage point and 5.5 percentage points, respectively. Additionally, the efficiency of investment in driving economic growth has changed a lot since the reform. However, the average annual growth rate of total investment has not

Table 3.5 CVs for the GDP growth arising from four expenditure categories and for their contributions calculated using the expenditure method

	CVs for the GDP growth arising from four expenditure categories			
Period	*1953–1977*	*1978–2016*	*1978–2001*	*2002–2016*
Household consumption	1.06	0.41	0.34	0.18
Government consumption	2.13	0.55	0.52	0.32
Total investment	3.11	0.64	0.93	0.43
Net exports	6.16	3.70	14.51	3.36
	CVs for contributions to average annual GDP growth			
Period	*1953–1977*	*1978–2016*	*1978–2001*	*2002–2016*
Household consumption	15.55	0.39	0.39	0.29
Government consumption	−6.53	0.50	0.54	0.39
Total investment	2.50	0.71	0.92	0.37
Net exports	6.48	4.75	5.24	3.96

changed much since the reform. Comparatively, the investment growth before the reform was even higher. However, the average annual growth of GDP driven by investment before the reform was only 2.54% and was lifted to 4.08% after the reform, up 1.54 percentage points. Despite lower GDP growth before the reform, the contribution of the higher investment growth to GDP growth before the reform was also lower than that of investment after the reform. This result may be related to the continuous increase in the proportion of investment over GDP. It can also be found by observing Figures 3.5 and 3.6 that the growth driven by the average annual growth rate of GDP and its contribution rate were more stable than those before the reform. The fact can be proved by using the CV to measure the fluctuations in the GDP growth driven by each factor and their contributions. Just take household consumption and total investment as examples. Before the reform, the CVs for the GDP growth driven by household consumption and total investment were 1.06 and 3.11 and those for their contributions were 15.5 and 2.5; after the reform, the CVs for the GDP growth driven by the two were 0.41 and 0.64 and those for their contributions were 0.39 and 0.71 (see Table 3.5). According to Formulas (3.5) and (3.6), it is not difficult to understand so many differences concerning the fluctuations in the growth driven by each factor and in their contributions, which is mainly due to the fluctuations in the GDP growth rates before and after the reform.

4 Changes in China's industrial structure and the industrial decomposition of GDP growth

This chapter analyzes the changes in the industrial structure of China's economy in terms of supply, and decomposes the industrial factors of China's real GDP growth rate from the perspective of changes in industrial structure. The structure of this chapter is arranged as follows: The first section studies the changes in the industrial structure of China's economy and the characteristics of economic growth from the supply side according to the industrial composition of GDP. Without regard for the relative price changes among industries, the second section excludes the inflation factor of the three industries according to the GDP deflator, decomposes China's real GDP growth rate by industry, and calculates the contribution of each industry to China's GDP growth. Taking into account the relative price changes of various industries, the third section decomposes China's real GDP growth rate by industry again, and analyzes how relative price changes affect the contribution rate of the growth of three industries to GDP growth.

Section 1 Growth of the three industries and changes in China's industrial structure

1.1 Data sources

The data sources for this chapter are as follows: Firstly, data on China's nominal GDP and the nominal output values of the three industries for the period 1952–2016 are available from the CEIC database. The proportions of the output values of the three industries over China's GDP can be calculated based on the above data, as shown in Figure 4.4. Secondly, the annual growth rate of China's real GDP from 1952 to 2016 can be obtained from the *China Statistical Yearbooks* and the *Collection of Statistical Data for New China during the 50 Years of Its Founding*. China's real GDP for the period 1952–2016 can be calculated by using the data of China's real GDP growth rate in 1952–2016 and China's nominal GDP in 1952. The real output value of each industry can be calculated by multiplying the real GDP by the proportion of the output value of each industry over GDP, as shown in

DOI: 10.4324/9781003261629-6

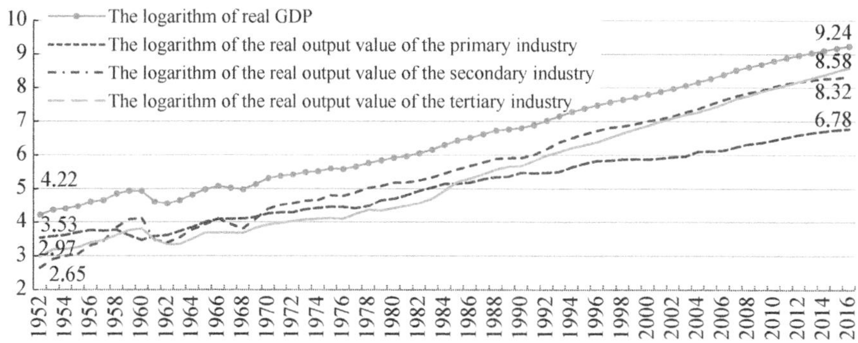

Figure 4.1 Changes in China's real GDP and real output values of the three industries: 1952–2016.

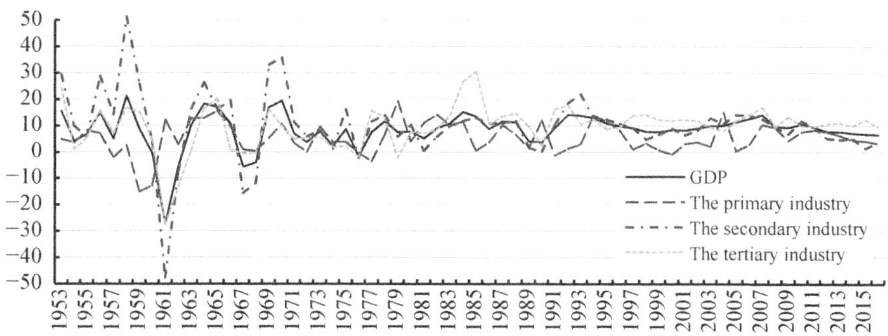

Figure 4.2 China's real GDP growth rate and real GDP growth rates of the three industries: 1953–2016.

Figure 4.1. China's real GDP growth rate and the real GDP growth arising from the output values of the three industries for the period 1953–2016 can be calculated by using the real GDP and the real output values of the three industries, as shown in Figure 4.2.

1.2 Overall changes in the industries: visual graphical analysis

During the period 1952–2016, all three industries in China grew at a fast pace. However, the unbalanced growth of the three industries caused changes in China's industrial structure. Figure 4.1 shows the changes in China's real GDP and in the real output values of the three industries adjusted according to the GDP deflator and at the constant prices of 1952. According to the data of Figure 4.1, during the period 1952–2016, the real output value of China's primary industry (hereinafter referred to as the "primary industry") increased from 34.29 billion yuan to 883.287 billion yuan, approximately up 25 times; that of China's secondary industry (hereinafter referred to as the "secondary industry") rose from 14.11 billion yuan to 4,109.61 billion yuan, approximately up 290 times; and that of China's tertiary industry (hereinafter referred to as the "tertiary industry") grew from 19.51 billion yuan to 5,330.19 billion yuan, approximately up 272 times. It can also be seen from Figure 4.1 that the growth of the real output value of the primary industry was always the smallest, with the smallest slope; the growth of the real output value of the secondary industry was faster than that of the tertiary industry before 1982 but slower than that of the latter after 1983.

Figure 4.2 shows the changes in the growth rate of real output values of the three industries during the period 1953–2016. As can be seen from the figure, there are significant differences in the growth rates of China's three industries. The growth rate of the primary industry was basically the lowest in the entire period except for a few years. The growth rate of the secondary industry was basically the fastest but fluctuated most before 1978 and witnessed a drop after 1978, with a decline in fluctuation range. The growth rate of the tertiary industry was always lower than the GDP growth rate before 1978 and basically the highest in most of the years after 1978, with the smallest fluctuation range.[1]

1.3 Overall changes in the industries: comparative analysis of data

Table 4.1 shows the growth multiples, average annual growth rates, and STDEVs and CVs for annual growth rates of China's three industries in different periods. The growth of the three industries is analyzed based on the aforementioned data.

1.3.1 Growth rate and fluctuations of each industry: 1953–2016

Table 4.1 shows that the average annual real growth rate of China's primary industry during the period 1952–2016 was 5.21%, which was far lower than the GDP growth rate (8.17%). In terms of the absolute fluctuation range, the STDEV for the growth rate of the primary industry (6.07) was slightly smaller than that for the GDP growth rate (6.97). However, since the primary industry had a lower average annual GDP growth rate than GDP, its relative fluctuation was much larger than that of GDP and its CV (1.13) was 36% larger than the CV for GDP growth rate (0.83). Among the three industries, the secondary industry grew fastest. During the period 1952–2016, it had an average annual growth of 9.27%, 1.1 percentage points higher than the average GDP growth rate. In the secondary industry, the construction segment grew faster than the industrial segment: the output value of the construction segment was up 311 times, with an average annual growth of 9.39%; and the output value of the industrial segment was up 286.5 times, with an average annual growth of 9.25%. In

Table 4.1 The growth of China's three industries in different periods: 1952–2016

	Total growth multiples (in times)											
Period	*GDP*	*Primary industry*	*Secondary industry*	*Industrial segment*	*Construction segment*	*Tertiary industry*	*Transportation, warehousing & postal service segment*	*Retail & wholesale segment*	*Catering & accommodation segment*	*Finance segment*	*Real estate segment*	*Other segments of the three industries*
1952–2016	151.0	24.8	290.3	286.5	311.3	272.2	158.6	139.7	124.3	735.7	476.0	388.8
1952–1977	3.22	1.42	8.49	9.22	4.51	2.57	4.03	1.46	1.25	4.19	3.64	2.96
1977–2016	35.00	9.63	29.69	27.14	55.71	75.47	30.75	56.31	54.69	141.0	101.8	97.32
1977–2001	8.18	3.43	7.81	7.53	10.66	14.58	10.20	11.59	16.23	19.33	16.25	17.75
2001–2016	2.92	1.40	2.48	2.30	3.86	3.91	1.83	3.55	2.23	5.98	4.96	4.24

	Average annual geometric growth rates (in %)											
Period	*GDP*	*Primary industry*	*Secondary industry*	*Industrial segment*	*Construction segment*	*Tertiary industry*	*Transportation, warehousing & postal service segment*	*Retail & wholesale segment*	*Catering & accommodation segment*	*Finance segment*	*Real estate segment*	*Other segments of the three industries*
1953–2016	8.17	5.21	9.27	9.25	9.39	9.16	8.25	8.04	7.84	10.87	10.12	9.77
1953–1977	5.93	3.61	9.42	9.74	7.06	5.22	6.67	3.66	3.30	6.81	6.33	5.66
1978–2016	9.62	6.25	9.18	8.93	10.91	11.76	9.27	10.94	10.86	13.55	12.61	12.48
1978–2001	9.68	6.40	9.49	9.34	10.78	12.12	10.59	11.13	12.59	13.37	12.60	12.99
2002–2016	9.53	6.01	8.68	8.29	11.12	11.19	7.19	10.63	8.13	13.83	12.64	11.68

(*Continued*)

Average annual arithmetical growth rates (in %)

Period	*GDP*	*Primary industry*	*Secondary industry*	*Industrial segment*	*Construction segment*	*Tertiary industry*	*Transportation, warehousing & postal service segment*	*Retail & wholesale segment*	*Catering & accommodation segment*	*Finance segment*	*Real estate segment*	*Other segments of the three industries*
1952–2016	8.42	5.38	10.12	10.05	11.35	9.52	8.93	9.77	8.28	12.73	10.48	10.05
1952–1977	6.48	3.87	11.43	11.65	11.51	5.83	8.19	5.31	3.87	10.51	6.76	6.14
1977–2016	9.66	6.36	9.27	9.03	11.26	11.88	9.41	12.63	11.12	14.15	12.87	12.56
1977–2001	9.72	6.54	9.60	9.44	11.29	12.30	10.77	13.83	12.96	14.09	12.89	13.10
2001–2016	9.48	5.89	8.61	8.26	10.83	11.27	7.35	10.62	8.26	13.67	12.75	12.09

STDEVs

Period	*GDP*	*Primary industry*	*Secondary industry*	*Industrial segment*	*Construction segment*	*Tertiary industry*	*Transportation, warehousing & postal service segment*	*Retail & wholesale segment*	*Catering & accommodation segment*	*Finance segment*	*Real estate segment*	*Other segments of the three industries*
1953–2016	6.98	6.07	12.79	12.65	18.57	8.53	11.58	20.60	9.66	19.61	9.15	7.66
1953–1977	10.48	7.35	19.79	19.55	27.85	11.04	17.28	18.82	10.65	27.61	9.91	9.99
1978–2016	2.70	4.95	4.69	4.59	9.04	5.37	5.76	21.41	7.87	12.27	7.86	4.21
1978–2001	3.02	5.86	5.03	4.76	11.04	6.53	6.56	27.36	9.42	13.35	8.39	5.15
2002–2016	2.12	3.81	4.01	4.28	4.35	2.28	2.83	3.90	2.94	10.25	7.14	2.12

CVs

Period	*GDP*	*Primary industry*	*Secondary industry*	*Industrial segment*	*Construction segment*	*Tertiary industry*	*Transportation, warehousing & postal service segment*	*Retail & wholesale segment*	*Catering & accommodation segment*	*Finance segment*	*Real estate segment*	*Other segments of the three industries*
1953–2016	0.83	1.13	1.26	1.26	1.64	0.90	1.30	2.11	1.17	1.54	0.87	0.76
1953–1977	1.62	1.90	1.73	1.68	2.42	1.89	2.11	3.55	2.76	2.63	1.47	1.63
1978–2016	0.28	0.78	0.51	0.51	0.80	0.45	0.61	1.70	0.71	0.87	0.61	0.33
1978–2001	0.31	0.90	0.52	0.50	0.98	0.53	0.61	1.98	0.73	0.95	0.65	0.39
2002–2016	0.22	0.65	0.47	0.52	0.40	0.20	0.39	0.37	0.36	0.75	0.56	0.18

terms of fluctuations in growth rate, the growth rate of the secondary industry fluctuated most among the three industries. During this period, the STDEV for the growth rate of the secondary industry (12.79) was almost twice of that for the GDP growth rate, and the CV for the former (1.26) was 52% larger than the latter. In the two segments within the secondary industry, the growth rate of the construction segment fluctuated more than that of the industrial segment. The CV for the growth rate of the construction segment was 1.64, 30% higher than that of the industrial segment (1.27). During the same period, the tertiary industry had an average annual growth of 9.16%, almost the same as that of the secondary industry. However, the tertiary industry had the smallest relative fluctuations (CV: 0.90), which were larger than those of the primary industry (STDEV: 8.52). Among the segments within the tertiary industry, the finance and real estate segments had the fastest growth of real output values. During the period 1952–2016, the output value of the finance segment was up 735.7 times, with an average annual growth of 10.9%; that of the real estate segment was up 476 times, with an average annual growth of 10.12%; that of the transportation, warehousing & postal service segment was up 158.6 times, with an average annual growth of 8.25%. The real growth rates of the three segments were faster than the real GDP growth rate. The growth rates of other segments such as retail, wholesale, catering, and accommodation were slower than the GDP growth rate. Figure 4.3 shows the changes in the growth rates of China's industrial, construction, transportation, warehousing & postal service, retail & wholesale, catering &accommodation, finance, real estate segments, and other segments of the three industries during the period 1953–2016.

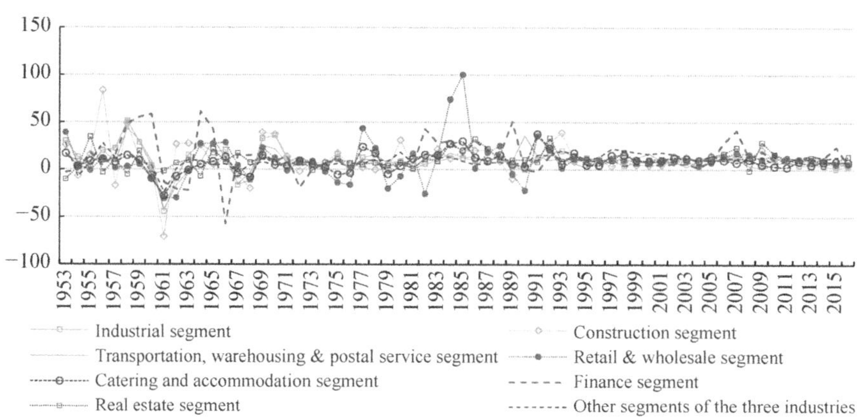

Figure 4.3 Changes in the real growth rates of output values of China's seven major segments: 1953–2016.

Table 4.2 CVs for the growth rates between China's GDP growth rate and the growth rates of the three industries during the period 1953–2016

	Primary industry	*Secondary industry*	*Tertiary industry*
Secondary industry	−0.0288 (0.82)		
Tertiary industry	−0.0987 (0.44)	**0.6620***** **(0.00)**	
GDP	0.1779 (0.16)	**0.9068***** **(0.00)**	**0.8215***** **(0.00)**

Note: The values in parentheses are P values of CVs; and "*", "**" and "***" indicate significance at the levels of 1%, 5%, and 10%.

The correlation among the growth rates of China's various segments from 1953 to 2016 shows an interesting phenomenon. Table 4.2 shows that there was almost no correlation among the growth rates of the primary, secondary, and tertiary industries and little correlation between the growth rates of the three industries and the GDP growth rate during this period. However, there was a highly significant correlation between the growth rates of the secondary and tertiary industries, and between the growth rates of the secondary and tertiary industries and the GDP growth rate. Table 4.3 further shows the correlations among the growth rates of the seven segments, and between these growth rates and those of GDP and the primary industry. As can be seen from the table, during the period 1953–2016, there was a significant positive correlation between the GDP growth rate and the growth rates of all industries and segments except the primary industry and the real estate segment, and the GDP growth rate has a strong correlation of more than 70% with the growth rates of the industrial, construction, transportation, warehousing & postal service segments. The growth rates of the industrial and transportation, warehousing & postal segments were significantly correlated with those of all the other industries and segments except the real estate segment and the primary industry, with a very large CV. The growth rate of the catering & accommodation segment was not correlated with the growth rates of the primary industry and the finance segment; the growth rate of the retail & wholesale segment was not correlated with the growth rates of the primary industry, the finance and real estate segments only, and was significantly and positively correlated with the other industries and segments. Additionally, the growth rate of the primary industry was not correlated with the growth rates of all the other industries and segments, and the growth rate of the real estate segment was only weakly correlated with that of the catering & accommodation segment (CV: 27%). The finance segment was significantly correlated with the industrial and transportation, warehousing & postal service segments.

Table 4.3 CVs for growth rates of different industries and segments of China during the period 1953–2016

	Primary industry	*Industrial segment*	*Construction segment*	*Transportation, warehousing & postal service segment 1*	*Retail & wholesale segment 2*	*Catering & accommodation segment 3*	*Finance segment 4*	*Real estate segment 5*	*Other segments of the three industries 6*
GDP	0.18	**0.88*****	**0.73*****	**0.75*****	**0.53*****	**0.66*****	**0.28****	0.15	**0.67*****
	(0.16)	**(0.00)**	**(0.00)**	**(0.00)**	**(0.00)**	**(0.00)**	**(0.02)**	(0.24)	**(0.00)**
Primary industry	1	−0.05	0.04	−0.11	−0.03	−0.07	−0.20	−0.02	−0.06
		(0.69)	(0.76)	(0.40)	(0.83)	(0.59)	(0.12)	(0.86)	(0.64)
Industrial segment		1	**0.68*****	**0.78*****	**0.38*****	**0.52****	**0.25****	−0.05	**0.53*****
			(0.00)	**(0.00)**	**(0.00)**	**(0.00)**	**(0.05)**	(0.67)	**(0.00)**
Construction segment			1	**0.53*****	**0.24***	**0.38*****	0.11 (0.40)	0.03	**0.62*****
				(0.00)	**(0.06)**	**(0.00)**		(0.80)	**(0.00)**
Transportation, warehousing & postal service segment				1	**0.31*****	**0.54*****	**0.34*****	0.09	**0.52*****
					(0.01)	**(0.00)**	**(0.01)**	(0.50)	**(0.00)**
Retail & wholesale segment					1	**0.74*****	0.08	0.20	**0.27****
						(0.00)	(0.51)	(0.11)	**(0.03)**
Catering & accommodation segment						1	0.11	**0.27****	**0.58*****
							(0.41)	**(0.03)**	**(0.00)**
Finance segment							1	0.15	0.13
								(0.24)	(0.32)
Real estate segment								1	0.02
									(0.86)

Note: The values in parentheses are P values of CVs; and "*", "**" and "***" indicate significance at the levels of 1%, 5% and 10%.

1.3.2 Changes in industrial structure: 1952–2016

Figure 4.4 shows the changes in the real output values of China's three industries during the period 1952–2016. As can be seen, in 1952, China's primary industry accounted for 50% of GDP, secondary industry 21%, and tertiary industry 29%. During the period 1952–1977, China implemented the strategy of prioritizing the development of heavy industry and vigorously developed the industrial segment. During this period, except for a few years, the secondary industry witnessed a rapid growth, and the real output value of the secondary industry had an average annual real growth of 9.24%. In 1978, China's secondary industry had a share of 48% over GDP, and its output value was close to half of the total. During the same period, the growth rates of the primary and tertiary industries were lower than the GDP growth rate. In 1978, the proportions of the primary and tertiary industries over GDP dropped to 28% and 25%, respectively. During the period of reform and opening-up, 1978–2016, the tertiary industry developed rapidly to satisfy the growing material and cultural needs of the Chinese people through the introduction of a market economy mechanism. In 2016, China's tertiary industry accounted for 52% of GDP and the output value of this industry exceeded half of GDP. Due to the role of economic development law and the characteristics of industries, the proportion of the primary industry over GDP witnessed a rapid drop since the reform and opening-up. In 2016, the primary industry accounted for 9% of GDP only. Since the reform and opening-up, the proportion of the secondary industry over GDP witnessed fluctuations and showed a slightly downward trend. In 2016, the proportion of the output value of the secondary industry over GDP reached 40%.

Not only the structures of the primary, secondary, and tertiary industries but also the internal structures of the three industries have undergone tremendous changes. Figure 4.5 shows the changes in the proportions

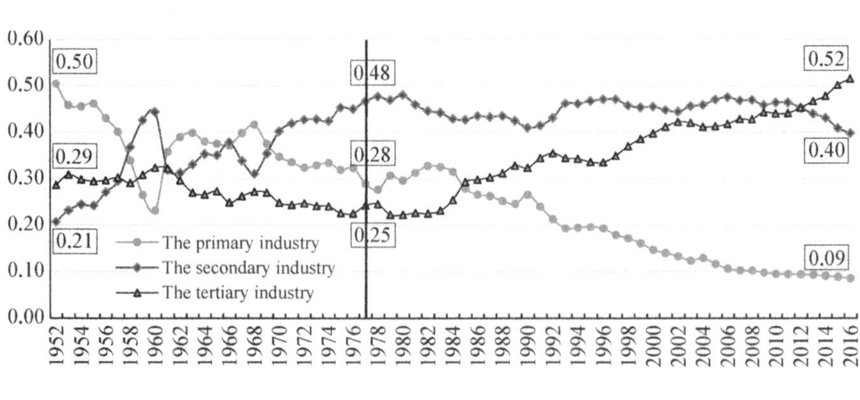

Figure 4.4 Changes in the proportions of China's three industries over GDP: 1952–2016.

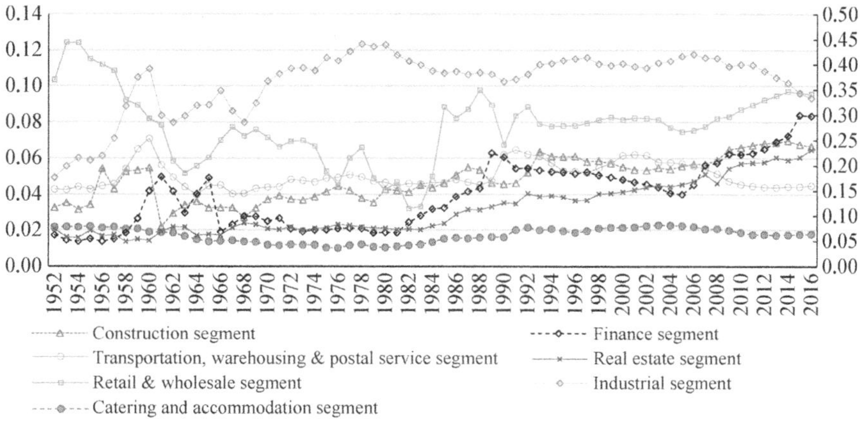

Figure 4.5 Changes in the proportions of China's seven major segments over GDP: 1952–2016.

of the output values of China's seven major industries during the period 1952–2016. Table 4.4 shows the specific proportions of the output values of China's three industries and segments over GDP within the industries in several important years. As can be seen from Figure 4.5 and Table 4.4, the proportion of China's industrial segment over GDP had identical changes with that of the secondary industry over the same. The proportion of the industrial segment over GDP witnessed a rapid, fluctuated rise during the period 1952–1977, from around 17.6% to 44%; showed a wave-like decline after 1978, with a value of 33.3% in 2016. Before the reform, the proportion of the construction segment over GDP showed a trend of ups and downs and slightly decreased. The proportion of the construction segment over GDP reached 3.2% in 1952 and approximately 4.2% in 1978. After the reform, the proportion of the construction segment over GDP saw an upward trend, reaching 6.67% in 2016. Before the reform, all segments within the tertiary industry basically witnessed a sharp rise and then a rapid decline. Among them, the retail & wholesale segment declined fastest, with its proportion over GDP rising from 10.3% in 1952 to 12% in 1954 and then dropped to 6% in 1977. The proportion of transportation, warehousing & postal service segment over GDP rose from 4.27% in 1952 to 7% in 1960, and then dropped to 5.1% in 1977. The proportion of catering and accommodation over GDP dropped from 2.16% to 1.15%. And the proportions of the finance and real estate segments over GDP rose slightly amid the volatility, to 2.12% and 2.26% in 1977. During the period 1978–2016, the proportions of almost all segments within the tertiary industry over GDP showed an upward trend; however, the proportion of transportation, warehousing & postal service segment experienced a sharp downward trend after 2002.

Table 4.4 Changes in the proportions of China's three industries over GDP: 1952–2019

Period	*Primary industry*	*Secondary industry*	*Industrial segment*	*Construction segment*	*Tertiary industry*	*Transportation, warehousing & postal service segment*	*Retail and wholesale segment*	*Catering and accommodation segment*	*Finance segment*	*Real estate segment*	*Other segments of the three industries or other segments of the tertiary industry*
1952	50.49	20.78	17.61	3.24	28.73	4.27	10.32	2.16	1.72	2.06	8.19
1977	28.99	46.70	42.62	4.22	24.31	5.08	6.00	1.15	2.12	2.26	7.69
2001	13.98	44.79	39.56	5.36	41.22	6.20	8.23	2.16	4.69	4.25	15.69
2016	8.06	39.58	32.88	6.90	52.36	4.43	9.88	1.82	8.03	6.69	21.51
2017	7.46	39.85	33.07	6.96	52.68	4.46	9.75	1.81	7.79	6.86	22.01
2018	7.04	39.69	32.75	7.12	53.27	4.39	9.67	1.80	7.68	7.03	22.70
2019	7.11	38.97	32.00	7.16	53.92	4.32	9.67	1.82	7.78	7.03	23.30

Source: The CEIC database.

Section 2 Contributions of the three industries to GDP growth without regard for relative price changes

2.1 Calculating method and formula

In order to analyze the impact of the growth of the three industries over the real GDP growth, this section decomposes the GDP growth rate by industry according to the method similar to the analysis of the breakdown of demand factors in GDP growth as mentioned in the previous chapter, without regard for the changes in the relative prices of industries. The third section reexamines the impact of relative price changes of industries over the breakdown of the economic growth rate.

Similar to the previous chapter, here we assume:

$$Y_t = X_{1t} + X_{2t} + X_{3t}$$

where Y refers to the real GDP, and X_i refers to the real output value of Industry i. Thus,

$$g_t^Y = \alpha_{t-1}^1 g_t^1 + \alpha_{t-1}^2 g_t^2 + \alpha_{t-1}^3 g_t^3 \tag{4.1}$$

where g^Y refers to the real GDP growth rate; g^i refers to the growth rate of the real output value of Industry i; and α_i refers to the proportion of the output value of Industry i over GDP. Therefore, g^{iY}, the GDP growth arising from the growth of Industry i, and R^i, the contribution of the industrial growth to the GDP growth rate, can be represented as follows:

$$g_t^{iY} = \alpha_{t-1}^i g_t^i = (X_{it} - X_{it\text{-}1})/Y_{t-1}, \quad i = 1,2,3 \tag{4.2}$$

$$R_t^i = g_t^{iY} / g_t^Y = \alpha_{t-1}^i g_t^i / g_t^Y, \quad i = 1,2,3 \tag{4.3}$$

2.2 Overview of the contributions of the three industries to the real GDP growth

According to the data introduced above, the real GDP growth and percentage points arising from the growth of China's three industries and the contributions of the three industries to the real GDP growth can be calculated by using Formulas (1.8) and (1.9), as shown in Figures 4.6 and 4.7. We can come to the following conclusions for the two figures: (1) In most of the years during the period 1953–2016, the growth of the secondary industry contributed more to China's GDP growth than the growth of the primary industry did. (2) The tertiary industry contributed less to GDP growth than the secondary industry and the primary industry before the reform, but more to GDP growth than the primary industry all the time after the reform, and even more to the same than the secondary industry after 1995. (3) In

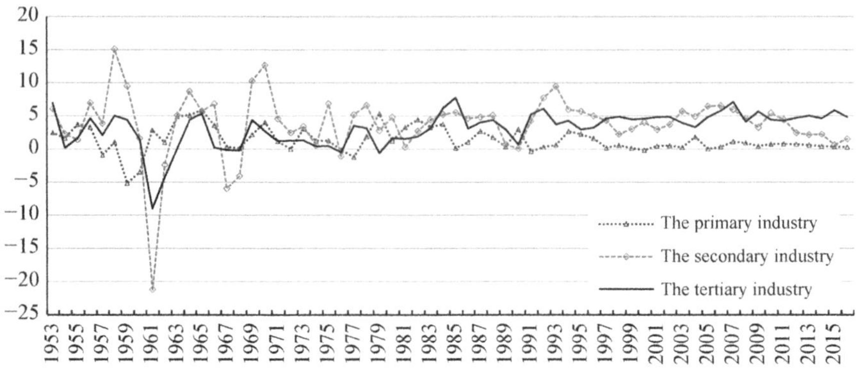

Figure 4.6 The annual GDP growth arising from the growth of the three industries: 1953–2016.

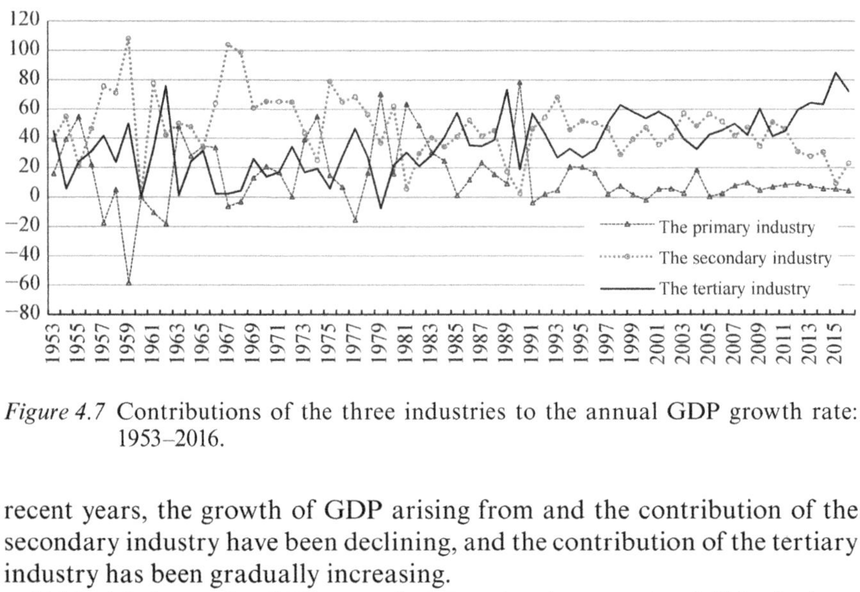

Figure 4.7 Contributions of the three industries to the annual GDP growth rate: 1953–2016.

recent years, the growth of GDP arising from and the contribution of the secondary industry have been declining, and the contribution of the tertiary industry has been gradually increasing.

Table 4.5 shows the GDP growth driven by the growth of China's three industries in different periods. As can be known from Table 4.5, (1) China's real GDP arising from the primary industry during the period 1952–2016 was up 12.5 times, with a contribution of 8.27%; China's real GDP arising from the secondary industry was up 60.3 times, with a contribution of 39.8%, in which the GDP arising from the industrial segment was up 50.46 times and that from the construction segment was up 10.08 times; and the real GDP arising from the tertiary industry was up 78.2 times, with a contribution of 51.7%. (2) So, in terms of the contribution to the total growth multiple, the tertiary industry contributed most, over 50%, to China's GDP

Table 4.5 Annual GDP growth arising from the growth of the industries and segments and their contributions

Growth multiples for the contributions of the growth of the industries and segments to annual GDP growth (in times)

Period	*GDP*	*Primary industry*	*Secondary industry*	*Industrial segment*	*Construction segment*	*Tertiary industry*	*Transportation, warehousing & postal service segment*	*Retail & wholesale segment*	*Catering & accommodation segment*	*Finance segment*	*Real estate segment*	*Other segments of three industries or tertiary industry*
1953–2016	151.2	12.50	60.31	50.46	10.08	78.20	6.77	14.4	2.69	12.68	9.81	31.83
1953–1977	3.23	0.72	1.76	1.62	0.15	0.74	0.17	0.15	0.03	0.07	0.08	0.24
1978–2016	35.1	2.79	13.87	11.57	2.35	18.35	1.56	3.38	0.63	2.98	2.31	7.48
1978–2001	8.20	0.99	3.65	3.21	0.45	3.54	0.52	0.70	0.19	0.41	0.37	1.36
2002–2016	2.92	0.20	1.11	0.91	0.21	1.61	0.11	0.29	0.05	0.28	0.21	0.67

Average annual GDP growth arising from the growth of the industries and segments (in %)

Period	*GDP*	*Primary industry*	*Secondary industry*	*Industrial segment*	*Construction segment*	*Tertiary industry*	*Transportation, warehousing & postal service segment*	*Retail & wholesale segment*	*Catering & accommodation segment*	*Finance segment*	*Real estate segment*	*Other segments of the tertiary industries*
1953–2016	8.42	1.40	3.87	3.40	0.49	3.15	0.42	0.65	0.14	0.43	0.35	1.16
1953–1977	6.48	1.55	3.40	3.09	0.32	1.53	0.32	0.36	0.06	0.15	0.12	0.52
1978–2016	9.66	1.30	4.18	3.60	0.59	4.18	0.49	0.83	0.19	0.62	0.49	1.56
1978–2001	9.72	1.71	4.28	3.75	0.54	3.73	0.56	0.80	0.21	0.51	0.39	1.27
2002–2016	9.48	0.63	3.95	3.32	0.65	4.90	0.38	0.89	0.17	0.76	0.63	2.07

	Contributions of the growth of the industries and segments to GDP growth multiples (in %)											
Period	*GDP*	*Primary industry*	*Secondary industry*	*Industrial segment*	*Construction segment*	*Tertiary industry*	*Transportation, warehousing & postal service segment*	*Retail & wholesale segment*	*Catering & accommodation segment*	*Finance segment*	*Real estate segment*	*Other segments of the tertiary industries*
1953–2016	100	8.27	39.87	33.36	6.67	51.71	4.48	9.54	1.78	8.38	6.49	21.04
1953–1977	100	22.28	54.66	50.30	4.52	22.90	5.33	4.66	0.84	2.24	2.32	7.52
1978–2016	100	7.96	39.55	32.99	6.71	52.33	4.46	9.64	1.80	8.51	6.58	21.34
1978–2001	100	12.13	44.51	39.14	5.50	43.23	6.33	8.49	2.29	4.99	4.49	16.65
2002–2016	100	6.69	38.04	31.12	7.09	55.11	3.89	10.0	1.65	9.59	7.22	22.77
	Contributions of the growth of industries and segments to the average annual GDP growth (in %)											
Period	*GDP*	*Primary industry*	*Secondary industry*	*Industrial segment*	*Construction segment*	*Tertiary industry*	*Transportation, warehousing & postal service segment*	*Retail & wholesale segment*	*Catering & accommodation segment*	*Finance segment*	*Real estate segment*	*Other segments of the three industries*
1953–2016	100	16.58	46.03	40.39	5.78	37.39	5.01	7.70	1.67	5.16	4.11	13.74
1953–1977	100	23.88	52.44	47.64	4.95	23.68	4.98	5.52	0.96	2.24	1.92	8.08
1978–2016	100	13.44	43.27	37.27	6.14	43.29	5.03	8.64	1.98	6.41	5.06	16.18
1978–2001	100	17.59	44.06	38.58	5.60	38.36	5.72	8.20	2.12	5.26	4.02	13.03
2002–2016	100	6.64	41.64	35.00	6.82	51.72	4.06	9.35	1.78	8.00	6.69	21.84

Source: *China Statistical Yearbooks* and the CEIC database. This table is obtained by the author according to the raw data.

growth during the same period. The secondary industry also contributed much to the real GDP growth but nearly 10 percentage points less than the tertiary industry did, whose growth was mainly driven by the growth of the industrial segment. And the primary industry contributed little, less than 10%, to the real GDP growth.

Just like with the deposition of demand factors for the GDP growth rate in the previous section, this method of calculating the contributions of the three industries based on the total growth multiple within the interval only considers the impacts of changes in the industrial structure at the beginning and end of the period on the growth structure rather than the changes and fluctuations in the annual GDP growth driven by the growth of each industry and their annual contributions added during the economic growth process. As can be seen from Table 4.6, the annual growth of GDP driven by the growth of the three industries differs greatly. During the period 1953–2016, the STDEV for the annual GDP growth driven by the secondary industry was 4.68%, 2.5 times larger than that driven by the primary industry and 1.7 times larger than that driven by the tertiary industry. The CV for the annual GDP growth driven by the secondary industry was 1.21, slightly smaller than that from the primary industry (1.37) and larger than that from the tertiary industry (0.87). In order to reflect the impact of the fluctuations in the growth of the three industries, Table 4.5 also gives the real GDP growth driven by the growth of the three industries and their contributions. As can be seen from Table 4.5, during the period 1953–2016, the average annual real GDP growth driven by the primary industry was 1.40%, with a contribution of 16.6%; the average annual real GDP growth from the secondary industry was 3.87%, with a contribution of 46.03%, in which that driven by the industrial segment was 3.40% and that driven by the industrial segment was 0.47%; and that driven by the tertiary industry was 3.15%, with a contribution of 37.39%. Thus, if the impact of short-term economic fluctuations is taken into account, the contributions of the primary and secondary industries to GDP will increase while the contribution of the tertiary industry will decrease.[2]

2.3 The contributions of the growth of the three industries to real GDP growth: comparisons before and after the reform

The differences in the contributions of the growth of the three industries to China's GDP growth before and after the reform are discussed below. As known from Table 4.6, during the period 1952–1977 before the reform, China's real GDP was up 3.22 times. The real GDP arising from the primary industry was up 0.72 times, with a contribution of 22.28%; the real GDP arising from the secondary industry was up 1.76 times, with a contribution of 54.66%, in which the real GDP arising from the industrial segment was up 1.62 times and that from the construction segment was up 0.15 times; the real GDP arising from the growth of the tertiary industry was up 0.74 times,

Table 4.6 Fluctuations in the growth of China's GDP arising from the growth of the industries and their contribution rates

Period	*GDP*	*Primary industry*	*Secondary industry*	*Industrial segment*	*Construction segment*	*Tertiary industry*	*Transportation, warehousing & postal service segment*	*Retail & wholesale segment*	*Catering & accommodation segment*	*Finance segment*	*Real estate segment*
STDEVs for the contributions of the growth of the industries to annual GDP growth											
1953–2016	1.91	4.68	4.08	0.81	2.73	0.63	1.24	0.16	0.73	0.32	0.91
1953–1977	2.57	7.10	6.19	1.17	3.28	0.94	1.38	0.19	0.93	0.17	0.89
1978–2016	1.36	2.07	1.82	0.43	1.65	0.29	1.12	0.12	0.50	0.31	0.66
1978–2001	1.65	2.17	1.84	0.52	1.81	0.32	1.41	0.14	0.47	0.25	0.65
2002–2016	0.44	1.89	1.78	0.24	0.93	0.17	0.29	0.07	0.51	0.33	0.36
CVs for the contributions of the growth of industries to annual GDP growth											
1953–2016	1.37	1.21	1.20	1.66	0.87	1.49	1.91	1.15	1.69	0.91	0.79
1953–1977	1.66	2.09	2.01	3.65	2.14	2.92	3.85	3.00	6.44	1.38	1.71
1978–2016	1.05	0.49	0.50	0.73	0.39	0.60	1.35	0.64	0.81	0.63	0.43
1978–2001	0.96	0.51	0.49	0.95	0.48	0.58	1.77	0.68	0.92	0.64	0.51
2002–2016	0.70	0.48	0.54	0.37	0.19	0.44	0.33	0.41	0.67	0.52	0.17

with a contribution of 22.90%. If calculated in terms of the average annual growth rate, China's real GDP had an average annual growth of 6.48% before the reform. The real GDP arising from the primary industry had an average annual growth of 1.55%, with a contribution of 23.88%; the real GDP arising from the secondary industry had an average annual growth of 3.40%, with a contribution of 52.44%, in which the real GDP arising from the industrial segment had an average annual growth of 3.09% and that from the construction segment 0.32%; the real GDP arising from the tertiary industry had an average annual growth of 1.53%, with a contribution of 23.68%. And in the tertiary industry, the transportation, warehousing & postal service segment, and the retail & wholesale segment, which serve the flow of commodity, grew the most. The growth arising from both segments above accounted for 43% of the growth contributed by the three industries to the real GDP growth.

It can be seen that the rapid growth of the secondary industry during the period 1952–1977, with an average annual growth of 9.42%, especially the high growth of the industrial segment, with an average annual growth of 9.74%, represented the major driver for China's economic growth. Despite the large contribution of the tertiary industry to the real GDP growth during the period 1952–2016, the contribution of this industry to GDP growth was almost the same as that of the primary industry during 1953–1977, with the total contributions of both industries to the real GDP growth approximately 8 percentage points lower than the contribution of the secondary industry to the same. Of course, the primary and tertiary industries differ in the mechanism of impact on GDP. Before the reform, the growth of the output value of China's tertiary industry was not low, with an average annual growth of 5.22%, but the contribution of this industry to real GDP growth was not large due to the small proportion of its output value over GDP. The low contribution rate of the primary industry was mainly due to its low growth rate. During the period 1952–1977, the average annual growth rate for the real output value of China's primary industry was only 3.61%, far lower than the average annual growth rates of real GDP and the real output value of the tertiary industry. Moreover, the primary industry contributed almost the same to GDP as the tertiary industry did due to the fact that the former accounted for a large proportion of GDP. Additionally, the absolute fluctuations in the growth of the secondary industry were the largest. Its STDEV (7.10%) was 2.16 times more than that of the tertiary industry (3.28%), and the CV (2.09) was almost the same as that of the tertiary industry (2.14) but far larger than that of the primary industry (1.66). Overall, during the period 1952–1977, China's GDP growth mainly relied on the growth of the tertiary industry, particularly the industrial segment. As the GDP growth was mainly driven by the secondary industry, the large fluctuations of the growth rate of the secondary industry also caused the fluctuations of China's economic growth to a large extent.

During the period 1978–2016 after the reform, China's real GDP was up 35.1 times. Among the three industries, the real GDP arising from the primary industry was up 2.79 times, with a contribution of 7.96%; the real GDP arising from the secondary industry was up 13.87 times, with a contribution of 39.55%, in which the real GDP arising from the industrial segment was up 11.57 times and that arising from the construction segment was up 2.23 times; and the real GDP arising from the tertiary industry was up 18.35 times, with a contribution of 52.33%. In terms of average annual growth rate, during the same period, China had a real GDP growth of 9.66%. The real GDP arising from the primary industry had an average annual growth of 1.30%, with a contribution of 13.44%. The real GDP arising from the secondary industry had an average annual growth of 4.18%, with a contribution of 43.27%, in which the real GDP arising from the industrial segment had an average annual growth rate of 3.6% and that from the construction segment 0.59%. And the real GDP arising from the tertiary industry had an average annual growth of 4.18%, with a contribution of 43.29%, in which the five segments including transportation, warehousing & postal service, retail & wholesale, catering & accommodation, finance, and real estate accounted for 52% of the GDP growth arising from the tertiary industry.

After the reform, China's economic growth pattern shifted from the GDP growth solely driven by the secondary industry to that jointly by the secondary and tertiary industries, which was the biggest change relative to the period before the reform. Also, the role of the tertiary industry in driving economic growth was even larger than that of the secondary industry. Firstly, after the reform, the role of the tertiary industry in driving economic growth was improved to a large extent, and its contribution to the real GDP growth increased from the pre-reform less than 25% to the post-reform nearly 50%. The rise in the contribution of the tertiary industry to GDP growth was mainly derived from the rapid growth of the tertiary industry itself. Although China's tertiary industry accounted for only 25% in the early period of the reform, the real growth of the output value of the tertiary industry during the period 1978–2016 was up 75.47 times, 2.5 times more than the real GDP growth multiple of GDP, and 2.15 times more than the real output value growth multiple of the secondary industry. The tertiary industry had an average annual growth of up to 11.76%, far higher than the average annual real GDP growth of 9.66% and the average annual real output value of the secondary industry of 9.22%. Secondly, despite the still large contribution of the secondary industry to economic growth after the reform, its contribution was even 0.78 percentage point higher than that after the reform. However, due to the greatly improved effect of the tertiary industry on economic growth, the average annual GDP growth driven by the tertiary industry was up 2.6 percentage points, making the role of the secondary industry in driving economic growth relatively decline after the reform. Within the secondary industry, the real GDP growth was mainly driven by the industrial segment, and the role of the construction segment also saw a significant increase, with the proportion of the real GDP growth driven by such segment increasing from 9.4% before the reform and 14.1% after the reform. Secondly, the average annual GDP growth driven by the primary industry growth decreased from 1.55% before the reform to 1.30% after the reform, and the absolute value for the real GDP growth driven by such segment also decreased, making the greatly reduced effect of the primary industry on China's economic growth after the reform. However, the real growth of the output value of the primary industry was increasing after the reform, with the average annual growth rate increasing from the pre-reform 3.61% to the post-reform 6.25%. However, due to the greatly reduced proportion of GDP driven by the primary industry after the reform, the average annual growth of real GDP driven by the primary industry increased as well. Additionally, in terms of fluctuations, the annual GDP growth driven by each industry after the reform became more stable. As can be seen in Table 4.6, although the average annual GDP growth driven by the tertiary industry since the reform was long on the rise, both its STDEV and CV decreased.

Section 3 Contributions of the three industries to GDP growth in consideration of relative price changes

Section 2 calculates the GDP growth driven by the three industries by assuming the prices of the three industries change in the same proportion. Thus, the price changes in the three industries can be eliminated according to the GDP deflator. However, in reality, the prices of the three industries did not change in the same proportion. Figure 4.8 shows the annual inflation rates measured by GDP deflator and of three industrial product prices in China during the period 1953–2016. According to Figure 4.8, during the years 1952–2016, the rise in the prices of the secondary industry was basically

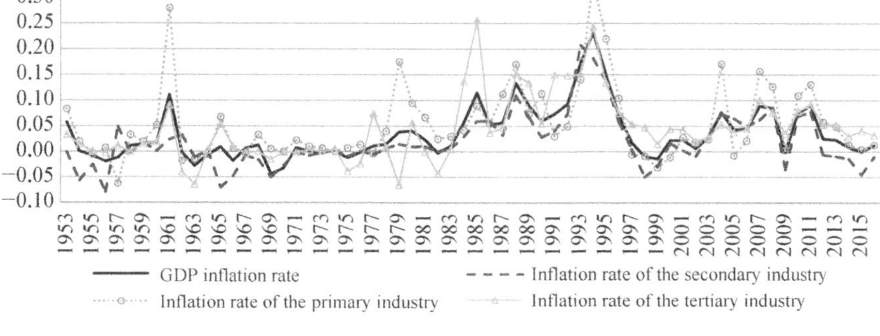

Figure 4.8 The inflation rates of China's GDP deflator and of price indexes for the three industries: 1953–2016.

lower than the GDP deflator; the price rise of the primary industry was basically higher than the GDP deflator; and that of the tertiary industry was higher in some years and lower in some other years than the GDP deflator. In the case of inconsistent price changes, in the calculation of the real GDP growth rate, the real GDP is not equal to the simple addition of the real output values of the three industries, but to one weighted average of the real output values of the three industries with each price proportion as weight. Since price structure changes are not taken into account, the formula on the decomposition of the real GDP growth rate, as shown in Formula (1.7), was not accurate. Thus, there will be bias from the contributions of the three industries to GDP growth calculated using Formulas (1.8) and (1.9).

3.1 The real GDP calculation formula in the case of price structure changes

Firstly, derive the formula for the decomposition of real GDP growth rates when there are different proportions of price changes. Assume:

$$P_t Y_t = \sum_{i=1}^{m} P_{it} X_{it} \Leftrightarrow Y_t = \sum_{i=1}^{m} (P_{it}/P_t) X_{it} \tag{4.4}$$

Y refers to GDP; P refers to the price index of real GDP; X_i refers to the real output value of Industry i; P_i refers to the price index of Industry i; and t refers to the year. There are four industries in the economy.

According to Formula (4.4), we can get:

$$(P_t Y)_t / (P_{t-1} Y_{t-1}) = \sum_{i=1}^{m} (P_{it} X_{it}) / (P_{t-1} Y_{t-1})$$

Let $\pi_t = (P_t - P_{t-1})/P_{t-1}$ represent the inflation rate of GDP; $\pi_{it} = (P_{it} - P_{it-1})/P_{it-1}$ the price inflation rate of Industry I; $g_t = (Y_t - Y_{t-1})/Y_{t-1}$ real GDP growth rate; and $g_{it} = (X_{it} - X_{it-1})/X_{it-1}$ the growth rate of the real output value of Industry i.

The following formula can be obtained using the above formula:

$$\pi_t + g_t + \pi_t g_t = \sum_{i=1}^{m} (\alpha_{it-1}\pi_{it} + \alpha_{it-1} g_{it} + \pi_{it} g_{it} \alpha_{it-1})$$

where $\alpha_{it} = (P_{it} X_{it})/(P_t Y_t)$ refers to the proportion of the nominal output value of Industry i over nominal GDP. In order to obtain the formula of calculating the real GDP growth rate, the following formulas can be obtained by further adjusting the formula above:

$$\begin{aligned} g_t &= \sum_{i=1}^{m} \alpha_{it-1} g_{it} + \sum_{i=1}^{m} \alpha_{it-1}(\pi_{it} - \pi_t) + \sum_{i=1}^{m} \alpha_{it-1}(\pi_{it} g_{it} - \pi_t g_t) \\ &= \sum_{i=1}^{m} \left[\alpha_{it-1} g_{it} + \alpha_{it-1}(\pi_{it} - \pi_t) + \alpha_{it-1}(\pi_{it} g_{it} - \pi_t g_t)\right] \end{aligned} \tag{4.5}$$

The first equation in Formula (4.5) indicates that the growth rate of real GDP can be decomposed into the following three parts: real GDP growth arising from the real growth of each industry (hereinafter referred to as the "industrial growth effect"), the real GDP growth arising from relative price changes caused by the difference in the price growth rate of each industry (hereinafter referred to as "price structure change effect"), as well as real GDP growth arising from the interaction between price structure changes and real output value changes of the three industries (hereinafter referred to as "growth-price structure cross effect"). The second equation in Formula (4.5) further decomposes the overall price structure change effect and the growth-price structure cross effect into each industry. That means the overall effect of each industry over real GDP growth includes three parts, namely the effect of the industry's real growth on real GDP growth, the effect of price changes of each industry over real GDP growth relative to the difference in the overall price changes of GDP, and the interaction effect of the industry's real growth-relative price changes on real GDP growth.

In the calculation of the annual GDP growth rate, both annual inflation rate and the growth of the real output value of each industry are quite small, and the last term in Formula (4.5) is an infinitely small quantity of a higher order relative to the previous two items. Thus, when calculating the annual real GDP growth rate, we can get the following formula by omitting higher-order items:

$$g_t = \sum_{i=1}^{m} \alpha_{it-1}(\pi_{it} - \pi_t) + \sum_{i=1}^{m} \alpha_{it-1} g_{it} \tag{4.6}$$

The error item for the real GDP calculated after omitting higher-order items is as follows:

$$\begin{aligned}\Delta &= \sum_{i=1}^{m} n_{it} g_{it} \alpha_{it-1} - n_t g_t = \sum_{i=1}^{m} n_{it} g_{it} \alpha_{it-1} - n_t g_t \sum_{i=1}^{m} \alpha_{it} \\ &= \sum_{i=1}^{m} (g_{it} n_{it} - g_t n_{it}) \alpha_{it-1}\end{aligned}$$

Let $\underline{ng}_{it} = \min_i : \{n_{it} g_{it}\}_{i=1}^{m}$, $\overline{ng}_{it} = \max_i : \{n_{it} g_{it}\}_{i=1}^{m}$, then:

$$\underline{ng}_{it} - n_t g_t \le \Delta = \sum_{i=1}^{m} (g_{it} n_{it} - g_t n_t)\, \alpha_{it-1} \le \overline{ng}_{it} - n_t g_t$$

If both growth rates π and g are percentiles, it is evident that the error item Δ is an infinitely small quantity of a higher order relative to the previous items. Therefore, the error of the real GDP growth rate calculated according to Formula (4.6) lies within the interval of $\left(\underline{ng}_{it} - n_t g_t, \overline{ng}_{it} - n_t g_t\right)$. R^i, the contribution of the real output value growth of Industry i to real GDP growth, and R^C, the contribution of price structure changes to real GDP growth, can be calculated according to Formula (4.5).

$$R_t^i = g_t^{iY} / g_t^Y = \alpha_{t-1}^i g_t^i / g_t^Y, \quad R_t^C = \sum_{i=1}^{m} \alpha_{it-1}(\pi_{it} - \pi_t) \Big/ g_t^Y \tag{4.7}$$

3.2 Data sources and calculation result of the growth rates by industry

As is known from Formulas (4.6) and (4.7), in order to decompose the real GDP growth under industrial price structure changes, it is necessary to know the real GDP growth rate (g), real growth rates of the three industries (g_i), inflation rate measured by GDP deflator (π), and the price inflation rates of the three industries (π_i), as well as the proportions of the nominal output values of the three industries over GDP (α_i). Data on the real GDP growth rate (g) and the growth rates of real output value of the three industries (g_i), as calculated at the prices of the previous year, are available from the *China Statistical Yearbooks* and the *Collection of Statistical Data for New China During the 50 Years of Its Founding*, as shown in Figure 4.9. According to the data of Section 2, the nominal GDP growth rate and the growth rates of the nominal output values of the three industries can be calculated. Based on the above, the inflation rate measured by GDP deflator (π), the inflation rates of the tertiary industries (πi), and proportions of the nominal output values of the three industries over GDP (αi) can be calculated. Thus, the GDP growth driven by the growth of the three industries and by changes in relative price changes and their contributions can be calculated using Formula (4.6), as shown in Figures 4.11 and 4.12.

In terms of the impact on the annual real GDP growth rate, price structure changes produced little effect on it. As can be seen from Figure 4.11, the annual real GDP growth driven by price structure changes was basically

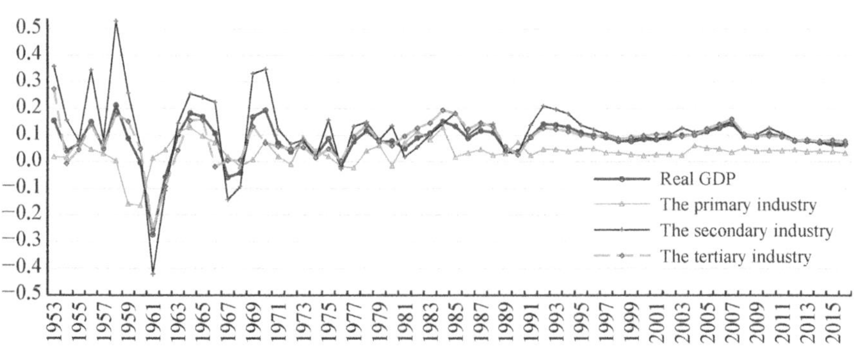

Figure 4.9 China's real GDP growth rate and the real output value growth rates of the three industries: 1953–2016.

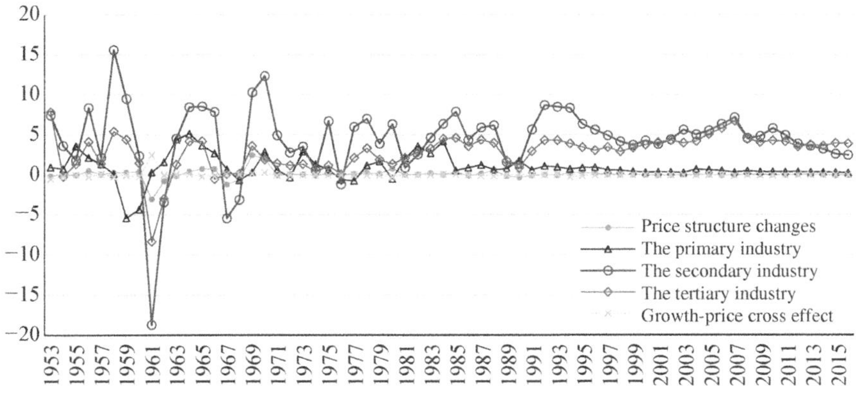

Figure 4.10 Price structure changes and contributions of the three industries to GDP growth.

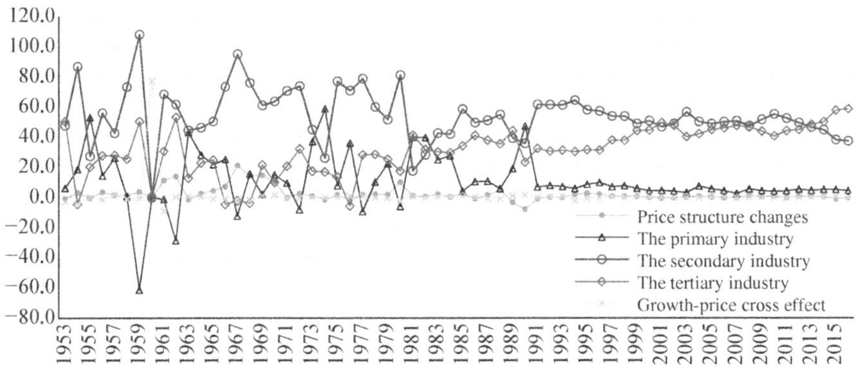

Figure 4.11 Contributions of each industry to the annual GDP growth rate in consideration of price structure changes.

kept between −1% and 1%. Especially since 1990, price structure changes produced an even smaller effect, with GDP growth arising therefrom kept between −0.1% and 0.1%, and their contributions to the annual real GDP growth rate were maintained between −1% and 1%. However, the annual GDP growth driven by the three industries and their contributions to annual GDP growth changed a lot in consideration of price changes rather than without regard for the same. Figure 4.12 compares the annual real GDP growth driven by the three industries before and after the price structure changes. As can be seen from the figure, the GDP growth driven by the primary industry was slower in most of the years in consideration of price structure adjustments compared to that without regard for the same. The annual real GDP growth driven by the three industries basically increased

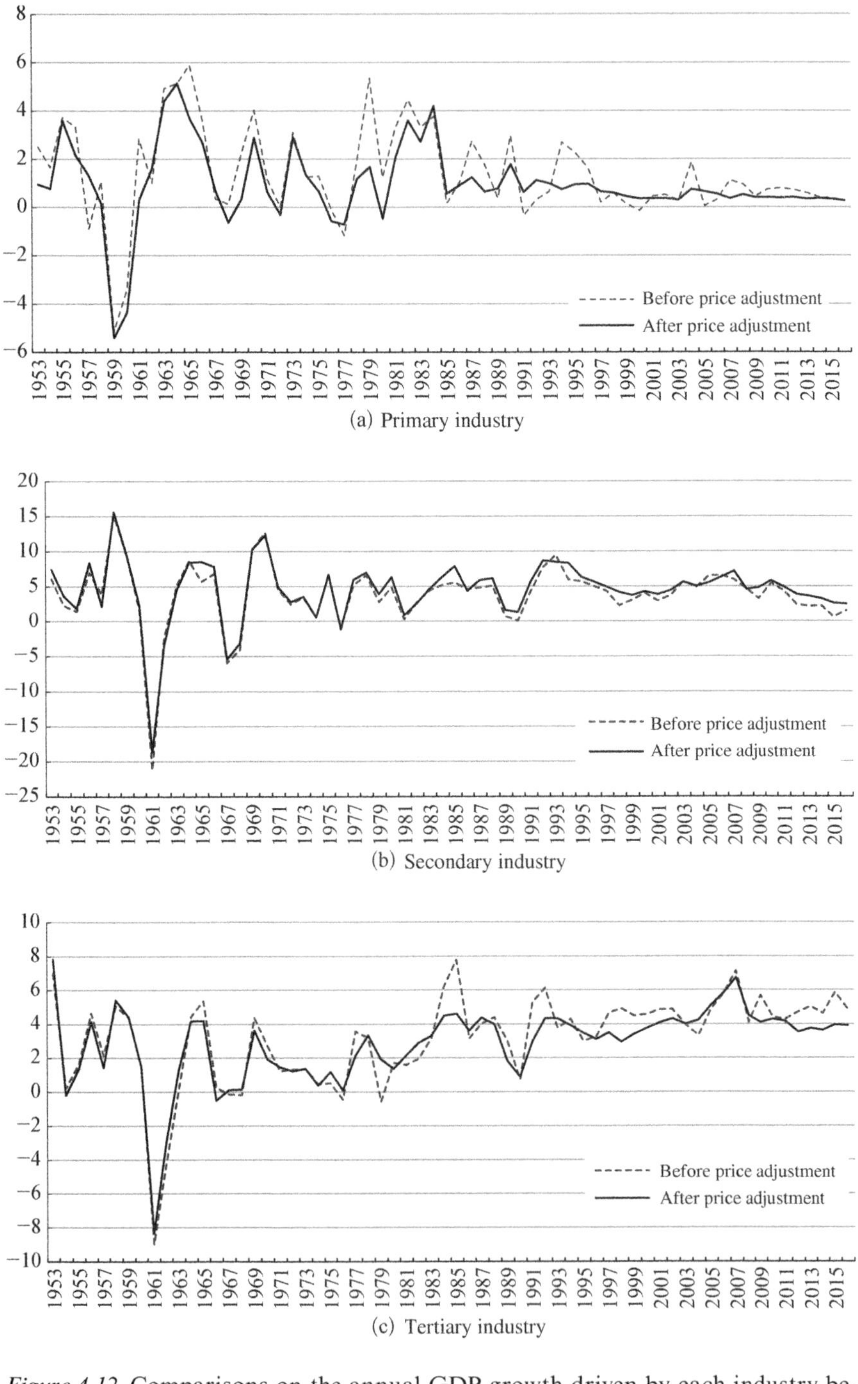

Figure 4.12 Comparisons on the annual GDP growth driven by each industry before and after price structure changes: 1953–2016.

Table 4.7 GDP growth driven by each factor and their contributions without regard for price structure changes

Period	*Growth effect*			*Price structure effect*	*Growth-price structure cross effect*	*Total GDP*
	Primary industry	*Secondary industry*	*Tertiary industry*			
			Growth driven by each factor			
1952–2016	3.92	158.23	51.24	7.21	−69.60	151.01
1952–1977	0.32	2.54	0.72	0. 22	−0.58	3.22
1977–2016	**1.27**	**26.44**	**12.18**	**1.18**	**−6.06**	**35.00**
1977–2001	0.56	5.78	2.68	0.22	−1.06	8.18
2001–2016	0.12	1.48	1.34	0.04	−0.05	2.92
			Contribution of each factor to GDP growth (in %)			
1952–2016	2.6	104.8	33.9	4.8	−46.1	100
1952–1977	9.9	78.9	22.4	6.8	−17.9	100
1977–2016	**3.6**	**75.5**	**34.8**	**3.4**	**−17.3**	**100**
1977–2001	6.8	70.6	32.7	2.7	−12.9	100
2001–2016	4.0	50.8	45.9	1.3	−1.9	100

Source: *China Statistical Yearbooks* and the CEIC database; the data here are calculated by the author according to the raw data.

before the reform and decreased after the reform. The annual GDP growth driven by the secondary industry basically increased in all years. The reason mainly lies in the faster growth of the prices in the primary and tertiary industries relative to the GDP deflator and slower growth of the price index of the secondary industry. As a result, the calculation weight of the real output values for the primary and tertiary industries increased and that for the secondary industry reduced. Additionally, the annual GDP growth driven by the three industries appeared more stable in consideration of relevant price structure changes compared with that without regard for the same.

Although both the price structure change effect and growth-price structure cross effect do not produce a great impact on the real GDP growth each year, the two effects are not small for China's long-term economic growth due to the cumulative effect of economic growth. By applying Formula (4.5), Table 4.7 calculates the growth multiples and contributions of the growth effect, price structure change effect, and growth-price structure cross effect of the three industries during different periods for China's real GDP growth.

3.3 Impact on the industrial breakdown of GDP growth rate in consideration of relative price changes

Firstly, as Table 4.7 shows, during the entire period 1952–2016, the real GDP growth of China driven by the secondary industry was up to 158.23 times if the effect of price changes is taken into consideration, far larger than the growth effect of the secondary industry (60.31 times) without regard for price structure changes, as shown in Table 4.5. During this period, the growth effect of the secondary industry was even larger than the growth multiple of real GDP, with its contribution to GDP growth of 104%. During the same period, the real GDP arising from the tertiary industry was up 51.24 times, with a contribution of 33.9%. The growth effect of the tertiary industry was 74.5% lower than that without regard for price structure changes, with its contribution down 17.2 percentage points. The growth effect of the primary industry was only 3.92 times, 23.6% of that without regard for price structure changes, with its contribution down from 8.27% to 2.6%. Additionally, the price structure change effect made the real GDP up 7.21 times during the same period, with a contribution of 4.8%. During the growth process, the secondary industry, with the fastest decline in prices, actually had the highest growth rate and the growth-price structure cross effect made the real GDP down 69.60 times, with a contribution of −46.1%.

Secondly, in consideration of the price structure change effect, similar changes occurred to the GDP growth effect driven by the three industries before and after the reform and opening-up (i.e., larger growth effect in the secondary industry and smaller growth effect in the primary and tertiary industries). Actually, during the period 1952–1977 before the reform, the effect of GDP growth driven by the primary industry was only 0.32, with a contribution of 9.9%; that driven by the secondary industry was 2.54 times, with a contribution of 78.9%; and that driven by the tertiary industry was 72%, with a contribution of 22.4%. The effect of price structure changes made China's real GDP grow by 22%, with a contribution of 6.8%; the growth-price structure adjustment cross effect made the real GDP drop by 58%, with a contribution of −17.9%. The overall effect caused a 36% decline in real GDP, and the overall effect on economic growth was −11.1%. Thus, China's real GDP growth during this period was basically driven by the secondary industry. During the period 1978–2016, the real GDP arising from the primary industry was up 1.27 times, with a contribution of 3.6%; that arising from the secondary industry was up 26.44 times, with a contribution of 75.5%; and that arising from the tertiary industry was up 12.18 times, with a contribution of 34.8%. The price structure change effect caused China's real GDP to be up 1.18 times, with a contribution of 3.4%. The growth-price structure adjustment cross effect made the real GDP down 6.06 times, with a contribution of −17.3%. The overall effect caused real GDP to be down 4.98 times, and the overall effect on economic growth was −13.9%. Thus, although the secondary industry remained a major driver for economic growth since the reform, the tertiary industry also played a big role, with a contribution of over one third. On the whole, the role of the primary industry on GDP growth declined, that of the tertiary industry greatly improved, and that of the secondary industry slightly dropped.

There is a permanent conclusion that the growth effects of the primary and secondary industries have been declining and the role of the tertiary industry in driving GDP growth has been increasing during China's economic growth in consideration of price structure changes when compared with those without regard for price structure changes. For the two stages before and after the reform, the contribution of the secondary industry after the reform was 3.4 percentage points lower than that before the reform; the contribution of the primary industry was cut by 6.3 percentage points; and the contribution of the tertiary industry rose by 12.2 percentage points. During the two periods 1977–2001 and 2001–2016 after the reform, the primary and secondary industries also witnessed a drop in the contribution to the GDP growth and the tertiary industry a rise in the same. Table 4.7 shows, compared with the period 1977–2001, the contributions of China's primary industry and secondary industry dropped by 2.8 percentage points and 19.8 percentage points, and the contribution of the tertiary industry rose by 13.2 percentage points. Additionally, the contributions of the price structure change effect and the growth-price structure adjustment cross effect also decreased during the period 1952–2016. During the three periods 1952–1977, 1977–2001, and 2001–2016, the contribution of the price structure change effect was 6.8%, 2.7%, and 1.3%, respectively, and that of the growth–price structure adjustment cross effect was −17.9%, −12.9%, and −1.9% separately.

Finally, although the impact of the price structure changes on real GDP growth is not large, if the impact of relevant price changes is ignored, the growth effect and contribution of the secondary industry will be seriously underestimated while the effects and contributions of the primary and secondary industries overestimated. That's because, during the economic growth, the rapid growth of the secondary industry did not only lower the product price of this industry but also expanded the demand of residents for products of the primary and tertiary industries through the increase in residents' income. This resulted in relative rise in the product prices of the primary and tertiary industries and further enlarged product price gaps in the secondary, primary, and tertiary industries. Therefore, if the impact of the supply and demand mechanism on relative price changes during the economic growth is taken into account, the growth effect of the secondary industry driving economic growth should be much larger than that based on the real output value of the tertiary industry.

Notes

1 It is impossible to eliminate the impact of changes in the relative prices of various industries on the real growth rate of each industry by using the calculation method of adjusting the prices of each industry based on the GDP deflator. Compared with the real growth rate calculated at the constant prices of each industry, the real growth rate of each industry calculated here exaggerates the fluctuation range of each industry, and also overestimates the real growth rate of the industry whose price rise is higher than GDP growth. Additionally, since changes in relative prices are also a response to the supply-demand relationship in economic development, the real growth rate of each industry adjusted

according to the GDP deflator may reflect the changes in the output value of each industry arising from economic development more. So, the first section analyzes the changes in the industrial structure of GDP according to the real growth rate of each industry adjusted using the GDP deflator.

2 The reason lies in the difference in the positive or negative correlation between the annual growth rates of the three industries and the annual GDP growth rate. For example, where there occurs negative GDP growth in a specific year and the secondary industry also sees negative growth, the secondary industry will still make a positive contribution to annual GDP growth but the negative growth of the secondary industry that year will obviously make a long-term negative contribution to GDP in the long run. If, the annual growth rate of the primary or tertiary industry is positive during the same period, its annual contribution to GDP calculated at the annual growth rate will be negative but that to the long-term GDP growth will be obviously positive. Therefore, the contribution calculated at the annual growth rate can better reflect the impact and relevance of the growth of the three industries on or with the short-term GDP growth rate, while the contribution calculated according to the total growth multiple takes into account the cumulative effect of the growth of the three industries on GDP growth. The difference in the results calculated using these two methods of calculating the contributions of the growth of the three industries to GDP growth shows that the contribution of the growth of the tertiary industry to economic growth was larger than the secondary industry in terms of the contribution within the entire interval during the period 1952–2016. But, judged from the short-term annual growth of GDP, the impact of the growth of the secondary industry on economic growth would be greater than that of the tertiary industry.

5 Changes in employment structure of industries and decomposition of industrial structure for real GDP growth per labor force

This chapter examines the impacts of the growth of productivity per labor force for the three industries and of changes in the employment price structure on China's real GDP growth per labor force. The structure of this chapter is arranged as follows: The first section introduces the changes in China's total population and demographic structure, as well as in the country's total employed population and the industrial structure in relation to the employed population; the second section analyzes China's real GDP growth per labor force and the growth of output values for the three industries per labor force; and the third section decomposes China's real GDP growth per labor force by industry, and discusses the impacts of changes in price structure and employment structure over China's real GDP growth per labor force.

Section 1 Changes in China's total population and employed population: 1952–2016

1.1 Changes in China's total population and demographic structure: 1952–2016

As known from Figure 5.1, the total population of Mainland China (excluding Hong Kong, Macao, and Taiwan) was approximately 575 million in 1952, rose to 950 million in 1977, representing an increase of 65% over that of 1952, and an average annual increase of about 2.03%. During the period 1952–1970, all the other years except 1951–1961, in which the negative population growth was caused by the food shortage brought by the three-year difficult period, had a population growth rate of more than 2%. During the period 1970–1977, China's population growth rate fell from 2.8% to 1.4%, showing a slight downward trend. After 1978, the birth rate started to drop to a large extent and the net population growth rate showed a downward trend due to the impact of the family planning policy, as shown in Figure 5.2. However, in view of China's large population base, the initial population decline caused by family planning policy was not so obvious. According to Figure 5.2 and Table 5.1, the population growth rate of China during the

DOI: 10.4324/9781003261629-7

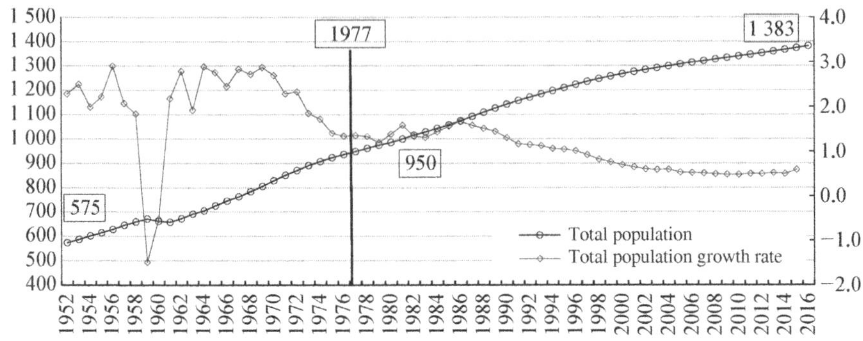

Figure 5.1 Changes in China's total population and population growth rate: 1952–2016.

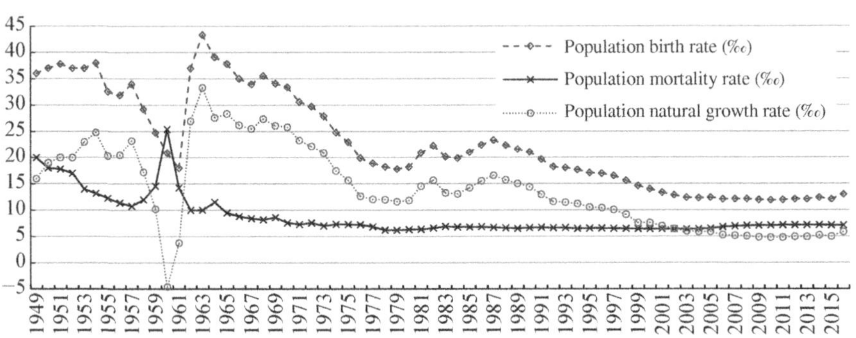

Figure 5.2 China's population death rate, birth rate, and natural birth rate: 1952–2016.

period 1978–1990 was basically maintained between 1.3% and 1.6%, without an obvious downward trend. Probably after 1990, the figure showed a significant downward trend, dropping from 1.30% in 1990 to 0.48% in 2011. After 2011, the population growth rate saw a slight upward trend. In the years 2016 and 2017, the population growth rate of Mainland China was 0.58% and 0.53%, respectively. Overall, since the reform and opening-up, especially the implementation of the family planning policy in China, the total population of the country has been on the rise and the absolute growth has remained high despite the declined growth rate. In 2016, Mainland China had a total population of roughly 1.383 billion, an increase of 420 million over that of 1978. During the period 1978–2016, China's total population had an average annual growth of 0.97%.

China's population age structure has changed along with the rapid growth of the total population. As known from Figure 5.3, the proportion of the Chinese working-age population (15–64 years old) over the total

Table 5.1 Growth multiples of China's total population and employed population: 1952–2016

Period	*Total population*	*Total employed population*	*Employed population of the primary industry*	*Employed population of the secondary industry*	*Employed population of the tertiary industry*
1952–2016	1.41	2.74	0.24	13.60	16.95
1952–1977	0.65	0.90	0.69	2.81	1.24
1977–2016	0.46	0.97	−0.27	2.83	7.03
1977–2001	0.34	0.85	0.24	1.78	3.79
2001–2016	0.08	0.07	−0.41	0.38	0.67

Source for raw data: the CEIC databases; the data here are calculated by the author according to the raw data.

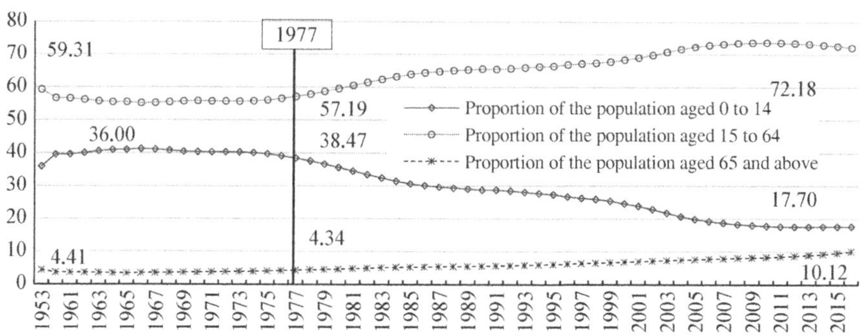

Figure 5.3 Changes in the proportions of the population of different ages over China's total population: 1953–2016.

population (hereinafter referred to as the "proportion over the total population") was 59.3%; the proportion of children (0 to 14 years old) over the total population was approximately 36%; and the proportion of the elderly (above 64 years old) was only 4.41%. The entire population was mostly children and working-age population, the total proportion of which hit 95.59%. During the period 1953–1977, both the elderly and the working-age population showed U-shaped changes, while children saw an inverted U-shaped change. In 1977, China's elderly population accounted for 4.34%; working-age population 57.2% and children 38.47%, with not much change in the demographic structure compared with that of 1953. During the period 1978–2016, China underwent significant changes in the demographic structure due to the impact of the family planning policy. As the most obvious change, the proportion of children in the total population dropped significantly, from 38.47% to 17.70%; that of the elderly also increased significantly, from 4.34% to 10.12%; and that of the working-age population also rose to a large extent, from 57.19% to 72.18%. Currently, China may have already been at the stage when the proportion of the working-age population is the largest and may face a serious problem of population aging in the future. In fact, as known from Figure 5.3, probably since 2010 or so, the proportion of the working-age population in China has started to decline, and that of the elderly shows a rising trend with an accelerating speed.

Additionally, according to the data released in the *Statistical Communiqué of the People's Republic of China on the 2019 National Economic and Social Development*, the total population of Mainland China in 2019 reached 1.4 billion, including 250 million at the ages of 0 to 15 (17.8%), 896 million at the ages of 16 to 59 (64.0%), and 254 million at the ages of 60 and above (18.1%), and 176 million at the ages of 65 and above (12.6%). In 2019, China had 14.65 million births, with a birth rate of 1.048%, and 9.98 million deaths, with a death rate of 0.714%. The natural population growth rate of the year was 0.334%.

1.2 Changes in the employed population and the employed population of the three industries

The rapid growth of China's total population has added abundant labor resources to the country's economic development, and the sustained rapid economic growth since the reform and opening-up has offered a huge demand market for China's labor forces. The growth of the total population and the demand for economic development has jointly contributed to the rapid growth of China's working-age population. Figure 5.4 shows changes in China's employed population and the growth rate of the employed population. Figures 5.5 and 5.6 show the changes in the share of the employed

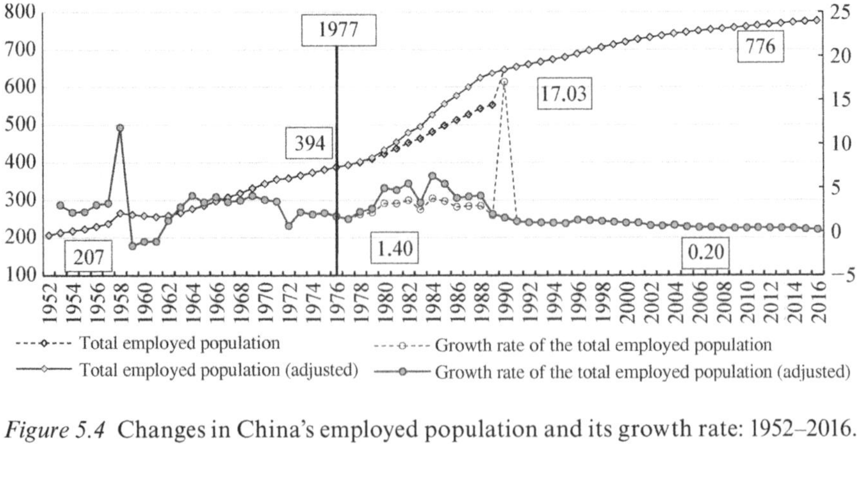

Figure 5.4 Changes in China's employed population and its growth rate: 1952–2016.

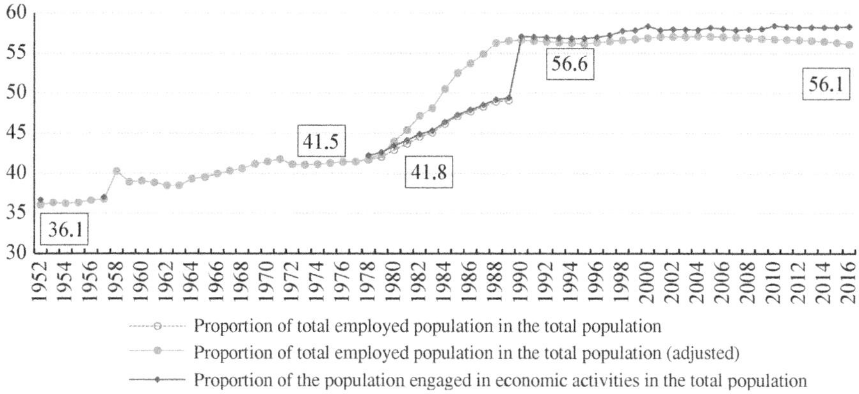

Figure 5.5 China's total population growth rate, growth rate of the employed population, and employment-to-population ratio: 1952–2016.

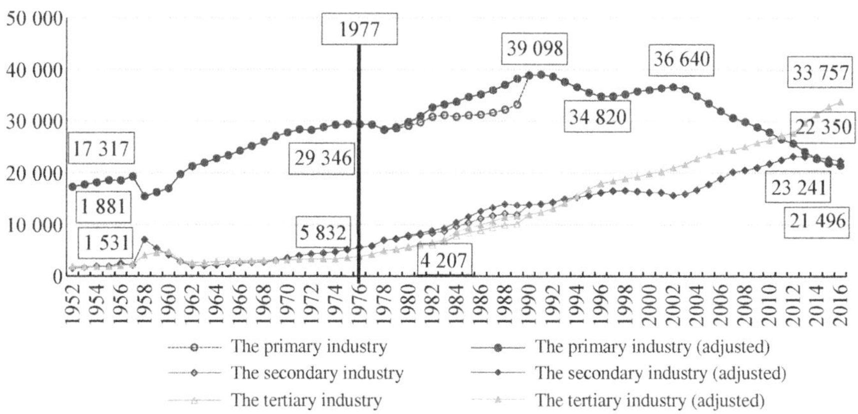

Figure 5.6 Changes in the employed population of China's three industries: 1952–2016.

population over the total population in China and the employed population in the three industries. Tables 5.1 and 5.2 list China's employed population and its growth multiple, and compare each of the employed populations in the three industries and their growth multiples during different periods. In Table 5.3, the average annual growth rates of the total employed population in China's three industries and their CVs are calculated and compared. Table 5.4 gives the contributions of the growth of the total employed population in the three industries during different periods to the growth rate of the total employed population. The following analysis will be made based on such data below.

Table 5.2 Added employed population of China during different periods: 1952–2016, in ten thousand

Period	*Total added employed population*	*Added employed population from the primary industry*	*Added employed population from the secondary industry*	*Added employed population from the tertiary industry*	*Proportion of the primary industry*	*Proportion of the secondary industry*	*Proportion of the tertiary industry*
1952–2016	56874	4179	20819	31876	7.35	36.61	56.05
1952–1977	18656	12029	4301	2326	64.48	23.06	12.47
1977–1991	26106	9752	8183	8171	37.36	31.34	31.30
1991–1996	3459	−4278	2188	5549	−123.68	63.26	160.42
1996–2002	4330	1820	−521	3031	42.03	−12.03	70.00
2002–2016	4323	−15144	6668	12799	−350.3	154.2	296.1
1977–2016	38218	−7850	16518	29550	−20.54	43.22	77.32

Source for raw data: the CEIC databases; the data here are calculated by the author according to the raw data.

Table 5.3 Average annual growth rates and STDEVs for China's total population and total employed population: 1952–2016

Period	*Total population*	*Total employed population*	*Employed population from the primary industry*	*Employed population from the secondary industry*	*Employed population from the tertiary industry*
	Average annual growth rates of total employed population (%)				
1952–2016	1.38	2.08	0.34	4.28	4.61
1952–1977	2.03	2.60	2.13	5.49	3.27
1978–2016	0.97	1.75	−0.79	3.51	5.49
1978–2001	1.24	2.59	0.90	4.36	6.75
2008–2016	0.54	0.43	−3.45	2.15	3.49
	STDEVs for average annual growth rates of total employed population (%)				
1952–2016	0.88	2.10	4.42	29.80	11.17
1952–1977	1.01	2.47	5.53	47.01	17.16
1978–2016	0.40	1.75	2.96	4.38	3.95
1978–2001	0.27	1.76	2.29	4.83	4.42
2002–2016	0.05	0.14	1.66	3.07	1.56

Source for raw data: the CEIC databases; the data here are calculated by the author according to the raw data.

1.2.1 Changes in employed population of the three industries before the reform: 1952–1977

According to Figures 5.4 and 5.6, China had a total employed population of only 207 million in 1952, 36.1% of the total population. Among them, the total employed population in the primary, secondary, and tertiary industries was 173 million, 15 million, and 18 million, with their proportions being 83%, 7.4%, and 9.1%, respectively. It can be seen that a majority of the Chinese population got jobs in the primary industry in that year. During the period 1952–1977, China had a total added employed population of 186.6 million, with an average annual growth of 2.60%. In 1977, the total employed population reached 394 million. Due to the rapid growth of the total population during the same period, the proportion of the employed population over the total only increased from 36.1% to 41.5%, representing an increase of 4.4 percentage points.

The total employed population of the secondary industry grew fastest during the period 1952–1977, and reached 58.31 million in 1977, with an increase of 43.01 million over that of 1952 and an average annual growth of 5.49%. The total employed population of the tertiary industry also grew fast during the same period and reached 42.06 million in 1977, with an increase of 23.26 million and an average annual growth of 3.27%. However, due to the small base of the total employed population of the secondary and tertiary industries in 1952, the total newly added employed population of both industries occupied a small proportion in the total added population of the three industries, only 35.5%. Additionally, the growth rates of the total employed population of the secondary and tertiary industries were large, with their STDEVs being 29.8% and 11.2%, respectively.

During the period 1952–1977, the primary industry was the one with the largest increase in employment. In 1977, the total employed population in the primary industry was 293 million, representing an increase of 120.3 million over that of 1952 and a contribution to the growth rate of the employed population of 64.5%. The growth rate of the total employed population in the primary industry also fluctuated most, with its STDEV being 14.8% and 39.6% of those in the secondary and tertiary industries, as shown in Tables 5.3 and 5.4. It is evident that, during the period 1952–1977, the growth of China's total employed population was mainly attributed to the primary industry. This conclusion is in line with the reality of China's economic development before the reform, when China's urban household registration system had restricted rural laborers from getting jobs in urban areas. Additionally, the policy of going down to the countryside to encourage or even force urban youths to work in rural areas and the agricultural field resulted in added labor forces, and sometimes even the stock of the unemployed in urban areas, who mainly got employed in the agricultural field. Additionally, due to the adoption of the people's commune system featuring collective operation in agriculture, it was also easy for the rural area to absorb or arrange for the employment of new laborers. Together, both factors sled the primary industry, which was dominated by agriculture, to become the main source of employment growth.

By 1978, at the beginning of the reform, the total employed population in China had reached 403 million, accounting for 41.8% of the total population. Among them, the employed population in the primary, secondary, and tertiary industries accounted for 70.4%, 17.4%, and 12.2% of the total employed population, respectively. This employment structure had not undergone fundamental changes compared to that of 1952. China was still a major agricultural country, and a vast majority of the population was still employed in the primary industry, which was dominated by agriculture. During the period 1952–1977, the primary industry, especially agriculture, was the most important industry to solve the employment issue in China.

1.2.2 Changes in the employment of China's three industries after the reform: 1978–2016

The rapid growth of more than 40 years since the adoption of reform and opening-up in 1978 brought about a sharp rise in the employment of the secondary and tertiary industries. During the period 1977–2016, China's newly added employed population was 419.9 million, an average annual growth of 1.75%, much higher than the 0.46% growth of the total population during the same period. The proportion of the employed population in the total population increased from 41.4% to 56.1%. During this process, the contribution of the three industries to employment growth was also quite different from that

Table 5.4 Growth multiples and contributions of the growth of employed population in China's three industries to the increase in the total employed population

	Growth multiple of total employed population	*Growth multiple of employed population for each industry*			*Contribution of each industry to the increase in total employed population*		
		Primary industry	*Secondary industry*	*Tertiary industry*	*Primary industry*	*Secondary industry*	*Tertiary industry*
1952–2016	2.74	0.20	1.00	1.54	7.35	36.61	56.05
1952–1977	0.90	0.58	0.21	0.11	64.48	23.06	12.47
1977–2016	0.97	−0.20	0.42	0.75	−20.54	43.22	77.32
1977–2001	0.85	0.18	0.26	0.41	21.11	31.13	47.76
2001–2016	0.07	−0.20	0.08	0.19	−310.1	127.26	282.8

Source for raw data: the CEIC databases; the data here are calculated by the author according to the raw data.

before the reform (as shown in Table 5.4). During the period 1978–2016, the tertiary industry was always the one with the fastest-growing employed population, with an average annual growth of 5.49%. The tertiary industry was also the one with the largest increase in employment, contributing 77.32% to the growth of the total employed population. The employed population in the secondary industry also grew rapidly, with an average annual growth of 3.51%, and its contribution to the growth of the total employed population was 43.22%. The absolute number of people employed in the primary industry began to decline. During this period, the employed population fell from 293 million to 215 million. It can be seen that, in terms of employment structure, the Chinese were mainly employed in the secondary and tertiary industries, especially the tertiary industry, since the reform rather than mainly in the primary industry before the reform.

In conclusion, over 40 years of economic growth in reform and opening-up, in terms of employment structure, the Chinese were mainly employed in the secondary and tertiary industries, especially the tertiary industry. Currently, among the three industries, the employed population of the tertiary industry accounts for the largest proportion of the total population, over 40%; that of the primary and secondary industries was almost the same, basically 30% each. Thus, in terms of employment structure, China basically got rid of its economic status as a major agricultural country and become a developing country in which the three industries go hand in hand, and agriculture, industry, and service segments jointly develop. However, China's industrialization is far from complete. In 2018, the employed population of the primary industry still accounted for 26.1%, with a large share of the employed agricultural population and agricultural population. More than 40% of the total population still relies on agriculture and rural areas for living.

Section 2 Changes in GDP per labor force and output value per labor force of the three industries: 1952–2016

2.1 Two data issues to be explained

The first issue that needs to be explained is the calculation of the real output value of each industry. Generally, there are two ways to calculate this. One is to exclude price hikes measured by GDP deflator, and the other is to exclude price hikes based on the prices of each industry. The nominal output value of each industry, nominal GDP, and the real GDP growth rate calculated at the prices of the period 1952–2016 are available from the *China Statistical Yearbooks*. We calculate the real GDP for the same period at the prices of 1952 using the real GDP growth rate and the nominal GDP of 1952. Then, we divide the nominal GDP by the real GDP to obtain the GDP deflator for the period 1952–2016. Next, we divide the nominal output value of each industry by the GDP deflator for the same period to obtain the real output value of each industry at the GDP deflator after excluding price hikes. The real growth rate for the output value of each industry calculated at the constant prices of the previous year for the industry can also be obtained from the *China Statistical Yearbooks*. Multiply the nominal output value of each industry in 1952 by the real growth rate of the output value of the industry, and then we can obtain the real output value of the industry at its constant prices during the period 1952–2016. The real output value of each industry per labor force can be obtained by dividing the real output value of each industry calculated using the above two methods by the employed population in each industry. As can be known from both methods of calculating the real output value per labor force above, different from the other, the real output value of each industry calculated at its constant prices is the real labor productivity (output value per labor force) at the input of each industry and the invariable prices of the output articles, without regard for changes in the relative prices of products among industries due to the market supply and demand factor. It can be understood as calculating the real productivity per labor force purely based on the changes in the input-output ratio of the industry itself and can reflect the technical changes of the labor productivity of an industry in a more accurate way. The real output value of each industry, calculated by excluding price hikes and at the GDP deflator, is the real output value of the industry calculated using the output value of the industry and at the constant prices of the GDP deflator. This calculation method takes into account the changes in the production conditions of each industry (including changes in technology and the role of the law of diminishing marginal productivity of input factors), and also the impact of changes in the relative prices of industrial products caused by the market supply and demand. In the analysis below, both methods above will be used to calculate the real output value of each industry. Then, the actual employed population of each industry is divided by the real output value of the industry to obtain the real output value of the industry per labor force.

The other issue to be explained is the statistics regarding China's employed population. As can be known by observing Figure 5.3, there are obvious statistical errors in the raw data of the employed population for 1990. The employed population increased by 94.19 million that year, with a growth of up to 17.3%, far higher than that in other years. It can be found from the data of the *China Statistical Yearbooks*, probably since 2002, adjustments have been made to the employed population data of 1990–2001, rather than that before 1990, in this book. In the *China Statistical Yearbooks* for the year 2002 and subsequent years, the employed population data for the year 1990 and later years, rather than that before 1990, were adjusted. The data following the year 1990 were adjusted based on the *China Statistical Yearbooks*. Thus, in this book, the newly employed population for the year 1990 and later years is smoothly adjusted to the period 1978–1990. The specific method is as follows: first, estimate the employed population growth rate in 1990 according to the weighted average of the employed population growth rate in 1989 and 1991 (0.183 and 0.114, respectively), (0.183+0.114)/2=0.149; then, readjust the growth rate of the employed population each year according to the growth of the population participation rate of the year. Specifically, the adjusting formula is as follows:

$$\text{Adjusted population growth rate} = \text{original population growth rate} \times (1 + \alpha \text{ the increase in the employed population participation rate of the year}) \quad (5.1)$$

where α is an adjustment coefficient. The value of the adjustment coefficient should be taken so that the employed population of China in 1990 calculated at the adjusted population growth rate on the basis of the employed population in 1977 is just equal to the employed population of 1990 included in the raw data. According to the calculation, the value of α should be 61.38. The increase in the employed population may be related to that in the working-age population. According to the adjustment method for the employed population growth rate of 1978–1990 above, if the 16-year-old population is regarded as the new working-age population, we can find that the adjusted growth rate of the new employed population quite matches the changes in the growth rate of the working-age population, as shown in Figure 5.7.

2.2 Changes in the output values of the three industries per labor force

Figure 5.8 shows the changes in China's real output value per labor force and real output values of the three industries per labor force during the period 1952–2016. A shows the real output values of the three industries per labor force at the GDP deflator and by excluding price hikes; and B shows the value obtained at the price index of each industry and after excluding price

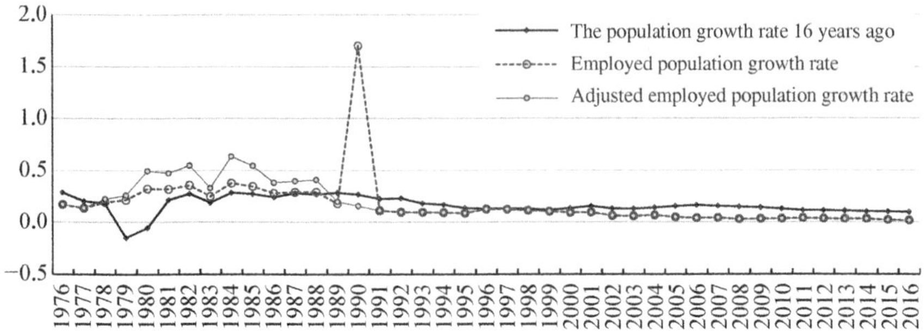

Figure 5.7 Comparisons between the adjusted employed population growth rate and the population growth rate 16 years ago.

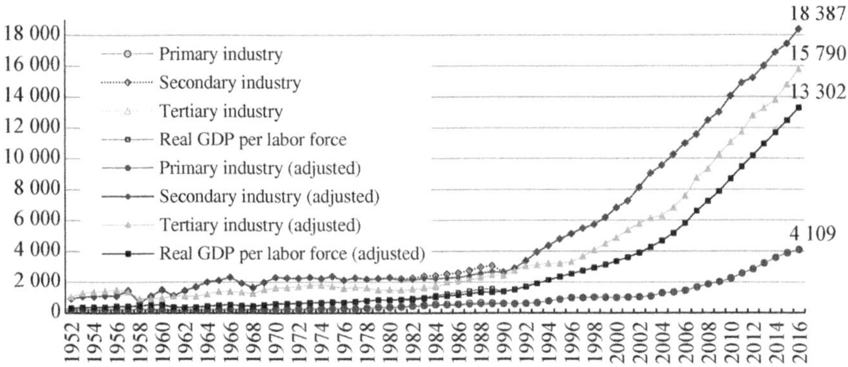

(a) Real output value calculated the constant prices of 1952 based on the GDP deflator

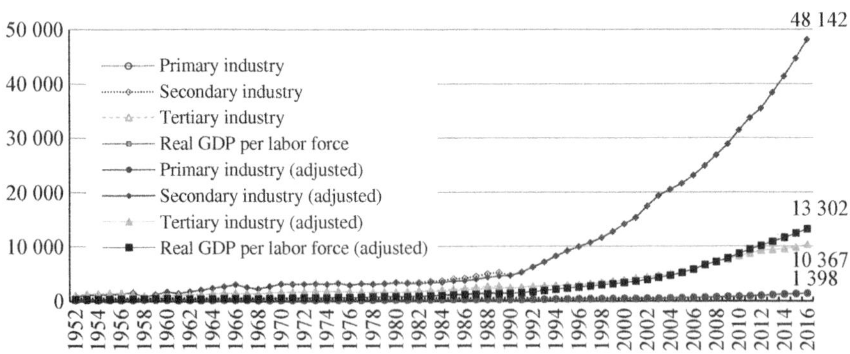

(b) Real output value calculated the constant prices of 1952 for each industry

Figure 5.8 China's real GDP per labor force and real output values of the three industries per labor force: 1952–2016.

Table 5.5 China's real GDP per labor force and real output value of the three industries per labor force: 1952–2016

Period	*At the prices of 1952 adjusted by the GDP deflator*				*At the constant prices of 1952 for each industry*		
	Real GDP per labor force	*Output value of the primary industry per labor force*	*Output value of the secondary industry per labor force*	*Output value of the tertiary industry per labor force*	*Output value of the primary industry per labor force*	*Output value of the secondary industry per labor force*	*Output value of the tertiary industry per labor force*
1952	328	198	922	1037	198	922	1037
1977	728	283	2297	1657	191	3203	1629
2001	3618	1012	7267	5384	450	15379	4086
2016	13302	4109	18387	15790	1398	48142	10367
	At the prices adjusted by the GDP deflator				*At the constant prices of the previous year for each industry*		
	Real GDP per labor force	*Output value of the primary industry per labor force*	*Output value of the secondary industry per labor force*	*Output value of the tertiary industry per labor force*	*Output value of the primary industry per labor force*	*Output value of the secondary industry per labor force*	*Output value of the tertiary industry per labor force*
Period	*Total growth multiple (in times)*						
1952–2016	39.60	19.75	18.95	14.22	6.06	51.24	8.99
1952–1977	1.22	0.43	1.49	0.60	−0.04	2.48	0.57
1977–2016	17.27	13.50	7.01	8.53	6.34	14.03	5.37
1977–2001	3.97	2.57	2.16	2.25	1.36	3.80	1.51
2001–2016	2.68	3.06	1.53	1.93	2.10	2.13	1.54
Period	*Average annual growth rate (in %)*						
1952–2016	5.96	4.85	4.79	4.35	3.10	6.38	3.66
1952–1977	3.24	1.44	3.72	1.90	−0.16	5.11	1.82
1977–2016	7.73	7.10	5.48	5.95	5.24	7.20	4.86
1977–2001	6.91	5.45	4.91	5.03	3.64	6.75	3.91
2001–2016	9.07	9.79	6.38	7.43	7.83	7.90	6.41

hikes. Tables 5.4 and 5.6 further show the real output values of the industries for different periods calculated by using the two methods above, and their growth multiples and average annual growth rates. As known from Figure 5.8, no matter which method is used to exclude price hikes, there are huge differences in the growth of the three industries, and the gap among the three industries in terms of real output value has always been increasing.

2.2.1 *Overview of changes in the output values of China's three industries per labor force*

According to the data of the *China Statistical Yearbooks*, the growth of China's real GDP per labor force and of real output value of the three industries per labor force takes on the following characteristics: Firstly, despite varying growth rates, all the real output values of the three industries have seen tremendous growth. During the period 1952–2016, China's real GDP per labor force was up 39.6 times, with an average annual real growth of 5.96%. If seen from the real output value per labor force calculated at the GDP deflator and by excluding price hikes, the real output values of the primary, secondary, and tertiary industries during this period had an average annual growth of 4.85%, 4.79%, and 4.35%, respectively. During the period 1952–2016, the primary industry had the fastest average annual growth of real output value per labor force, and the tertiary industry had the slowest growth. In 1952, the gap between the secondary and tertiary industries was not large, and the secondary industry had a higher growth rate of real output value per labor force than the tertiary industry. Therefore, the secondary industry was always the industry with the highest real output value per labor force. Although the primary industry did not only have the slowest growth rate of productivity per labor force, but also the lowest value of output value per labor force at the beginning. It has always been the industry with the lowest real output value per labor force in China.

Secondly, the absolute gap among the three industries in terms of real output value per labor force during the period 1952–2016 was expanding. At the constant prices of 1952, the gaps of the primary industry from the secondary and tertiary industries in terms of real output value per labor force rose from 724 yuan and 839 yuan to 14,278 yuan and 11,681 yuan, and the gap between the secondary and tertiary industries rose from 116 yuan to 2,598 yuan. The relative gaps of the primary industry from the secondary and tertiary industries in terms of real output value per labor force were narrowing. The output value per labor force of the primary industry was 21% and 19% of those of the secondary and tertiary industries in 1952, and rose to 22% and 26%, respectively, in 2016. The real output values per labor force of the secondary and tertiary industries did not only reverse in size but also widened in terms of the relative gap. The real output value per labor force of the tertiary industry was 1.125 times more than that of the secondary industry in 1952, but the real output value per labor force of the secondary industry was 1.164 times more than that of the tertiary industry in 2016.

Thirdly, the gaps among the three industries in terms of the growth rate of real output value calculated at the GDP deflator and by excluding price hikes were much smaller than those calculated at constant prices of each industry. That's mainly due to the Baumol effect in which the growth rate of the prices of each industry is exactly opposite to the rate of technological progress of the industry (i.e., an industry with slower technological progress

Table 5.6 The growth of China's real GDP per labor force and real output values per capita of the three industries: 1952–2016

	At the prices adjusted by the GDP deflator				*At the constant prices of the previous year for each industry*		
	Real GDP per labor force	*Output value of the primary industry per labor force*	*Output value of the secondary industry per labor force*	*Output value of the tertiary industry per labor force*	*Output value of the primary industry per labor force*	*Output value of the secondary industry per labor force*	*Output value of the tertiary industry per labor force*
Period	*Total growth multiple (in times)*						
1952–2016	39.60	19.75	18.95	14.22	6.06	51.24	8.99
1952–1977	1.22	0.43	1.49	0.60	−0.04	2.48	0.57
1977–2016	17.27	13.50	7.01	8.53	6.34	14.03	5.37
1977–2001	3.97	2.57	2.16	2.25	1.36	3.80	1.51
2001–2016	2.68	3.06	1.53	1.93	2.10	2.13	1.54
Period	*Average annual growth rate (in %)*						
1952–2016	5.96	4.85	4.79	4.35	3.10	6.38	3.66
1952–1977	3.24	1.44	3.72	1.90	−0.16	5.11	1.82
1977–2016	7.73	7.10	5.48	5.95	5.24	7.20	4.86
1977–2001	6.91	5.45	4.91	5.03	3.64	6.75	3.91
2001–2016	9.07	9.79	6.38	7.43	7.83	7.90	6.41

will have a faster rise in its relative prices). As known from Table 5.6, the real output value per labor force of China's secondary industry during the period 1952–2016 had an average annual growth of 6.38%, far higher than the real GDP growth rate per labor force in the same period. The average annual growth rates of real output values of the primary and secondary industries were 3.10% and 3.66%, respectively, almost half as much as that of the primary industry. Both growth rates of the real output values per labor force in the primary and secondary industries were lower than the real GDP growth rate per labor force and also much lower than the growth rate of the real output value per labor force at the GDP deflator and after excluding price hikes. This indicates that the rise in the relative prices of the primary and tertiary industries has compensated for the shortage of low productivity growth to a large extent.

2.2.2 Characteristics of changes in the output values per labor force of the three industries in different periods: comparative analysis

There were significant differences between the growth of China's real GDP per labor force and that of the real output values of the three industries in the two periods before and after the reform and opening-up. Such differences were mainly reflected in the following two aspects. Firstly, regardless of real GDP per labor force or real output value per labor force for each industry, the average annual growth rate after 1978 was higher than that before the reform, and such growth rate in the late of the reform period (2002–2016) was higher than that in the early period of reform (1978–2001). As can be known from Table 5.6, China's real GDP per labor force in the period 1952–1977 had an average annual growth of 3.24%, and that in the period 1978–2016 7.73%, more than double that before the reform. The country's real GDP per labor force had an average annual growth of 9.07% in the late period of the reform (2002–2016), 2.16 percentage points higher than that in the early period of the reform (1978–2001). The average annual growth rates of real output values per labor force of the primary, secondary, and tertiary industries during the period 1952–1977 were 1.44%, 3.72%, and 1.90%, respectively, and those after the reform rose to 7.10%, 5.41%, and 5.95%, 5.64, 1.76, and 4.05 percentage points higher respectively than those before the reform. The growth rates of real output values per labor forces for the three industries in the late period of the reform (2001–2016) were also significantly higher than those in the early period of the reform (1978–2001), 1.34, 1.47, and 2.40 percentage points higher than the latter.

Secondly, the growth rate of the real output value per labor force of the secondary industry after the reform did not change much relative to that before the reform, but those of the primary and tertiary industries changed a lot, especially the primary industry. Both average annual growth rates of real output values per labor force of the primary and tertiary industries in the period 1952–1977 were not higher than 2%. Without regard for relative price changes among industries, if calculated at the prices of 1952 and excluding price hikes based on the price index of each industry, the average real output value per labor force of the primary industry even registered a negative growth and the average annual growth rate of the real output value per labor force of the tertiary industry was lower than 1% before the reform. During the period 1978–2016, the real output value per labor force of the primary industry had an average annual growth of 5.24% at its constant prices and 7.10% at the constant prices measured by the GDP deflator. At the constant prices of the GDP deflator, the average annual growth rate of the real output value per labor force of the tertiary industry increased from 1.90% before the reform to 5.95% after the reform, and that of the secondary industry from 3.72% to 5.84%. At the constant prices of the industry, the average annual growth rate of the real output value of the tertiary industry increased from 1.82% to 4.86%, and that of the secondary industry from 5.11% to 7.22%. Through comparisons on the two periods after the reform, which were before and after China's accession to WTO, there was also a continuous increase in the growth rate of the real output value of the primary industry and a relative decline in that of the secondary industry. During the period 1978–2001 in the early period of the reform, if calculated at the constant prices of the GDP deflator, the growth rates of real output values of the primary, secondary, and tertiary industries did not differ much, at around 5%; if calculated at the constant prices of each industry, the growth rate of the real output value of the secondary industry was almost half as high as that of the primary and tertiary industries. During the period 2002–2016 after the reform, if calculated at the constant prices of the GDP deflator, the real output value per labor force of the primary industry had an average annual growth of 9.79%,4.34 percentage points higher than that in the early period of the reform; and the real output values per labor force of the secondary and tertiary industries were 1.47 and 2.40 percentage points higher than those before the reform. If calculated at the constant prices of the industries, the growth rates of real output values of the primary, secondary, and tertiary industries were 4.19, 1.15, and 2.50 percentage points higher, respectively, than those in the early period of reform.

It is also easy to understand the relative increase in the productivity per labor force of the primary industry from the perspective of economic intuition. **After the reform**, particularly in the late period of the reform, the rural household contract responsibility system greatly improved agricultural productivity and increased the real output value per labor force of the primary industry, possibly due to the fact it increased farmers' enthusiasm for production. Also, the more important reason may lie in the fact that a large number of the employed population of the primary industry moved to the secondary and tertiary industries following the economic development after the reform. Under the effect of the law of diminishing marginal productivity of labor, a decline in the employed population of the primary industry will naturally increase the output value per labor force. Additionally, if calculated at the constant prices measured by the GDP deflator, the growth rate of the real output value of the tertiary industry also saw an upward trend, which may be due to the increasing demand for products and services of the tertiary industry together with the rise in economic growth and in residents' income level, which contributed to the rapid rise in product prices of the tertiary industry.

Finally, whether in the entire period 1952–2016 or in two different stages before and after the reform, all the growth rates of real output values of the three industries calculated at the constant prices measured by GDP deflator were significantly different from those of the industries calculated at their constant prices. As known from Figure 5.9, firstly, whether before or after the reform, the growth rate of the real output value of the secondary industry calculated at its constant prices was higher than that calculated at the constant prices of the GDP deflator. The primary and tertiary industries were just the opposite (i.e., the growth rate of the real output value of the industry calculated at its constant prices was higher than that calculated at the constant prices of the GDP deflator). As shown in Table 5.6, the real output value per labor force of the secondary industry calculated at its constant prices during the period 1952–2016 had an average annual growth of 6.38%, with a growth of 5.11% before the reform and of 7.20% after the reform. And the real output value per labor force of the secondary industry calculated

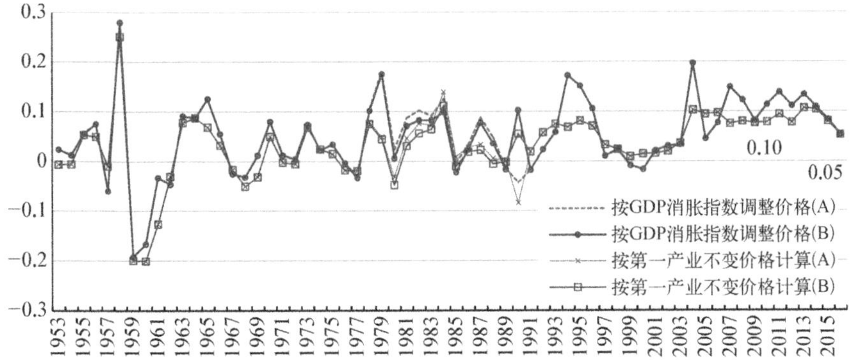

(a) The growth rate of real output value per labor force for the primary industry

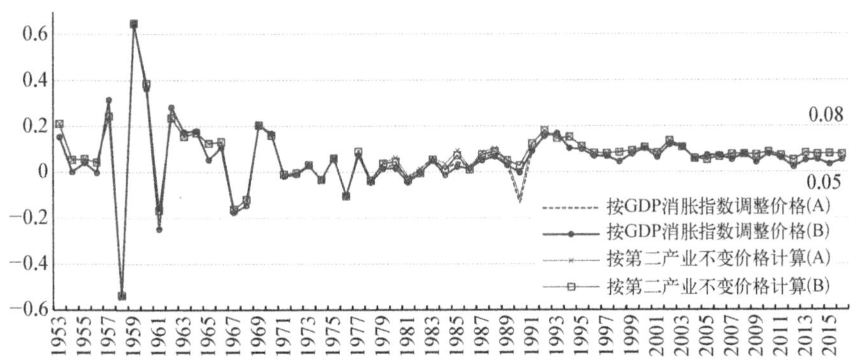

(b) The growth rate of real output value per labor force for the secondary industry

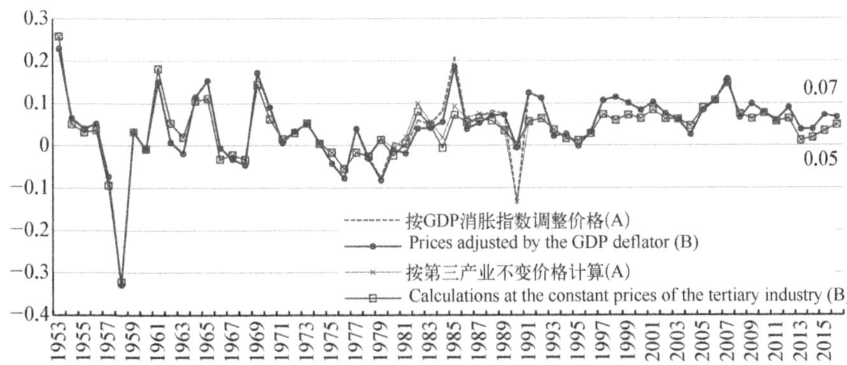

(c) The growth rate of real output value per labor force for the tertiary industry

Figure 5.9 Changes in the growth rates of real output values per labor force of China's three industries: 1952–2016.

at the constant prices measured by GDP deflator had an average annual growth of 4.79%, with a growth of 3.72% before the reform and 5.48% after the reform. In the same period, the average annual growth rates of real output values per labor force of the primary and tertiary industries had average annual growth rates of 3.10% and 3.66% at their constant prices,1.75 and 0.69 percentage points lower than those calculated at the constant prices of the GDP deflator. Secondly, regardless of industry, the annual growth rate of the real output value per labor force calculated at the constant prices measured by the GDP deflator fluctuated more than that calculated at the constant prices of the industry, and the primary and tertiary industries fluctuated more than the secondary industry, which was mainly due to the larger price weight of the secondary industry in the GDP deflator.

Section 3 Decomposition of China's real GDP growth rate per labor force: 1952–2016

Two phenomena can be found from the analysis above. Firstly, different speeds of rise in product prices in various industries have led to the continuous rise in the relative prices of the primary and tertiary industries and that in the relative prices of the secondary industry. Changes in the relative prices of the three industries have caused a big gap between the growth rate of the average real output value per labor force for each industry adjusted based on the GDP deflator and that adjusted at the constant prices of each industry, as shown in Figure 5.9. Since the real GDP per labor force is the sum of the weighted average of the real output values of the three industries per labor force, changes in relative prices of the three industries will lead to changes in the weights of output values per labor force of the three industries during the calculation of the real GDP per labor force, and then changes in real GDP. The changes in real GDP per labor force caused by those in relative prices of the three industries is hereinafter referred to as the effect of relative price structure on economic growth or price structure change effect. Secondly, the employment structure of China's employed population of the three industries is always changing. Since the real GDP per labor force is the weighted average sum of real output values of the three industries with the proportion of the population in each industry as weight, changes in the structure of employed population of the three industries will also cause those in real GDP per labor force. Actually, in Table 5.6, there were several periods when the growth multiples (or annual growth rates) of real output values per labor force of the three industries were smaller than those of real GDP per labor force. The reason lies in the changes in the calculation weights of the three industries caused by those in the employed population structure of the three industries. Thus, the effect of changes in the proportions of the population in the three industries on the real GDP per labor force will be called the growth effect of changes in the employed population structure or abbreviated as the "employment structure change effect."

3.1 Breakdown of economic growth rate: price structure change effect and employment structure effect

The nominal GDP of a country in any period t is equal to the sum of nominal output values of individual industries, namely:

$$P_t N_t y_t = \sum_{i=1}^{m} P_{it} N_{it} y_{it} \tag{5.2}$$

where nominal P refers to the price level of the entire economy, measured by the GDP deflator; N refers to the total employed population; y refers to real GDP per labor force; i (=1, 2, 3) refers to the industry; t refers to the time; x_{it} refers to the real output value of Industry i in period t; P_i refers to the price level of Industry i; and N_i refers to the employed population of Industry i. The left side of Formula (5.1) represents the nominal GDP in the period t, and the right side of Formula (5.2) represents the sum of nominal output values of the specific industry in period t. Dividing both sides of Formula (5.2) by the country's $(t-1)^{\text{th}}$ nominal GDP calculation formula, we can get:

$$\frac{P_t N_t y_t}{P_{t-1} N_{t-1} y_{t-1}} = \sum_{i=1}^{m} \frac{P_{it} N_{it} x_{it}}{P_{it-1} N_{t-1} y_{t-1}} \tag{5.3}$$

Define a country's employed population growth rate as n, inflation rate as π, and the growth rate of real GDP per labor force as:

$$n_t = (N_{t+1} - N_t)/N_t, \quad \pi_t = (P_{t+1} - P_t)/P_t, \quad g_t = (y_{t+1} - y_t)/y_t \tag{5.4}$$

In terms of Industry i of the country, the employed population growth rate n_{it}, price change rate π_{it}, and growth rate of real output value per labor force g_{it} is expressed as follows:

$$n_{it} = (N_{it+1} - N_{it})/N_{it}, \quad \pi_{it} = (P_{it+1} - P_{it})/P_{it}, \quad g_{it} = (y_{it+1} - y_{it})/y_{it} \tag{5.5}$$

According to the above definitions and Formula (5.3), the following formula can be obtained through simple calculation:

$$(1+n_t)(1+g_t)(1+\pi_t) = \sum_{i=1}^{m} \alpha_{it-1}(1+n_{it})(1+g_{it})(1+\pi_{it}) \tag{5.6}$$

where $\alpha_{it} = (P_{it} N_{it} x_{it})/(P_t N_t y_t)$ refers to the proportion of the output value of Industry I over nominal GDP (hereinafter referred to as the "proportion of nominal output value of Industry i"). According to Formula (5.6), the following formula can be obtained through simple calculation and sorting:

$$
\begin{aligned}
g_t = & \sum_{i=1}^{m} \alpha_{it-1} g_{it} + \sum_{i=1}^{m} \alpha_{it-1}(n_{it} - n_t) + \sum_{i=1}^{m} \alpha_{it-1}(\pi_{it} - \pi_t) \\
& + \sum_{i=1}^{m} \alpha_{it-1}(n_{it} g_{it} - n_t g_t) + \sum_{i=1}^{m} \alpha_{it-1}(\pi_{it} g_{it} - \pi_t g_t) \\
& + \sum_{i=1}^{m} \alpha_{it-1}(n_{it}\pi_{it} - n_t \pi_t) + \sum_{i=1}^{m} \alpha_{it-1}(n_{it}\pi_{it} g_{it} - n_t \pi_t g_t)
\end{aligned} \tag{5.7}
$$

As can be seen from Formula (5.7), the real GDP growth rate per labor force of a country can be decomposed into seven parts. The first part, $\left(\sum_{i=1}^{m} \alpha_{it-1} g_{it}\right)$, is the increase in real GDP per labor force arising from the increase in the real output value of each industry, where the growth rate of real GDP per labor force of Industry *I* is equal to the growth rate of real output value per labor force of the industry *I* multiplied by the proportion of the nominal output value of the industry for the previous period. The growth effect of the real output value of Industry *i*on the real GDP per labor force is abbreviated as the **growth effect of Industry *i*.**

The second part, $\left(\sum_{i=1}^{m} \alpha_{it-1}(n_{it} - n_t)\right)$, refers to the changes in real GDP per labor force caused by those in the employed population of the industries arising from different employed population growth rates of the industries. This part is only related to changes in the employment structure of each industry. It is just the employment structure change effect defined above or the effect of changes in the employment structure of each industry on the real GDP growth per labor force. It is easy to understand the economic intuition so defined. We might as well consider the calculating formula for real GDP per labor force with constant relative prices (i.e., $P_t = P_{it}$). Thus:

$$
N_t y_t = \sum_{i=1}^{m} N_{it} x_{it} \Leftrightarrow y_t = \sum_{i=1}^{m} x_{it}\left(N_{it}/N_t\right) = \sum_{i=1}^{m} \beta_{it} x_{it}
$$

where $\beta_{it} = N_{itt}/N_t$ refers to the proportion of the employed population in Industry *i*. If the real output value per labor force of each industry (x_{it}) remains unchanged, the real GDP growth per labor force is equal to the change rate of the proportion of the employed population of each industry (β_{it}) multiplied by the proportion of the real (nominal) output value of the industry for the previous period ($\beta_{it}x_{it}/y_t$=$N_{it}x_{it}/N_t y_t$). And the change rate of the proportion of the employed population of each industry (or $\beta_{it} = N_{itt}/N_t$) is equal to the employed population growth rate of the industry (n_{it}) minus the growth rate of the total employed population (n_t). So, $\sum_{i=1}^{m} \alpha_{it-1}(n_{it} - n_t)$ is actually the economic growth brought about by changes in the employment structure of various industries.

In fact, the employment structure change effect can be further decomposed into various industries. Here the employment structure change effect of Industry *i* is $\alpha_{it-1}(n_{it} - n_t)$. It represents the percentage increase in real

GDP per labor force arising from the growth of employment for Industry i is equal to the difference between the employment growth rate of the industry and the total employment growth rate $(n_{it} - n_t)$, then multiplied by the nominal output value of the industry for the previous period, α_{it-1}. As the total employment growth rate is equal to the weighted average of the growth rates of the industries, there must be some industries whose employment growth rate is higher than the total employment growth rate, and other industries whose employment growth rate is lower than the total employment growth rate. Industries whose employment growth rate is faster than the total employment growth rate can bring a positive employment structure change effect; industries whose employment growth rate is slower than the total employment growth rate have a negative employment structure change effect. If the employment structure change effect of an industry with a fast employment growth rate exceeds that of an industry with a slow employment growth rate in absolute value, the employment structure change effect in the entire economy will be positive; otherwise, it will be negative.

The third part, $\left(\sum_{i=1}^{m} \alpha_{it-1}(\pi_{it} - \pi_t)\right)$, is mainly due to the exchange of relevant prices among various industries arising from different change rates of product prices of the industries, thus causing changes in the real GDP per labor force. This part is only related to changes in the relative prices of products among different industries. It is just the **price structure change effect** defined above or the effect of changes in the relative price structure in the economy on the growth of real GDP per labor force. Also, the economic intuition in this definition can also be understood by examining the calculating formula of real GDP per labor force under the same employed population structure as before (i.e., N_{it}/N_t and x_{it} remain unchanged). We might as well assume:

$$P_t y_t = \sum_{i=1}^{m} P_{it} x_{it} \beta_{it} \Leftrightarrow y_t = \sum_{i=1}^{m} \beta_{it} x_{it} \left(P_{it}/P_t\right) = \sum_{i=1}^{m} \beta_{it} \gamma_{it} x_{it}$$

where $\gamma_{it}=P_{it}/P_t$ indicates the proportion of the price index of Industry I over the overall price index (hereinafter referred to as the "proportion of product prices of Industry i"). Similarly, if the real output value per labor force (x_{it}) and employment structure (β_{it}) of each industry remain unchanged, the real GDP growth rate per labor force will be equal to the change rate of product prices of each industry multiplied by the proportion of the real (nominal) output value per labor force of the industry for the previous period ($\gamma_{it}\beta_{it}x_{it}/y_t=P_{it}N_{it}x_{it}/P_tN_ty_t$). And the change rate of the proportion of product prices of each industry is equal to the change rate of product prices of the industry (π_{it}) minus the change rate of the price index of the entire economy (π_t).

The price structure change effect can also be decomposed into each industry. The relative price change effect of Industry i is expressed as $\alpha_{it-1}(\pi_{it} - \pi_t)$, which indicates the added percentage of the real GDP growth per labor force driven by the price change of Industry i is equal to the difference between the price change rate of the industry and the overall inflation rate $(\pi_{it} - \pi_t)$ multiplied by the proportion of the nominal output value of the industry for the previous period. Similarly, as the total price index is equal to the weighted average of the prices of each industry, there must be some industries whose prices increase faster than the total price and other industries having the opposite result. The price structure change effect of the industry whose price increases faster than the total price is positive, and that whose price increases slower is negative. If the price structure change effect of the industry with faster price hikes exceeds the industry with slower price hikes, the overall price structure change effect will be positive; otherwise, the effect will be negative.

The fourth to seventh parts are the cross effects among the growth effect of the real output value of each industry, the employment structure change effect, and the price structure change effect on the real GDP growth per labor force. The fourth part, $\sum_{i=1}^{m} \alpha_{it-1}(n_{it}g_{it} - n_t g_t)$, describes the interaction effect between changes in the employment structure and the growth of the three industries (hereinafter referred to as the "**growth-employment cross effect**"); the fifth part, $\sum_{i=1}^{m} \alpha_{it-1}(\pi_{it}g_{it} - \pi_t g_t)$, describes the cross effect between relevant price changes and the growth of the three industries (hereinafter referred to as the "**growth-price cross effect**"); the sixth part, $\sum_{i=1}^{m} \alpha_{it-1}(n_{it}\pi_{it} - n_t\pi_t)$, describes the cross effect between relevant price changes and changes in employment structure (hereinafter referred to as the "**employment-price cross effect**); the seventh part, $\sum_{i=1}^{m} \alpha_{it-1}(n_{it}\pi_{it}g_{it} - n_t\pi_t g_t)$, is the cross effect between changes in employment structure, relative prices changes, the growth of the real output value of each industry, and real GDP growth per labor force (hereinafter referred to as the "**growth-employment-price cross effect**"). As the four cross effects mentioned here are aggregated by industries, they may also be classified into different industries. When the growth rate of the real output value of each industry, price change rate, and employment growth rate are all small values, it can be proved that the four cross effects are the high-order infinitely small items for the growth effect of real output value, the employment structure change effect, and the price structure change effect. Among them, the fourth to sixth terms are two-order infinite small and the last term is three-order infinite small.

The contributions of various effects to the real GDP growth rate per labor force can be further calculated according to the result of decomposing the real GDP growth rate per labor force according to Formula (5.7). The specific calculation formulas are as follows:

Contribution of the growth of Industry *i*:

$$R_{it} = \alpha_{it-1}g_{it}/g_t, \quad i = 1,2,3 \tag{5.8a}$$

Contribution of the employment structure change effect:

$$R_{nt} = \sum_{i=1}^{m} \alpha_{it-1}(n_{it} - n_t) \Big/ g_t \tag{5.8b}$$

Contribution of the price structure change effect:

$$R_{Pt} = \sum_{i=1}^{m} \alpha_{it-1}(\pi_{it} - \pi_t) \Big/ g_t \tag{5.8c}$$

Contribution of the growth-employment cross effect:

$$R_{ngt} = \sum_{i=1}^{m} \alpha_{it-1}(n_{it}g_{it} - n_t g_t) \Big/ g_t \tag{5.8d}$$

Contribution of the growth-price cross effect:

$$R_{Pgt} = \sum_{i=1}^{m} \alpha_{it-1}(\pi_{it}g_{it} - \pi_t g_t) \Big/ g_t \tag{5.8e}$$

Contribution of the employment-price cross effect:

$$R_{nPt} = \sum_{i=1}^{m} \alpha_{it-1}(\pi_{it}n_{it} - \pi_t n_t) \Big/ g_t \tag{5.8f}$$

Contribution of the growth-employment-price cross effect:

$$R_{Pgnt} = \sum_{i=1}^{m} \alpha_{it-1}(n_{it}\pi_{it}g_{it} - n_t\pi_t g_t) \Big/ g_t \tag{5.8g}$$

3.2 Industrial decomposition of China's real GDP growth rate per labor force: calculation of the annual growth rate

According to the decomposition formula (5.7) in relation to the real GDP growth rate per labor force and Figure 5.10, the growth effect of each industry, the price structure change effect, the employment structure change effect, and the growth of annual real GDP driven by four types of cross effects can be calculated using the data concerning the growth rate of total employed population and the population growth rates of the three industries introduced in Sections 1 and 3 of this chapter (see Figure 5.7), the increase rate of the GDP deflator and the price growth rates of the three industries introduced in Chapter 4, as shown in Figure 4.8 of Chapter 4, and real GDP growth rate per labor force and the growth rates of real output values per labor force of the three industries (as shown in Figure 5.11). Here Figure 5.10A shows the breakdown of the growth rate of the output value per labor force during the period 1953–2016. For ease of comparison, Figure 5.10B shows the breakdown before the reform, and Figure 5.10C shows the breakdown after the reform. The contributions of various effects to the growth of real

GDP per labor force can be calculated using Formula (5.8), as shown in Figure 5.14. Similarly, Figure 5.10A shows the contributions for the period 1953–1977; Figure 5.10B shows the contributions for the period 1978–2016; and Figure 5.10C the contributions for the period 1953–2016. Additionally, the cross effect is minimal in the calculation each year as it is a higher-order term. In order to make the graphs much clearer, Figure 5.10 only shows the contributions of growth effects of the three industries and the growth rates

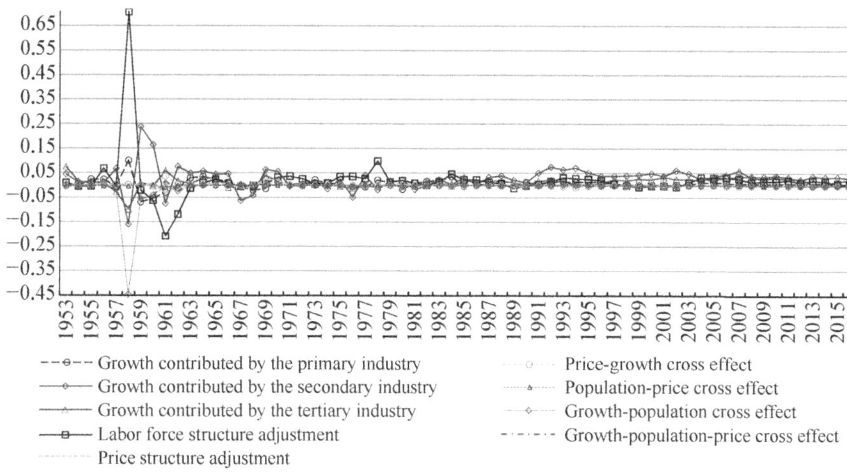

(a) 1953—2016

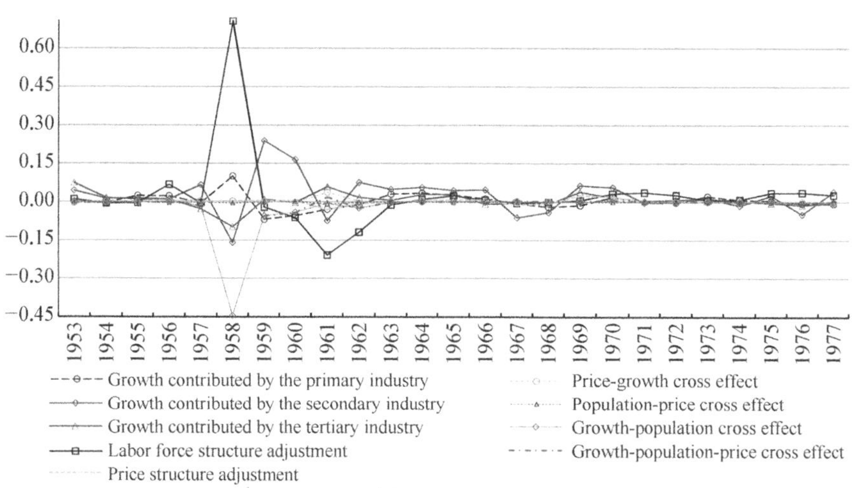

(b) 1953—1977

Figure 5.10 Annual real GDP growth of China per labor force driven by the three industries and structure changes: 1953–2016.

(Continued)

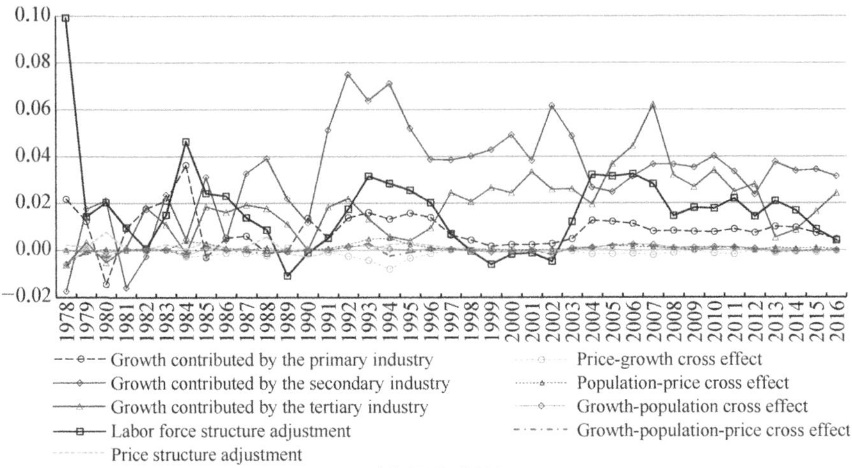

(c) 1978–2016

Figure 5.10 (Continued).

of two structural adjustment effects. Various effects are analyzed and discussed based on the breakdown data below.

According to decomposition formula (5.7) in relation to the growth rate, the growth of the three industries and Figure 5.10, the price structure change effect, the employment structure change effect, and the growth of annual real GDP driven by cross terms can be calculated using the data concerning total employment growth rate and the population growth rates of the three industries introduced in Sections 1 and 2 of this chapter (see Figure 5.7), the increase rate of the GDP deflator and the price growth rates of the three industries (see Figure 4.8 of Chapter 4), and the real GDP growth rate per labor force and the growth rates of real output values per labor force of the three industries (as shown in Figure 5.9). Figure 5.10A shows the breakdown of the growth rate of the output value per labor force during the period 1953–2018. For ease of comparison, Figures 5.10B and 5.10C show the breakdown of China's output values per labor force before and after the reform. Then, according to Equation (5.8), the contributions of various effects to real GDP growth per labor force can be calculated, as shown in Figure 5.11. Similarly, Figure 5.11A shows the contributions for the period 1953–1977; Figure 5.11B shows the contributions for the period 1978–2018; and Figure 5.11C the contributions for the period 1953–2018. Additionally, the cross effect is minimal in the calculation each year as it is a higher-order term relative to other ones. In order to make the graphs much clearer, Figure 5.11 only shows the contributions of growth effects of the three industries and the growth rates of two structural adjustment effects. Table 5.7 shows the annual average of the breakdown of the annual real GDP growth rate per labor force during different periods.

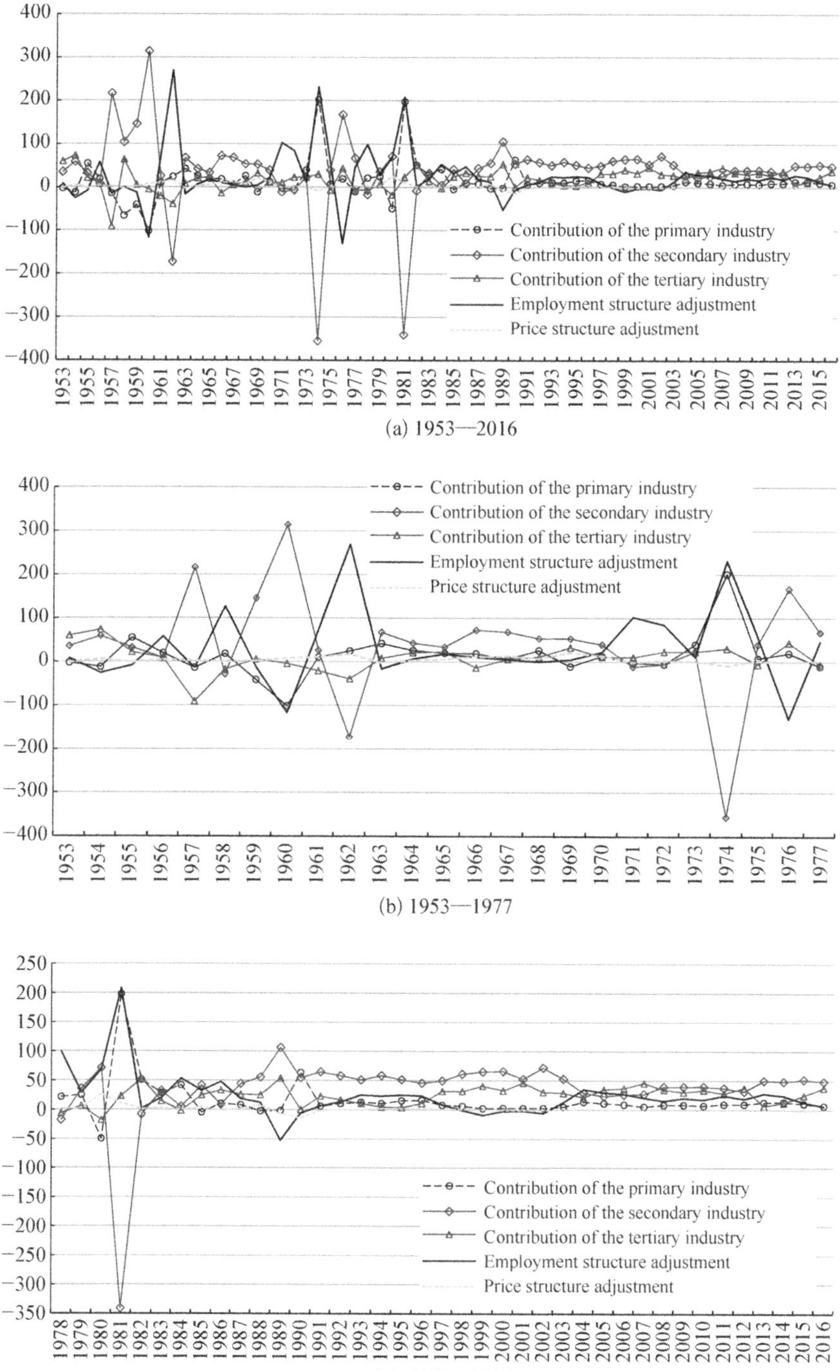

Figure 5.11 Contributions of the three industries and structure changes to China's real GDP growth per labor force: 1953–2016.

Table 5.7 Average annual growth of real GDP per labor force arising from various effects, in %

Period	Growth effect of the primary industry	Growth effect of the secondary industry	Growth effect of the tertiary industry	Employment structure effect	Price structure effect	Growth-employment cross effect	Growth-price cross effect	Employment-price cross effect	Triple cross effect
	Average annual growth of real GDP per labor force arising from various effects, in %								
53–16	0.67	2.96	1.40	1.97	0.09	−0.8942[a]	−0.0049	0.0281	−0.0090
53–77	0.33	2.49	0.69	2.42	0.10	−2.32[b]	0. 177[c]	−0.0882	−0.0267
78–16	0.88	3.26	1.86	1.70	0.08	0.02	−0.122	0.103	0.0024
	STDEVs for average annual real GDP growth per labor force driven by various effects								
53–16	2.07	4.98	2.28	9.53	0.62	5.62d	0.4988	0.1876	0.0467
53–77	3.17	7.62	3.11	15.24	0.99	8.92e	0.745	0.202	0.0710
78–16	0.81	2.03	1.39	1.85	0.184	0.142	0.162	0.133	0.009
	CVs for average annual GDP growth per labor force driven by various effects								
53–16	3.090	1.682	1.629	4.838	6.889	−112.400	−101.796	6.676	5.189
53–77	8.703	3.202	4.342	6.488	10.100	−56.813	4.011	−2.047	−2.623
78–16	0.920	0.623	0.747	1.088	2.300	7.100	−1.328	1.291	3.750

Note: ①The high employment-structure-growth cross effect of a and b are mainly due to the extremely high employed population growth rate in the secondary and tertiary industries caused by the Great Leap Forward in the period 1958–1960 (the employment growth rate in the secondary industry during this period was 230% and −23.7% and −23.8% respectively, and that of the tertiary industry was 74%, 11.5%, and 5.6%, respectively.) The extremely high annual growth rate of employed population made the employment-structure cross effect in 1958 as high as −44.6%. If the data for 1958 are removed, these two values are only −0.19% and −0.53%, respectively. If the data for these three years are removed, the employment-structure-growth cross effect is only −0.05% and −0.16%, respectively. ② The data at point c are mainly affected by the high inflation in 1961. The inflation rate that year reached 15%, and the price growth rate of the primary industry was as high as 27%. This made the price adjustment effect of the year as high as 3.66%. If the data for that year are removed, this average is only 0.031%. ③ These two values are very large and were also affected by the Great Leap Forward from 1958 to 1960.

3.2.1 Overall characteristics: 1953–2016

The following conclusions can be drawn according to the decomposition results shown in Figure 5.10 and Table 5.7. Firstly, in the decomposition of the annual growth rate of real GDP per labor force, only the growth of GDP per labor force driven by the growth effects of the three industries and two structure change effects are large, and the effect of the four cross effects is low. As known from Figure 5.10, the annual growth of GDP per labor force driven by GDP per labor force of the primary, secondary, and tertiary industries significantly deviates from the position of point 0 but is positive in most of the years. The employment structure change effect also significantly deviates from the position of Point 0, sometimes being positive and sometimes being negative. The price structure change effect is almost 0. The GDP growth driven by real GDP per labor force due to four types of cross effects is nearly 0. In fact, as known from Table 5.9, the average annual real GDP growth per labor force driven by the growth effects of the three industries, the employment structure change effect, and the price structure change effect is 0.67%, 2.96%, 1.40%, 1.97% respectively, and 0.09%, and the average annual GDP growth per labor force driven by the employment-growth cross effect, price-growth cross effect, employment-price cross effect, and employment-price-growth cross effect is only −0.89%, −0.0049%, 0.0281%, and −0.0090% respectively. Obviously, the latter four types of cross effects are not of the same order of magnitude with the first five types of direct effects but are much smaller than the latter. These specific figures also indicate that the three main effects that contribute most to the real GDP growth rate per labor force for the period 1953–2016 were the growth effect of the secondary industry, growth effect of the tertiary industry, and employment structure change effect. The growth effect of the primary industry, although it existed, was much smaller than the first three types of effects but the price adjustment effect was one level lower in terms of quantity. Only the first five types of first-order direct effects are taken into account in the analysis of the annual real GDP growth rate per labor force.

Secondly, in terms of volatility, the effect of employment structure change fluctuates most in absolute terms, followed by the growth rate of the secondary industry, the growth rate of the tertiary industry, the growth rate of the primary industry, and the price structure change effect. The growth rate of the secondary industry is the largest one and also fluctuates significantly in absolute terms, and the STDEV for the real GDP growth per labor force driven by such effect is 4.98. The employment structure change effect fluctuates most. Its average value is smaller than that of the growth rate of the secondary industry but its STDEV (9.53) is about 91% higher than that of the growth rate of the secondary industry, and its CV (4.84) is almost three times that of the growth rate of the secondary industry. The growth rate of the tertiary industry is more than twice the growth rate of the primary industry and its STDEV is almost the same as that of the primary industry.

The price structure change effect has a small average value and the smallest STDEV. In terms of CV, both price structure change effect and employment structure change effect fluctuate significantly, with CVs being 6.89 and 4.84; while the growth effects of the three industries fluctuate little relatively, with CVs being 3.09, 1.68, and 1.63, respectively. Either in terms of relative fluctuations or in terms of absolute fluctuations, the employment structure change effect fluctuates significantly; the price structure change effect has small absolute fluctuations but the largest relative fluctuations.

Finally, there are some interesting features of the correlations among the five first-order direct effects. Table 5.8 lists the coefficients of correlation for the annual growth rate of the real GDP per labor force contributed by the five effects from 1953 to 2016. According to the table, the growth rate of the primary industry is significantly, negatively correlated with the growth effects of the secondary and tertiary industries; significantly, positively correlated with the employment structure change effect, but is poorly and also insignificantly correlated with the price structure change effect. This phenomenon may be related to the flow of the employed population from the primary industry to the secondary and tertiary industries, when the output value per labor force of the primary industry will increase and those of the secondary and tertiary industries will decrease under the effect of the law of diminishing marginal productivity of labor. The growth effect of the secondary industry is significantly, positively correlated with the growth rate of the tertiary industry and also the price structure change effect, but significantly, negatively correlated with the employment structure population effect. This may be related to the close correlation between the secondary and tertiary industries, as the development of the secondary industry will promote the development of the tertiary industry. The growth rate of the tertiary industry is significantly correlated with the employment structure change effect in addition to the growth effects of the primary and secondary

Table 5.8 Coefficients of correlation among the five effects: 1953–2016

	Growth rate of the primary industry	*Growth rate of the secondary industry*	*Growth rate of the tertiary industry*	*Price structure effect*
Growth rate of the primary industry	**−0.5440***** **(0.000)**	1.00		
Growth rate of the tertiary industry	**−0.3458***** **(0.0051)**	**0.3414***** **(0.0058)**	1.00	
Employment structure effect	**0.6939***** **(0.0013)**	**−0.4562***** **(0.0002)**	**−0.6438***** **(0.0000)**	1.00
Price structure effect	0.1649 (0.1928)	**0.3370***** **(0.0065)**	−0.1232 (0.3321)	**0.5870***** **(0.0000)**

Note: The values in parentheses are P-values; "*", "**" and "***" indicate significance at the level of 10%, 5%, and 1% respectively.

industries, but insignificantly correlated with the price structure change effect. Thus, the employment structure change effect is significantly correlated with the growth effects of the primary, secondary, and tertiary industries, but the price adjustment effect is only correlated with the growth rate of the secondary industry, and there is also a significant correlation between the employment structure change effect and the price structure change effect. The above analysis shows that, during China's economic development, the adjustment of the employment structure among industries will not only directly promote economic growth but also may affect economic growth by affecting changes in the productivity of each industry per labor force, and may even affect economic growth by impacting the changes in the relative price structure among industries. So, changes in the industrial structure on economic growth produce an important, far-reaching effect.

Additionally, there exist interesting characteristics of correlation between various growth effects with the employment growth rates and the price change rates of the three industries, as shown in Table 5.9. First, the total employment growth rate and total price changes have the characteristics distinct from the five first-order growth effects. The total employment growth rate is significantly correlated with all five first-order growth effects; significantly, positively correlated with the growth rate of the primary industry and the price structure change effect and negatively correlated with the growth effects of the secondary and tertiary industries and the employment structure change effect. The total inflation rate is only positively correlated with the growth rate of the tertiary industry, negatively correlated with the price structure change effect, and insignificantly correlated with the other three first-order direct effects. The employment growth rates of the secondary and tertiary industries are almost significantly correlated with the five first-order direct effects. Among them, the employment growth rate of the primary industry is significantly, positively correlated with the growth rate of the secondary industry, but significantly, negatively correlated with the other five effects; the employment growth rate of the secondary industry is only insignificantly, positively correlated with the growth effect of the tertiary industry; significantly, negatively correlated with the growth effect of the secondary industry, and significantly, positively correlated with the other three effects; the employment growth rate of the tertiary industry is not correlated with the growth effect of the primary industry, negatively correlated with the growth effect of the tertiary industry, and significantly, positively correlated with the other three first-order effects. However, the employment growth rate of the tertiary industry is significantly, negatively correlated with the industry's own growth effect. This shows that labor force growth in a certain industry will indeed lead to the decline in the industry's productivity per labor force, and there exists diminishing marginal productivity of labor in all three industries. The price growth rates of the secondary and tertiary industries are not significantly correlated with almost all the five first-order direct effects; only the price growth rate of the primary industry is negatively

Table 5.9 Coefficients of correlation of five effects with the employment growth rate and the price growth rate: 1953–2016

	Growth effect of the primary industry	*Growth effect of the secondary industry*	*Growth effect of the tertiary industry*	*Employment structure effect*	*Price structure effect*
Total employment growth rate	**0.57*** (0.000)**	**−0.53*** (0.000)**	**−0.54*** (0.000)**	**0.63*** (0.0000)**	**0.29** (0.0201)**
Employment growth rate of the primary industry	**−0.60*** (0.0000)**	**0.23* (0.0724)**	**0.33*** (0.0069)**	**−0.76*** (0.0000)**	**−0.25** (0.0485)**
Employment growth rate of the secondary industry	**0.71*** (0.0000)**	**−0.56*** (0.000)**	**−0.60*** (0.0000)**	**0.97*** (0.0000)**	*0.20 (0.1090)*
Employment growth rate of the tertiary industry	**0.57*** (0.0000)**	**−0.24* (0.0588)**	**−0.73*** (0.0000)**	**0.91*** (0.0000)**	**0.36*** (0.0035)**
Total inflation	*−0.05 (0.7025)*	*0.03 (0.8099)*	**0.21* (0.0941)**	*−0.10 (0.4309)*	**−0.31** (0.0127)**
Price growth rate of the primary industry	*−0.05 (0.6741)*	*−0.04 (0.7780)*	*0.19 (0.1338)*	*−0.09 (0.4716)*	**−0.23* (0.0695)**
Price growth rate of the secondary industry	*0.00 (0.9935)*	*0.14 (0.2671)*	*0.09 (0.5005)*	*−0.04 (0.7391)*	*−0.17 (0.1871)*
Price growth rate of the tertiary industry	*−0.04 (0.7452)*	*0.13 (0.3246)*	**0.21* (0.0986)**	*−0.07 (0.5587)*	*−0.12 (0.3576)*

Note: The values in parentheses are P-values; "*", "**" and "***" indicate significance at the level of 10%, 5%, and 1% respectively.

correlated with the price structure change effect; and the price growth effect of the tertiary industry is positively correlated with the growth effect of the tertiary industry. Since correlation may imply mutual impacts, the above analysis shows again that, during the period 1953–2016, China's employment structure adjustment not only had a direct effect on the growth rate of real GDP per labor force, but also may produce an indirect effect through other effects. The price structure adjustment not only produced a small direct effect on the real GDP growth per labor force but also little impact on other economic effects. Thus, the adjustment of the employment structure from 1953 to 2016 produced an important impact on China's real GDP growth per labor force, but the effect of changes in price structure was insignificant.

3.2.2 Comparative analysis for the period before and after reform: 1953–1977 & 1978–2016

Either in terms of growth or volatility, there are significant differences in the average annual growth of real GDP per labor force driven by various effects before and after the reform. According to Table 5.7, firstly, the average annual growth of real GDP per labor force driven by the growth effects of the three industries after the reform was significantly higher than that before the reform; and both structure change effects before the reform were higher than those after the reform. Secondly, the contributions of the output values of the three industries to the growth of the real GDP per labor force before the reform were smaller than those after the reform, with two structure change effects before the reform being larger. Actually, without regard for the temporary impact of the Great Leap Forward 1958–1960, the contribution of the growth effects of the three industries to the real GDP growth rate per labor force was 58.4%, with the proportion of the two structure adjustment effects being 41.5%; and the effect of the growth of the three industries after the reform being 77.1% of the average annual growth rate for real GDP per labor force, with the proportion of the two structure adjustment effects being 22.9%. Finally, the influence of the employment structure change effect on the real GDP per labor force before the reform was greater than that after the reform and was related to the Great Leap Forward. If the influence of the Great Leap Forward in 1958 was ignored, the contribution of employment structure change effect to the real GDP per labor force before there form was not large.

In terms of volatility, the fluctuations of the real GDP growth per labor force driven by the five first-order direct effects before the reform were larger than those after the reform. The STDEV for the annual real GDP growth per labor force driven by the growth effect of the secondary industry before the reform was 7.26%, up more than twice compared with that after the reform (2.03); and its CV was 3.20, which was more than five times higher compared with that after the reform (0.62). The annual growth rate of real GDP per labor force driven by the employment structure change effect before the reform fluctuated greatly, with a STDEV of 15.24, 8.4 times more than that after the reform (1.85), and a CV of 6.49, 5.96 times more than that after the reform (0.47). The STDEVs and CVs for the growth effect of the primary industry, the growth effect of the tertiary industry, and the price structure change effect were all larger than those after the reform, with the former being 3.98 times, 2.28 times, and 5.49 times more than those after the reform, and the latter being 9.45 times,5.81 times, and 4.39 times more than those after the reform.

In terms of the correlation among the growth effects and their correlation with the employment growth rate and the inflation rate, different characteristics were shown before and after the reform. According to Table 5.10, some significant changes occurred to the correlation among the five first-order

Table 5.10 Coefficients of correlation among five first-order direct effects: comparisons for the period before and after the reform

	Growth effect of the primary industry		*Growth effect of the secondary industry*		*Growth effect of the tertiary industry*		*Employment structure effect*	
	Before the reform	*After the reform*	*Before the reform*	*After the reform*	*Before the reform*	*After the reform*	*Before the reform*	*After the reform*
Growth effect of the secondary industry	**−0.60***** **(0.00)**	−0.23 (0.16)	1.00	1.00				
Growth effect of the tertiary industry	**−0.44**** **(0.03)**	−0.23 (0.16)	**0.34*** **(0.10)**	**0.33**** **(0.04)**	1.00	1.00		
Employment structure effect	**0.72***** **(0.00)**	**0.51***** **(0.00)**	**−0.47**** **(0.02)**	**−0.30*** **(0.06)**	**−0.74***** **(0.00)**	−0.22 (0.18)	1.00	1.00
Price structure effect	0.203 (0.33)	**−0.27*** **(0.10)**	**0.37*** **(0.07)**	0.01 (0.96)	−0.10 (0.62)	**−0.31**** **(0.05)**	0.28 (0.179)	0.26 (0.11)

Note: The values in parentheses are P-values; "*", "**" and "***" indicate significance at the level of 10%, 5%, and 1% respectively.

direct effects before and after the reform. **Firstly,** the correlation and significance among the five first-order effects before the reform were much greater than those after the reform. Before the reform, only the price structure change effect was insignificantly correlated with the growth effects of the primary and tertiary industries; and the other seven relationships among the five first-order effects were all significantly correlated. After the reform, five relationships among the five-order effects were significantly correlated with each other, and the other five were insignificantly correlated with each other. **Secondly, compared with that before the reform,** the correlation between the growth effects of industries after the reform and their correlation with the employment structure change effect did not only decrease in significance but also declined in the coefficient of correlation. Among them, the coefficients of correlation of the growth effect of the primary industry with those of the secondary and tertiary industries before the reform were −0.60 and −0.40, respectively, and were significant at the level of 5%; and the coefficient of correlation after the reform was only −0.23 and was insignificant at the level of 10%. The correlation between the growth effects of the secondary and tertiary industries has slightly declined as well. The correlation of the growth effects of the primary, secondary, and tertiary industries with the employment structure change effect has also decreased. Among them, the coefficient of correlation between the growth rate of the primary industry and the employment structure change effect dropped from 0.72 to 0.51; that between the growth rate of the secondary industry and the employment structure change effect dropped from −0.47 to −0.30; and the tertiary industry changed most, which was insignificant in correlation and whose coefficient of correlation decreased from −0.74 to −0.22. Thirdly, **the correlation between the price structure change effect and the growth effects of the three industries** has undergone an opposite change **since the reform**. Before the reform, the price structure change effect was only significantly, positively correlated with the growth effect of the secondary industry, and was insignificantly, positively correlated with the growth effects of the primary and tertiary industries. After the reform, it was significantly, negatively correlated with the growth effects of the primary and tertiary industries, and was almost not correlated with the secondary industry in terms of significance, with the coefficient of correlation dropping from the previous 0.37 to 0.01. On the whole, the overall correlation among the five effects before the reform was stronger than that after the reform. This may be mainly because of the overall planning of economic development under the system of planning economy before the reform. Moreover, the decentralized decision-making under the market economy after the reform may weaken the overall integrity of various effects.

Finally, according to Table 5.11, the correlations of the five first-order direct effects with the employment growth rate and the inflation rate have undergone significant changes since the reform. Firstly, in terms of the correlation between the five first-order direct effects and the growth rate of the employed population, the correlation of the growth rate of the employed population with the growth effects of the three industries and the employment structure change effect fell after the reform. Before the reform, they were basically significantly correlated with each other. As an only exception, the growth effect of the secondary industry was not correlated with the growth rate of the employed population in the tertiary industry. Since the reform, the correlations of the growth effect of the primary industry with the total population and the employment growth rate of the primary industry, of the growth effect of the tertiary industry with the population growth rate of the secondary industry, and of the total population growth rate with the employment structure change effect became insignificant. The correlation between the price structure change effect and the growth rate of the employed population became even more significant than before. Before the reform, the price structure change effect was only correlated with the growth rates of the employed population in the primary and tertiary industries; after the reform, it was significantly, positively correlated with the growth rate of the total employed population and the growth rates of the employed population in the secondary and tertiary industries. Secondly, in terms of the effect of the price change rate, the effect of price changes on the five effects also changed greatly after the reform. Before the reform, only the total inflation and the price growth rate of the primary industry were significantly, positively correlated with the growth effect of the tertiary industry. After the reform, the total inflation and the price growth

Table 5.11 Coefficients of correlation of the five effects with the employment growth rate and the price growth rate: 1953–2016

	Growth effect of the primary industry		Growth effect of the secondary industry		Growth effect of the tertiary industry		Employment structure effect		Price structure effect	
	Before the reform	After the reform	Before the reform	After the reform	Before the reform	After the reform	Before the reform	After the reform	Before the reform	After the reform
Growth rate of the total employed population	1.0.84***	2.0.08	−0.57***	−0.54***	−0.56***	−0.47***	0.84***	0.11	0.31	0.44***
	(0.00)	3.(0.64)	(0.00)	(0.00)	(0.00)	(0.00)	(0.00)	(0.52)	(0.13)	(0.00)
Growth rate of the employed population in the primary industry	−0.70***	−0.23	0.41**	−0.31*	0.75***	−0.29*	−0.96***	−0.42***	−0.37*	0.21
	(0.00)	(0.15)	(0.04)	(0.06)	(0.00)	(0.08)	(0.00)	(0.01)	(0.07)	(0.21)
Growth rate of the employed population in the secondary industry	0.77***	0.36**	−0.57***	−0.58***	−0.67***	−0.23	0.98***	0.81***	0.20	0.39***
	(0.00)	(0.02)	(0.00)	(0.00)	(0.00)	(0.15)	(0.00)	(0.00)	(0.34)	(0.01)
Growth rate of the employed population in the tertiary industry	0.57***	0.52***	−0.23	−0.33**	−0.81***	−0.68***	0.94***	0.67***	0.35*	0.42**
	(0.00)	(0.00)	(0.26)	(0.03)	(0.00)	(0.00)	(0.00)	(0.00)	(0.08)	(0.01)
Total inflation	−0.29	0.08	−0.24	−0.41***	0.34*	−0.10	−0.24	0.20	−0.78***	0.24
	(0.15)	(0.65)	(0.25)	(0.01)	(0.09)	(0.56)	(0.25)	(0.22)	(0.00)	(0.14)
Price growth rate of the primary industry	−0.24	0.08	−0.23	0.20	0.42**	−0.20*	−0.21	0.22	−0.57***	0.36**
	(0.25)	(0.61)	(0.28)	(0.22)	(0.04)	(0.23)	(0.32)	(0.18)	(0.00)	(0.02)
Price growth rate of the secondary industry	−0.28	0.16	0.05	0.34**	−0.06	−0.01	−0.16	0.25	4.−0.54***	0.17
	(0.17)	(0.33)	(0.82)	(0.03)	(0.76)	(0.93)	(0.43)	(0.11)	(0.00)	(0.30)
Price growth rate of the tertiary industry	−0.24	−0.08	−0.09	0.49***	0.30	−0.02	−0.18	0.11	−0.38***	0.19
	(0.26)	(0.66)	(0.65)	(0.00)	(0.14)	(0.89)	(0.37)	(0.51)	(0.06)	(0.24)

rates of the secondary and tertiary industries were significantly correlated with the growth effect of the secondary industry, with significant, negative correlation for the former and significant, positive correlation for the latter. Thirdly, in terms of the effect of price changes on the price adjustment effect itself, the total inflation and the price growth rates of the three industries were significantly, negatively correlated with the price adjustment effect before the reform. After the reform, they were positively correlated with each other. However, only the price growth rate of the primary industry was significantly, positively correlated with the price change effect. The correlations of the total inflation and the price growth rates of the three industries with the growth rate of the primary industry and the employment structure change effect were weak, either before or after the reform; but almost all signs of the coefficients of correlation changed. For example, the growth rate of the employed population in the primary industry was significantly, positively correlated with the growth effects of the secondary and tertiary industries before the reform, and was significantly, negatively correlated with the latter since the reform. The price growth rate of the primary industry was significantly, negatively correlated with the price structure effect and was significantly, positively correlated with the latter since the reform. In summary, the effect of the growth of the employed population over real GDP per labor force was greater than the effect of price changes on the real GDP per labor force; the effect of the growth of employed population on the economy before the reform was greater than that after the reform, with little difference between them; and the effect of price changes on economic growth was much lower, which differed greatly before and after the reform.

Part 2

6 The high savings, investment, and economic growth of China

Section 1 China's high savings and investment rates: basic facts

China's economy grew at an average annual growth rate of 9.3% during the period 1978–2018. Such rapid economic growth was mainly driven by investment. In fact, during the past 70 years, China has always been characterized as high savings and investment, which are one of the typical characteristics for China's economic growth. As shown in Figure 6.1, the proportion of China's investment in GDP shows an increasing trend. Even when both investment growth rate and real GDP growth rate dropped significantly after 2010, the proportion of China's investment over GDP remained at a high level of around 45%.

The other side of high investment is high savings. As can be seen in Figure 6.2, China's savings rate remained at a high level and continued to rise during the period 1952–2018. Figure 6.3 shows that only China's domestic savings rate showed an upward trend during the period 1968–2017; China has become the country with the highest savings rate among the countries listed in the figure since 2001. Actually, there are huge differences in the savings rates of countries and of one country in different periods. Generally, the

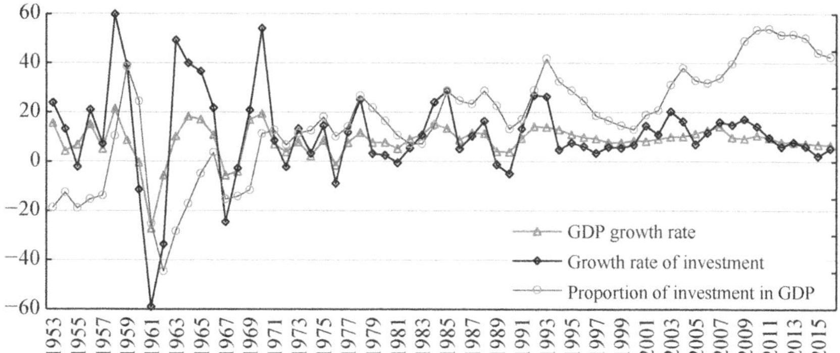

Figure 6.1 Changes in the proportion of China's investment in GDP, investment growth rate, and real GDP growth rate: 1952–2019.

DOI: 10.4324/9781003261629-9

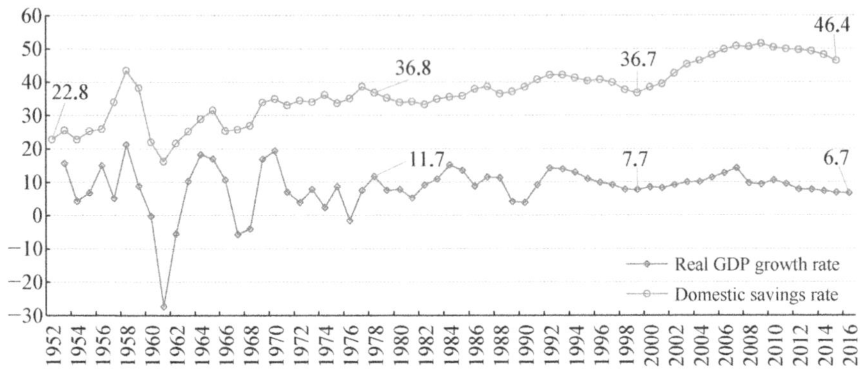

Figure 6.2 China's national savings rate and real GDP growth rate: 1952–2019.

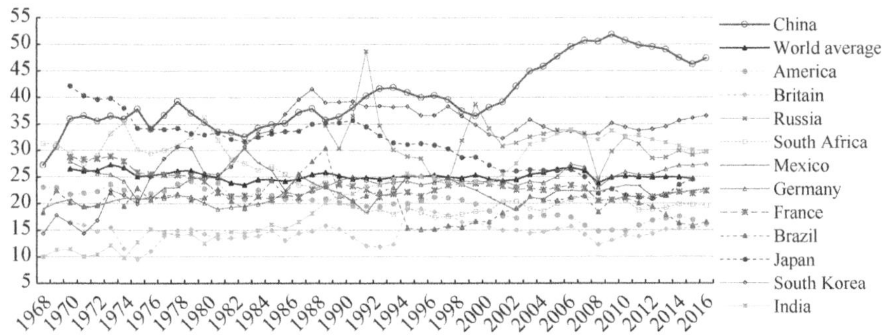

Figure 6.3 Actual changes in the domestic savings rate of some major countries: 1968–2017.

savings rate of a rich country is higher than that of a poor country, though this not necessarily so. As can be seen from Table 6.1, the world's average savings rate has not changed much since the 1970s, being basically around 25%. The average savings rate of upper-middle-income countries was mostly maintained at around 30% during the 1970s to the 1990s last century, and slightly rose this century, reaching about 35% during the period 2010–2017. The average savings rate of middle-income countries was basically kept at around 28% during the 1970s to 1990s, and slightly rose this century, reaching about 33% during the period 2010–2017. The savings rates of lower-middle-income countries and high-income countries were quite different last century, only 15.1% for the former and 25.8% for the latter in the 1970s. However, the savings rates of the two have shown an opposite trend, and the gap between the two has been narrowing. Since the beginning of this century, the savings rate of lower-middle-income countries has been higher than that of high-income ones. During the period 2010–2017, the average savings

Table 6.1 Savings rates of different countries in the world: 1970–2017 Unit: %

Country or region	*1970–1979*	*1980–1989*	*1990–1999*	*2000–2009*	*2010–2017*
China	36.6	35.0	39.7	44.5	49.0
World average	26.1	24.7	25.0	25.3	25.0
Upper-middle-income countries	30.6	29.7	30.4	33.8	35.0
OECD members	25.2	23.7	23.4	22.1	21.0
Middle-income countries	27.3	27.1	28.5	31.7	32.8
Lower-middle-income countries	15.1	18.2	21.5	24.4	25.2
Low-income countries	–	–	7.6	11.4	10.7
Low- and middle-income countries	27.1	26.8	28.1	31.4	32.5
High-income country	25.8	23.9	23.7	22.9	21.9
EU	23.6	21.0	22.4	22.8	22.5
America	22.5	21.6	20.2	17.4	16.3
Britain	13.8	14.2	15.6	14.8	14.6
Italy	24.8	22.4	22.4	21.3	19.5
Germany	23.6	20.8	24.2	24.6	26.2
France	27.0	22.0	22.6	22.9	21.6
Canada	24.3	24.1	21.4	25.2	22.3
Australia	28.7	25.5	24.3	25.1	25.7
Russian Federation	–	34.7	31.8	32.7	29.9
Mexico	21.3	25.7	22.8	21.4	22.5
Brazil	20.8	23.4	18.6	19.4	**18.5**
South Africa	30.7	27.3	18.5	19.8	**19.7**
Singapore	28.8	42.9	49.0	48.5	53.6
Malaysia	25.1	32.1	40.6	43.0	35.1
Republic of Korea	22.6	33.3	38.0	33.8	35.1
Japan	37.0	33.3	32.2	26.0	22.3
Indonesia	19.9	26.7	28.4	28.3	33.9
India	12.4	15.7	23.8	29.6	31.7
Hong Kong of China	30.8	33.6	32.0	31.6	25.5
Iran	32.4	16.9	32.2	44.1	42.9

Source: World Bank, *World Development Indicators*, World Bank Online Database, 2018. The savings rate listed in the table above refers to the average annual savings rate for the period and is equal to the arithmetic average of the savings rates for all years within the period.

rate of lower-middle-income countries was 25.2% and that of high-income countries was only 21.9%. The average savings rate of low-income countries has been maintained at around 10% since the beginning of this century. Table 6.1 shows that, although high-income countries and middle-income countries have higher savings rates than low-income countries, middle-income countries and upper-middle-income countries have higher savings rates than high-income countries and OECD members and the average savings rate of lower-middle-income countries have been higher than that of high-income countries since the beginning of this century. In terms of the average savings rate of a single country during the period 2010–2017, the figure was 18.5% and 19.7% in Brazil and South Africa, both of which are among BRICS countries, lower than the average of high-income countries; savings rates were up to 31.7% and 29.9% in India and Russia, significantly higher than the average level of high-income countries and regions. Singapore (53.6%), Hong Kong (25.5%), and South Korea (35.1%), among the list of Four Asian Tigers, had quite different savings rates. Malaysia, a developing country, and South Korea, a developed country, share the same savings rate, 35.1%. So, the difference in savings rates of different countries cannot be explained by their income level.

Some scholars also believe that high economic growth rates will bring about high savings rates. For example, in 1995, Korea had a savings rate of 36%, Taiwan 27%, Hong Kong 32%, and Singapore up to 50.8%. In the 1980s, Thailand, Malaysia, Indonesia, and other countries experienced rapid economic growth, and their savings rates were also quite high. For example, in 1992, Thailand had a savings rate of 36.2% and Malaysia 37.2% (Xu et al., 2005). However, some countries or regions almost had the same economic growth rate, and their savings rates also differed greatly. South Korea and Taiwan in the 1990s are just examples. Thus, it is not enough to explain the difference in savings rates by the economic growth rate alone.

This chapter will study the decision on the savings rate, and explain China's high savings and investment. The subsequent structure of this chapter is arranged as follows: the second section describes the basic model; the third section discusses the existence, uniqueness, and stability of the balanced growth path under short-sighted expectations and fully rational expectations; the fourth section analyzes the decision on consumption and savings rates under short-sighted expectations and fully rational expectations; the fifth section estimates the consumption and savings rates in China, America, and other economies using the estimated values of the parameters in the existing literature, explains China's high savings rate on the basis of the above, and makes a simple forecast of changes in China's future savings rate; and the last section discusses whether the economic growth mode of high savings and investment in China can continue, and its impact on the lives of Chinese residents.

Section 2 Basic model setup

2.1 Basic model and assumptions

Assume that there is a heterogeneous consumer economy: there is only one product in the economy and it can be consumed and invested in. There are many agents with infinite life expectancy in the economy, represented by $j=1,2,3 \dots J$. Due to the large number of agents, the impact of an individual's behavior on aggregate economy is negligible. Individuals may differ in their initial wealth but share the same preferences and abilities. For an individual's maximization of its utility level within its lifetime, the individual's utility function within its lifetime is expressed as follows:

$$E\sum_{t=0}^{\infty}\rho^{t}u(c_{j}(t)),0<\rho<1 \tag{6.1}$$

where u (.) represents the single-period utility function. For the convenience of analysis, assume $u(c)$=ln c. $c_j(t)$ refers to the consumption of individual j in period t. t refers the time, and ρ refers to the subjective discount rate of the individual.

Personal income arises from labor and capital. Let $k_j(t) \in R^+$ represent the wealth level of individual j in period t. Let $r(t)$ and $w(t)$ represent the total rate of return on capital (1 plus the interest rate) and the rate of return on labor (wages), both of which are determined by the labor market and the capital market. The constraint equation for the budget of individual j is expressed as follows:

$$k_j(t+1)=r(t)k_j(t)+w(t)L_j(t)-c_j(t) \tag{6.2}$$

where $L_j(t)$ represents the labor capacity of individual j in period t. Assuming the personal capacity is the same, $L_j(t)$ is unitized into 1. Also, assume that the individual meets the conditions for non-Ponzi countermeasures.

Assume there is a representative manufacturer in the economy and the manufacturer determines the labor and capital it hires by maximizing profits. The production function is Harold's neutral technological advancement function:

$$Y(t)=F\left(K(t),A(t)L(t)\right) \tag{6.3}$$

where totally refers to output, K refers to total capital, L refers to total labor input, and $A(t)$ refers to technology. The production function $F(.,.)$ has the following properties:

$$\begin{aligned}&F(\lambda K,\lambda L)=\lambda F(K,L),\forall\lambda>0;\quad F_1>0,F_{11}<0,F_2>0,F_{22}<0;\\&F(0,L)=F(K,0)=0,\ \lim_{x_i\to 0}F_i(x_1,x_2)=+\infty,\ \lim_{x_i\to+\infty}F_i(x_1,x_2)=0,i=1,2\end{aligned} \tag{6.4}$$

Assume the rate of technological advancement is g. Since the assumed constant returns to scale, the production function in an intensive form is expressed as follows:

$$\hat{y}=F\left(K(t)/[A(t)L(t)],1\right)=f(\hat{k}) \tag{6.5}$$

where $\hat{k}=K/AL$refers to the capital per effective labor, and $\hat{y}$refers to the output per effective labor. According to the assumption of production function $F(.)$, the function $f(.)$ satisfies the following formula:

$$f(0)=0, f'(k)>0, f''(k)<0, \lim_{k\to\infty} f(k)=0, \lim_{k\to 0} f(k)=\infty \tag{6.6}$$

Assume the goods market and the factor market are perfectly competitive and are always in the state of market clearing. Assume the capital depreciation rate δ is 0. The following equation can be obtained from the profit maximization behavior of the manufacturer:

$$r(t)=1+f'(\hat{k}(t)), w(t)=A(t)f(\hat{k}(t))-\hat{k}(t)A(t)f'(\hat{k}(t)) \tag{6.7}$$

2.2 Model solution and personal consumption function

The optimum behavior of representative consumer j can be expressed as follows:

$$\begin{aligned} &V_j(k(t_0))=E_{t0}\sum_{t=t0}^{\infty}\rho^t u(c_j(t)) \\ &s.t.\ k_j(t+1)=r(t)k_j(t)+w(t)-c_j(t), \quad given\ k_j(t_0) \end{aligned} \tag{6.8}$$

The following equation can be obtained under the assumption of $u(c)=\ln c$ and according to the principle of optimum solution:

$$1/c_j(t)=\rho r(t+1)/c_j(t+1) \tag{6.9}$$

Equation (6.9) is the Euler equation of the consumer. It is not difficult to deduce the recursive equation of consumption and capital as follows:

$$c_j(t)=(1-\rho)\left[r(t)k_j(t)+w(t)\right]+b_j(t) \tag{6.10}$$

$$k_j(t+1)=\rho\left[r(t)k_j(t)+w(t)\right]-b_j(t) \tag{6.11}$$

where

$$b_j(t)=(1-\rho)\sum_{j=1}^{\infty}w(t+j)\Big/\prod_{i=1}^{j}r(t+i) \tag{6.12}$$

According to Equations (6.10) and (6.11), for any period t, personal consumption is determined by three parts: $k(t)$, wealth level of the period; $(r(t)-1)k(t)+w(t)$, net income level of the period; and $b(t)$, the fixed consumption level that is the same for everyone and determined by the future wage level. According to this conclusion, in consideration of a group of people at the same income level, the consumption function obtained when the income level is regressed with the consumption of cross-sectional data will definitely satisfy the Keynesian form. However, considering the consumption function of time series data with increasing wealth level, the fixed items will change along with future wages due to the correlation between the wealth levels of the two periods. So, the consumption form obtained through the regression of consumption along with consumption does not necessarily satisfy the Keynesian form. Additionally, Equations (6.10) and (6.11) also indicate that the marginal propensity to consume and the marginal propensity to save are both constants at any time,[1] but the average propensity to consume will decrease along with income level, and the average savings will increase along with income level. If an individual's current labor capacity increases, he/she will increase his/her consumption and savings level at the same time but the ratio of consumption increment to savings increment, $(1-\rho)/\rho$, will remain unchanged.

Taking the expectation value at each side of Equation (6.11), and according to the consumption function, production function, and market conditions above, we can get the recursive equation of effective capital per capita as follows:

$$(1+g)\hat{k}(t+1) = \rho\left[\hat{k}(t) + f(\hat{k}(t))\right] - (1+g)\hat{b}(t) \tag{6.13}$$

where $\hat{b}(t) = b(t)/A(t+1) = (1-\rho)\sum_{j=1}^{\infty}\left[\left(w(t+j)/A(t+1)\right)\Big/\prod_{i=1}^{j} r(t+i)\right]$.

Section 3 Dynamic behavior of aggregate economy

3.1 Aggregate economy and consumption function under short-sighted expectations

Firstly, assume consumers are of short-sighted expectations, or individuals regard the wages and interest rates of next period as wages and interest rates in all future periods. Under this assumption, $\hat{b}(t) = (1-\rho)w(t+1)/A(t+1)$ $\left(r(t+1)-1\right)$. Thus, Equation (6.13) can be transformed as follows:

$$(g+1)\hat{k}(t+1) + \frac{(g+1)(1-\rho)}{\rho}\left[\frac{f(\hat{k}(t+1))}{f'(\hat{k}(t+1))}\right] = \hat{k}(t) + f(\hat{k}(t)) \tag{6.14}$$

Theorems 6.1 and 6.2 can be obtained according to Equation (6.14).[2]

Theorem 6.1 For the production function that satisfies Equation (6.6), the economy determined by recursive equation (6.14) has one and only one balanced effective capital per capita, $\hat{k}_s^*$, and it satisfies:

$$f'(\hat{k}_s^*) = g\varepsilon_{yk}(\hat{k}_s^*) + \left[(g+1)(1-\rho)/\rho\right] \tag{6.15}$$

where $\varepsilon_{yk}(\hat{k}) = \hat{k}f'(\hat{k})/f(\hat{k})$ represents the elasticity of capital output.

Theorem 6.1 shows that, under short-sighted expectations, there is only one balanced growth path in the economy. And on the balanced growth path, both effective capital per capita and return on capital remain unchanged. It can thus be concluded that the dynamic path for capital per capita on the balanced growth path under short-sighted expectations is as follows:

$$k_s(t) = A_0 \hat{k}_s^*(1+g)^t \equiv k_s^*(1+g)^t \tag{6.16}$$

The rate of return on capital and the wage level are expressed as follows:

$$\begin{aligned} r_s^* &= f'(\hat{k}_s^*) + 1 = g\varepsilon_{yk}(\hat{k}_s^*) + \frac{(g+1)(1-\rho)}{\rho} + 1; \\ w_s^*(t) &= A_0\left[f(\hat{k}_s^*) - \hat{k}_s^* f'(\hat{k}_s^*)\right](1+g)^t \end{aligned} \tag{6.17}$$

The consumption function is as follows:

$$\begin{aligned} c_s(t) &= (1-\rho)\left[r_s^* k_s(t) + w_s(t)\right] + \frac{(1-\rho)w_s^*(t+1)}{r_s^* - 1} \\ &= y_s(t) + \frac{(1-\rho r_s^*)y_s(t)}{r_s^* - 1} + \frac{g w_s^*(t)(1-\rho)}{r_s^* - 1} \end{aligned} \tag{6.18}$$

where $w_s^*(t) = A(\mathrm{t})\left[f(\hat{k}_s^*) - \hat{k}_s^* f'(\hat{k}_s^*)\right]$.

According to the consumption function (6.18) derived through the above analysis, the consumption puzzle related to the form of consumption function can be explained. In the empirical study on the consumption function, economists have previously used multinational cross-sectional data and time series data to check whether the consumption function has any constant term, reaching a contradictory conclusion. The consumption function obtained in the case of regressing multinational cross-sectional data satisfies the Keynesian assumption (i.e., the consumption function has a constant term). But when the consumption function is rechecked using time series data, the consumption function obtained through regression does not have a constant term. Therefore, the Keynesian consumption function is untenable for time series data, which is called the "consumption puzzle" by economists (Romer, 2001, p.334). The "consumption puzzle" can be easily understood according to the consumption function form obtained through the analysis in this chapter. Firstly, for cross-sectional data, there is a constant term in the consumption function (6.18) as different individuals share the same rate of return on capital and future wage level in different periods. However, in consideration of the time series data with economic growth, wages on the balanced growth path will continue to rise. Thus, the constant term in the consumption function (6.18) is no longer a constant but will change with the passage of time. The consumption function will also lose the stable relationship expressed as Equation (6.18). Actually, consumption and income will permanently maintain a fixed ratio, as expressed in Equation (6.19) below.

$$\frac{c(t)}{y(t)} = \frac{(1-\rho)r^*}{r^*-1} + (1-\rho)\frac{gw(t)}{\left(r^*-1\right)y(t)} = 1 - \frac{g\varepsilon_{ky}}{r^*-1}$$
$$= \left[\frac{(g+1)(1-\rho)}{\rho}\right] \Big/ \left\{ g\varepsilon(\hat{k}^*) + \left[\frac{(g+1)(1-\rho)}{\rho}\right]\right\} \tag{6.19}$$

If $g=0$, then $c(t)/y(t)=1$. If $g\neq 0$, $\rho=0.9$, $\varepsilon=1/3$, and $g=0.0$, then $r^*=1.1244$ and $c(t)/y(t)\approx 0.9196$. For those groups at different wealth levels at the same time, Equation (6.18) also indicates that they will have the same slope but different cross-sectional terms. Therefore, the consumption function obtained based on the model of this chapter can well explain the results of some empirical research on consumption functions.[3]

Theorem 6.2 Under short-sighted expectations, if $\varepsilon_{yk}{}'(\hat{k}) \le 0$ applies near equilibrium point $\hat{k}_s^*$, then $\hat{k}_s^*$ is a local stable point of recursive equation (6.14); if $\varepsilon_{yk}{}'(\hat{k}) \le 0$ applies for all $\hat{k}$, $\hat{k}^*$ is also a global stable point of recursive equation (6.14).

Theorem 6.2 indicates that if capital output elasticity is a non-increasing function of capital per capita (or $\varepsilon_{yk}{}'(\hat{k}) \le 0$), the economy will converge to a balanced growth path no matter which state it starts. However, it can be proved that if non-increasing conditions cannot be met (or $\varepsilon_{yk}{}'(\hat{k}) > 0$), the economy may diverge. However, in the Cobb-Douglas production function, when $\varepsilon_{yk}{}'(k) = 0$, and the CES production function, when $\varepsilon_{yk}{}'(k) < 0$, the economy is globally stable.

3.2 Aggregate economy and consumption function under fully rational expectations

When an individual has fully rational expectations of the future wage and the interest rate, the following theorems 6.3 and 6.4 will apply according to Equation (6.13).

Theorem 6.3 Under the assumption that an individual has fully rational expectations, for the production function that satisfies Equation (6.6), the economy given in Equation (6.13) has and only has one balanced effective capital per capita, which satisfies:

$$\rho f'(\hat{k}^*) = (1+g-\rho) \tag{6.20}$$

Theorem 6.3 shows that, under fully rational expectations, there is also only one balanced growth path in the economy. And on this path, both effective capital per capita and its rate of return will remain unchanged. Additionally, the accumulation path of capital per capita on the balanced growth path under fully rational expectations can also be obtained as follows:

$$k_L(t) = A_0 \hat{k}_L^{\,*}(1+g)^t \equiv k_L^{\,*}(1+g)^t \tag{6.21}$$

At this time, the rate of return on capital and the wage level are expressed as follows, respectively:

$$r_L^{\,*} = (g+1)/\rho; \quad w_L^{\,*}(t) = A_0\left[f(\hat{k}_L^{\,*}) - \hat{k}_L^{\,*} f'(\hat{k}_L^{\,*})\right](1+g)^t \tag{6.22}$$

It is not difficult to calculate the consumption function on the balanced growth path under fully rational expectations, which is shown as follows:

$$\begin{aligned} c_L(t) &= (1-\rho)\left[r_L^{\,*} k_L(t) + w_L(t)\right] + \frac{(1-\rho)w_L^{\,*}(t+1)}{r_L^{\,*}-1} \\ &= y_L(t) + \frac{(1-\rho r_L^{\,*})y_L(t)}{r_L^{\,*}-1} + \frac{g w_L^{\,*}(t)(1-\rho)}{r_L^{\,*}-1} \end{aligned} \tag{6.23'}$$

where $w_L^{\,*}(t) = A(t)\left[f(\hat{k}_L^{\,*}) - \hat{k}_L^{\,*} f'(\hat{k}_L^{\,*})\right]$.

Theorem 6.4 Under fully rational expectations, the effective capital per capita that satisfies Equation (6.20), $\hat{k}_L^{\,*}$, is both local and global stable points of recursive equation (6.13).

It can be seen that the aggregate economy under the assumption of fully rational expectations has exactly the same dynamic nature as that under short-sighted expectations. However, the decisions on interest and consumption rates under both consumptions above are different.

Section 4 Decisions on consumption and savings rates: short-sighted expectations and fully rational expectations

As known from the above analysis, under either short-sighted or fully rational expectations, the aggregate economy has a stable, balanced growth path. However, the determining equations of interest rates and consumption paths under different forms of expectations are different, so are long-term consumption and savings rates. The decisions on consumption and savings rates on the balanced growth path will be discussed below.

Under fully rational expectations, the long-term consumption rate is expressed as follows according to Equations (6.10) and (6.20):

$$\frac{c(t)}{y(t)} = 1 - \frac{gk(t)}{y(t)} = 1 - \frac{gk(t)f'(k(t))}{f(k(t))f'(k(t))} = 1 - \frac{g\varepsilon_{ky}}{r^*-1} = 1 - \frac{g\rho\varepsilon_{ky}}{g+1-\rho} \tag{6.24}$$

Thus, the consumption and savings rates on the balanced growth path under fully rational expectations are constant terms, which are only determined by economic growth rate g, personal subjective discount rate ρ, and capital output elasticity ε.

Under short-sighted expectations, the long-term consumption rate is expressed as follows according to Equations (6.10) and (6.15):

$$\frac{c(t)}{y(t)} = 1 - \frac{g\varepsilon_{ky}}{r^* - 1} = \left[\frac{(g+1)(1-\rho)}{\rho}\right] \Big/ \left[g\varepsilon(\hat{k}^*) + \frac{(g+1)(1-\rho)}{\rho}\right] \tag{6.25}$$

So, the consumption and savings rates on the balanced growth path under short-sighted expectations are also constant terms, which are also determined by the economic growth rate g, the personal subjective discount rate ρ, and the capital output elasticity ε. Additionally, the following Theorem 6.5 applies no matter the expectations.

Theorem 6.5 Whether under short-sighted or fully rational expectations, an increase in economic growth rate g, in capital output elasticity ε, in personal subjective discount rate ε or a decrease in interest rate r will cause the decrease in the consumption rate on the balanced growth path and the increase in the savings rate on the balanced growth path.

Section 5 Numerical simulation: explanation of China's high savings rate

5.1 Numerical simulation: comparisons on the model and the real economy

According to Equations (6.24) and (6.25), if we know the values of g, ε, ρ, and other parameters in the real economy, we can then estimate the consumption and savings rates. In this section, the consumption and savings rates of countries are estimated according to the actual estimated values of g, ε, ρ, and other parameters of the countries in the existing literature, and are also compared against the actual values of the countries, in order to test the rationality of the explanations concerning the real consumption and savings rates. Table 6.2 gives the estimated values of consumption and savings rates under short-sighted expectations and fully rational expectations that correspond to various subjective discount rates, with the US economy as an example. Based on the reality of the US economy, take the economic growth rate as 0.03 and capital output elasticity as 1/3 in Table 6.2. As known from Table 6.2, if ρ=0.95, the estimated values under short-sighted expectations are quite close to the average savings rate of 0.163 during the period 2010–2017 and 0.174 during the period 2000–2009 for America. Thus, the model is very proper for the savings rate of America. Of course, in order to obtain the savings rate that is consistent with that of America last century, higher

Table 6.2 The slope, interest rate, and subjective discount rate of consumption function (g=0.03, ε=1/3)

ρ	*0.95*	*0.9*	*0.88*	*0.85*	*0.8*	*0.7*	*0.6*
R_f	1.084	1.144	1.171	1.212	1.288	1.471	1.717
C_f	0.881	0.931	0.941	0.952	0.965	0.979	0.986
S_f	0.119	0.069	0.059	0.048	0.035	0.021	0.014
R_s	1.064	1.124	1.150	1.192	1.268	1.451	1.697
C_s	0.844	0.920	0.934	0.948	0.963	0.978	0.986
S_s	0.156	0.08	0.066	0.052	0.037	0.022	0.014

Note: C_f: consumption rate under fully rational expectations; Sf: savings rate under fully rational expectations; R_f: rate of return on capital under fully rational expectations; C_s: consumption rate under short-sighted expectations; S_s: savings rate under short-sighted expectations; R_s: rate of return on capital under short-sighted expectations (the letters in the following tables have the same meanings as above).

Table 6.3 The slope, interest rate, and subjective discount rate of consumption function (g=0.09, ε=2/3)

ρ	*0.95*	*0.9*	*0.88*	*0.85*	*0.8*	*0.7*	*0.6*
R_f	1.1474	1.2111	1.2386	1.2824	1.3625	1.5571	1.81667
C_f	0.5927	0.7158	0.7485	0.7875	0.8345	0.8923	0.9265
S_f	0.4073	0.2842	0.2515	0.2125	0.1655	0.1077	0.0735
R_s	1.1174	1.1811	1.2086	1.2524	1.3325	1.5271	1.7867
C_s	0.4885	0.6687	0.7124	0.7622	0.8195	0.8862	0.9237
S_s	0.5115	0.3313	0.2876	0.2378	0.1805	0.1138	0.0763

capital output elasticity, economic growth rate or subjective discount rate, and intertemporal elasticity of substitution are required.

According to the estimation by Zou Zhizhuang (Chow, 2002, p. 95), China's capital output elasticity is about 0.61 and China's average growth rate in the past 40 years is about 0.09. Taking China's economy as an example, Table 6.3 indicates the estimated values of consumption and savings rates under short-sighted expectations and fully rational expectations of the economy at various subjective discount rates, where g=0.09 and ε=2/3. As known from Table 6.3, if the subjective discount rate is set to be 0.95, the savings rate of China's economy in the model of short-sighted expectations is estimated to be 0.5115, which is quite close to China's average savings rate for the period 2008–2013, average savings rate for the period 2000–2009, 0.44, and average annual savings rate for the period 2010–2017, 0.49. Additionally, Table 6.4 also estimates the savings rate when the GDP growth rate is 0.07, which is close to the savings rate of 0.45–0.47 when China's GDP growth rate has declined in recent years. Thus, the estimated values of the model well explain the savings rates in China's real economy. Table 6.5 shows the savings rates estimated when g=0.06 and ε=1/3. These values and the estimated savings rates under short-sighted expectations are quite close to the economic situation of Japan and South Korea in the 1970s.

Table 6.4 The slope, interest rate, and subjective discount rate of consumption function (g=0.07, ε=2/3)

ρ	*0.95*	*0.9*	*0.88*	*0.85*	*0.8*	*0.7*	*0.6*
R_f	1.1263	1.1889	1.2159	1.2588	1.3375	1.5286	1.7834
C_f	0.6305	0.7528	0.7839	0.8197	0.8617	0.9117	0.9404
S_f	0.3695	0.2472	0.2161	0.1803	0.1383	0.0883	0.0596
R_s	1.1040	1.1656	1.1926	1.2355	1.3142	1.5052	1.76
C_s	0.5513	0.7181	0.7576	0.8018	0.8514	0.9076	0.9386
S_s	0.4487	0.2819	0.2424	0.1982	0.1486	0.0924	0.0614

Table 6.5 The slope, interest rate, and subjective discount rate of consumption function (g=0.06, ε=1/3)

ρ	*0.95*	*0.9*	*0.88*	*0.85*	*0.8*	*0.7*	*0.6*
R_f	1.1158	1.1778	1.2045	1.2471	1.325	1.5143	1.766667
C_f	0.8272	0.8875	0.9022	0.9190	0.9385	0.9611	0.973913
S_f	0.1727	0.1125	0.0978	0.0810	0.0615	0.03889	0.026087
R_s	1.0758	1.1378	1.1645	1.2071	1.285	1.4742	1.726667
C_s	0.7361	0.8548	0.8785	0.9034	0.9298	0.9578	0.972477
C_s	0.2639	0.1451	0.1215	0.0966	0.0702	0.0422	0.027523

It can be found through the numerical analysis above that the main reason for the differences in the savings rates of various countries may lie in different economic growth rates and capital output elasticity in these countries. The result of numerical analysis shows that short-sighted expectations and rational expectations may have little effect on the differences in the savings rates of different countries in the case of low economic growth rates and low capital output elasticity. However, in the case of high economic growth rates and high capital output elasticity, short-sighted expectations may widen the gaps among different countries in the savings rate. This may be very important to understand the differences in the savings rates of Southeast Asian countries and some undeveloped countries. Additionally, the difference in the rates of return of various countries caused by other exogenous factors may constitute an important reason for the differences in the savings rates of these countries.

5.2 *Explanation on China's high savings rate and prediction of changes in the future savings rate*

According to the above analysis, both consumption and savings rates of a country or region are mainly determined by the economic growth rate, subjective discount rate (or rate of return on capital), and capital output elasticity. Additionally, the form of an individual's expectations of future wages is also an important factor affecting consumption and savings rates. It can be seen from the numerical simulation results in the previous sub-section that the following may cause the sustained rise in China's savings rate:

Firstly, the high economic growth rate may be one of the reasons for China's high savings rate. It is not difficult to draw the following conclusions based on the analysis of the previous sub-section: when the subjective discount rate is 0.95, the capital output elasticity is 1/3 and the economic growth rate increases from 0.03 to 0.09, the savings rate will rise from 0.12 to 0.20 under fully rational expectations, representing an increase of 69.9% and from 0.15 to 0.34 under short-sighted expectations, representing an increase of 129%. In addition, it can also be seen from Figure 6.2 that the years when China's savings rate fell corresponded to those when the economic growth rate declined. So, the high economic growth rate may be one of the main factors resulting in China's current high savings rate. However, as investment and savings are two sides of the same coin, high growth rate requires high investment rate, which must be sustained by high savings rate. Therefore, it is difficult to determine which is the cause and which is the effect between the high growth rate and the high savings rate. However, it is certain that a high economic growth rate will inevitably require a high savings rate.

Secondly, the high economic growth rate alone will not increase China's savings rate up to 45% or above. The second factor for China's high savings rate may be high capital output elasticity. Numerical simulation results show that, when the subjective discount rate is 0.95, the economic growth rate is 0.09 and the capital output elasticity increases from 1/3 to 2/3, the savings rate will rise from 0.20 to 0.40 under fully rational expectations, representing a two-fold increase; from 0.34 to 0.51 under short-sighted expectations, representing an increase of 50%. The main reason the capital output elasticity reduces the savings rate lies in the fact that higher capital output elasticity means lower proportion of wages in the economy. In the case of constant national income, this means lower wages. And the wages determine the individual's fixed consumption level. So, the higher the capital output elasticity, the lower the personal fixed consumption level. Thus, a lower consumption rate means a higher savings rate.

The third reason for China's high savings rate may be the short-sighted expectations of individuals for future wages. Under the low economic growth rate and the low capital output elasticity, the form of individuals' expectations of wages does not produce a significant impact on the savings rate. As shown in Table 6.2, when the economic growth rate is 0.03 and the capital output elasticity is 1/3, which corresponds to those of the US economy, the savings rate under short-sighted expectations is 0.156 and that under fully rational expectations is 0.12, with a difference of only 3 percentage points. However, in the case of high economic growth rate and high capital output elasticity, people's short-sighted expectations for future wage growth will cause a great increase in the savings rate. Table 6.3 shows that, when the economic growth rate is 0.09 and the capital output elasticity is 2/3, which correspond to those of China's economy, the savings rate under short-sighted expectations is 0.51 and that under fully rational expectations is 0.40, with a difference of 10 percentage points.

The fourth factor for China's high savings rate may be the high subjective discount rate and high risk aversion (intertemporal elasticity of substitution) of Chinese residents. The numerical simulation results in this chapter do not indicate that the difference in personal preferences (subjective discount rate and high risk aversion) is the reason for the difference in the saving rates of China and America. However, China is now in the era of reform, where the existing insurance system has lost its effect and the new social insurance system has not been completely established, which will virtually raise the risks of Chinese residents. Additionally, the uncertainty brought about by the reform has raised the risks of residents. So, the high risks and high uncertainty of China's reform may be one of the main reasons for China's high savings rate. The continuous increase in China's savings rate may be related to this factor.

Of course, due to the simplified assumptions for the analysis in this chapter, there are still many factors that may affect the savings rate that are not reflected in the model, and there remains a lot of space for improvement. Firstly, population growth and changes in population structure are obviously an important factor affecting the savings rate. Since there is no population growth in the model of this chapter, there is no way to analyze the impact of population changes over the savings rate. Secondly, the model of this chapter only analyzes the private savings rate, but the total savings rate of a country should include government and private savings. Discussing the differences in the total savings of countries by applying this conclusion may cause deviations from the practical conditions. Additionally, this chapter mainly analyzes the decision on balancing the savings rate on the balanced growth path. So, analyzing China's reality by using the result may cause doubt about whether China's actual economy must follow a balanced growth path. Thus, incorporating any of the above factors into the model of this chapter can make the analysis result much closer to the reality of the actual economy, which will thus be regarded as the aspect for further expansion of this chapter. Nevertheless, through the simple analysis of the model in this chapter, we can basically give some explanations on the main reasons for China's high savings rate. Also, according to the analysis of the model in this chapter, it is not difficult for us to make some predictions about the future changes in China's savings rate.

Firstly, as China mainly adopts a labor-intensive production technology in the current stage, the country has an extremely high capital output rate, which is one of the main reasons for its high savings rate. If the production technology will gradually shift from the labor-intensive type to the capital-intensive type with the development of China's economy in the future, the capital output elasticity is expected to gradually decrease. Thus, the shifting of production technology will be an important factor driving China's consumption to increase in the future. Secondly, if China can still maintain a high economic growth rate in the future, changes in other factors will cause the decrease in the savings rate, and the high economic growth rate will also cause China's savings rate to maintain a high level. Thirdly, as China's reform deepens, if social insurance systems and other social distribution systems can be gradually improved, the uncertainties in life can be reduced, and people's risk aversion (or intertemporal flexibility of substitution) may be reduced. This can also cause a decline in China's future savings rate and drive China's consumption growth.

Section 6 Brief comment: is the high savings and high investment growth pattern sustainable?

The previous analysis indicates that China's savings rate has stayed high and continued to rise since the reform and opening-up. China's savings rate was basically maintained at around 35% in the early 1980s, and exceeded 40% in the late 1990s. It had been above 50% since 2005 and declining since 2010, and was as high as 44.8% in 2018. The issue of high savings rate has always been the concern of all walks of life. The possible reasons for China's high savings have been analyzed and discussed through the model above. In this section, two issues will be discussed. First, is China's high savings and high investment growth pattern sustainable? Second, what impact does the growth pattern produce on the lives of Chinese residents?

6.1 High savings rates may produce three impacts on the macro economy

The first effect of high savings on the macro economy is the economic growth effect. For individuals, the division of income between consumption and savings is actually that of personal consumption between the present and the future. More savings today is for spending more in the future, which does not apply to misers. For the overall economy of a country, all products produced by the country can only be used for two aspects, namely consumption and investment. The national income formed by the total value of a country's products can only be used for consumption and investment as well. Thus, without regard for import and export, the total investment afterwards is equal to the total investment, which is the principle of "total investment is equal to total savings." Consumption is what happens today and does not produce a big impact on the economy tomorrow. Savings represent today's investment and may improve tomorrow production capacity. From this point of view, today's high savings promise tomorrow's higher production capacity. Conversely, a country must also maintain a high savings rate and a high investment rate in order to obtain a high economic growth rate. Thus, high savings and high investment will inevitably occur during a period of rapid economic growth, which has been demonstrated by the model analysis in this chapter.

The second impact that high savings produce on the macro economy is the economic structure effect. Different from personal savings, the savings rate of a country will, as far as its overall economy is concerned, directly impact its future economic structure. If the current savings rate is very high, it will mean a large part of the demand is for investment goods, and the demand for consumption goods will have a relatively low proportion. Manufacturers focus on demand when carrying out production. As far as the current production investment is concerned, high savings will also contribute to the current production of the investment goods and there is little investment in the production of consumption goods. As a result, there will be high production capacity of investment goods and low production capacity of consumption goods. Therefore, if the current savings rate is very high, the production capacity of consumption goods cannot be improved in a relatively short period of time, and tomorrow's production capacity cannot be improved. It can be seen that a country with a high savings rate today will surely have an economic structure featuring a large proportion of investment goods production capacity and a small proportion of consumption goods production capacity. For example, since China's fiscal expenditure of four trillion yuan was used for roads, bridges, and other infrastructures in 2008, the operation capacity of these infrastructures will inevitably be improved to a large extent within the subsequent period of time. Also, it will be proved later that, as a large part of such fiscal expenditure has flown into the real estate industry, a large number of houses are supplied within a period of time after 2009 (see Figures 7.1 and 7.3 in Chapter 7). However, the production capacity of some consumption goods may not be much improved in the short term.

The accelerated investment effect is the third macroeconomic effect produced by high savings. The impact of a country's high savings rate on its overall economy may not end here. We may need to be more cautious if we further consider the impact of the investment today over the economic structure of the day after tomorrow through tomorrow's investment goods. When there is a high savings rate in today's economy, there will be more investment goods produced tomorrow due to the increase in the investment goods production capacity then. In order to make the investment goods produced tomorrow be fully absorbed, it is necessary to have a higher savings rate and investment demand tomorrow than today to absorb tomorrow's investment goods. If tomorrow's economy can continue its stable development, the savings rate and investment demand tomorrow are sufficient to absorb the output of tomorrow's investment goods. So, there will be a higher investment goods production capacity on the day after tomorrow than that of tomorrow. It can be seen that, in order to maintain stable and balanced development of the entire economy, the excessively high savings rate may produce the dynamic acceleration effect that enables the self-expansion of savings investment in addition to the economic growth effect and the economic structure effect; otherwise, economic growth will not continue.

6.2 High savings rates are not conducive to sustained and stable economic development

Although countries with high economic growth rates generally have high savings rates, no country except Singapore, a small country where re-export dominates, can maintain a savings rate of more than 40% for long, according to the historical development experience of various countries. However, China can do so for long. Of course, in the case of reasonable economic structure, China's current economic structure may continue, the consumption level of residents can still be improved, and the future standards of living and welfare will not be deteriorated at all. However, as mentioned above, high savings and high investment may produce an economic structure effect and an accelerated investment effect. In the case of high savings rate today, there may be a higher investment demand. Therefore, a higher savings rate may be required in the future to maintain the current economic situation, which can be verified by the fact that China's high savings rate has been growing since 1978. However, the future consumption level or living standards may not necessarily improve (the consumption level may not necessarily increase together with output due to the decrease in the percentage of consumption). This is also the issue concerning China's high savings rate that macroeconomists worry about. In other words, the current economic pattern of self-expanding high savings and high growth will not continue some day. If the growth pattern is not shifted, high economic growth may be interrupted in the near future. More importantly, once the high economic growth rate becomes interrupted, many other issues, such as employment and social security, will become even more serious. Thus, in terms of sustained, stable economic development, the current high savings rate is detrimental to long-term economic growth.

In terms of the impact of the economic development model of high savings rate on the living standards of residents, the economy featuring a low savings rate always means a higher welfare level than the economy featuring a high savings rate under the same economic growth rate as the welfare level of residents depends on their consumption level. High savings and high investment can lift the social welfare level as long as they continuously bring about rapid economic growth and continuously increase the consumption level of residents. Only the high GDP growth presented by such high savings and high investment is of practical significance for the lives of ordinary people. However, as far as our current situation is concerned, the real wage level of ordinary residents has almost not changed at least in the past 10 years, although China's GDP per capita has reached 8.5% since 1978. This means that residents' consumption level has almost not improved. The significance of this high economic growth pattern that cannot increase the consumption level of residents is also open to deliberation.

Notes

1 This conclusion relies on the assumption on the logarithmic utility function. In the utility function of CRRA, the marginal propensity to consume (MPC) and marginal propensity to save (MPS) are no longer fixed. More specifically, the MPC and MPS then are both a recursive form and depend on the rate of return on capital, relative risk aversion coefficient, and MPC of the next period.
2 To save space, all the proofs in this book are omitted. Readers may contact the author if necessary.
3 This result does not rely on the assumption of short-sighted expectations and is also true under fully rational assumptions. The interest rate and consumption rate are determined in a different way.

References

[1] Chow, G. C. (2002). *China's Economic Transformation.* Malden, MA: Blackwell Publishers Inc.
[2] Romer, D. (2001). *Advanced Macroeconomics*, second ed., New York: McGraw-Hill Companies, Inc.
[3] Xu, D. Q., Gao, N., & Zhang, Q. W. (2005). How long will high national savings rate last? Retrieved from http://finance.sina.com.cn/economist/jingjixueren/20050602/ 182116 50887.shtml.

7 China's real estate development and economic growth

Since 1978, the proportion of the output value of the real estate industry over China's GDP (hereinafter referred to as the "proportion of the real estate industry over China's GDP") has been on the rise. As can be seen in Figure 7.1, the proportion of the real estate industry in GDP in China was around 2% during the period 1952–1978, and was approximately 2.2% in 1978. Since 1983, this proportion has basically shown an upward trend. In 2019, the proportion of the real estate industry in GDP reached 7.03%. From the perspective of China's current economic structure and in consideration of the multiplier effect, the real estate industry has become one of the most important industries that can produce a direct impact on China's overall economic growth. In fact, China has been facing such a dilemma in the past 10 years. The government has relaxed its control over the real estate industry, resulting in a surge in housing prices. The economic growth rate has dropped sharply as long as the government exercises control over the real estate industry. In this chapter, the relationship between China's real estate industry development and its economic growth will be discussed.

The structure of this chapter is arranged as follows: the first section analyzes the development status of China's real estate industry; the second section theoretically studies the relationship of housing and land supply with

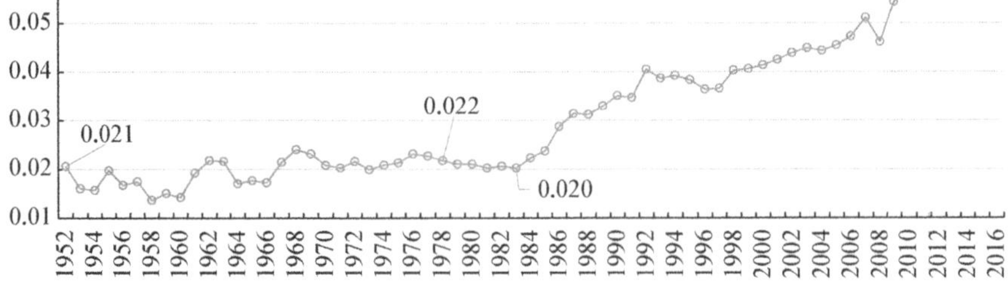

Figure 7.1 Changes in the proportion of the output value of the real estate industry in China's GDP: 1952–2019.

DOI: 10.4324/9781003261629-10

economic growth and housing prices; the third section analyzes the impact of China's housing supply on economic growth and the rise in housing prices by applying China's inter-provincial panel data; and the fourth section empirically discusses the reasons for China's sustained rise in housing prices and the dilemmas faced by the government in regulation.

Section 1 Status quo and features of China's real estate industry

As the income of Chinese urban and rural residents continues to rise, people turn to the housing and transportation needs at a higher level when their food and clothing needs are continuously satisfied. As a commodity that meets residential needs, housing has come to be the most important consumer demand of Chinese residents, and thus China's real estate industry has continued to grow up and develop. The increase in the residential demand of Chinese residents and the development of the real estate industry has been significantly reflected in two macro indicators, namely housing quantity and price. As shown in Figures 7.2 and 7.3, China's urban and rural housing area per capita and area of newly built residential building area have grown rapidly during the period 1978–2017. Since real estate is also part of the gross domestic product (GDP), increasing housing investment is also an important driver for China's economic growth. Actually, China's economic growth has reached a point where it heavily depends on the development of the real estate industry. As shown in Figure 7.4, the changes in the growth rate of China's real estate investment are highly synchronous with the economic growth rate. Of course, the causal relationship between real estate investment and economic growth cannot be determined by this simple trend chart alone. However, unlike other investments, land is one of the most critical elements in real estate development and housing development, and changes in land supply may constrain the development of real estate investment and the real estate industry to a large extent. Since the land in

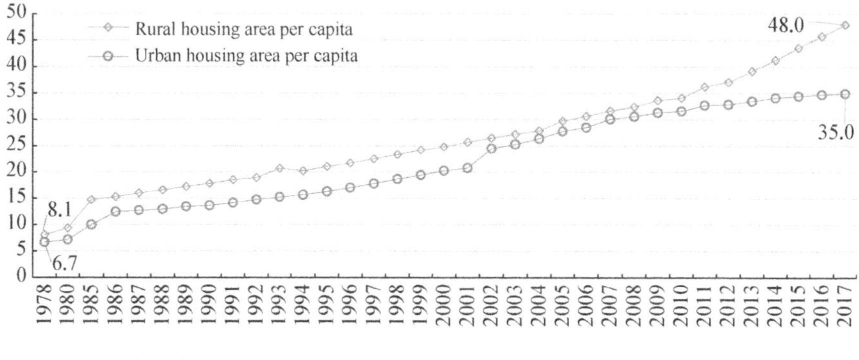

Figure 7.2 China's urban and rural housing area per capita: 1978–2017.

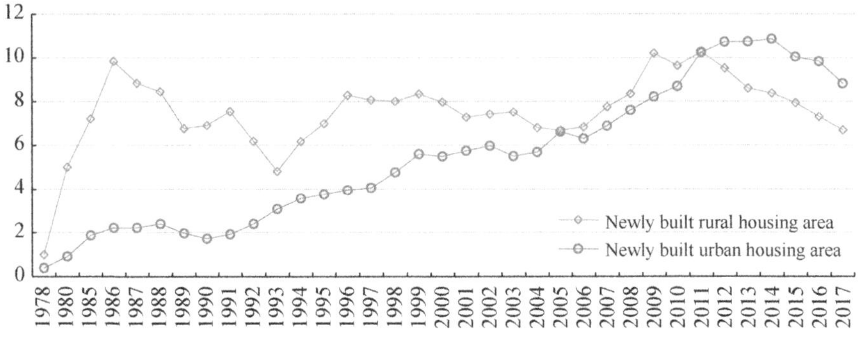

Figure 7.3 The area of newly built urban and rural houses in China: 1978–2017.

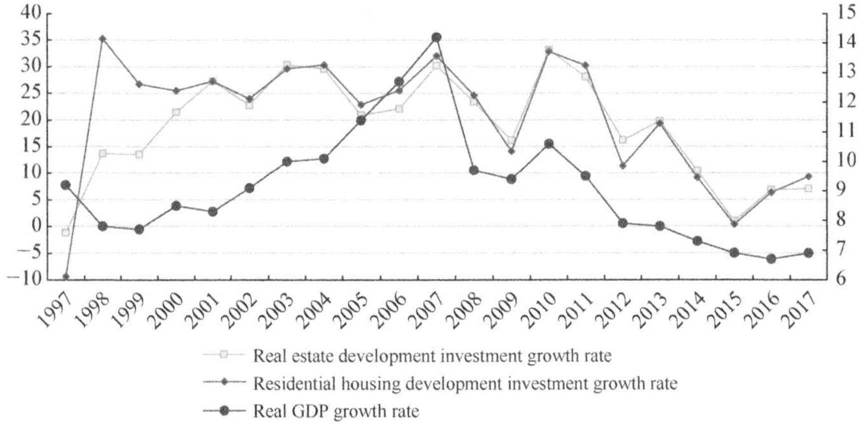

Figure 7.4 China's real estate investment growth rate and real GDP growth rate: 1997–2017.

China is legally owned by the state, the country's real estate development is not a complete market, and land supply and new housing supply may be determined by the local government. In this sense, China's land supply may be exogenously determined by the government to a large extent.[1] Is China's economic growth affected by land supply? Does land and housing supply affect China's economic growth?

People's ever-increasing housing demand is more apparent in terms of housing prices. As shown in Figures 7.5a and 7.5b, China's housing prices have been rising at an almost crazy speed in the past 30 years. The rate of increase in housing prices is much higher than the rate of increase in the GDP deflator and also higher than the wage growth rate, the growth rate of the disposable income per capita, and the real GDP growth rate per capita in the same period. In fact, in order to control the rapid rise in housing prices,

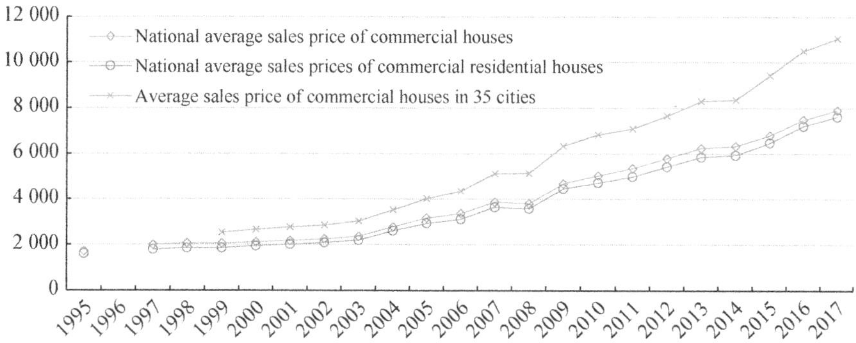

Figure 7.5a Changes in the national average sales price of commercial houses in China: 1995–2017.

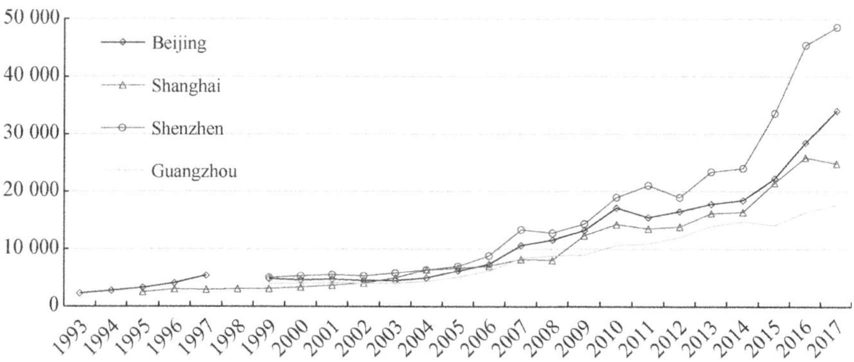

Figure 7.5b Changes in the average sales price of residential commercial houses in China's four major first-tier cities: 1993–2017.

the Chinese central government has issued real estate regulation policies several times since 2005. However, under stringent housing price regulation policies, China's housing prices have remained at a high level and keep rising. Why do the government's real estate regulation policies produce almost no effect on housing prices and their rising trend? What factor determines the long-term changes in housing prices during the economic growth process?

In addition, China's housing supply has also been increasing alongside the sustained sharp rise in China's housing prices. However, the growth rate of China's housing prices is also much faster than that of housing supply. As known from Figure 7.6, in most years, China's housing prices and housing area per capita are growing, and the growth rate of housing prices is faster than that of housing area per capita. Moreover, in terms of growth rate, the growth rate of housing area per capita shows a downward trend, while that of housing prices goes in the opposite direction. According to Figure 7.7,

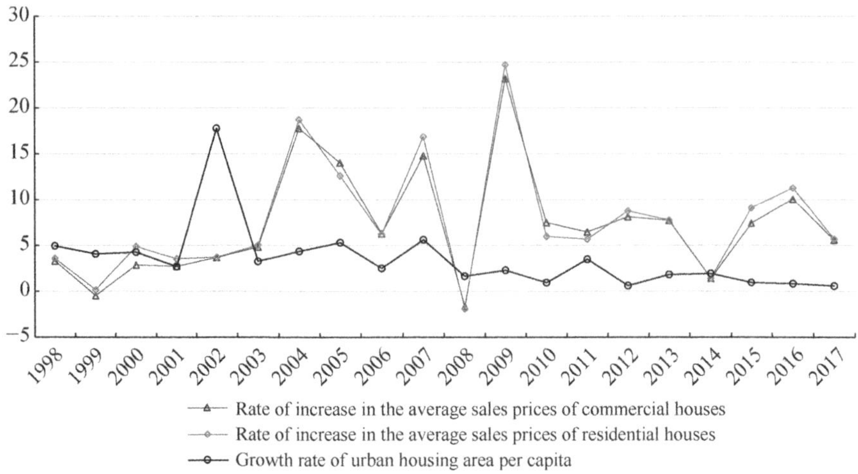

Figure 7.6 The increase in China's housing area per capita and urban housing price growth rate: 2002–2016.

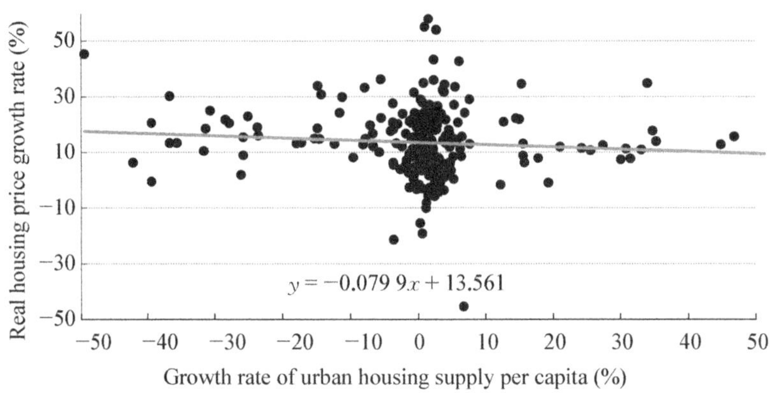

Figure 7.7 The scatter plot of housing price growth rates and the growth rates of housing area per capita in the provinces of China.

during the period 2004–2011, the growth rate of housing prices in China's provinces was negatively correlated with the growth rate of housing area per capita of these provinces. Why is there a negative relationship between the growth rate of housing prices and that of housing supply? In terms of the principle of supply and demand, added housing supply will cause a decrease in housing prices. It seems that the continued rise in housing prices of China can be attributed to the lack of housing supply. However, it is not enough to conclude that a decrease in the growth rate of supply will lead to an increase in the growth rate of housing prices. That's because the housing supply is still on the rise as long as the growth rate is positive despite a decline in the growth rate. Thus, when the principle of supply and demand cannot explain the continuous increase in housing supply, China's housing prices are still rising at a faster speed than that of housing supply. From the macro perspective of general equilibrium analysis, land and housing supply will not only impact housing supply but also affect housing demand by influencing economic growth and people's income level. Therefore, it is necessary to take into account the impact of land and housing supply on economic growth and people's income level and make a comprehensive analysis of the overall effect of land supply on housing supply and economic growth in order to study the overall effect of the increase in land and housing supply on housing prices and understand the relationship between the housing price growth rate and the land supply growth rate. In view of the above, this chapter will study the impact of land supply on housing prices by taking a comprehensive account look at the impact of land and housing supply on the supply and demand of housing supply and demand (economic growth and income level) from the macro perspective of general equilibrium.

However, the impact of land and housing supply on economic growth is also related to the impact of land and housing supply on housing prices. Firstly, the increase in the supply of land as a factor of production will contribute to economic growth. However, land and housing supply will also impact the substitution of people's consumption between housing consumption and general commodity consumption, and people's savings substitution between housing investment and physical investment, thus affecting the material capital investment and material accumulation process of the whole society and producing an indirect impact on long-term economic growth. The effect of land and housing supply on economic growth through this indirect mechanism will be much more important than the direct impact produced on economic growth as a factor of production. In terms of the second effect, the increase in land and housing supply will enable people to invest more savings in housing when the housing prices remain unchanged, which is not conducive to material capital accumulation and constrain economic growth. However, if the increase in land supply can control the increase in housing prices and even promote the decline in housing prices, the price effect may cause people to reduce the percentage of housing consumption over the total consumption and enable the selection of investment in kind to replace "housing investment," which will facilitate material capital accumulation and long-term economic growth. However, according to the scatter plot between the economic growth rate of each province of China and the growth rate of housing area per capita during the period 2004–2011, as shown in Figure 7.8, there seems to be a relationship of reverse change between the urban housing supply growth rate of each province of China and the economic growth rate. Why is there a negative correlation between the housing supply growth rate and the economic growth rate? This is another puzzling and interesting question to be analyzed in this chapter.

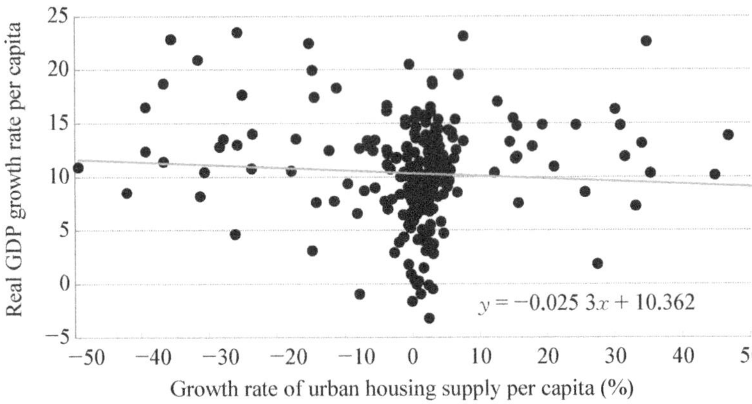

Figure 7.8 The scatter plot of the economic growth rate of each province of China and the growth rate of housing area per capita.

To sum up, the following section of this chapter will study the relationship of land supply with economic growth and changes in housing prices within the general macroeconomic equilibrium analysis framework of land and housing supply and economic growth and housing demand, and probe into the long-term impact of housing supply on housing prices and economic growth from the perspective of dynamic economics. Based on this analytical perspective, this chapter will first establish an Over Lapping Generation (OLG) model for housing consumption and endogenous economic growth, and apply the dynamic macroeconomic method of general equilibrium to analyze the impact of land supply on housing price changes and economic growth during the dynamic process of long-term economic growth. Then, this chapter will test the theoretical research conclusions of the chapter by using China's inter-provincial panel data, and verify the impact of China's housing supply on the changes in China's housing prices and economic growth; it will then analyze the root cause and endogenous mechanism for the sustained rise in China's housing prices by applying the mechanism and principle of theoretical analysis. The research on the theoretical model of this chapter shows that in an economy where consumers have housing consumption, the growth of land and housing supply is also one of the major factors affecting housing prices and economic growth even if there is no speculative housing demand and housing price bubbles. In particular, on the balanced growth path, the housing price growth rate is equal to the economic growth rate (also equal to the growth rate of income per capita) plus the population growth rate, minus the growth rate of land supply per capita, which is also shown as the growth rate of income housing supply per capita. In particular, on the balanced growth path, the housing price growth rate is equal to the economic growth rate (also equal to the growth rate of income per capita) plus the population growth rate, then minus the growth rate of land supply per capita (also expressed as housing supply per capita in the model). Additionally, and more importantly, since the service arising from the provision of housing is not completed in one period, its future value enables it to become both consumption goods and investment goods. Due to this characteristic of housing, it is possible for people to become engaged in speculative housing purchase under certain conditions, thus leading to unstable equilibrium in the economy. This unstable equilibrium means that it is extremely easy for the economy to deviate from the equilibrium state, resulting in a housing bubble. Once the economy deviates from such state and a bubble appears, the economy will return to its equilibrium state only when it undergoes an extreme depression and forces the bubble to burst. The empirical research results in this chapter show that the growth rate of China's housing supply indeed has a significant positive impact on the economic growth rate and a significant negative impact on the housing price growth rate. Moreover, there is indeed a bubble in China's housing prices due to the speculative demand.

Section 2 Basic model and theoretical analysis

2.1 Basic model: invariable land and housing supply

2.1.1 Basic assumptions

Assume there are many individuals in an economy, each of whom lives for two periods: they earn labor income when they are young and have no labor income when they are old. There are two types of goods in the economy, namely general goods and housing. The former is produced with capital and labor and can be used for consumption and the latter is produced on land and provides residential services to individuals for the purpose of effect. The entire economy continues in an indefinite way. The specific assumptions are as follows:

Assume that one unit of housing is produced on one unit of land and the housing depreciation rate is 0. Also, assume both land and housing are freely competitive markets, and land price P_t^X is equal to housing price P_t^H. For the sake of simplicity, both housing price and land price in period t are expressed by P_t. The housing price is determined by the supply and demand in the housing market. Additionally, land supply and the total population on the land are assumed to be fixed in this section. The housing supply in the market of any period t is H; the total population is L; and the housing supply per capita is $h_t^S = \bar{h} = H/L$. The variable population growth and land supply are discussed in the following section.

Assume that general goods are produced by numberless manufacturers and have a production function in the Arrow-Romer form, i.e.:

$$Y_{it} = AK_{it}^{\alpha}\left(EL_{it}\right)^{1-\alpha} \tag{7.1}$$

where Y_{it}, $K_{it,}$ and L_{it} represent the total output, capital input, and labor input of manufacturer *i* in period *t*; A and α are parameters that reflect the level of technology; and *E* represents the production efficiency per unit amount of labor. Assume *E* is determined by the capital per labor force of the whole society, i.e.:

$$E = k_t = K_t / L_t = \sum_{i=1}^{N} K_{it} \Big/ \sum_{i=1}^{N} L_{it} \tag{7.2}$$

where k_t represents the capital stock per labor force in the entire economy in period *t*. Assume that the capital market, labor market, and product market are all perfect competitive markets, where profit maximization is adopted by manufacturers. The interest rate and wage in period *t* are r_t and $w_{t,}$ respectively, and then the optimization behavior of manufacturer *i* is expressed as follows:

$$\max_{K_{it}, L_{it}} : \Pi = AK_{it}^{\alpha}\left(EL_{it}\right)^{1-\alpha} - \left(r_t + \delta\right)K_{it} - w_t L_{it} \tag{7.3}$$

Assume the utility function within the whole life of an individual as follows:

$$U = \theta \ln c_t^y + \rho \ln h_t + \left(1 - \theta - \rho\right)\ln c_{t+1}^o$$

where c_t^y, c_{t+1}^o, and h_t represent the two-period consumption level and housing demand of a young person in period *t*; θ, ρ, and 1-θ-ρ are all positive numbers less than 1 and represent the individual's preference for consumption and housing when he/she is young and for consumption when he/she is old. s_t represents the savings of the young person in period *t*, and then the optimization behavior of the young person in period *t* is expressed as follows:

$$\begin{aligned} &\max_{\{c_t^y, h_t, c_{t+1}^o, s_t\}} : \quad \theta \ln c_t^y + \rho \ln h_t + \left(1 - \theta - \rho\right)\ln c_{t+1}^o \\ &s.t.: c_t^y + s_t + p_t h_t = w_t,\ c_{t+1}^o = \left(1 + r_{t+1}\right)s_t + p_{t+1} h_t,\ c_t^y, c_{t+1}^o, s_t \geq 0 \end{aligned} \tag{7.4}$$

2.1.2 Optimality conditions and market equilibrium

The following equation is obtained according to the manufacturer optimization behavior equation (7.3):

$$r_t = \alpha AK_{it}^{\alpha-1}\left(EL_{it}\right)^{1-\alpha} - \delta,\ w_t = \left(1 - \alpha\right)AEK_{it}^{\alpha}\left(EL_{it}\right)^{-\alpha} \tag{7.5}$$

Since the interest rates and wages of all manufacturers are the same, all manufacturers have the same capital per labor force, which is equal to the stock of capital per labor force in the economy, as known from Equation (7.5). Thus, Equation (7.5) can be expressed as follows:

$$r_t = \alpha A - \delta, w_t = (1-\alpha) A k_t \tag{7.6}$$

According to the consumer optimization equation (7.4), the first-order condition for housing demand h_t can be obtained as follows:

$$\rho / h_t + p_{t+1}(1-\theta-\rho)/c_{t+1}^o = p_t \theta / c_t^y \tag{7.7}$$

According to the Kuhn-Tucker theorem, the first-order condition of S_t in the customer optimization problem can be obtained as follows:

$$\begin{aligned} &\frac{(1+r_{t+1})(1-\theta-\rho)}{(1+r_{t+1})s_t + p_{t+1}h_t} \le \frac{\theta}{w_t - s_t - p_t h_t}, s_t \ge 0, \\ &s_t \left[\frac{(1+r_{t+1})(1-\theta-\rho)}{(1+r_{t+1})s_t + p_{t+1}h_t} - \frac{\theta}{w_t - s_t - p_t h_t} \right] = 0 \end{aligned} \tag{7.8}$$

According to Equations (7.7) and (7.8), if and only if:

$$1 + r_{t+1} \ge (p_{t+1}/p_t)\left[(1-\theta)/(1-\theta-\rho)\right], \tag{7.9}$$

an individual makes a positive saving. The individual's savings levels and two-period consumption level are expressed as follows:

$$s_t = (1-\theta) w_t - p_t h_t, \quad c_t^y = \theta w_t, \quad c_t^o = (1-\theta-\rho)(1+r_{t+1}) w_t \tag{7.10}$$

When Equation (7.9) is untenable, i.e.

$$1 + r_{t+1} < (p_{t+1}/p_t)\left[(1-\theta)/(1-\theta-\rho)\right], \tag{7.11}$$

personal saving s_t=0 and the material capital of the next period is also 0, then the economy will not be sustainable at this time. Thus, Equation (7.9) is a necessary condition for economic sustainability. It can be proved that the Equation (7.9) on the balanced growth path will be definitely satisfied as long as the parameters meet certain conditions.

In order to better understand the meaning of Equation (7.9) in economics, we make a simple transformation of the equation as follows:

$$\frac{(1-\theta-\rho)}{h_{Mt} p_{t+1}}(1+r_{t+1}) \ge \frac{\rho}{h_{Mt}} \frac{1}{p_t} + \frac{(1-\theta-\rho)}{h_{Mt} p_{t+1}} \frac{p_{t+1}}{p_t} \tag{7.12}$$

where h_{Mt} refers to the maximum number of houses that an individual can purchase without any savings when he/she is young.

When the savings rate is greater than 0, the following equation can be obtained according to Equations (7.8) and (7.10):

$$h_t = \rho w_t (1 + r_{t+1}) / \left[(1 + r_{t+1}) p_t - p_{t+1}\right] \tag{7.13}$$

and the housing supply per capita is $\bar{h} = H/L$. Substitute Equation (7.13) into the housing market equilibrium condition $h_t = h_t^s$, and then we can get:

$$p_t = \frac{\rho w_t}{\bar{h}} + \frac{p_{t+1}}{(1+r_{t+1})} \tag{7.14}$$

According to the goods market equilibrium condition, we can get:

$$K_{t+1} - K_t + \delta K_t = I_t = S_t = s_t L$$

Substitute Equation (7.11) into the above formula, and then we can get the following equation through simple sorting:

$$k_{t+1} = (1-\delta)k_t + s_t = (1-\delta)k_t + (1-\theta)w_t - p_t h_t \tag{7.15}$$

2.1.3 Dynamic behavior and equilibrium status of aggregate economy

When the savings are greater than 0, the following equations can be obtained as follows according to Equations (7.7), (7.14), and (7.15):

$$k_{t+1} = (1-\delta)k_t + (1-\theta)(1-\alpha)Ak_t - p_t\bar{h} \tag{7.16a}$$

$$\bar{h}\left(p_t - p_{t+1}/(\alpha A + 1 - \delta)\right) = \rho(1-\alpha)Ak_t \tag{7.16b}$$

Equations (7.16a) and (7.16b) jointly determine the dynamic behavior of capital and housing price per labor force in the economy.

Let $G_{pt} = p_{t+1}/p_t$ and $G_{kt} = k_{t+1}/k_t$, then $g_{kt} = G_{kt} - 1$ and $g_{pt} = G_{pt} - 1$ represent the growth rate of capital per labor force and the growth rate of housing prices; let $z_t = k_t/(p_t\bar{h})$ represent the ratio of capital per labor force to housing value.[2] The following formula can be obtained after sorting Equations (7.16a) and (7.16b):

$$G_{kt+1} = (1-\delta) + (1-\theta)(1-\alpha)A - 1/z_t \tag{7.17a}$$

$$G_{pt+1} = (\alpha A + 1 - \delta)(1 - \rho(1-\alpha)Az_t) \tag{7.17b}$$

According to the definition $z_t = k_t/(p_t\bar{h})$ and Equations (7.17a) and (7.17b), the dynamic behaviors of the growth rate of capital per labor force and of the growth rate of housing prices can be determined.

Definition 7.1 If both growth rate of capital per labor force and growth rate of output per labor force in the economy remain unchanged, then this state is called the **dynamic equilibrium state** of the economy or the **unbalanced growth path** of the economy.

Note: In the model of this chapter, it can be known from the production function Equation (7.1) and Equation (7.2) for defining E that the output per labor force of all manufacturers is $y_{it} = Ak_{it}^{\alpha}k_t^{1-\alpha}$. Since the capital per labor force of all manufacturers in the whole society in any period t is the same, the output level per capita of the whole society in any period t is $y_t = Ak_t$. Additionally, according to Equation (7.6), there is $w_t = (1-\alpha)Ak_t$. So, the growth rate of output per labor force in any period t is equal to the growth rate of capital per labor force and also to the growth rate of wages. Also, it can be known from Equations (7.17a) and (7.17b) that if the growth rate of capital per labor force, g_{kt}, remains unchanged, the ratio of capital to housing value will also remain the same. Since $z_t = k_t/(p_t\bar{h})$ and the housing supply per capita $\bar{h}$ is invariable, the invariable z value will change at the same pace. This shows that the growth rate of capital per labor force under a dynamic equilibrium state must be equal to the growth rate of housing prices (i.e., $g_{kt} = G_{kt} - 1 = g_{pt} = G_{pt} - 1$).

According to Equations (7.17a) and (7.17b), the dynamic behavior of the economy can be analyzed according to Figure 7.9. In Figure 7.9, the horizontal axis represents the ratio of capital per labor force to housing value and the vertical axis represents G_{kt} or G_{pt}. The straight line EB represents the relationship between G_{pt} and z_t (see Equation (7.17b)) and the abscissa at the intersection point B between the line and the horizontal axis is $z_t = 1/\left[\rho(1-\alpha)A\right]$. Curve AE represents the relationship between G_{kt} and z_t (see Equation (7.17a)) and the abscissa at the intersection point A between the curve and its horizontal axis is $z_t = 1/\left[(1-\delta)+(1-\theta)(1-\alpha)A\right]$. Additionally, since $(1-\delta) > 0 > (\rho+\theta-1)(1-\alpha)A$, then:

$$1/\left[(1-\delta)+(1-\theta)(1-\alpha)A\right] < 1/\left[\rho(1-\alpha)A\right]$$

So, Curve AE and the straight line BE must intersect in the first quadrant, which indicates that there must be a positive equilibrium value $z*$ and G_{pt} is equal to G_{kt} at this intersection point.

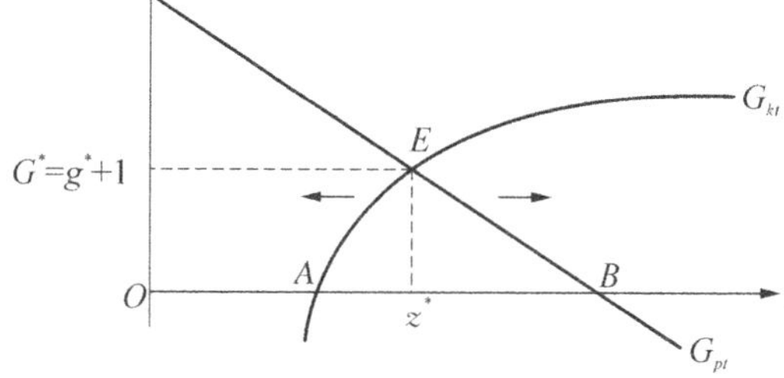

Figure 7.9 Changes in capital per labor force and housing prices: basic model.

It can be known from the above analysis and Figure 7.9 that, when the ratio of capital per labor force to housing value is z^* (or Point E in Figure 7.9), $G_{kt}=G_{pt}$, the growth rate of capital stock per labor force, g_{kt}, is equal to the growth rate of housing prices, g_{pt}. At this time, the ratio of capital per labor force to housing price p_t remains unchanged, so does the ratio of capital per labor force to housing value z_*. And according to Equations (7.17a) and (7.17b), both growth rate of capital stock per labor force and growth rate of housing prices remain unchanged, along with the growth rate of output per labor force and the growth rate of wages. Thus, Point E is the dynamic equilibrium state of the economy. Theorem 7.1 is obtained as follows:

Theorem 7.1 The economic system determined by Equations (7.17a) and (7.17b) has a unique dynamic equilibrium state (z_*, g^*). z_* and g^* are determined by the following two equations:

$$g^* + 1 = (1-\delta) + (1-\theta)(1-\alpha)A - 1/z^* \tag{7.18a}$$

$$g^* + 1 = (\alpha A + 1 - \delta)\left(1 - \rho(1-\alpha)Az^*\right) \tag{7.18b}$$

Under this state, the economic growth rate g^* and the ratio of capital per labor force to housing value, z^*, must be larger than 0. And when the parameters satisfy $\alpha A + 1 - \delta > (1-\theta)(1-\delta)/(1-\theta-\rho)$, an individual selects a positive savings level under the state of equilibrium.[3]

According to Figure 7.9, when the initial state of the economy is on the left side of Point E or the ratio of capital per labor force to housing value, z_t, is lower than the z_*, under the equilibrium state (or in the case of excessively high housing prices), the growth rate of housing prices will continue to be higher than that of capital per labor force; the ratio of capital per labor force to housing value will continue to drop; and the economy will continue to move away from Point E to the left. In this case, it is considered that a housing price bubble will appear in the economy. As the growth rate of the real economy (including capital per labor force, output per labor force, wage level, and consumption level) will gradually decline or may even witness negative growth, the economy will collapse and housing prices will not be maintained once Equation (7.9) cannot be met due to the sustained negative growth. When the initial state of the economy is on the right side of Point E or the ratio of capital per labor force to housing value, z_t, is higher than z_* (in the case of excessively low housing prices), the growth rate of capital per labor force will continue to be higher than that of housing prices; the ratio of capital per labor force to housing value, z, will continue to increase; and the economy will continue to move away from Point E to the right. At this time, the real economy will continue to grow at a high pace; the growth rate of housing prices will slow down, and housing prices may even fall. Therefore, Point E under the dynamic equilibrium state is an unstable equilibrium state of the economic system.

The stability of the equilibrium state of the economic system can also be simply understood through the phase image within the $\overline{G_{kt-z}}$ coordinate plane. Firstly, according to the definition $z_t = k_t/(p_t\bar{h})$, there is $z_{t+1} = G_{kt+1}z_t/G_{pt+1}$. The following equation can be further obtained according to Equation (7.17b):

$$z_{t+1} = \frac{G_{kt+1}}{(\alpha A + 1 - \delta)(1 - \rho(1-\alpha)Az_t)} z_t \tag{7.19}$$

Equations (7.17a) and (7.19) jointly determine the dynamic behavior of the growth rate of labor per labor force, *Gk*, to the ratio of capital per labor force to housing value, *z*. According to Equation (7.17a), *Gk* and *z* should satisfy the following relationship:

$$G_k = (1-\delta) + (1-\theta)(1-\alpha)A - 1/z,$$

as indicated by Curve AE in Figure 7.10. G_k will gradually decrease on the top part of Curve AE and gradually increase on the top of the curve. According to Equation (7.19), G_k and z should satisfy the following relationship when z keeps unchanged:

$$G_k = (\alpha A + 1 - \delta)(1 - \rho(1-\alpha)Az)$$

This relationship is indicated by the straight line BE in Figure 7.10. z will gradually increase on the upper part of BE and decrease on the lower part of the straight line. The phase images of G_k and z are shown in Figure 7.10. As known from the phase images in Figure 7.10, the equilibrium state point *E* is stable at the saddle point. Thus, Theorem 7.2 is obtained as follows:

Theorem 7.2 In a system composed of g_{kt} and z_t, the dynamic equilibrium state *E* described in this model is stable at the saddle point.

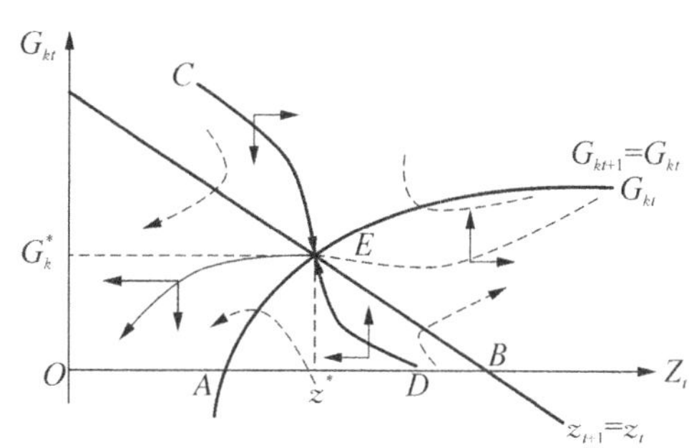

Figure 7.10 Phase images of the growth rate of capital per labor force and the ratio of capital per labor force to housing value.

2.2 Extended model: population growth and variable land supply

2.2.1 Model setup and assumptions

Assume that the government supplies land at a fixed growth rate of g_X and that the population growth rate is n, or

$$X_t = X_0(1+g_X)^t,\ L_t = L_0(1+n)^t$$

Assume that one unit of housing is produced on one unit of land and that the new housing supply in any period t is equal to the new land area ($\Delta H_t = X_t$). Thus:

$$\Delta H_t / H_t = X_t / H_t = \Delta X_t / \Delta H_t = g_H$$

Also, as $\Delta H_t / H = (g_H \Delta H_t)/(g_H H_t) = \Delta X_t / X_t = g_X$, the growth rate of total housing supply in any period t, g_H, is also equal to the growth rate of land supply, g_X. The growth rate of housing supply per capita, hs, is equal to the growth rate of total housing supply minus the population growth rate, or

$$g_{h^s} = g_H - n = g_X - n$$

When the government supplies land ($X_t = \Delta H_t$) to the market in any period t, the government will receive an income of $X_t p_t = \Delta H_t p_t = g_H H_{t-1} p_t$ through the new land supply. The impact of government's actions on the economy is not studied here. For the sake of simplicity, assume that the government equally distributes the income resulting from the land it receives in each period to young people in the form of transfer payment. Let b_t represent the transfer payments by the government to young people per capita during period t, then:

$$b_t L_t = g_H H_{t-1} P_t \Leftrightarrow b_t = g_X H_{t-1} p_t / L_t = p_t g_X h_t^s / (1+n)(1+g_h) = v p_t h_t^s \quad (7.20)$$

where $v = g_X/(1+n)(1+g_h) = g_X/(1+g_X) < 1$, $h_t^s = H_t / L_t$ represents the housing supply per capita in period t.

The assumptions about the behaviors of consumers and manufacturers are completely the same as those described in Section 7.3.1. Since individuals can obtain transfer income from the government when they are young, the budget constraint equation of young people in period t is expressed as follows:

$$c_t^y + s_t + P_t h_t = w_t + b_t, c_{t+1}^o = (1+r_{t+1}) \cdot s_t + p_{t+1} h_t$$

The individual's optimization problem is expressed as follows:

$$\max_{\{c_t^y, h_t, c_{t+1}^o, s_t\}}: \quad \theta \ln c_t^y + \rho \ln h_t + (1-\theta-\rho)\ln c_{t+1}^o$$
$$s.t. c_t^y + s_t + P_t h_t = w_t + b_t, \ c_{t+1}^o = (1+r_{t+1})s_t + p_{t+1}h_t \tag{7.21}$$
$$c_t^y, c_{t+1}^o, s_t \geq 0$$

The behavior of general goods manufacturers is still determined by the optimization problem Equation (7.3).

2.2.2 Dynamic equations of optimal conditions, market equilibrium, and aggregate economy

Just like the calculation process described in Section 2.1, the first-order condition about h_t in the individual's optimization problem Equation (7.21) is as follows:

$$\frac{\rho}{h_t} + \frac{p_{t+1}(1-\theta-\rho)}{(1+r_{t+1})s_t + p_{t+1}h} = \frac{p_t\theta}{w_t + b_t - s_t - p_t h_t} \tag{7.22}$$

The first-order condition about S_t is as follows:

$$\frac{(1+r_{t+1})(1-\theta-\rho)}{(1+r_{t+1})s_t + p_{t+1}h_t} \leq \frac{\theta}{w_t + b - s_t - p_t h_t}, s_t \geq 0,$$
$$s_t\left[\frac{(1+r_{t+1})(1-\theta-\rho)}{(1+r_{t+1})s_t + p_{t+1}h_t} - \frac{\theta}{w_t + b_t - s_t - p_t h_t}\right] = 0 \tag{7.23}$$

It can be obtained according to Equations (7.22) and (7.23) that,

$$\text{When } 1 + r_{t+1} > \frac{(1-\theta)}{1-\theta-\rho}\frac{p_{t+1}}{p_t}, \ s_t = (1-\theta)(w_t + b_t) - p_t h_t > 0 \tag{7.24a}$$

$$\text{When } 1 + r_{t+1} \leq \frac{(1-\theta)}{1-\theta-\rho}\frac{p_{t+1}}{p_t}, \ s_t = 0, \quad h_t = (1-\theta)(w_t + b_t)/p_t \tag{7.24b}$$

As can be known by comparing Equations (7.10) and (7.24), in the case of the given income of an individual when he/she is young, the transfer payment behavior of the government does not affect his/her personal consumption, savings, and housing purchase.[4] According to Equations (7.23) and (7.24), when an individual has positive savings, his/her housing demand is expressed as follows:

$$h_t = \frac{(1+r_{t+1})\rho(w_t + b_t)}{(1+r_{t+1})p_t - p_{t+1}} \tag{7.25}$$

There is one more transfer payment b_t in Equation (7.25) compared with Equation (7.13).

When the housing market is under an equilibrium state, the housing supply per capita is equal to housing demand per capita (or $h_t = h_t^s$). Substitute housing supply per capita, $h_t^s = h_0^s(1+g_h)^t$, and the housing demand equation (7.25) into the housing market equilibrium condition, and then we can get:

$$h_0^s(1+g_h)^t[p_t - p_{t+1}/(1+r_{t+1})] = \rho(w_t + b_t) \tag{7.26}$$

The optimal behavior of a manufacturer is the same as that of Section 7.3.1, and the interest rate and wages under the state of market equilibrium are still determined by Equation (7.6). Similarly, the dynamic equation of capital per labor force is as follows:

$$k_{t+1}(1+n) = (1-\delta)k_t + s_t = (1-\delta)k_t + (1-\theta)(w_t + b_t) - p_t h_t \tag{7.27}$$

Substitute Equation (7.20) for determining the transfer payment b_t and Equation (7.6) for determining the interest rate and wages into Equations (7.26) and (7.27) as follows:

$$h_t^s[p_t - p_{t+1}/(\alpha A + 1 - \delta)] = \rho(1-\alpha)Ak_t + \rho v p_t h_t^s \tag{7.28a}$$

$$k_{t+1}(1+n) = (1-\delta)k_t + (1-\alpha)(1-\theta)Ak_t + \left[(1-\theta)v - 1\right]p_t h_t^s \tag{7.28b}$$

Equations (7.28a) and (7.28b) jointly determine the dynamic behaviors of capital per labor force and housing prices.

2.2.3 Dynamic behavior of the economy: decisions on economic growth and housing prices

Since h_t^s is a function of time t, the dynamic system composed of Equations (7.28a) and (7.28b) is not an autonomous dynamic system. In order to analyze the dynamic characteristics of the economy, it is necessary to transform Equations (7.28a) and (7.28b) into an autonomous dynamic system. Let $V_t = p_t h_t^s$ denote housing value per capita, which also indicates the housing consumption of an individual measured by general goods when the individual is young. Equations (7.28a) and (7.28b) are transformed as follows:

$$V_t - \frac{V_{t+1}}{(\alpha A + 1 - \delta)(1-\rho v)(1+g_h)} = \frac{\rho(1-\alpha)}{(1-\rho v)}Ak_t \tag{7.29a}$$

$$k_{t+1}(1+n) = (1-\delta)k_t + (1-\alpha)(1-\theta)Ak_t - \left[1-(1-\theta)v\right]V_t \tag{7.29b}$$

Let $G_{Vt} = V_{t+1}/V_t$ and $G_{kt} = k_{t+1}/k_t$, then $g_{kt} = G_{kt} - 1$ and $g_{Vt} = G_{Vt} - 1$ represent the growth value of capital per labor force and the growth rate of housing value per capita. Let $z_t = k_t/V_t$ represent the ratio of capital per labor force to the value of housing per capita, which also represents the reciprocal of the percentage of housing consumption per capita.[5] The following equations can be obtained through simple sorting of Equations (7.29a) and (7.29b):

$$G_{Vt+1} = (\alpha A + 1 - \delta)(1 + g_h)\left[(1 + \rho v) - \rho A(1 - \alpha)z_t\right] \tag{7.30a}$$

$$(1 + n)G_{kt+1} = (1 - \delta) + (1 - \alpha)(1 - \theta)A - (1 - (1 - \theta)v)/z_t \tag{7.30b}$$

The dynamic behaviors of the growth rate of capital per labor force and of the growth rate of housing value per capita can be determined according to the definition $z_t = k_t/V_t$ and Equations (7.30a) and (7.30b). In order to analyze the dynamic behavior of the economy, the dynamic equilibrium state of the economy is defined as follows:

Definition 7.2 If both growth rate of capital per labor force and growth rate of output per labor force in the economy remains unchanged, this state is called the **dynamic equilibrium state** of the economy or the balanced growth path of the economy.

Just like in Section 2.1, under the assumption of the production function in this chapter, the growth rate of output per labor force is equal to the growth rate of capital per labor force and also equal to the growth rate of wages. Equation (7.30b) further demonstrates that, under the dynamic equilibrium state, if the growth rate of capital per labor force remains unchanged, the ratio of capital per labor force to housing value, z, will remain the same. And according to Equation (7.30b), the growth rate of housing value per capita under the dynamic equilibrium state will remain the same. Additionally, according to the definition $z_t = k_t/V_t$, the invariable z value also means the same growth rate of k and V.

Just like in Section 2.1, the dynamic behavior of the economy can be analyzed with the aid of Figure 7.11 according to Equations (7.30a) and (7.30b).

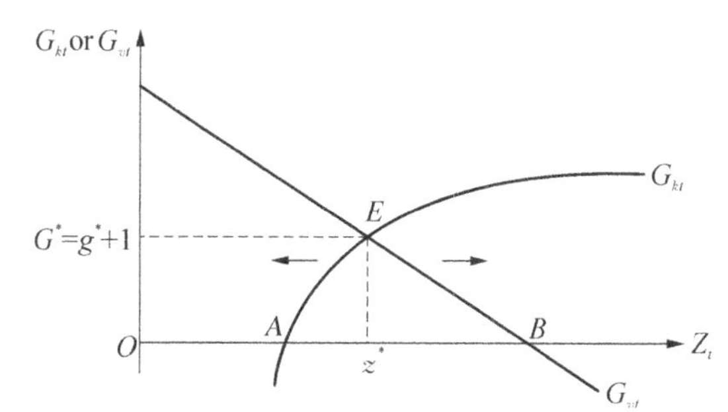

Figure 7.11 Changes in capital per labor force and in housing value per capita: extended model.

In the figure, the abscissa axis represents the ratio of capita per labor force to housing value, and the vertical axis represents G_{kt} or G_{Vt}. The straight line EB represents the relationship between G_{vt} and z_t (or Equation (7.30a)) and the abscissa of the intersection point between the straight line and the horizontal axis is $z_t = (1+\rho v)/[\rho(1-\alpha)A]$. The straight line AE represents the relationship between G_{vt} and z_t (see Equation (7.30b)) and the abscissa of the intersection point between the straight line and the horizontal axis is $z_t = (1-(1-\theta)v)/[(1-\delta)+(1-\theta)(1-\alpha)A]$. Additionally, it can be known according to $1-\delta > (\rho+\theta-1)(1-\alpha)A$ that

$$(1-(1-\theta)v)/[(1-\delta)+(1-\theta)(1-\alpha)A] < (1+\rho v)/[\rho(1-\alpha)A]$$

So, the curve AE and the straight line BE must intersect in the first quadrant. This indicates that there must be a positive equilibrium value z^* at this point, when G_{vt} is equal to G_{kt}. Alternatively, the growth rate of capital per labor force at z^* is equal to that of housing value per capita. Thus, at z^*, the ratio of capital per labor force to housing value, z^*, remains unchanged, and the growth rate of housing value per capita, g_{Vt}, is equal to that of capital per labor force, g_{kt}, which remains unchanged (or $g_{Vt} = g_{kt} = g^*$). Thus, Theorem7.3 below can be obtained:

Theorem 7.3 The economic system composed of Equations (7.30a) and (7.30b) has a unique dynamic equilibrium state (z^*, g^*), z^* and g^* satisfy the following equations:

$$g^* + 1 = (\alpha A + 1 - \delta)(1 + g_h)[(1+\rho v) - \rho A(1-\alpha)z^*] \quad (7.31a)$$

$$(g^* + 1)(1+n) = (1-\delta) + (1-\alpha)(1-\theta)A - (1-(1-\theta)v)/z^* \quad (7.31b)$$

And both the economic growth rate under the dynamic equilibrium state, g^*, and the ratio of capital per labor force to housing value, z^*, are larger than 0. When the parameters in the economy satisfy the inequality,[6]

$$\alpha A + 1 - \delta > \frac{(1-\theta)(1-\delta)}{(1+n)(1+g_h)(1-\theta-\rho)}$$

the individual selects a positive savings level under the equilibrium state.

It is not difficult to observe from Figure 7.11 that the equilibrium state E is unstable.[7] That means, when the housing prices in the economy are so high that the ratio of capital per capita to housing value (or the reciprocal of the housing consumption per capita), z_t, is smaller than the z^* under the equilibrium state, the economy will deviate from the equilibrium state and be located at the left of the equilibrium state E. At this time, as the growth rate of housing value is continuously higher than that of capital per labor force, the ratio of capital per labor force to housing value or the ratio of housing consumption per capita, z_t, will continue to drop and the economy will move farther and farther away from the point *E* and to the left. In this case, due to the excessively high growth rate of housing prices, housing investment will have a higher rate of return than savings; there will be an increasingly higher speculative demand for housing in the economy; and the accumulation of material capital and then the growth of the real economy, measured by capital per labor force and output per labor force, will slow down and even witness negative growth. This will enable the housing value in the entire economy to account for an increasing proportion of social wealth. When this situation continues until Equation (7.9) cannot be satisfied, zero saving will cause the zero material capital stock of the next period to fail to be produced, and the economy will collapse and force the house price bubble to burst.[8] Thus, when the economy is on the left side of point *E*, the depression or even collapse of the real economy will surely cause the sudden drop in prices, although the sustained rise in prices can be sustained for a short period of time, which is completely in line with the characteristics of a bubble. Thus, it is believed that there is actually a housing price bubble under this situation. Conversely, if the housing prices in the economy are so low that the ratio of capital per capita to housing value or the reciprocal of housing consumption per capita, z_t, is higher than the z^* under the equilibrium state, the economy will continue to grow and expand when the economic deviation equilibrium appears on the right side of Point *E*. The continued development of the situation will lead to negative growth of housing prices. When housing prices fall below the marginal effect of housing service, this economic expansion will be compulsorily broken. Overall, both situations above will lead to economic crisis in the long term. Thus, only when housing prices are at such a reasonable level that the ratio of capital per labor force to housing value is exactly at z^*, the economy will maintain long-term stable growth. If it is assumed that people have perfectly rational expectations, then Point *E* will be the only long-term equilibrium state. If it is assumed that people cannot have perfectly rational expectations but short-sighted expectations, the economy is likely to deviate from Point *E* and then witness a housing bubble or economic expansion in the short term, but will still return to the equilibrium state of Point *E* in the long run.

Finally, as can be known according to the definition of balanced growth path and the analysis above, the growth rate of capital per labor force, the growth rate of output per labor force, the growth rate of housing value per capita, and the growth rate of wages remain unchanged and are equal on the balanced growth path (or Point *E*). Since the growth rate of housing value per capita is equal to the growth rate of housing prices and that of housing supply per capita, and the growth rate of housing supply per capita is equal to the growth rate of land supply minus the population growth rate,

$$g_P = g_V - g_{h^s} = g_V - g_X + n = g^* - g_X + n = g_w - g_X + n \tag{7.32}$$

Equation (7.32) shows that, if both population growth rate and the growth rate of land supply are invariable, the growth rate of housing prices on the balanced growth path will remain unchanged and be equal to the economic growth rate (also equal to the growth rate of young people's wages), plus the population growth rate minus the growth rate of land or housing supply per capita. So, in the long run, changes in the housing prices of a country or region are determined by its economic growth rate (income growth rate), land supply growth rate, and population growth rate. As long as the land supply growth rate is smaller than the sum of the economic growth rate and the population growth rate, housing prices will definitely rise.

Based on the above theoretical conclusions, it is not hard to understand China's continuously rising housing prices. On the one hand, as China is currently promoting urbanization, it has a high growth rate of urban population, which is one of the main reasons for the increase in the housing price of Chinese cities. On the other hand, the continuous economic growth and income growth since the reform and opening-up has caused the continuous rise in individuals' demand for housing, which is another reason. Additionally, in the long run, the growth rate of housing prices should be equal to the economic growth rate plus the population growth rate minus the growth rate of housing supply. Due to the land finance of the local government, major cities have extremely low growth rates of land supply. And China's economic growth rate plus population growth rate are higher than its interest rate level, which makes people rationally expect that the growth rate of housing prices is far higher than the interest rate.[9] So, borrowing money from banks to purchase a house is profitable for everyone. In this case, the speculative demand for housing will inevitably arise. The emergence of the speculative demand will further contribute to the rise in housing prices. This is reflected by the fact that the economy will move towards the left of equilibrium point *E* in Figure 7.11, and the housing bubble and the decline in economic growth rate will appear in the economy. This process may continue till the growth rate of the real economy decreases to a certain level so that the sum of the economic growth rate and the population growth rate is lower than the interest rate. At this time, as the growth rate of housing prices is lower than the interest rate, the speculative demand for housing will disappear; the housing price bubble in the economy will burst; and the economy will return to the equilibrium state *E*. Of course, whether there is any bubble in China's current housing prices is mainly determined by whether the economy is on the balanced growth path or not. According to theoretical analysis, if the economy is on a balanced growth path, both growth rate of housing prices and economic growth rate are independent of the ratio of capital per labor force to housing value or the reciprocal of housing consumption per capita and are only correlated with the population growth rate, the growth rate of land, and housing supply per capita. If the economy is not at the equilibrium growth path, especially when it is located in an area with any housing price bubble on the left of point E in Figure 7.11 (or if the capital per labor force-housing value ratio is smaller), there will be a higher economic growth rate and higher growth rate of housing prices. The empirical analysis of the fourth part in this chapter will demonstrate China's economy at this time is indeed located in the left area of point E with a housing price bubble.

2.2.4 *Factors affecting economic growth and housing prices: comparative statistical analysis*

This subsection discusses how factors such as land and housing supply, population growth rate, etc., affect the long-term economic growth rate and the growth rate of housing prices. The following equations are obtained by differentiating Equations (7.31a) and (7.31b):

$$\partial g^*/\partial g_h = \frac{-(\alpha A+1-\delta)\left[(1+\rho v)-\rho A(1-\alpha)z^*\right](1-(1-\theta)v)}{|\mathrm{H}|} > 0 \tag{7.33a}$$

$$\partial g^*/\partial n = \frac{\left(g^*+1\right)z^{*2}(\alpha A+1-\delta)(1+g_h)\left[\rho A(1-\alpha)\right]}{|\mathrm{H}|} < 0 \tag{7.33b}$$

$$\partial z^*/\partial g_h = \frac{-(1+n)z^{*2}(\alpha A+1-\delta)\left[(1+\rho v)-\rho A(1-\alpha)z^*\right]}{|\mathrm{H}|} > 0 \tag{7.33c}$$

$$\partial z^*/\partial n = (1+n)z^{*2}/|\mathrm{H}| < 0 \tag{7.33d}$$

where $|H| = -(1-(1-\theta)v)-(\alpha A+1-\delta)(1+g_h)[\rho A(1-\alpha)](1+n)z^{*2}$.

The following equation can be obtained according to the equation $(1+g_h)(1+n)=1+g_X$:

$$\partial g_h/\partial n = -(1+g_X)/(1+n)^2 = -(1+g_h)/(1+n) \tag{7.34}$$

The following equation can be obtained according to the housing value per capita $V_t = p_t h_t^S$:

$$g_p + 1 = p_{t+1}/p_t = (g_{Vt}+1)/(1+g_h)$$

So, the following equation on the balanced growth path can be obtained:

$$g_p + 1 = \left(g^*+1\right)/(1+g_h) \tag{7.35}$$

We can get the following equation by differentiating Equation (7.35) and sorting Equations (7.33a), (7.33b), and (7.34) as follows:

$$\frac{dg_p}{dg_h}=-\frac{-z^{*2}\rho A(1-\alpha)(1+g_h)(1+n)(\alpha A+1-\delta)}{(1+g_h)|\mathrm{H}|} \times(\alpha A+1-\delta)\left[(1-\rho v)-\rho A(1-\alpha)z_t\right]<0 \tag{7.36}$$

$$dg_p/dn=-\left(g^*+1\right)\left(1-(1-\theta)v\right)/[|H|(1+g_h)(1+n)]>0 \tag{7.37}$$

The following theorem can be obtained according to Equations (7.33a) to (7.33b) and Equations (7.36) and (7.37):

Theorem 7.4 If other conditions remain unchanged on the balanced growth path, increasing the growth rate of land and housing supply per capita will increase the economic growth rate, reduce the growth rate of housing prices, and increase the ratio of capital per capita to housing value per labor force (or the percentage of housing consumption will decrease); and increasing the population growth rate will reduce the economic growth rate, increase the growth rate of housing prices, and decrease the ratio of capital per labor force to housing value per capita (or the percentage of housing consumption will increase).

Section 3 Empirical study—taking the inter-provincial panel data of China as examples

3.1 Econometric model and regression equation

The theoretical analysis in Section 2 shows the following. Firstly, on the balanced growth path, both the long-term economic growth rate and the growth rate of housing prices are related to the growth rate of land and housing supply and the population growth rate. Secondly, it can be known from Equations (7.30a) and (7.30b) and Figure 7.11 that if the economy is not on the balanced growth path, the economic growth rate and the growth rate of housing prices are not only correlated with the growth rate of land and housing supply but also with the ratio of capital per labor to housing value (or the reciprocal of the percentage of housing consumption per capita), z. And if the growth rate of housing prices is positively correlated with z but the economic growth rate is negatively correlated with it, then the housing prices will have bubbles, as shown in Figure 7.11. This section will test the effect of land and housing supply growth rates on economic growth and the housing price growth rate by using China's inter-provincial panel data, and judge whether there is a housing price bubble in China by testing the effect of the ratio of capital per capita to housing value (or the reciprocal of the proportion of housing consumption per capita) over the economic growth rate and the housing price growth rate. Additionally, in view of the fact that

China is still a developing country, the current economic growth has not reached a balanced growth path yet. Thus, the economic growth rate will also be affected by material capital accumulation, while the growth rate of housing prices will be affected by the increase in people's income. For this reason, the following basic econometric regression equations are established for the economic growth rate and the housing price growth rate respectively:

$$\text{Model 1: } g_{it}^{y} = a_0 + a_1 g_{it}^{h} + a_2 g_{it}^{L} + a_3 g_{it}^{k} + a_4 R_{it} + \sum \beta_{1i} X_{it} + \varepsilon_{it} \quad (7.38)$$

$$\text{Model 2: } g_{it}^{P} = b_0 + b_1 g_{it}^{h} + b_2 g_{it}^{L} + b_3 g_{it}^{w} + b_4 R_{it} + \sum \beta_{2i} X_{it} + u_{it} \quad (7.39)$$

where i represents the province; t represents the time; g_{it}^{y} represents the growth rate of GDP per capita; g_{it}^{h} represents the growth rate of housing supply per capita; R_{it} represents the ratio of housing value per capita to income per capita (or the percentage of housing consumption per capita in the third part of this chapter, $1/z$); g_{it}^{L} represents the population growth rate; g_{it}^{k} represents the growth rate of wages; a^j, $b^j (j=0,1,2,3,4)$, β_{1i} and β_{2i} are the parameters to be estimated; ε and u represent random disturbance items; and X_{it} represent other control variables. According to the theoretical analysis in the third part of this chapter, the growth rate of housing supply per capita and that of capital per capita produce a positive effect on the economic growth rate, and the population growth rate produces a negative effect on the growth rate of housing prices; the growth rate of housing supply per capita produces a negative effect on the growth rate of housing prices, and both the population growth rate and the growth rate of income per capita produce a positive effect on housing prices. Thus, a_1, a_2, a_3, and b_3 are expected to be positive, while a_2 and b_1 negative. Additionally, if there is any bubble in the economy, according to Equations (7.17) and (7.30), a_4 should be significantly smaller than 0 and b_4 should be significantly larger than 0.

3.2 Data sources and statistical descriptions

The econometric analysis in this chapter only takes into account the impact of housing land supply and housing supply per capita on housing prices and economic growth. In this chapter, the total urban housing floor area of each province (hereinafter referred to as the "housing area") is adopted in this chapter as a proxy variable for the land and housing supply in the model. According to the completed urban housing area of each province in China for the period 2003–2011, the actual urban housing area and aggregate population of each province in the years 2002 and 2006, and other data obtained from the CEIC database, the urban housing area per capita of each province (PHS), the population growth rate of each province (GP), and the growth rate of urban housing area per capita of each province (GPHS) can be calculated. This data are used in this chapter as a proxy variable for the growth rate of land and housing supply per capita in the following empirical research. The real GDP, real disposable income per capita of urban residents, consumer price index of urban residents, and average sales price of urban housing for each province in years are also available from the CEIC database. Based on the above, the growth rate of real GDP per capita, growth rate of urban housing prices, growth rate of real urban disposable income per capita, and the ratio of housing value per capita to disposable income per capita (hereinafter referred to as the "housing-income ratio") for each province in years can be calculated. Additionally, the growth rate of urban doctors per capita (GPDC) and the percentage of state-owned enterprises can also be obtained from the CEIC database. Finally, the capital stock per capita and the capital growth rate per capita of each province in years can be obtained by reference to Zhang Jun et al. (2004) and the total capital formation and population data of each province in the *China Statistical Yearbooks*. In order to match the data of the growth rate of housing area per capita (GPHS), all the above data are available from the panel data of 31 provinces in China during the period 2004–2011.

The names, economic meanings, and statistical characteristics of the ten major variables used in this chapter are shown in Table 7.1. The global financial crisis in 2008 may produce an impact on China's economic growth and housing price-related behavior. In order to analyze the impact of the global financial crisis, a dummy variable representing the impact of the financial crisis, Dum, is also introduced in this chapter. The value setting method of this dummy variable is as follows: if the time is earlier than 2007, Dum is 0; and if the time is later than or equal to 2008, Dum is 1.

3.3 Econometric methods and regression results

Firstly, this chapter carries out regression of the fixed effects (FE) model and the random effects (RE) model and the applicability of FE and RE is judged through the Hausman test. Secondly, for the purpose of comparison, regardless of the result of Hausman test, the FE, RE, and OLS regression results are listed at the same time in this chapter. Finally, in order to test the robustness of the regression results, the maximum likelihood estimate (MLE), the population-averaged estimator (PA), and the panel-corrected standard errors (PCSE) are also used in this research for regression. The results of these regression methods are basically in line with the RE model. For the sake of simplicity, only the PCSE estimation results are listed in this chapter. The four regression results of OLS, FE, RE, and PCSE in this chapter are highly consistent with each other.

First of all, the test result of the theoretical model on the economic growth rate is analyzed below using provincial panel data in China, as shown in Table 7.2. In Table 7.2, there are a total of eight regression results in two sets of equations, and each equation shows the regression results of four econometric methods, namely OLS, FE, RE, and PCSE. Columns 1–4 show the

Table 7.1 Names, meanings, and data statistics characteristics of the variables used in this chapter

Variable	*Economic meaning of the variable*	*Sample size*	*Average*	*STDEV*	*Minimum*	*Maximum*
GPRGDP	Growth rate of real GDP per capita (%)	248	10.4	4.62	−3.19	23.5
GRHP	Growth rate of real urban housing price per capita (%)	248	13.5	12.47	−45.5	57.9
GPHS	Growth rate of urban housing area per capita (%)	248	0.63	13.17	−49.5	51.3
GPRDI	Growth rate of urban disposable income per capita (%)	248	11.0	4.03	−4.55	22.2
RHVDI	Ratio of urban housing value per capita to disposable income	248	4.70	1.83	2.10	13.1
GPC	Growth rate of capital per capita (%)	248	19.9	6.14	−7.40	42.7
GPOP	Growth rate of population (‰)	248	5.47	2.80	−0.34	11.8
GCPI	Growth rate of consumer price index (%)	248	3.33	2.27	−2.30	10.1
GPDC	Growth rate of the number of doctors per capita	248	2.50	12.8	−66.8	96.6
RSOE	Percentage of state-owned enterprises (%)	248	46.8	15.6	15.8	89.3
Dum	Dummy variable representing the financial crisis 2008	248	0.5	0.25	0	1

regression results of Equation (7.38). The explained variable is the growth rate of real GDP per capita, and the explanatory variables include five variables, namely the growth rate of material capital per capita, the growth rate of housing supply per capita, the population growth rate, the ratio of housing value per capita to urban disposable income per capita, and the i financial crisis shock. Columns 5–8 show the regression results of the extended model for the robustness test of the basic model Equation (7.38). For the robustness test method used here, see Levine & Renelt (1992). In the test, some new explanatory variables that may affect the economic growth rate are incorporated into the basic regression equation to test if the regression results of the basic model are robust. According to data availability and the significance of its impact on inter-provincial economic growth, the new variables newly incorporated mainly include the growth rate of the number of doctors per capita, the percentage of state-owned enterprises, and the growth rate

Table 7.2 Econometric regression results: the explained variable is the growth rate of GDP per capita (GPRGDP)

Model	*(I)*				*(II)*			
Econometric regression method	*OLS*	*FE*	*RE*	*PCSE*	*OLS*	*FE*	*RE*	*PCSE*
GPC	0.267***	0.227***	0.263***	0.267**	0.279***	0.238***	0.273***	0.278***
	(5.36)	(3.58)	(5.15)	(5.46)	(7.02)	(4.05)	(5.63)	(7.13)
GPHS	0.06**	0.061**	0.064**	0.062**	0.028	0.016	0.028**	0.028**
	(2.08)	(2.00)	(2.12)	(2.09)	(0.99)	(0.57)	(2.09)	(1.94)
GPOP	−0.190**	−0.598	−0.189*	−0.190**	−0.176*	−0.814*	−0.192*	−0.176**
	(−1.97)	(−1.25)	(−1.08)	(−2.01)	(−1.76)	(−1.87)	(−1.63)	(−1.79)
RHVDI	−0.369**	−0.236	−0.354**	−0.369**	−0.377**	−0.410	−0.295*	−0.377**
	(−2.09)	(−0.63)	(−1.90)	(−2.13)	(−1.89)	(−1.18)	(−1.67)	(−1.93)
Dum	−2.75***	−3.03***	−2.75***	−2.75***	−2.19***	−2.90***	−2.17***	−2.19***
	(−5.07)	(−5.23)	(−5.11)	(−5.16)	(−7.49)	(−4.40)	(−4.25)	(−4.31)
GPDC					−0.036**	−0.024	−0.033*	−0.036**
					(−1.97)	(−1.31)	(−1.87)	(−2.01)
RSOE					−0.011	−0.229	−0.021	−0.012
					(−0.47)	(−0.44)	(−0.76)	(−0.48)
GCPI					−0.712***	−0.739***	−0.714***	−0.712***
					(−6.73)	(−7.11)	(−6.93)	(−6.86)
Intercept	8.79***	9.12***	8.78***	8.80***	86.4***	87.3***	86.5***	86.4***
	(4.48)	(2.93)	(4.67)	(5.03)	(7.49)	(7.49)	(7.69)	(7.63)
Sample size	248	248	248	248	248	248	248	248
R-square	0.31	0.191	0.311	0.31	0.40	0.35	0.42	0.42
F- or W-value	21.8***	9.97***	98.5***	107.5***	21.87***	14.00***	155.23***	181.6***

Note: (1) The value in parenthesis below each coefficient in the table is the t-statistic (FE and OLS) or *z*-statistic (other) value of the coefficient; (2) "***", "**" and "*" indicate the significance at the statistical levels of 1% and 5% and 10%; (3) F-value is for testing the overall significance of the OLS model or FE model; W-value is the Wald value for testing the overall significance of the RE and PCSE models, and F-u_i is for the fixed effects test in the FE model; (4) The p-values of the Hausman test of RE vs. FE in (I) and (II) are 0.48 and 037 respectively, so the random effects model (i.e. RE) cannot be rejected. The F-values of the fixed effects test in the FE model of (I) and (II) are 1.25 and 1.57 respectively, which are not significant at the level of 10%.

of consumer price index. Wang et al. (2006), Yang et al. (2006), and Wang et al. (2008) have demonstrated that the three variables produce a significant impact on the economic growth of the provinces in China. The first points can be seen from Table 7.2. Firstly, the regression results of the basic model show that, although the Hausman test shows that the random effect model cannot be rejected, RE and FE are basically identical in terms of signs of the coefficients of variables in relation to the regression results except for the differences in the size of the coefficients and the significance level of regression. The results of the panel-corrected standard errors (PCSE) and OLS regression carried out in order to overcome the problems of heteroscedasticity and autocorrelation are basically consistent with the regression results of FE and RE. On the whole, the regression results of OLS, PCSE, and RE are very close in terms of the regression coefficients and the significance level. Through comparison, the significance of the variables in the FE regression results is weaker; the regression coefficients of the three variables, namely GPC, GPHS, and RHVDI, are smaller, while those of GPOP are much smaller but insignificant. However, neither Hausman test nor the F-test without FE (i.e., F-u_i in Table 7.2) supports the assumption of the existence of FE. Secondly, all the regression results show that the growth rate of material capital per capita and the growth rate of housing area per capita have a significant positive effect on economic growth, and the population growth rate and the ratio of housing value per capita to disposable income per capita produce a significant negative effect on the economic growth rate, which is completely identical with theoretical predictions, where the growth rate of housing area per capita and the population growth rate are the main factors that determine the economic growth rate on the balanced growth path as predicted in the theoretical model of Section 3. The significance of the regression coefficient of the growth rate of material capital per capita shows that China's economic growth has not reached the balanced growth path yet, and the growth of material capital remains the mainly driving factor for China's economic growth. The ratio of housing value per capita to disposable income per capita has a significant negative effect on economic growth, indicating that China's housing prices are not under the state of equilibrium. Being too high relative to income per capita, China's housing prices and their rapid growth have suppressed the country's economic growth. Finally, the robustness test in the extended model shows that the regression results of the four regression methods are very consistent with those of the basic model. After new variables are incorporated, the signs of all variables remain unchanged. Among them, the four basic explanatory variables in the regression results of OLS, RE, and PCSE still have a significant impact on economic growth. The regression coefficients of GPOP and RHVDI in the FE model are not very significant, and those of GPC, GPHS, and RHVDI are even smaller, with a larger GOPO coefficient. Similarly, the Hausman test does not support the assumption of fixed effects. Overall, the characteristics of the above regression results show that the regression results of Equation (7.38) are quite robust and consistent with the prediction results of the theoretical model mentioned above. In addition, all the regression results show that the global financial crisis 2008 had a significant negative impact on China's economic growth. According to the regression coefficients, the financial crisis in 2008 cut China's average annual economic growth rate by about 2 to 3 percentage points.

Secondly, the econometric results on housing prices are also consistent with the theoretical model. Table 7.3 gives the regression results of the econometric model Equation (7.39), in which the second and third columns give the estimated results of the FE model and the RE model, respectively. The Hausman test indicates that the RE estimation is rejected, but the F-test regarding whether there are any fixed effects among individuals in fixed effects estimation shows that there are no significant fixed effects among individuals. However, regardless of the FE model or the RE model, the signs of the regression coefficients of all variables are the same as the theoretical prediction results, but the population growth rate in the FE model has no significant impact on housing prices, just the same as the theoretical prediction result. In order to further test the robustness of the regression results, Table 7.3 further provides the estimation results of the overall average model (Column 4) and the panel-corrected standard errors (PCSE) (Column 5).

Table 7.3 Econometric regression results: the explained variable is the growth rate of urban real housing prices

Estimation method	*OLS*	*FE*	*RE*	*PA*	*PCSE*
GPRDI	1.57***	1.57***	1.57***	1.54***	1.57***
	(9.17)	(8.94)	(9.17)	(9.04)	(7.71)
GPHS	−0.16***	−0.21***	−0.16***	−0.162***	−0.161***
	(−3.10)	(−3.86)	(−3.10)	(−3.13)	(−2.84)
GPOP	0.57**	0.75	0.57**	0.508***	0.570*
	(2.19)	(0.57)	(2.19)	(2.43)	(1.75)
RHVDI	1.77***	5.74***	1.77**	1.519***	1.77***
	(4.43)	(5.52)	(4.43)	(4.67)	(3.52)
Dum	−3.43***	−5.60***	−3.43***	−3.27**	−3.43***
	(−2.51)	(−3.86)	(−2.51)	(−2.38)	(−2.58)
Intercept	−70.6***	−81.3***	−70.6***	−65.4***	−70.6***
	(−3.61)	(−3.92)	(−3.61)	(−3.37)	(−2.64)
Sample size	248	248	248	248	248
R-square	0.28	0.35	0.28	0.28	0.30
F- or W-value	20.3***	23.55***	93.2***	99.78***	55.95***

Note: (1) The value in parenthesis below each coefficient in the table is the t-statistic (FE and OLS) or *z*-statistic (other) value of the coefficient; (2) "***", "**" and "*" indicate the significance at the statistical levels of 1% and 5% and 10%; (3) F-value is for testing the overall significance of the OLS model or FE model; W-value is the Wald value for testing the overall significance of the RE and PCSE models, and F-u_i is for the fixed effects test in the FE model; (4) The p-value of the Hausman test of RE vs. FE is 0.0002, so the random effects model (i.e. RE) cannot be rejected. The F-value of the fixed effects test in the FE model is 1.19, which is not significant at the level of 10%.

Additionally, for the sake of comparison, the results of the ordinary least squares method are also given (Column 1). The results of all these estimation methods are basically consistent with those of the FE model and the RE model. All these estimation results show that there are significant positive effects between the growth rate of the urban disposable income per capita and the housing value per value, between the population growth rate and the growth rate of housing prices; and there is a significant negative effect between the growth rate of housing area per capita and the growth rate of housing prices. These results are entirely consistent with the prediction results of the theoretical model in Section 3. According to the theoretical model, the ratio of housing value per capita to urban disposal income per capita produces a significant positive effect on the growth rate of housing prices, indicating China's housing prices are not under the equilibrium state (or on the balanced growth path) and the excessively high housing prices further aggravates the growth rate of housing prices. Thus, in addition to the economic growth rate, the population growth rate, and the growth rate of housing supply, the expectation of rising housing prices plays a crucial role in the rise of housing prices. According to the conclusion of the theoretical model, the rise in housing prices caused by such factors may require the compulsory burst of the bubble and the return of the price path to the balanced growth path. Finally, all the regression results also show that the global financial crisis in 2008 had a significant inhibitory effect on the growth rate of China's housing prices, and significantly reduced the growth rate of the housing prices.

Overall, the regression results of the determining Equation (7.38) about the economic growth rate (Table 7.2) and those of the determining Equation (7.39) about the growth rate of housing prices in China are completely consistent with the prediction results of the theoretical model in the third section of this chapter. This means the growth rate of land and housing supply produce a positive effect on the economic growth rate, and a negative effect on the rise in housing prices; the population growth rate produces a negative effect on the economic growth rate, and a positive effect on the rise in housing prices; and the economic growth rate produces a positive effect on housing prices by increasing the income level per capita. Additionally, since China's economy and housing prices are not under the equilibrium state (or on the balanced growth path), the percentage of housing consumption over income per capita (or the ratio of housing value per capita to urban disposable income per capita in the econometric model, RHVDI) has a significant negative effect on the economic growth rate, and a significant positive effect on the rise in housing prices. This indicates the rapid rise in housing prices will not only further aggravate their rise, but also suppress the economic growth. Thus, curbing the rapid rise in housing prices by increasing the supply of land and housing will not only help curb the rapid rise in housing prices, but also help promote economic growth.

Section 4 Reasons for high housing prices in China and the government's regulation dilemmas

As mentioned previously, China's housing prices have been rapidly rising in the past 30 years. Although the central government has been regulating housing prices by various means, few achievements have been made. What are the reasons for the persistently high and rising housing prices in China? What are the economic consequences of high housing prices? And how does the government respond to the ever-lasting high and rising housing prices?

4.1 Three conditions for balanced development of the real estate industry

From a macro perspective, a healthy, stable real estate industry should meet the following equilibrium conditions. Firstly, the partial equilibrium of supply and demand in the real estate market, also the most important condition. If we view the housing market only, housing prices and their changes are mainly determined by the supply status of the housing market and its relative changes. Housing prices will rise as long as supply exceeds demand in the entire housing market and vice versa. However, this partial equilibrium analysis method is only suitable for the industries that produce little impact on the entire national economy. For any industry that occupies an important position in the entire national economy, whether the housing prices under the state of partial equilibrium can sustain in the long run is affected by the overall macroeconomic equilibrium or the said general equilibrium, in addition to the industry's supply and demand. This equilibrium includes the equilibrium of the supply structure among different industries on the supply side and the equilibrium of the consumption demand structure on the demand side.

Secondly, the equilibrium of interest rates among different industries. The equilibrium of the housing market must enable the supply structure of the entire economy to reach equilibrium, which means the equilibrium price of the housing market must enable manufacturers of other industries to share the same profit margin as the real estate industry. As an industry that occupies a large proportion in the gross national product and to which manufacturers can freely have access, its long-term housing equilibrium price must maintain the equilibrium between the profit margin of the industry and the average interest rate of the entire economy. If the existing housing prices make the real estate industry more profitable than other industries, manufacturers in other industries will continue to enter the industry. Consequently, the manufacturers in the real estate industry will increase, and the goods supply in other industries will decrease. Also, the demand for land, a production factor of the real estate industry, will increase, and the demand for the factors in other industries will decrease. Thus, this will break the equilibrium of supply and demand of the housing market and all the other markets, resulting in changes in housing prices and other goods prices.

Thirdly, the equilibrium in the consumption demand structure. Long-term balanced, stable housing prices should also allow consumers to maintain reasonable proportions of consumer spending on clothing, food, housing, transportation, and other aspects, or a demand structure equilibrium. Generally, an individual will maintain fixed proportions in those aspects. For the housing consumption that occupies a large proportion in the total personal consumption expenditure, a balanced housing price must enable itself not to squeeze out other expenditures of consumption demand, and the structural equilibrium between housing expenditure and other consumption demands is reflected in the fact that the housing price-to-income ratio should fall within a certain scope in the macro economy. Just as the theoretical model shows, a too high or too low housing price-to-income ratio will destroy the structural equilibrium of an individual in food, clothing, housing, accommodation, and other aspects, and produce a serious impact or even distort the total consumption demand and consumer price index in macroeconomic entities, thus seriously affecting the welfare of residents and the long-term growth of the entire economy.

4.2 Reasons for persistently high housing prices in China

Firstly, the housing marketization caused by China's housing reform, the expansion of urban population by the urbanization process, the continuous increase in residents' income by rapid economic growth, and other factors have resulted in the continuous increase in people's demand for housing, which is the initial reason for the rise in China's housing prices and also a fact common to a country that is in the midst of an economic boom. This idea has been recognized by a majority of scholars, but it is not enough for China's housing prices to reach the current state only due to the growth of income and the expansion of the urban population.

Secondly, the land supply policy caused by the mechanism of maximizing the fiscal revenue of land is the direct cause for the excessively rapid rise in the housing prices of China. The principle of supply and demand shows that, even if people's income level and urban population expansion lead to the rapid growth in housing demand, housing prices will not increase at a too fast rate if housing supply can grow at the same speed as the housing demand. However, since the local government is the sole land supplier under the current fiscal system of China, the government will increase the land transfer price by controlling land supply in order to maximize land revenue, thus raising housing prices and gaining monopoly income. More importantly, the impact of the local government's land monopoly pricing policy on housing prices is not only the impact of the land monopoly pricing on housing prices. When the government's monopoly land prices make the growth rate of housing prices higher than the interest rate, there will be a large amount of funds either from the real economy or from bank credit, which will flow into the housing market following the speculative housing demand and cause a bubble in the real estate market.

Thirdly, the housing loan mortgage system according to which residents purchase houses by installments adopted in China's financial system and the expansion of a large amount of credit in the housing market by the banking system represented by the mortgage loan system constitute a strong guarantee that China's high housing prices will be sustained and continue to rise. As far as the housing loan mortgage system featuring repayment by installments is concerned, if individuals are rich people without credit constraints, the system will not actually affect housing prices. That's because the housing demand of an individual will still depend on his/her income level when it is not constrained by credit. However, for those poor people who are constrained by credit, the housing loan mortgage featuring repayment by installments directly increases the consumer demand for housing and directly raises housing prices. More importantly, when housing prices are above the loan rate, housing loan mortgages will further increase the rate of return on housing investment, thus generating speculative housing demand and accelerating the rise in housing prices. With respect to the substantial credit expansion of the banking system towards the housing market, the credit expansion of the banking system towards the housing market produces little effect on the housing market when the growth rate of housing prices is lower than the bank loan interest rate in the market. That's because there is neither possibility of arbitrage between the housing market and other capital markets, nor possibility of speculative housing demand. However, there is a possibility of arbitrage in the housing market and other capital markets when the government's land supply is so small that housing prices rise faster than the bank loan interest rate. So, the credit expansion of the banking system towards the housing market will make all possible funds available to create speculative housing purchase demand so as to make housing prices continue to rise and become a bubble.

4.3 The impact of high housing prices on the macro economy and the dilemma of government regulation

The above analysis shows that a long-term reasonable housing price should be reflected in three aspects, namely the equilibrium of supply and demand in the housing market, the equilibrium of supply structure, and of consumption demand structure among different industries. China's current high and persistently rising housing prices are mainly reflected in their imbalance in the equilibrium of the last two aspects above. This kind of persistently high and rising housing prices will produce an impact on the macro economy from the following aspects:

Firstly, squeezing out the funds utilized for the development of other industries and slowing down the growth of the entire economy. Due to the high profit margin brought about by the persistently high housing prices, the funds of other industries will start to flow into the real estate industry, thus causing other real economies to shrink. And the real estate industry may experience a bubble, which may cause harm to the financial industry when the bubble bursts and may even cause a financial crisis.

Secondly, reducing the total consumption demand of the public, making the entire macro economy exhibit insufficient effective demand. Generally, the effect of high housing prices on personal consumption is divided into income effect and substitution effect. The former tends to reduce the demand of residents for all consumption goods, and the latter tends to increase the demand of residents for other goods. However, if the demand of residents for housing is rigid, it can be proved theoretically that the income effect of rising housing prices on other consumption is greater than the price effect. As a result, the increase in housing prices will increase people's expenditure on housing demand and reduce their consumption of other goods, thus leading to a decline in total consumer demand of the public. Additionally, in the case of persistently rising housing prices, a higher rate of return than the interest rate will encourage residents to reduce their current personal consumption and increase their savings in the form of housing investment. Consequently, the excessively high increase in housing prices will further reduce residents' consumption behavior and the total consumption demand of the public.

Thirdly, intensifying the inequality of wealth distribution in China. Due to the persistently high and rising housing prices and the resulting high rents, the proportion of housing expenditure over the total personal expenditure has continued to increase; housing prices have rapidly risen; and housing, as part of personal wealth, has become the largest part in the stock of personal wealth. During China's economic development in recent years, the persistently high housing prices have inherently made the speculative housing capital to gain the income whose rate of return is higher than the average interest rate, and the housing credit system featuring repayment by installments has magnified the rate of return for this kind of speculative capital by several times through the effect of leverage. As a result, the continuously high and rising housing prices and the housing credit system featuring repayment by installments have greatly intensified the inequality of wealth distribution.

Fourthly, reducing people's living welfare. The damage to the living welfare of residents due to the persistently high and rising housing prices is mainly reflected in the following three aspects. Firstly, the sustained rise in housing prices will cause a large amount of speculative housing demand, which will leave a large number of houses vacant. This will inevitably cause a waste of housing resources and reduce the living welfare of people in the whole society. Secondly, due to the constraints of high housing prices and relatively low wages, most people either can not afford to buy houses or buy houses by borrowing high debts. Either way, an individual will finally become a mortgage slave and suffer from both material and spiritual pressures, or live in poverty due to their unimproved housing conditions. All these will cause harm to the welfare of residents. Finally, the extremely unequal distribution of wealth resulting from high housing prices will bring great dissatisfaction to the public, which may even cause social instability. This kind of dissatisfaction and instability can cause potential harm to anyone in the society, regardless of income status. Thus, it will inevitably reduce the welfare level of the whole society.

Finally, possibly reducing the stability of the financial system or prices. On the one hand, the system of repayment by installments is adopted by Chinese residents to purchase houses. Housing mortgage loans account for a large proportion in Chinese commercial banks and its proportion in the total housing price is also high. Once housing prices fall too fast and the current bubble caused by high housing prices bursts, this will endanger the stability of the country's financial system. On the other hand, since the persistently high housing prices mainly rely on China's housing credit system and housing credit expansion, it will be hard for the high housing prices resulting from speculative housing demand to sustain if the credit expansion of the housing market does not continue. If this kind of high housing price increase is sustainable at present and cause the continuous expansion of credit in the housing market, such credit expansion will surely be passed to the prices of the whole goods, thus resulting in inflation.

4.4 Future trend of the real estate market: dilemmas and the direction for government regulation

Although the current real estate market has caused great damage to the lives and social welfare of residents, the development of the real estate market promoted by the housing reform and the resulting development of the real estate related industries has made an undeniable contribution to China's economic growth. The domestic demand expanded by housing reform and the development of the real estate market through the multiplier effect has been the main growth point of China's economy in recent years. Therefore, whether for residents, manufacturers, or the government, the future trend of housing prices is the focus of attention albeit for different purposes. Whether from the supply side (policy support and regulation for land supply and developers) or the demand side (credit regulation for residents' housing purchase), China's real estate market has been strongly influenced by the government's regulatory policies from the very beginning, and the trend of housing prices in the next few years will be still determined by the government's policy orientation. However, this does not mean that the government can regulate the real estate market at its own will. In the face of the current macroeconomic situation and the situation of real estate market, the government faces at least three dilemmas in regulating the real estate market:

One of the dilemmas for the government is the contradiction between the rapid growth of the real estate market that stimulates effective demand in the short term and hinders economic growth in the long run. The biggest contribution of China's real estate development to the economy lies in its rapid rise in the demand for domestic investment in real estate-related industries, thereby increasing the effective demand of the public. If the state adopts the policy of lowering housing prices, the development of the real estate industry and other related industries may be affected due to the reduced profitability of the real estate industry. This may cause the insufficiency of the investment demand in these industries in the short term, thus causing insufficient effective demand of the whole society and slower economic growth. Additionally, the high profit margin of the real estate industry caused by the existing high housing prices will make the real estate market squeeze out the development funds of other industries. Meanwhile, high housing prices will also cause residents to lower their demand for consumption in other goods, leading to a decline in the total consumer demand. Thus, if the government continues to maintain the existing high housing prices, the over-development of real estate-related industries and under-development or even shrinkage of other industries may occur in the long run, which is very likely to cause the slowdown or even stagnation of economic growth.

The second dilemma for the government is the contradiction between maintaining the stability of the financial system and curbing inflation. The above analysis shows that, once the current high housing prices cannot be maintained, a credit crisis is very likely to occur, which will thus endanger the stability of the banking system. Additionally, if the government continues to maintain the existing high housing prices, inflation may follow as the expansion of credit will be reflected in the price level sooner or later.

The third dilemma for the government is the contradiction between the fiscal revenue of local government resulting from land and residents' welfare. As local fiscal revenues are heavily dependent on land transfer fees, the fiscal revenues of the local government will be directly affected once it is hard for the high housing prices to be sustained. And the decline in housing prices may also affect the growth of local GDP. Thus, whether aimed at maintaining its local GDP or fiscal revenue, the local government has the motivation to maintain the existing high housing prices. Additionally, if the government continues to maintain the existing high housing prices, the social welfare level will be greatly lowered due to the waste of resources brought by vacant housing and the living, financial, and spiritual burdens caused by high housing prices on residents. Meanwhile, high housing prices may also become a factor of social instability.

Based on the above analysis, the government should take the following measures to regulate the future direction of the real estate market. Firstly, curbing the continued rise in housing prices and stabilizing while reducing housing prices should be the primary goal of government regulation. The former aims to curb the continuation of the speculative behavior in the real estate market, and the latter can not only prevent the excessively rapid decline in housing prices from a huge impact on the development of the financial system and the real estate industry, but also help maintain equilibrium between the development of the real estate industry and that of other industries, thus avoiding stagnant economic growth and inflation. Secondly, in order to achieve the above goals, it is necessary to adopt fiscal policies, monetary policies, and other policies so that these policies match each other and are regulated in a coordinated way. Specifically, first, it is necessary to control the credit expansion of the banking system towards the real estate market, especially to prevent the one that has speculative demand from enhancing its speculative behavior by using the leverage of the mortgage system featuring repayment by installments. This is the only way to eliminate inflation and the bubbles in the real estate market. Second, since it is impossible for housing prices to fall too fast in the short term, it is necessary to improve the affordable housing and low-rent housing systems as soon as possible in order to meet the growing housing demand of residents. Third, it is necessary to accelerate the implementation of real estate tax in order to avoid the waste of resources caused by vacant housing, the decline in land prices, and the shortage of local fiscal revenue caused by the decrease in housing prices. This can increase the cost of vacant housing for speculators, and also the local fiscal revenue. Finally, it is necessary to end the situation where the fiscal revenue of the local government is directly dependent on the land transfer fee, thus fundamentally removing the incentive of the local government to raise housing prices.

Notes

1 Of course, if the local government adjusts economic growth through land supply after understanding the impact of land supply on economic growth, land supply may become endogenous again.
2 In consideration of output per capita, $y=Ak$, the wage of an individual when he/she is young, $w=(1-\alpha)Ak$, and the proportion of personal housing consumption in his/her total income when he/she is young, V/w, $1/z=p_t\bar{h}/k=(1-\alpha)A\left(p_t\bar{h}/w\right)$ actually represents the proportion of housing consumption in the total income for a young person.
3 When $\alpha A+1-\delta\leq(1-\theta)(1-\delta)/(1-\theta-\rho)$, savings are equal to 0. However, there are few circumstances when savings are 0. So, the assumed condition is basically reasonable.
4 If y_t is used to represent the income of a young person in period t, according to Equations (6.10) and (6.24), the individual's savings, two-period consumption and housing demand are expressed as follows:
$s_t=(1-\theta)y_t-p_th_t$, $c_t^y=\theta y_t$, $c_t^o=(1-\theta-\rho)(1+r_{t+1})y_t$ and $h_t=(1+r_{t+1})\rho y_t/\left[(1+r_{t+1})p_t-p_{t+1}\right]$
However, in the basic model without government transfer, the income when he/she is young, y_t, is equal to w_t. But in the extended model that contains government transfer, the income when he/she is young, y_t, is equal to w_t+b_t.
5 Like Section 7.3.1, $1/z=V/k=(1-\alpha)A\left(V/w\right)$ also represents the proportion of young person's housing consumption in the total income (hereinafter referred to as the "proportion of housing consumption per capita").
6 Obviously, when the condition in Theorem 7.1 is satisfied, the condition in Theorem 7.3 must be satisfied.

7 Similarly, the stability of the saddle point under the equilibrium state in Section 3.2 can also be discussed through the phase image.
8 Of course, for the actual economy, it is impossible for the housing price bubble to burst till the real economy completely collapses. Maybe, most people would expect housing prices will collapse when the bubble cannot continue when the economic depression reaches a certain level.
9 According to the data of *China Statistical Yearbooks*, during the period 1978–2013, the average annual growth rate of China's GDP per capita was about 10%, while the country's deposit interest rate was about 3%, and the commercial loan interest rate was only 6% to 7%. Since the growth rate of housing prices is equal to the growth rate of GDP per capita plus the population growth rate, and then minus the growth rate of land supply. However, the growth rate of China's new housing supply is less than 1% (see Table 7.1 of this chapter). Thus, even without regard for the urban population growth rate, the expected housing price growth rate of China will also be higher than its interest rate.

8 Education development in China's economic growth process

This chapter analyzes the education development of P.R. China since its founding, including national education funding, education scale, number of graduates at different levels of education, as well as the development and status quo of the overall education human capital. It also probes into the problems that exist in China's education development through international horizontal comparisons. The structure of this chapter is arranged as follows: the first section analyzes the changes in China's education expenditure; the second section discusses the changes in the scale and quality of China's education at different levels, including changes in the number of teachers and students at all levels of education, as well as student-teacher ratio in schools; and the third section studies the development of China's education human capital.

Section 1 Trends and status quo of China's education expenditure

1.1 Changes in the scale and composition of China's education expenditure

Since the founding of P.R. China, the absolute scale of the Chinese government's investment in education has witnessed a gradual increase. During the period 1952–1978, China's public fiscal education expenditure[1] showed an upward trend on the whole, from 1.162 billion yuan to 7.623 billion yuan and was approximately 7.343 billion yuan at the constant prices of 1952, with an average annual real growth rate of 7.3%. Since 1978, the investment in education has grown even faster. In 2018, the public fiscal education expenditure was 3,244.6 billion yuan and approximately 382.43 billion yuan at the constant prices of 1952, up 50.7 times compared with that of 1978, with an average annual growth of 10.4%, up 329.1 times compared with that of 1952, with an average annual growth of 8.9%, significantly higher than the real GDP growth rate in the same period.

As shown in Figure 8.1, during the period 1952–1978, the proportions of China's public fiscal education expenditure over the national fiscal revenue

DOI: 10.4324/9781003261629-11

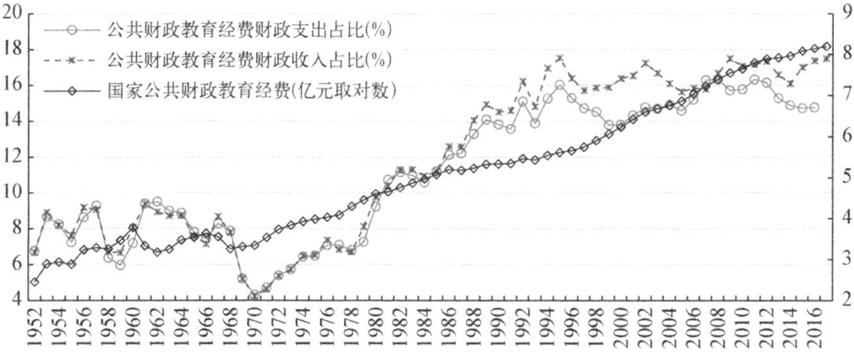

Figure 8.1 China's public fiscal education expenditure and its proportions over the fiscal revenue and expenditure: 1952–2018.

and over the national fiscal expenditure increased from 6.68% and 6.75% to 6.73% and 6.79%. During this period, these two proportions fluctuated greatly due to the impact of the changes in the macroeconomic situation, the fiscal budget system, and the education funding management system. For the two proportions, the minimum values were 4.23% and 4.24% (1970), and the maximum values were 9.39% (1960) and 9.50% (1961). Since 1978, China has proactively promoted the reform of the education funding management system. The *Decision of the Central Committee of the Communist Party of China on Education System Reform*, issued in 1985, clarified the principles of personnel and administrative powers featuring "local responsibility and hierarchical management" for basic education, and proposed that "the increase in education funds contributed by the central and local governments shall be higher than that of regular fiscal revenues and the gradual increase in the average education expenses per capita according to the number of current students shall be realized." *The Outline of China's Education Reform and Development*, issued in 1993, clearly stated that "we shall continue to improve the level-by-level school running and management system" and proposed two more important goals, namely, the percentage of fiscal education funds over GDP reached 4% and the percentage of education funds in the total fiscal expenditure at all levels 15%. Promoted by such policies, the proportion of public fiscal education expenditure in fiscal revenues of 1995 rose to 17.51%, and that of fiscal expenditure to 16.02%. The tax-sharing system reform implemented after 1995 has affected local fiscal revenues, but the power of the central and local governments on education investment has not changed. The *Decision of the State Council on the Reform and Development of Basic Education*, issued in 2001, further clarified the education management system featuring "local responsibility, hierarchical management and county-based." Affected by both aspects above, the proportion of public education funds in fiscal revenues during the period 1995–2018 has been maintained at 15.5%–17.7%, and that of public education expenditure in fiscal expenditure remained at 13.8%–16.3%.

The proportion of education expenditure in GDP is another indicator commonly used to measure the relative scale of the fiscal education expenditure. In the first few years of the founding of New China, the proportion of the country's public fiscal education expenditure in GDP was maintained at 1.5% to 2.5%, rose to 3.1% in 1960, saw a decline for the first time due to the impact of the subsequent three-year difficult period, and then continued to drop to 1.3% due to the impact of the Cultural Revolution. At the National Education Work Conference in 1971, Zhou Enlai ordered at the Meeting Minutes that, "the expenditure shall not be reduced but increased year by year." That year, the Planning Commission and the Ministry of Finance added 350 million yuan as education expenses. Since 1972, the central government has listed education expenditure as a separate item and allocated for special purposes when arranging the national fiscal budget. After that, the share of education expenditure over GDP started to recover. However, despite the rapid economic growth driven by the reform and opening-up, the growth rate of tax revenue in the same period clearly lagged behind the economic growth rate, and the proportions of fiscal revenues and fiscal expenditure in GDP continued to decline (see Figures 8.2 and 8.3). Thus, the proportion of public fiscal education in GDP decreased to varying degrees. Since 1997, the proportion of China's public fiscal education expenditure in GDP has recovered its upward trend. In 2018, this proportion reached 3.60%.

For China's fiscal education expenditure[2] and total education expenditure, only the data after 1990 are available. According to Figure 8.2, changes in the proportions of the two in GDP are basically the same as changes in the proportion of the public fiscal education expenditure in GDP. The share of the country's fiscal education expenditure over GDP reached 2.96% in 1990 and dropped to the minimum of 2.29% in 1995. Since then, this share

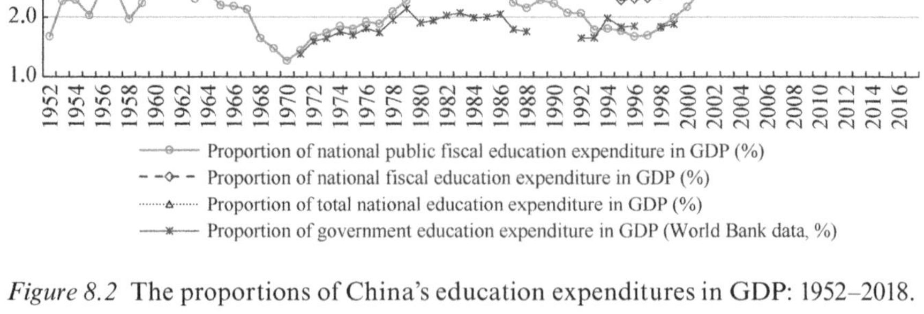

Figure 8.2 The proportions of China's education expenditures in GDP: 1952–2018.

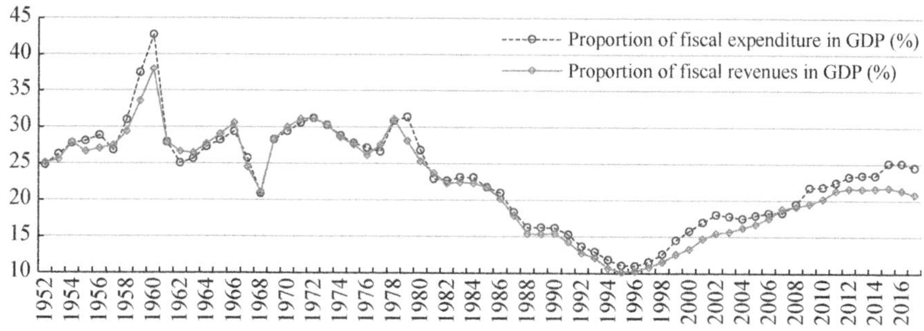

Figure 8.3 The proportions of China's public fiscal revenue and expenditure in GDP: 1952–2018.

has risen like waves. It exceeded 4% in 2012, achieving for the first time the goal that the proportion of the national fiscal education expenditure account for 4% of GDP as stipulated in the *Education Law* of China. Then, the figure hit 4.11% in 2018. The proportion of the total education expenditure in GDP was 3.46% in 1990 and reached the minimum of 2.95% in 1994. The figure has showed an upward trend since then. It exceeded 4.5% in 2002 and reached 5.12% in 2018. The reason for the substantial increase in the proportion of the total education expenditure in GDP is related to the dramatic increase in national non-public fiscal education expenditure in addition to the rapid rise in the public fiscal education expenditure (see Figure 8.4). The non-fiscal education expenditure increased from 7.65 billion yuan to 28.33 billion yuan in 2012, and has continued to maintain a relatively high level

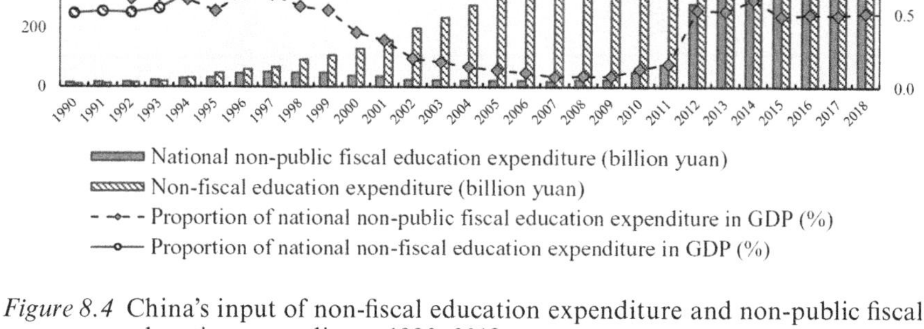

Figure 8.4 China's input of non-fiscal education expenditure and non-public fiscal education expenditure: 1990–2018.

since then, with its proportion in GDP basically maintained at around 0.5%. However, the growth of the national non-public fiscal education expenditure has started to be lower than that of the GDP since 2006. During the period 2012–2018, its share over the GDP was basically maintained at about 1.0%.

1.2 International comparisons regarding public education expenditure

According to World Bank data, the proportion of China's fiscal education expenditure in GDP was 4.08% in 2014. In the same period, the average of the world was 4.9%, that of OECD members and high-income countries was 5.2%, and that of upper-middle-income countries and middle-income countries was 4.1%. It can be seen that, over 40 years of development, the proportion of China's fiscal education expenditure in GDP was basically the same as the average for upper-middle-income countries, but lower than the average of high-income countries and the world average. In terms of proportion, among major European and American countries, China exceeded Japan (3.6%) alone; and among BRICS countries, the proportions in India and Russia were lower than China but those of Brazil and South Africa were higher than China (see Figure 8.5).

In terms of the proportion of national fiscal education expenditure over the government's public expenditure, the proportion in China was 14.9% in 2014. In the same year, the average of the world was 14.0%, that of OECD members and high-income countries was 12.7% and 13.0%, and that of

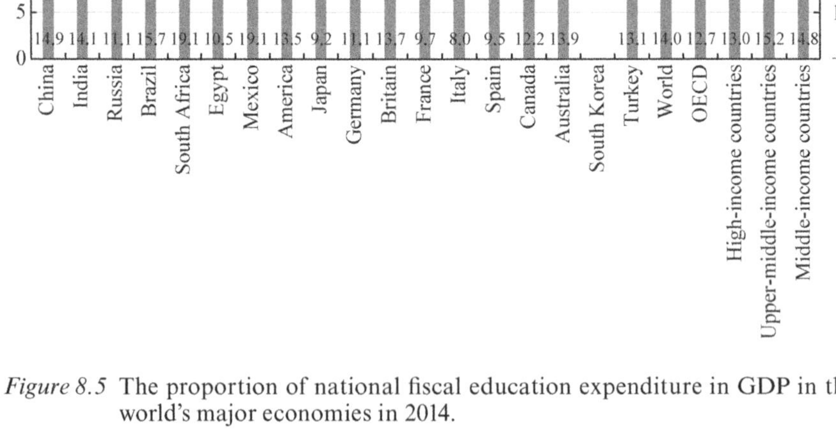

Figure 8.5 The proportion of national fiscal education expenditure in GDP in the world's major economies in 2014.

upper-middle-income countries and middle-income countries was 15.2% and 14.8%. In 2014, the proportion of national fiscal education expenditure over the government's public expenditure in European and American developed countries was not high, basically 9% to 14%, lower than the average of China and the world. In terms of this proportion, among BRICS countries, India and Russia were inferior to China, which was not better than Brazil and South Africa. It can be seen that, compared with other countries in the world, the proportion of China's fiscal education expenditure over the government's public expenditure was lower than the average of upper-middle-income countries, equivalent to the average of middle-income countries, but higher than the average of the world, high-income countries, and developed countries.

In terms of the absolute level of the fiscal education expenditure per capita, China's fiscal education expenditure is still low, not only lower than that of developed countries but also lower than the average of upper-middle-income countries and of the world. As can be seen from Figure 8.6, China's fiscal education expenditure per capita in 2014 was only US$ 313, lower than the world average (US$ 532) and the average of upper-middle-income countries (US$ 346). In the same year, this expenditure was above US$ 1,000 for developed countries; US$ 2,018 and US$ 2,146 for OECD members and high-income countries on average, respectively, far higher than that of China. Among BRICS countries, the other three countries except India exceeded China with respect to the same.

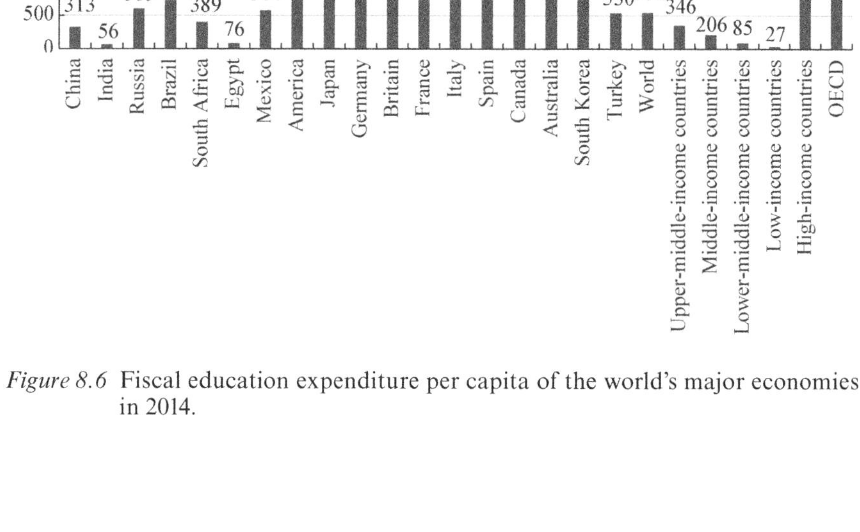

Figure 8.6 Fiscal education expenditure per capita of the world's major economies in 2014.

Section 2 Education development trends and status quo of China's education at all levels

2.1 The development trend and status quo of primary education

In the early years of the founding of P.R. China, universal education was regarded as the focus of education. The *Common Program of the Chinese People's Political Consultative Conference* adopted in 1949, which had interim constitutional significance, proposed to implement universal education in a planned, step-by-step manner. In some important documents closely related to education, such as the *Instructions on Education* issued in 1958, the central government regarded universal primary education as the primary task of China's social and educational development. In the first half of the 1970s, the central government not only attached great importance to universal primary education, but also tried to popularize junior secondary education and even senior secondary education (Liao, 2019). Under this guidance, the scale of primary education showed a trend of rapid growth but underwent adjustments and fluctuations in its rapid development due to policy changes from the founding of New China until the launch of the reform and opening-up. The number of primary schools was 346,800 in 1949, reached its first peak of 777,000 in the Great Leap Forward period, slightly dropped in the following five years, and then dropped to the local minimum of 708,000 in 1963. The figure grew rapidly from 1963 to 1965, reached a historical peak of 1.682 million in 1965, and dropped to 1.007 million in 1966. It resumed growth after the start of the Cultural Revolution in 1967, continued to drop after 1975, and reached 949,000 in 1978, up 1.74 times over that of 1949 (see Figure 8.7).

The number of full-time primary school teachers has also witnessed a similar volatile growth.[3] This number showed a rapid upward trend during the period 1949–1978, except for the years 1960–1962, 1965–1970, and 1949–1978, and grew from 830,000 in 1949 to 5.23 million in 1978, up 5.26

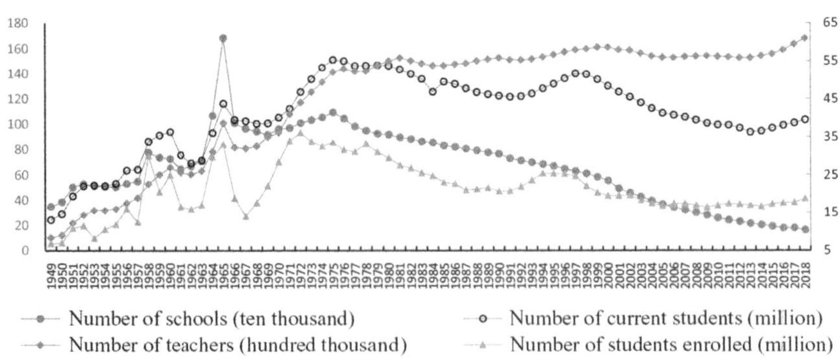

Figure 8.7 Changes in the number of primary schools, students, and full-time teachers of China: 1952–2018.

times in 39 years, with an average annual growth of 4.8%. During the period 1949–1978, the number of primary school students enrolled and current students in primary schools also witnessed the same trend of changes. Except for the years 1960–1962 and 1965–1970, other years saw a rapid increase in such numbers. The number of primary school students was 6.8 million and that of current students in primary schools was 24.391 million in 1949. In 1978, the former increased to 33.15 million, representing an average annual increase of 4.15%; and the latter increased to 146.2 million, representing an average annual increase of 4.93%. Accordingly, the student-teacher ratio rose from 29 in 1949 to 35.6 in 1952, and then dropped to 28.4 in 1978. In terms of the popularization rate of primary education, the net enrollment rate for primary schools was approximately 20% in 1949,[4] increased to 49.2% in 1952, 67.1% in 1957, 90.0% in 1970, and reached 95.5% in 1978. The ratio of the number of primary school students to the school-age population (hereinafter referred to as the "enrollment rate of school-age population") was as high as 107.6%[5] in 1970 and 112.1% in 1978. It can be seen that China's primary education has basically covered all school-age population.

Since the reform and opening-up, the size of primary schools in China first declined, then rose and fell (see Figures 8.7 and 8.8). The main reasons are described as follows. Firstly, under the collective production mode of the people's communes before the reform, many rural schools were set up by collective organizations, which would grant some tuition subsidies to students. After the reform and opening-up, the household contract responsibility system was implemented in rural areas and the income of collective organizations dropped and was not guaranteed. As a result, many schools that had been originally established by collective organizations were merged or cancelled, and the tuition subsidies for students were also cancelled (Zhang, 2006), which led to a rapid decline in the number of primary schools in

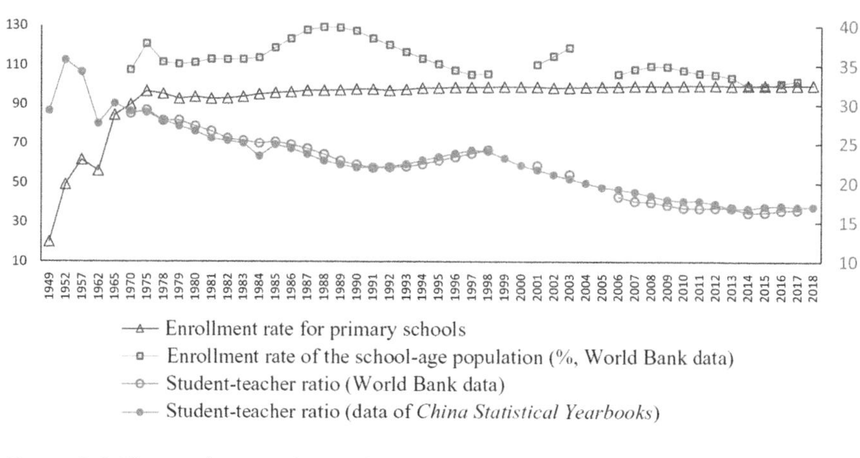

Figure 8.8 The student-teacher ratio, enrollment rate, and proportion of current students in the school-age population of China: 1952–2018.

the early years of the reform and opening-up. Secondly, the decline in the fertility rate caused by the family planning policy was the main reason for the decline in the number of primary schools in the later years of the reform and opening-up. Thirdly, the promulgation of the *Compulsory Education Law* in 1986 and the full implementation of the nine-year compulsory education have also affected the development of primary schools within a period of time. Under the joint effect of the three factors, the number of primary school students enrolled and current primary school students during the period 1978–1990 dropped from 33.15 million and 146.2 million to 20.6 million and 122.4 million, respectively. Under the influence of the gradual and comprehensive implementation of national compulsory education, the two figures above during the period 1991–1998 rose to 24.6 million and 140 million, and that during the period 1998–2018 dropped to 18.7 million and 103.4 million, respectively.

During the period 1978–2018, the number of primary school teachers was basically stable, increasing only from 5.204 million to 6.092 million, representing a 40-year growth of 16.6% and an average annual growth of 0.38%; the number of primary school students decreased from 949,000 to 162,000; and the student-teacher ratio was reduced from 28.0 to 17.0. The enrollment rate for primary schools has been on the rise. It reached 99.1% in 1999, remained above 99% afterwards, and hit 99.95% in 2018. The enrollment rate of school-age population in primary schools was basically maintained at above 100%. And primary school education has been fully universalized.

Overall, China's primary education has achieved rapid development in the past 70 years. It kept growing even during the period of Cultural Revolution. The development of primary education before the reform and opening-up was mainly reflected in the growth in the number of schools, teachers, and students. Universal education was basically achieved. However, as the number of teachers was not growing as fast as student scale, the student-teacher ratio has been large for a long period of time. The shortage of teachers, too many students, and too large-scale classes seriously affected teaching quality. Since the 1980s, the decline in the fertility rate and changes in the demographic structure have caused a decline in the number of primary schools and students. The development of primary education is mainly reflected in the increase of the number of teachers and student-teacher ratio, as well as other improvements.

2.2 *The development trend and status quo of secondary education development*

The development of secondary education from 1949 to 2018 can be roughly divided into the following four stages (see Figures 8.9, 8.10, and 8.11).

The first stage is the initial development period from 1949 to 1957. In the early period of the founding of New China, the state regarded the popularization of education for a majority of rural population as the focus of

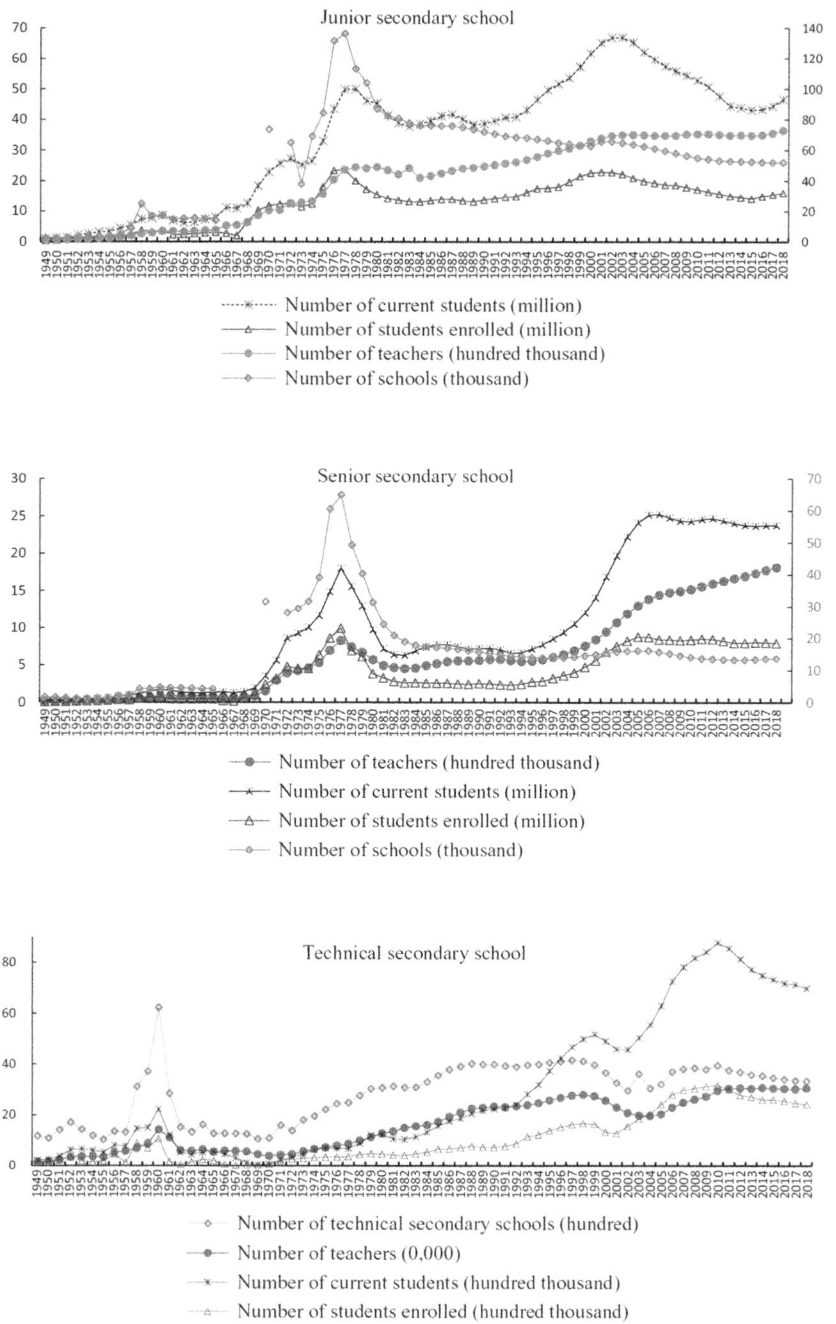

Figure 8.9 Changes in the number of schools, students, and full-time teachers at various types of secondary schools in China: 1949–2018.

(Continued)

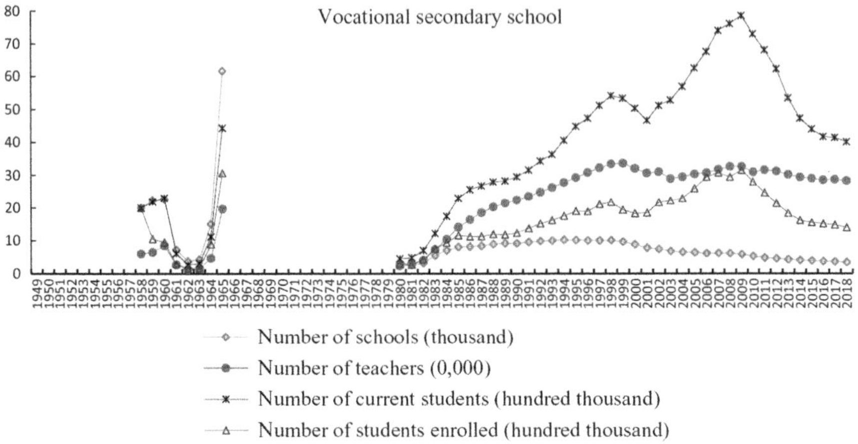

Figure 8.9 (Continued).

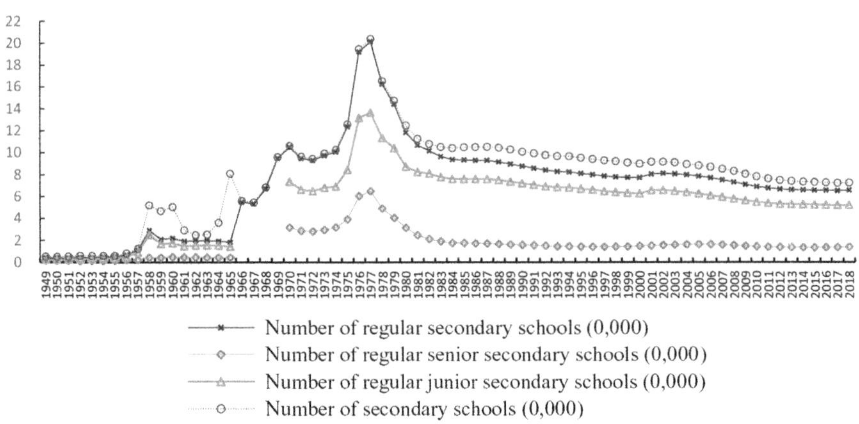

Figure 8.10 Changes in the number of various types of secondary schools in China: 1949–2018.

education, and proposed the goal of "popularizing primary education for children in a planned, step-by-step manner." The focus of rural education was to popularize primary education then. Moreover, rural secondary schools in this period also achieved rapid development in the context that both knowledge and skills of primary school graduates cannot meet the requirements for agricultural production. According to the data from the Ministry of Education of China, the country had 5,261 secondary schools in 1949, including 4,045 regular secondary schools, 1,597 regular senior secondary schools, 2,448 junior secondary schools, and 216 technical secondary schools. In 1957, the total number of secondary schools increased to

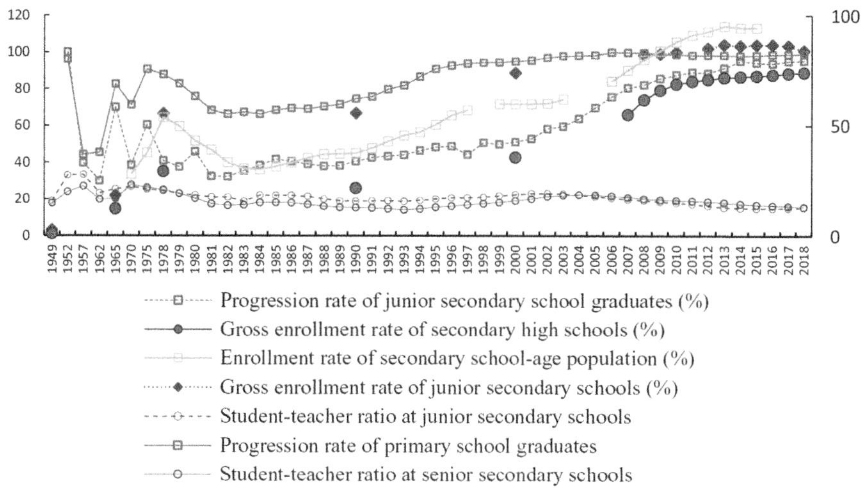

Figure 8.11 Changes in the student-teacher ratio, enrollment rate, and regression rate of secondary school graduates in China: 1952–2018.

12,400, including 11,100 regular secondary schools, 2,184 regular senior secondary schools, and 8,912 junior secondary schools, with few changes in the number of other schools.[6] During the period 1949–1957, at junior secondary schools, the number of teachers increased from 52,000 to 194,000, the number of current students from 832,000 to 5.377 million, and the number of students enrolled from 341,200 to 2.17 million; at senior secondary schools, the number of teachers increased from 14,000 to 40,000, the number of students from 320,000 to 904,000, and the number of students enrolled from 71,100 to 323,000; at technical secondary schools, the number of teachers increased from 16,000 to 58,000, and the number of students enrolled and current students from 97,000 and 229,000 to 123,000 and 778,000. Due to the far higher growth rates of the number of schools and students than the growth rate of the number of teachers, the student-teacher ratio at junior secondary schools and senior secondary schools during this period rose from 15.8 and 14.8 in 1949 to 27.2 and 22.6 in 1957, respectively. Due to the rapid development of primary and junior secondary schools relative to the education at the corresponding higher levels, the progression rate of primary school graduates (the percentage of primary school graduates admitted to junior secondary schools) and that of junior secondary school graduates (the percentage of junior secondary school graduates admitted to senior secondary schools) dropped from 96% and 100% in 1952 to 44.2% and 39.7% in 1957.

The second is the adjustment stage from 1958 to 1965. Under the guidance of Mao Zedong's education policy of 1957 that "Education must serve proletarian politics, and get integrated with productive labor," secondary schools experienced a fluctuating process of expansion, adjustment, reduction, and expansion in scale, especially vocational secondary schools, during this period. During the Great Leap Forward in 1958, the number of secondary schools soared to 50,600. The number of regular secondary schools grew to 28,900, that of regular junior secondary schools to 24,800, that of regular senior secondary schools to 4,144, and that of technical secondary schools to 3,113. The number of vocational high schools grew most, by 20,000. During the period 1959–1960, the total number of secondary schools was maintained at around 50,000, with a slight decline in the number of regular secondary schools. In 1961, the total number of secondary schools was reduced to 29,100, including 19,000 regular secondary schools and 14,600 junior secondary schools, with almost no changes in the number of senior secondary schools and technical secondary schools and the number of vocational secondary schools cut by 15,000. During the period 1962–1963, the total number of secondary schools was basically maintained at around 25,000, but surged to 81,000 in 1965, including 18,100 regular secondary schools, 14,600 junior secondary schools, 4,100 senior secondary schools, and 1,265 technical secondary schools; the number of vocational secondary schools grew most, to 62,000 in 1965. During this period, the number of teachers and student scale in junior secondary schools, senior secondary schools, and non-regular secondary schools also changed in a similar way. At junior secondary schools, the number of teachers increased to 254,000 in 1958, to 346,000 in 1960, then dropped to 318,000 in 1962, and rose to 379,000 in 1965; the number of new students enrolled and that of current students increased from 3.783 million and 7.341 million in 1958 to 3.648 million and 8.585 million in 1960, were adjusted to 2.383 million and 6.189 million in 1962, and grew to 2.998 million and 8.03 million in 1965; and the student-teacher ratio was reduced from 28.9 in 1958 to 21.2 in 1965. At senior secondary schools, the number of teachers was adjusted from 51,000 in 1958 to 78,000 in 1965; the number of new students enrolled and current students were adjusted from 562,000 and 1.179 million to 459,000 and 1.308 million; and the student-teacher ratio dropped from 22.6 to 16.8. At technical secondary schools, the number of teachers increased from 69,000 in 1958, to 142,000 in 1960, and then was adjusted to 55,000 in 1962; the number of new students enrolled and current students increased from 895,000 and 1.47 million in 1958 to 1.06 million and 2.216 million in 1960, and were then adjusted to 208,000 and 547,000. The biggest changes occurred to vocational secondary schools. At these schools, the number of teachers decreased from 60,000 in 1958 to 13,000 in 1962, and then increased to 197,000 in 1965; the number of new students enrolled and current students was changed from 2 million each in 1958 to 612,000 and 2.19 million in 1961, and then increased to 3.06 million and 4.433 million in 1965. In 1965, the progression rates of primary and junior high school graduates increased to 86.5% and 70%, respectively; and the gross enrollment rates of junior secondary schools and senior secondary schools increased from 3.1% and 1.1% in 1949 to 22.0% and 14.6% in 1965.[7]

The third stage is the rapid development phase during the Cultural Revolution period from 1966 to 1976. Driven by the education revolution and guided by the school-running policy of "village-run primary schools, production team-run junior secondary schools and commune-run senior secondary schools," secondary education, especially rural secondary education, developed rapidly during this period. The development of secondary schools during this period had two characteristics. First, the total number of regular rural secondary schools achieved great development; second, the number of non-regular secondary schools was greatly reduced, and vocational secondary schools were canceled in particular. Through adjustments during the period 1966–1967, the number of secondary schools decreased from 81,000 in 1965 to 54,800 in 1967 but the number of regular secondary schools increased from 18,000 to 53,500, with the share of regular secondary schools accounting for 97.6% of all secondary schools. During this period, many rural vocational secondary schools were merged into regular secondary schools. During the years 1968–1977, a large number of vocational secondary schools were cancelled or merged, with only regular secondary schools and a few technical secondary schools left. In 1977, the number of secondary schools increased to 203,800 and that of regular secondary schools to 201,200, including 136,400 junior secondary schools, 64,900 senior secondary schools, and 2,485 technical secondary schools. In 1978, at junior secondary schools, the number of teachers increased to 2.441 million; the number of new students enrolled and current students increased to 20.06 million and 49.952 million; and the student-teacher ratio was 20.45. At senior secondary schools, the number of teachers increased to 741,000, the number of new students enrolled and current students increased to 6.929 million and 11.531 million, and the student-teacher ratio rose to 20.96 compared with that of 1975. At technical secondary schools, the number of teachers was 87,000; the number of new students enrolled and current students was 366,000 and 689,000, respectively. The progression rates of primary schools and junior secondary schools increased by 87.7% and 40.0%; the enrollment rate at primary schools and senior high schools increased to 66.4% and 35.1%, respectively. According to World Bank data, the enrollment rate of the secondary school-age population was 54.89%. It shows that China's secondary education had achieved great development by 1978; more than two thirds of the school-age population had entered junior high schools, and nearly two thirds of the school-age population was studying at secondary schools. However, the development of secondary education was still insufficient, with a low popularization rate in the school-age population.

The fourth stage is the compulsory education popularization after 1978. During this period, secondary schools were basically regular schools on the whole; the number of schools showed a downward trend; the number of teachers increased; the number of junior secondary school students increased first and then decreased, while the number of senior secondary school students showed an upward trend (see Figure 8.9). In the early years of the reform and opening-up, just like primary schools, the income of rural collective economic organizations was low due to the implementation of the household contract responsibility system in rural areas. Many secondary schools run by collective economic organizations before the reform and opening-up were forced to merge or close due to the decrease in the revenues of the collective economic organizations. Consequently, the number of regular secondary schools witnessed a rapid decrease during the period 1978–1985, with the number of junior and senior secondary schools falling from 113,100 and 49,500 to 75,900 and 17,300. At the same time, vocational secondary education institutions started to be built and expanded; the number of technical secondary schools increased from 2,760 to 3,557; and vocational secondary schools also started to be rebuilt and expanded in 1980, with 3,314 that year and 8,070 in 1985. During this period, the number of teachers and students at various types of secondary schools also witnessed similar changes. At junior secondary schools, the number of teachers, current students, and students enrolled dropped from 2.441 million, 49.952 million, and 20.06 million to 2.16 million, 39.648 million, and 13.494 million, respectively; at senior secondary schools, the number of teachers, current students, and the students enrolled dropped from 741,000, 15.531 million, and 6.929 million to 492,000, 7.411 million, and 2.575 million, respectively[8]; at technical secondary schools, the number of teachers, current students, and students enrolled increased from 99,000, 889,000, and 447,000 to 174,000, 668,000, and 1.571 million, respectively; and at vocational secondary schools, the number of teachers, students, and enrolled students increased from 23,000, 307,000, and 454,000 in 1980 to 141,000, 1.161 million, and 2.295 million, respectively. The promulgation of the *Compulsory Education Law* and the full implementation of the nine-year compulsory education in 1986 controlled the trend of decline in regular secondary education. However, due to the decline in the number of newborns, the number of secondary schools has continued to decline since 1986, but with a slower rate of decrease. By 2018, the total number of secondary schools had reached 72,500, a decrease of 32,400 compared with that of 1985. There were 13,700 regular senior secondary schools, 52,000 junior secondary schools, 3,431 vocational secondary schools, and 3,322 technical secondary schools, a decrease of 3,618, 28,500, 4,639, and 235, respectively, over that of 1985. In 2018, the number of teachers, current students, and students enrolled at junior secondary schools was 3.639 million, 46.526 million, and 16.026 million, respectively; that at senior secondary schools was 1.813 million, 23.754 million, and 7.928 million, respectively; that at vocational secondary schools was 283,000, 4.011 million, and 1.403 million, respectively; and that at technical secondary schools was 305,000, 6.994 million and 2.419 million, respectively. The number of current students and students enrolled at non-regular secondary schools was 31.0% and 32.5% of that at senior secondary schools, respectively. During this period, the student-teacher ratio at junior and senior secondary schools witnessed a volatile downward trend, dropping to 12.79 and 13.10, respectively, in 2018.

The progression rates of primary school and junior secondary school graduates increased to 99.1% and 95.2% in 2018; and the gross enrollment rates of junior and senior secondary schools rose to 100.1% and 88.8%, respectively. The proportion of current secondary school students in the total secondary school-age population reached the minimum of 30.17% in 1984, and showed an upward trend afterwards, reaching 94.30% in 2015, as shown in Figure 8.10. Currently, almost all secondary school-age population can receive junior secondary school education and about 90% of the population can receive senior secondary school education.

Overall, as shown in Table 8.1, the development of China's secondary education before the reform was mainly reflected in the rapid growth of scale (including number of schools, teachers, and students); the rapid increase in the number of students and student scale was mainly attributed to the rapid growth of the school-age population and China's emphasis on secondary education; and the increase in the number of students was based on the impact of the dual demand increase brought by the increase in the number of both schools and students. Since the reform, as the number of schools has shown a downward trend and the needs of junior secondary school education for scale expansion in terms of the number of teachers and students have been met, the development of education has been mainly reflected in the improvement of teaching quality, including student-teacher ratio. Since

Table 8.1 Changes in education indicators of China's secondary schools: 1949–2018

Period	*Number of schools (ten thousand)*	*Number of teachers (hundred thousand)*	*Number of current students (million)*	*Number of students enrolled*	*Student-teacher ratio*	*Progression rate (%)*	*Gross enrollment rate (%)*
Changes in junior secondary schools							
1949–1978	110.68	23.89	49.95	20.06	4.66	40.90	63.30
1949–1957	6.46	1.42	5.38	2.17	11.92	39.70	−3.10
1957–1965	5.08	1.85	2.65	0.83	−6.53	30.30	22.00
1965–1978	99.14	20.62	41.92	17.06	−0.72	−29.10	44.40
1978–2001	−47.61	9.45	15.19	2.82	−1.22	12.00	−66.40
2001–2018	−13.53	2.53	−18.62	−6.85	−6.45	42.30	100.90
1978–2018	−61.13	11.98	−3.43	−4.03	−7.67	54.30	34.50
Changes in senior secondary schools							
1949–1978	47.62	7.27	15.53	6.93	6.16	5.89	34.00
1949–1957	0.59	0.26	0.90	0.32	7.80	56.15	−1.10
1957–1965	1.93	0.38	0.40	0.14	−5.83	−10.59	14.60
1965–1978	45.10	6.63	14.22	6.47	4.19	−39.67	20.50
1978–2001	−34.31	0.99	−1.48	−1.35	−4.23	72.91	−35.10
2001–2018	−1.21	9.73	9.70	2.35	−3.63	−78.80	88.80
1978–2018	−35.52	10.72	8.22	1.00	−7.86	−5.89	53.70

Source: Calculations by the author.

the reform, senior secondary education has achieved development in terms of the number of schools, teachers and students, student-teacher ratio, and other aspects.

2.3 The development trend and status quo of higher education

Beginning at the founding of New China, China's higher education development can be divided into five stages.

First, the initial development stage from 1949 to 1957. The scale of China's higher education was very small in the early years of the founding of New China. In 1949, there were only 205 colleges and universities in the country, with 16,100 college students. That year, the number of undergraduate and junior college students enrolled and current college students was only 31,000 and 119,000; the number of postgraduates enrolled and current postgraduates was 242 and 629, respectively; the student-teacher ratio at colleges and universities was 7.3; and the gross enrollment rate for higher education was 0.26%. In 1949, the separate enrollment method, which had been adopted before the liberation, was still in place in various regions. In 1950, the joint enrollment by colleges and universities was implemented in the same regions. In 1951, unified enrollment was executed nationwide (Fan, 2011). In 1952, in order to satisfy the needs for socialist industrialization construction, colleges/universities, and departments throughout the country were adjusted; a large number of engineering colleges and universities were built and merged; the number of engineering students enrolled was increased to a large extent; and the number of comprehensive universities and liberal art universities was greatly cut. That year, the total number of colleges and universities in China was adjusted to 201; the number of university teachers increased to 27,000; the number of undergraduates and junior college students enrolled and current students increased to 79,000 and 191,000; and the student-teacher ratio fell to 7.07. In 1957, the number of colleges and universities rose to 229; the number of teachers increased to about 70,000; the number of undergraduates and junior college students enrolled was only 106,000 and 441,000; and the student-teacher ratio continued to drop to 6.06. As the number of students who participated in college entrance examinations increased from 73,000 in 1952 to 252,000 in 1957, the admission rate of colleges and universities dropped from 91.0% to 41.67%, and the progression rate of senior secondary school graduates reached 56.1% (Figure 8.12).[9]

Second, the Great Leap Forward period from 1958 to 1960 and the adjustment period from 1961 to 1965. In 1957, the central government started to decentralize its administrative authority for some agricultural and medical colleges, and increased the local's government's hierarchical management authority over the colleges and universities affiliated to the central government, motivating the local government's enthusiasm for running higher education institutions. This factor, together with the Great Leap Forward period from 1958 to 1960, led to the blind increase in the number of higher

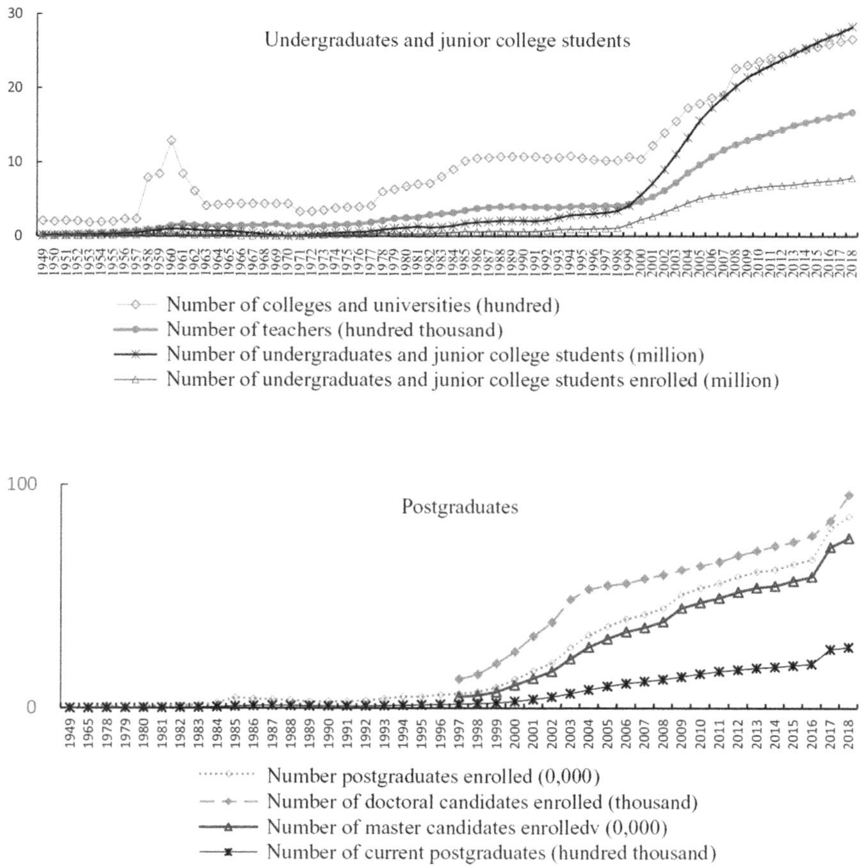

Figure 8.12 Changes in China's colleges and universities, students and full-time teachers: 1949–2018.

education institutions and the expansion of enrollment scale for higher education, thus causing related issues such as added difficulty in employment and poorer teaching quality. After that, the guidelines of "adjustment, consolidation, enrichment and improvement" in terms of higher education proposed by the central government in the economic field also started to be implemented (Li Shuohao & Tao Wei, 2017). For this reason, the number of colleges and universities surged from 791 in 1958 to 1,289 in 1960 and was adjusted to 434 in 1965; the number of university teachers surged from 70,000 in 1957 to 158,100 in 1961 and was adjusted to 138,000 in 1965; the number of undergraduate and junior college students enrolled and current students increased from 106,000 and 439,600 to 320,000 and 960,000 in 1960, and then was adjusted to 164,000 and 674,600, respectively; the number of postgraduates enrolled and current postgraduates reached 1,456 and 4,546

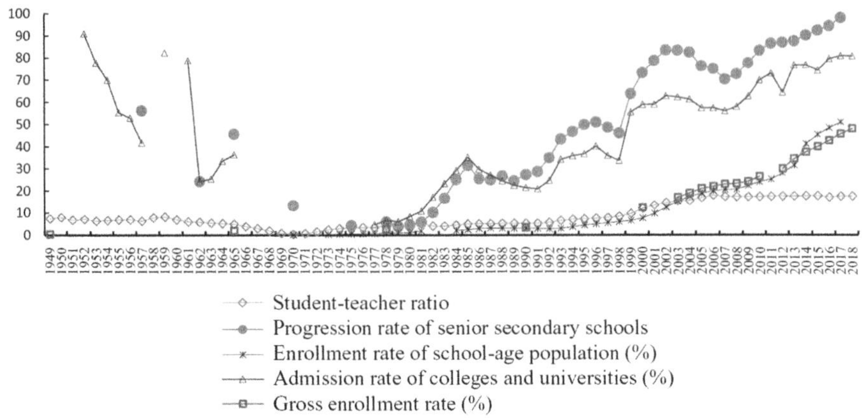

Figure 8.13 Changes in the student-teacher ratio and enrollment rate of school-age population and gross enrollment rate of Chinese colleges and universities: 1949–2018.

in 1965; and the student-teacher ratio rose from 6.3 to 8.1 in 1960, and then dropped to 4.9. In 1965, the number of students who participated in college entrance examinations continued to rise to 450,000; the admission rate of colleges and universities dropped to 36.3%; the progression rate of senior secondary school graduates dropped to 45.6%; and the gross enrollment rate at colleges and universities reached 1.95 (Figure 8.13).

Third, the stagnation period of the Cultural Revolution from 1966 to 1976. In 1966, Chairman Mao called for shortening the academic length and revolutionizing education. The Ministry of Education also issued a notice on postponing college and university enrollment in the same year. In 1968, Mao requested in the "July 21" instructions the selection of outstanding talents from the workers and peasants to study at colleges and universities, and also called for a wide range of intellectual youths to go to the countryside for further receiving education from poor and lower-middle peasants. Under the influence of these major policies, the number of colleges and universities in China was maintained at 434 during the period 1965–1970 and was reduced to 404 in 1977; little change occurred in the number of college teachers during the same period, basically 130,000 to 160,000. In terms of college student enrollment, the college entrance examination was abolished during the period 1966–1976 and college enrollment was suspended during the years 1966–1971. In 1970, 42,000 college students were enrolled through recommendations and interviews, and the number of college students reached 48,000. During the years 1972–1976, China resumed the student enrollment at colleges and universities but by recommending workers, peasants, and soldiers to receive higher education, and a total of approximately 820,000 such students were enrolled from 1970 to 1976. During this period, the postgraduate enrollment was also suspended. Due to the sharp decline in the number of students enrolled, the student-teacher ratio then was quite low, basically below 3.0; the enrollment rate of the school-age population at colleges and universities was also very low. It was only 0.12% in 1970 and rose slightly to 0.57% in 1976.

Fourth, the phase of restoration, development, and reform from 1977 to 1998. China's education has initiated its new stage of development and reform under the background of socialist economic construction since the reform and opening-up and the direction of the education reform and development direction that "Education must orient towards modernization, the world and the future." In 1977, China resumed its unified national college entrance exam. The number of applicants for colleges and universities that year was 5.73 million and 270,000 students were enrolled, with an admission rate of 4.7%; the number of undergraduates and junior college students was 626,800, and the enrollment rate of the college-age population was 0.65%; there was 18,400 university teachers and 404 colleges and universities that year. In 1978, the number of undergraduates and junior college students enrolled increased to 402,000, with an admission rate of 6.6% and the progression rate of senior secondary school graduates of 5.89%; the number of undergraduates and junior college students increased to 856,000, and the gross enrollment rate of higher education hit 2.7%; the number of university teachers increased to 20,600, and the number of colleges and universities surged to 598; the number of postgraduates enrolled that year was 10,708, and the number of current postgraduates was 10,934. Moreover, the enrollment rate of the school-age population in Chinese colleges and universities was still only 0.72%; the number of students enrolled by colleges and universities was 1.21%, 2.00%, and 5.80% of that enrolled by primary, junior secondary, and senior secondary schools, respectively, and the number of current students was 0.59%, 1.71%, and 5.51% of that at primary, junior secondary, and senior secondary schools, respectively, in the same year. It can be seen that Chinese colleges and universities seriously lagged behind primary and secondary schools in seeking development.

Following the restoration and reconstruction of higher education in the early period of reform and opening-up, the *Decision of the Central Committee of the Communist Party of China on Education System Reform* issued in 1985 further proposed reforms and extended the autonomy of higher education institutions. Since then, China has entered the first stage of rapid development of higher education in the early period of reform and opening-up. In 1985, the number of Chinese higher education institutions increased to 1,016 in 1985, was basically maintained at 1,020 to 1,080 during the period 1986–1998, and was 1,022 in 1998. The number of university teachers increased from 344,000 to 407,000, with an average annual growth of 3.46% over the past 20 years. The number of students enrolled and current students grew from 619,000 and 1.703 million to 1.084 million and 3.409 million, with an annual growth of 5.08% and 7.15%. The corresponding student-teacher ratio also rose from 4.95 to 8.38. The enrollment rate of colleges and universities, progression rate of senior secondary school graduates, and enrollment rate of college-age population increased from 35.2%, 31.5% and 2.42% to 33.8%, 46.1%, and 5.96%, respectively.

Fifth, the stage of deepened reform and rapid development from 1999 to 2018. Around 1998, China's higher education development entered a new stage. During this period, China made two breakthroughs in the direction of higher education development. First, it was emphasized in terms of quality that world-class universities should be built. With the "211" and "985" projects as symbols, the state increased its support for the two types of selected engineering universities. Second, it was emphasized in terms of quantity that the scale of colleges and universities should be expanded and higher education entered a stage of popularization. In 1999, the *Resolution on Deepening Education Reform and Fully Promoting Quality Education* issued explicitly proposed that China entered the climax of college and university student enrollment after the gross enrollment rate of colleges and universities reached the goal of 15%, represented by college and university student enrollment expansion and merger of colleges and universities. As a result, the number of colleges and universities, teachers, and students entered the fastest growing period after 2000. During the period 1998–2018, the number of Chinese colleges and universities increased from 1,022 to 2,663, up 1.61 times; the number of university teachers from 407,000 to 1.673 million, up 3.11 times, with an average annual growth of 7.32%; the number of undergraduates and junior college students enrolled increased to 7.91 million and 28.31 million, with average annual growth rates of 10.4% and 11.2%, respectively; and the number of postgraduates enrolled and current postgraduates increased from 72,500 and 199,000 to 858,000 and 2.731 million, with an annual growth of 13.1% and 14.0%. The admission rate and gross enrollment rate of colleges and universities rose to 80.9% and 48.1%, respectively, and the enrollment rate of college-age population in 2017 was 51.0%. However, due to the rapid expansion of college students and the relatively slow increase in the number of teachers, the student-teacher ratio at colleges and universities rose to 17.56 in 2018. On the whole, both student scale and popularization rate indicate that the number of Chinese colleges and universities has grown at an amazing speed since the reform and opening-up, especially since 1998, and the fastest growing period just coincided with the period following 2000, when China implemented higher education industrialization reform and acceded to the WTO. Thus, the increase in the number of colleges and universities may be related to China's reform and opening-up policy, national economic development, and degree of reform and opening-up to the outside world.

2.4 The development trend and status quo of early childhood education

Due to misunderstandings, China has mistaken early childhood education as childcare work for the purpose of reducing the workload of women

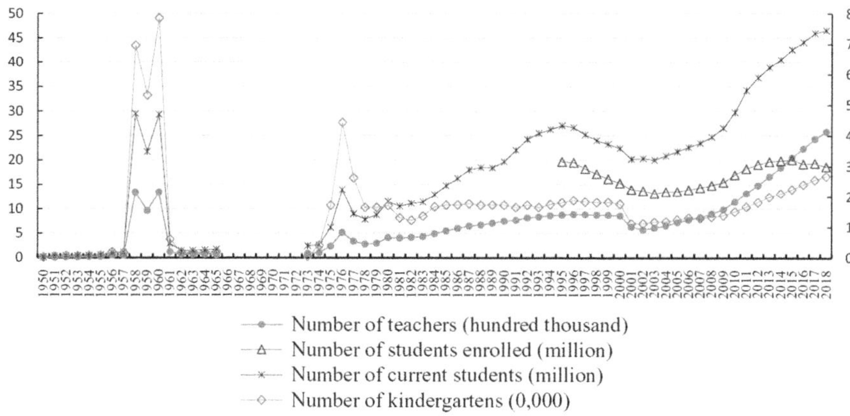

Figure 8.14 Changes in the number of kindergartens and their students and teachers in China: 1950–2018.

(Lv Qin, 2008). Thus, compared with other levels of education, China's early childhood education has been more backward in its development. Firstly, in terms of the number of kindergartens (see Figure 8.14), there were about 1,799 kindergartens in China in 1950, and the number of teachers and current students was 2,000 and 140,000, respectively, less than those of secondary and primary schools in terms of absolute scale. For early childhood education, the student-teacher ratio was 82.4, and the enrollment rate of children was only 0.4%. During the period 1951–1957, the number of kindergartens witnessed a rapid increase, from 1,799 to 16,420, and the number of teachers and current students grew from 50,000 to 1.088 million, respectively, with the student-teacher ratio down 21.76. Affected by the Great Leap Forward and the People's Commune Movement during the years 1958–1960, a climax of education expansion was set off in rural areas. Guided by the slogan "kindergartens and primary schools were everywhere in teams, junior secondary schools in communes, and senior secondary schools in counties," the number of kindergartens throughout the country, especially rural ones, witnessed a dramatic increase, and surged to 695,000 in 1958. The number of teachers and students increased to 1.34 million and 29.501 million, and the student-teacher ratio was only 22.0, with few changes. In 1960, there were 785,000 kindergartens, 1.34 million and 29.331 million teachers and current students, respectively, with the student-teacher ratio being 21.9. As the number of kindergartens grew too fast, and both faculty and material resources, etc., failed to keep up with the times, kindergartens were reduced and adjusted after 1960. In 1961, the number of kindergartens was adjusted to 60,300; the number of teachers and students sharply decreased to 117,000 and 2.896 million; and the student-teacher ratio rose to 24.8. During the period 1962–1965, the number of kindergartens was maintained at 17,000 to 19,000; the number of teachers basically at around 70,000 and the number of current students at around 1.5 million, with the student-teacher ratio rising to 27.6 and the enrollment rate of children reaching 4.2%. Under the influence of the Cultural Revolution after 1966, early childhood education was almost interrupted, and the data on early childhood education for this period were also missing. By 1973, the number of kindergartens had dropped to 4,528, close to the level of 1953; there had been 85,000 and 2.45 million teachers and current students at kindergartens, with the student-teacher ratio rising to 28.8. During the period 1974–1976, the scale of early childhood education saw dramatic expansion. The number of kindergartens increased to 442,700; the number of teachers and current students surged to 514,000 and 13.955 million; and the student-teacher ratio dropped to 27.1. From 1977 to 1978, kindergartens were adjusted again, and the scale of early childhood education was reduced almost by half. In 1978, the number of kindergartens was reduced to 164,000; the number of teachers and current students dropped to 277,000 and 7.877 million; the student-teacher ratio rose to 28.44; and the rate of admission of children to kindergartens was 10.6%.

Overall, during the period 1950–1978, the number of kindergartens increased by approximately 162,000, with an average annual growth of 17.5%; the number of kindergarten teachers grew by 275,000, with an average annual growth of 19.3%; and the number of children at kindergartens increased by 7.73 million, with an average annual growth of 15.5%. Moreover, compared with other levels of education, early children education was still small. The number of current students at kindergartens was 5.4%, 15.8%, and 50.7% of those at primary, junior secondary, and senior secondary schools, respectively, in the same period; the number of children and teachers at kindergartens was 5.3%, 11.3%, and 37.4% of those at primary, junior secondary, and senior secondary schools, respectively; and the enrollment rate of kindergarten-age population was far lower than that of secondary and primary education in the same period (see Table 8.2).

Since the reform and opening-up, China has maintained a rapid growth in childhood education on the whole, with its growth rate far higher than the primary and secondary education in the same period. China's early childhood education following 1978 can be roughly divided into two periods. The first period is 1978–1996 (Figure 8.15). In the early years of the reform and opening-up, the state placed its focus on the popularization of the nine-year compulsory education, and early childhood education was excluded from the scope of compulsory education. Although it was proposed at the National Nursery Work Conference held in 1979 that it was necessary to adhere to the principle of "walking on two legs" and restore, develop, rectify, and improve all types of nursery organizations, early childhood education remained to be positioned at the "childcare" level that reduced the burden over women. Although early childhood education was restored during this period, it achieved little development. The number of kindergartens

Table 8.2 Number of students enrolled and current students at all levels of education of China for previous years: 0,000; %

year	*Kindergartens*	*Primary schools*	*Junior secondary schools*	*Senior secondary schools*	*Colleges and universities*
	Number of schools				
1949	0.180[a]	34.68	0.2448	0.1597	0.0205
1965	1.923	168.19	1.3990	0.4112	0.0434
1978	16.40	94.93	11.3130	4.9215	0.0598
2000	17.58	55.36	6.2704	1.4564	0.1042
2018	26.67	16.18	5.2000	1.3700	0.2663
	Number of teachers				
1949	0.2[a]	83.5	5.2	1.4	1.61
1965	6.2	385.7	37.9	7.8	13.8
1978	27.7	522.6	244.1	74.1	20.6
2000	85.6	586.0	328.7	75.7	46.3
2018	258.1	609.2	363.9	181.3	167.3
	Number of students enrolled				
1949	–	680	34.12	7.11	3.1
1965	–	3,296	299.9	45.9	16.4
1978	–	3,315	2,006.0	692.9	40.2
2000	1,531	1,947	2,263.3	472.7	220.6
2018	1,864	1,867	1,602.6	792.8	791.0
	Number of current students				
1949	14[a]	2,437.5	83.2	20.7	11.9
1965	171.3	11,621	803.0	130.8	67.5
1978	787.7	14,624	4,995.2	1,553.1	85.6
2000	2,244	13,013	6,167.8	1,201.3	556.1
2018	4,656	10,034	4,652.6	2,375.4	2,831

Enrollment rate of school-age population

	Kindergartens	*Primary schools*	*Secondary schools (including junior and senior secondary schools)*	*Colleges and universities*
1970	2.28[b]	107.6	28.00	0.13
1978	8.77	111.6	53.63	0.72
2000	44.07	110.3[c]	59.65	7.62
2017	85.96	102.1	94.3[d]	51.0

Source: *World Development Indicators* of World Bank for the enrollment rate of the school-age population, the CEIC database for other data.

[a] The data of 1952

[b] The data of 1974

[c] The data of 2001

[d] The data of 2015.

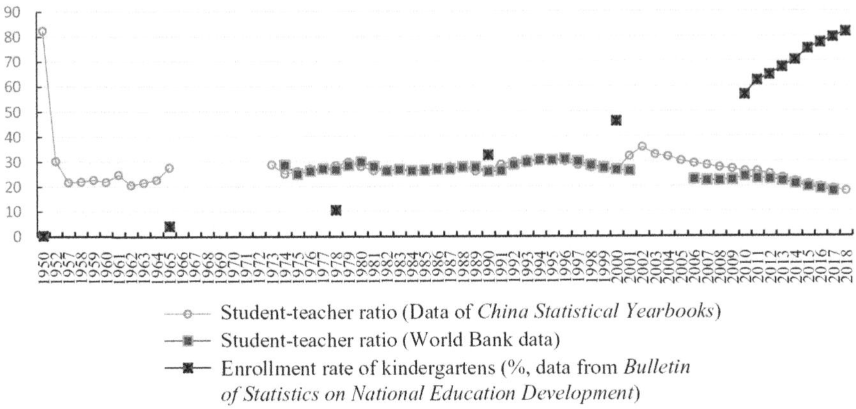

Figure 8.15 Changes in the student-teacher ratio and enrollment rate of China's early childhood education: 1950–2018.

basically fluctuated at around 170,000 and was reduced to around 120,000 to 130,000 during the period 1981–1983. During this period, the number of teachers and students at kindergartens slightly increased; the number of teachers grew from 277,000 in 1978 to 889,000 in 1996; and the number of current students grew from 7.877 million to 46.564 million. The enrollment rate of children at kindergartens reached 32.6% in 1990. The second period is 1997–2001. With economic development and the decrease in the family fertility rate during this period, families paid more and more attention to early childhood education, the orientation of childhood education was lifted from "childcare" to "preschool education," and early childhood education was highlighted by all levels. In fact, the state determined early childhood education to be an important part of socialist education, but also regarded it as part of welfare services as early as 1987 (Lv Ping, 2008) and did not give insufficient attention and support in economics. The *Working Rules for Kindergartens* promulgated by the National Education Commission of China in 1996 formally lifted early childhood education to the level of basic education. However, due to the adjustment of some private kindergartens during the regularization of early childhood education, the number of children at kindergartens in China dropped instead during the period 1997–2001. The number of kindergartens dropped by 175,600, the number of teachers decreased by 259,000, and the number of current students was reduced by 6.445 million. The *Decision on the Deepening of Educational Reform and the Full Promotion of Quality Education* promulgated by 1999 proposed that it is necessary to proactively develop community-based public and private education, formulate favorable policies by catering them to local conditions (such as preferential use of land, exemption of supporting fees), and support private organizations in running schools. Since then, due to the rise of private organizations and private early childhood education, the scale of childhood education has been on the rise, and the number of kindergartens, kindergarten teachers, current students, and students enrolled ushered in a new round of rapid growth. In 2018, the number of kindergartens in China reached 267,000, an increase of 155,000 over that of 2001; the number of kindergarten teachers hit 2.581 million, an increase of 1.951 million over that of 2001; and the number of children enrolled and current students arrived at 18.639 million and 46.564 million, an increase of 1.657 million and 26.346 million over that of 2001. In 2000, the student-teacher ratio in early childhood education dropped from 26.22 in 2000 to 18.04, and the rate of admission of children to kindergartens rose to 81.7%.

Overall, China has achieved tremendous development since the reform and opening-up. During the period 1978–2018, the number of kindergartens in China increased by 62.7%; the number of kindergarten teachers was up 8.3 times; the number of children at kindergartens was up 4.9 times; and the popularization rate of early childhood education was above 80%. However, there was still a gap between early childhood education and other levels of education in terms of quality and popularization rate. According to World Bank data, the enrollment rate of primary school-age population was 102% and that of kindergarten school-age population was 86% in 2017; the number of kindergarten teachers was only 70% of that of junior secondary and 42% of primary secondary school teachers in 2018. And the student-teacher ratio for early childhood education was also the highest among all levels of education, 6.1%, 4.9%, and 34.5% higher than that of primary, junior secondary, and senior secondary schools, respectively. Additionally, the percentage of private education in childhood education was also the highest. According to the data of the *Bulletin of Statistics on National Education Development 2018*, in terms of the current student scale structure of the year, private kindergartens accounted for 49.1% of all kindergartens, and private primary, junior secondary, senior secondary schools, and higher education institutions had a share of 16.4%, 11.8%, 6.1%, and 12.1% of all primary, junior secondary, senior secondary schools, and higher education institutions, respectively.

2.5 Multinational comparisons among all levels of education in China

In terms of the enrollment rate of the school-age population for each level of education, the early childhood education and primary education have basically reached the level of developed countries but there is some development space for secondary and higher education. Overall, the enrollment rate of the school-age population at all levels of education in China was basically at the average of upper-middle income countries but lower than that of high-income countries and EU members (see Table 8.3) in 2016. Specifically, the enrollment rate of kindergarten-age population was 83.7%, lower than the average of EU members, slightly lower than the average of OECD members

Table 8.3 The enrollment rate of the school-age population at all levels of education in major economies of the world, 2016, in %

Country	*Early childhood education*	*Primary education*	*Secondary education*	*Higher education*
China	83.7	100.9	95.0[a]	48.4
India	12.9	114.5	75.2	26.9
Russia	88.7	102.1	104.8	81.8
Brazil	95.7	113.9	101.5	50.5
South Africa	25.5	102.3	100.4	20.5
Egypt	29.9	103.6	85.9	34.4
Mexico	70.6	103.9	97.3	36.9
America	71.9	101.4	98.8	88.8
Japan	86.8	98.2	102.4	63.6
Germany	108.5	103.0	101.9	68.3
Britain	110.9	101.4	152.2	59.4
France	105.1	102.0	103.1	64.4
Italy	98.2	100.4	102.8	63.0
Spain	95.4	103.9	127.9	91.2
Canada	–	101.4	113.0	67.0
Australia	168.6	101.3	153.8	121.9
South Korea	97.9	97.0	99.7	93.8
Turkey	30.3	101.3	103.0	103.7
World average	49.3	104.1	76.8	37.5
Upper-middle income countries	74.1	103.0	93.0	50.7
Middle-income countries	50.4	105.1	78.1	35.0
Lower-middle income countries	34.5	106.4	69.6	24.2
Low-income countries	21.2	100.3	40.9	8.7
Low and middle income countries	44.9	104.3	72.6	31.7
High-income countries	83.2	102.6	108.5	77.1
EU	96.1	102.5	114.3	68.4
OECD	79.7	101.9	106.6	74.4

Source: *World Development Indicators* of World Bank.
[a] The data of 2013.

and upper-middle income countries, and far higher than the average of middle-income countries and the world. In terms of the same, China was inferior to Russia and Brazil, but better than India and South Africa among BRICS countries. The enrollment rate of the primary school-age population in the world was above 104.1%, and that in almost all countries was above 100%. China had the same enrollment rate of primary school-age population with other countries in the world and basically reached the status of saturation. The enrollment rate of secondary schools in China was 95.0%. This figure is lower than the level of European and American developed countries, the average of EU members, high-income countries, and OECD members and even the level of Russia, Brazil, South Africa, and other BRICS countries, and only two percentage points higher than that of upper-middle income countries. The enrollment rate of the school-age population for higher education in China was also significantly low. The figure is generally lower than the level of European and American developed countries, much lower than the average of EU members, high-income countries, and OECD members and the levels of Russia and Brazil among BRICS Countries, and even higher than the average of upper-middle income countries.

Compared with the student-teacher ratios at all levels of education in major economies of the world (see Table 8.4), the student-teacher ratios in

Table 8.4 Student-teacher ratios at all levels of education for major economies in the world, 2016

Country	*Early childhood education*	*Primary school education*	*Secondary education*	*Junior secondary school education*	*Senior secondary school education*	*Higher education*
China	19.1	16.5	13.5	12.3	15.1	16.8
India	20.1[a]	35.2	28.5	27.0	30.2	23.7
Russia	–	20.6	8.8[d]	–	–	10.3
Brazil	16.6	20.3	16.6	17.4	15.6	19.5
South Africa	29.6[b]	30.3[a]	26.8	11.2[e]	–	–
Egypt	26.9	23.1	14.8	16.9	12.6	23.9[b]
Mexico	25.0	26.7	16.3	20.0[a]	11.9[a]	9.7[a]
America	13.8[a]	14.5[a]	14.7[a]	14.7[a]	14.7[a]	12.4[a]
Japan	27.3	15.9	11.2	12.4	10.3	6.9
Germany	7.2	12.1	12.0	11.0	14.5	7.6
Britain	20.0[b]	15.1	19.4	21.3	18.2	15.8
France	20.3[c]	18.2[c]	12.9[c]	14.7[c]	11.2[c]	21.3[c]
Italy	12.0	11.1	10.0	10.2	10.0	20.3
Spain	13.6	13.0	11.6	11.9	11.3	12.0
Canada	–	–	–	–	8.8	9.2
South Korea	13.3	16.3	13.8	14.2	13.6	14.6
Turkey	17.0[a]	18.4[a]	18.5	17.8[a]	19.1[a]	40.7[a]
World average	17.7	23.5	17.1[a]	16.9	17.5	–
Upper-middle income countries	17.3	18.5	14.4	13.8	15.3	–
Middle-income countries	18.1	23.8	18.1	17.2	19.4	–
Lower-middle income countries	19.4	28.7	22.5	21.1	24.5	–
Low-income countries	29.2	39.5	21.9	26.0	16.7	–
High-income countries	14.4	14.2	12.8	13.1	12.5	–
EU	12.7	13.3	12.1	11.9	12.4	–
OECD	15.1	15.5	13.8	14.3	13.4	–

Source: *World Development Indicators* of World Bank.

[a] The data of 2015

[b] The data of 2014

[c] The data of 2013

[d] The data of 2012

[e] The data of 2010.

primary and secondary schools of China were at a more reasonable level and that for early childhood education and higher education were obviously higher. In 2016, the student-teacher ratio for early childhood education in China was obviously higher than the average of high-income countries, EU members, and OECD members, higher than the average of upper-middle income countries and middle-income countries, 1.4 percentage points higher than the world average, slightly lower than the average of middle-income countries, and lower than the level of other BRICS countries except Brazil. At China's primary schools, the student-teacher ratio was 16.5, slightly higher than the average of high-income countries, EU members, and OECD members (15.7), but slower than the average of upper-middle income countries and far lower than the world average, being the lowest among BRICS countries. At China's secondary schools, the student-teacher ratio was 13.5, lower than the average of the world and upper-middle income countries, slightly lower than the average of middle-income countries and EU members but slightly lower than the average of OECD members. At China's colleges and universities, the student-teacher ratio was 16.8, higher than that of other major European and American economies except France and Italy. In terms of the student-teacher ratio, Russia was inferior to China, which was not better than India, Brazil, and South Africa.

Section 3 Changes in education human capital of China

3.1 Changes in the number of graduates from primary, secondary, and technical secondary schools

During the period 1949–1978, the number of primary school graduates in China increased from 646,000 to 22.879 million, with an average annual increase of 13.1%. After 1978, due to changes in the demographic structure, the number of primary school graduates tended to first drop, then rise, and finally decline (see Figure 8.16). In 2018, there were 16.165 million primary school graduates, a decrease of more than six million over 1978.

During the period 1949–1978, the number of junior secondary school graduates increased from 219,000 to 16.926 million, with an average annual growth of 16.2%. During the period 1978–2018, this figure showed a volatile downward trend. In 2018, the number of junior secondary school graduates was 16.165 million, with a decrease of 3.248 million over that of 1978.

During the period 1974–1978, the number of senior secondary school graduates showed an overall upward trend and grew from 61,000 to 6.852 million, with an average annual growth of 22.4%. In the early years of the reform and opening-up, the number of senior secondary school graduates started to decline, reaching a local minimum of 1.966 million in 1985, was basically maintained at 2.2 million to 2.5 million during the period 1986–1997, grew from 2.049 million to 8.361 million from 1997 to 2008, and saw a downward trend afterwards. In 2018, the number of senior secondary school

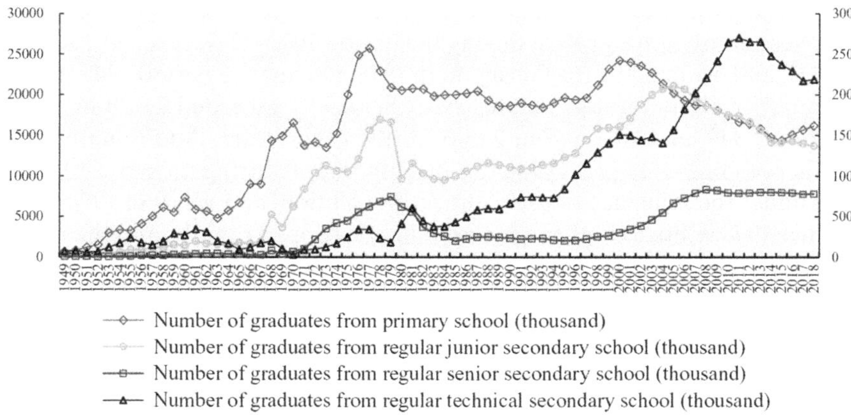

Figure 8.16 Number of graduates from primary, secondary, and technical secondary schools in China: 1949–2018.

graduates reached 7.792 million, an increase of 965,000 compared with that of 1978. However, the number of senior secondary graduates in China, 1979 was abnormal under the impact of the Cultural Revolution and the reform and opening-up. If compared with the minimum of 1985 in the early period of the reform and opening-up, the number of senior secondary graduates in 2018 was up 2.96 times, and the increase was still very significant.

Before the reform and opening-up, the number of graduates from technical secondary schools in China was relatively small, with a large fluctuation range. The number of such graduates was approximately 72,000 in 1949, rose to 340,000 in 1961, dropped to the historical minimum of 28,000 in 1970, rose again to 340,000 in 1977, and reached 232,000 in 1978. Since 1978, the number of graduates from technical secondary schools has increased significantly, also with a lot of volatility. The number of such graduates grew to 605,000, dropped to 375,000 in 1983, rose again to 1.507 million in 2000, dropped to 1.406 million in 2004, increased to the historical peak value of 2.702 million in 2011, and declined again to 2.185 million in 2018. During the period 1978–2018, the number of technical secondary school graduates was up 8.42 times, with an average annual growth of 5.77%. In 2018, it was equivalent to around 28% of the students who graduated from regular senior secondary schools.

3.2 Changes in the number of higher education graduates

Higher education graduates are a symbol of China's technological development and scientific progress. During the period 1949–1978, the number of higher education graduates fluctuated greatly, with a small scale on the whole. In 1949, there were 21,000 undergraduates and junior college graduates, and 107 postgraduates. The number of undergraduate and junior college graduates reached 204,000 in 1964, dropped to 6,000 in 1971, saw a six-year consecutive growth during the period 1972–1977, reached 194,000 in 1977, and dropped to 165,000 again in 1978. During the period 1949–1978, the number of doctoral graduates every year only exceeded 2,000 in 1956, reached 2,349, and was within 2,000 for the other years. Additionally, the number of graduated postgraduates in China was 0 during the period 1970–1977 under the influence of the Cultural Revolution, and was 9 in 1978.

Since 1978, China's higher education has developed rapidly, and the number of undergraduates and junior college graduates was on the rise. The period 1978–2001 was a time when interest in China's higher education resumed but experienced low-speed development. Accordingly, the number of graduated undergraduates, junior college students, and postgraduates during this period witnessed a fluctuating upward trend. The number of undergraduates and junior college students increased from 165,000 to 1.036 million, representing an average increase of 8.32%. After 2001, China's higher education entered a period of rapid growth. Affected by the industrialization of higher education and the enrollment expansion of colleges and universities that started in 1998, the number of undergraduate and junior college graduates has grown at a rate of geometric series. The figure reached 7.533 million in 2018, up 4.47 times over that of 1978, with an average annual increase of 10.0%, and up 6.27 times over that of 2001, with an average annual increase of 12.4% (Figure 8.17).

After the reform and opening-up, the development of postgraduate education in China almost started from scratch. In 1978, the number of graduated postgraduates was only 9, surged to 11,700 in 1981, dropped to 2,756

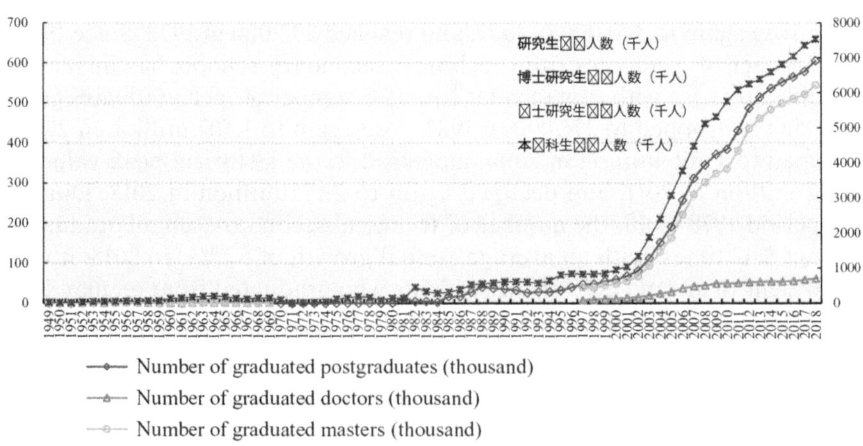

Figure 8.17 Number of graduated undergraduates, junior college students, and postgraduates in China: 1949–2018.

during the period 1982–1984, jumped to 17,000 in 1985, and reached 408,000 in 1988. The number of graduated postgraduates consecutively dropped during the period 1989–1992, dropped to 25,700 in 1992, and then resumed growth afterwards. In 2001, there were 67,800 graduated postgraduates, including 12,900 doctoral graduates and 54,900 master graduates. During the period 1992–2001, the number of graduated postgraduates was up 1.64 times, with an average annual growth of 11.1%. Since China has started to expand its postgraduate enrollment since 1998, the number of graduated postgraduates has also grown at a rate of geometric series since 2001. In 2018, the number of graduated postgraduates reached 604,000, up 7.91 times compared with that of 2001 and representing an average annual growth of 14.7%, including 60,700 doctors, up 3.71 times compared with that of 2001 and representing an average annual growth of 9.54%; and 544,000 masters, up 8.90 times compared with that of 2001 and representing an average annual growth of 14.4%.

3.3 National average length of education

With the expansion of education at all levels in China and the increase in the number of students enrolled and graduates, the average length of education for China's working population has gradually increased and the country's education human capital has continued to increase. Using the data of the *China Statistical Yearbooks* and *Collection of Statistical Data for New China during the 50 Years of Its Founding*, two methods were used to estimate the average length of education for the population over 15 years old during the period 1982–2017 (see Figure 8.18). It can be seen that, no matter which calculation method is adopted, the increase in the average length of education of China was quite obvious. According to the calculation results of China's provincial aggregate data, the average length of education for the population over 15 years old in 1982 was approximately 5.27 years, equivalent to

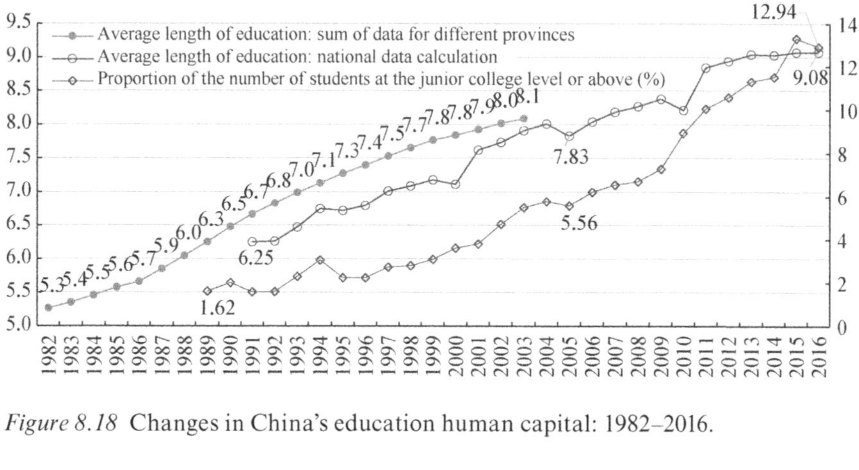

Figure 8.18 Changes in China's education human capital: 1982–2016.

the level of graduates from Grade 5 of the primary school; and rose to 8.09 years in 2003, equivalent to the second-year level for the junior secondary school in the 9-year education program. According to the calculation results based on the national data from the *China Statistical Yearbooks*, the average annual length of education for the population over 15 years old was 6.25 years in 1991, 0.41 year less than the result (6.66 years) calculated by summing the province-wise data; rose to 7.91 years in 2003, 0.18 year less than the result calculated by summing the province wise data; and increased to 9.08 years in 2016, approximately equivalent to the compulsory education level in the 9-year program. The average length of education for the population over 15 years old in 2016 increased by 70% compared with that of 1982.

Barro and Lee (2013) calculated the average length of education for the population over 15 years old in the world's major economies during the period 1950–2010 (see Figure 8.19). Compared with the author's calculation results based on the data of the *China Statistical Yearbooks*, the value of Barro and Lee (2013) was much higher in early years, and the author's calculation data was higher in recent years, with the error between the two basically within one year. According to the calculation results of Barro and Lee (2013), the average length of education for the population over 15 years old in China was 1.61 year in 1955 and rose to 5.31 years in 1980. The figure shows that, during the early period of the reform and opening-up, the population above 15 years old in China reached the level of graduation from primary schools, and the 5-year primary school education was basically popularized before the reform and opening-up. Through the calculations by Barro and Lee (2013), the average length of education for the population over 15 years old in 2010 was 7.95 years, with an increase of 50% compared with that of 1980. All the above calculation results show that, since the reform and opening-up, the average length of education for the population over 15 years old in China has greatly increased, showing the significant improvement in China's education human capital.

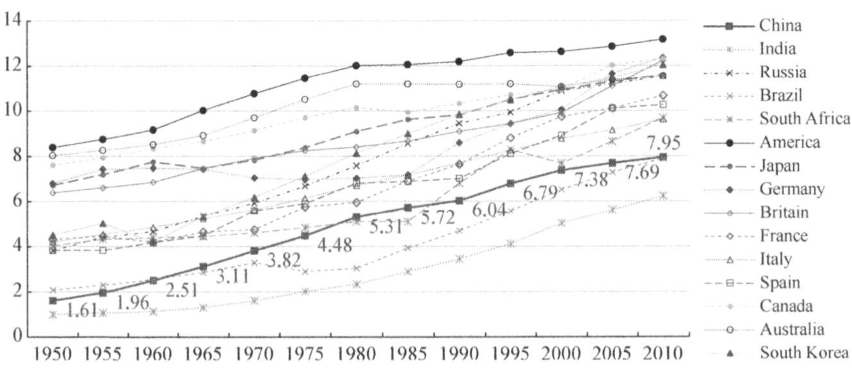

Figure 8.19 Changes in the average length of education for the population over 15 years old in major economies of the world.

3.4 Multinational comparisons on the average length of education

According to the calculation results of Barro and Lee (2013), the average length of education for 24 developed countries in 2010 was 11.30 years. Among these countries, the figure of America was 13.18 years; that of Germany, Britain, Canada, South Korea, and other developed countries was all above 12 years; and that of Italy was short, only 9.62 years. According to the author's calculations, in 2016, the average length of education for people over 15 years old in China was only 9.08 years, which was only equivalent to the level of America during the period 1955–1960, the level of Australia and Canada during the period 1965–1970, the level of Japan during the period 1975–1980, and the level of Britain, Russia, and South Korea during the period 1985–1990. Among the BRICS countries, in 2010, the average length of education for the population over 15 years old in Russia reached the average level of developed countries, 11.53 years; that of South Africa was 9.69 years, higher than that of Italy in developed countries; that of Brazil was 7.89 years, close to the level of 2010 in China; and that of India was quite short, only 6.24 years. Additionally, in 2010, the average length of education for the population over 15 years old in the world was 7.89 years and that in developing countries was 7.20 years. It can be seen according to the data of Barro (2013) that China's average length of education in 2010 remained low, only 0.06 year higher than the average of the world (Figure 8.20).

The calculation results of Barro and Lee (2013) are only up to 2010. According to the previous analysis, China's education level per capita was still developing rapidly during the period 2010–2016. Is China's average

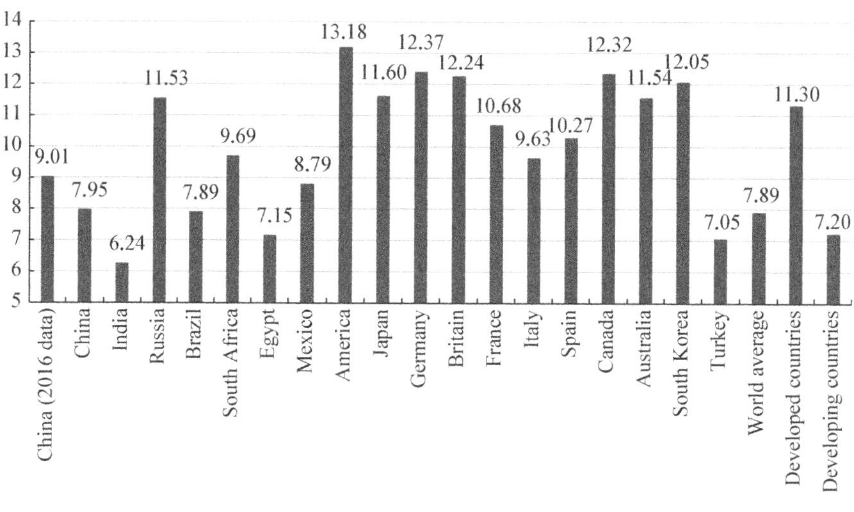

Figure 8.20 The average length of education for the population over 15 years old in the world's major economies of 2010.

current education level close to that of developed countries? As can be known from Figure 8.18, in 2016, the average length of education for the population over 15 years old in China was 9.07 years. Even without regard for the fact that the estimated data in the *China Statistical Yearbooks* was much higher than that of Barro and Lee (2013), China's average length of education of 9.07 years was 2.25 years less than the average of developed countries in 2010. Additionally, according to Figure 8.20, the education level per capita of developed countries in 2016 may still have been improving. Even if China's average length of education in 2016 was 9.07 years, this was only equivalent to the level of America during the period 1955–1960; that of Australia and Canada during the period 1965–1970; that of Japan during the period 1975–1980; and that of Britain, Russia, and South Korea during the period 1985–1990. Also, compared with developed countries, China still has a shorter average length of education, which should be vigorously increased.

Notes

1 The public fiscal education expenditure for the period 1952–1992 refers to the education expenditure within the national fiscal budget, including education expenses, research funds, infrastructure costs, and other expenditures. The public fiscal education expenditure for the period 1992–2012 includes education expenses, infrastructure costs, education surcharges, research funds, and other expenditures. Since 2012, it has included education expenses, infrastructure expenditures, and education surcharges.

2 According to the *China Statistical Yearbook 2017*, the national fiscal education expenditure includes public fiscal budget for education, taxes, and fees collected by governments at all levels for the purpose of education, appropriations by enterprises to the schools they run, the education expenditure resulting from the income of school-run industries and social services, as well as other government expenditures on education. And according to the calculation method in the table of the *China Statistical Yearbook 2017*, the total national education expenditure investment includes national fiscal education expenditure, sponsors' investments in private schools, social donations, institutional fees, and other education expenditures.

3 Full-time teachers refer to teachers who teach students, excluding school administration and logistics service personnel (hereinafter referred to as "teachers").

4 The net primary enrollment rate for primary schools refers to the percentage of the school-age population receiving primary education over the total population of the age group receiving primary education specified by the state. It is calculated according to the different ages of admission and education systems of different regions.

5 The enrollment rate of school-age population at each level of school refers to the number of registered students at each level of school divided by the total population suitable for the education level. The over 100% enrollment rate of the primary school-age population may be due to China's relative deficiency in early childhood education. In many places, a lot of children went to primary school before they reached the age. Another possible reason lies in the fact that many over-age students continued their primary education as the grade-repetition system remained in the early period of the reform.

6 Other schools include vocational secondary schools and secondary specialized schools (or technical secondary schools and secondary normal schools).
7 The gross enrollment rate refers to the percentage of the total number of current students regardless of age at the corresponding level of education in the total population of the age group specified by the state. Due to the inclusion of students in informal age groups (lower or over-aged), the gross enrollment rate may exceed 100%. The data in the article come from *Bulletins of Statistics on National Education Development*.
8 During the period 1978–1985, the number of primary and secondary school students dropped sharply. There are three main reasons behind it. First, the implementation of the rural household contract responsibility system reduced the revenues of rural collective organizations, which caused many primary and secondary schools initially set up by rural collectives to be merged or cancelled. The far distance from school causes many rural students to drop out. Second, the decline in revenues of rural collective organizations also made the tuition subsidies initially provided by collective organizations cancelled, and schools' tuition and miscellaneous fees were almost entirely borne by students themselves. The financial burden of students going to school increased. Third, the household contract responsibility system allowed children to engage in agricultural work as family labor, which also caused students to drop out of school. Under the influence of these factors, the number of primary and secondary schools and kindergartens in China, especially the number of secondary schools and their teachers, also experienced a rapid decline in the early period of the reform.
9 The admission rate of colleges and universities is equal to the number of students admitted to colleges and universities divided by the number of the applicants, and the progression rate of senior secondary school graduates is equal to the number of students admitted to colleges and universities divided by the number of senior secondary school graduates. Due to the existence of repeat students and senior secondary school graduates who did not take the college entrance examination that year, both data are not necessarily equal.

Reference

[1] Zhang, C. W. (2006). Changes in return rate of human capital and income disparities: Matthew's effect and its policy implications. *Economic Research Journal*, Issue 12.

9 Contribution of China's education development to economic growth

Section 1 Why education makes less significant contribution to China's economic growth

The analysis in Chapter 8 showed that China has achieved great development in education since 1949, especially since the reform and opening-up in 1978. According to the new growth theory human capital is one of the main drivers for a country's economic growth, and the difference in human capital among countries in the world is one of the major factors causing a gap in the income per capita among the countries (Lucas, 1988). A lot of empirical studies have also demonstrated that, during the economic development of countries, the improvement of human capital, as measured by the average length of education, produces a significant positive effect on economic growth, as shown in Table 9.1. According to both theories above, China's education development should result in an important contribution to its economy. However, many empirical studies on Chinese education believe that the increase in the average length of education of China produces no significant effect on China's output per capita, and some studies even hold that the increase in China's education level has a negative impact on the economic growth. For example, Shen and Geng (2001) and Lin and Liu (2003) et al. all believe that the increase in China's human capital produces no significant promoting effect on economic growth. Zhang et al. (2010) even believe that the increase in China's average length of education produces an inhibitory effect on output per capita. Does the improvement of China's education level really produce no promoting effect on the country's economic growth? What is the reason China's human capital plays an insignificant effect on the country's economic growth?

It should be pointed out that both the human capital theory and the new economic growth theory emphasize that human capital refers to the one entering the field of production when it produces an effect on output and economic growth. If the education level of the whole society is improved but the added human capital does not really enter the field of production, the improvement of education level may not help promote economic growth but may produce a negative impact on economic growth from the perspective of the whole society (Romer, 1999, p.149). Baumol (1990) also believes that

DOI: 10.4324/9781003261629-12

Table 9.1 Estimated results on the effect of the average length of education on economic growth in the foreign literature

Author	*Number of countries (or regions)*	*Period of survey*	*Main conclusions*
Barro and Lee (1994)	116	1965–1975 (85) 1975–1985 (95)	Once the average length of education for men at secondary schools (initial value) increases by one year, the GDP growth rate per capita will increase by 1.4 percentage points.
Barro (1998)	100	1965–1990	For men aged 25 years and above, once the average length of education at secondary schools and above increases by one year, the GDP growth rate per capita will increase by 1.2 percentage points.
Krueger and Lindahl (2001)	42	1988–1992 (different years in different countries)	Once the length of education per capita increases by one year, the GDP growth rate per capita will grow by 0.7 to 0.9 percentage point.
Temple (2002)	78	1960–1987	Once the average length of education for workers increases by one year, the output per capita will increase by 1.3%.

if the most talented people in society are engaged in activities such as military conquests, political and religious leadership, tax collection, criminal activities, financial transactions, and manipulation of law, the production efficiency of such human capital will be quite low. This is because not only do these activities produce few social benefits, some of which are even negative, but these activities are also generally rent-seeking behaviors. They are essentially trying to grab rather than create wealth; so, they are of negative externality for the whole production process. Baumol also points out that how society guides talents with human capital to enter different sectors of the society is key to determining whether the talents with high human capital can play a productive role. From this point of view and with regard to the craze for being civil servants in China during the past 10 years, as well as the fact that talents with high education backgrounds are keen to enter government departments, state-owned enterprises, and public institutions, etc., the increase in China's human capital has no significant promoting effect on economic growth. Is it also related to the fact that China's talents with high education backgrounds are keen to enter these sectors or to the configuration of human capital in the public sector and the production departments?

Judged from the changes in China's labor market, the wage gap and labor structure between China's public and private sectors in the past 20 years

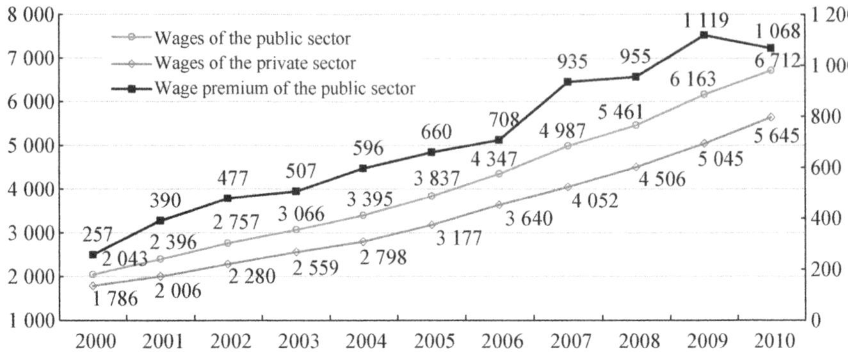

Figure 9.1 Changes in the average real wages of public and private sectors of China during the period 2000–2010.

have undergone significant changes. On the one hand, the wage gap between the public and private sectors has widened year by year.[1] Figure 9.1 shows the average wage level of the public and private sectors in China, as well as the wage gap between the public and private sectors (hereinafter referred to as the "wage premium of the public sector") during the period 2000–2010.[2] As can be seen from the figure, the average wage of the public sector was always higher than that of the private sector during the period 2000–2010, and the absolute gap between the two was gradually widening. On the other hand, due to the wage premium of the public sector, the proportion of talents with high- and mid-level backgrounds in the public sector has continued to increase; more talents with higher education backgrounds would like to enter the public sector, and frequent applications for civil servants have occurred. The incomplete segmentation of the labor market between the public and private sectors has caused the long-term existence of the wage premium of the public sector. As a result, highly educated talents have continued to flow into the public sector, and the proportion of human capital in the public sector in the total human capital of the economy (hereinafter referred to as the "proportion of human capital in the public sector") has gradually improved. Since the productivity of human capital in China's public sector is generally lower than that of the private sector,[3] will the changes in the human capital allocation structures of the country's public and private sectors affect the effect of China's education over economic growth? Or, more specifically, will the wage premium of the public sector relate to the low effect of China's education on the economic growth aforementioned? This chapter will begin by looking at the new research perspective on the effect of the department allocation structure of human capital, use the wage premium of the public sector as a proxy variable to estimate the effect of the increase in the length of education on economic growth, and make a comparative analysis of the rate of return on education between China and other countries, and among different regions in China.

Compared with previous studies, the research in this chapter has the following two characteristics. Firstly, the analysis in this chapter shows that the allocation structure of human capital between the public and private sectors is very important for the effect of education on economic growth. China's persistent wage premium of the public sector has caused a continuous increase in the proportion of human capital in the public sector, a decrease in the proportion of the laborers with a longer length of education for the production department in the entire economy, and decreased the contribution of education to economic growth as a whole. In previous studies, ignoring the impact of changes in the allocation structure of human capital in the public and private sectors on the contribution to the growth of the education economy may be the main reason why the conclusion that the rate of return on China's education is too low is drawn. Secondly, after excluding the impact of the wage premium of the public sector on the human capital allocation structure and other factors, the research in this chapter shows that the increase in the length of education of China produces a significant positive effect on economic growth. The structure of the subsequent parts of this chapter is as follows: the second part establishes the econometric model studied in this chapter describes and explains the main proxy variables used in econometric analysis and the sources and characteristics of the data in this chapter; the third part gives the results of the econometric analysis along with economics explanations; the fourth part analyzes the gap between China and other countries in terms of the rate of return on education based on the studies in the third part, and estimates the difference in the rate of return in education among different regions of China; and the fifth part is the main conclusions of this chapter, the possible deficiencies in the research of this chapter, and the problems to be studied in the future.

Section 2 Basic assumptions, theoretical models, econometric equations, and data descriptions

2.1 Main assumptions

For facilitation of analysis, this chapter makes two theoretical assumptions according to China's reality:

Firstly, in the labor market, there is a significant difference in the contribution of human capital to productivity in the public and private sectors. The studies in the existing literature show that only the increase in the level of human capital that directly enters the field of production can promote output and economic growth (Schundeln & Playforth, 2008). Most of the human capital in the public sector is engaged in non-productive activities, which would not directly affect output per capita and economic growth.

Table 9.2 Average wages of the public and private sectors in all regions during the period 2000–2010, in yuan

	Wage of the public sector	*Wage of the private sector*	*t-value in one-tailed test*	*p-value in one-tailed test*
2000	2043.0 (89.61)	1786.2 (93.34)	1.985	0.026
2001	2396.0 (111.78)	2005.7 (105.71)	2.536	0.007
2002	2757.3 (128.70)	2279.9 (112.63)	2.791	0.004
2003	3066.1 (154.75)	2558.9 (125.63)	2.545	0.007
2004	3394.6 (180.98)	2798.2 (133.59)	2.651	0.005
2005	3836.7 (207.70)	3176.9 (148.25)	2.586	0.006
2006	4347.2 (231.46)	3639.6 (171.04)	2.459	0.009
2007	4987.2 (258.67)	4052.2 (200.91)	2.855	0.003
2008	5460.5 (281.62)	4505.8 (233.67)	2.609	0.006
2009	6163.0 (311.92)	5044.5 (250.05)	2.798	0.004
2010	6712.4 (335.43)	5644.9 (279.64)	2.444	0.009
All the years	4105.8 (106.47)	3408.4 (86.64)	5.080	0.000

Note: ①The values in the brackets of the second and third columns are the corresponding standard deviations; ② The last two columns give the results of the overall mean difference test. Zero assumption: wages of the public sector=wages of the private sector, alternative assumption: wages of the public sector>wages of the private sector.

For simplification of the model, assume that the human capital of the public sector is not included in the production function.

Secondly, as mentioned earlier, there has been a significant gap in wages between the public and private sectors of China, and this gap has continued to widen in nearly 10 years from 2000 to 2010. Table 9.2 gives the statistical test of the wage premium of the public sector in China during the period 2000–2010. The results show that the p-value of the one-tailed test for the wage premium of the public sector each year was less than 0.01 and indicate that the wage level of China's public sector continued to be higher than that in the private sector. The theory of personal rational choice suggests that labor forces will flow into high-wage sectors. Thus, this chapter assumes that the wage premiums of the public sector and private sector are the main factors affecting the flow of human capital into the public sector. Additionally, due to the incomplete flow of labor forces between the public and private sectors in China, this chapter assumes that the mobility of labor force lags behind wage adjustment (i.e., the amount of human capital flowing into the public sector in the current period is affected by the wage premium of the public sector for the previous year). The higher the wage premium in the previous period the more human capital flowing into the public sector in the current period and the lower proportion of human capital in the private sector.

2.2 Theoretical models and econometric equations

Based on the two assumptions, further assume the aggregate production function takes the form of Cobb-Douglas.

$$Y_t = A_t K_t^{\beta_1} (H_t^p)^{\beta_2} L_t^{\beta_3} \tag{9.1}$$

where *Y* refers to output; *K* refers to material capital; *Hp* refers to human capital in the private sector; *L* refers to labor; and *t* refers to the period. Assuming that the returns to scale for the production function are constant,

$$\beta_1 + \beta_2 + \beta_3 = 1 \tag{9.2}$$

Assuming the total amount of human capital of the whole society is *H*, and the proportion of human capital in the private sector is θ, or

$$H_t^p = \theta_t H_t \tag{9.3}$$

Since θ_t is mainly determined by the proportions of workers at all levels of education entering the private sector, the total human capital in the private sector can be constructed if the data on the average length of education in the public sector or its change are available in order to directly test the impact of the human capital allocation structure in the public and private sectors on output and economic growth. Unfortunately, there is no way for us to obtain the data related to $\theta_{t.}$ However, the impact of θ_t can be indirectly investigated according to the wage premium of the public sector. According to the second basic assumption above, the wage premium of the public sector for the previous period is an important factor determining θ_t. Due to the incomplete flow of labor forces between the public and private sectors, the total human capital of the public sector for the previous period is also one of the main factors affecting the education human capital for the current period. Additionally, θ_t may also be affected by other factors. Thus, assume:

$$\theta_t = f(\theta_{t-1}, \Delta w_{t-1}, Z_t) \tag{9.4}$$

where Δw_{t-1} represents the wage premium of the public sector for the period t_1 and Z_t represents other factors. Without prejudice to generality, assume:

$$\ln\theta_t = \alpha\ln\theta_{t-1} + \gamma\Delta w_{t-1} + \delta Z_t \tag{9.5}$$

According to the assumptions above, $\gamma<0$ applies. Substitute Equation (9.3) into Equation (9.1), and then we can get:

$$Y_t = A_t K_t^{\beta_1} (\theta_t H_t)^{\beta_2} (L_t)^{\beta_3} \tag{9.6}$$

Divide both sides of Equation (9.6) by L and take the logarithms, and then get the following equation by using Equation (9.5):

$$\begin{aligned}\ln y_t = \alpha\ln y_{t-1} + \beta_1\ln k_t - \alpha\beta_1\ln k_{t-1} + \beta_2(\ln\theta_t - \alpha\ln\theta_{t-1})\\ + \beta_2(\ln h_t - \alpha\ln h_{t-1}) + \ln A_t - \alpha\ln A_{t-1}\end{aligned} \tag{9.7}$$

By subtracting $\ln y_{t-1}$ from both sides of Equation (9.7), we can get the determination equation for the economic growth rate:

$$\begin{aligned}g_{y,t} = (\alpha-1)\ln y_{t-1} + \beta_1\ln k_t - \alpha\beta_1\ln k_{t-1} + \gamma\beta_2 wd_{t-1} + \delta\beta_2 Z_{t-1}\\ + \beta_2\ln h_t - \alpha\beta_2\ln h_{t-1} + \ln A_t - \alpha\ln A_{t-1}\end{aligned} \tag{9.8}$$

where g_y represents the growth rate of output per capita. If the proportion of human capital in the public sector remains unchanged (or $\theta_t=\theta_{t-1}$; i.e., $\alpha=1$, $\gamma=0$ and $\delta=0$), Equation (9.8) is simplified as follows:

$$g_{y,t} = \beta_1 g_{k,t} + \beta_2 g_{h,t} + g_A \tag{9.9}$$

where g_k, g_h, and g_A represent the growth rate of material capital per capita, the growth rate of human capital per capita, and the rate of technological advancement, respectively. Thus, if the proportion of human capital in the public sector remains unchanged, the total human capital of the whole society can also be used to estimate the contribution of education to economic growth. However, θ_t will change in general cases. Thus, there will be deviations if Equation (9.9) is applied to estimate the contribution of education to economic growth.

If the proportion of human capital in the public sector remains unchanged, the econometric equation I can be obtained according to Equation (9.9):

$$g_{y,it} = \alpha_0 + \alpha_1 g_{k,it} + \alpha_2 g_{h,it} + \sum_{i=1}^{n} \beta_i X_{i,t} + \mu_i + \varepsilon_{i,t} \tag{9.10}$$

where i refers to the province; $\varepsilon_{i,t}$ refers to the time-varying error term; α_0, α_1, α_2, and β_i are all parameters to be estimated; and $X_{i,t}$ is a group of control variables and also a non-observational effect of province i that does not change with time.

If the proportion of human capital in the public sector changes and θ_t is determined by Equation (9.5), the econometric equation II can be obtained according to Equation (9.8):

$$g_{yi,t} = \alpha_0 + \alpha_1 \ln y_{i,t-1} + \alpha_2 \ln k_{it} + \alpha_3 \ln k_{i,t-1} + \alpha_4 h_{i,t} + \alpha_5 h_{i,t-1} + \alpha_6 \Delta w_{i,t-1} + \sum_{i=1}^{n} \beta_i X_{i,t} + \mu_i + \varepsilon_{i,t} \tag{9.11}$$

According to the above analysis, the coefficient α_6 of $\Delta w_{i,\ t-1}$ in Equation (9.11) represents the effect of the public sector premium on the proportion of human capital in the private sector, which should be significantly less than 0; the coefficient $\alpha 4$ of $hi,\ t$ represents the contribution of education to economic growth, which should be significantly larger than 0.

When the assumption condition Equation (9.5) is tenable, without regard for the difference of public and private sectors in human capital productivity or the fact that the econometric regression Equation (9.10) is used to estimate the contribution of human capital on economic growth, serious endogenous problems would be caused due to the omission of variables. That's because, as seen from the econometric Equation (9.11), higher wage premium of the public sector for the previous period means lower proportion of human capital in the production field, thus lowering the effect of education on output level and economic growth. Thus, the wage premium of the public sector would affect the economic growth correlation. Also, statistical analysis indicates that the coefficient of correlation between the length of education and the wage premium of the public sector for the previous period is 0.1107, which is significant at the level of 10%. Thus, higher wage premium of the public sector in the previous period means higher education level per capita in the economy. The positive correlation between the length of education and the wage premium of the public sector in the previous period may be due to the fact that the high wage premium of the public sector has intensified the competition for workers to enter the public sector, thus increasing the educational background requirements for entering the public sector. Also, due to the attraction of the high wage premium, laborers have the desire for higher education in order to get employed in the public sector and reach the education background threshold for employment in the public sector or obtain an educational advantage over other applicants. Certainly, there may be other factors in the economy that enable the positive correlation between the length of education and the wage premium in the previous period.

2.3 Data sources, main variables, and their statistical characteristics

In this chapter, the inter-provincial panel data of 29 provinces in China during the period 2000–2010 is selected for research. Due to the lack of the data for years in the Tibet Autonomous Region, this data are excluded from the sample data. Considering the historical origin and in order to maintain the consistency with the estimated results of the existing material capital stock, Chongqing and Sichuan are combined into one region.

There are four main variables in the regression model of this chapter, namely output per capita (ln*y*), wage premium of the public sector (Δw), human capital per capita (*h*), and material capita per capita (In*k*). Output per capita (In*y*) is directly used as a proxy variable in the form of the logarithm of the real GDP per capita of each province in China. The data on real GDP per capita in each province before 2008 can be obtained from the *Collection of Statistical Data for New China During the 60 Years of Its Founding* and the data for the period after 2008 from the *China Statistical Yearbooks*. For material capital per capita, the material capital for each province in China is directly used as its proxy variable and is not directly available. Starting from the data on the material capital of each province in 2000, estimated by Zhang et al. (2004), this chapter uses the estimation method of Zhang et al. (2004) to estimate the real material capital stock per capita of each province during the period 2000–2010 by reference to the data on the investment amount of each province released in the *China Statistical Yearbooks*. GDP growth rate per capita (g_y) and the growth rate of material capital per capita can be obtained according to the data above. The proxy variables of the wage premium of the public sector and their data are easy to obtain. In this chapter, the premium of the public sector relative to the national average wage is used as a proxy variable for the variable.[4] It is calculated by using the number of employees and average labor remunerations and adjusted by using the price index. The raw data on this variable come from the *China Labor Statistical Yearbooks*. Since the wage premium of the public sector adopts the wage premium of the public sector for the previous period, the wage premium for the previous period is represented by $L\Delta w$. For any variable, the one for the previous period is expressed by this variable plus *L*.

In the existing literature, the length of education is generally used to measure human capital, but there is debate over the specific form of its proxy variable. In some of the early literature, the average weighted length of education per capita is used as the proxy variable of human capital (h) in the production function. However, Topel (1999) believes that the human capital based on micro aggregation should take the linear form of the length of education rather than be included in the regression equation Formula (9.9) in the logarithmic form. Thus, if education level per capita is represented by *sch*, human capital per capita will be represented by h=exp $\{sch\}$. In this chapter, the research by Krueger and Lindahl (2001) and Canton et al. (2005) is also used and exp$\{sch\}$ is used as the proxy variable of human capital per capita.[5] Thus, the growth rate of human capital per capita is expressed by the increment of the average length of education, or $\Delta \ln h$=Δsch. Regarding the specific calculation of the average length of education (*sch*), the method of Chen et al. (2004) is adopted in this chapter, i.e. in terms of the average length of education, 16 years for laborers graduating from college and above, 12 years for laborers graduating from senior secondary school (including technical secondary school), 9 years for laborers graduating from junior secondary school, 6 years for laborers graduating from

Table 9.3 Descriptive statistics of variables

Variables	*Observed value*	*Average*	*STDEV*	*Minimum*	*Maximum*
g_y	290	0.1078	0.2399	0.0237	0.2119
g_k	290	0.1392	0.0443	−0.0027	0.3298
Δsch	290	0.1200	0.2213	−0.5791	0.8141
LΔw	290	2.9573	4.6009	−1.809	34.821
patent	319	8.6445	1.4672	4.8203	12.371
pteacher	319	2.7259	0.1744	2.24314	3.1757
rexpgdp	319	0.17412	0.2053	0.01483	0.9053

Note: The wage is measured in ten thousand yuan.

primary school, and 0 for illiterate laborers. Find the number of labor forces at different education levels in each province in the *China Labor Statistical Yearbooks*, and then multiply the number of people at each education level by the corresponding length of education, which is divided by the total population of each region after summation to get the length of education per capita.

According to the research on the factors affecting China's economic growth by Wang et al. (2006), Qian et al. (2010), Zhang et al. (2010), and Wang et al. (2008) and in consideration of the availability of related data, three variables including technological advancement, education quality, and degree of openness are mainly selected in this chapter as control variables in the robustness test. With respect to technological advancement, the logarithm of the number of patent applications in each region is used as a proxy variable and can accurately reflect the level of technological advancement in a region. For education quality, the logarithm of the student-teacher ratio (pteacher) that lags behind for ten years is used as a proxy variable (Zhang et al., 2010). Both data are sourced from the *Collection of Statistical Data for New China During the 60 Years of Its Founding*. The degree of opening-up to the outside world (rexpgdp) refers to the proportion of the total value of imported and exported goods in GDP and is sourced from the *China Statistical Yearbooks*. Table 9.3 gives the statistical characteristics of some key variable data and their correlations.

Section 3 Empirical research results

3.1 Benchmark model

First, this section is arranged according to the existing literature. Under the assumption of ignoring the changes in the human capital allocation structure, Equation (9.10) is used to estimate the contribution of human capital to economic growth. The columns of Table 9.4 give the results obtained by using four methods including OLS regression, fixed effects (FE), random effects (RE), and instrumental variable (IV). Table 9.4 shows that, in terms

Table 9.4 Regression results without regard for the wage premium of the public sector: the explained variable is g_y.

Model	①*Regression equation (9.10): basic variable*				②*Regression equation (9.10): incorporation of control variables*			
Econometric method	*OLS*	*FE*	*RE*	*IV*	*OLS*	*FE*	*RE*	*IV*
g_k	0.346***	0.277***	0.304***	0.274***	0.354***	0.284***	0.306***	0.278***
	(15.758)	(9.687)	(12.031)	(9.671)	(14.752)	(9.578)	(11.544)	(9.471)
!sch	0.006	0.007	0.007	0.017**	0.006	0.006	0.006	0.017**
	(1.224)	(1.589)	(1.521)	(2.239)	(1.185)	(1.415)	(1.469)	(2.331)
Patent					0.002**	0.004	0.002	0.003
					(1.975)	(1.213)	(1.416)	(0.935)
Pteacher					−0.008	−0.003	−0.006	−0.001
					(−1.396)	(−0.235)	(−0.679)	(−0.134)
Rexpgdp					−0.001	−0.001	−0.005	−0.004
					(−0.222)	(−0.066)	(−0.554)	(−0.208)
_cons	0.074***	0.084***	0.066***		0.066***	0.022	0.047**	
	(16.931)	(17.075)	(12.939)		(3.734)	(0.539)	(2.042)	
N	290	290	290	290	290	290	290	290
F	41.347	34.201		33.718	33.330	26.823		26.385
LM value				85.6***				89.4***
Wald F−value				60.766				64.16
				(19.930)				(19.930)
Sargan value				0.816				1.21
				(0.366)				(0.271)

Note: ①"***", "**" and "*" indicate significance at the levels of 1%, 5% and 10% respectively; ② The LM value corresponds to the Anderson canon corr. LM statistic in the identifiable test, and its p-values are in parentheses. The Wald F-value corresponds to the Cragg-Donald Wald F-statistic in the weak instrumental variable test, and the threshold value of the test at the significance level of 10% is in parentheses. The p-value of Sargan value is in its parentheses. The other numbers in parentheses are the corresponding *t*-statistics (the same as below). ③ The null hypothesis of the equation identifiable test is that the instrumental variable is not identifiable; the null hypothesis of the weak instrumental variable test is that the instrumental variable is weakly correlated with the endogenous variable; the null hypothesis of the Sargan test is that the instrumental variable is over-identified. ④ The p-value in the Hausman's test is 0.87, indicating that random effects are more appropriate. ⑤ In the instrumental variable method, the added value of the number of graduates from colleges and universities and the lag and difference terms of the education level are used as instrumental variables. The notes in Table 9.5 below are the same and are omitted here. It is the same case with the following tables.

of the results of OLS, FE, and RE, regardless of whether the control variable is added, there will not be much change to the coefficient and significance of each key variable. And the same with the regression result of the existing literature; the regression coefficient of the increment for the length of education is insignificant. According to the previous analysis, the reason may lie in the fact that the total social human capital is used in the regression equation as the proxy variable of human capital for the output department. Since the proportion of human capital in the public sector will remain unchanged, there are serious endogenous problems when using Equation (9.10) for regression. Thus, although this result is not in line with economic intuition, it is consistent with the theoretical prediction result of this chapter.

Since the omission of variables in the econometric Equation (9.10) may cause endogenity, the IV method is used in this chapter to estimate Equation (9.10). The regression results are shown in the fourth column of Models ① and ② in Table 9.4. Table 9.4 shows that, first, the instrumental variable is identifiable and not weakly identified, so it can be assumed that there is no over-identification (the p-value in the Sargan test is larger than 0.05), with a reasonable instrumental variable; second, regardless of whether other control variables are added, the effect of the increase in the length of education on economic growth is significantly positive, and the regression coefficients do not change much. This shows again that the counterintuitive results of the first three columns of regression coefficients are due to the fact the endogenous problem caused by the omission of variables is ignored.

3.2 Considering the changes in the proportion of effective human capital

The effect of the increase in the length of education on economic growth following the incorporation of the human capital department allocation structure is examined below. That is, the econometric regression Equation (9.11) is used to estimate the contribution of education to economic growth. The regression results are shown in Table 9.5. The p-value in the Hausman test is 0.1265, indicating the FE model may be more appropriate. However, for the purpose of comparison, the regression results of FE are also given in Table 9.5. The table shows the following: firstly, the coefficient of the wage premium of the public sector in the previous period is significantly negative. That means higher wage premium of the public sector for the previous period means lower economic growth rate for the current period. This is consistent with the expectations of the theoretical model. That's because the increase in the wage premium of the public sector will attract more high-level human capital into the public sector, which will reduce the human capital of the private sector and thus inhibit the growth of output and income. Secondly, the coefficients for the variables in relation to the length of education listed in the table above are significantly positive, and compared with the corresponding columns in the benchmark model, their significance has

Table 9.5 Regression results in consideration of the wage premium of the public sector: the explained variable is g_y.

Model	①*Regression equation (9.11): basic variable*				②*Regression equation (9.11): incorporation of control variables*			
Regression method	*OLS*	*FE*	*RE*	*IV*	*OLS*	*FE*	*RE*	*IV*
Llny	0.017***	−0.019	−0.016***	−0.050	0.015***	−0.058**	−0.011*	−0.064
	(−5.057)	(−0.825)	(−3.700)	(−1.386)	(3.689)	(−2.197)	(−1.899)	(−1.642)
lnk	0.379***	0.312***	0.359***	0.283***	0.395***	0.319***	0.373***	0.291***
	(16.408)	(9.438)	(14.034)	(9.990)	(15.170)	(9.009)	(12.780)	(9.318)
Llnk	−0.386***	−0.293***	−0.366***	−0.261***	−0.402***	−0.277***	−0.377***	−0.262***
	(−16.209)	(−7.332)	(−13.707)	(−6.578)	(−14.932)	(−7.330)	(−12.413)	(−6.691)
L!w	−0.048*	−0.071	−0.050*	−0.123***	−0.051	−0.128***	−0.064*	−0.142***
	(−1.779)	(−1.638)	(−1.653)	(−2.777)	(−1.643)	(−2.866)	(−1.856)	(−3.013)
sch	0.008*	0.010*	0.008*	0.017**	0.008*	0.010**	0.008*	0.013**
	(1.656)	(1.890)	(1.727)	(2.464)	(1.765)	(2.034)	(1.841)	(1.999)
Lsch	−0.012**	−0.007	−0.012***	−0.003	−0.013***	−0.006	−0.013***	−0.003
	(−2.514)	(−1.168)	(−2.600)	(−0.553)	(−2.732)	(−1.105)	(−2.853)	(−0.526)
patent					0.001	0.007	0.001	0.009**
					(0.576)	(1.614)	(0.580)	(2.012)
pteacher					−0.01	−0.008	−0.006	−0.010
					(−1.478)	(−0.579)	(−0.728)	(−0.549)
rexpgdp					0.008	0.097***	0.016*	0.043*
					(1.074)	(5.472)	(1.704)	(1.931)
_cons	0.016***	0.030***	0.019***		0.054**	0.085*	0.050*	
	(1.098)	(0.711)	(1.119)		(1.098)	(0.711)	(1.119)	
Adjusted R^2	0.512***	0.293***		0.334	0.513	0.369		0.354
N	290	290	290	232	290	290	290	232
F	51.531	25.597		12.561	34.761	22.903		10.996
LM value				193.796				194.316
				(0.000)				(0.000)
Wald F-value				783.30				818.96
				(10.830)				(10.830)
Sargan value				7.637				4.954
				(0.106)				(0.292)

Note: The values in parentheses are P-values; "*", "**" and "***" indicate significance at the level of 10%, 5%, and 1% respectively.

been obviously improved. Considering the possible omission of allowance, reputation and other variables in the first three columns of Model ①, the variables of the length of education may still be endogenous. For the sake of prudence, the lag term and the difference of each period are used again as the instrumental variables of the length of education for estimation, and the results are listed in the fourth column of Model ①.[6] The regression results show that the significance of the length of education and wage premium has further increased, although the overall regression results after the adoption of instrumental variables do not change much. Thirdly, in the fourth columns of Model ①, except for the wage premium, the coefficients of the current term for the other variables are positive, but those of the lag terms are negative. Additionally, the coefficients of both current and lag terms for material capital per capita are significant, indicating that material capital promotes the increase in income per capita. All these results are in line with theoretical predictions.

In order to test the robustness of the regression results, for Model ② in Table 9.5, some other variables that are believed to affect the economic growth rate in the existing research literature are added based on Model ①. By comparing the regression results of ① and ② in Table 9.5, it can be found that the coefficients and significance of each variable almost do not change, which shows that the regression results have sound robustness. At the same time, the signs of the three newly added variable coefficients are also consistent with the conclusions of the literature and the same as the results in Table 9.4. This shows that technological advancement, education, and the degree of opening-up to the outside world all have a positive effect on economic growth.

Additionally, the difference between the average wages in the public sector and those in the non-public sector is used in this chapter as the proxy variable of the wage premium of the public sector. The regression results are shown in Table 9.6. According to Table 9.6, first, the Hausman test still shows that the RE model is better than the FE model; second, the estimated values of the coefficients do not change much compared to those of Table 9.5. The coefficients of the newly added wage premium variables are basically significant (as mentioned above, in terms of data quality, the calculation method of the second wage premium variable is relatively rough, which may be one reason its coefficient is not as significant as the first form). At the same time, all coefficients of education variables in the second column of ① and ② show ideal significance. Therefore, the regression results have sound robustness.

3.3 Comparisons between China and other countries in terms of the rate of return on education output

According to the econometric regression Equation (9.11) and its theoretical Equation (9.8), the regression coefficient α_4 of *sch* in Table 9.5 (or Table 9.6)

Table 9.6 Regression results in consideration of the wage premium of the public sector and with the adoption of wd_2: the explained variable is g

Model	①*Regression equation (9.11): basic variable*				②*Regression equation (9.11): incorporation of control variables*			
Econometric method	*OLS*	*FE*	*RE*	*IV*	*OLS*	*FE*	*RE*	*IV*
Llny	0.016***	−0.021	0.015***	−0.051	0.015***	−0.060**	0.011*	−0.065*
	(4.915)	(−0.944)	(3.561)	(−1.386)	(3.690)	(−2.274)	(1.935)	(−1.657)
lnk	0.381***	0.318***	0.363***	0.296***	0.398***	0.328***	0.378***	0.306***
	(16.543)	(9.733)	(14.221)	(9.408)	(15.326)	(9.352)	(13.024)	(9.805)
Llnk	−0.389***	−0.298***	−0.369***	−0.271***	−0.405***	−0.286***	−0.382***	−0.275***
	(−16.334)	(−7.508)	(−13.868)	(−6.831)	(−15.10)	(−7.563)	(−12.655)	(−7.004)
sch	0.008	0.010*	0.008*	0.016**	0.008*	0.011**	0.008*	0.013**
	(1.628)	(1.881)	(1.700)	(2.364)	(1.739)	(2.085)	(1.819)	(1.964)
Lsch	−0.012**	−0.007	−0.012**	−0.003	−0.013***	−0.006	−0.013***	−0.003
	(−2.504)	(−1.149)	(−2.572)	(−0.539)	(−2.706)	(−1.071)	(−2.799)	(−0.488)
Lwd2	−0.025	−0.038	−0.025	−0.064**	−0.025	−0.071**	−0.030	−0.071**
	(−1.371)	(−1.275)	(−1.235)	(−2.077)	(−1.231)	(−2.338)	(−1.316)	(−2.173)
patent					0.000	0.006	0.001	0.008*
					(0.405)	(1.372)	(0.348)	(1.725)
pteacher					−0.011	−0.005	−0.007	−0.004
					(−1.625)	(−0.381)	(−0.810)	(−0.203)
rexpgdp					0.007	0.096***	0.015	0.045**
					(0.958)	(5.370)	(1.591)	(2.010)
_cons	0.019	0.038	0.023		0.059**	0.089*	0.055**	
	(1.361)	(0.895)	(1.395)		(2.286)	(1.873)	(2.004)	
Adjusted R^2	0.510	0.290		0.324	0.510	0.362		0.341
N	290	290	290	232	290	290	290	232
F	51.087	25.318		12.144	34.485	22.366		10.539
LM value				193.838				194.455
				(0.000)				(0.000)
Wald F-value				787.036				832.873
				(10.830)				(10.830)
Sargan value				7.302				5.512
				(0.121)				(0.239)

Note: The values in parentheses are P-values; “*”, “**” and “***” indicate significance at the level of 10%, 5%, and 1% respectively.

is the elasticity of output in relation to human capital in the production function Equation (9.1), β_2. According to the definition of human capital per capita, h=exp{sch}:

$$\alpha_4 = \beta_2 = (dy/y)/(dh^p/h^p) = (dy/y)/dsch \tag{9.12}$$

So, α_4 means the percentage of output per capita added every one additional year for the average length of education *sch*.

According to the economic meaning of α_4, the regression results in Table 9.5 show that, once every one year is added to the average length of education in China's production sector, output per capita will increase by about 0.8–1.7 percentage points. It can be seen from Table 9.1 that the rate of return on education in other countries estimated in the existing literature is as follows: once every one year is added to the average length of education in China's production sector, GDP growth rate per capita will increase by about 0.7–1.4 percentage points. Thus, if human capital in the public sector is excluded and only the contribution of human capital in the private production sector to economic growth is considered, the contribution of China's education to economic growth is not low relative to the contribution of education to economic growth in OECD countries and the world average in the second half of the last century (see Table 9.1).

Notes

1 Note: according to the data of *China Statistical Yearbooks*, the gap between the average wages in China's public sector and those in the private sector has been narrowing in recent years.
2 According to Ma (2000), Xu et al. (2010) and Zhang (2012), the public sector is defined as state-owned organizations, including government authorities, state-owned public institutions and state-owned enterprises. This definition is also adopted in the author's research.
3 The public sector defined in this chapter includes state-owned enterprises. Although state-owned enterprises are also engaged in production, the existing researches show that the production efficiency of state-owned enterprises in China is generally lower than that of non-state-owned enterprises, such as Liu (2000) and Mou (2012) et al.
4 In the research of this chapter, the wage premium of the public sector relative to the private sector is used as a proxy variable for the wage premium of the public sector. And the result of analysis obtained is the same.
5 This chapter also attempts to use the average length of education (sch) to represent human capital per capita, *h*. The conclusions of this paper basically keep unchanged.
6 Considering that the logarithm of output per capita in the previous period may be endogenous, this chapter uses its lag and difference terms as instrumental variables in the estimation of instrumental variables. The corresponding results are relatively close to the fourth column in Table 9.6.

References

[1] Canton, E., Minne, B., Nieuwenhuis, A., Smid, B., & Steeg, M. (2005). Human Capital, R&D and Competition in Macroeconomic Analysis. *ENEPRI, Working Paper*, No. 38.

[2] Chen, Z., Lu, M., & Jin, *Y.* (2004). Regional Differences of Human Capitals and Education Development in China: An Estimation of the Panel Data. *The Journal of World Economy*, No. 12, 25–31.

[3] Krueger, A. B., & Lindahl, M. (2001). Education for Growth: Why and for Whom? *Journal of Economic Literature*, 39(4), 1101–1136.

[4] Liu, X. X. (2000). The impact of the structure of China's industrial enterprise's ownership on its efficiency. *Economic Research Journal*, No. 2, 17–25.

[5] Lucas, R. (1988). On the Mechanics of Economic Development. *Journal of Monetary Economics*, 22, 3–42.

[6] Ma, S. Y. (2000). An empirical analysis of China's public capital and economic growth of private sectors. *Economic Science*, No. 6, 21–26.

[7] Mou, J. L. (2012). Differential research on China's SoEs and non-SoEs. *Economic Survey*, No. 3, 55–59.

[8] Qian, X. *Y.*, Chi, W., & Li, B. (2010). The Role of Human Capital in Regional Innovation Activities and Economic Growth. *The Journal of Quantitative and Technical Economics*, 107–121.

[9] Romer, D. (1999). *Advanced macroeconomics*. Beijing: The Commercial Press.

[10] Topel, R. (1999). Labor Market and Economic Growth. *Handbook of Labor Economics*, 3, 2943–2984.

[11] Romer, D. (1999). *Advanced macroeconomics*. Beijing: The Commercial Press.

[12] Wang, Z. G., Gong, *L.* T. & Chen, *Y. Y.* (2006). China's Regional Differences in Technical Efficiency and the Decomposition of Total Factor Productivity Growth: 1978–2003. *Social Sciences in China*, No. 2, 55–66.

[13] Wang, D. H., Gong, L. T., & Li, H. Y. (2008). Healthy human capital, investment and economic growth. *Management World*, No. 3, 27–39.

[14] Xu, Z., Zhang, X. C., Ding, Z. J., & Tang, T. (2010). Public finance and the high saving trend of national income in China. *Social Sciences in China*, No. 6, 97–107.

[15] Zhang, H. F., Yao, X. G., & Zhang, J. S. (2010). The Impact of School Quality on Regional Labor Productivity. *Economic Research Journal*, No. 7.

[16] Zhang, J., Wu, G. Y., & Zhang, J. P. (2004). The Estimation of China's Provincial Capital Stock: 1952–2000. *Economic Research Journal*, No. 10, 35–44.

[17] Zhang, Y. B. (2012). The change of income differentials between public and nonpublic sector in China. *Economic Research Journal*, No. 4, 77–88.

10 Medical and healthcare development in China's economic growth

This chapter analyzes the changes in and status quo of China's medical conditions and the overall health status of residents in the 70 years since the founding of New China. The analysis in this chapter shows that, since 1949, the health conditions of Chinese residents have been significantly improved in terms of the investment of medical and healthcare expenditure or health indicators of residents. However, there remains a gap between China and developed countries in terms of medical and healthcare conditions, which still needs to be improved. The structure of the following parts of this chapter is as follows: the first section analyzes the changes in China's medical and healthcare expenditure; the second section discusses the changes in the supply of medical and healthcare resources for Chinese residents; and the third section studies the changes in the health status of Chinese residents.

Section 1 China's medical and healthcare expenditure

1.1 China's total medical and healthcare expenditure and its share in GDP

In 1949, when New China was founded, China's medical and health resources and national health fund were quite limited, and both health status of residents and national medical and healthcare facilities were outmoded. At the first National Health Work Conference in 1950, the sanitation policy of "orienting towards workers, peasants and soldiers, focusing on prevention, combining western medicine and traditional Chinese medicine" was identified. Since then, Mainland China has gradually established a government-led low-level welfare medical security system composed of free medical care, labor medical care, and cooperative medical care, and the total medical and healthcare expenditure (hereinafter referred to as the "total healthcare expenditure") has been increasing. Tables 10.1 and 10.2 show the changes in China's total healthcare expenditure and in the proportion of the total healthcare expenditure in GDP. As can be seen from the tables, China's total healthcare expenditure was only 854 million yuan, 1.26% of GDP, in 1952; and increased to 11.021 billion yuan or 10.617 billion yuan at the

DOI: 10.4324/9781003261629-13

Table 10.1 Total healthcare expenditure of China in major years and its average annual growth rates

Year	*Nominal value (hundred million yuan, at the prices of the year)*	*Real nominal value (hundred million yuan, at the prices of 1952)*	*Real growth multiple (times)*	*Average annual real growth rate (%)*	*Real GDP growth rate*	*Proportion in GDP (%)*
1952	8.54	8.54	–	–	–	1.26
1958	23.24	23.64	1.77	18.50	11.93	1.78
1968	35.16	32.38	0.37	3.19	1.87	2.04
1978	110.21	106.17	2.28	12.61	8.23	3.02
1990	747.39	365.89	2.45	10.86	8.31	4.00
2000	4586.63	1061.83	1.90	11.24	9.65	4.62
2010	19980.39	2953.27	1.78	10.77	10.13	4.98
2018	57998.30	6833.30	1.31	11.06	7.18	6.39

Note: Source: The internet for the data of 2018; Du Lexun et al. (2009) for the data on the healthcare expenditure of 1952–1977; and *China Statistical Yearbooks* for other data.②The growth multiple means the growth multiple of the year in relation to the column over the year of the previous column, and the average annual growth rate means the average growth rate of the year in relation to the column over the year of the previous column.

Table 10.2 Average annual growth rates for the number of health workers and the number of beds in China, in %

Period	*Urban health workers*	*Health technicians*	*Practicing (assistant) physicians*	*Practicing doctors*	*Nurses*	*Total number of beds*	*Number of beds at hospitals*
1949–1978	6.21	5.62	3.67	2.31	9.05	11.59	9.43
1978–2001	2.58	2.66	3.13	4.39	5.13	1.68	2.61
2002–2018	4.98	5.15	4.28	4.61	7.72	6.35	6.96

constant prices of 1952, representing an average annual growth of 10.18%, 3.02% of GDP, in 1978. In 2018, the total healthcare expenditure was 5799.83 billion yuan or 683.33 billion yuan at the constant prices of 1952, up 64.36 times over that of 1978 and with an annual real growth of 10.97%, 6.39% over GDP. During the period 1952–2018, the total healthcare expenditure had an average annual real growth of 10.66%.

Table 10.1 shows the growth of China's total healthcare expenditure in different periods. As can be seen from Table 10.1, during the "First Five-Year Plan" period (1952–1957) and the period 1968–1978, the growth rate of China's total healthcare expenditure exceeded 10%, far higher than the economic growth rate of the same period. Moreover, the growth rate of the total healthcare expenditure during the period 1958–1968 was only 3.2%, which still exceeded the real economic growth rate in the same period (Figure 10.1). Since the reform, the total healthcare expenditure has grown faster, and the real growth rate in any period has exceeded 10%. In fact, the

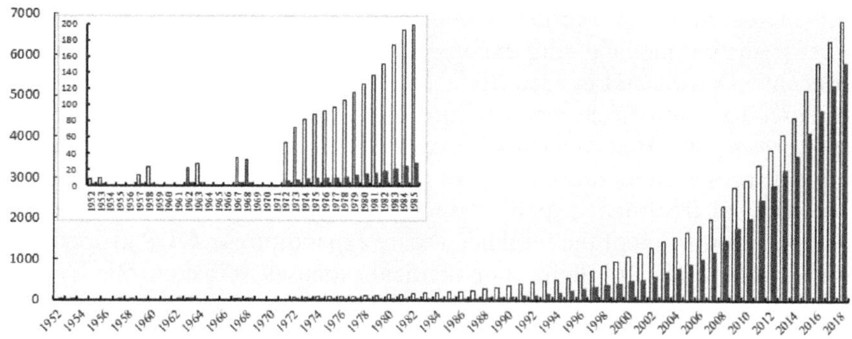

Figure 10.1 Changes in China's total healthcare expenditure: 1952–2018.

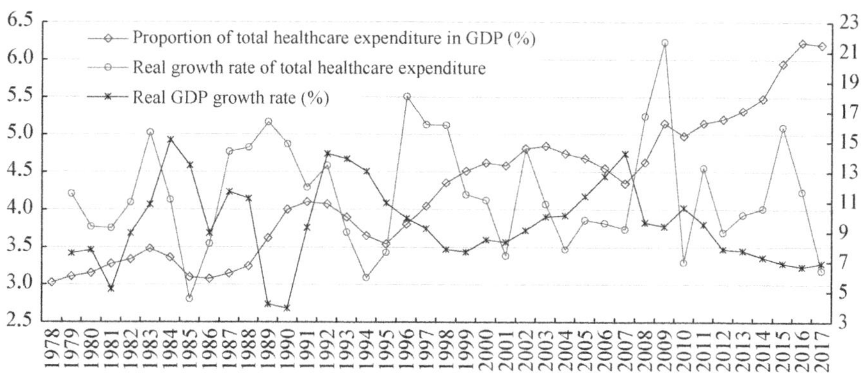

Figure 10.2 Changes in the proportion of China's total healthcare expenditure in GDP: 1978–2018.

growth rate of the total healthcare expenditure in other years, except for a few years such as 1984–1985, 1993–1995, and 2003–2007, was higher than the real economic growth rate. Figure 10.2 also shows that the real growth rate of the total healthcare expenditure within 40 years of the reform has been relatively stable compared with that before the reform.

In terms of the proportion of the total healthcare expenditure in GDP, Figure 10.2 shows that the proportion of China's healthcare expenditure in GDP during the period 1952–2018 showed an upward trend on the whole. In 1952, the total healthcare expenditure accounted for only 1.26% of GDP. During the "First Five-Year Plan" period, with the establishment and implementation of the free medical care system for workers in government departments and institutions and the labor medical care system for enterprise employees, the proportion of the total healthcare expenditure in GDP gradually increased to 1.77% in 1958 and then to 2.5% in 1963. With the gradual increase in free medical care expenses and the continued increase in the government's financial burden, the state has started to adopt some policy measures to control free medical care expenses. For example, the *Notice on Improving the Management of Free Medical Care* issued in 1965 specified measures such as rational use of medications and saving expenditure. Free medical treatment expenses were controlled to a certain extent. In 1968, the proportion of the total healthcare expenditure in GDP dropped to 2.06%. After 1968, although urban medical expenses were controlled, rural cooperative medical care was quickly promoted nationwide and the total healthcare expenditure has been on the rise, according to Mao Zedong's instruction on focusing on medical and healthcare in the countryside. In 1978, the proportion of the total healthcare expenditure in GDP increased to 3.02%, which was still lower than the international standard of 5% specified by the World Health Organization (WHO).

Despite several major fluctuations, the total healthcare expenditure as a percentage of GDP grew faster during the period 1978–2018. As shown in Figure 10.2, during the period 1978–1983, the increase in the wages of residents contributed to the increase in the demand for medical and healthcare services and the rapid rise in the total healthcare expenditure, with its share over GDP rising from 3.02% to 3.48%. However, the household contract responsibility system adopted in rural areas after the reform and opening-up led to the continued decrease in the revenues of rural collective organizations, and the gradual decline, shrinkage, and even disappearance of the rural cooperative medical care system supported by the rural collective economy, resulting in the decline in the total healthcare expenditure. During the period 1984–1986, the proportion of total healthcare expenditure in GDP dropped to 3.07%. After 1986, economic growth and income increase enabled residents to pay more and more attention to health, and the demand for medical services and medical treatment continued to increase. Additionally, following the market-oriented reform of the medical and healthcare system, the autonomy of medical and health authorities and organizations was gradually expanded; the medical services supplied continued to rise, so did the prices of medical services and supplies. Both factors led to a rapid rise in residents' medical expenses and in the total healthcare expenditure. The economic growth rate also declined in the same period. Thus, the proportion of total health expenditure in GDP rose from 3.07% to 4.10% during the period 1986–1991. The *Opinions on Deepening Medical and HealthCare System Reform*, issued by the State Council in September 1992, proposed that "we rely on the state for construction and ourselves for living." The Ministry of Health also requested hospitals to "support health centers with the aid of township enterprises and supplement the auxiliary one with the major one." The growth rate of total healthcare expenditure witnessed a sharp decline during the period 1992–1996, despite the decrease in the economic growth rate and the decline in the percentage of total health expenditure over GDP in the same period. In 1996, the reform on the medical security system for employees started to be implemented. In the subsequent years, the government healthcare expenditure, social healthcare expenditure, and personal healthcare expenditure all increased to a large extent; the growth rate of total healthcare expenditure suddenly and significantly increased and was higher than the GDP growth rate in the same period, during which the percentage of total healthcare expenditure rose from 3.81% (1995) to 4.85% (2002). During the years 2002–2007, the economy resumed rapid growth, but the growth rates of personal health expenditure and social health expenditure declined and that of total health expenditure dropped rapidly, following the completion and promotion of the medical system reform. In 2007, the proportion of total healthcare expenditure in GDP fell to a local minimum of 4.35%. During the period 2007–2017, the growth rate of total healthcare expenditure continued to drop but was still higher than the GDP growth rate, and the proportion of total healthcare expenditure in GDP rose again. This proportion rose to 5.15% in 2011, reaching the international standard of 5% for the first time, and reached 6.39% in 2018.

1.2 Changes in China's total healthcare expenditure structure

According to the classification in the *China Statistical Yearbooks*, China's healthcare expenditure is comprised of three parts, namely personal cash healthcare expenditure, government healthcare expenditure, and social healthcare expenditure. Government healthcare expenditure refers to the expenditures of governments at all levels used for medical and healthcare service, medical security subsidy, administrative management of medical and healthcare insurance, population and family planning expenditure, and other aspects. Social health expenditure refers to capital investments of all walks of life in health services, including social medical security expenditure, commercial health insurance premium, social medical expenditure, social donations and assistance, income resulting from administrative fees, etc. Personal cash health expenditure refers to the cash payment by urban and rural residents when receiving various medical and healthcare services, including the expenses paid by residents entitled to the benefits of various medical insurance systems when seeking medical treatment, reflecting the burden of medical and healthcare expenses for urban and rural residents. Since there is only post-1978 data in the *China Statistical Yearbooks*, Figures 10.3 and 10.4 show the growth rates of China's personal cash healthcare expenditure, government healthcare expenditure, and social healthcare expenditure and their share over the total health expenditure during the period 1978–2018.

As known from Figure 10.3, during the period 1978–2018, the proportion of China's personal cash healthcare expenditure in the total healthcare

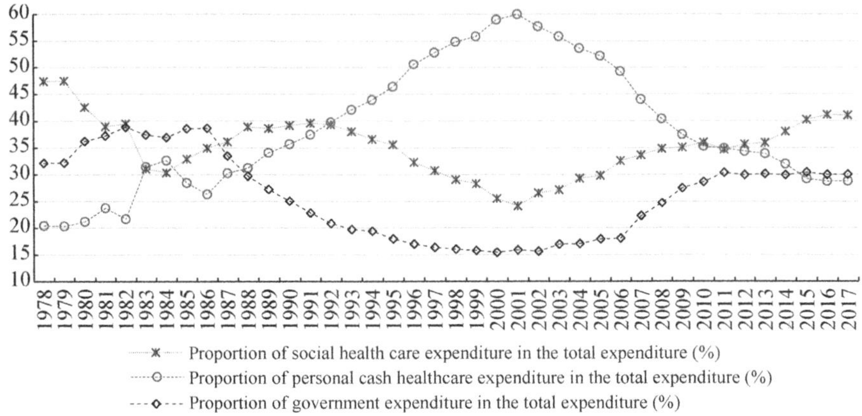

Figure 10.3 Changes in China's total medical and healthcare expenditure: 1978–2018.

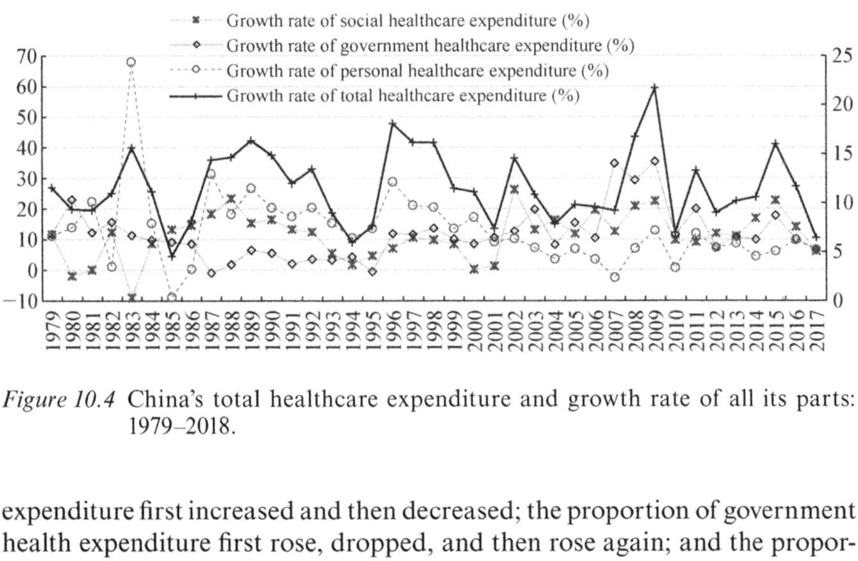

Figure 10.4 China's total healthcare expenditure and growth rate of all its parts: 1979–2018.

expenditure first increased and then decreased; the proportion of government health expenditure first rose, dropped, and then rose again; and the proportion of social healthcare expenditure first dropped and then rose. In 1978, China's total healthcare expenditure was mainly borne by the government and society. Social healthcare expenditure had a share of 47.7%; government health expenditure and personal cash health expenditures were 32.16% and 20.4%, respectively. In the early years of the reform, due to the decline in the revenues of rural collective organizations, the medical expenses borne by collective organizations in rural medical cooperation could not be guaranteed; the healthcare expenses arising from the government's fiscal expenditure and personal consumption expenditure continued to increase, along with the proportion of personal cash health expenditure and government health expenditure. In 1987, the total healthcare expenditure of residents was essentially equally divided among the government, society, and individuals according to the proportions of 33.53%, 36.16%, and 30.31%, respectively. From then until 2001, the market-oriented reform of the urban medical care system led to the sustained decrease in healthcare expenses contributed by the government and state-owned enterprises. Basically, personal cash healthcare expenditure grew at a rate of more than 10% each year, and the proportions of government healthcare expenditure and social healthcare expenditure dropped. In 2001, the proportion of personal cash healthcare expenditure reached a peak of 60%; the proportions of government healthcare expenditure and social healthcare expenditure were 16% and 24%, respectively, at nearly the lowest levels in history. During the period 2001–2017, with the implementation and promotion of the three medical insurance systems, namely urban employee medical insurance, new rural cooperative medical insurance system, and medical insurance system for urban and rural residents, China gradually formed a socialized "universal medical insurance" system. The proportion of personal cash healthcare expenditure declined again, that of social healthcare expenditure continued to rise, and that of government healthcare expenditure increased from 2003 to 2011 but basically remained unchanged during the period 2011–2017. Around 2011, China's healthcare expenditure was equally divided among individuals, society, and the government. In 2018, the proportions of China's government healthcare expenditure, social healthcare expenditure, and personal cash healthcare expenditure were 28.3%, 43.0%, and 28.7%, respectively. Through 40 years of medical reforms, China's healthcare expenditure structure basically returned to the level of 1978, but the proportion of personal contribution was about eight percentage points higher than that of 1978, and the proportion of private contribution dropped by approximately four percentage points.

1.3 Healthcare expenditure per capita and its proportion in personal consumption expenditure

In the early period of the founding of New China, China's healthcare expenditure per capita and its proportion in personal consumption was quite limited. In 1952, China's healthcare expenditure per capita was about 1.5 yuan, and the total consumption expenditure per capita accounted for 1.86% of consumption expenditure per capita. In 1957, the healthcare expenditure per capita rose to 2.18 yuan or 2.12 yuan at the constant prices of 1952, representing an average annual real growth of 7.4%, and the proportion of consumption per capita rose to 2.02%. In 1963, the healthcare expenditure per capita increased to 4.51 yuan or 3.89 yuan at the constant prices of 1952, and the proportion of consumption per capita rose to 3.63%. This proportion was 10.04 yuan in 1976 or 9.87 yuan at the prices of 1952, and the proportion of consumption per capita was 5.87%. By 1987, China's healthcare expenditure per capita had reached 11.03 yuan at the constant prices, up 6.42 times over those of 1952 in real terms and with an average annual real growth of 8.0%, and the proportion of healthcare expenditure in consumption expenditure per capita increased to 6.22%.

Since the reform and opening-up, both personal cash healthcare expenditure and total healthcare expenditure per capita have grown rapidly, and the proportion of personal cash healthcare expenditure in personal cash consumption expenditure and that of total healthcare expenditure per capita in consumption expenditure per capita increased. Figures 10.5a and 10.5b show that China's total healthcare expenditure per capita in 1978 was 11.45 yuan, in which personal cash health expenditure was 2.34 yuan, and the proportion of total healthcare expenditure per capita in consumption expenditure per capita and that of personal cash expenditure in cash consumption expenditure per capita were 6.22% and 1.55%, respectively. In 1990, the total healthcare expenditure per capita and personal cash health expenditure grew to 65.4 yuan and 23.4 yuan, respectively, or 36.31 yuan and 12.97 yuan at the constant prices of 1978, with both proportions rising to 7.85% and 3.04%. In

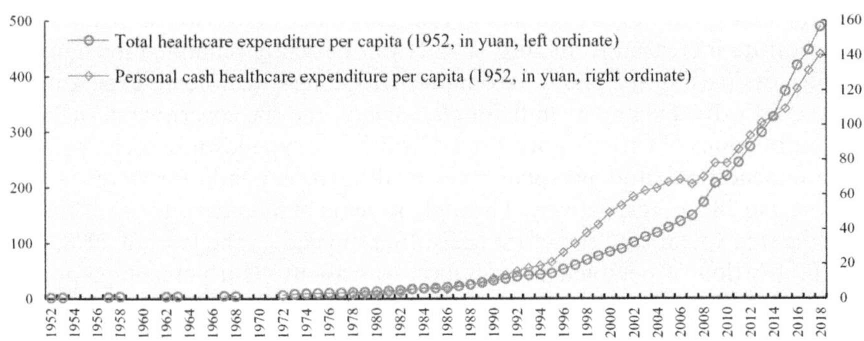

Figure 10.5a Changes in the medical and healthcare expenditure per capita of China: 1952–2018.

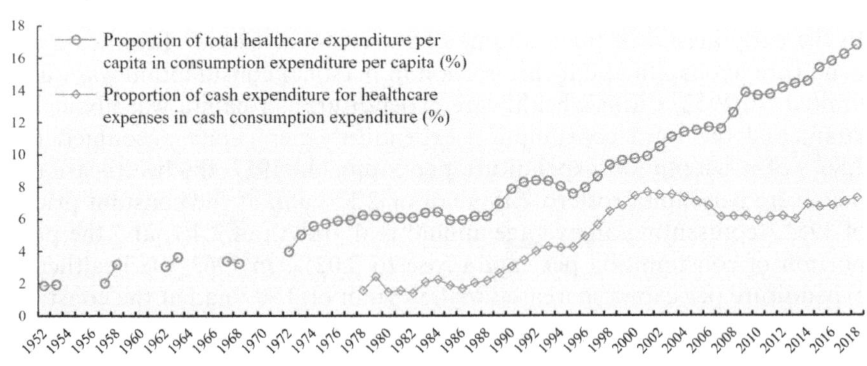

Figure 10.5b Changes in the proportion of healthcare expenditure per capita: 1952–2018.

2001, the total healthcare expenditure per capita and personal cash expenditure increased to 393.80 yuan and 236.15 yuan, respectively, or 108.81 yuan and 65.25 yuan at the constant prices, with both proportions rising to 9.88% and 7.66%. In 2018, the total healthcare expenditure per capita and personal cash healthcare expenditure continued to grow to 4,148.10 yuan and 1,195.50 yuan, or 620.01 yuan and 177.94 yuan at the constant prices; the proportion of healthcare expenditure per capita in consumption expenditure per capita increased to 16.77%, and that of personal cash expenditure in personal cash consumption dropped to 7.29%. At the constant prices, during the period 1978–2018, the proportion of consumption expenditure per capita and cash consumption expenditure per capita had an average annual growth of 7.82% and 6.67%, and that of total healthcare expenditure per capita and personal cash healthcare expenditure had an average annual growth of 10.49% and 11.43%, respectively.

Due to the lack of data, Figures 10.6a and 10.6b only show the changes in personal cash healthcare expenditures of Chinese urban and rural residents

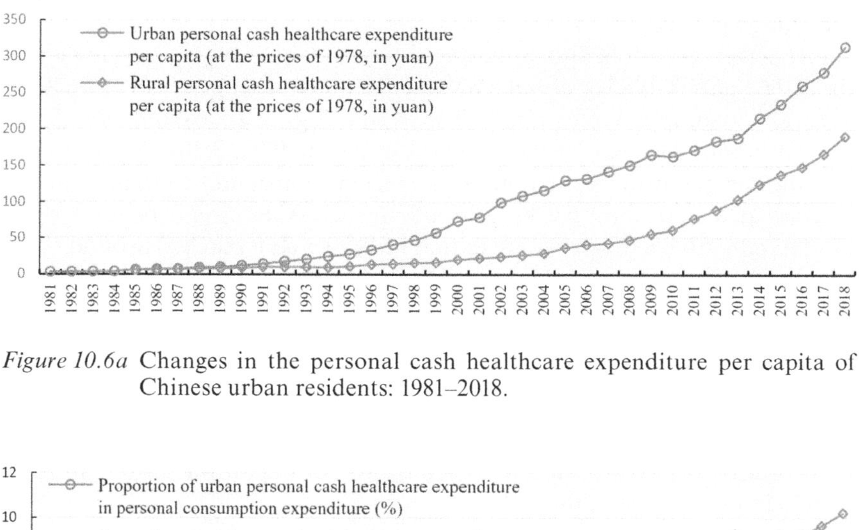

Figure 10.6a Changes in the personal cash healthcare expenditure per capita of Chinese urban residents: 1981–2018.

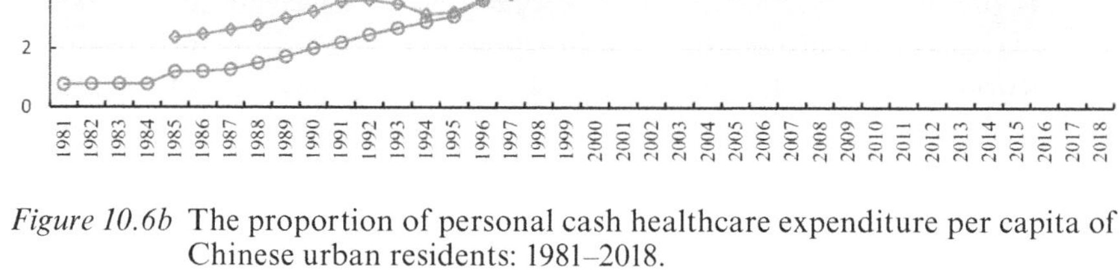

Figure 10.6b The proportion of personal cash healthcare expenditure per capita of Chinese urban residents: 1981–2018.

and their proportions in cash consumption expenditure per capita since the mid-1980s. As known from Figure 10.6, since the 1980s, the cash healthcare expenditure per capita of residents and its proportion in cash consumption expenditure per capita have been increasing, in both urban and rural areas. The personal cash healthcare expenditure of urban residents was about 3.5 yuan in 1981, or about 3.2 yuan at the constant prices of 1978, and its proportion in cash consumption expenditure per capita was 0.77%; it grew to 26 yuan in 1990, or about 12 yuan at the constant prices of 1978, and its proportion in cash consumption expenditure per capita was 2%; it rose to about 318 yuan in 2000, or about 73 yuan at the constant prices, and its proportion in cash consumption expenditure per capita was 3.1%; and it increased to around 2,046 yuan, or about 314 yuan at the constant prices of 1978, and its proportion in cash consumption expenditure was 7.84%. During the period 1981–2018, the personal cash health expenditure of urban residents was up 99.6 times in real terms, with an average annual real growth of 13.27%; the consumption expenditure per capita of urban residents had an increase of 8.83% in real terms; and the proportion of personal cash healthcare expenditure for residents in cash consumption expenditure per capita grew by seven percentage points.

The personal cash healthcare expenditure of Chinese rural residents was about 7.6 yuan in 1985 or about 5.8 yuan at the constant prices of 1978, 2.8% of rural consumption expenditure per capita; it grew to around 19 yuan in 1990, or about 8.8 yuan at the constant prices of 1978, 3.26% of rural consumption expenditure per capita; it increased to around 88 yuan, or about 20 yuan at the constant prices, 3.1% of rural consumption expenditure per capita, indicating a drop relative to that of 1990; and it reached around 1,240 yuan in 2018, or about 190 yuan at the constant prices of 1978, 10.23% of cash consumption expenditure per capita. During the period 1981–2018, the personal cash healthcare expenditure of Chinese rural residents was up 32.9 times in real terms, representing an average annual real growth of 11.2%; cash consumption expenditure per capita had an average annual real growth of 6.38%; and the proportion of rural personal cash healthcare expenditure in cash consumption expenditure per capita increased approximately 10 percentage points.

1.4 Government healthcare expenditure and its proportion in the government's fiscal expenditure

During the period 1952–1978, China's total government healthcare expenditure and government health expenditure per capita grew steadily, and the proportions of government healthcare expenditure in the government's fiscal expenditure, in the total healthcare expenditure, and in GDP showed a volatile rise. When P.R. China was initially founded, the absolute level of its total government healthcare expenditure and government healthcare expenditure per capita was very low. The total government healthcare expenditure and government healthcare expenditure per capita were approximately 245 million yuan and only 0.43 yuan in 1952, with the proportions of government healthcare expenditure in the government's fiscal expenditure, GDP, and total healthcare expenditure being 0.68%, 0.57%, and 28.7%; The total government healthcare expenditure and government healthcare expenditure per capita grew to 488 million yuan and 0.74 yuan in 1958, representing an increase of 99.5% and 73.8%, with the proportions of government healthcare expenditure in the government's fiscal expenditure increasing to 0.91%, in GDP decreasing to 0.45%, and in total healthcare expenditure decreasing to 20.7%. The total government healthcare expenditure and government healthcare expenditure per capita increased to 945 million yuan and 1.11 yuan in 1968, representing a ten-year increase of 93.6% and 62.7%, with the proportions of government healthcare expenditure in the government's fiscal expenditure and in GDP rising to 1.54% and 0.69%, and in the total healthcare expenditure to 29.2% In 1978, the total government healthcare expenditure and government healthcare expenditure per capita reached 3.544 billion yuan and 3.68 yuan or 3.414 billion yuan and 3.55 yuan at the constant prices of 1952, with the average annual real growth rates for the period 1952–1978 being 10.67% and 8.49%, respectively. The proportions of the government's healthcare expenditure in the government's fiscal expenditure, GDP, and total healthcare expenditure rose to 3.16%, 0.96%, and 32.16%, respectively.

Since the reform, China's government healthcare expenditure and government healthcare expenditure per capita still maintained rapid growth, but the proportions of government healthcare expenditure in the government's fiscal expenditure, GDP, and total healthcare expenditure has not grown on the whole and at one point declined due to the impact of the medical system reform. The total government healthcare expenditure and government healthcare expenditure per capita increased to 18.73 billion yuan and 16.38 yuan, respectively, in 1990 or 10.4 billion yuan and 9.10 yuan at the constant prices of 1978, representing an average annual real growth of 9.39% and 7.83% for the period 1978–1990, with the proportions of government healthcare expenditure in the government's fiscal expenditure, GDP, and total healthcare expenditure being 6.07%, 0.98%, and 25.6%, respectively. The total government healthcare expenditure and government healthcare expenditure per capita grew to 70.95 billion yuan and 55.98 yuan in 2000 or 20 billion yuan and 15.78 yuan at the constant prices of 1978, representing an average annual real growth of 6.75% and 5.66% for the period 1990–2000, with the proportions of government healthcare expenditure in the three being 4.47%, 0.71%, and 15.47%, respectively. Due to the medical system reform, the government healthcare expenditure during this period was declining relative to economic growth. All three proportions of government healthcare expenditure reached their lowest points around 2000. The medical system reform was basically completed in 2002, and the government healthcare expenditure has witnessed a substantial increase since 2000. By

2018, China's total government healthcare expenditure and government healthcare expenditure per capita had grown to 1,639.07 billion yuan and 1,174.6 yuan or 244.838 billion yuan and 175.46 yuan at the constant prices of 1978, representing an average real growth of 14.9% and 14.3% for the period 2000–2018, with the three proportions of government healthcare expenditure rising to 7.43%, 1.82%, and 28.3%. At the constant prices, during the period 1978–2018, China's GDP was up 36.8 times in real terms, representing an average annual real growth of 9.43%; total fiscal expenditure was up 29.4% in real terms, representing an average annual real growth of 8.82%; government healthcare expenditure was up about 78.5 times in real terms, representing an average annual growth of 11.5%; government healthcare expenditure was up 47.7 times in real terms, representing an average annual growth of 10.1%. The real growth rates of government healthcare expenditure and personal government health expenditure was much higher than those of GDP and fiscal expenditure. However, the proportions of government healthcare expenditure in the government's total fiscal expenditure, GDP, and total healthcare expenditure basically returned to the level of 1982 (Figure 10.7).

1.5 Multinational comparisons on medical and healthcare expenses and their structure

Although China's medical and healthcare expenditure has witnessed tremendous growth since 1949, the healthcare expenditure per capita is still low, and the proportion of total healthcare expenditure in GDP is not high relative to that of developed countries. As shown in Figure 10.8, at the purchasing power parity, the figure was approximately US$ 762 in 2015. In the same year, the total healthcare expenditure of America was about US$ 9,540; that of Japan, Germany, Britain, France, Canada, Australia, and

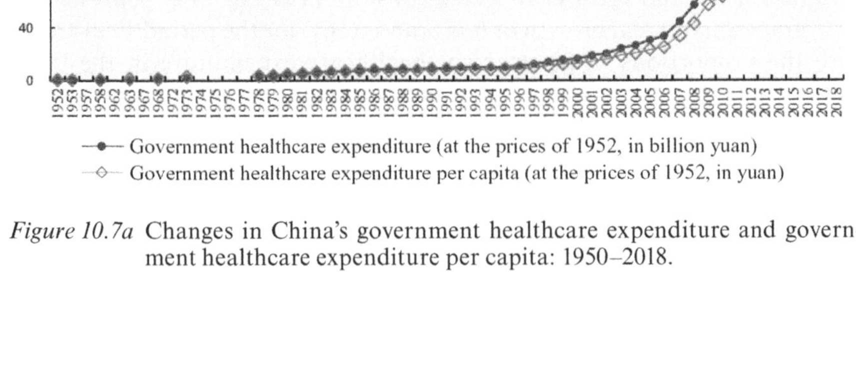

Figure 10.7a Changes in China's government healthcare expenditure and government healthcare expenditure per capita: 1950–2018.

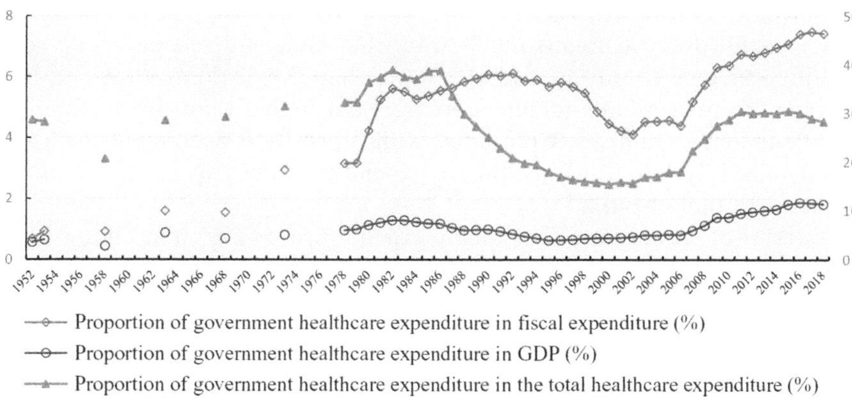

Figure 10.7b Changes in the proportions of China's government healthcare expenditures: 1952–2018.

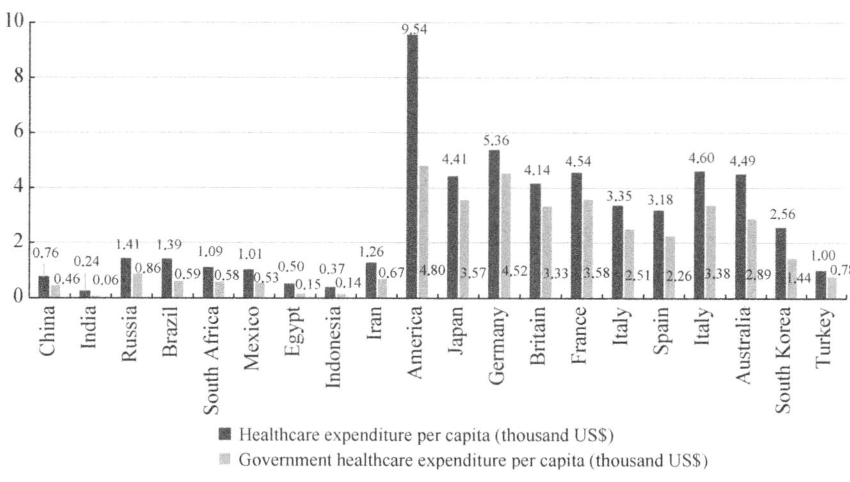

Figure 10.8 The total healthcare expenditure per capita and government healthcare expenditure per capita of different countries in 2015.

other countries was all above US$ 4,000; that of Spain and Italy was above US$ 3,000; and that of South Korea was US$ 2,556. The healthcare expenditure per capita of Russia, Brazil, and South Korea, among BRICS countries, Mexico, Iran, Turkey, etc., among developing countries, was all above US$ 1,000; and that of other developing countries and populous countries such as Egypt (US$ 495), India (US$ 237), and Indonesia (US$ 369) was all below US$ 500. In the same period, the healthcare expenditure per capita of the world was approximately US$ 1,300 on average; that of high-income countries was about US$ 5,280; that of middle-income countries was about

US$ 560; that of upper-middle-income countries was US$ 903; and that of low-income countries was about US$ 98. It can be seen that the total healthcare expenditure of China is much lower than that of developed countries and high-income countries, and also lower than the world average and the average of upper-middle-income countries but higher than the average of middle-income countries. Compared with other BRICS countries, China has a relatively low total healthcare expenditure per capita, and is only higher than that of India.[1]

In terms of the source of healthcare expenditure, as shown in Figure 10.9, China had a total healthcare expenditure per capita of US$ 762 in 2015, including the part paid by the government, US$ 456 (59.8%), and the part paid by individuals, US$ 307 (40.2%). In developed countries other than America and South Korea the public healthcare expenditure accounted for more than 60% of the total healthcare expenditure: above 70% in France, Italy, Spain, and Canada and above 80% in Germany, Brazil, and Japan. For BRICS countries, the proportion exceeded 55% in Russia and South Africa and was around 40% in Brazil and India. For other developing countries and populous countries, the proportion was above 50% in Mexico and Iran; 30.3% and 38.8%, respectively, in Egypt and Indonesia; and below 30% almost in all the other countries. It can be seen that in the composition of the total healthcare expenditure of residents, the proportion of government healthcare expenditure in China is lower than that of developed countries, but with a small gap. The figure is slightly lower in China than in Russia but higher than other BRICS countries. China ranks second among the tenth most populous countries in the world. So, compared with other developing countries and

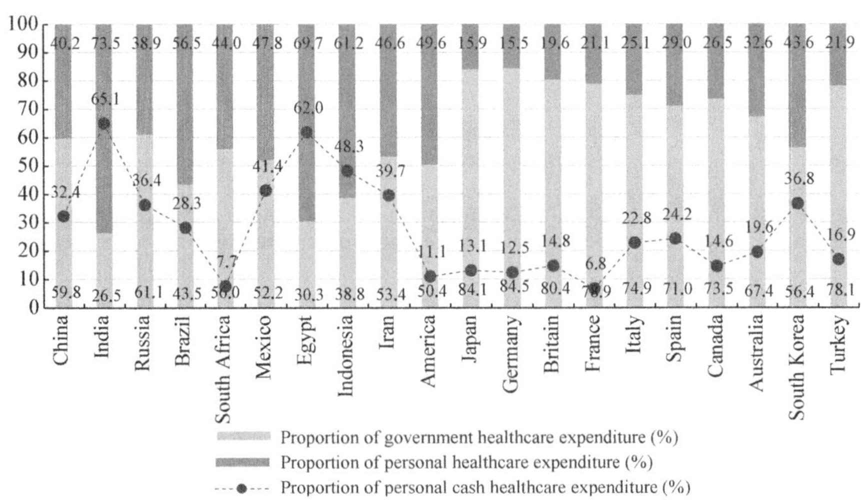

Figure 10.9 Proportions of government expenditure and personal expenditure in the total healthcare expenditure of different countries in 2015.

BRICS countries, China has a higher proportion of healthcare expenditure in total healthcare expenditure. In addition, for the part paid by individuals, the out-of-pocket payments in China were US$ 246, 32.4% of the healthcare expenditure per capita, as shown in Figure 10.9. This proportion was 20.0% in developed countries, 11.1% for America. Among the BRICS countries, this figures in South Africa and Brazil were lower than that of China, differed little in Russia from that of China, and were higher in India than in China. It can be seen that, although the proportion of personal contribution in personal health expenditure in China does not differ much from that of developed countries, the out-of-pocket payments in China are relatively high.

As can be seen in Figure 10.10, in 2015, the proportion of total healthcare expenditure in the GDP of development countries generally ranged from 9% to 10%. The proportion in China was 5.3%, significantly lower than that in developed countries. This figure in Russia, Brazil, and South Africa, all of which were among BRICS countries, was higher than that in China; however, India was an exception. In 2015, the average of the total healthcare expenditure in the world was 10.57%; that in high-income countries was 12.28%; that in middle-income countries was 5.38%; that in upper-middle-income countries was 5.77%; and that in low-income countries was 6.21%.[2] Thus, the proportion of total healthcare expenditure in GDP of China was far lower than that of developed countries, slightly lower than the average level of upper-middle-income countries and low-middle income countries, and only a little higher than that of India among BRICS countries. Moreover, China ranked in the middle relative to Asian, American, and African developing countries in this respect.

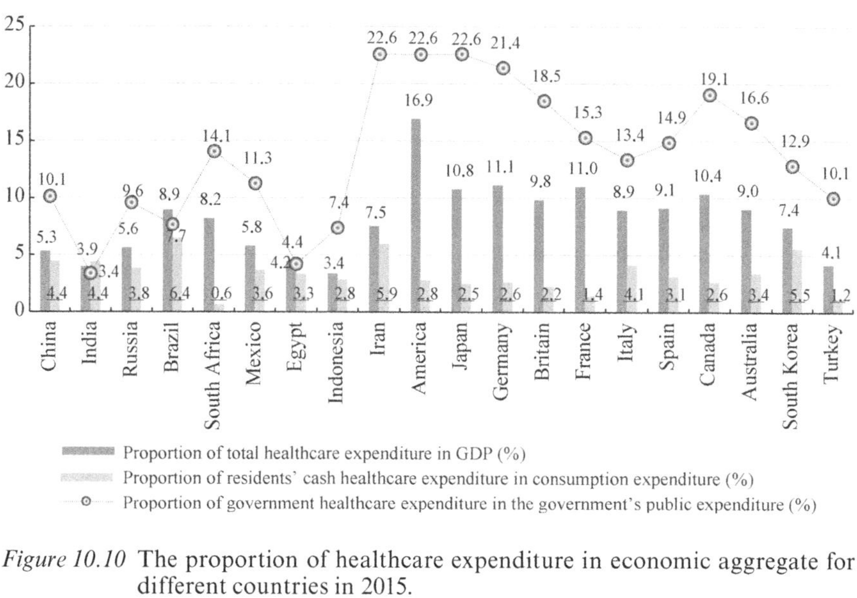

Figure 10.10 The proportion of healthcare expenditure in economic aggregate for different countries in 2015.

Figure 10.10 also shows that, for developed countries, the proportion of government healthcare expenditure in the government's public expenditure was generally above 15% and the proportion of personal cash expenditure in personal consumption expenditure generally ranged between 2% and 4%. The first proportion of developing countries was lower than that of developed countries, generally below 15%; the second proportion of developing countries was even higher than that of developed countries; for example, 6.4% in Brazil, 5.9% in Iran, 4.4% in China and India, 3.8% in Russia, and only 0.6% in South Africa. In 2015, the average of the two indicators in the world was 3.06% and 15.53%,[3] respectively; the average of the two indicators in high-income countries was 2.82% and 18.64%; and the average of both indicators in upper-middle–income countries was 3.81% and 9.97%, respectively. The two proportions in China were 4.42% and 10.1%, respectively, and both were higher than the corresponding average level of upper-high-income countries. Compared with developed countries, China had a much higher proportion of personal cash healthcare expenditure in personal consumption expenditure but slightly lower proportion in the government's public expenditure.

Overall, firstly, China's total healthcare expenditure and its composition are close to the average level of upper-middle-income countries in the world, which is in line with the country's GDP per capita among upper-middle-income countries. Secondly, the proportion of China's total healthcare expenditure per capita and its percentage in GDP are far below the average level of developed countries, and the proportion of total healthcare expenditure in GDP is even lower than the average level of middle-income countries. Thirdly, although the government-funded part in China's total healthcare expenditure does not appear low relative to its economic development level, the proportion of out-of-pocket payments in personal consumption and the proportion of personal cash expenditure in the total healthcare expenditure are both high, indicating China's medical insurance system remains to be improved.

Section 2 Changes and status quo of China's medical and healthcare resources

2.1 Changes in the number of medical institutions

Figure 10.11 shows the changes in the number of China's medical institutions during the period 1949–2018. According to the data in the figure, in 1949, China had a total of 3,670 medical and health institutions, including 2,600 hospitals, 9 maternity and child health centers, 11 specialized disease prevention & treatment institutes, 769 grass-roots outpatient clinics, and 251 other types of medical institutions. In 1952, the total number of medical and health institutions increased to 38,987, including 3,658 hospitals, 2,379 maternity and child health centers, 188 specialized disease

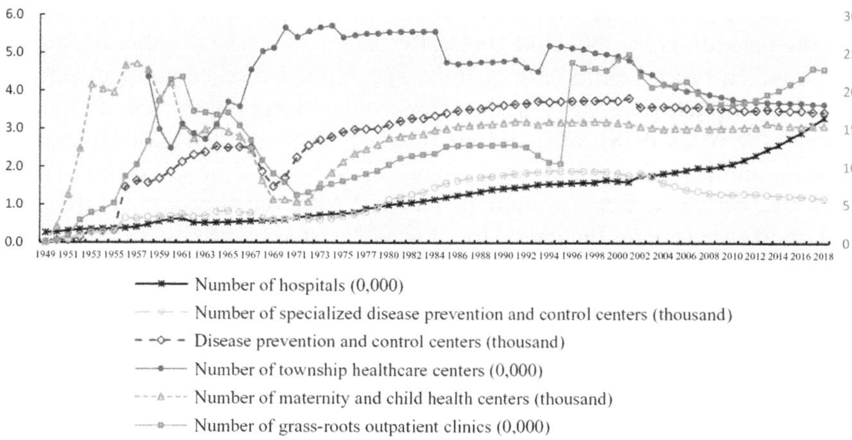

Figure 10.11 Changes in the number of various medical institutions in China: 1950–2018.

prevention & treatment institutes, 29,050 grass-roots outpatient clinics, and 147 disease prevention and control centers. During the period 1952–1961, the total number of medical institutions and number of various medical institutions rose rapidly and reached a local peak during the Great Leap Forward period. Among them, the number of maternity and child health hospitals in 1957 reached 4,695; the number of grass-roots outpatient clinics, hospitals, and specialized disease prevention and treatment institutes in 1961 reached 217,600, 6,339, and 735, respectively; and the number of disease prevention and control centers reached 2,530. Afterwards, the number of these medical institutions declined rapidly, reached the lowest value around 1965 or 1970, and then rose rapidly again. In 1978, the total number of Chinese medical and health institutions increased to 169,732, representing an increase of 46.2% over that of 1950 and an average annual growth of 14.67%. Among them, the number of hospitals increased to 9,293, representing an average annual growth of 4.37%; the number of maternity and child care centers increased to 2,571, representing an average annual growth of 6.63%; the number of specialized disease prevention & control centers increased to 887, representing an average annual growth of 12.86%; and the number of disease prevention and control centers increased to 2,989, representing an average annual growth of 14.91%. The number of other grassroots medical institutions such as township healthcare centers and grassroots outpatient clinics also witnessed a significant increase.

Since the reform and opening-up, various types of medical institutions in China have continued to grow steadily. Due to changes in the statistical criteria after 2002 and the fact that the year 2002 was also the year China's medical system reform was complete, this year is used as a cut-off point and the two stages are discussed separately. As known from Figure 10.10, during the periods 1978–2001 and 2002–2018, changes in the number of hospitals, maternity and child care centers, specialized disease control centers as well as disease prevention and control centers were completely different. During the years 1978–2001, all four types of medical institutions basically took on an upward trend. Among them, the number of hospitals increased to 16,197, with an average annual growth of 2.44%; the number of maternity and child care centers increased to 3,132, with an average annual growth of 0.87%; the number of specialized disease control centers increased to 1,783, with an average annual growth of 3.08%; and the number of disease prevention and control centers increased to 3,813, with an average annual growth of 0.06%. Actually, the number of maternity and child care centers as well as specialized disease control centers started to drop in 1999 and 1997, respectively. During the years 2002–2018, the number of hospitals grew even faster, from 17,800 (2002) to 33,000 (2018), with an average annual growth of 4.28%; the number of maternity and child care centers changed little and was basically maintained at around 3,000, and slightly increased possibly due to the statistical reason after 2013, reaching 3,080 in 2018; the number of disease prevention and control centers decreased from 3,580 (2002) to 3,443 (2018); and the number of specialized disease control centers dropped from 1,839 (2002) to 1,161 (2018). The decline in the number of the latter three institutions may be related to the population aggregation during the process of industrialization and urbanization as the number of beds at maternity and child care centers and specialized disease control centers was increasing, according to the number of beds at various types of medical institutions in the *China Statistical Yearbooks*. Thus, it can be judged that the total number of beds in the country has not decreased but only been adjusted.

2.2 Changes in the number of medical technicians and medical beds

Figures 10.12a and 10.12b show the changes in the number of health workers and the number of health workers per capita in China. Figure 10.13 shows the changes in the total number of medical beds and the number of medical beds per capita in China during the same period. According to the data in the figures, in 1949, the number of urban health workers, health technicians, practicing (assistant) doctors, practicing doctors, physicians, and nurses was 541,000, 505,000, 363,000, 314,000, and 33,000 respectively (no statistical data on rural doctors and health workers is available), and the total number of medical beds at various medical institutions and the number of medical beds at the medical institutions at the county level or above were all about 80,000. During the period 1949–1978, the number of health workers and the number of medical beds basically increased. Both the number of health workers and the number of beds grew rapidly during the periods 1949–1958

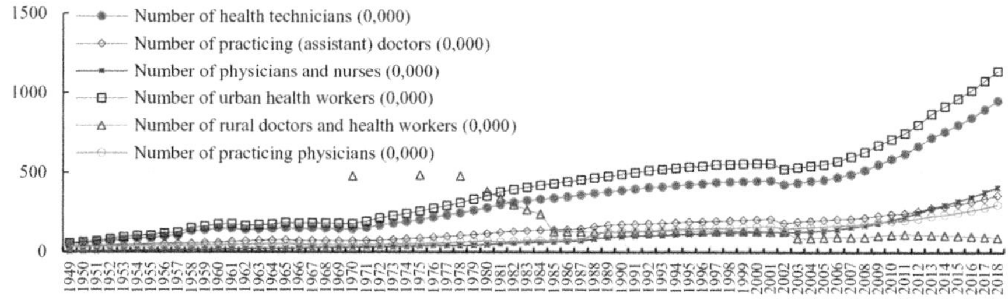

Figure 10.12a Number of health technicians, physicians, and nurses in China: 1949–2018.

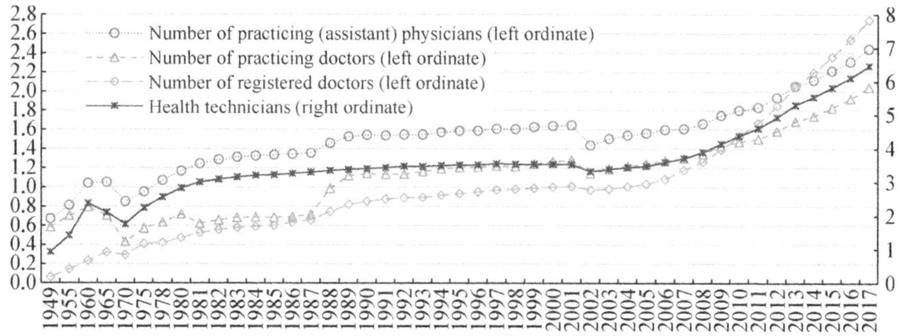

Figure 10.12b The number of health technicians, physicians, and nurses per thousand persons in China: 1949–2018.

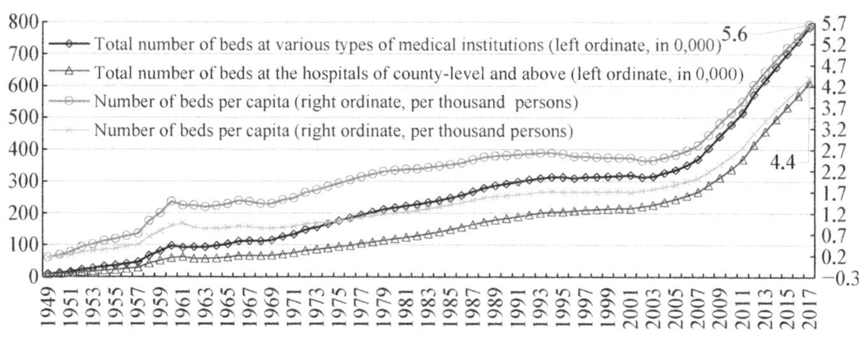

Figure 10.13 Changes in the total number of medical beds and the number of beds per capita in China: 1949–2018.

and 1970–1978. There was a significant fluctuation around 1960 due to the impact of the Great Leap Forward. The first statistics on rural doctors and health workers were reported in 1970. That year, the total number of rural doctors and health workers was 4.788 million, which stayed the same until 1978. In 1978, the number of urban health workers, health technicians, practicing (assistant) doctors, practicing doctors, as well as physicians and nurses was 3.106 million, 2.464 million, 1.033 million, 610,000, and 407,000, respectively. During the period 1949–1978, their average annual growth rates were 6.21%, 5.62%, 3.67%, 2.31%, and 9.05%, respectively; the number of rural doctors and health workers dropped to 4.777million; and the number of beds at various medical hospitals and the number of beds at the medical hospitals at the county level or above increased by 2.042 million and 1.093 million, respectively, with average annual growth rates of 11.59% and 9.43%.

In terms of per capita level, in 1949, the number of health workers, practicing doctors, practicing (assistant) physicians, and registered nurses per thousand persons was 0.93, 0.58, 0.67, and 0.06 in China; the number of beds per thousand persons in the country was 0.16; and the number of beds at hospitals was 0.15. China witnessed an overall increase in the number of medical and health technicians per capita and the number of beds per capita during the period 1949–1778, saw an obvious peak in 1960, and experienced a slight decline during the period 1960–1970. The peak in 1960 was caused by the Great Leap Forward Movement in 1958, and the decline in 1960–1970 was due to the dual effect of the country's adjustments after the Great Leap Forward and the rapid population growth during this period.[4] In 1978, the number of health workers, practicing doctors, practicing (assistant) physicians, and registered nurses per thousand persons increased to 2.56, 0.63, 1.07, and 0.42, respectively, with average annual growth rates for the period 1949–1978 being 3.55%, 0.30%, 1.63%, and 6.95%, respectively; and the total number of beds at various types of medical institutions and the number of beds at hospitals per thousand persons also increasing to 2.12 and 1.14, with average annual growth rates for the period 1949–1978 being 9.40% and 7.29%, respectively.

As can be seen in Figures 10.10 and 10.11, the number of health workers and the number of medical beds in China has been rising since 1978 and has grown even faster since 2005. Similarly, in order to avoid the changes in the statistical criteria, analysis will be made in two stages based on the cut-off point in 2002. According to the data in both figures, the number of urban health workers, health technicians, practicing (assistant) doctors, practicing

Table 10.3 Average annual growth rates for the number of medical and health workers per capita and the number of beds per capita, in %

	Health technicians	*Practicing (assistant) physicians*	*Practicing doctors*	*Nurses*	*Number of beds*	*Number of beds at hospitals*
1949–1978	3.55	1.63	0.30	6.95	9.40	7.29
1978–2001	1.41	1.87	3.12	3.85	0.73	1.74
2002–2018	4.60	4.26	3.74	7.17	5.80	6.40

doctors, physicians, and nurses was 5.584 million, 4.508 million, 2.1 million, 1.637 million, and 1.287 million, respectively, in 2001, and their average annual growth rates during the period 1978–2001 were 2.58%, 2.66%, 3.13%, 4.39%, and 5.13%, respectively; the number of beds at various types of medical institutions and the number of medical beds at the medical institutions at the county level and above increased to 3.2012 million and 2.1556 million, and their average annual growth rates were 1.97% and 3.00%. Except for practicing doctors, their growth rates were all smaller than those for the period 1949–1978. The number of rural doctors and health workers declined rapidly during the period 1978–1985. The number was 1.293 million in 1985, and did not change much until 2001, when the number was 1.2906 million. In terms of per capita level, the number of health workers, practicing doctors, practicing (assistant) physicians, and registered nurses per thousand persons in 2001 was 3.53, 1.28, 1.65, and 1.01, respectively, and their average annual growth rates for the period 1978–2001 were 1.41%, 3.12%, 1.89%, and 3.87%, respectively. The number of practicing doctors per capita and the number of practicing (assistant) physicians grew faster than that of 1949–1978. The number of beds per thousand persons of China increased to 2.51 in 2001 and the number of beds per thousand persons at the hospitals of China increased to 1.69, and their average annual growth rates were 0.73% and 1.74%, respectively, for the period 1978–2001, both being slower than those of 1949–1978.

The medical system reform was completed in 2002, when the number of health workers and medical beds increased rapidly once again. During the period 2002–2018, the number of urban health workers increased from 5.238 million to 11.393 million, an average annual increase of 4.98%; the number of health technicians increased from 4.270 million to 9.529 million, an average annual increase of 5.15%; the number of practicing (assistant) doctors increased from 1.844 million to 3.607 million, an average annual increase of 4.28%. The number of practicing doctors increased from 1.465 million to 3.011 million, an average annual increase of 4.61%; and the number of doctors and nurses increased from 1.247 million to 4.099 million, an average annual increase of 7.72%. However, the total number of rural doctors and health workers dropped from 1.291 million to 907,000 during this period. During the same period, the total number of beds at various medical institutions increased from 3.136 million to 8.404 million, an average annual increase of 6.35%; and the number of beds in hospitals at the county level or above increased from 2.222 million to 6.5197 million, an average annual increase of 6.96%. In this period, the growth rates of the total number of medical and health workers and the number of medical beds were much higher than those of 1978–2001, and not far from those of 1949–1978. In terms of per capita level, the total number of health workers per thousand persons increased from 3.32 to 6.83, an average annual increase of 4.60%; the number of practicing doctors per thousand persons increased from 1.44 to 2.22, an average annual increase of 4.26%; the number of practicing (assistant) physicians per thousand persons increased from 1.44 to 2.58, an average annual increase of 3.74%; and the number of registered nurses per thousand persons increased from 0.97 to 2.94, an average annual increase of 7.17%. These growth rates were much higher than those of 1978–2001, and also higher than those of 1949–1978. During the same period, the number of beds at various medical institutions per thousand persons increased from 2.44 to 6.02 and the number of medical beds in hospitals nationwide per thousand persons from 1.93 to 4.67, with average annual growth rates of 5.80% and 6.40%, respectively. Both growth rates were also higher than those of 1978–2001, and close to those of 1949–1978.

2.3 Status quo of China's medical and healthcare facilities: country-wise comparisons

Figure 10.14 shows the number of doctors per capita and the number of nurse midwives per capita in major economies and populous countries in the world in 2015. As can be seen from the figure, the number of doctors per thousand persons in European and American developed countries ranged between 2.5 and 4.0. This figure was the largest in Germany, 4.2; that in Russia was 4.0 and in Brazil was 1.9 (both are BRICS countries); and that in other developing countries and populous countries was very low, generally below 1. In 2015, China had 3.6 doctors per thousand persons, exceeding the level of many developed countries. According to the data of *World Development Indicators*, the world average in 2013 was 1.86; the level in high-income countries was 3.00; the level in OECD members was 2.86; and that in upper-middle-income countries and middle-income countries was 3.00 and 1.78. In 2013, China had 3.33 doctors per thousand persons. Thus, China had more doctors per capita than the other countries.

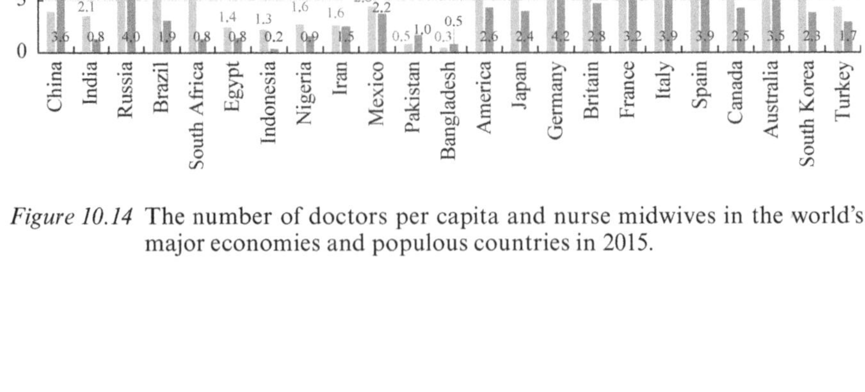

Figure 10.14 The number of doctors per capita and nurse midwives in the world's major economies and populous countries in 2015.

In 2015, the number of nurse midwives per thousand persons in European and American countries was more than 5.0. Among them, the figure in Germany, Australia, and Japan was all above 10, and that in America was 9.4. This figure was above 6 in Russia, Brazil, and South Africa and 2.1 in India; around 1.0 in other populous countries and developing countries. China had 2.3 nurse midwives per thousand persons, far lower than the level of European and American countries and, as compared with the other BRICS countries, also lower than that of Russia, Brazil, and South Africa, and almost the same as that of India. According to the data of *World Development Indicators*, the world average was 3.14%; the number of nurse midwives per thousand persons was 8.68; that in OECD members was 7.90; and that in upper-middle-income countries and mid-income countries was 3.35 and 2.50, respectively. In 2013, China had 2.03 nurse midwives per thousand persons. Thus, the number of China's nurse midwives per capita is still small.

Additionally, by observing the ratio of the number of doctors per capita to the number of nurse midwives per capita, it can be found that, in general countries, especially developed countries, the former is less than the latter, with the exception of China. The number of doctors per capita in China is more than 1.5 times of the nurses and midwives, which is opposite of the case in developed countries. In the latter, the number of nurses and midwives is twice to four times that of doctors. In developing countries, only Bangladesh and Pakistan have more doctors per capita than nurse midwives. Thus, the doctor-nurse ratio is extremely low in China (Figure 10.15).

Using the data of *World Development Indicators*, Figure 10.15 shows the number of hospital beds per capita in each country during the most recent years. As can be seen from the figure, the number of hospital beds per

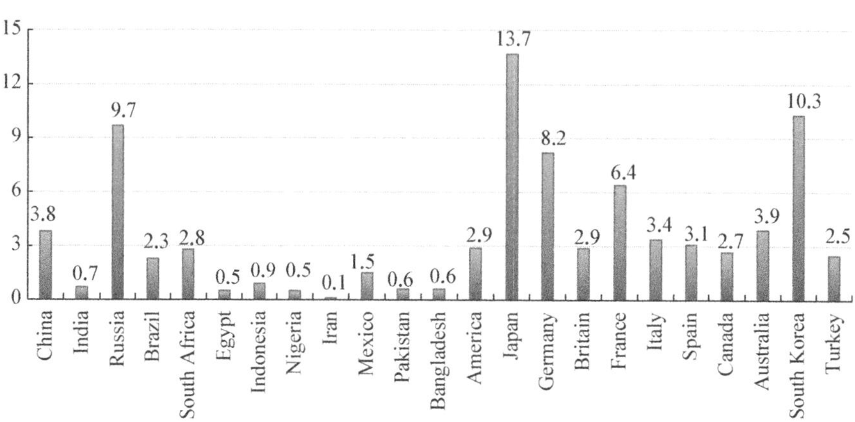

Figure 10.15 Number of hospital beds per capita in major economies and populous countries of the world.

thousand persons in China, 2011 was 3.8. During the same period, the gap among European and American countries was quite large. America, Britain, Italy, Spain, Canada, and other countries had only about three hospital beds per 1,000 persons, but Japan, Germany, France, and South Korea had 6–13 hospital beds per thousand persons each. Generally, developing countries had less than one bed per thousand persons, more than two for Brazil and South Africa, and 9.7 for Russia (2006). In 2001, the number of hospital beds per thousand persons was 4.23 in high-income countries, 3.77 in OECD members, and 2.18 in middle-income countries. Thus, the number of hospital beds per capita in China is large, exceeding the average level of middle-income countries and OECD members and not far from the average level of high-income countries.

Section 3 Changes and status quo of Chinese residents' health status

3.1 Population mortality rate

Figure 10.16 shows the changes in China's population mortality rate since 1949. As can be seen from Figure 10.16, in the years except the Great Leap Forward period and the 3-year difficult period (1958–1961), China's population mortality rate has basically declined. In 1949, when New China was founded, the country's population mortality rate was 2.0% and dropped to 1.7% in 1952 and to 1.08% in 1957. Due to the impact of natural disasters, the population mortality rate began to rise, to 1.198% in 1958 and 1.459% in 1959, and reached the peak of 2.543% in 1960. The mortality rate started to decline in 1961, reaching 1.42%, still higher than that of 1957. During the period 1962–1963, the mortality rate returned to normal, 1.00%, but rose again to 1.15% in 1964. Since 1965, China's population mortality rate has returned to normal and been declining. In 1977, the rate dropped to 0.687%

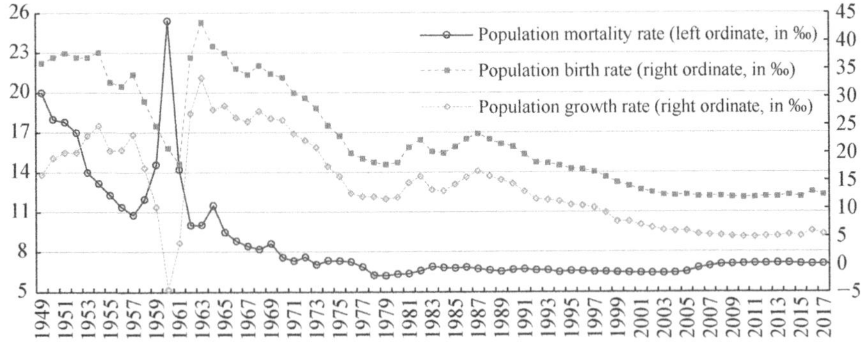

Figure 10.16 Changes in the population birth rate and mortality rate of China: 1949–2018.

in 1977, and continued to drop to 0.64% in 2003. After 2003, affected by the demographic structure changes, China's population mortality rate began to rise slightly, reaching the post-reform peak of 0.718% in 2014. In 2018, the country's population mortality rate reached 0.713%.

3.2 Infant and maternal mortality rates

Table 10.4 shows China's infant mortality rate and life expectancy by gender in different periods. As can be seen in Table 10.4, the infant mortality rate of China was 20% before 1949, dropping to 4.7% in the 1970s, to 3.47% in 1981, and to 1.9% in 2005, reaching 0.64% in 2018. The country's infant mortality rate dropped by 57.0% during the period 1957–1981 and by 82.4% during the period 1981–2018.

Figure 10.17 shows, according to World Bank data, the mortality rate of male and female adults (15–60 years old) and of infants under one year in China during the period 1960–2017. As can be known from Figure 10.17, due to the impact of the three-year natural disaster caused by the Great Famine, the mortality rate of adult males in China was about 50% and that of adult females about 40% during the period 1960–1962. For this period, the mortality rate data of infants under one year is not available. In 1969, the infant mortality rate reached 8.43%, and the mortality rates of male adults and female adults were 28.01% and 24.03%, respectively. In 1978, the infant mortality rate dropped to 5.30% and the mortality rates of male adults and female adults dropped to17.74% and14.40%, respectively, by 37.1%, 36.8%, and 40.0% than those of 1969. Mortality indicators continued to drop after 1978. In 2017, the mortality rate of infants under one year in China

Table 10.4 China's infant mortality rate and life expectancy by gender in different periods

Year	*Infant mortality rate (unit: 1/1000)*	*Life expectancy (year)*		
		All	*Gender*	*Male/Female*
Before the liberation	Around 200	35	...	...
1957	80.6	57	...	...
1973–1975	47.0	...	63.6	66.3
1981	34.7	67.9	66.4	69.3
1990	...	68.6	66.9	70.5
2000	32.2	71.4	69.6	73.3
2005	19.0	73.0	70.8	75.3
2010	13.1	74.8	72.4	77.4
2015	8.1	76.3	73.6	79.4
2018	6.1	77.0	...	...

Source: The life expectancy data for men and women in 2015 are taken from *China Statistical Yearbook 2017*, the data of 2018 are taken from *Bulletin of Statistics on China's Medical and Healthcare Development 2018*, and the data for other years are taken from *China Health and Family Planning Statistical Yearbook 2017*.

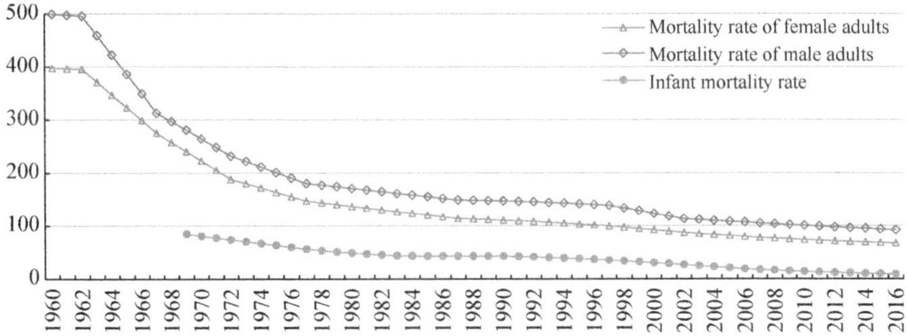

Figure 10.17 Changes in the mortality rates of infants and adults in China.

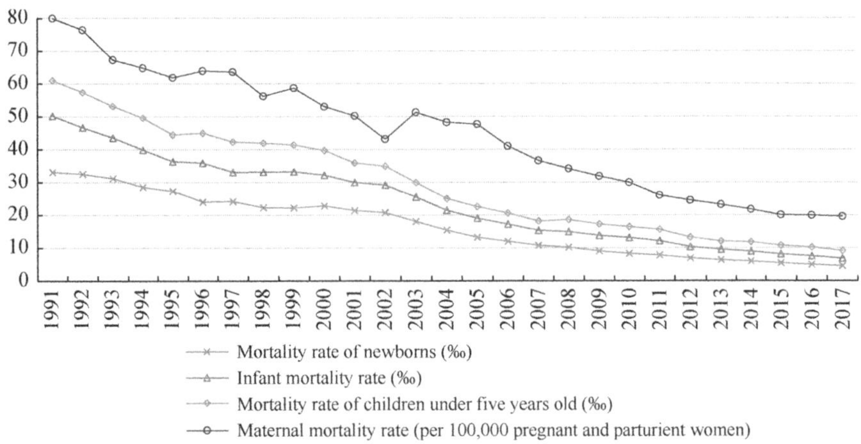

Figure 10.18 China's infant, child and maternal mortality rates: 1991–2018.

fell to 8.0%, and the mortality rates of adult men and women declined to 9.08% and 6.61%, respectively. The three rates decreased by 90.5%, 67.7%, and 72.5%, respectively, from those of 1969. These rates dropped by 37.1%, 36.8%, and 40.0% during the period 1969–1978, and by 84.9%, 48.8%, and 54.1%, respectively.

Figure 10.18 shows the changes in the newborn, infant, child (under 5 years old), and maternal mortality rates during the period 1991–2018. As shown in Figure 10.18, during the period 1991–2018, the newborn mortality rate dropped from 3.31% to 0.39%, a decrease of 88.2%; the infant mortality rate from 5.02% to 0.61%, a decrease of 87.8%; the mortality rate of children under 5 years old from 0.61% to 0.84%, a decrease of 86.2%; and the maternal mortality rate from 80 per 100,000 to 18.6 per 100,000, a decrease of 77.1%. The rate of decline in mortality rate of all above has exceeded 80%. Additionally, as seen in Figure 10.18, except for a few years when the maternal mortality rate increased, almost all mortality rates decreased every year. Among them, the maternal mortality rate increased significantly in 2003, which may be related to the outbreak of SARS in China that year.

3.3 Average life expectancy

According to the data of Table 10.4 and Figure 10.19, the average life expectancy of Chinese residents was about 35 years before 1949; rose to 57 years around 1957; and dropped to 43.7 years around 1960 due to the impact of food shortage. The average life expectancy rose rapidly after 1962, to 59.1 in 1970, slightly higher than that of 1957, and an increase of 15.4 years over that of 1962. In 1978, this figure increased to 65.9 years, 64.5 years for men and 67.3 years for women. During the period 1949–1978, the average life expectancy of Chinese residents increased by 30.9 years. Even compared with 1957, the average life expectancy in 1958 also increased by 6.4 years, representing an increase of 15.6%. After 1978, the average life expectancy continued to rise. It reached 72.0 years in 2000 and increased to 73.0 years in 2005. In 2017, the average life expectancy of Chinese residents reached 76.4 years, 75.0 for men and 78.0 for women. During the years 1978–2017, the average life expectancy increased by 10.6 years, 10.5 years for men and 10.67 years for women. According to the latest data in the *Bulletin of Statistics on China's Medical and Healthcare Development 2019*, the average life expectancy of Chinese residents reached 77.3 years in 2019.

3.4 Incidence and mortality rates of infectious diseases

Figure 10.20 shows the changes in the incidence of and mortality rates resulting from notifiable Class A and B infectious diseases in China. According to the data in the figure, in 1950, the incidence rate of Class A and B

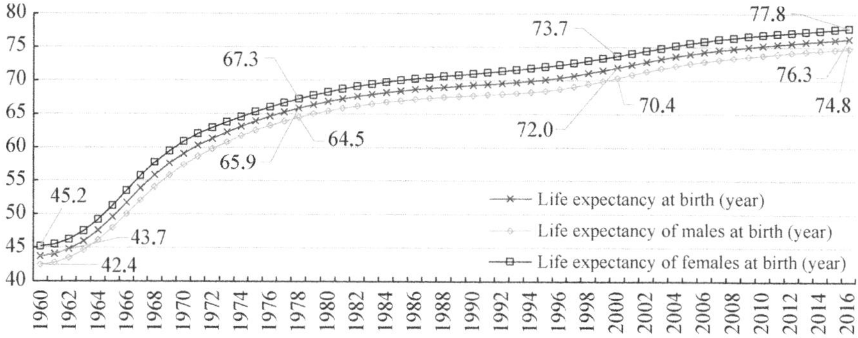

Figure 10.19 Life Expectancy of Chinese residents at birth: 1960–2017.

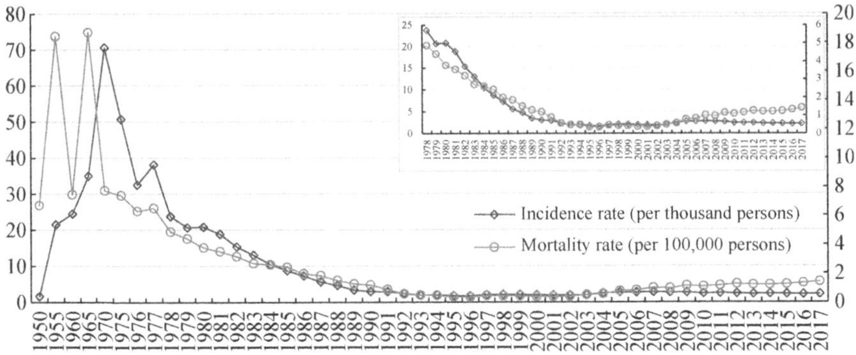

Figure 10.20 The incidence and mortality rates of Class A and Class B notifiable infectious diseases in China: 1950–2018.

notifiable in China was roughly 0.163%, and the resulting mortality rate was approximately 6.7 per 100,000. From the 1950s to 1970s, both rates were rising. The incidence rate of notifiable Class A and B infectious diseases rose to 70.6% (1970), and the mortality rate was also as high as 18.43 per 100,000 and 18.71 per 100,000 in 1955 and 1965. Both rates above witnessed a significant decrease during the period 1970–1978, with the former down 2.37% and the latter down 4.86 per 100,000. And the former was up 13.5 times, and the latter down 27.5%. Since 1978, both rates basically have showed a downward trend, which can be divided into two stages. First, the period 1978–1996, which was the stage of rapid decline in the incidence rate of infectious diseases and rapid decrease in the resulting mortality of these diseases. During this period, the incidence rate of infectious diseases dropped from 2.37% to 0.166%, a decrease of 93.0%; the resulting mortality rate dropped from 4.86 per 100,000 to 0.33 per 100,000, a decrease of 93.2%. Both rates reached their bottom again in 1996. Second, the period 1997–2018, when the incidence rate of infectious diseases showed a fluctuating trend, with a small fluctuation range, basically between 0.2 and 0.3%. In 2018, the incidence rate of infectious diseases was 0.22%, representing a slight increase over that of 1996. In the same period, the mortality rate resulting from infectious diseases showed a slight upward trend, but the range of increase was not large. In 2018, the mortality rate as a result of the disease was 1.66 per 100,000, up 4.25 times compared with that of 1996. The increase in the death rate of infectious diseases of China after 1996 was mainly due to the following two reasons: first, the rise in the mortality rate caused by the evolution and mutation of viruses for some infectious diseases (the number of deaths divided by the number of patients). For example, the mortality rate resulting from epidemic cerebrospinal meningitis rose from 5.58% in 1996 to 7.2% in 2014; the mortality rate resulting from malaria rose from 0.07% in 1996 to 0.82% in 1996; and the mortality rate resulting from AIDS rose from 0.02%

to 29.3% in 2018. Second, the rising incidence rate (or infection rate) of some infectious diseases. For instance, the incidence rate of HIV (AIDS virus) infectors rose from 015 per 100,000 in 1997 to 6.4 per 100,000 in 2016, and the incidence rate of AIDS rose from 0.15 per 100,000 in 1997 to 4.60 per 100,000 in 2018.

Table 10.5 lists, for certain years, the incidence rates of the top 18 infectious diseases in China in 2018. Since not all data are complete for all these years, Figure 10.21 shows the changes in the incidence rates of some infectious diseases with relatively complete annual data in order to reflect

Table 10.5 Incidence rates of various types of Class A and B notifiable infectious diseases in China (unit: 1/100,000)

Disease\year	*1950*	*1960*	*1970*	*1978*	*1980*	*1990*	*2000*	*2010*	*2018*
Viral hepatitis		61.84*	32.23	*92.39*	111.47	117.57	64.91	98.74	91.73
Tuberculosis						**39.21[a]**	**43.75**	**74.27**	**59.0**
Syphilis					**0.01[b]**	**0.23**	**6.43**	**28.90**	**35.46**
Bacterial and amoebic dysentery	46.37	438.88	352.15	*676.06*	568.99	127.44	40.79	18.9	9.53
Gonorrhea					**0.02[c]**	**9.49**	**22.92**	**8.07**	**9.54**
Scarlet fever	0.59	6.38	7.22	*14.69*	10.95	2.7	1.08	1.56	5.65
AIDS						**0.01[a]**	**0.02**	**2.56**	**4.60**
Brucellosis	0.23[d]	0.33	0.99	*0.24*	0.17	**0.07**	**0.17**	**2.53**	**2.72**
Typhoid fever and paratyphoid fever	8.17	37.75	9.96	*15.58*	11.94	10.32	4.19	1.05	0.77
Epidemic hemorrhagic fever		0.1	0.41	*1.58*	3.12	3.66	3.05	0.71	0.86
Pertussis	133.82[d]	87.77	152.23	*125.95*	62.82	1.8	0.46	0.13	1.58
Dengue						0.03	0.03	0.02	0.37
Measles	44.08	157.51	450.47	*249.44*	114.88	7.71	5.93	2.86	0.28
Malaria	**1027.7[d]**	**1553.9**	**2961.1**	*325.37*	337.83	10.56	2.02	0.55	0.18
Epidemic encephalitis B	2.3[d]	2.18	18.02	*5.39*	3.31	3.43	0.95	0.19	0.13
Rabies	0.32[d]	0.03	0.18	*0.25*	0.69	0.32	0.04	0.15	0.03
Anthrax	0.46[d]	0.21	0.23	*0.54*	0.43	0.21	0.05	0.02	0.02
Leptospirosis		19.73*	11.14	*2.14*	3.67	2.59	0.32	0.05	0.01
Epidemic cerebrospinal meningitis	1.94	6.91	20.97	*32.18*	23.44	0.89	0.19	0.02	0.01
Schistosomiasis							0.24[e]	0.32	0.01

Source: *China Health and Family Planning Statistical Yearbook 2017* and *Bulletin of Statistics on China's Medical and Healthcare Development 2018*.

* indicates the data of 1965,

[a] indicates the data of 1998

[b] indicates the data of 1981

[c] indicates the data of 1982

[d] indicates the data of 1955

[e] indicates the data of 2005.

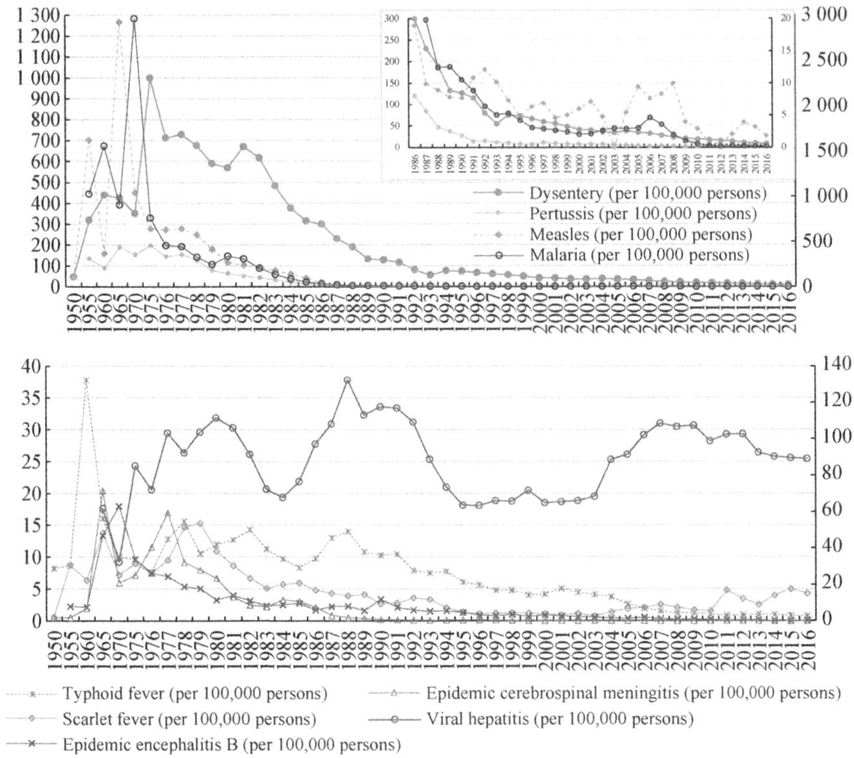

Figure 10.21 Incidence rates of several types of major Class A and B notifiable infectious diseases in China: 1950–2018.

the changes of various infectious diseases. As known from Figure 10.21, the nine representative infectious diseases listed show a trend of first rising and then declining from 1950 to 1978. With the exception of viral hepatitis, the incidence rates of other infectious diseases declined significantly from 1978 to 2018. Among all the infectious diseases listed in Table 10.5, only a few types witnessed a drop in the incidence rate during the years 1950–1978. Among them, the incidence rate of malaria dropped from 1,027 per 10,000 to 337.8 per 100,000; that of pertussis from 133.8 to 125.4 per 100,000; and that of rabies also declined significantly, from 0.332 to 0.25 per 100,000. The incidence rates of the other infectious diseases were all on the rise, and the increase in the incidence rates of some infectious diseases was even up ten to tens of times. For example, during the period 1950–1978, the incidence rates of bacterial and amoebic dysentery rose from 46.4 to 676.1 per 100,000, up nearly 14 times; the incidence rate of measles from 44.1 to 249.4 per 100,000, up around five times; that of epidemic cerebrospinal meningitis from 1.94 to 32.2 per 100,000, up more than 15 times; that of scarlet fever from 0.59 to 14.7 per 100,000, up nearly 24 times; and epidemic hemorrhage also from 0.1 per 100,000 in 1960 to 1.58 per 100,000 in 1978, up more than 15 times. Nevertheless, during this period, except for rabies, whose mortality rate rose from 29.76% (1955) to 99.7%, other infectious diseases saw a significant decrease in the mortality rate. For example, the mortality rate resulting from viral hepatitis B dropped from 0.33% in 1965 to 0.20%; that resulting from bacterial and amoebic dysentery from 4.22% in 1950 to 0.12%; that resulting from measles from 6.46% to 0.4%; and those resulting from scarlet, fever cerebrospinal meningitis, epidemic cerebrospinal meningitis, pertussis, and brucellosis also decreased from 8.34%, 16.54% , 27.35% (1955), 0.74% (1955), and 0.12% (1955) to 0.08%, 4.17%, 11.01%, 0.11%, and 0.04%, respectively, but the mortality rate of rabies rose from 26.8% to 98.9%.

During the period 1978–2008, among the nine infectious diseases listed in Figure 10.21, except for viral hepatitis B, which showed a cyclical fluctuation, and scarlet fever, which saw an upward trend after 2003, the other infectious diseases saw a significant downward trend in the incidence rate. For example, the incidence rate of bacterial and amoebic dysentery dropped from 676.6 to 9.53 per 100,000; that of scarlet fever from 14.69 to 5.65 per 100,000; that of measles from 249.44 to 0.28 per 100,000; that of pertussis from 125.95 to 1.58 per 100,000; and that of malaria from 325.37 to 0.18 per 100,000. Other epidemics such as epidemic cerebrospinal meningitis, rabies, and epidemic encephalitis B saw a significant increase in the incidence rate. Among the 17 infectious diseases listed in Table 10.5, except for tuberculosis, brucellosis, and three sexually transmitted diseases (syphilis, gonorrhea, and AIDS), other infectious disease saw a decrease in the incidence rate. Even for those diseases with rising incidence rates, their overall mortality rate basically declined due to the declining mortality of these diseases from 1978 to 2018, and the larger decrease in the mortality rate than the rise in the incidence rate. As the sole exception, AIDS saw a rising mortality rate, as shown in Figure 10.22.

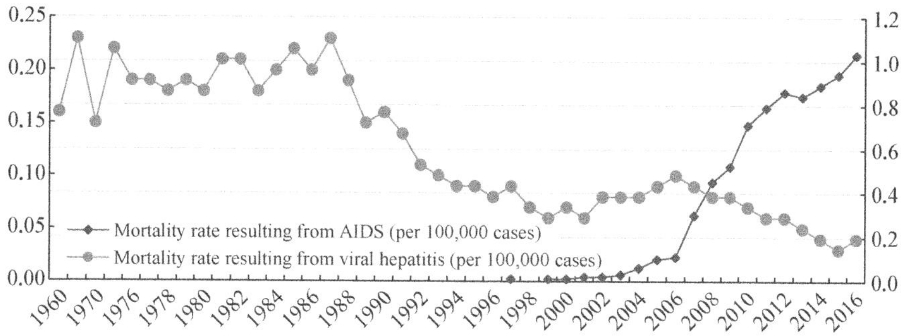

Figure 10.22 The mortality rates of viral hepatitis and AIDS in China: 1960–2018.

3.5 Multinational comparisons over the health status of Chinese residents

Although China has seen a significant improvement in the health status of its residents since 1949, the country, as a developing one, still lags far behind developed countries in this respect. Firstly, in terms of the child mortality rate, as shown in Figure 10.23, the mortality rates of China's newborns, one-year-old infants, and children under five years were 0.55%, 0.92%, and 1.07% in 2015, and the mortality rate of the children above five was 0.29%. In developed countries, the first three rates were all below 0.7%, and the mortality rate of the children between 5 and 14 years old was above 0.15%. China's infant mortality rate was far higher than that of developed countries. Among the five BRICS countries, the four indicators of Russia were all lower than those of China. Brazil was not much different than China, with the first three indicators being higher than those of China. Moreover, the mortality rate of 5-year-old children was lower than that of China. And the four indicators of India and South Africa were higher than those of China. Among the ten most populous countries in the world, only America, Japan, and Russia had lower infant mortality rates than China. The indicators for Mexico and Brazil were similar to those of China. The other five countries had higher infant mortality rates than China. In 2015, the mortality rates of newborns, one-year-old infants, children above 5, and children between 5 and 14 years old were 3.14%,1.91%, 4.22%, and 0.78%, respectively, in the world;0.46%, 0.31%, 0.56%, and 0.11%, respectively, in high-income countries;0.46%, 0.75%, 1.48%, and 0.30%, respectively, in upper-middle-income

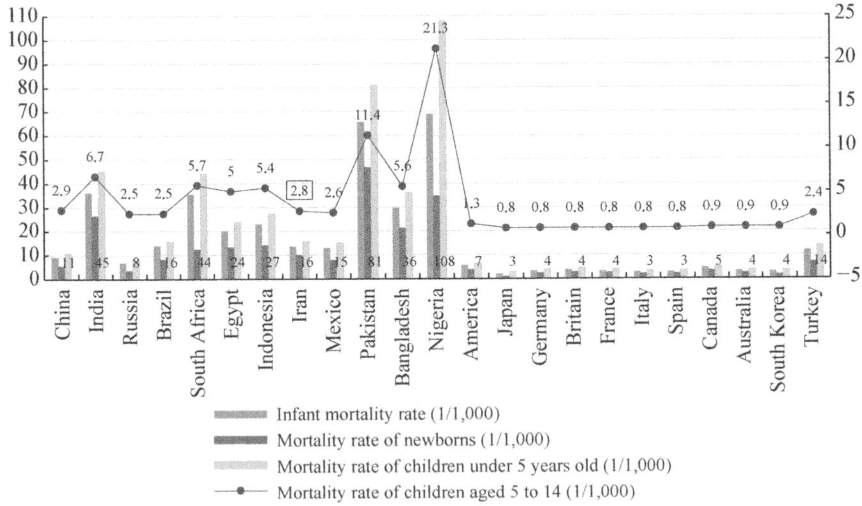

Figure 10.23 The infant and child mortality rates of major economies and populous countries in the world.

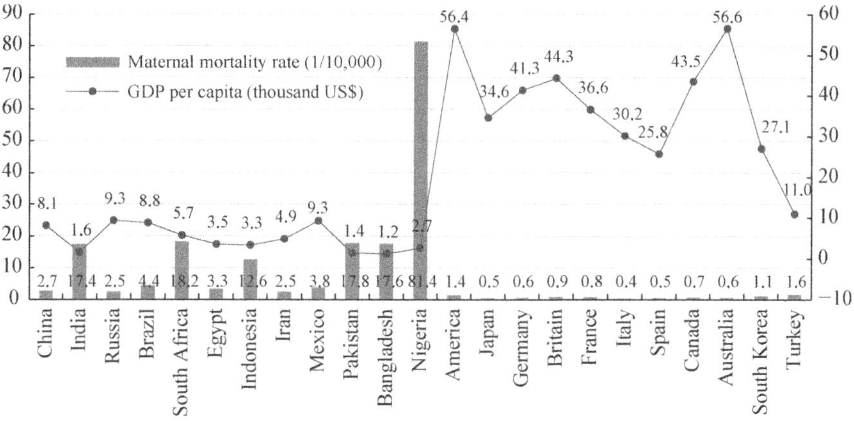

Figure 10.24 The domestic income per capita and maternal mortality rate in different countries of 2015.

countries; and 3.18%, 1.92%, 3.92%, and 0.66%, respectively, in middle-income countries. So, the infant mortality rate in China is relatively low among developing countries and is lower than the average of upper-middle-income countries but much higher than that of developed countries.

Secondly, in terms of the mortality rate, as shown in Figure 10.24, in 2015, this figure was 0.027% in China, 0.014% in America, and below 0.01% in developed countries such as Australia, Germany, Japan, and France, 0.011% in South Korea. Compared with developed countries, China still had a high maternal mortality rate, almost two to seven times of that of developed countries. Among BRICS countries, only Russia had a slight lower maternal mortality rate (0.027%) than China. The maternal mortality rate of Brazil (0.044%) was more than 1.6 times that of China; that of South Africa (0.182%) and India (0.174%) was much higher than that of China. Among the ten most populous countries in the world, only America and Russia had lower maternal mortality rates than China. In 2015, the maternal mortality rate was 0.216% for the world on average, 0.013% for high-income countries, 0.041% for upper-high-income countries, and 0.180% for middle-income countries. Just like with the infant mortality rate, the maternal mortality rate of China is higher than that of developed countries and high-income countries but lower than the average of developing countries and lower-middle income countries.

Finally, in terms of life expectancy per capita, as shown in Figure 10.25, except for American whose residents' average life expectancy is less than 80 years, the life expectancy of other developed countries basically was basically above 80 years, above 81 years for females and above 78 years for men (76.3 for America). In 2015, the average life expectancy of residents in China was 76.1 years, 2.6 years less than that of America; 77.7 years for women and

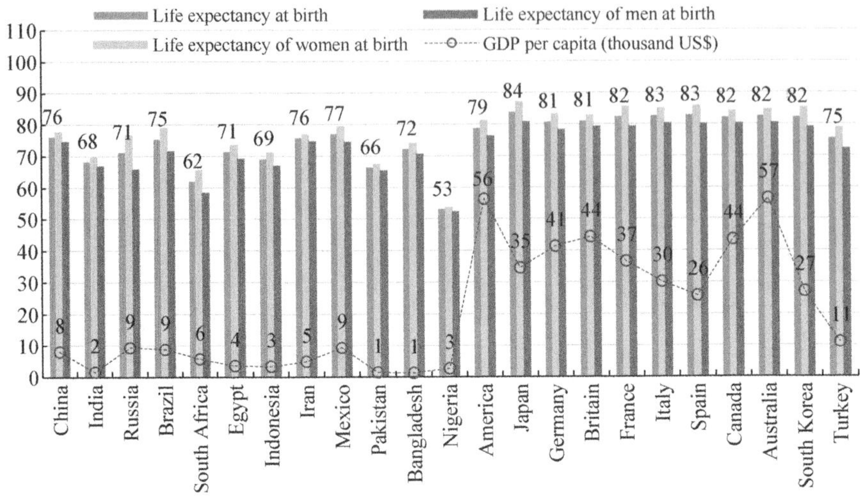

Figure 10.25 Life expectancy per capita and number of population in different countries, 2015.

74.6 for men, two years less than that of developed countries. China ranked the top among BRICS countries. Only Brazil (75.2 years) was close to China in this respect. The average life expectancy of other countries, such as Russia (71.2 years), India (68.3 years), and South Africa (62.0 years), was 5 to 12 years less than that of China. Among other developing countries, only Iran and Mexico had an average life expectancy that was close to that of China. In 2015, the life expectancy for men, life expectancy for women, and overall average life expectancy was 69.8, 74.1, and 71.9 in the world on average; 77.8, 83.1, and 80.3, respectively, for high-income countries; 72.9, 77.5, and 75.1, respectively, for upper-high-income countries; and 69.1, 73.3, and 71.1, respectively, for upper-middle-income countries. Thus, the average life expectancy of China is significantly less than that of developed countries but higher than the average level of developing countries, especially the average level of upper-middle-income countries into which China's is classified in terms of income per capita.

Notes

1 At the official exchange rate 2015, China's medical and healthcare expenditure per capita was only US$425; the world average was about US$1,002; that in high-income countries was about US$4,874; that in upper-middle-income countries was about US$457; that in middle-income countries was US$257, and that in low-income countries was about US$ 37. The total healthcare expenditure per capita in China is still between the average level of middle-income countries and that of upper-middle-income countries.

2 The healthcare expenditure of low-income countries includes the healthcare expenditure resulting from foreign aid, and the total healthcare expenditure accounts for a high proportion in GDP instead.
3 It is true for the world average data of the proportion of government public health expenditure in the government's public expenditure in 2015, but the world average was 15.53% in both 2011 and 2013.
4 According to the Collection of China's Population Statistics, the 1960s was a period when China's population grew fastest. During the period 1962-1972, China's annual population growth rate exceeded 2.2%, reaching 3.3% in the peak year.

11 The impact of health on China's economic growth

Section 1 Is health important to economic growth?

Like education, health is also a type of human capital (Schultz, 1961; Mushkin, 1962, etc.). Will China's increasing health investment and health human capital promote economic growth? It is understandable that economic growth helps increase people's demand for health, thereby promoting the added investment in the health of the entire economy and the improvement of residents' health status. But how can health investment and residents' health status promote economic growth? What are the mechanisms by which health human capital and health investment affect economic growth? Particularly, under the interaction between health and economic growth, how will the investment in health and the health status of residents affect economic growth?

This chapter will first theoretically study the mechanism of interaction between economic growth and health. In a model that contains the Arrow-Romer production function and the Grossman (1972) utility function, considering the impact of health human capital on the economy, this chapter probes into the dynamic behavior of material capital accumulation and health human capital investment and their impact on economic growth. Then, using China's inter-provincial panel data, this chapter empirically studies the impact of China's health human capital and health investment on China's economy. It is found through research in this chapter that, theoretically, economic growth is not only related to the growth rate of health investment, but also to the stock of health human capital. The overall effect of the stock of health human capital on economic growth depends on how it affects material capital accumulation. If the crowding-out effect of material capital is excluded, the stock of health human capital will surely promote economic growth as it will improve individuals' labor productivity. However, as health investment may squeeze out material capital accumulation, excessive health human capital and health investment may suppress economic growth. Additionally, considering the positive externality of health investment for labor productivity through its effect on material capital investment, introducing health human capital into the economy may cause a

DOI: 10.4324/9781003261629-14

poverty trap during economic development. In this case, the initial state of the economy produces an important effect on the long-term development of the economy. The empirical research in this chapter shows that, in terms of China's inter-provincial panel data, there is a significant positive correlation between China's health investment growth rate and the country's economic growth rate; when the ratio of health human capital and material capital remains unchanged, both health human capital (measured by the number of beds in hospital per capita) and health investment (measured by the growth rate of the number of beds in hospital per capita) produce a positive promoting effect on China's economic growth rate. However, the increase in the ratio of health human capital to material capital produces a negative effect on the economic growth rate. Thus, the analysis on the overall effect of China's health investment on economic growth should be determined by the sum of these triple effects.

A lot of existing literature (including empirical research and theoretical research literature) has studied the relationship between health and economic growth. Most of the existing literature believes that, as one type of human capital that shares the same nature as education human capital, health human capital can also improve labor productivity and promote economic growth. However, health does differ from education in some aspects. Grossman (1972) believes that due to the effect of good health for individuals, health investment is not only a human capital investment but one type of service-oriented consumption necessary in individuals' lives. Thus, if "health" is a normal commodity, health investment and the stock of health human capital will continue to increase during the economic growth process, which may squeeze out material capital investment and hinder the sustained growth of the economy. This characteristic of health has actually been proved in the research of Baumol (1967) and Zon and Muysken (2001, 2003). In a Lucas (1988) endogenous growth model with health investment, Zon and Muysken (2001, 2003) studied this effect of health human capital on economic growth. They believe in their research that, as health investment may increase together with income per capita, the increase in individuals' health status of the economy may lead to population aging. Thus, health human capital may slow down economic growth in the long run, while long-term economic growth may eventually disappear due to increasing investment in health human capital. By assuming the capacity of health to improve individuals' labor capacity and utility level, this chapter re-examines the effect of health human capital on economic growth in an Arrow-Romer (Arrow, 1962; Romer, 1986) endogenous growth model with health human capital. And the following conclusions that are consistent with those of Zon and Muysken (2001, 2003) are drawn. Firstly, health human capital will gradually increase together with the increase in income; secondly, it is more important that a higher health investment cause the reduction of material capital investment under the given output as maintaining a higher health status requires a higher health investment level. Therefore, if health investment does not play an enough large role in the improvement of production capacity, the increase in health human capital may cause harm to economic growth. Based on the conclusions deduced from the Grossman-Arrow-Romer model, this chapter tests the effect of health investment on economic growth based on China's inter-provincial panel data, and discusses the effect of the country's health human capital and health investment on its economic growth. The empirical research in this chapter shows that the negative effect of health investment on economic growth is related to the ratio of health investment to material capital. The higher the ratio, the greater the negative effect of human investment on economic growth. Additionally, the research in this chapter also shows that, in the economy with the Arrow-Romer production function, health human capital may affect material capital accumulation by affecting the rate of return on material capital as the material capital is of externality. Thus, it is also externality for economic growth. The consequence of this effect is that there may be a poverty trap in the Grossman-Arrow-Romer model. This result is different from that of Zon and Muysken (2001, 2003).

The structure of the subsequent parts of this chapter is arranged as follows: the second part is the theoretical model of this chapter, which mainly analyzes the relationship between health and economic growth in theory; the third part tests the conclusions of the second part by applying China's inter-provincial panel data; and the fourth part is the conclusions of this chapter.

Section 2 Basic model and theoretical analysis: health and economic growth

2.1 Consumers' behavior

Assume health human capital produces two effects on individuals. First, since healthy people always have a higher happiness index than unhealthy people, it is assumed in the following analysis that health can produce a positive utility on individuals. So, health is included in the utility function Grossman (1972). Second, as pointed out in the literature review, since health can improve individuals' labor productivity, the analysis in this chapter also assumes that health is included in the production function for individuals. Additionally, in order to make the analysis simple, like Zon and Muysken (2001, 2003), assume that health human capital is completely depreciated. So, the current health status is only determined by the health investment of the current period.[1] Without loss of generality, suppose the utility function of an individual is:

$$u(c,h) = \ln c + \ln h \tag{11.1}$$

where c refers to the individual's consumption level and h refers to the current health status (or health human capital) of the individual.

In the analysis of this chapter, the mechanism of interaction between health and economic growth mainly reflects the fact that health investment can increase health human capital and personal labor capacity, thereby promoting economic growth. In fact, there are at least two methods for improving personal health status (or h). Firstly, the improvement of consumption level and nutrition can improve personal health status. Fogel (1994a, b, 2002) and Straus & Thomas show in their research that, if height and weight are used as indicators for measuring health human capital, the improvement of consumption level and then nutrition level will be the main factor for the improvement of health human capital in many countries in the long run. Secondly, the approach that may help improve health is health investment (Grossman, 1972; Strauss & Thomas, 1998; Zon & Muysken, 2001, 2003). Grossman (1972) believes that health investment, such as medical treatment, medical care, physical exercise, rest and health consumption goods, would produce a significant effect on health improvement. The third method of improving health conditions is related to individuals' knowledge. In their research, Howitt (2005) and Sanso and Asia (2006) et al. hold that the improvement of an individual's personal knowledge about physiology and health care can improve his/her personal health. An individual's health status is affected by a lot of factors. Moreover, as the research in this chapter mainly highlights the effect of health investment on economic growth, it is assumed below that an individual's health status is mainly determined by his/her health investment level. It is further assumed that an individual's health cost function is expressed as follows:

$$T = T(h) \tag{11.2}$$

where T refers to health investment cost. Equation (11.2) shows that an individual will have to make a health investment at the level of $T(h)$ in order to reach the health status of h.

Finally, it is also assumed that the individual's income mainly comes from his/her capital income and labor income. Since better health status of an individual promises higher production capacity, the individual's wage level is directly determined by the individual's health human capital according to the principle that marginal productivity determines the wage level. It is assumed in this research that an individual with h health human capital has a wage level of $w(h)$. Thus, the material capital accumulation equation of the individual is as follows:

$$\dot{k} = w(h) + rk - c - T(h) \tag{11.3}$$

where k represents the individual's material capital stock and r represents the interest rate. The individual's optimization behavior is as follows:

$$\max_{c,h} : \int_0^{+\infty} u(c,h)e^{-\beta t}dt$$
$$s.t.: \dot{k} = w(h) + rk - c - T(h), \ \ given\ k_0$$

where β refers to the individual's subjective discount rate.

2.2 Production function and manufacturers' behavior

Assume the production function takes the form of Arrow-Romer; i.e.:

$$Y = A(K)^{\alpha}(EL)^{1-\alpha} \tag{11.4}$$

where Y represents total output, L represents the total output, L represents the total amount of capital, and A and α are both invariable parameters. E represents the production efficiency per labor force, which is directly related to the stock of capital per capita of the society: i.e.:

$$E_t = K_t / N_t = \bar{k}_t \tag{11.5}$$

where N refers to total population and $\bar{k}$ refers to capital per capita.

Health human capital is another important way health can affect individuals' labor productivity and thus economic growth. A large number of micro and macro data have also demonstrated that labor productivity has a significant positive correlation with health human capital, which becomes even more obvious in low-income countries (Strauss & Thomas, 1998; Bloom et al., 2004, etc.). The fact that health can affect personal productivity can be well understood. Firstly, healthier workers obviously have more energy so that they can do longer, more intensive work. Also, healthy people are less likely to become ill and can provide more working time. Therefore, just as Barro (1996) and Zon and Muysken (2001, 2003), et al. believe, it is quite natural and reasonable to assume that health is included in the production function. Fogel (2002, p. 24) believes that the contribution of health to economic growth can be considered as one type of labor-expanding technological advancement. Zon and Muysken (2001, p. xiii) also believe that health improvement is equivalent to the neutral technological advancement of Harrod. In this chapter, the production function of health human capital is expressed as follows:

$$P = f(h) \tag{11.6}$$

where p represents an individual's production capacity. Equation (11.6) shows that a person with health human capital being h can provide the total labor equal to $f(h)$. Under this assumption, the total labor input of the entire economy, L, is expressed as follows:

$$L = Nf(h) \tag{11.7}$$

N refers to the total population. To simplify the analysis, assume that there is no population growth in the economy. N is a constant and is further unitized into 1. According to Equations (11.4), (11.5), and (11.7), the production function can be expressed as follows:

$$y = Y/N = A(f(h)\bar{k})^{1-\alpha}(k)^{\alpha} \tag{11.8}$$

Assume that enterprises maximize profits, and all markets are perfectively competitive. Since the capital per capita of all manufacturers is the same in the case of equilibrium, the profit maximization behavior of manufacturers enables:

$$r = \alpha A\phi(h),\ w = (1-\alpha)\phi(h)Ak \tag{11.9}$$

where $\phi(h) = (f(h))^{1-\alpha}$. Without loss of generality, assume:

$$\begin{aligned}&\phi'(h) > 0, \phi''(h) < 0\text{: } \phi(0) = 0,\ \lim_{h\to 0}\phi'(h) = +\infty,\ \lim_{h\to\infty}\phi'(h) = 0,\\ &2\beta/(\alpha A) > \lim_{h\to\infty}\phi(h) = \bar{\phi} \geq \beta/(\alpha A)\end{aligned} \tag{11.10}$$

Equation (11.10) shows that, when health human capital increases, the productivity of health human capital will increase, but its marginal productivity will decrease. Also, $\phi(0) = 0$ indicates that health human capital is necessary for production, and the person without health human capital will not have any production capacity. The others are a few technical assumptions. $2\beta/(\alpha A) > \bar{\phi}$ allows the convergence of the individual's effect level, and $\bar{\phi} \geq \beta/(\alpha A)$ guarantees the existence of sustained economic growth.

2.3 Dynamic behavior of the economy

The following equations can be obtained by seeking the optimization problem for individuals:

$$c/c = r - \beta = \alpha A\phi(h) - \beta \tag{11.11}$$

$$\left(\frac{1}{h}\right)\left[\frac{1}{T'(h) - (1-\alpha)A\phi'(h)k}\right] = \frac{1}{c} \tag{11.12}$$

To facilitate the analysis, assume $T(h) \equiv (1-\alpha)A\varphi(h)$. The inclusion of technical level A into the health cost function indicates that technological advancement may be of some externality for individuals' health. Also, assume $\varphi'(h) > 0$ and $\varphi''(h) > 0$, which indicates the health investment function is an increasing function of increasing marginal cost.

According to Equation (11.12), the determination equations for the ratio of health expenditure to the total consumption expenditure and for the ratio of health investment to the total output are as follows:

$$\frac{T}{T+c}=1-\frac{1}{\left(1/\varepsilon_{\varphi h}+1\right)+(1-\alpha)(y/c)(\varepsilon_{\phi h}/\varepsilon_{\varphi h})} \tag{11.13}$$

$$\frac{T}{y}=\frac{1}{\varepsilon_{\varphi h}}\frac{c}{y}+(1-\alpha)\varepsilon_{\phi h} \tag{11.14}$$

where $\varepsilon_{\varphi h}=\varphi'(h)h/\varphi(h)$represents the elasticity of the health cost function and $\varepsilon_{\phi h}=\phi'(h)h/\phi(h)$ represents health output elasticity. Equations (11.13) and (11.14) show that an increase in health output elasticity (or $\varepsilon_{\phi h}$) will result in a decrease in the proportion of healthcare expenditure in the total consumption and the proportion of healthcare expenditure in total output; and an increase in the health cost elasticity (or $\varepsilon_{\varphi h}$) will lead to an increase in the proportion of healthcare expenditure in the total consumption and in the proportion of healthcare expenditure in the total output. However, an increase in the pure consumption-output ratio (or c/y) will lead to a decrease in the proportion of healthcare expenditure in the total consumption and the proportion of healthcare expenditure in the total output.

According to Equation (11.12), the health human capital accumulation equation is obtained as follows:

$$\left[1+\varepsilon(h,k)\right]\frac{\dot{h}}{h}=\frac{\dot{c}}{c}+\tau_{hk}\frac{\dot{k}}{k} \tag{11.15}$$

where $\varepsilon(h,k)=\left[\varphi''(h)-\phi''(h)k\right]h/\left(\varphi'(h)-\phi'(h)k\right)s$ and $\tau_{hk}=\phi'(h)k/\left[\varphi'(h)-\phi'(h)k\right]$. Equation (11.15) reflects the relationship among the growth rate of health human capital, the consumption growth rate, and the growth rate of material capital. According to this equation, if both material capital per capita and consumption per capita increase, health human capital will inevitably increase, and vice versa. These conclusions are obviously in line with the actual economy.

According to the material capital accumulation Equation (11.13) and Equation (11.14), we can get:

$$\dot{k}/k=A\phi(h)\left[1+(1-\alpha)\varepsilon_{\phi h}\right]-(\varepsilon_{\varphi h}+1)\left[T(h)/k\right] \tag{11.16}$$

Equation (11.16) indicates that health human capital has two effects on material capital accumulation. On the one hand, since the increase in health human capital can increase labor productivity and the total output level, health human capital will benefit material capital accumulation. The positive effect of health on material capital accumulation is reflected in the first item on the right side of Equation (11.16). On the other hand, maintaining high health human capital requires high health investment, which will squeeze out material capital investment under the fixed total output. Thus, health human capital has a negative crowding-out effect on material capital accumulation. The crowding-out effect of health human capital is reflected in the second term on the right side of Equation (11.16). Also, Equation (11.16) shows that the crowding-out effect of health human capital is related to health cost elasticity and the stock of material capital. That is, larger health cost elasticity or smaller material capital stock means higher crowding-out effect of health human capital on material capital accumulation. The studies by Baumol (1967) and Zonand Muysken (2001, 2003) also show that health has a negative crowding-out effect on material capital. However, their models cannot analyze what factors may affect the crowding-out effect of health on material capital accumulation.

According to Equations (11.11), (11.15), and (11.16), the health human capital accumulation equation can be obtained as follows:

$$\frac{\dot{h}}{h}=\frac{-\beta}{1+\varepsilon(h,k)}+\frac{A\left[\tau_{hk}+\tau_{hk}(1-\alpha)\varepsilon_{\phi h}+\alpha\right]}{1+\varepsilon(h,k)}\phi(h)-\frac{\tau_{hk}(\varepsilon_{\varphi h}+1)}{1+\varepsilon(h,k)}\left[\frac{T(h)}{k}\right] \tag{11.17}$$

According to the above analysis, in the Grossman-Arrow-Romer economy with health investment and material capital investment, the following Theorem 11.1 and Theorem 11.2 apply:

Theorem 11.1 When the health human capital under the equilibrium state, h^*, satisfies $T'(h^*)>(1-\alpha)A\phi'(h^*)k^*$, there will be a unique equilibrium point (k^*, c^*, h^*), which is determined by the following equations:

$$\alpha A\phi(h^*)-\beta=0 \tag{11.18}$$

$$k^*=\left[\left(1+\varepsilon_{Th}{}^*\right)/\left(1+(1-\alpha)\varepsilon_{\phi h}{}^*\right)\right]\left[T(h^*)/A\phi(h^*)\right] \tag{11.19}$$

$$c^*=h^*\left[T'(h^*)-(1-\alpha)A\phi'(h^*)k^*\right]=A\phi(h^*)k^*-T(h^*) \tag{11.20}$$

where $\varepsilon_{Th}{}^*=T'(h^*)h/T(h^*)$ and $\varepsilon_{\phi h}{}^*=\phi'(h^*)h/\phi(h^*)$

Theorem 11.2 If

$$\frac{\varepsilon_{\phi h}}{(1+\varepsilon(h,k))}\left\{\alpha\left[1+\frac{1}{1-\phi'(h)k/\varphi'(h)}\right]-1\right\}+1\geq 0 \tag{11.21}$$

,then the equilibrium point (c^*,h^*,k^*) is not stable. At this time, if the economy is above the equilibrium point, there will be sustained economic growth in the economy; and if the output of the economy is below the equilibrium point, the economy will converge to zero. If Equation (11.21) is not satisfied, the equilibrium point in the economy will be a stable one.

Theorem 11.2 is of great significance in theory and for explaining the actual economy. Firstly, Theorem 11.2 shows that there will be a poverty trap in the economy if Equation (11.21) is satisfied. The economy whose initial state is higher than the equilibrium point will witness sustained economic growth, and have ever-increasing levels of consumption, health, and output. Conversely, if the initial state is below the equilibrium point, the economy will continue to deteriorate in terms of the consumption, health, and output levels. This theorem shows that even two economies located near the equilibrium state and with very similar initial states will witness huge differences in all aspects with the passage of time as long as they are located in different directions of the equilibrium point. Thus, compared with the Lucas (1988) endogenous growth economy that involves health investment in Zon and Muysken (2001, 2003), in the Grossman-Arrow-Romer endogenous growth economy with health investment, the externality of material capital may produce a poverty trap through health human capital. Equation (11.21) also indicates that, in the case of bigger material capital output elasticity (α) and $\phi'(h)k/\varphi'(h)$or smaller health output elasticity ($\varepsilon_{\phi h}$), the economy is more likely to fall into a poverty trap. Secondly, Theorem 11.22 also indicates that the poverty trap mentioned in this chapter differs from the one in previous literature. In the previous literature (Chakraborty, 2004; Hemmi et al., 2006), the poverty trap mainly comes from multiple equilibriums in the economy. Thus, in these models, the economies with different initial states will converge to different equilibrium points. And when these equilibrium points are reached, the differences between the economies will remain unchanged. According to predictions on these models, the differences between developed and developing countries will remain the same after they reach a certain degree. The poverty trap mentioned in this chapter is mainly derived from the instability of economic equilibrium points. The differences determined by the initial state may make the differences among different economies last forever and gradually intensify. This conclusion is apparently in line with the ever-increasing differences between developed and developing countries in the real world. So, the poverty trap analyzed in this chapter may better explain reality. Additionally, this chapter also predicts the possibility of the existence of a sustained growth economy, and like the conclusions of Zon and Muysken (2001, 2003), Equation (11.11) indicates that health investment also tends to inhibit economic growth. Finally, Theorem 11.2 shows that, if Equation (11.21) is not satisfied, the economy will converge to the same stable point, regardless of the initial state. Additionally, the smaller the capital output elasticity (or α) and $\phi'(h)k/\varphi'(h)$ are or the smaller the health output elasticity ($\varepsilon_{\phi h}$) is, the more likely the economy is to have a stable equilibrium solution.

Section 3 Empirical study on China's inter-provincial panel data

The above theoretical analysis shows that both the level of health human capital and health investment produce an effect on material capital accumulation, thus affecting economic growth. The determination formula for economic growth is deduced below based on the theories above. Then, China's inter-provincial panel data are used for testing. According to the production function, we can get:

$$x_y = \dot{y}/y = \dot{k}/k + \varepsilon_{\phi h}\dot{h}/h \tag{11.22}$$

And according to Equations (11.16) and (11.17), we can get:

$$x_y = A\phi(h)\left[1+(1-\alpha)\varepsilon_{\phi h}\right] - (\varepsilon_{\varphi h}+1)\frac{T(h)}{k} + \varepsilon_{\phi}\frac{\dot{h}}{h} \tag{11.23}$$

and

$$x_y = \frac{\varepsilon_{\phi h}(1-\beta)}{1+\varepsilon(h,k)} + \frac{\left(\varepsilon_{\phi h}\tau_{hk}+1\right)\left[(1-\alpha)\varepsilon_{\phi h}+1\right]+\varepsilon_{\phi h}\alpha}{1+\varepsilon(h,k)}A\phi(h) - \frac{\left(\tau_{hk}\varepsilon_{\phi}+1\right)(\varepsilon_{\varphi h}+1)}{1+\varepsilon(h,k)}\frac{T(h)}{k} \tag{11.24}$$

Equations (11.23) and (11.24) indicate that the growth rate of health investment always produces a positive effect on economic growth. However, the effect of the stock of health human capital (or health investment) may be either positive or negative, which depends on the scale of its crowding-out effect on material capital. Actually, we have pointed out in the analysis of the previous section that health investment produces two effects on economic growth. On the one hand, health investment can increase health human capital and labor productivity, thus improving the output level; on the other hand, as health investment may squeeze out material capital accumulation, increasing health investment can reduce material capital accumulation, which is detrimental to economic growth. Health investment may produce a positive effect on economic growth as long as it does not produce a crowding-out effect on material capital accumulation; otherwise, health investment and health human capital may produce a negative effect on economic growth. Turning to empirical research, this section tests the theoretical results above by applying China's inter-provincial panel data.

3.1 Data descriptions

In this chapter, it is assumed that the current health status is mainly attributed to health investment. So, the health investment of each province may be used as a proxy variable for the health human capital of each province. According to the *China Statistical Yearbooks*, data on the total number of beds and total population in each province of China can be obtained. On such basis, the data on the number of beds in each province of China (*PCMB*) can be obtained and are used as a variable for the province's health investment and a proxy variable for the province's health human capital.

The data used in this chapter are sourced from Yang et al. (2005) and Wang et al. (2006). The raw data on the number of beds for each province are sourced from the *China Health Statistical Yearbooks.* The total population of each province is derived from the *China Population Statistical Yearbook 2003.* The data on the number of beds per capita for each province can be obtained based on the two sources of data. The current data on the number of beds per capita include the data of China's 28 provinces from 1978 to 2003. And the data of four provinces including Tibet, Hainan, Taiwan, and Chongqing are excluded. It is panel data with a sample observation value of 728. According to the current data on the number of beds per capita (*PMCB*), the data on the growth rate of the number of beds for each province (*GPCMB*) can be obtained. Obviously, it is panel data with a sample size of 700. In this chapter, the data on the growth rate of the number of beds per capita (*GPCMB*) are used to represent the growth rate of health investment.

The other data used in the subsequent research of this chapter also include each province's GDP per capita (*PGDP*), GDP growth rate per capita (*GPGDP*), growth rate of material capital per capita (*PCRPC*), and the ratio of the number of beds per capita to material capital (*RABEDCAP*). In the stability test, the proportion of the total value of state-owned industry over that of the industry (*RSOE*), proportion of exports in GDP (*GEXPORT*), and growth rate of labor population (*GLAB*) are also used. Specifically, the data on inter-provincial GDP per capita (*PGDP*) are calculated mainly based on the GDP per capita in the statistical yearbooks of each province in China (with the year 1952 as the base period) (Yang et al., 2006). Thus, the index of the GDP growth rate per capita (*GPGDP*) can be further obtained. The raw inter-provincial panel data on *PCRPC*, *RSOE*, *GEXPORT*, and *GLAB* are sourced from each province's statistical yearbooks, the *Collection of Statistical Data for New China during the 50 Years of Its Founding* (1999), and *China's Statistical Yearbooks* (Wang et al., 2006). The inter-provincial panel data of *GPCRPC* and *RABEDCA* can be calculated according to the data of *TPOP*, *PCRPC*, and *PCMB*. To balance *GPCMB*, the above data are the panel data for 28 provinces of China during the period 1978–2003. Table 11.1 gives some statistical characteristics of inter-provincial panel data on five main variables (*PCMB, GPCMB, GPGDP, GPCRPC,* and RABEDCAP).

Table 11.1 Statistical characteristics of *PCMB, GPCMB, GPGDP, GPCRPC,* and *RABEDCAP*

Variable	*Sample size*	*Average*	*STDEV*	*Minimum*	*Maximum*
PCMB	700	28.13	10.10	14.67	63.33
GPCMB	700	-0.135	0.128	0.007	0.026
GPGDP	700	0.088	0.048	-0.109	0.260
GPCRPC	700	0.122	0.093	-0.029	0.099
RABEDCAP	700	210.22	158.05	11.28	908.13

3.2 Econometric models and regression results

The empirical research in this chapter mainly aims to test the effects of health investment, the stock of health human capital, and the growth rate of health investment on the economic growth rate, and tries to investigate the relationship between China's health investment and its economic growth from a macro perspective through this research. The theoretical analysis of the previous section has shown that health human capital level, the growth rate of health investment, and the growth rate of material capital produce effects on economic growth. In the analysis of this section, the inter-provincial panel data of China from 1979 to 2003 are used to test this theoretical conclusion. Also, it is hoped that health human capital and health investment can be separated from the positive and negative crowding-out effect of economic growth. This chapter first highlights the overall impact of health investment and health human capital on the economic growth rate, including the significance of the coefficients and whether the coefficient signs are positive or negative when conducting regression of health investment, the growth rate of health investment, and the ratio of health human capital to material capital with the economic growth rate. Second, this research also intends to check if the above results apply when the growth rate of material capital is controlled.

Both FE and RE models are mainly taken into account during the econometric analysis. For the FE model, this chapter reports the F-statistic to test if the FE parameter is statistically significant. For the RE model, the Hausman test is mainly used to determine if there is any random effect. Moreover, the econometric results of this chapter demonstrate that almost all Hausman tests reject the RE model. Even if one or two RE models are not rejected, the regression results then are very similar to those of the FE model. So, the results of the FE model are mainly reported in the analysis below.

Firstly, according to Equations (11.23) and (11.24), the regression equations of the economic growth rate for health investment and the growth rate of health investment are discussed without controlling the growth of material capital. The regression equations are as follows:

$$\text{Model 1 } g_{it}^{y} = a + a_1 h_{it} + a_2 x_{it} + u_{it} \tag{11.25}$$

$$\textit{Model 2}\ g_{it}^{y} = a + a_1 h_{it} + a_3 g_{it}^{h} + u_{it} \quad (11.26)$$

$$\textit{Model 3}\ g_{it}^{y} = a + a_1 h_{it} + a_2 x_{it} + a_3 g_{it}^{h} + u_{it} \quad (11.27)$$

where i (i = 1, 2, …, N) represents the province, t (t =1, 2, …, T) represents the time, and u_{it}represents the error term. The explained variable g_{it}^{y}represents the growth rate of GDP per capita (GPGDP),the explanatory variable h_{it} represents health investment level per capita (PCMB), x_{it}represents the ratio of health human capital stock to material capital stock (RABEDCAP),and g_{it}^{h}represents the growth rate of health investment (GPCMB). According to the analysis in Section 2, it can be predicted that α1 and α3 should be significantly positive, and $\alpha 2$ should be significantly negative. Columns (I), (II), and (V) in Table 11.2 are the regression results of Equations (11.25), (11.26), and (11.27).

The regression results of Table 11.2 show the following: firstly, the FE models for the three equations match data well, and FE is statistically significant; secondly, except for the growth rate of health investment in the second model (*GPCMB*),the coefficients of all variables are statistically significant at the level of 10%; finally, for the sign of the estimated value of each coefficient, the statistical significance for the signs of the coefficients in relation to *PCMB* and *GPCMB* is positive, and that in relation to *RABEDCAP* is negative. These results are completely the same as the theoretical predictions.

Since the stock of material capital is also an endogenous variable of economic growth and is directly related to health human capital and the economic growth rate in the models, this chapter further takes into account material capital and re-examines the relationship between health investment and economic growth. The equations considered mainly include:

$$\text{Model 4}\ g_{it}^{y} = a + a_1 h_{it} + a_4 g_{it}^{p} + u_{it} \quad (11.28)$$

$$\text{Model 5}\ g_{it}^{y} = a + a_1 h_{it} + a_2 x_{it} + a_4 g_{it}^{p} + u_{it} \quad (11.29)$$

$$\text{Model 6}\ g_{it}^{y} = a + a_1 h_{it} + a_3 g_{it}^{h} + a_4 g_{it}^{p} + u_{it} \quad (11.30)$$

$$\text{Model 7}\ g_{it}^{y} = a + a_1 h_{it} + a_2 x_{it} + a_3 g_{it}^{h} + a_4 g_{it}^{p} + u_{it} \quad (11.31)$$

Where g_{it}^{p}refers to the growth rate of material capital per capita (GPCRPC) and the meanings of the other variables are the same as above. Columns (III), (IV), (VI), and (VIII) in Table 11.2 are the regression results of Equations (11.28), (11.29), (11.30), and (11.31). According to Table 11.2, firstly, in all equations, the coefficients of regression of GPCMB and GPCRPC for economic growth are positive and statistically significant, indicating the positive effect of the growth rate of health investment and the growth rate of material capital on economic growth; secondly, the coefficient of

Table 11.2 Econometric regression results: the explained variable is GPGDP

Model	*I*	*II*	*III*	*IV*	*V*	*VI*	*VII*
method	fixone	fixone	fixone	fixone	fixone	fixone	fixone
Intercept	0.0187	−0.0142	0.0264	−0.0179	0.0493	−0.021	0.0073
	(0.62)	(−0.51)	(0.87)	(−0.65)	(5.29)	(−0.76)	(0.24)
PBED	0.0011*	0.0017***	0.0010*	0.0015***		0.0016***	0.0012*
	(1.77)	(2.76)	(1.68)	(2.56)		(2.70)	(1.94)
RABEDCAP	−3E−5**		−4E−5***				−3E−5**
	(−2.48)		(−3.68)				*(−2.03))*
GPBED		0.0987	0.1777**		0.1253*	0.1378**	0.184***
		(1.44)	(2.45)		(1.83)	(2.01)	*(2.56)*
GPCAP				0.0727***	0.0791***	0.078***	0.066***
				(3.86)	(4.15)	(4.11)	(3.29)
NOB	25×28	25×28	25×28	25×28	25×28	25×28	25×28
R-Square:	0.1395	0.1342	0.1471	0.1504	0.1463	0.156	0.161
Pr1 > F[a]	<.0001	<0.0001	<0.0001	<0.0001	<0.0001	<0.0001	<0.0001

Note: ① The software used for regression is SAS 9.1, and the regression program used is TSCSREG. ② The R-Square reported in the table is the adjusted goodness of fit found by Buse (1973). ③ The values in parentheses below each coefficient are the values of *t*-statistic for such coefficient. ④ *Pr1* > F^a is the p-value of F-statistic for testing FE, and *Pr2* >F^b is the p-value of F-statistic with joint significance for testing all explanatory variables except dummy variables.

regression of RABEDCAP with the economic growth rate is negative and statistically significant, indicating the negative effect of health investment on economic growth indeed, which is related to the ratio of health human capital to material capital. A higher ratio of health human capital to material capital means larger negative effect of health investment on economic growth. Additionally, the coefficient of regression of PCMB with the economic growth rate is either significantly positive and or insignificantly negative in statistics, indicating the positive effect of health human capital per capita or health investment on economic growth. So, on the whole, whether health investment produces a promoting effect on economic growth is determined by the aggregation of the two effects above. All these regression results are completely the same as those of the theoretical analysis.

3.3 Robustness test of regression results

In this section, a stability test is conducted on the above measurement results. The main purpose of the robustness test is to test whether the regression results are sensitive to the newly added explanatory variables. If a conclusion that is completely opposite to the previous regression results is drawn after the incorporation of these variables, then the previous regression results can be considered as not robust. For the robustness test method used in this chapter, see Levine and Renelt (1992). The test here is mainly to test whether the regression results in Section 4.2 are robust by adding some new explanatory variables that may affect the economic growth rate in the regression equation in Section 4.2. The new variables mainly include *GRNLP*, *RSOE*, and *GRNLP*. Among them, *RSOE* represents the proportion of the output value of the state-owned industry in total output value of the industry, which measures the degree of market reform in each province; *GEXPORT* represents the proportion of foreign exports in GDP, which measures the degree of opening-up of each province to the outside world; and *GRNLP* represents the number of labor forces in each province. The effect of these three variables on the per capita GDP growth rate of each province is obvious. The data on the three variables are taken from Wang et al. (2006). In the test process, at least one new explanatory variable is added to the basic regression equation each time, and the regression results are shown in columns (I) to (VII) in Table 11.3.

In the robustness test of this research, we are most concerned about whether the regression coefficients of *PCMB*, *RABEDCAP*, and *GPCMB* are significantly different from the previous regression results after adding new explanatory variables. The regression results of (I) to (VII) in Table 11.4 show that, in the FE regression model of all the seven equations, the regression coefficients of *GPCMB* and *GPCRPC* are significantly positive in statistics, while the coefficients of *PCMB* and *RABEDCAP* are sometimes significantly positive in statistics, sometimes insignificantly negative

Table 11.3 Econometric regression results of robustness analysis: the explained variable is GPGDP

Variable	*I*	*II*	*III*	*IV*	*V*	*VI*	*VII*
Intercept	0.0169	0.0969	0.0079	0.0172	0.0969	0.0957	0.0957
	(0.53)	(2.47)	(0.23)	(0.52)	(2.47)	(2.44)	(2.44)
PBED	0.0009	0.00022	0.0013**	9.5E−4	0.0002	0.00027	0.00026
	(1.36)	(0.33)	(1.99)	(1.41)	(0.32)	(0.39)	*(0.38)*
RABEDCAP	−2.0E−5	−2.12E−6	−0.00003**	−2.0E−5*	−2.07E−6	−3.01E−6	−2.97E−6
	(−1.56)	(−0.13)	(−2.08)	(−1.61)	(−0.13)	(−0.10)	*(−0.19)*
GPBED	0.179**	0.20***	0.1720**	0.167**	0.20***	0.19***	0.19***
	(2.48)	(2.81)	(2.40)	(2.33)	(2.80)	(2.66)	(2.65)
GPCAP	0.067***	0.07***	0.065**	0.066***	0.065***	0.064***	0.064
	(3.38)	(3.31)	(3.25)	(3.32)	(3.30)	(3.27)	1. (3.26)
GExport	0.0302			0.0290	0.0005		0.0004
	(1.25)			(1.23)	(0.02)		2. (0.02)
GRNLP			−0.0506	−0.0497		−0.0447	−0.0448
			(−1.19)	(−1.17)		(−1.06)	(−1.06)
RSOE		−0.07***			−0.07***	−0.07***	−0.07***
		(−3.65)			(−3.42)	(−3.60)	(−3.38)
NOB	25×28	25×28	25×28	25×28	25×28	25×28	25×28
R-Square:	0.1627	0.1771	0.1635	0.1653	0.1771	0.1794	0.1794
Prl > F[a]	0.0001	0.2863	<0.0001	<0.0001	0.2884	0.2414	0.2433
Pr2 > *F*[b]	0.0001	0.0001	0.0001	0.0001	0.0001	0.0001	0.0001

Note: ① The software used for regression is SAS 9.1, and the regression program used is TSCSREG. ② The R-Square reported in the table is the adjusted goodness of fit found by Buse (1973). ③ The values in parentheses below each coefficient are the values of *t*-statistic for such coefficient. ④ *Prl* > *F*[a] is the p-value of F-statistic for testing FE, and *Pr2* >*F*[b] is the p-value of F-statistic with joint significance for testing all explanatory variables except dummy variables.

in statistics. In addition, even for the model including all three variables of *GRNLP*, *RSO*, and *GRNLP*, the regression results did not appear statistically contrary to the conclusions in Section 3.2. Therefore, the robustness test shows that *PCMB* and *GPCMB* are positively correlated with economic growth, and *RABEDCAP* is negatively correlated with economic growth. This regression result is robust.

In addition, the robustness test result also finds that the progress of reform and marketization (*RSOE*) is significantly, positively correlated with the economic growth rate in statistics. The export dependence (*GEXPORT*) is also positively correlated with economic growth, but is insignificant in statistics. The non-working population (*GNLP*) is insignificantly, negatively correlated with economic growth. These results are also consistent with general economic intuition.

Note

1 For more discussions regarding this assumption, see Zon and Muysken (2001).

References

[1] Arrow, K. J. (1962). The Economic Implications of Learning by Doing. The Review of Economic Studies, 29(3), 155–173.

[2] Barro, R. J. (1996). Health and Economic Growth, paper presented at the "Senior Policy Seminar on Health, human Capital and Economic Growth: Theory, Evidence and Policies", Pan American Health Organization and Inter-American Development Bank, Washington, DC.

[3] Baumol, W. J. (1967). Macroeconomics of Unbalanced Growth: The Anatomy of Urban Crisis. *American Economic Review*, 57, 415–426.

[4] Buse, A. (1973). Goodness of Fit in Generalized Least Squares Estimation. *American Statistician*, 27, 106–108.

[5] Chakraborty, S. (2004). Endogenous Lifetime and Economic Growth. *Journal of Economic Theory*, 116(1), 119–137.

[6] Fogel, Robert W. (1994a). Economic Growth, Population Theory, and Physiology: The Bearing of Long-term Processes on the Making of Economic Policy. *American Economic Review*, 84(3), 369–395.

[7] Fogel, R. W. (1994b). The Relevance of Malthus for the Study of Mortality Today: Long-run Influences on Health, Mortality, Labor Force Participation, and Population Growth, *NBER Working Paper*, h0054.

[8] Fogel, R. W. (2002). *Nutrition, Physiological Capital, and Economic Growth*, paper presented at the "Senior Policy Seminar on Health, Human Capital and Economic Growth: Theory, Evidence and Policies," Pan American Health Organization and Inter-American Development Bank, Washington, DC.

[9] Grossman, M. (1972). The Demand for Health: A Theoretical and Empirical Investigation. *NBER, Occasional Paper* 119, Columbia University Press.

[10] Hemmi, N., Tabata, K., &Futagami, K. (2006). The Long-term Care Problem, Precautionary Saving, and Economic Growth. *Journal of Macroeconomics*, In Press, Corrected Proof, Available online 22 December 2006.

[11] Howitt, P. (2005). Health, Human Capital, and Economic Growth, In *Health and Economic Growth: Findings and Policy Implications*, edited by Guillem Lopez-Casasnovas, Berta Rivera and Luis Currais. Cambridge, MA: MIT Press, 2005, 19–40.

[12] Levine, R., & Renelt, D. (1992). A Sensitivity Analysis of Cross-Country Growth Regressions. *American Economic Review*, 82, 942–963.

[13] Lucas, R. (1988). On the Mechanics of Economic Development. *Journal of Monetary Economics*, 22, 3–42.

[14] Mushkin, S. J. (1962). Health as an Investment. *Journal of Political Economy*, 70(5), 129–157.

[15] Romer, P. M. (1986). Increasing Returns and Long-Run Growth. The Journal of Political Economy, 94(5), 1002–37.

[16] Sanso, M., & Aisa, R. M. (2006). Endogenous Longevity, Biological Deterioration and Economic Growth. *Journal of Health Economics*, 25, 555–578.

[17] Schultz, *T.* (1961). Investment in Human Capital. *American Economic Review*, 51(1), 1–17.

[18] Strauss, J., & Thomas, D. (1998). Health, Nutrition and Economic Development. *Journal of Economic Literature*, 36, 766–817.

[19] Wang, Z. G., Gong, L. *T.*, & Chen, Y. Y. (2006). China's Regional Differences in Technical Efficiency and the Decomposition of Total Factor Productivity Growth: 1978–2003. *Social Sciences in China*, Issue 2.

[20] Yang, J. F., Gong, L. T., & Zhang Q. H. (2005). Human Capital Formation and Its Effect on Economic Growth, *Management World*, 5, 10–18.

[21] Zon, A. H. van, & Muysken, J. (2001). Health and Endogenous Growth. *Journal of Health Economics*, 20, 169–185.

[22] Zon, A. H. van, & Muysken, J. (2003). Health as a Principal Determinant of Economic Growth. Working Paper, *MERIT-Infonomics Research Memorandum*.

Part 3

12 Changes and status quo of the income distribution in China

Since the reform and opening-up, China has achieved rapid economic development and the income gap among Chinese residents has been widening. The income distribution issue in China has been receiving widespread attention, from academic and political circles and also from ordinary people. What changes have occurred in China's income distribution pattern since the reform? What about China's current income distribution situation? All these aspects will be analyzed in this chapter. The structure of this chapter is as follows: Section 1 compares income distribution inequality between China and other countries from the perspective of the Gini coefficient; Section 2 discusses the current income distribution situation of China and its changes; Section 3 analyzes the changes and status quo of the income gap between urban and rural residents in China; Section 4 analyzes the evolution and status quo of China's regional income gap; Section 5 probes into the internal income gaps in China's urban and rural areas; Section 6 analyzes the industry income gap and the proportions of capital and labor income; and Section 7 summarizes the status quo and characteristics of China's income distribution.

Section 1 Comparison of income distribution inequality between China and other countries

As shown in Figure 12.1 and Table 12.1, the Gini coefficient of common developed countries in 2015 ranged from 0.30 to 0.40 according to World Bank data. China's Gini coefficient was 0.422 in 2015, a little higher than America (0.15). Among the major economies and populous countries in Figure 12.1, only a few developing countries such as South Africa, Brazil, Mexico, Nigeria, and Turkey have larger Gini coefficients than China. According to the data of the National Bureau of Statistics of China, China's Gini coefficient is even larger, up to 0.49 during the period 2008–2009, above 0.46 during the period 2010–2016 and 0.467 in 2017. According to universal international standards, a Gini coefficient of smaller than 0.3 was the best average state; that between 0.3 and 0.4 was a normal state; that of larger than 0.4 was a warning state; and that of 0.6 was a dangerous state in which social unrest

DOI: 10.4324/9781003261629-16

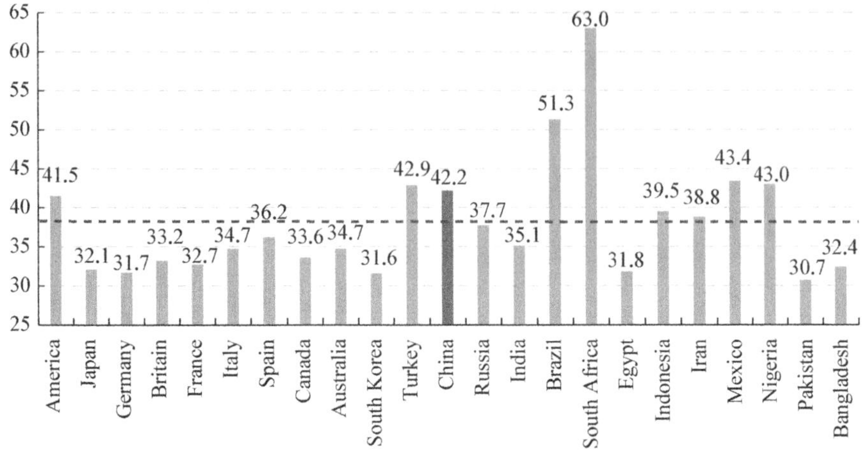

Figure 12.1 The Gini coefficients of major economies and populous countries around 2015.

may happen at any time. Thus, according to international practice, the value 0.4 is usually regarded as the "warning line" for an excessively large income gap. Judged by this standard, China has now exceeded the international warning line and entered the ranks of countries with excessively large income gaps, which is an alert state that could cause huge income disparity and affect social stability.

According to Table 12.1, all the Gini coefficients of developed countries in the 1980s to 1990s were low and have been increasing since 2000. By contrast, since China only has the Gini coefficient data following the year 2009, it seems that the country's Gini coefficient has always been around 0.42. Actually, the Gini coefficient of China in the early period of the reform and opening-up was very small, smaller than that of developed countries and other developing countries. This figure started to increase only from the mid-to-late 1980s. The evolution of China's income distribution after 1978 is discussed in detail in the following.

Section 2 Status quo and changes of China's income distribution: overview and trends

Since the reform and opening-up in 1978, China's income distribution inequality has shown a wave-like, sharp rise in general. And there has been a slight downward trend since 2010. Taking the Gini coefficient as an example, Figure 12.2 shows the estimated value of China's Gini coefficient of income distribution given by different scholars since 1978. Although the absolute values estimated by these scholars are different, the Gini coefficient has basically followed the same trend of changes. According to Figure 12.2,

Table 12.1 The Gini coefficients of major economies and populous countries in different periods (%)

Period	*1980–1989*	*1990–1999*	*2000–2009*	*2010*	*2015*
America	37.5	38.2~40.8	40.4~41.1	40.4	41.54[h]
Japan			32.1	32.1[a]	32.1[a]
Germany		29.2	28.8~31.3	30.2	31.7
Britain			34.1–36	34.4	33.2
France			29.7~33	33.7	32.7
Italy			32.9~34.9	34.7	34.7[g]
Spain			31.8~34.9	35.2	36.2
Canada	31.5~32.4	31~33.2	33.3~33.8	33.6	33.6[c]
Australia	31.3~33.2	32.5	33.5~35.4	34.7	34.7[c]
South Korea			31.7~32.3	32	31.6[e]
Turkey	43.5	41.3	38.4~42.6	38.8	42.9
China			42.8	42.2[e]	42.2[e]
Russia		37.4~48.4	36.9~42.3	39.5	37.7
India				35.1[d]	35.1[d]
Brazil	55.6~63.3	53.2~60.1	53.7~58.4	52.9[b]	51.3
South Africa		59.3~60.7	57.8~64.8	63.4	63[g]
Egypt		30.1~32.8	31.1~31.8	31.5	31.8
Indonesia				-	39.5[f]
Iran	47.4	43~44.1	42.1~44.8	42.1[b]	38.8[g]
Mexico	48.9	48.2~50.3	44.6~51.4	45.3	43.4[h]
Nigeria	38.7	45~51.9	40.1~43	43b	43[b]
Pakistan	33.3	28.7~33.1	30.4~32.7	29.8	30.7[f]
Bangladesh	25.9~28.8	27.6~32.9	33.2~33.4	32.1	32.4[h]

Source: *World Development Indicators* of World Bank.

Due to the incomplete data on the Gini coefficient of each country, the data for the periods 1980–1989, 1990–1999 and 2000–2009 refer to the range of changes in the existing data in the *World Development Indicators*.

a The data for the year 2008
b For the year 2009
c For the year 2010
d For the year 2011
e For the year 2012
f For the year 2013
g For the year 2014
h For the year 2016.

the Gini coefficient showed a downward trend from 1978 to 1985; basically exhibited a fluctuating upward trend from 1985 to 2008, with a short-term decline during the period 1994–1997; reached its peak from 2008 to 2009; showed a slight downward trend after 2010; and slightly rose in 2017. Generally, China's Gini coefficient of income distribution in the early period of the reform was approximately 0.3, dropped to around 0.25 in the 1980s, approached 0.4 in the mid-1990s, exceeded 0.4 after 2000, and came close to 0.5 around 2008. And the figure has hovered around 0.46 in recent years.

Additionally, according to World Bank data, China's Gini coefficient was 0.17 to 0.18 in the 1960s and 0.21 to 0.27 in the 1980s. Since 2000, this figure has surpassed the warning line of 0.4 and been rising year by year.

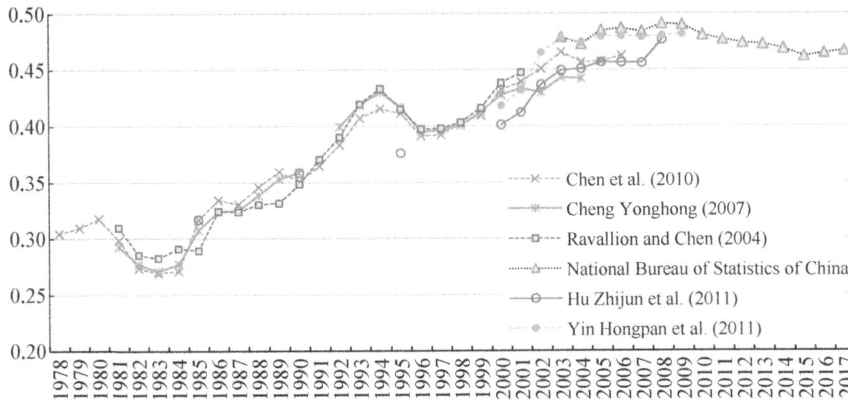

Figure 12.2 Changes in China's Gini coefficient: 1978–2017.

The figure rose to 0.496 in 2006 and reached 0.48 in 2007. According to the Gini coefficient published by the National Bureau of Statistics, China's Gini coefficient reached the highest value of 0.491 in 2008 and was declining in subsequent years, reaching about 0.465 in 2016. However, it is generally believed by the academic circle that, among the data obtained by the National Bureau of Statistics, there may be deviations and omissions in the income statistics of high-income groups.[1] In brief, based on the estimates by different scholars, it is an indisputable fact that China's Gini coefficient of income distribution has crossed the international warning line of 0.4. In fact, since 2000 or so, China's Gini coefficient has crossed this line and kept increasing year by year. Now, a lot of scholars believe that China's current total Gini coefficient may have reached or exceeded 0.5.

According to the research data of Piketty et al. (2017), Figure 12.3 shows the changes in the income share of different income groups in China's total income during the period 1978–2015. As can be seen from the figure, the income gap in China tended to widen before 2008 and has slightly narrowed since 2008. Specifically, in 1978, the income of the 1% highest income group accounted for around 6.3% of the total income; the income of the 9% second highest income group and that of the 40% middle income group accounted for about 20.8% and 45.8% of the total income; and the income of the 50% lowest income group accounted for about 27.1% of the total income. In 1985, the income share of the 1% highest income group and of the 9% second highest income group rose to 8% and 21.3%, respectively, and that of the 40% middle income group and of the 50% lowest income group dropped to 45.1% and 25.6%, respectively. During the period 1978–1985, the income share of the 1% highest income group and of the 9% second highest income group increased by 1.7 and 0.5 percentage points, and that of the 40% middle income group and of the 50% lowest income group decreased

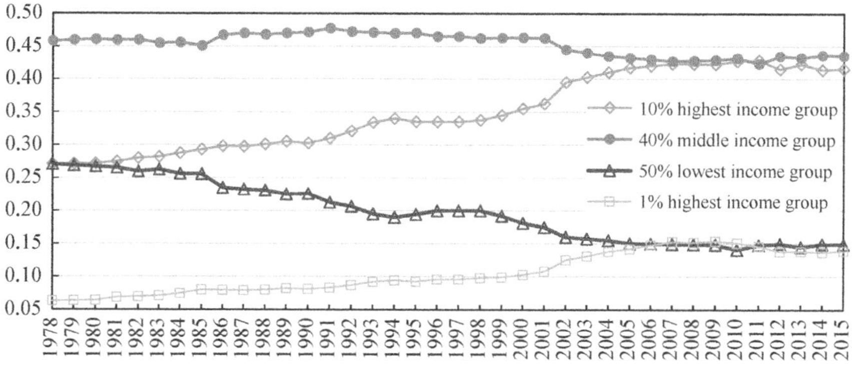

Figure 12.3 Changes in the income share of different income groups in China: 1978–2015.

by 0.7 and 1.4 percentage points. So, the widening income gap during this period was mainly reflected in the increase in the income of the 1% highest income group and other groups. In 1995, the income share of the 1% highest income group, of the 9% second highest income group, and of the 40% middle income group rose to 9.3%,24.3%, and 47% respectively; and the proportion of the 50% lowest income group dropped to 19.5%. During the period 1985–1995, the income share of the 1% highest income group, of the 9% second highest income group, and of the 40% middle income group increased to 1.3, 3, and 1.9 percentage points, and that of the 50% lowest income group decreased by 6.1 percentage points. Thus, the widening income gap during the ten years was mainly reflected in the sharp increase in the income of the 9% second highest income group and in the income of the lowest income group and other groups. In 2008, the income share of the 1% highest income group and of the 9% second highest income group in China rose to 15.2% and 27.1%, respectively, and that of the 40% middle income group and of the 50% lowest income group decreased by 42.8% and 14.9%, respectively. During the period 1995–2008, the income share of the 1% highest income group and of the 9% second highest income group in China increased by 5.9 and 2.8 percentage points, and that of the 40% middle income group and the 50% lowest income group decreased by 4.3 and 4.6 percentage points, respectively. Thus, the widening income gap in China during this period was mainly demonstrated by the 10% highest income group, especially the 1% highest income group and lower-middle income groups. By 2015, the income share of the 1% highest income group decreased to 13.9%; that of the 9% second highest income group and the 40% middle income group rose to 27.7% and 43.6% respectively; and that of the 50% lowest income group was still maintained at 14.9%. During the period 2008–2015, China's income gap became slightly narrowed. The income share of the 1% highest income group and of the 10% highest income group witnessed a slight drop and that of the 40% middle income group and of the 50% lowest income group slightly increased.

As known from Figure 12.3, the income share of the 1% highest income group and of the 10% highest income group in China was basically rising during the period 1978–2015. The proportion of the total income of China's 1% highest income group in the country's total income was approximately 6.3% in 1978, rose to around 8.1% in 1990, further increased to 10.3% in 2000, and reached 13.9% in 2015. The income share of the 50% lowest income group was declining, from around 27.1% in 1978, to 22.6% in 1990, and then to about 18.1% in 2000 and to only 14.9% in 2015. In 1978, the income share of the 10% highest income group and of the 50% lowest income group was basically the same, about 27% each. In 2015, the income share of the 10% highest income group increased to about 27.7%, 1.85 times that of the 50% lowest income group. The proportion of the 40% middle income group in 1995 reached 47% of the highest value of the same year, slightly dropped afterwards, and dropped by about 1.5 percentage points in 2015 relative to that of 1978.

Moreover, according to the estimates by Li and Luo (2011), in 2007, the income share of the 20% lowest income group of the total income in China was only 3.45%–3.87%, and that of the 20% highest income group of the total income in China was from 51.8% to 56.7%. The World Bank report also shows that the ratio of the average income of the 20% highest income group to that of the 20% lowest income group is 10.7 times in China, 8.4 times in America, 4.5 times in Russia, 4.9 times in India, and 3.4 times in Japan (at the lowest level).

Table 12.2 further shows the income and wealth distribution statuses of China in 2015 as estimated by Piketty et al. (2017). According to the latest research data of Piketty et al. (2017), the inequality of wealth distribution among Chinese residents was more severe than that in income distribution in 2015. For example, for the 10,635 Chinese people with the highest income or the 0.001% highest income group, its total income accounted for 1.36% of the total income of the entire country, but the total wealth of these 10,635 richest people had a share of 5.76% over the total wealth, 4.23 times the corresponding income share. For the 0.01% highest income group, its total income accounted for 3.2% of the total income, but the total wealth of the 0.01% richest people had a share of 10.98% over the total wealth, 3.4 times the corresponding income share. For the 1% highest income group, its total income accounted for 13.93% of the total income, but the total wealth of the 1% richest people had a share of 29.64% over the total wealth, 2.13 times the income share. For the 50% lowest income group, its total income accounted for 14.85% of the total income, one percentage point higher than that of the 1% highest income group and 2.31 times the wealth share of the corresponding group; but the total wealth of the 50% poorest people had a share of only 6.44% over the total wealth, about one fifth of the wealth share of the 1% richest people.

Table 12.2 China's income and wealth distribution status in 2015

Income group	*Total adult population*	*Income distribution status*			*Wealth distribution status*		
		Lowest income (yuan)	*Average income (yuan)*	*Income share (%)*	*Lowest wealth (yuan)*	*Average wealth (yuan)*	*Wealth share (%)*
Total population	1.063 billion	0	57807	100	0	281718	100
0.001% highest income group	10,635	30,203,833	78,833,979	1.36	465,654,285	1,623,209,327	5.76
0.01% highest income group	106,354	6,207,479	18,503,392	3.20	67,744,170	309,247,711	10.98
0.1% highest income group	1,063,543	1,071,112	3,641,463	6.30	7,988,140	46,156,982	16.39
1% highest income group	10,635,426	345,520	804,886	13.93	2,979,431	8,347,004	29.64
10% highest income group	106 million	117,812	239,476	41.34	420,197	1,899,019	67.41
40% middle income group	425 million	34,442	63,210	43.72	84,932	184,173	26.14
50% lowest income group	532 million	0	17,150	14.85	0	36,293	6.44

Source: Piketty et al. (2017);
The adult population refers to the population aged 20 and above, and a married couple is counted as two persons.

In brief, whether in terms of the Gini coefficient or the income share of each income group, China has transformed from one of the countries with the most average residents' income to one of the countries with the largest residents' income gap in the world since the reform and opening-up.

Section 3 Changes and status quo of China's income gap between urban and rural residents

The analysis in Section 2 shows that the overall income gap of Chinese residents has been widening since 1978. However, the degrees of changes in income gap in different aspects are different, and so are their impacts on the overall income inequality. Wang and Xu (2006) indicate that income inequality between urban and rural areas plays a crucial role in China's expanding income gap, followed by regional income inequality. The former contributes more than 60% of the total income inequality, and the latter about 25%, with the two having a total share of more than 80%. Hu et al. (2011) also believed that the contribution of China's income gap between urban and rural areas to the overall income gap rose from 50.6% to 60.7% during the period 1985–2000 and remained at around 60% during the period 2001–2008. It can be seen that the continuous widening of such gap is one of the most important factors that led to the aggravated income inequality in China since the reform. As shown in Table 12.3, the annual disposable income per capita of urban residents and the annual net income per capita of rural residents (hereinafter referred to as "annual income of urban residents" and "annual income of rural residents," respectively) in China in 1978 were only 343.4 yuan and 134.6 yuan, respectively, with an absolute

Table 12.3 Changes in the annual income per capita of Chinese urban and rural residents: 1978–2019

	1978	*1985*	*1990*	*1995*	*2000*	*2005*	*2010*	*2015*	*2017*	*2018*	*2019*
Income of urban residents (yuan)	343.4	739.1	1510	4283	6280	10493	19109	31195	36396	39251	36396
Income of rural residents (yuan)	133.6	397.6	686.3	1578	2253	3255	5919	11422	13432	14617	13432
Absolute difference (yuan)	209.8	341.5	823.9	2705	4027	7238	13190	19773	22964	24634	26338
Income ratio	2.57	1.86	2.20	2.71	2.79	3.22	3.23	2.73	2.71	2.69	2.64

Source: *China Statistical Yearbooks*;
Disposable income is adopted for urban residents; net income is adopted for rural residents before 2010 and disposable income is adopted after 2010 (at the prices of the current year).

difference of 109.8 yuan and urban-rural income ratio of 2.57 times; and that in 1990 increased by 1,510 yuan and 686 yuan, with the absolute difference rising to 824 yuan and urban-rural income ratio dropping to 2.20. In 2000, the absolute income difference between urban and rural areas rose to 4,027 yuan and the urban-rural income ratio to 2.79. In 2010, the absolute income difference increased to 13,190 yuan and the urban-rural income ratio to 3.23. According to the *Statistical Communiqué of the People's Republic of China on National Economic and Social Development in 2019*, the annual income of Chinese urban and rural residents was 42,359 yuan and 16,021 yuan, respectively, in the year, with the absolute income difference being 26,338 yuan and the urban-rural income ratio dropping to 2.64.

Price hikes will affect the income gap between urban and rural areas. To exclude the impact of price hikes, Figure 12.4 shows the changes in the annual income of urban and rural residents in China and the urban-rural income gap calculated at the constant prices of 1978. According to Figure 12.4, even at constant prices, the absolute income gap between urban and rural areas in China also tended to widen during the period 1978–2016 but narrowed in the early years of the reform in the 1980s. During the entire period 1978–2016, the real income of Chinese urban and rural residents basically grew at the same rate, and the absolute urban-rural income gap also increased almost at the same rate as the real income growth rate of urban and rural residents. Thus, the widening absolute urban-rural income gap in China may be mainly due to China's economic growth.

The absolute income gap ignores the impact of price hikes and economic growth on the income gap. To exclude the impact of income hikes on the urban-rural income gap during the process of economic growth, Figure 12.5 shows the changes in the ratio of urban income to rural income, including the urban-rural income ratio calculated at the prices of the current year and that at the constant prices. As known from Figure 12.5, similar to the changes in China's Gini coefficient, the relative income gap between China's urban and rural areas widened like waves during the period 1978–2009 and

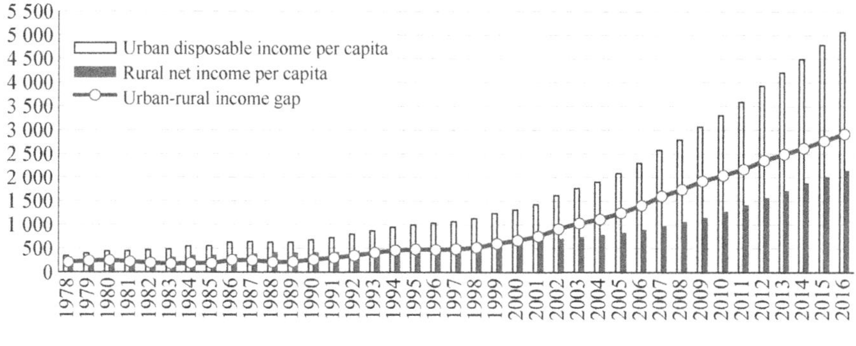

Figure 12.4 Urban disposable income per capita, rural net income per capita, and urban-rural income gap: 1978–2017.

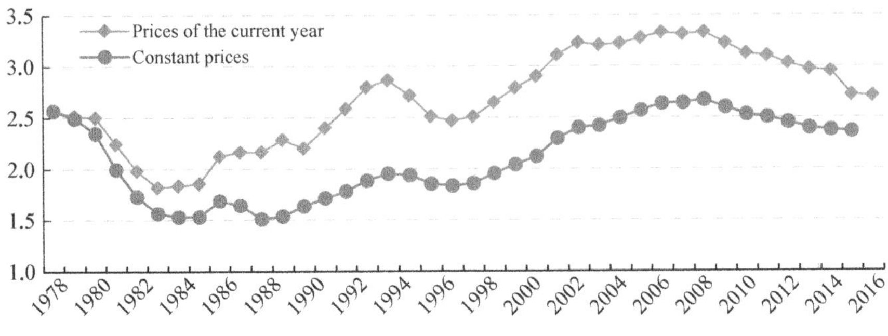

Figure 12.5 The ratio of urban disposable income to rural net income: 1978–2017.

then declined after 2009. At the prices of the current year, the implementation of the rural household contract responsibility system during the period 1978–1985 greatly increased the income of farmers and the urban-rural income ratio fell from 2.56 to 1.86. However, from 1985, when the urban economic reform started, to 1994, the urban-rural income ratio rose from 1.86 to 2.86, exceeding 2.57 in 1978. During the period 1994–1997, due to the reform of state-owned enterprises, increasing laid-off workers, and the slowdown of the urban income growth rate, the urban-rural income ratio dropped from 2.86 to 2.47, close to the level of 1978. During the period 1998–2009, a new round of economic growth and China's accession to the WTO greatly facilitated industrialization and urbanization. As a result, the urban economy witnessed rapid development, the income of urban residents increased fast relative to that of rural residents, and the urban-rural income ratio rose from 2.47 to 3.3. The urban-rural income ratio tended to decrease again after 2009, dropped to 2.97 in 2014, and further dropped to 2.71 in 2016, still 5.4% larger than that of 1978. If measured by the urban-rural real income ratio, the change in China's urban-rural income gap follows the same trend as that in the nominal income ratio. However, the urban-rural income gap measured by the urban-rural real income ratio for the period 1978–2016 was not larger than that for the initial period of the reform but smaller than that in 1978 in most of the years during this period instead. Only during the period 2006–2010 was the urban-rural real income ratio slightly larger than that of 1978. In 2016, this figure even dropped to 2.36, slightly smaller than that of 1978. If measured at the constant prices of urban and rural areas, the post-reform economic growth of China has narrowed the relative urban-rural real income gap due to the faster rise in the urban and rural consumer price indexes.

The current urban-rural real income ratio in China is even smaller than that in 1978. So, does it mean China's urban-rural income gap is not large? No, in fact. The International Labor Organization (ILO) has released statistics on the urban-rural income ratios of 36 countries in 1985, 1990, and

1995. The statistical data show that, in most countries, the ratio of the income of urban residents per capita to that of rural residents per capita was smaller than 1.5 in the above three years. In the years 1985, 1990, and 1995, there were only four, five, and three countries, respectively, whose ratios of income of urban residents to that of rural residents exceeded 2 (Zeng & Hu, 2008). Since 1992, the ratio of the nominal income of urban residents to that of rural residents has been above 2 and even exceeded 3 during the period 2002–2013. Currently, the urban-rural real income ratio in China has exceeded 2, reaching 2.36. It can be seen that, whether in terms of the nominal income ratio or the real income ratio, China is now basically the country with the largest urban-rural income gap in the world. After the reform, the urban-rural real income gap in China was smaller than that of 1978, which was due to the fact that such gap was already large in 1978. The narrowed real income gap after the reform only indicates that the real urban-rural income gap has been narrowed due to economic development, which does not mean the current urban-rural income gap in China is not large.

Section 4 Changes and status quo of China's regional income gaps

The widening of regional income gaps is also one of the important reasons for the increase in income distribution inequality and in the Gini coefficient in China. Although the income gaps among residents of China's provinces (municipalities) were previously narrowed, they had continued to widen since 1982. The income gaps were not narrowed till 2006.

4.1 Changes in the disposable income gaps among urban residents of China's provinces (municipalities)

In terms of the income gap among urban residents, Shanghai, Beijing, and Zhejiang, which had the highest disposable income per capita of urban residents in 2016, are compared with Gansu, Qinghai, and Heilongjiang, which had the lowest disposable income per capita of urban residents in the same year, as shown in Table 12.4. During the period 1978–2016, the urban disposable income per capita in Shanghai, Beijing, and Zhejiang increased from 560 yuan, 365.4 yuan, and 332 yuan to 57,692 yuan, 57,275 yuan, and 47,237 yuan, respectively. The urban disposable income per capita of the three provinces (municipalities) was up by 102 times, 156 times, and 142 times, with average annual growth rates of 12.97%, 14.23%, and 13.94%, respectively. In the same period, the urban disposable income per capita of Gansu, Qinghai, and Heilongjiang increased from 407 yuan in 1978, 418.7 yuan in 1981, and 742 yuan in 1985 to 25,693 yuan, 26,757 yuan, and 25,736 yuan, respectively, in 2016, with average annual growth rates of 11.52%, 12.61%, and 12.12%, all of which were lower than those of Shanghai, Beijing, and Zhejiang.[2] During the period 1978–2016, the ratios of urban disposable income

Table 12.4 Changes in the urban disposable income per capita of China's provinces and municipalities during the period 1978–2016 (unit: yuan)

Year	*1978*	*1990*	*1995*	*2000*	*2005*	*2010*	*2013*	*2016*
National average	341.4	1487.3	4258.3	9421.6	10195.8	18067	25531	32291
STDEV	61.1	286.4	1135.9	2590.9	2883.6	4701	6251	8126
CV	0.179	0.193	0.267	0.275	0.283	0.260	0.245	0.252
Maximum	560 (Shanghai)	2303.2 (Guangdong)	7438.7 (Guangdong)	16683 (Shanghai)	18645 (Shanghai)	31838 (Shanghai)	43851 (Shanghai)	57692 (Shanghai)
Minimum	261 (Guizhou)	1119.1 (Qinghai)	2845.7 (Inner Mongolia)	7218 (Ningxia)	7990 (Xinjiang)	13189 (Gansu)	18965 (Gansu)	25693 (Gansu)
Range	299	1184.1	4593	9465	10654	18649	24887	31999
Maximum-minimum ratio	1.873	2.058	2.614	2.311	2.334	2.414	2.312	2.245

Source: The author's calculations based on the data from *China Statistical Yearbooks*.

per capita in Shanghai, Beijing, and Zhejiang, which were the most economically developed, to that in Gansu rose from 1.374, 0.897, and 0.815 to 2.245, 2.29, and 1.839, respectively. In 2008, the year when the largest income gap occurred, these three ratios reached 2.432, 2.254, and 2.072, respectively. In 2016, the ratios of urban disposable income per capita in Gansu, Heilongjiang, and Jilin, to the national average rose from 0.728 in 1978, 0.657 in 1981, and 0.690 in 1985 to 0.764, 0.766, and 0.789, respectively. In 2008, such three ratios were 0.695, 0.737, and 0.745, respectively. It can be seen that the absolute income gap between urban residents in the richest regions and those in the poorest regions has been gradually widening. The relative income gap widened before 2008, and has narrowed since then.

In terms of the general conditions of the country, the absolute gap in the disposable income of urban residents in China's provinces and municipalities during the period 1978–2016 also widened, and the relative gap first increased and then decreased. Figures 12.6 and 12.7 show the changes in the average, STDEV, and CV of urban disposable income per capita of Chinese provinces (municipalities) during the period 1978–2016. According to Figure 12.6, whether calculated at the current prices or at the constant prices, the STDEV for the average urban income of all provinces (municipalities) in China has been widening during this period, showing the widening absolute income gap of urban residents in different provinces (municipalities). Actually, the average disposable income of urban residents in China was 341.4 yuan in 1978, with a STDEV of 61.1 yuan, and 32,290.9 yuan in 2016, with a STDEV of 8,126.3 yuan. If the price hike factor is excluded using the urban consumer index, the national average disposable income of urban residents in 2016 was 4,773.2 yuan, with a STDEV of 1,201.2 yuan. The average was up 12.98 times but the STDEV was up 18.67 times compared to that of 1978. During the period 1978–2016, the CV for the relative income of Chinese

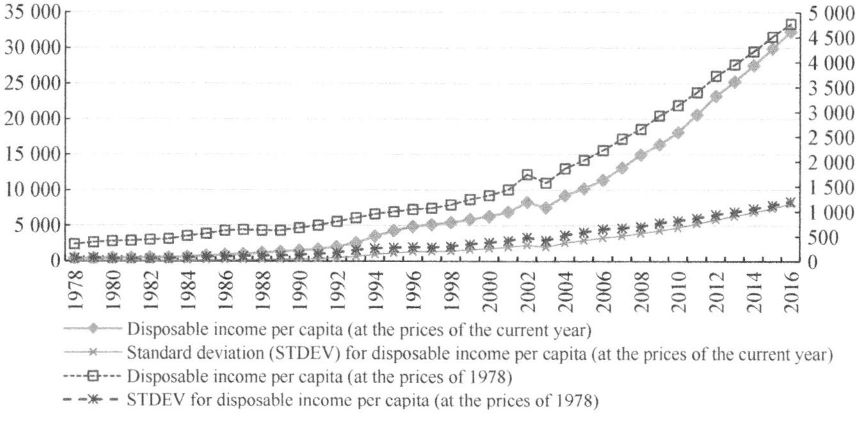

Figure 12.6 The average and standard deviation (STDEV) for the urban disposable income per capita of China' provinces (municipalities): 1978–2016.

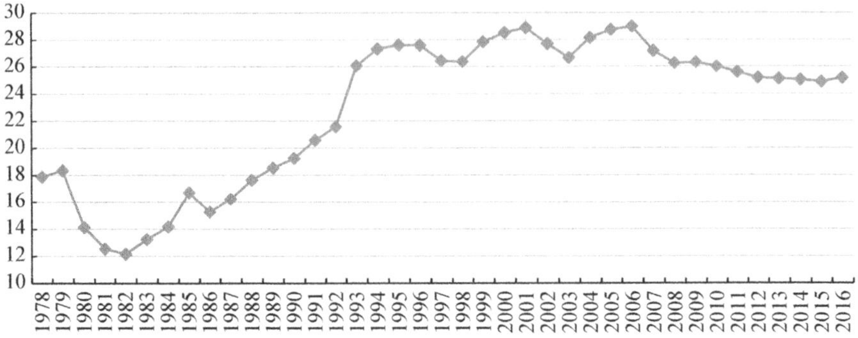

Figure 12.7 The coefficient of variance (CV) for the urban disposable income per capita of China's provinces (municipalities): 1978–2016.

urban residents also showed an upward trend. This figure was 17.88% in 1978, dropped to 12.15% in 1982, basically kept rising from 1983 to 1994, and remained at around 17.5% from 1994 to 1997. During the period 1994–2007, the CV fluctuated between 26% and 29% and showed three obvious fluctuation cycles. This figure reached 17.18% in 2007, was basically the same with that of 1994, kept dropping during the period 2007–2015, reached a local minimum of 24.88% in 2015, and rose to 25.17% in 2016.

4.2 Changes in the net income gap of rural residents in China's provinces (municipalities)

In terms of net income per capita of rural residents, Shanghai, Beijing, and Zhejiang, which had the highest net income per capita in 2016, are compared with Gansu, Guizhou, and Yunnan, which had the lowest net income per capita in the same year again. During the period 1978–2016, the rural net income per capita in Shanghai, Beijing, and Zhejiang increased from 281 yuan, 244.8 yuan, and 165 yuan to 19,595 yuan, 18,337 yuan, and 16,106 yuan, respectively, up 69 times, 75 times, and 67 times and representing an average annual growth of 12.8%, 12.0%, and 12.8%; that in Gansu, Guizhou, and Yunnan increased from 100.9 yuan, 109.3 yuan, and 130.6 yuan to 5,107 yuan, 5,434 yuan, and 6,141 yuan, respectively, up 50 times, 49 times, and 46 times and representing an average annual growth of 10.8%, 11.8%, and 13.2%. During the same period, the ratios of rural net income per capita of Shanghai, Beijing, and Zhejiang to that in rural areas of Gansu changed from 2.78, 2.42, and 1.63 to 3.84, 3.59, and 3.15, respectively, with the three ratios being 4.20, 3.91, and 3.40 in 2008; and the ratios of rural net income per capita of Gansu, Qinghai, and Guizhou, which were the poorest then, to that of the whole country decreased from 0.359, 0.389, and 0.465 to 0.261, 0.277, and 0.313, respectively, with the three ratios being 0.238, 0.244, and

0.271 in 2008. It can be seen that the absolute income gap between rural residents in the richest provinces and those in the poorest ones is widening; the relative income gap showed an upward trend before 2008 and has been narrowing in recent years.

From a national perspective overall, the absolute gap in rural net income of China's provinces (municipalities) during the period 1978–2016 widened, and the relative gap first widened and then narrowed, which is the same as the situation of Chinese urban residents in the same period. Figure 12.8 and Figure 12.10 show the changes in the average, STDEV, and CV of the net income per capita of rural residents in 31 provinces (municipalities) throughout China. As known from Figure 12.8, regardless whether calculated at the prices of the current year or at the constant prices, the STDEV for rural net income per capita of China's provinces (municipalities) has been increasing, showing the widening absolute gap. Actually, the average net income of rural residents in China's provinces (municipalities) in 1978 was 144.54 yuan, with a STDEV of 41.46 yuan, and that in 2016 was 12,877 yuan, with a STDEV of 4,423.6 yuan. At the constant prices of 1978, the average was 2,096 and the STDEV was 720 yuan in 2016, with the former being up 13.5 times and the latter up 16.4 times compared with those of 1978. During the period 1978–2016, the CV for rural net income per capita of China's provinces (municipalities) showed a wave-like upward trend in the early period of the reform, but has witnessed a downward trend since 2006. Specifically, this figure was 28.67% in 1978 and declined continuously from 1978 to 1981, reaching a local high of 19.57% in 1981. It exhibited a step-like upward trend from 1981 to 1993, reaching a local maximum of 37.95% in 1993; and continuously dropped from 1994 to 1998, reaching a local minimum of 36.22% in 1998. The figure started to rise again from 1999 to 2006, reaching the historical maximum of 46.18% in 2006.

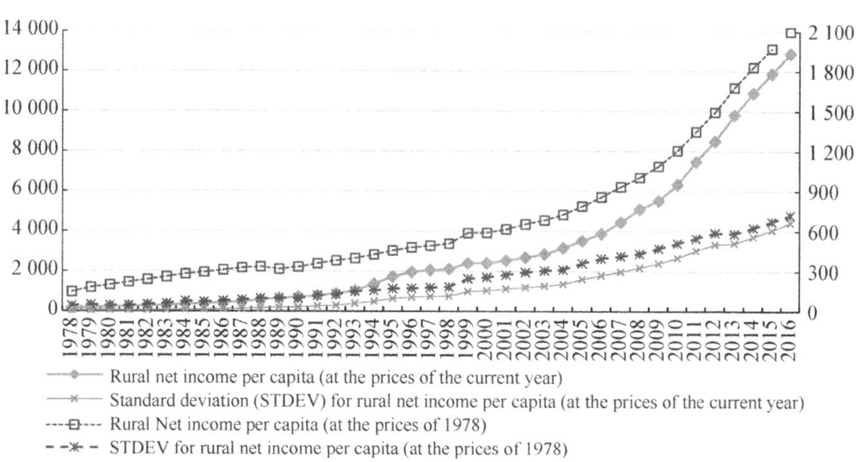

Figure 12.8 The average and standard deviation (STDEV) for rural net income per capita of China's provinces (municipalities): 1978–2016.

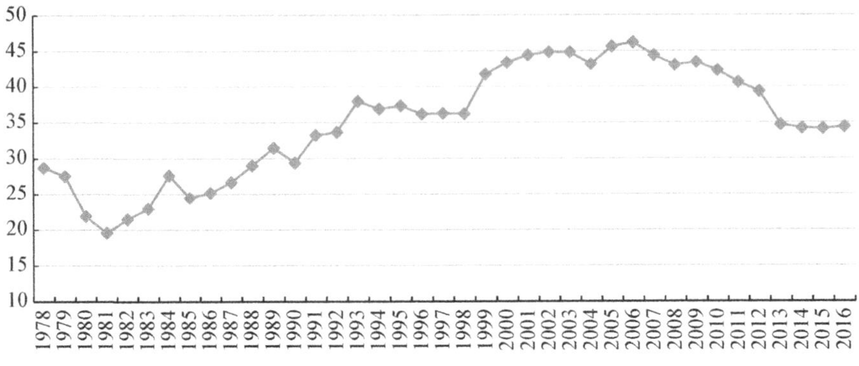

Figure 12.9 The coefficient of variation (CV) for rural net income per capita of China's provinces (municipalities): 1978–2016.

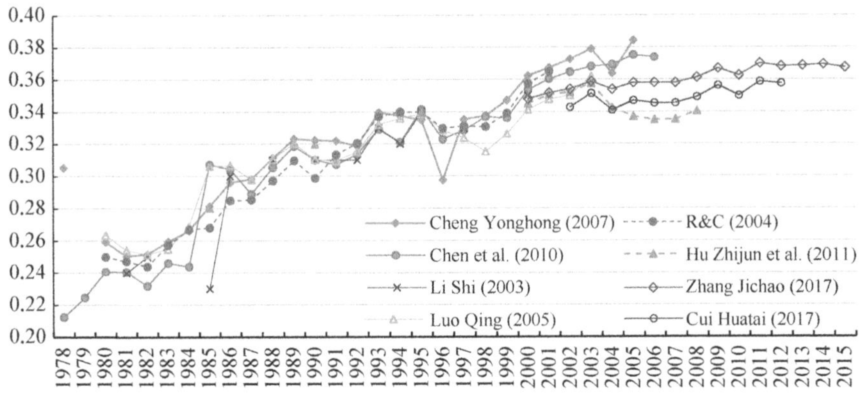

Figure 12.10 Changes in the Gini coefficient of income distribution in rural China: 1978–2015.

During the period 2007–2016, the CV decreased for ten consecutive years, reaching 34.35% in 2016, the same level as that of 1993. Overall, the absolute gap in the rural net income per capita of China's provinces (municipalities) has been widening since the reform, and the relative inequality firstly widened and narrowed since 2006 (Figures 12.9 and 12.10 and Table 12.5).

4.3 Changes in the income gaps of eastern, middle, and western regions of China

Finally, let's have a look at the changes in the income gap among residents in central, eastern, and western China.[3] Since the division of the East, Central, and West started in 1986, the changes for the period 1986–2016 are analyzed below. According to Table 12.6, in terms of annual rural net income per

Table 12.5 Changes in the rural net income per capita of regions (unit: yuan)

Year	*1978*	*1990*	*1995*	*2000*	*2005*	*2010*	*2013*	*2016*
Average	144.5	747.48	1636.27	2525.46	3511.55	6326.77	9429.6	12362.4
STDEV	41.5	294.66	739.42	1103.72	1575.31	2628.97	3401	4423.59
CV	0.2868	0.3942	0.4519	0.4370	0.4486	0.4155	0.3607	0.3578
Maximum	281 (Shanghai)	1907 (Shanghai)	4245.61 (Shanghai)	5870. 87 (Shanghai)	8247.77 (Shanghai)	13977.96 (Shanghai)	19208.3 (Shanghai)	25520.4 (Shanghai)
Minimum	100.93 (Gansu)	430.98 (Gansu)	880.34 (Gansu)	1404.41 (Tibet)	1873.96 (Guizhou)	3424.65 (Gansu)	5107.8 (Gansu)	7546.85 (Gansu)
Range	180.07	1476.02	3365.27	4466.46	6373.81	10553.31	14100.5	17973.55
Maximum-minimum ratio	2.784	4.425	4.823	4.180	4.401	4.082	3.761	3.382

Note: The data in the table are sorted by the author based on the data from *China Statistical Yearbooks*.

Table 12.6 The gap in annual rural net income per capita in eastern, central and western China: 1986–2016 (unit: yuan)

Region	*Indicator*	*1986*	*1999*	*2003*	*2008*	*2011*	*2016*
China	Average	425.35	2210.3	2622.2	4760.6	6977.3	12362.4
Eastern region	Average	580.24	3344.6	4160.4	7238. 8	9585.0	17135.1
	Difference from the national average	154.89	1134.2	1538.2	2478.2	2607.7	4772.7
	Ratio to the national average	1.36	1.51	1.59	1.52	1.374	1.39
Central region	Average	411.03	2065.2	2407.4	4551.0	6529.9	11780.9
	Difference from the national average	−14.32	−145.1	−214.9	−209.6	−447.4	−581.5
	Ratio to the national average	0.966	0.934	0.918	0.956	0.936	0.953
Western region	Average	342.88	1604.0	1921.0	3481.2	5246.8	9706.4
	Difference from the national average	−87.47	−606.3	−701.3	−1279.4	−1730.5	−2656
	Ratio to the national average	0.806	0.726	0.733	0.731	0.752	0.785

Note: The data in the table above are calculated by the author based on the data of *China Statistical Yearbooks* and *Collection of Statistical Data for New China during the 60 Years of Its Founding.* According to *China Statistical Yearbook 2017*, the rural disposable income per capita is included in the year 2016.

capita, eight of the 11 eastern provinces (municipalities) were among the top ten with the highest annual rural net income per capita in 1986; the per capita value of these regions was 580.24 yuan, 36% higher than the average level of the country (435.35); and all these provinces (municipalities) had higher annual rural net income per capita than the national average. In the same year, among the 11 western provinces (municipalities), eight ranked among the bottom ten in terms of rural net income per capita and the last four were all within the 11 western provinces (municipalities); the rural average net income per capita of these 11 provinces (municipalities) was 342.8 yuan, 80.6% of the national average. The rural net income per capita of the eight central provinces was 411.03 yuan, 96.6% of the national average, and their average level was almost the same with the national average. Among the eight provinces, two were listed among top ten of the whole country; two among the last ten; and only three were higher than the national average, indicating the large gap among the provinces (municipalities) in central China.

In 1999, 10 of the 11 eastern provinces (municipalities) ranked among the top ten in China in terms of annual rural net income per capita, and only Hainan Province ranked 16th in the country in this respect; the average annual rural net income per capita in the eastern region was 3,344.58 yuan, 51% higher than the national average (2,210.33 yuan) and 15 percentage points higher than that of 1986. Nine of the 12 western provinces ranked among the bottom nine in China in terms of the same; the average rural net income per capita of the 12 western provinces was 1,604.05 yuan, 72.57% of the national average and a decrease of 10 percentage points compared with that of 1986. The average annual rural net income per capita of the eight central provinces was 2,065.22 yuan, 93.4% of the national average and a decrease of 3.2 percentage points compared with that of 1986. During the period 1986–1999, the growth rate of rural income per capita in the 11 eastern provinces (municipalities) of China was higher than the national average; in the central region except Shanxi, whose level was lower than the national average, the growth rate of rural net income per capita in the other seven provinces was basically the same with the national average; and the growth rates of rural net income per capita in the 12 western regions were all lower than the national average. The rural net income ratios per capita of the eastern, central, and western regions were 1.692: 1.199: 1 in 1986 and 2.085: 1.287: 1 in 1999. During the period 1986–1999, the gap among the eastern, central, and western regions was widening.

In 2008, nine of the 11 eastern provinces (municipalities) ranked among top nine in terms of annual rural net income per capita, with Hebei and Henan dropping by 11th and 18th places; the rural net income per capita of the eastern region was 7,238.78 yuan, 52% higher than the national average (4,760.62 yuan) and still one percentage point higher than that of 1999. Among the 12 western provinces (municipalities), nine ranked among bottom nine in the country in terms of annual rural net income per capita; the average annual rural net income per capita was 3,481.26 yuan, 73.1% of the national average and an increase of 0.53 percentage point compared with that of 1999. The average annual net income per capita of the eight central provinces was 4,551.04 yuan, 95.59% of the national average and 2.19 percentage points higher than that of 1999, basically returning to the level of 1986. In 2008, the average level of rural areas in eastern China except Hainan was generally better than the national average; the level of the 12 western provinces except Inner Mongolia, whose level approached the national average, had a large gap from the national average. In 2008, the ratio of annual rural net income per capita in the eastern, central, and western regions decreased to 2.079: 1.307: 1. The gap between the eastern and central & western regions was narrowed but that between the central and western regions widened in 2008 compared with that of 1999.

The rural net income per capita of China's provinces and municipalities is not included in the *China Statistical Yearbook 2017* any longer; instead, their rural disposable income per capita is included. According to the data in the book, in 2016, nine of the 11 eastern provinces (municipalities) ranked among top nine in the country in terms of annual rural disposable income per capita (Hebei and Hainan ranked 14th and 15th, respectively, in this respect); the annual rural disposable income per capita of these 11 provinces was 17,135 yuan, 39% higher than the national average (12,362 yuan). The annual rural disposable income per capita of the 12 western provinces was

9,706 yuan, 78.5% of the national average. The average level of the eight central provinces was 11,781 yuan, 95.3% of the national average. In 2016, the ratio of annual rural disposable income per capita in the eastern, central, and western regions was 1.77:1.21:1. The relative gaps in income per capita in the eastern, central, and western regions were further narrowed in the year compared with those of 2008.

In terms of annual urban income per capita, as shown in Table 12.7, in 1986, eight of the 11 eastern provinces (municipalities) ranked among the top ten in China, one province ranked the last but four and another the last but 13; the average of the 11 provinces was 981.28 yuan, 11% higher than the national average (881.60). In 1986, in terms of the same, four of the 11 western provinces (municipalities) ranked from last and the last but nine in China, two ranked among the top ten, and five ranked between the top ten to top 15; and the average of the western region was 852.97 yuan, 96.8% of the national average. The average of the eight central provinces was 783.88 yuan, 88.9% of the national average, making the central region the one with the lowest urban income.

In 1999, seven of the 11 eastern provinces (municipalities) ranked among the top ten in China in terms of annual urban disposable income per capita, with five provinces ranking among the top five; the annual urban disposable income per capita of the eastern provinces was 7,284.2 yuan, 23.8% higher

Table 12.7 The gaps in urban net income per capita in eastern, central and western China: 1986–2016 (unit: yuan)

Region	*Indicator*	*1986*	*1999*	*2003*	*2008*	*2011*	*2016*
China	Average	881.60	5884.2	82948	14941	20607	32291
Eastern region	Average	981.28	7284.2	10367	18788	25917	39705
	Difference from the national average	99.68	1400.8	2071	3847	5310	7414
	Ratio to the national average	1.113	1.238	1.250	1.258	1.258	1.230
Central region	Average	783.88	4845.4	7406	13598	18783	29451
	Difference from the national average	−97.72	−1038.8	−889	−1343	−1824	−2840
	Ratio to the national average	0.889	0.823	0.893	0.910	0.911	0.912
Western region	Average	852.97	5338.5	7235	12741	17551	28242
	Difference from the national average	28.63	−645.7	−1059	−2199	−3057	−4048
	Ratio to the national average	0.967	0.890	0.872	0.853	0.852	0.875

Note: The data in the table above are calculated by the author based on the data of *China Statistical Yearbooks* and *Collection of Statistical Data for New China during the 60 Years of Its Founding.*

than the national average (5,884 yuan), representing an increase of 13 percentage points than that of 1986. Five of the eight central provinces in the central region ranked among the bottom ten in the country in this respect; the annual urban disposable income per capita of the central region was 4,845.4 yuan, 82.3% of the national average, representing a decrease of 6.6 percentage points compared with that of 1986; and the levels of all central provinces were lower than the average of the country. The average level of the 12 western provinces was 5,238.5 yuan, 89.0% of the national average, representing a decrease of 7.8 percentage points compared with that of 1986. The disposable income ratio of urban residents in the eastern, central, and western regions was 1.15:0.92:1 in 1986, and was changed to 1.39:0.92:1 in 1999. During the period 1986–1999, the gap between the eastern region and the central & western regions widened, but that between the central and western regions basically remains unchanged.

In 2008, nine of the 11 eastern provinces (municipalities) ranked among the top nine in China, but Hainan ranked among the bottom ten in the country; the average annual urban disposable income per capita of 11 provinces was 18,878 yuan, 25.8% of the national average (14,941 yuan), an increase of 2.5 percentage points compared with that of 1999. Three of the eight central provinces ranked among the top ten in the country, with Hunan ranking 11th alone; the average annual urban disposable income per capita of the eight provinces was 13,598 yuan, 91.0% of the national average, an increase of 8.7 percentage points compared with that of 1999. The average level of the 12 western provinces was 12,741 yuan, 85.3% of the national average, a decrease of 3.7 percentage points compared with that of 1999. In 2008, the ratio of the urban disposable income per capita of the eastern, central, and western regions increased to 1.475:1.067:1. During the period 1999–2008, the level of the eastern region was even higher than the national average; the level of the western region increasingly lagged behind the average of the whole country; and that of the central region became increasingly closer to the national average, with the central region surpassing the western region in particular.

In 2016, eight of the 11 eastern provinces (municipalities) ranked among the top eight in the country; the annual urban disposable income per capita in the eastern region was 39,705 yuan, 23% higher than the national average (32,291 yuan) and a decrease of 2.8 percentage points compared with that of 2008, basically returning to the level before 1999. Four of the eight central provinces (municipalities) ranked among the last ten, and the other four ranked 11th to 15th; the annual urban disposable income per capita of the central region was 29,451 yuan, 91.2% of the national average, basically at the same level with that of 2008. The average of the 12 western provinces (municipalities) was 28,242 yuan, 87.5% of the national average, with a slight increase. The ratio of the annual urban disposable income per capita in the eastern, central, and western regions was 1.406:1.043:1. The income gap of urban residents between the eastern and central & western regions widened but that between the central and western regions slightly narrowed relative to that of 2008.

In conclusion, the income gap between regions in China was decreasing from 1978 to the mid-1980s; after that, it was increasing until around 2007; and the regional income gap was decreasing from 2007 to 2016.

Section 5 Internal income gaps of China's rural and urban residents

Since 1978, internal income gaps of urban and rural residents in China have also continued to widen. In particular, from the mid-1980s to 2010, such gaps widened significantly, as shown in Figures 12.10 and 12.12. However, the Gini coefficients in China's urban and rural areas were not high and were both below 0.4. Take the year 2006, which had the largest Gini coefficient in China, as an example. Figure 12.10 shows that all the estimated values of the Gini coefficient in China's rural areas that year were between 0.3349 and 0.3737, and Figure 12.12 indicates that those in China's urban areas that year were between 0.309 and 0.392. However, the sustained widening of internal gaps of urban and rural areas is also one of the important reasons for the widening of China's overall income gap. Hu (2011) believes that the contribution of the internal urban-rural gap to the overall gap was approximately 35.5% to 45.6% during the period 1985–2000 and around 35% during the period 2001–2008. Additionally, the internal income gaps of urban and rural residents may be more important for people's sense of justice and social stability.

5.1 The internal income gap of rural residents

Figure 12.10 shows the changes in the internal Gini coefficients of rural areas in China as estimated by different scholars. According to Figure 12.10, the internal income gap of the rural areas obviously widened from 1978–2006, and the Gini coefficient of rural residents' income distribution increased except for a few years; and since 2006, the Gini coefficient has mostly remained a stable trend. In the early years of the reform, the Gini coefficient in rural China was not large, probably 0.21–0.25 in 1978. For example, the sampling survey data of the Rural Survey Team from the National Bureau of Statistics of China showed that the Gini coefficient of rural China was 0.21–0.22 (Rural Survey Team of the National Bureau of Statistics of China, 1987; Rural Social and Economic Survey Team of the National Bureau Statistics of China, 2001; Tang, 1995, etc.), and was estimated by Adelman and Sunding (1987) to be 0.22. In Figure 12.10, other scholars' estimates of the Gini coefficient in rural China for the 1980s may be slightly larger, but all below 0.25. By 2000, all the internal Gini coefficients in the rural areas estimated by scholars had exceeded 0.3, which was generally believed to be around 0.35, nearly ten percentage points larger than that of 1978. According to the survey data of the Chinese Academy of Social Sciences, the Gini coefficient of rural residents in China reached about 0.37 (Khan & Riskin, 2008; Beyon

Gustafsson et al., 2008) in 2002. This figure reached the peak around 2006. Chen et al. (2010) believe that the Gini coefficient in the rural areas of 2006 was approximately 0.37. After 2006, the rural Gini coefficient remained stable and slightly declined. According to the estimates from different literature in Figure 12.10, the internal coefficient of China's rural areas since 2010 has been between 0.35 and 0.37. In summary, the current internal Gini coefficient in rural China is about 0.36, similar to that in developed countries around 2010 (see Table 12.1), below the international warning line of 0.4.

The following is an analysis of the changes in the income gap between different groups in rural China after 2002 based on data from the *China Statistical Yearbook*. Figure 12.11 shows the ratio of income per capita of different groups to the national average income in rural China during the period 2000–2018. According to the data in this figure, the income per capita of the low income group in rural China was 820 yuan in 2000, 35.6% of the national income per capita (2,553 yuan). The income per capita of the lowest income group was 1,870 yuan in 2010, with its ratio to the national income per capita (5,919) dropping to 31.6%. In 2018, the income per capita of the lowest income group was 3,302 yuan and its ratio to the national income per capita (12,363 yuan) was 25.1%. The income per capita of the lower-middle income group was 1,440 yuan in 2000, 63.9% of the national income per capita; 3,621 yuan in 2010, 61.2% of the national income per capita; and 8,509 yuan in 2018, 58.2% of the national income per capita. The net income per capita of farmers in the high income group was 5,190 yuan in 2000, with its

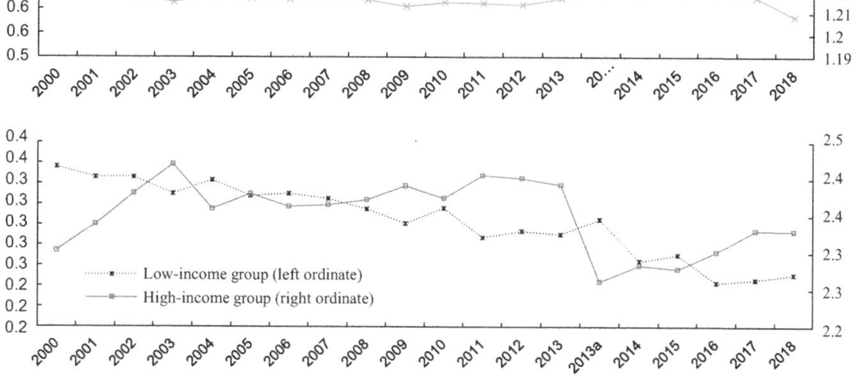

Figure 12.11 Ratios of income per capita in different groups to average income in rural China: 2000–2018.

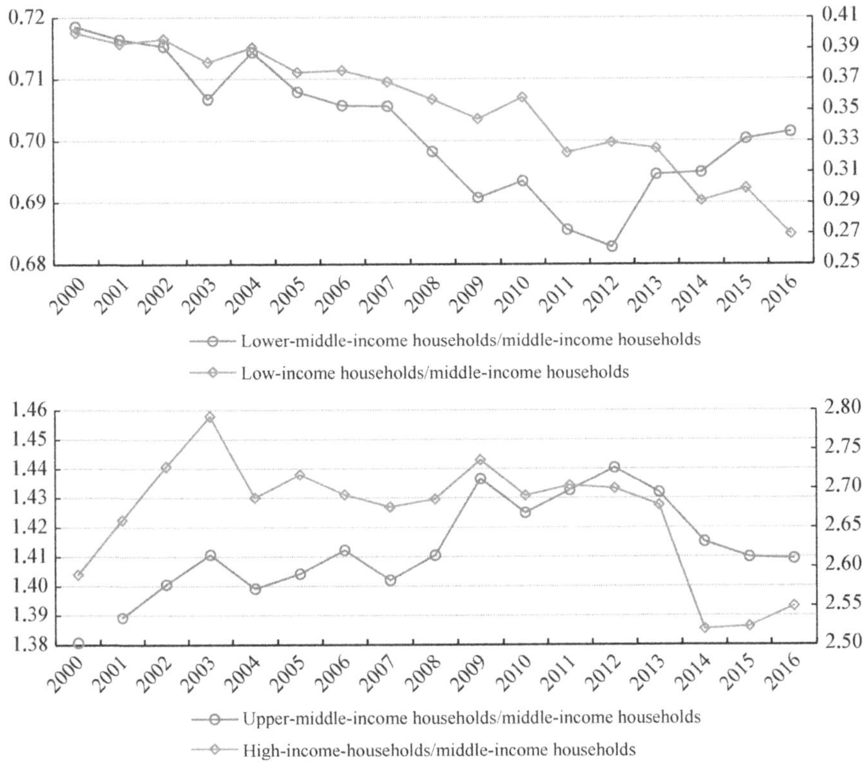

Figure 12.12 Ratios of the annual net income per capita of different income groups to that in the middle income group in rural China: 2000–2016.

ratio to the national income per capita being 2.30; 14,050 yuan in 2010, with its ratio to the national income per capita rising to 2.37; and 34,042 yuan in 2018, with its ratio to the national income per capita dropping to 2.33. The ratio of the net income per capita of the upper-middle income group to the national income per capita has been rising. It reached 1.23 in 2000, rose to 1.26 in 2010, and became 1.24 in 2018.

Figure 12.12 further shows the changes in the ratios of the income per capita of rural middle income residents to that of other income groups. As can be seen in the top chart of this figure, the gap between the annual net income per capita of farmers in the low income group and that of the middle income group has been widening from 2000 to 2016. In 2000, the ratio of the annual net income per capita of the low income group to that of the middle income group was 40%. During the period 2000–2016, the annual nominal net income per capita of the low income group was up 2.75 times, and that of the middle income group up 4.57 times, with the ratio of the former to the latter decreasing to 26.9%. The income gap between the lower-middle income group and the middle income group first widened and then narrowed. In 2000, the ratio of the annual net income per capita of the lower-middle income group to that of the middle income group was 71.9%, decreased by 68.2% in 2012, rose again after 2012, and increased to 70.1% in 2016, still decreasing by two percentage points compared with that of 2000.

The bottom chart of Figure 12.12 shows that, during the period 2000–2016, the gap between the annual net income per capita of farmers in China's high income group and that in the middle income group first widened and then declined steadily. It has slightly widened recently. The annual net income per capita of the high income group was 2.59 times that of the middle income group in 2000, was up 2.79 times in 2003, was maintained at 2.65 to 2.75 during the period 2004–2013, slightly decreased to 2.52 in 2014, and increased to 2.55 in 2016, a slight decrease compared to that of 2000. The gap between the annual net income per capita of farmers in the upper-middle income group and that in the middle-income group widened during the period 2000–2012 and narrowed during the period 2012–2016. In 2000, the annual net income per capita of farmers in the upper-middle income group was 1.38 times that of the middle income group, increased by 1.44 times in 2012, and declined after 2012, to 1.41 in 2016, still up by 0.132 times compared with that of 2000.

In summary, the internal income gap in rural China takes on the following characteristics. First, the Gini coefficient of the internal income gap of rural residents is still lower than the international warning line of 0.4. Second, China's rural internal income gap showed a continuous widening trend during the period 1978–2006, a narrowing trend during the period 2006–2012, but a widening trend in recent years. Third, the income gap among different classes has different trends. The income gap between the low income group and other income groups has been widening and that among the other income groups has basically tended to widen and then narrow. However, in recent years, the income gap of the highest income group and the lowest income group from the middle income group has tended to widen. In particular, the gap between the low income group and other groups has tended to sharply widen.

5.2 The income gap among urban residents

Figure 12.13 shows the Gini coefficient values of the income distribution of Chinese urban residents during the period 1978–2015 estimated by different scholars. As known from Figure 12.13, the Gini coefficient of China's urban areas basically tended to widen during the period 1978–2016, and basically remained stable after 2006 but showed a slight downward trend. In 1978, the Gini coefficient of China's urban areas was 0.16. This figure was about 0.165 according to the estimate of Adelman and Sunding (1987) and around 0.16 according to the estimates of other scholars. In 1988, the

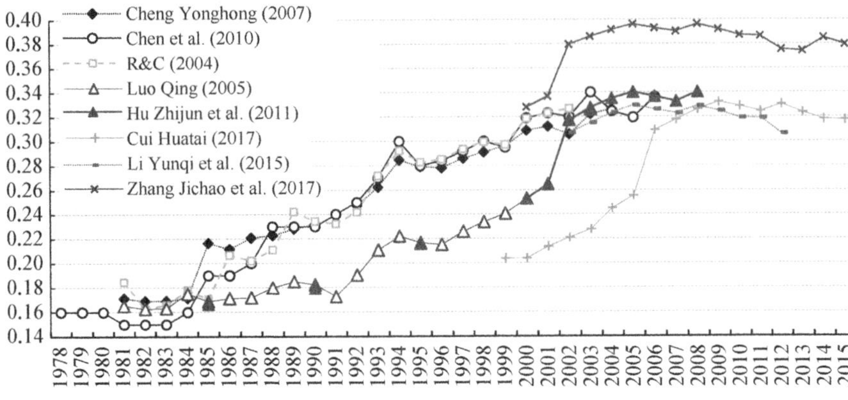

Figure 12.13 Changes in the Gini coefficient of China's urban income distribution: 1978–2015.

figure rose to 0.23 according to the estimate of the National Bureau of Statistics of China, with the same result as that estimated by Khan and Riskin (1998) and Gustafsson and Li (1998), and above 0.18 according to the estimates of other scholars. In 2002, all the other scholars listed in Figure 12.13 thought the value exceeded 0.3 except Cui (2017), who believed that the value exceeded 0.22.

In terms of the income gap among different income groups, the annual disposable income gap per capita of Chinese urban residents has also continued to widen, despite the slight narrowing in recent years and varying trends of the income gaps among different income groups. According to the data of the *China Statistical Yearbooks*, in 1985, the annual disposable income per capita of the highest income group, the lowest income group, and the extreme poor group was 1,276.2 yuan, 394.8 yuan, and 437.4 yuan, respectively, and that of the highest income group was 3.23 and 2.91 times that of the lowest income group and the poor group, with an absolute difference of 8,881 yuan and 838 yuan, respectively. The ratios of the annual disposable income per capita of the highest income group to that of the lowest income group and the difficult group were up 5.15 times and 4.19 times in 1999, with the absolute gaps increasing to 9,501 yuan and 9,791 yuan, and up 9.17 times and 11.68 times, with the absolute gaps being 38,860 yuan and 39,879 yuan. In 2016, the absolute gaps were still increasing, to 55,609 yuan and 57,304 yuan, respectively, with slightly narrowed absolute gaps. The ratios decreased to 7.78 times and 9.78 times, respectively.

Figure 12.14 shows the changes in the ratios of the annual disposable income per capita of different income groups to the national annual disposable income per capita during the period 1985–2018 by dividing Chinese urban

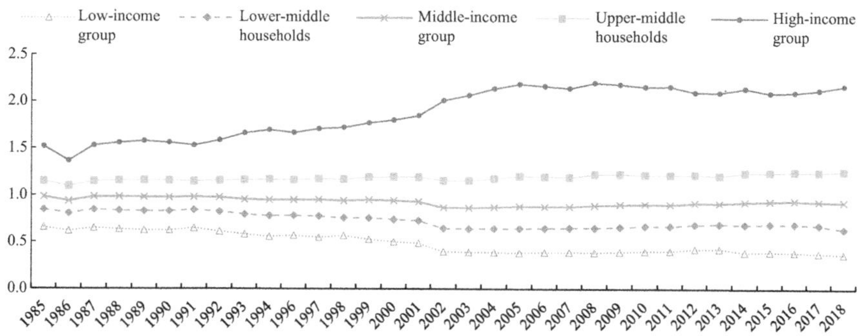

Figure 12.14 Ratio of the disposable income per capita of Chinese urban residents in each group to the national average: 1985–2018.

residents into five equal parts. As known from the data of Figure 12.14, the ratio of the annual disposable income per capita of residents in China's low income group to the national disposable income per capita first dropped, then rose, and then declined again during this period. This ratio reached 65.2% in 1985, dropped to 38.3% in 2005, rose to 42.4% in 2013, and declined to 36.7% in 2018, reaching the lowest level in history. The ratio of the disposable income per capita of the high income group to the national average reached 1.52 in 1985, rose to the historical high of 2.20 in 2008, dropped to 2.09 in 2015, and grew to 2.16 in 2018. The ratio of the disposable income per capita of the middle income group to the national average reached 0.98 in 1985, lower than 1, indicating that there were more people at the national average level. In 2013, this ratio dropped to the historical low of 0.859, indicating an increase in the number of people in the low income group and a decrease in the number of people in the high income group. This ratio was rising during the period 2014–2016 and reached 0.938 in 2016, approximately returning to the level of 1998 (0.922). Figure 12.14 also shows that the relative gap between the lower-middle income and upper-middle income households and the national disposable income per capita has tended to drop first and then rise.

In conclusion, since the reform and opening-up, the internal income gap among Chinese urban residents has taken on the following characteristics. First, the internal income gap in the urban areas of China has basically continued to widen since 1978, but tended to narrow since 2008. Second, through the comparison of different income groups it can be seen that the income gap in China's urban areas has been widening in recent years. Third, in terms of the Gini coefficient, the current internal income gap in China's urban areas has not exceeded the international warning line of 0.4 and its Gini coefficient does not differ much from that of developed countries, basically within the normal range of the income gap.

Section 6 Income gaps of industries and capital-labor income ratio

6.1 Income gaps among industries

Table 12.8 shows the differences in average wages of various industries in China during the period 1978–2016, including wage difference of highest and lowest income industries, wage ratio of the highest to lowest income industries, ratio of the average wage of the highest income industry to the national average, ratio of the average wage of the lowest income industry to the national average, and STDEV and CV for industry wages. According to this table, the industry income inequality measured by relative income gap indicators such as wage ratio of the highest to lowest income industries, ratio of the average wage of the highest income industry to the national average, and CV also indicate that China's industry income inequality was showing a wave-like widening trend during the period 1978–2016. Firstly, the wage ratio of the highest to lowest income industries was declining until 1989, gradually widened after 1990, and slightly narrowed after 2008 but widened in 2016. According to the data of Table 12.8, the average wage of China's highest income industry (electricity, gas, water production, and supply) was 850 yuan and that of the country's lowest income industry (social service) was 392 yuan, with their difference being 458 yuan and ratio being 2.17. In 1990, the average wage of the highest income industry (extractive industry) was 2,378 yuan and that of the lowest income industry (agriculture, forestry, animal husbandry, and fishery) was 1,541 yuan, with their difference rising to 1,177 yuan and ratio to 1.764 in 1978. In 2000, the average wage of the highest income industry (scientific research and technical service) was 13,620 yuan and that of the lowest income industry (agriculture, forestry, animal husbandry, and fishery) was 5,184 yuan, with their difference rising to 8,436 yuan and ratio to 2.63 in 1978. In 2016, the average wage of the highest income industry (information transmission, software, and information technology service) was 122,478 yuan and that of the lowest income industry (agriculture, forestry, animal husbandry, and fishery) was 33,612 yuan, with their difference increasing to 88,866 yuan and ratio to 3.64 in 1978. During the period 1978–2016, the absolute gap between the maximum and minimum wages in China's industries was up 226 times and their ratio between the two increased by 67.7%. Secondly, the ratio of the average wage of highest income industry to the national average and that of the lowest income industry to the national average also showed the same trend. The former was 1.382 in 1978, 1.27 in 1992, 1.453 in 2000, and 1.813 in 2016 and the latter was 0.636 in 1978, 0.504 in 2000, and 0.497 in 2016. Thus, the average wage of the highest income industry has been increasingly higher than the national average and that of the lowest income industry increasingly lower than the national average. Finally, as shown in Figure 12.15, the CV for average industry wages was 0.1745 in 1978; it had been narrowing during the period

Table 12.8 Changes in the average wages of industries during the period 1978–2016

Year	*National average wage*	*Highest income industry*	*Lowest income industry*	*Wage difference of the highest and lowest income industries*	*Wage ratio of the highest to the lowest income industry*	*Ratio of the highest industry wage to the national average wage*	*Ratio of the lowest industry wage to the national average wage*	*Average wage of industries*	*STDEV for industry wages*
1978	615	850(water, electricity, coal and gas)	392(social service)	458	2.168	1.382	0.636	617	108
1980	762	1035(water, electricity, coal and gas)	475(social service)	560	2.179	1.358	0.620	766	128
1985	1148	1406(geology and water conservancy)	777(social service)	629	1.810	1.225	0.676	1150	169
1989	1935	2378(extractive industry)	1389(agriculture, forestry, animal husbandry and fishery)	989	1.712	1.229	0.702	1979	241
1990	2140	2718(extractive industry)	1541(agriculture, forestry, animal husbandry and fishery)	1177	1.764	1.270	0.691	2229	293
1991	2340	2942(extractive industry)	1652(agriculture, forestry, animal husbandry and fishery)	1290	1.781	1.257	0.679	2432	331
1992	2711	3392(water, electricity, coal and gas)	1828(agriculture, forestry, animal husbandry and fishery)	1564	1.856	1.251	0.640	2857	396
1993	3371	4320 (real estate)	2042(agriculture, forestry, animal husbandry and fishery)	2278	2.116	1.282	0.573	3562	585

(*Continued*)

Year	*National average wage*	*Highest income industry*	*Lowest income industry*	*Wage difference of the highest and lowest income industries*	*Wage ratio of the highest to the lowest income industry*	*Ratio of the highest industry wage to the national average wage*	*Ratio of the lowest industry wage to the national average wage*	*Average wage of industries*	*STDEV for industry wages*
1994	4538	6712 (finance and insurance)	2819(agriculture, forestry, animal husbandry and fishery)	3893	2.381	1.479	0.551	5120	978
1995	5500	7843(water, electricity, coal and gas)	3522(agriculture, forestry, animal husbandry and fishery)	4321	2.227	1.426	0.588	5993	1099
1996	6210	8816(water, electricity, coal and gas)	4050(agriculture, forestry, animal husbandry and fishery)	4766	2.177	1.420	0.598	6774	1285
1997	6470	9734(finance and insurance)	4311(agriculture, forestry, animal husbandry and fishery)	5423	2.258	1.505	0.586	7356	1540
1998	7479	10633(finance and insurance)	4528(agriculture, forestry, animal husbandry and fishery)	6105	2.348	1.422	0.548	8258	1675
1999	8346	12046(finance and insurance)	4832(agriculture, forestry, animal husbandry and fishery)	7214	2.493	1.443	0.524	9219	1976
2000	9371	13620(scientific research and technical service)	5184(agriculture, forestry, animal husbandry and fishery)	8436	2.627	1.453	0.504	10286	2288
2001	10870	16437(scientific research and technical service)	5741(agriculture, forestry, animal husbandry and fishery)	10696	2.863	1.512	0.483	11893	2818

2002	12422	19135(finance and insurance)	6398(agriculture, forestry, animal husbandry and fishery)	12737	2.991	1.540	0.473	13525	3320
2003	13969	30897(software information and technical service)	6884(agriculture, forestry, animal husbandry and fishery)	24013	4.488	2.212	0.493	15496	4991
2004	15920	33449(software information and technical service)	7497(agriculture, forestry, animal husbandry and fishery)	25952	4.462	2.101	0.471	17556	5530
2005	18200	38799(software information and technical service)	8207(agriculture, forestry, animal husbandry and fishery)	30592	4.728	2.132	0.451	20116	6594
2006	20856	43435(software information and technical service)	9269(agriculture, forestry, animal husbandry and fishery)	34166	4.686	2.083	0.444	23012	7680
2007	24721	47700(software information and technical service)	10847(agriculture, forestry, animal husbandry and fishery)	36853	4.398	1.930	0.439	26995	8970
2008	28898	54906(software information and technical service)	12560(agriculture, forestry, animal husbandry and fishery)	42346	4.371	1.900	0.435	31468	10750
2009	32244	60398(finance)	14356(agriculture, forestry, animal husbandry and fishery)	46042	4.207	1.873	0.445	34663	11614
2010	36539	70146(finance)	16717(agriculture, forestry, animal husbandry and fishery)	53429	4.196	1.920	0.458	39114	13176

(Continued)

Year	*National average wage*	*Highest income industry*	*Lowest income industry*	*Wage difference of the highest and lowest income industries*	*Wage ratio of the highest to the lowest income industry*	*Ratio of the highest industry wage to the national average wage*	*Ratio of the lowest industry wage to the national average wage*	*Average wage of industries*	*STDEV for industry wages*
2011	41799	81109(finance)	19469(agriculture, forestry, animal husbandry and fishery)	61640	4.166	1.940	0.466	45046	14701
2012	46769	89743(finance)	22687(agriculture, forestry, animal husbandry and fishery)	67056	3.956	1.919	0.485	50200	16162
2013	51483	99653(finance)	25820(agriculture, forestry, animal husbandry and fishery)	73833	3.860	1.936	0.502	55670	18137
2014	56360	108273(finance)	28356(agriculture, forestry, animal husbandry and fishery)	79917	3.818	1.921	0.503	60503	19753
2015	62029	114777(finance)	31947(agriculture, forestry, animal husbandry and fishery)	82830	3.593	1.850	0.515	66053	21298
2016	67569	122478(information and computers)	33612(agriculture, forestry, animal husbandry and fishery)	88866	3.644	1.813	0.497	71114	22659

Source: *China Statistical Yearbooks*. Due to the adjustment of industries in *China Statistical Yearbooks* following the year 2003, there are differences between the data before 2003 and that after the year.

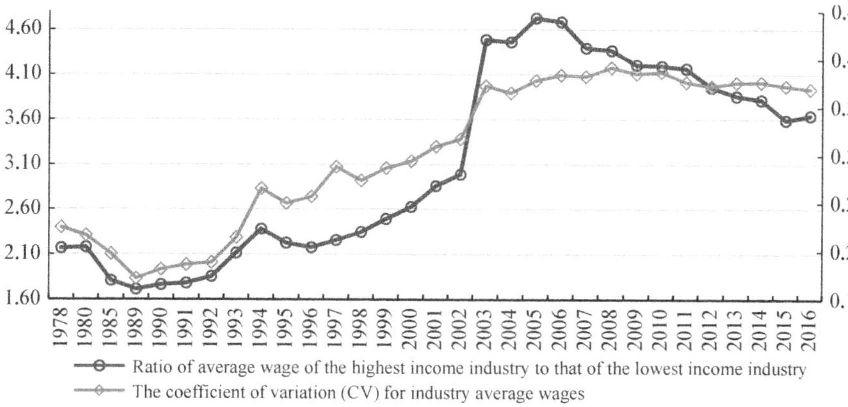

Figure 12.15 Changes in the wage gaps among industries in China: 1978–2016.

1978–1989, reaching 0.1712 in 1989; it gradually increased in 1990, reached the maximum of 0.3416 in 2008; and it tended to slightly narrow afterwards and reached 0.319 in 2016.

6.2 Capital-labor income ratio

The sustained widening income gap in China is also reflected in the changes in the capital-labor income ratio. Regarding the proportion of labor income in China, an early study by Li (1992) argued that the labor income share largely increased during the early reform period. However, many scholars have found that the proportion of China's labor income has continued to decline since the 1990s (Zhou et al., 2010b; Bai & Qian, 2009a, b; Luo & Zhang, 2009b). The continuous increase in the capital-labor income ratio has attracted the attention of scholars and is also considered to be one of the important reasons for the widening income gap in China (Gong & Yang, 2010). According to the estimates of Luo and Zhang (2009a), the proportion of China's labor income fell from around 52% to 41% during the period 1987–2006. Figure 12.16 shows the changes in the proportion of China's labor income during the period 1987–2016. In the figure, the solid line marked by the diamond indicates the proportion of that labor income that is earned by the labor income in the *China Statistical Yearbooks* divided by the total value added, and the dotted line marked by the circle shows the proportion of the labor income that is earned by the labor remunerations through the aggregation of regional data in the *China Statistical Yearbooks* divided by GDP. As known from Figure 12.16, the proportion of China's labor income basically tended to first decline and then rise during the period 1987–2016. In terms of the proportion of labor income earned through regional aggregation, the proportion of China's labor income was 52% in 1987; it dropped

Figure 12.16 Changes in the proportion of China's labor income: 1987–2016.

to 50.1% in 1992; it increased to 53.4% in 1996; it kept decreasing during the period 1996–2007; it dropped to around 50% in 2003; it reached the lowest point of 39.7% in 2007; and it basically showed an upward trend during the period 2008–2016, reaching 50.9% in 2016 and close to the level of 2002. In terms of the proportion of the total labor income in the total value added, the proportion of labor income in China has also experienced the same trend. The proportion of labor income was about 59.9% in 1992, suddenly dropped to 56.7% in 1993, and slowly increased during the period 1994–1999, reaching the maximum value of 59.6% in 1999. This proportion started to decline after 2000, reaching 47.0% in 2011; it rose after 2012, and reached 51.8% in 2015, almost at the same level as that of 2003.

Section 7 Status quo and features of China's income distribution pattern

In conclusion, China's current income distribution mainly shows the following three features. Firstly, China's income distribution inequality has been widening on the whole. The Gini coefficient has now exceeded the internationally recognized warning line of 0.4, making China rank among the countries with huge income disparity in income distribution (the Gini coefficient exceeds 0.45). This indicates that it is very important and urgent to improve China's income distribution pattern. Secondly, China's income gap has been comprehensively and continuously widening since the reform, and the intensification of income inequality has been reflected in all areas of economy and life. It shows that we face an extremely complicated and difficult situation when improving China's income distribution pattern and narrowing the income gap among residents. Finally, there is also a fact worthy of attention. If we only look at the internal income gaps of urban and rural areas we see that they are both within the international warning line of 0.4, and China does not differ much from other developed countries in the world in terms of income distribution inequality. As China's current urban-rural segmentation is still serious, urban and rural areas can almost be regarded as two different living areas, and urban and rural residents mainly live in their own areas. Thus, in reality, the primary factor affecting one's sense of fairness is the internal income gaps of urban and rural areas. It is precisely due to the fact that the social and economic life remains stable and no social instability and turmoil have occurred in some countries with highly unequal income distribution, although the Gini coefficient of the overall income distribution in China is quite large. However, with the further deepening of urbanization, the integration between urban and rural residents has become increasingly deeper; the connection between urban and rural areas has gotten closer; and the urban-rural segmentation has not been as obvious as before. Thus, the excessive urban-rural gap and the impact of the overall Gini coefficient of the country over social stability may increase to a large extent. And it is more urgent to improve the income distribution pattern and narrow the overall income gap.

Furthermore, three additional characteristics of China's income distribution should also be paid attention to. First, the income gap between urban and rural areas is widening, which tends to accelerate. Second, the mobility of social classes or the possibility of the poor becoming the rich through hard efforts is becoming smaller. Thus, social stratification is forming and social classes emerging. Third, the gap in wealth distribution is much larger than that in income distribution. These three points are the reasons the current income gap is widely highlighted and instable social sediments occur. As China's reform goes deeper and urbanization continues to expand, the three characteristics of income distribution may become the most important factors affecting social instability and economic development.

Notes

1 According to data from the National Bureau of Statistics of China, China's Gini coefficient was about 0.467 in 2017, an increase of 0.002 over that of 2016. However, the data estimated by other scholars are higher than that of the National Bureau of Statistics. For example, the Gini coefficient 2007 estimated by Li and Luo (2011) and listed in the main text is higher than that announced by the state. The Survey and Research Center for China Household Finance of Southwestern University of Finance and Economics, according to the calculation results of its household survey data, announced in December 2012 that the Gini coefficient 2010 of national residents' income was 0.61. Of course, there are still controversies about the actual value of China's Gini coefficient, the reliability of the calculation results, and whether China's income gap has really narrowed in recent years, which will not be discussed here.

2 The data on urban disposable income per capita of Qinghai and Heilongjiang in 1978 are not available from *China Statistical Yearbooks*. The data of Qinghai started in 1981 and that of Heilongjiang started in 1985.

3 The classification of China into the eastern, central, and western regions started in 1986, and the Seventh Five-Year Plan passed at the Fourth Session of the Sixth National People's Congress was officially announced. At that time, there were 11 provinces (municipalities) in the eastern region; ten provinces (regions) in the central region; and nine provinces (regions) in the western region. After Chongqing was established as a municipality directly under the Central Government and included in the western region in 1997, the number of provinces (regions, municipalities) in the western region increased from nine to ten. Inner Mongolia and Guangxi were also included in the scope of provinces (regions, municipalities) entitled to favorable policies listed in the Western Development Plan 2000. As a result, the division of the eastern, central and west regions is changed as follows: the eastern region includes 11 provinces and municipalities, namely Beijing, Tianjin, Hebei, Liaoning, Shanghai, Jiangsu, Zhejiang, Fujian, Shandong, Guangdong, and Hainan; the central region includes eight provinces, namely Shanxi, Jilin, Heilongjiang, and Anhui, Jiangxi, Henan, Hubei and Hunan; the western region includes 12 provinces, regions and municipalities, namely Chongqing, Sichuan, Guizhou, Yunnan, Tibet, Shaanxi, Gansu, Qinghai, Ningxia, Xinjiang, Inner Mongolia, and Guangxi. This classification method is adopted in the analysis of this chapter below.

References

[1] Adelman, I., & Sunding, D. (1987). Economic Policy and Income Distribution in China, *Journal of Comparative Economics*. 62, 1021–1040.

[2] Bai, C. E., & Qian, Z. J. (2009a). Factor Income Share in China: The Story Behind the Statistics. *Economic Research Journal*, Issue 3, 27–41.

[3] Bai, C. E., & Qian, Z. J. (2009b). Who Is the Predator, Who the Prey? An Analysis of Changes in the State of China's National Income Distribution. *Social Sciences in China*, Issue 5, 99–115.

[4] Chen, B. K., Zhang, P. F., & Yang, R. D. (2010). Government Educational Expenditure, Human Capital Investment and Urban-Rural Inequality in China. *Management World*, Issue 1, 36–43.

[5] Chen, J., Dai, D., Hou, W., & Feng, Q. (2010). The Trend of the Gini Coefficient of China. *BWPI Working Paper 109*.

[6] Cui, H. T. (2017). An Analysis of the Change of the Gini Coefficient in China from the Dualistic Perspective of Both Urban and Rural Areas. *Comparative Economic & Social Systems*, Issue 3, 33–44.

[7] Gong, G., & Yang, G. (2010). On the Evolution of Wage Share in National Income – Another Explanation to Kuznets' Cure. *Management World*, Issue 5, 45–55.

[8] Gustafsson, B., & Li, S. (1998). Inequality in China at the End of the 1980s: Locational Aspects and Household Characteristics. *Asian Economic*, 12, 35–63.

[9] Gustafsson, B., Li, S., Sicular, T., & Yue, X. M. (2008). Income inequality in China and its regional differences. In *Research on income distribution in China III*, edited by S. Li, T. Sicular, & B. Gustafsson. Beijing: Beijing Normal University Press.

[10] Hu, Z. J., Liu, Z. M., & Gong, Z. M. (2011). Estimation of the Gini Coefficient for China's General Income: From 1985 to 2008. *China Economic Quarterly*, Issue 3, 1423–1436.

[11] Khan, A. R., & Riskin, C. (1998). Income and Inequality in China: Composition, Distribution and Growth of Household Income, 1988 to 1995. *The China Quarterly*, 154, 221–253.

[12] Khan, A. R., & Riskin, C. (2008). China's household income and its distribution. In S. Li, T. Sicular, & B. Gustafsson, *Research on income distribution in China III*. Beijing: Beijing Normal University Press.

[13] Li, S., & Luo, C. L. (2011). How Unequal Is China? *Economic Research Journal,* Issue 4, 68–79.

[14] Li, Y., (1992). Adjustment of income function distribution, *Economic Research Journal,* Issue 7, 34–44.

[15] Luo, C. Y., & Zhang, J. (2009a). An Economic Explanation of Declined Ratio of Labor Income: Analysis Based on China's Provincial Panel Data. *Management World*, Issue 5, 25–35.

[16] Luo, C. Y., & Zhang, J. (2009b). Labor Income Share and Economic Development: An Empirical Study Based on Chinese Industry-Level Data. *Social Sciences in China*, Issue 4, 65–79.

[17] Piketty, T. (1997). The Dynamics of the Wealth Distribution and the Interest Rate with Credit Rationing. *Review of Economic Studies*, 64, 173–189.

[18] Piketty, T., Yang, L., & Zucman, G. (2017). Capital Accumulation, Private Property and Rising Inequality in China, 1978–2015, *NBER Working Paper* No. 23368.

[19] Rural Social Economic Survey Branch of National Bureau of Statistics of China. (2001). *Research on Chinese Peasants' Income*. Beijing: China Statistics Press.

[20] Rural Survey Branch of National Bureau of Statistics of China. (1987). *Research on Chinese Peasants' Income*. Taiyuan: Shanxi People's Publishing House.

[21] Tang, P. (1995). Analysis of rural population's income level and differences in China. *Management World*, Issue 2, 173–181.

[22] Wang, H. L., & Xu, X. (2006). Interregional and Urban-Rural Income Inequality. *Management World*, Issue 11, 41–50.

[23] Zeng, A. G. and Hu, J. J. (2008), International Comparison of Urban-Rural Income Gap, *Shandong Social Science*, Issue 10, 47–53.

[24] Zhou, H. M., Xiao, W., & Yao, X. G. (2010). Declining of Labor Share in China: Measurement and Interpretation of Research Progress. *World Economic Papers*, Issue 6, 92–105.

13 Imperfect labor market, unbalanced regional economic development, and regional income gap

Existing research shows that the regional income gap constitutes one of the main factors for the widening income gap among Chinese residents. Other research literature holds that the widening income gap among regions in China is mainly due to the unbalanced development of the regional economy and the continuous widening of the regional economic gap that results. It is believed based on the research of this chapter that the widening regional income gap in China is not necessarily due to the unbalanced development of the regional economy and the continuous widening of the regional economic gap but regional labor market segmentation; but that it is quite likely that both the unbalanced regional economic development and the widening of the regional economic gap in China are the results of regional labor market segmentation. Thus, only by reforming the household registration system, labor employment system, and social security system that prevent the free flow of labor forces in the region and other economic systems that cause labor market segmentation and by continuously improving the labor market can China's regional income gap be narrowed. The structure of the following parts of this chapter is as follows. Section 1 considers why the regional income gap would widen. Section 2 analyzes the regional economic development and regional income gap in a perfect labor market. Section 3 discusses the regional economic development and regional income gap in an imperfect labor market.

Section 1 Why would the regional income gap widen?

Since the reform and opening-up, China has made significant progress in economic development but witnessed the gradual deterioration of its income distribution pattern. The income gap among residents has obviously widened and the income distribution inequality has continued to rise (Wang, 2012). According to the data of the National Bureau of Statistics of China, the overall Gini coefficient of income distribution of Chinese residents is approximately 0.47, exceeding the international warning line of 0.45. Although the widening income gap in China is reflected in all aspects and levels of social economy, existing research shows that the regional income gap and

DOI: 10.4324/9781003261629-17

the urban-rural income gap are the two most important factors causing income distribution inequality in China (Li & Zhao, 1999; Wang & Xu, 2006, etc.). Regarding the changes in China's regional income gap, early research has discovered that the income gap among regions in China was narrowing in the early period of the reform (Yang, 1992, etc.). However, subsequent research found that, with the continued deepening of the reform, the regional income gap has continued to widen. For example, Lin and Liu (2003), believed that the income gap among regions in China was narrowing from 1978 to 1990 but widening from 1990 to 1998. The analysis in Chapter 12 also shows that the regional income gap in China was widening until around 2010 and has slightly narrowed in recent years. Lin and Liu (2003), and Wang and Fan (2005) have also confirmed this conclusion in their research. Generally speaking, China's regional income gap has tended to widen rapidly over the past 40 years of the reform and opening-up, exhibiting the characteristics of step-like rise during the system reform.

There is a lot of empirical literature regarding China's regional income gap. In the existing research, most scholars attribute the continuous widening of China's regional income gap to the unbalanced development of the country's regional economy. For example, based on the neoclassical economic growth theory on the convergence of economic conditions in different countries, Lin and Liu (2003), Peng (2005), Xu and Li (2006), Liu et al. (2009), and Pan (2010) believed that the economic growth in China's provinces does not meet the conditions of convergence, which has caused divergent growth in different regions and led to the widening regional income gap in the country. Fan (2006), Liu and Yin (2008), and Jin et al. (2006) explained the widening of China's regional income gap from the perspective of spatial geo-economics. They believed that the regional economic agglomeration and regional productivity differences caused by spatial and geographical factors, such as industrial agglomeration caused by increasing returns to scale, industrial agglomeration caused by opening to the outside world, and the unbalanced geographical distribution of market potential led to the widening of regional income gap in China, which is related to unbalanced regional economic development. That is because the income levels in different regions will be basically the same if they develop at the same level. However, regional development inequality is not necessarily the root cause of the widening regional income gap. If the labor market is perfect or labor forces (residents) can flow freely among different regions without cost, both wage gap and income gap of laborers in different regions will also gradually narrow even if these regions are unbalanced in economic development. In other words, for the economy in which labor forces can flow freely without cost, labor forces will flow from a low income region to a high income one as long as there is a significant difference in the wages of both regions. And according to the two principles of "diminishing marginal productivity of labor" and "wages are determined by marginal productivity of labor", the wage income in different regions takes on a trend of convergence. Thus, it is impossible for the regional income gap to continue to widen in a perfect labor market. Existing theoretical literature also shows that there is no mechanism that allows the income gap to continue to widen in a perfect market economy; and in the long run, the income distribution pattern usually tends to reach a stable distribution state (Stiglitz, 1969; Lucas, 1992; Wang & Gong, 2006, 2008).

However, there is no perfect labor market among different regions of China. The existence of various socio-economic systems such as the household registration system and the "discriminatory employment policies" adopted by local governments to solve local employment problems has led to a certain degree of regional segmentation in the labor market in all regions. Non-local labor forces would be discriminated against in the local labor market, leading to the huge costs of labor force flow among regions and hampering the mobility of labor forces among regions and the formation of a perfect labor market throughout China. For example, Yao and Lai (2004) discovered that the discrimination against migrant workers in household registration is the main reason for the great shortage of laborers in the laborer-employer relations. Migrant workers are subject to household registration discrimination in terms of wages, pension insurance, medical insurance, unemployment insurance, participation in trade unions, etc., in addition to employment contracts. The research results of Wang (2005) showed that 43% of the wage difference between local and non-local urban labor forces is caused by factors that cannot be explained, such as discrimination. Yan (2006) believed in his research that, during the job hunting in a city, what type of department a laborer chooses and in what way he/she flows among different departments are mainly determined by the institutional factors, mainly household registration, and have little to do with human capital factors such as educational background and work experience. The data analysis of Yan (2007) further shows that, with the development of China's economy, there is a significant gap between the rates of return on human capital of local and non-local residents, and this gap is still widening. Of course, there is no empirical literature regarding the degree of labor market segmentation in China and the extent of labor mobility costs. However, the above research is sufficient to demonstrate that there is indeed labor market segmentation among different regions in China and the household registration system is the main cause for regional labor market segmentation in China.

Based on the above conclusions, this chapter will focus on the research on the causes for the regional income gap and for the unbalanced regional economic development from the perspective of the completeness of labor, analyze the changes in regional economic development and income gap under different labor market assumptions, and explain the regional economic development and regional income gap of China based on this theoretical research. Of course, for the sake of simplicity, this chapter only discusses the changes in regional economic development and regional income gap under two extreme situations where labor can move freely and cannot move freely in two regions. Through comparative analysis of the economy of both regions under the two circumstances, the research in this chapter shows that if the labor market is perfect, the free flow of regional labor will eliminate the imbalance of regional economic development and regional income gap. Only when regional labor cannot flow will the regional economy develop in an unbalanced way and will the regional income gap continue to widen. Thus, labor market segmentation produces a direct impact on the widening of regional income gap. In addition, the inequality of regional development and the widening of regional income gap may be caused by the restriction of the flow of labor among regions due to regional labor market segmentation.

Section 2 Regional economic development and income gap: perfect labor market

2.1 Model and assumptions

Assume there are two regions, regions 1 and 2. Region 1 is a developed region and region 2 is an undeveloped region. Manufacturers in each region satisfy the following neoclassical production function:

$$Y_i = K_i^{\alpha_i}(A_i L_i)^{1-\alpha_i}, \quad i=1,2 \tag{13.1}$$

where i represents the region; Y represents output; K represents the total capital input in production (measured by goods); L represents the total labor input in production (measured by the number of laborers); A represents the technological level; and α_i represents the capital output elasticity of region i. Rewrite Equation (13.1) into the production function in an intensive form as follows:

$$\hat{y}_i = \hat{k}_i^{\alpha_i}, \quad i=1,2 \tag{13.2}$$

where $\hat{k} = K/(AL)$ represents the capital input per unit of effective labor and $\hat{y} = Y/AL$ represents the output per unit effective labor.

The differences between developed region 1 and undeveloped region 2 are mainly reflected in two aspects. First, the capital output elasticity of the two regions may be different. In general, the capital output elasticity of developed countries is lower than that of developing countries. For example, it is estimated that the capital output elasticity of developed countries, including those in Europe and America, is generally around 1/3 (Romer, 1999, CHp.1), while the capital output elasticity of developing countries such as China and India is between 0.6 and 0.7 (Wang & Gong, 2007). However, no literature has estimated the capital output elasticity in different regions of China. Without loss of generality, assume the capital output elasticity of the developed region is lower than that of the undeveloped region,[1] or

$0<\alpha_1<\alpha_2<1$. Second, both regions differ in the technological level and the rate of technological advancement.[2] Without loss of generality, assume the rates of technological advancement in both regions are g_1 and g_2, respectively, but the rate of technological advancement in developed region 1 is faster ($g_1>g_2$), and the initial technological level in the developed region is also higher.[3] Thus,

$$A_1(t) = A_{10}e^{g_1 t}, \; A_2(t) = A_{20}e^{g_2 t} \tag{13.3}$$

where A_{i0} represents the initial technological level in region i and $A_{10}>A_{20}$. Assume the two regions have the same population growth rate and the initial population is standardized to 1. Then,

$$L_1(t) = L_2(t) = e^{nt} \tag{13.4}$$

In addition, assume the goods market and factor market inside both regions are perfectly competitive markets and their depreciation rates are both zero. Capital can flow freely in both regions, so the two regions share the same interest rate r. Use w_i to denote the wage of region i. The behaviors of manufacturers in the two regions are expressed as follows:[4]

$$\max_{K_i, L_i}: K_i^{\alpha_i}(A_i L_i)^{1-\alpha_i} - w_i L_i - rK_i, \; i = 1,2 \tag{13.5}$$

Consumers in each region obtain income through labor and assets. The income earned by consumers in region i in each period is expressed as follows:

$$y_i^d = w_i + a_i r, \; i = 1,2 \tag{13.6}$$

Assume the saving rate of all consumers is s, and then the asset accumulation equation of each consumer is expressed as follows:

$$\dot{a}_i = s y_i^d = s(w_i + a_i r), \; i = 1,2 \tag{13.7}$$

where the point above the letter represents the derivative of the variable represented by the letter with respect to time (or $\dot{a}_i = da_i/dt$) and also the increment of the variable per unit time.

2.2 *The gap between two regions in economic development and income per capita and its changes*

Under the assumption of a perfect labor market, labor can flow freely between two regions. Since laborers would choose to work in the regions with high wages, there will be no labor supply in the regions with low wages if the wages of both regions are different. Thus, when the labor market is in equilibrium, the two regions will have the same wages. According to the first-order condition of the profit maximization behavior formula (13.5) for manufacturers,

$$r = \alpha_1 \hat{k}_1^{\alpha_1 - 1} = \alpha_2 \hat{k}_2^{\alpha_2 - 1} \tag{13.8}$$

$$w_1 = (1-\alpha_1) A_1 \hat{k}_1^{\alpha_1} = w_2 = (1-\alpha_2) A_2 \hat{k}_2^{\alpha_2} \tag{13.9}$$

Equations (13.8) and (13.9) show that there is no wage gap between the two regions under the assumption of a perfect labor market. However, in order to obtain the same remuneration in relation to labor and capital in both regions, there will be capital and labor flow between the regions. As this chapter mainly focuses on regional economic development and regional income gap, the issue of capital and labor flow in the two regions will not be discussed here. The differences in the economic development and income gap of both regions and their changes are mainly analyzed here.

Divide Equation (13.8) by Equation (13.9). After simple sorting, we can get the following equation:[5]

$$\frac{k_1}{k_2} = \frac{A_1 \hat{k}_1}{A_2 \hat{k}_2} = \frac{(1/\alpha_2 - 1)}{(1/\alpha_1 - 1)} \tag{13.10}$$

Equation (13.10) shows that, when the interest rates and wages of the two regions are the same, the ratios of material capital per capita in both regions are related to the relative size of the capital output elasticity in the two regions. Thus, the following Theorem 13.1 can be obtained.[6]

Theorem 13.1 If both capital and labor can flow freely, the region with higher capital output elasticity (or capital income share) or the region with lower labor income share will have higher capital per capita.

Theorem 13.1 is actually quite a generalized conclusion, and has nothing to do with the assumed form of the production function. It is very easy to understand the economic intuition in Theorem 13.1. When capital can flow freely, the interest rates of both regions are the same so that the marginal output of capital per capita in the two regions ($f^{i\prime}(k_i)$) is also the same. Since the capital output elasticity is also equal to the marginal output of effective capital per capita divided by its average output (or $\alpha_i = f^{i\prime}(k_i) \big/ \left[f^i(k_i)/k_i \right]$) the region with high capital output elasticity must have lower output of capital per capita (or $f^i(k_i)/k_i$). If the two regions have the same capital per capita, the region with higher capital output elasticity will definitely have a lower level of output per capita ($f^i(k_i)$). Also, if the two regions have the same capital per capita, the free flow of capital means that the remuneration earned through per capita capital ($rk_i = k_i f^{i\prime}(\hat{k}_i)$) should also be the same in both regions. The wage is equal to the output per capita minus the remuneration earned through the capital per capita ($w=f(k)-kr$). Therefore, wages in regions with high capital output elasticity will definitely be lower. This shows that if the two regions have the same capital per capita, the region with lower capital output elasticity will definitely have higher wages, thus continuing to attract labor from the region with higher capital output elasticity to flow into the region with lower capital output elasticity. The continuous outflow of labor makes the capital per capita in the regions with higher capital output elasticity continuously increase, and this process continues until the two regions have the same wages. This theoretical analysis process is actually closer to that of the actual economy. In the actual economy, it can be seen that the wages of developing countries with higher capital output elasticity are generally much lower than those of developed countries, and all labor forces flow from the developing countries and/or regions with higher capital output elasticity to developed countries and/or regions.

One important inference of Theorem 13.1 is that, under the assumptions of a perfect capital market and labor market, the two regions must have the same capital per capita if they have the same capital output elasticity.

When the capital output elasticity of the two regions is fixed, the following equation can be further obtained according to Equation (13.10):

$$\left(\frac{\dot{A}_1}{A_1}+\frac{\dot{\hat{k}}_1}{\hat{k}_1}\right)-\left(\frac{\dot{A}_2}{A_2}+\frac{\dot{\hat{k}}_2}{\hat{k}_2}\right)=\frac{\dot{k}_1}{k_1}-\frac{\dot{k}_2}{k_2}=0 \tag{13.11}$$

Equation (13.11) indicates that two regions have the same growth rate of capital per capita if they are both production functions of fixed capital output elasticity.

Additionally, according to $y_i = A_i f^i(\hat{k}_i)$ and Equation (13.10), the ratio of the output per capita of the two regions is as follows:

$$\frac{y_1}{y_2}=\frac{A_1\hat{y}_1}{A_2\hat{y}_2}=\frac{A_1\hat{k}_1^{\alpha_1}}{A_2\hat{k}_2^{\alpha_2}}=\frac{\alpha_2 A_1\hat{k}_1\left(\alpha_1\hat{k}_1^{\alpha_1-1}\right)}{\alpha_1 A_2\hat{k}_2\left(\alpha_2\hat{k}_2^{\alpha_2-1}\right)}=\frac{\alpha_2 k_1}{\alpha_1 k_2}=\frac{1-\alpha_2}{1-\alpha_1} \tag{13.12}$$

By the Equation (13.12), Theorem 13.2 can be obtained as follows:

Theorem 13.2 When both capital and labor can flow freely, the region with higher capital output elasticity (or capital income share) will have higher output per capita.

Similar to Theorem 13.1, Theorem 13.2 is also quite a generalized conclusion, and has nothing to do with the form of the production function. It is easy to understand the economic intuition in Theorem 13.2 from the following two aspects. Firstly, according to the definition of capital output elasticity, when the interest rate is equal to the marginal returns to capital, capital output elasticity is actually equal to the share of capital income per capita in output per capita (or $\alpha_i = \hat{k}_i f^{i\prime}(\hat{k}_i) / f^i(\hat{k}_i) = k_i r / \left[A_i f^i(\hat{k}_i) \right]$). Except for the remuneration earned through capital in output per capita, the remaining part of output per capita is the remuneration earned through labor (i.e., wage). In other words, the income share obtained through labor is equal to 1 minus capital income share (i.e., $w_i / y_i = (1 - \alpha_i)$). The free flow of labor forces means wages in the two regions would be the same. So, in the region with higher capital output elasticity (or higher capital income share), the labor income share is lower. In the case of the same output, the region would have lower wages. In order to obtain the same wages as the region with low capital output elasticity, the region with high capital output elasticity (or high capital income share) must have higher output per capita. Actually, through a simple transformation of Equation (13.12), the meanings of Equation (13.12) and Theorem 13.2 can be understood in a more intuitive way. In the converted equation, α represents capital output elasticity, also capital income share, and 1-α represents labor income share. Therefore, Equation (13.12) actually means that the two regions have the same wages, which is exactly the equilibrium condition for the labor markets in the two regions.

Secondly, Theorem 13.2 can also be understood according to Theorem 13.1. Since output is distributed only between capital and labor, output per capita is equal to the income per unit of labor (i.e., wage) and the income earned through capital per capita (i.e., interest rate multiplied by capital per capita). When both capital and labor can flow freely, the two regions will have the same interest rate and wages. However, the region with high capital output elasticity has higher capital per capita and the region with high capital output elasticity even has higher income per capita earned through capital per capita, thus resulting in higher output per capita.

Let $\varepsilon_i = (1 - \alpha_i)$ represent labor output elasticity or labor income share. The following equation can be obtained according to Equation (13.12):

$$\dot{y}_1 / y_1 + \dot{\varepsilon}_1 / \varepsilon_1 = \dot{\varepsilon}_2 / \varepsilon_2 + \dot{y}_2 / y_2 \tag{13.13}$$

Equation (13.13) shows that the sum of the growth rate of output per capita and the rate of change in labor output elasticity is the same in the two regions. Thus, the region where the labor income share (labor output elasticity) increases or the capital income share (capital output elasticity) decreases would witness a slower economic growth rate. However, where the capital output elasticity in the two regions remains unchanged, the two regions will have the same growth rate of output per capita.

The differences in income per capita of the two regions and their changes are discussed as follows. As known from Equation (13.6), both absolute gap and relative gap of the income per capita of the two regions are as follows:[7]

$$y_1{}^d - y_2{}^d = (w + a_1 r) - (w + a_2 r) = (a_1 - a_2) r \tag{13.14}$$

$$y_1{}^d / y_2{}^d = (w + a_1 r)/(w + a_2 r) < a_1 / a_2 \tag{13.15}$$

Equation (13.14) shows that although the output per capita and wages of the two regions are the same, there is still a gap in the current income per capita of these regions as long as there is a gap in wealth per capita (a_i) for the two regions in the late of the previous period, which is due to the fact that a gap in the wealth per capita at the end of the previous period would result in a gap in the current income of capital per capita in the two regions. The last inequality of Equation (13.15) shows that the relative difference in income per capita caused by the gap in the wealth per capita between the two regions would be smaller than the relative gap of wealth per capita between the two regions in the previous period. In other words, the relative inequality of income per capita is smaller than the relative inequality of wealth. Equation (13.14) also indicates that whether the absolute difference in per capita income between the two regions will be greater than the difference in per capita income between the two regions in the previous period depends on whether the interest rate is greater than one or less than one. If the interest rate is larger than 1, the absolute difference in income per capita between the two regions will be larger than that in income; and if the interest rate is smaller than 1, the result will be opposite.

The following equation can be obtained according to Equations (13.7) and (13.15):

$$\dot{a}_1 / \dot{a}_2 = y_1{}^d / y_2{}^d < a_1 / a_2 \Leftrightarrow g_{a1} = \dot{a}_1 / a_1 < g_{a2} = \dot{a}_2 / a_2 \tag{13.16}$$

Equation (13.16) shows that the growth rate of wealth per capita of developed region 1 is smaller than the growth rate of wealth per capita of undeveloped region 2. Since the initial wealth level per capita in developed region 1 is higher than that in undeveloped region 2, the absolute gap between the two regions in wealth level per capita will be gradually narrowed. According to Equation (13.15), the income per capita between the two regions will also continue to narrow. Thus, with the development of the economy, the gap in wealth per capita and the absolute inequality and relative inequality of income per capita for the two regions will continue to narrow.

In brief, the analysis in this section shows that if capital and labor can move freely between the two regions, the following conclusions can be drawn. First, there is no wage gap between the two regions. Second, the high capital output elasticity of the undeveloped region will make the region have higher capital per capita and a higher level of output per capita. Third, the two regions have the same growth rate of output per capita. Fourth, the two regions would have different levels of income per capita due to their different initial wealth levels. Moreover, the gap in income per capita of the two regions will continue to narrow with economic development. Fifth, the gap in the technological level and its growth rate of the two regions produces no effect on the economic development and income gap of both regions. The free move of capital and labor can completely make up for the gap in the technological level between the two regions.

Section 3 Regional economic development and income gap: inter-regional labor segmentation

This section assumes that, due to regional labor market segmentation, labor forces in the two regions cannot flow freely. Other assumptions are the same with those in Section 2. Due to the existence of inter-regional labor market segmentation, labor forces cannot move freely between both regions and wages in the two regions are not necessarily equal. The free flow of capital between the regions makes the two regions have the same interest rate. According to the first-order condition of the profit maximization behavior formula (13.6) for manufacturers,

$$r = \alpha_1 \hat{k}_1^{\alpha_1 - 1} = \alpha_2 \hat{k}_2^{\alpha_2 - 1} \tag{13.8}$$

$$w_1 = (1-\alpha_1) A_1 \hat{k}_1^{\alpha_1}, \quad w_2 = (1-\alpha_2) A_2 \hat{k}_2^{\alpha_2} \tag{13.17}$$

It can be obviously known from Equation (13.17) that there may be both wage gap and wage inequality between the two regions. Additionally, in order to make the capital of the two regions receive the same remuneration, there will be capital flow between the two regions.

3.1 The wage gap, gap in output per capita, and income gap per capita between the two regions

As known from Equation (13.8), the following equation applies at any time t:

$$\alpha_1 \hat{k}_1^{\alpha_1 - 1} = \alpha_2 \hat{k}_2^{\alpha_2 - 1} \Leftrightarrow \alpha_1 / \alpha_2 = \hat{k}_1^{1-\alpha_1} \Big/ \hat{k}_2^{1-\alpha_2} \tag{13.18}$$

Since capital output elasticity is a positive number of less than 1 (i.e., $0<\alpha_1<\alpha_2<1$), Equation (13.18) proves that the region with larger capital output elasticity would have larger effective capital per capita and larger effective capital per capita.[8] This means the effective capital per capita of the developed region would be lower than that of the undeveloped region (i.e., $\hat{k}_1 < \hat{k}_2$).

The wage ratio of the two regions can be further obtained according to Equations (13.8) and (13.17) above:

$$\frac{w_1}{w_2} = \frac{(1-\alpha_1) A_1 \hat{k}_1^{\alpha_1}}{(1-\alpha_2) A_2 \hat{k}_2^{\alpha_2}} = \frac{(1/\alpha_1 - 1) A_1 \hat{k}_1}{(1/\alpha_2 - 1) A_2 \hat{k}_2} = \frac{(1/\alpha_1 - 1) k_1}{(1/\alpha_2 - 1) k_2} \tag{13.19}$$

As known from Equation (13.19), it is impossible for the two regions to have the same wages unless under some specific parameter conditions. That means the two regions would have wage differences. By Equation (13.19), it is not difficult to come to the following conclusions. First, if the two regions have the same capital per capita, the developed region with low capital output elasticity would have higher wages. Second, if the two regions have the same technological level, the undeveloped region with higher capital output elasticity would have higher wages.[9] Since the effective capital per capita of the two regions would maintain some relationship under general circumstances, which is determined by Equation (13.18), developed region 1 will have higher capital per capita than the undeveloped region and developed region 1 will have higher wages if the technological level of the region is high enough. In other words, the low capital output elasticity in the developed region tends to be lower wages in the region while the high technological level in the developed region tends to be higher wages in the region. Particularly, the two regions will have effective capital per capita when they have the same capital output elasticity. At this time, developed region 1 would definitely have higher material capital and wages per capita due to higher technology. Without loss of generality, the following assumes that developed regions are sufficiently technologically advanced and thus have higher physical capital per capita and higher wages.

According to $y_i = A_i f^i(\hat{k}_i)$ and Equation (13.18), the output per capita of the two regions is as follows:

$$\frac{y_1}{y_2} = \frac{A_1\hat{k}_1^{\alpha_1}}{A_2\hat{k}_2^{\alpha_2}} = \frac{\alpha_2 A_1 \hat{k}_1}{\alpha_1 A_2 \hat{k}_2} = \frac{\alpha_2 k_1}{\alpha_1 k_2} = \frac{(1-\alpha_2)w_1}{(1-\alpha_1)w_2} \tag{13.20}$$

Equation (13.20) shows that the gap in output per capita of the two regions is the same as that of the wages in the two regions. Generally, the developed region must have higher capital per capita as long as it has higher capital per capita.

Regarding the income gap per capita of the two regions, the following equations can be obtained according to Equation (13.6):

$$\begin{aligned} y_1^d - y_1^d &= (w_1 - w_2) + (a_1 - a_2)r \\ &= (a_1 - a_2) + (a_1 - a_2)\left(\frac{w_1 - w_2}{a_1 - a_2} + r - 1\right) \end{aligned} \tag{13.21}$$

$$\begin{aligned} \max\left(\frac{w_1}{w_2}, \frac{a_1}{a_2}\right) > \frac{y_1^d}{y_2^d} &= \frac{w_1}{w_2}\left(\frac{w_2}{w_2 + a_2 r}\right) + \frac{a_1}{a_2}\left(\frac{a_2 r}{w_2 + a_2 r}\right) \\ &> \min\left(\frac{w_1}{w_2}, \frac{a_1}{a_2}\right) \end{aligned} \tag{13.22}$$

Equation (13.21) shows that if the labor forces in the two regions cannot flow freely, the income gap per capita between the two regions will not only be related to the wage gap between the two regions but also related to the initial wealth gap between them. Equation (13.22) shows that the ratio of income per capita between the two regions ranges from the wage ratio and initial wealth ratio between the two regions. Thus, if the relative wage gap between the two regions is larger than their initial wealth gap, the relative income gap per capita between the two regions will be smaller than the wage gap but larger than the initial wealth gap. At this time, the wage gap between the two regions tends to widen the relative gap in income per capita between both regions. On the contrary, if the initial wealth gap between the two regions is larger than their wage gap, the income gap per capita between both regions will be larger than their wealth gap but smaller than their initial wealth gap and the wage gap will tend to narrow the relative gap in income per capita between the two regions.

3.2 Dynamic changes in the economic development level and income gap between the two regions

This subsection discusses the dynamics of wage differentials and differences in per capita output growth rates between the two regions. Taking the derivative of time at both sides of Equation (13.8), we get:

$$(1-\alpha_1)\dot{\hat{k}}_1/\hat{k}_1 = (1-\alpha_2)\dot{\hat{k}}_2/\hat{k}_2 \tag{13.23}$$

Equation (13.23) shows that the product of the growth rate of effective capital in the two regions and the labor output elasticity in the two regions (or 1 minus capital output elasticity) should be equal. Thus, the region with higher capital output elasticity (or capital income share) or the region with lower labor income share has a faster growth rate of effective capital per capita.

The following equation can be further obtained according to Equations (13.19) and (13.20):

$$\frac{\dot{y}_1}{y_1} - \frac{\dot{y}_2}{y_2} = \frac{\dot{w}_1}{w_1} - \frac{\dot{w}_2}{w_1} = \frac{\dot{k}_1}{k_1} - \frac{\dot{k}_2}{k_2} = \left(\frac{\dot{A}_1}{A_1} - \frac{\dot{A}_2}{A_2}\right) + \left(\frac{\dot{\hat{k}}_1}{\hat{k}_1} - \frac{\dot{\hat{k}}_2}{\hat{k}_2}\right) \tag{13.24}$$

Equation (13.24) shows that the difference in the growth rate of wages between the two regions is equal to the difference between the growth rates of output per capita of these regions and also to the difference between the growth rates of capital per capita between the two regions, which is also further equal to the difference between the rates of technological advancement of the two regions plus the difference of the growth rates of effective capital per capita. The last part of Equation (13.24) indicates that the faster technological advancement of the developed region tends to make the region have faster capital growth rate per capita and wage growth rate. However, the lower capital output elasticity of the developed region would tend to make this region have slower growth rate of capital per capita and growth rate of wages as the elasticity makes the region have a slower growth rate of effective capital per capita in the region. In general, as far as different regions in China are concerned, the developed region has a higher economic growth rate and capital growth rate per capita, and also a higher wage growth rate than the undeveloped region, as the difference in exogenous technological advancement plays a dominating role in the economic growth rate. However, if we compare developed countries with developing countries and if the difference in the economic growth of the two is mainly derived from technological advancement, developed countries will have higher economic growth and wage growth. For example, the exogenous technological advancement in European and American countries may occupy a more important position compared with that of Latin American countries and African countries, so the former has higher economic growth rates and wage growth rates than the latter. If the difference in capital output elasticity plays a dominant role in different countries, the economic growth rate and wage growth rate of developing countries will be higher than that of developed countries. For example, the difference in capital output elasticity of East Asian countries and India may play a more dominant role compared with that of European and American countries. Thus, these countries and regions have a faster economic growth rate and wage growth rate than that of European and American countries.

Finally, with respect to the changes in the income gap per capita between the two regions, the following equation can be obtained according to Formula (13.7):

$$\max\left(\frac{w_1}{w_2},\frac{a_1}{a_2}\right) > \frac{\dot{a}_1}{\dot{a}_2} = \frac{y_1{}^d}{y_2{}^d} > \min\left(\frac{w_1}{w_2},\frac{a_1}{a_2}\right) \tag{13.25}$$

The following formula can be obtained through further sorting:

$$\begin{cases} \dfrac{\dot{a}_1}{\dot{a}_2} = \dfrac{y_1{}^d}{y_2{}^d} > \dfrac{a_1}{a_2} \Leftrightarrow \dfrac{\dot{a}_1}{a_1} = \dfrac{y_1{}^d}{y_2{}^d} > \dfrac{\dot{a}_2}{a_2}, \quad if\ \dfrac{w_1}{w_2} > \dfrac{a_1}{a_2} \\ \dfrac{\dot{a}_1}{\dot{a}_2} = \dfrac{y_1{}^d}{y_2{}^d} < \dfrac{a_1}{a_2} \Leftrightarrow \dfrac{\dot{a}_1}{a_1} = \dfrac{y_1{}^d}{y_2{}^d} > \dfrac{\dot{a}_2}{a_2}, \quad if\ \dfrac{w_1}{w_2} < \dfrac{a_1}{a_2} \end{cases} \tag{13.26}$$

Formula (13.26) shows that if the wage ratio between the two regions is smaller than the ratio of wealth per capita in the previous period, the current growth rate of wealth per capita in developed region 1 will be lower than the growth rate of wealth per capita in undeveloped region 2 and the wealth gap per capita between the two regions will continue to narrow. If the wage ratio between the two regions is larger than the ratio of wealth per capita between the two regions in the previous period, the current growth rate of wealth per capita in developed region 1 will be higher than that in undeveloped region 2 and the gap of wealth per capita between the two regions will continue to widen. According to Equation (13.24), since the changes in the wage growth gap between the two regions are the same as those in their output growth rate gap per capita, developed region 1 will also have a higher wage growth rate than undeveloped region 2 if the former has a higher economic growth rate than the latter. Therefore, the regional wage gap will become increasingly larger. As a result, the income gap per capita between both regions will also become larger and larger.

Overall, the analysis in this section shows that if capital flows freely between the two regions and labor cannot flow move freely, we will arrive at the following conclusions: Firstly, there are gaps in wages and income per capita between the two regions. Secondly, the lower capital output elasticity in the developed region tends to make the region have lower output and wages per capita, but the higher technological level in the developed region tends to make the region have higher output and wages per capita. If the technological level of the developed region is sufficiently high, this region will have a higher output level and wages per capita. Thirdly, the lower capital output elasticity in the developed region tends to make the region have lower growth rates of output and wages per capita, but the higher technological advancement rate tends to make the region have higher growth rates of output and wages per capita. If the developed region has a higher economic growth rate due to technological advancement, the region must have a higher wage growth rate. Fourthly, when the developed region has a higher economic growth rate than the undeveloped region, the income gap per capita between the two regions will also widen due to the increasing wage gap between these regions.

Notes

1 This assumption is not a necessary condition for explaining the income gap and economic development in different regions of China, but it is essential for explaining the economic development and wage gap among different countries.

2 The difference in the technological level between the two regions discussed in this chapter does not necessarily refer to the technology in reality. As can be seen from the above assumption about A, the technological level referred to in this chapter is actually the Solow surplus in the theory of economic growth, which can actually include all factors that can affect productivity except labor and capital. Technology A in this chapter can not only refer to the actual technical gap, but also the difference in productivity between the two regions due to differences in taxation, geographical conditions, resource conditions, human capital, and other institutional differences.

3 If it is assumed that the two regions have the same rate of technological advancement but developed region 1 has a higher initial technological level than undeveloped region 2, most of the research conclusions in this chapter are also valid.

4 Since the manufacturer's decision is only related to the wages and interest rates of each period, it is a static optimization problem, so the time variable t is omitted in the formula (13.5). Although each variable in this chapter is actually a

function of time, the time variable t is omitted in the following analysis in order to simplify the formula.

5 Equation (13.10) is also valid for a more general production function. The specific derivation process is as follows: We must as well assume the production functions of the two regions are $Y_i = F^i(K_i, A_iL_i)$ and $F^i(\lambda K, \lambda L) = \lambda F^i(K, L), \forall \lambda > 0$ respectively. Thus, $y_i = f'(\hat{k}_i)$. As the wages and interest rates of both regions are the same, $r_1 = f'(\hat{k}_1) = r_2 = f'(\hat{k}_2)$ and
Divide the former by the latter, and then we can get:

$$\left[A_1 f(\hat{k}_1) - A_1\hat{k}_1 f'(\hat{k}_1)\right] / f'(\hat{k}_1) = \left[A_2 f(\hat{k}_2) - A_2\hat{k}_2 f'(\hat{k}_2)\right] / f'(\hat{k}_2) \Leftrightarrow A_1\hat{k}_1(1/\alpha_1 - 1) = A_2\hat{k}_2(1/\alpha_2 - 1)$$

Equation (13.10) can be obtained through further sorting.

6 Actually, Theorem 13.1 is also valid for different sectors in a perfect market economy. That is, for an economy in which labor and capital can move perfectly in different sectors, if the capital market and the labor market are both competitive markets (that is, remunerations are earned according to the marginal productivity of factors), then the sector with a high share of capital income will have a high capital per capita.

7 The proof for the last inequality of Equation (13.15) is as follows:

$$y_1^d / y_2^d = (w + a_1 r)/(w + a_2 r) = (a_1 - a_2)r/(w + a_2 r) + 1 < (a_1 - a_2)r/(a_2 r) + 1 = (a_1 - a_2)/a_2 + 1 = a_1/a_2.$$

8 This point can be proved as follows. Since the two regions share the same interest rate, i.e. $r = \alpha_i \hat{k}_i^{\alpha_1 - 1}$, while the interest rate r remains unchanged, $d\hat{k}_i / d\alpha_i = \left(\hat{k}_i^{\alpha_1 - 1} + \alpha_i \hat{k}_i^{\alpha_1 - 1}\ln \hat{k}_i\right) / \left[\alpha_i(1 - \alpha_1)\hat{k}_i^{\alpha_1 - 2}\right] > 0$ can be got by differentiating $r = \alpha_i \hat{k}_i^{\alpha_1 - 1}$. This shows that, in order to keep the interest rate unchanged, the region with higher capital output elasticity α_i must also has higher effective capital per capita.

9 This point can be proved as follows. Since the two regions share the same interest rate, for any region, $\bar{r} = \alpha_i \hat{k}_i^{\alpha_i - 1}$. Through differentiation, we can get:

$$0 = \hat{k}_i^{\alpha_i - 1} d\alpha_i + \alpha_i \hat{k}_i^{\alpha_i - 1} \ln \hat{k}_i d\alpha_i + \alpha_i(\alpha_i - 1)\hat{k}_i^{\alpha_i - 2} d\hat{k}_i \quad (13.a)$$

The two regions have the same technological level A, i.e.

$$w_i = (1 - \alpha_1)A\hat{k}_i^{\alpha_1}$$

Differentiate both sides at the same time, and then we can get:

$$dw_i = -A\hat{k}_i^{\alpha_1} d\alpha_1 + (1 - \alpha_1)A\hat{k}_i^{\alpha_1} \ln \hat{k}_i d\alpha_i + \alpha_i(1 - \alpha_1)A\hat{k}_i^{\alpha_i - 1} d\hat{k}_i \quad (13.b)$$

Multiply Equation (13.a) by $\alpha_i \hat{k}_i$ and plus Equation (13.b), and then we can get:

$$dw_i = -A\hat{k}_i^{\alpha_1} d\alpha_1 + (1 - \alpha_1)A\hat{k}_i^{\alpha_1} \ln \hat{k}_i d\alpha_i + \alpha_i(1 - \alpha_1)A\hat{k}_i^{\alpha_i - 1} d\hat{k}_i$$
$$0 = A\hat{k}_i^{\alpha_i} d\alpha_i + A\alpha_i \hat{k}_i^{\alpha_i} \ln \hat{k}_i d\alpha_i + \alpha_i(\alpha_i - 1)A\hat{k}_i^{\alpha_i - 1} d\hat{k}_i$$

$$dw_i/d\alpha_i = A\hat{k}_i^{\alpha 1} \ln \hat{k}_i > 0$$

This shows that if two regions have the same technological level, the region with higher capital output elasticity will have higher wages.

References

[1] Fan, J. Y. (2006). Industrial Agglomeration and Difference of Regional Productivity. *Economic Research Journal,* Issue 11, 72–81.

[2] Jin, Y., Chen, Z., & Lu, M. (2006). Industry Agglomeration in China: Economic Geography, New Economic Geography and Policy. *Economic Research Journal*, Issue 4, 79–89.

[3] Li, S., & Zhao, R. W. (1999). Re-research on Income Distribution of Chinese Residents. *Economic Research Journal*, Issue 4, 3–17.

[4] Lin, Y. F., & Liu, P. L. (2003). Analysis on the New Fluctuation Mode of China Economy Development. *Economic Research Journal,* Issue 3, 19–25.

[5] Liu, L. S., Wang, Y. H., & Hu, A. G. (2009). The effect of western development program and regional convergence in China. *Economic Research Journal*, Issue 9, 94–105.

[6] Liu, X. Y., & Yin, X. M. (2008). Spatial Externalities and Regional Wage Differences: A Dynamic Panel-Data Study. *China Economic Quarterly*, Issue 8(1), 77–98.

[7] Lucas, R. (1992). On Efficiency and Distribution. *Economic Journal*, 102, 233–247

[8] Pan, W. Q. (2010). Research on China's Regional Economic Differences and Convergence. *Social Sciences in China*, Issue 1, 72–84.

[9] Peng, G. H. (2005). Analysis of China's Regional Income Disparities, Total Factor Productivity and Convergence. *Economic Research Journal*, Issue 9, 19–29.

[10] Romer, D. (1999). *Advanced macroeconomics*. Beijing: The Commercial Press.

[11] Stiglitz, J. (1969). Distribution of Income and Wealth among Individuals. *Econometrica,* 37, 382–397.

[12] Wang, D. H. (2012). Current State and Changes of China's Income Distribution Pattern. *Social Science Journal*, Issue 3, 121–129.

[13] Wang, D. H., & Gong, L. T. (2006). Dynamics of Income and Wealth Distribution in a Neoclassical Growth Model. *China Economic Quarterly*, Issue 5(3), 777–802.

[14] Wang, D. H., & Gong, L. T. (2007). Consumption and Savings in Economic Growth. *Journal of Financial Research,* Issue 12, 1–16.

[15] Wang, D. H., & Gong, L. T. (2008). Overview of the Dynamics of Income and Wealth Distribution Inequality. *China Economic Quarterly*, Issue 7(2), 731–774.

[16] Wang, H. L., & Xu, X. (2006). Interregional and Urban-Rural Income Inequality. *Management World*, Issue 11, 41–50.

[17] Wang, X. L., & Fan, G. (2005). Income inequality in China and its influential factors. *Economic Research Journal*, Issue 10, 24–36.

[18] Wang, M. Y. (2005). Employment Opportunities and Wage Gaps in Urban Labor Market: A Study of the Employment and Wages of Migrant Laborers. *Social Sciences in China*, Issue 5, 36–46.
[19] Xu, Z. Y., & Li, S. T. (2006). Analysis on the Trend of Regional Income Disparity in China. *Economic Research Journal*, Issue 7, 106–116.
[20] Yan, S. P. (2006). Mobility of Urban Labor Market and Its Decision Mechanism. *Management World*, Issue 8, 8–17.
[21] Yan, S. P. (2007). Human Capital, Institution and Wage Disparities. *Management World*, Issue 6, 4–13.
[22] Yao, X. G., & Lai, P. Q. (2004). Urban and Rural Huji Differentials in Chinese Labor Relations, *Economic Research Journal*, Issue 7, 82–90.
[23] Yang, W. M. (1992). Empirical Analysis of the Changes in Regional Income Disparities. *Economic Research Journal*, Issue 3, 70–74.

14 Labor market monopoly, minimum wage restrictions and inequality

China has undergone reform and opening-up for more than 40 years since 1978. Due to the progressive reform, many fields have been highly monopolized during this process. Even today, industries such as finance, petroleum, and telecommunications are still highly monopolized by a few state-owned enterprises, making it difficult or even impossible for other enterprises to enter these fields. These highly monopolized industries do not only have a high degree of monopoly in the market where they sell products, they also have a huge monopoly over the labor forces they employ. This chapter will probe the impact of monopoly in the labor market over inequality as well as the effect of minimum wage restrictions on inequality. The structure of this chapter is as follows. Section 1 briefly discusses the possible impact of monopoly on the economy; Section 2 compares and analyzes the inequality of income and social welfare distribution in a monopolistic labor market and a perfect competitive labor market; Section 3 analyzes the impact of minimum wage restrictions on inequality in the perfect competitive labor market; and Section 4 discusses the impact of minimum wage restrictions on inequality in the monopolistic labor market.

Section 1 Why should we study monopoly and minimum wage restrictions?

Just as the analysis in Chapter 12 demonstrated, the inequality of income and wealth distribution, either in terms of urban and rural areas or in terms of between urban and rural areas, has sharply widened during China's 40 years of economic reform and development. The widening of the income gap among Chinese residents has come to the attention of many researchers. Existing research suggests that there are many reasons for increasing inequality in China. Monopoly, including that over the goods market and labor market, is one of the important reasons (Wang & Gong, 2006; Hao & Li, 2006). Theoretically, there are primarily two forms of monopoly, including monopoly over goods market and that over labor market. The monopoly in China is mainly reflected as industry monopoly, such as finance, petroleum, telecommunications, electric power, aviation, railway, and other

DOI: 10.4324/9781003261629-18

monopolized sectors, which controls not only the sales of these products but also the employment of workers in these sectors. For these types of sectors, the impact of monopoly over inequality may be derived from their monopoly over the goods market. Also, there is another type of monopoly that produces a bigger impact on inequality in China (i.e., the monopoly of manufacturers or enterprises over the labor market for migrant workers). As is known to all, there is a huge supply of migrant workers in China. In contrast with the migrant workers who have flooded into cities in large numbers and are also restricted by urban regulation systems, urban manufacturers or enterprises are undoubtedly in a monopoly position to some extent at all times.[1] The monopoly of urban manufacturers or enterprises on the labor market for migrant workers and the monopolized pricing on their wages[2] may be one of the most important factors causing increasing inequality during China's economic development. Additionally, in order to protect the interests of laborers, China has formulated a series of minimum wage systems. Can this system, initially designed for protecting the benefits of laborers, really increase the income of the working class and narrow the income gap between labor and capital? Regarding the impact of the monopolistic labor market on the aggregate economy and social welfare level, a very standard conclusion has been drawn in existing mainstream economics (i.e., monopoly will inevitably result in the loss of output and social welfare). However, there is not much literature on the impact of monopoly in the labor market over the inequality of income distribution. Moreover, with respect to the impact of wage restrictions on the aggregate economy and social welfare level in a monopolistic labor market and a perfect competitive labor market, the conclusions drawn in the modern mainstream economics are also very clear. It is generally believed that minimum wage restrictions would cause the loss of output and social welfare level in the perfect competitive market economy and minimum wage restrictions may improve the level of output and social welfare level in the monopoly market. These conclusions have been included in traditional textbooks. However, regarding the impact of minimum wage restrictions on the inequality of income distribution under these two market conditions, there is still no conclusion in the existing literature.

This chapter will mainly analyze how the monopolistic labor market affects the inequality of income distribution and what impact minimum wage restrictions have on the inequality of income distribution relative to a perfect competitive labor market. The analysis in this chapter demonstrates the following points. Firstly, compared with a perfect competitive labor market, a perfect monopolized market will definitely aggravate inequality. Secondly, in an economy where the labor market is perfectly competitive, the minimum wage restrictions that exceed the equilibrium wages will inevitably cause more people to lose jobs, thus intensifying the inequality of income distribution among laborers. That's because in an economy with a perfect competitive labor market, the minimum wages that exceed equilibrium wages will reduce labor demand and the number of the employed on the one hand, and it makes the wages of the employed higher, leading to a larger income gap between the unemployed and the employed on the other hand. However, the analysis in this chapter indicates that, under certain conditions, minimum wage restrictions may reduce the income percentage of capitalists and the inequality of income distribution between laborers and capitalists. Thus, minimum wage restrictions may also lower the inequality of income distribution in the entire society. It can be seen that, even in a perfect competitive labor market, the effect of minimum wage restrictions on inequality is uncertain, depending on the relative elasticity of the labor supply curve and the demand curve. This relative elasticity determines which of the two effects aforementioned dominates. Finally, the analysis in this chapter also shows that, in a buyer monopolistic labor market, the minimum wage restrictions that are higher than the wages in a perfect monopolized market will definitely reduce unemployment and inequality. This is because, in a monopolistic labor market, employees are faced with a horizontal labor supply curve rather than a perfect monopolized market supply after the adoption of minimum wage restrictions. In this case, minimum wage restrictions will increase jobs and reduce unemployment and the inequality among laborers on the one hand, but add the wages of laborers and reduce the income percentage of capitalists, thus reducing the income inequality between labor and capital on the other. Thus, in a perfect monopolized market, minimum wage restrictions would reduce income inequality.

Section 2 Impact of competition and labor market monopoly on income distribution

Assume that there are $\bar{N}$ laborers in the entire market and their sole income is wages earned from labor. There are N0 capital owners or capitalists, whose income is capital income arising from profits. We also assume that capitalists are always the class at the highest income level. For the sake of simplicity and without loss of generality, N0 is unitized into 1. As shown in Figure 14.1, the marginal output of labor and hence the demand curve of labor, DL, is BE and the supply curve of labor, SL, is AEC. This indicates that when the actual wage is lower than $\hat{w}$, the supply of labor is a diagonal line that increases with the wage, AE. When the wages are higher than $\hat{w}$, the supply of labor will no longer increase with wages as the number of laborers in the whole society is $\bar{N}$.

In a perfect competitive labor market, the market will reach equilibrium in the case of the same supply and demand of labor. Thus, *E*, the intersection point between the labor supply curve and the labor demand curve, is an equilibrium point. In this situation, the equilibrium wage in the economy is w^* and the number of employees in the whole economy is N^*. The total output of the society is SBEN**O*; the profit income of capitalists is

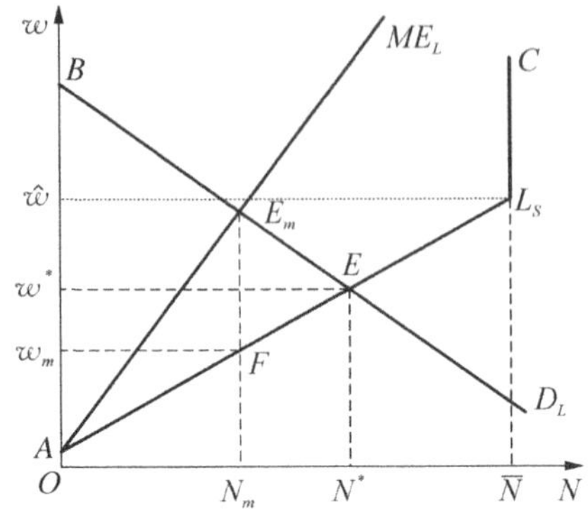

Figure 14.1 Equilibrium in an economy: a perfect competitive labor market and a perfect monopolistic labor market.

SEw*B; and all employed N^* laborers receive wages totaling SE w^*N^*O, with the total surplus of SEw*A. Additionally, $\bar{N} - N^*$ laborers are unemployed and their wages and surplus are both zero. In the equilibrium state, the $\left(\bar{N} - N_1\right)/(\bar{N}+1)$ of the unemployed people in the society earn the income and total surplus accounting for zero percent of the total output and surplus; the $\bar{N}/(\bar{N}+1)$ of the total laborers earn the income accounting for $S_{w^*EN^*O}/S_{BEN^*O}$ of the total output and the welfare level accounting for S_{w^*EO}/S_{BEO} of the total surplus. Therefore, in the perfect competitive labor market economy, the Lorenz curves of income distribution and total surplus distribution are as shown in Figure 14.2.

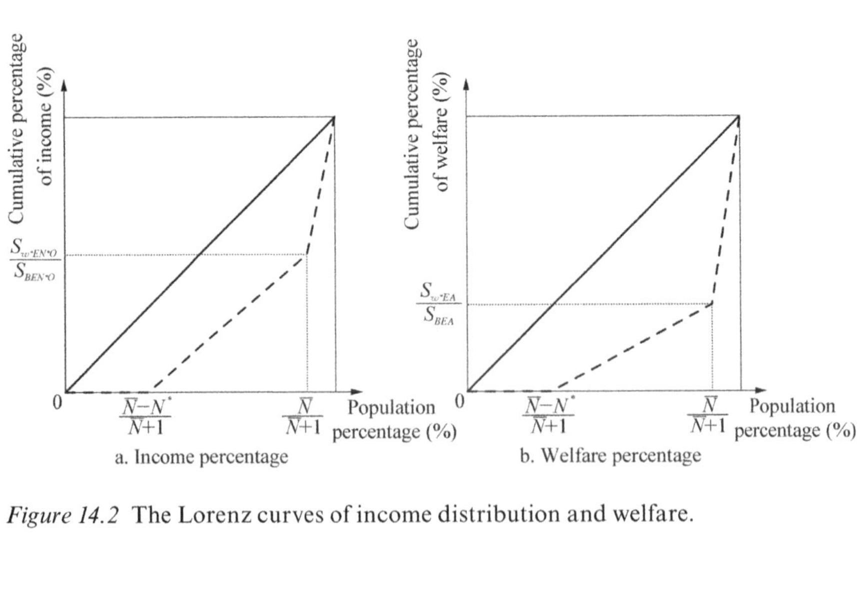

Figure 14.2 The Lorenz curves of income distribution and welfare.

In the monopolistic labor market, the equilibrium point is determined by Em, the intersection point between the marginal product value curve of labor forces (i.e., the labor demand curve) and the marginal expenditure curve of labor forces (i.e., AEm). The equilibrium employment is Nm and the equilibrium wage is wm, which is the corresponding wage w_m of the equilibrium employment (Nm) on the labor supply curve. In the situation, the number of employees is *Nm*; the total output of the society is $S_{BE_mN_mO}$; capitalists obtain a profit of $S_{BE_mFw_m}$; and all employed N^* laborers receive wages of $S_{w_mFN_mO}$ and total surplus of S_{w_mFA}. Additionally, $\bar{N} - N_m$ laborers are unemployed and their wages and surplus are both zero. In the equilibrium state, the $\left(\bar{N} - N_1\right)/(\bar{N}+1)$ of the unemployed people in the society earn the income and total surplus accounting for zero percent of the total output and surplus; the $\bar{N}/(\bar{N}+1)$ of the total laborers earn the income accounting for $S_{w_mFN_mO}/S_{BE_mN_mO}$ of the total output and the welfare level accounting for S_{w_mFO}/S_{BE_mFO} of the total surplus. Therefore, in the monopolistic labor market, the Lorenz curves of social income distribution and total surplus distribution are shown in Figure 14.3.

According to the relationship between points *Em* and *E* and the above analysis, Theorem 14.1 can be obtained as follows through simple geometric reduction:

Theorem 14.1 The percentage of total income earned by all laborers over the total income and the percentage of total surplus over the total surplus in a perfect competitive labor market are both higher than that in a monopolistic labor market, i.e.:

$$S_{w^*EN^*O}/S_{BEN^*O} > S_{w_mFN_mO}/S_{BE_mN_mO};S_{w^*EA}/S_{BEA} > S_{w_mFA}/S_{BE_mFA}.$$

(Proof: see Appendix 14.A1)

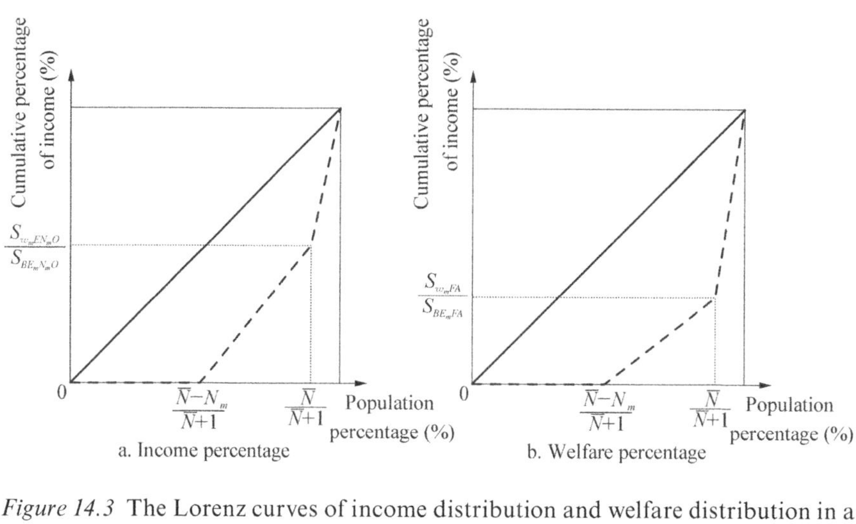

Figure 14.3 The Lorenz curves of income distribution and welfare distribution in a monopolistic labor market.

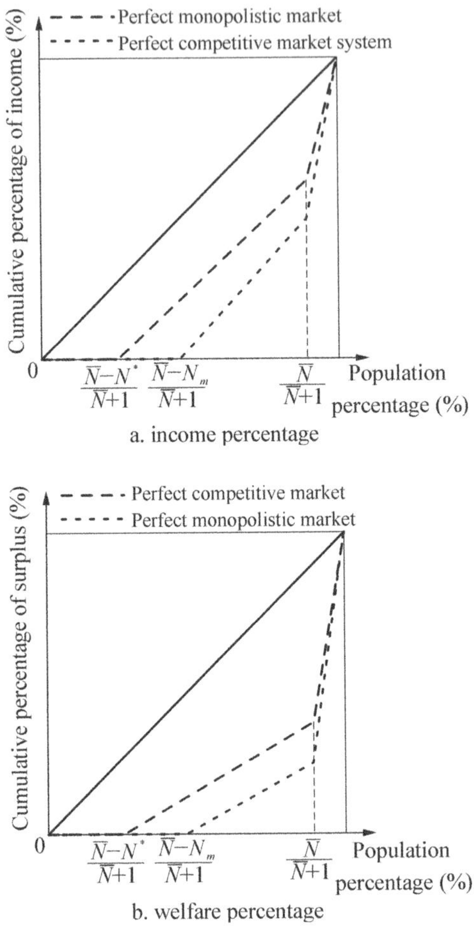

Figure 14.4 Comparisons of the Lorenz curves in a perfect competitive labor market and a perfect monopolistic labor market.

According to Theorem 14.1 above, we can place the Lorenz curves regarding the income distribution and surplus distribution under the perfect competition market and a monopoly market in a chart each, as shown in Figure 14.4.

Property 14.1 regarding income distribution inequality in a perfect competitive labor market and in a monopolistic labor market can be obtained according to Figure 14.4.

Property 14.1 Either in terms of the inequality of income distribution or in terms of the inequality of social welfare distribution, Lorenz dominates in the distribution of a perfect monopolized market with respect to the distribution in a perfect competitive market.

Property 14.1 shows that the monopolistic labor market has intensified the inequality of income and welfare distribution. The intensified inequality in the monopolistic labor market is mainly reflected in the following two aspects. On the one hand, the existence of labor market monopoly enables capitalists to impose monopoly pricing over labor, and hence lowers labor wages so that capitalists can obtain more income percentage and surplus percentage, which intensifies the inequality between laborers and capitalists. On the other hand, monopoly pricing causes a lower employment level of labor forces and leads to more unemployment. Thus, the income level of the lowest income group is lower, thereby widening the income gap between the lowest income earners and other income groups.

Section 3 Impact of minimum wage restrictions on inequality in a perfect competitive labor market

This section discusses the impact of minimum wage restrictions in a perfect competitive labor market on inequality. When there is a minimum wage restriction policy in the economy, we might as well assume that the authorities set a minimum wage of $\underline{w}$ or the minimum wage of laborers shall not be lower than $\underline{w}$. In this case, the labor supply curve for the manufacturer will be a horizontal straight line, as shown by the straight line $\underline{w}E_1$ in Figure 14.5 (the other lines of this figure have the same meanings as those in Section 1). When the minimum wage $\underline{w}$ exists, as shown in Figure 14.5, in the economy with a perfect competitive labor market, the equilibrium point of the labor market is E1, and the equilibrium labor employment level is N1. At this time, the total output of the society is $S_{BE_1N_1O}$, the profit income earned by capitalists is $S_{BE_1\underline{w}}$, and all $N1$ laborers employed obtained the wage income of $S_{\underline{w}E_1N_1O}$ and the total surplus they obtain is $S_{AE_1\underline{w}}$. A total of $\bar{N} - N_1$ laborers are unemployed in the economy and their wage income and surplus are

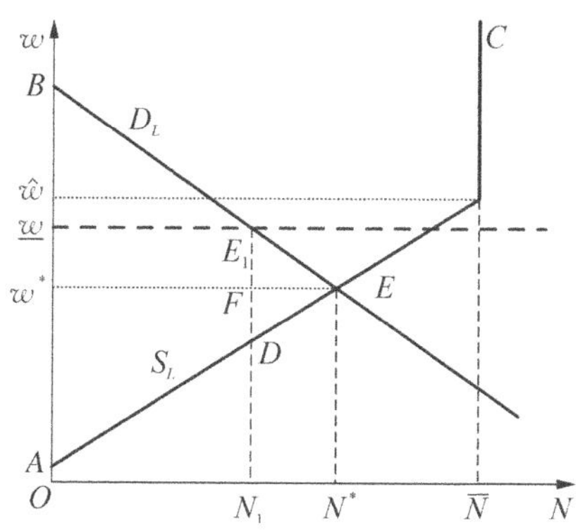

Figure 14.5 The impact of wage regulation on the economy in a perfect competitive labor market.

both zero. In the equilibrium state, the $(\bar{N}-N_1)/(\bar{N}+1)$ of the unemployed people in the society earn the income and total surplus accounting for zero percent of the total output; the $\bar{N}/(\bar{N}+1)$ of the laborers obtain the income accounting for $S_{\underline{w}E_1N_1O}/S_{BE_1N_1O}$ of the total output and the welfare level accounting for $S_{\underline{w}E_1DA}/S_{BE_1DA}$ of the total surplus. The following conclusions apply to the impact of minimum wage on output and welfare level. Firstly, due to the increase in the number of the unemployed due to wage regulation, the employment level decreases from N* to N1 and the total labor forces idle increases by N* N1. Thus, the output level will drop relative to the economy without minimum wage restrictions. Secondly, in terms of welfare level, due to minimum wage restrictions, the welfare level of S_{E_1ED} is lost in the whole society. Relative to the economy without minimum wage restrictions, in the economy, manufacturers' profit level decreases by $S_{\underline{w}E_1Ew^*}$ and the total surplus lost by laborers is $S_{\underline{w}E_1Ew^*}-S_{FED}$. This point has been well explained in general textbooks. The impact of minimum wage restrictions on the inequality of income and social welfare distribution is mainly discussed below.

According to the relationship between E_l and E and the above analysis, Theorem 14.2 can be obtained as follows:

Theorem 14.2 Let $\varepsilon_{DL}=\left(\Delta N/\left(N_1+N^*\right)\right)/\left(\Delta w/\left(w^*+\underline{w}\right)\right)$ represent the wage elasticity of labor demand. If the minimum wage restrictions are not too high (or $\underline{w}\le\frac{1}{2}\left(1-\varepsilon_{DL}\right)B\underline{w}$), which makes the percentage of the capitalist's income upon wage restrictions over the total output smaller than the reciprocal of the wage elasticity of labor demand (or $S_{B\underline{w}E_1}/S_{BE_1N_1O}\le 1/\varepsilon_{DL}$), the percentage of the total income earned by all laborers over the total output would be larger than that without minimum wage restrictions when minimum wage restrictions are imposed, or $S_{w^*EN^*O}/S_{BEN^*O}\le S_{\underline{w}E_1N_1O}/S_{BE_1N_1O}$, and vice versa. When minimum wage restrictions are adopted, the percentage of the surplus obtained by all laborers over the total surplus is always larger than that without minimum wage restrictions, or $S_{w^*EA}/S_{BEA}<S_{\underline{w}E_1DA}/S_{BE_1DA}$.

According to Theorem 14.2, the Lorenz curves of income distribution and surplus distribution with and without minimum wage restrictions in a perfect competitive labor market can be placed in a chart, respectively, as shown in Figures 14.6 and 14.7.

Figure 14.6a shows that, in a perfect competitive market, the minimum wage restrictions[3], which are not quite large, produce two effects on the inequality of income distribution. On the one hand, due to the minimum wage restrictions, the employment level of the society decreases and the wages of laborers increases. Therefore, the inequality between unemployed and employed laborers will increase. On the other hand, when the minimum wage restrictions are not too high, due to the increase in laborers' wages, the percentage of the income earned by laborers over the total output of the society will increase and the share of the income earned by capitalists will decrease. So, the income inequality between laborers and capitalists will decrease.

a. The minimum wage is not too high $\underline{w} \leqslant \frac{1}{2}(1-\varepsilon_{D_L})B\underline{w}$

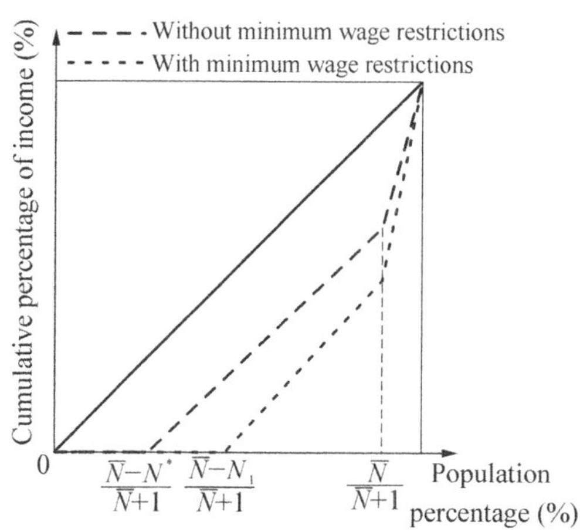

b. he minimum wage is too high $\underline{w} > \frac{1}{2}(1-\varepsilon_{D_L})B\underline{w}$

Figure 14.6 The impact of minimum wage restrictions on the Lorenz curve of income distribution in a competitive labor market.

Therefore, whether the minimum wage restrictions will increase or reduce income inequality depends on the sum of the two effects. In this case, if the income inequality between laborers and capitalists dominates in the society and social inequality is mainly derived from different income sources, the implementation of minimum wage restrictions may not help solve income inequality and may even intensify income inequality. Figure 14.6a shows that excessively high minimum wage restrictions will not only aggravate the income gaps among laborers and between laborers and capitalists. So, such limit will definitely aggravate the inequality of social income distribution.

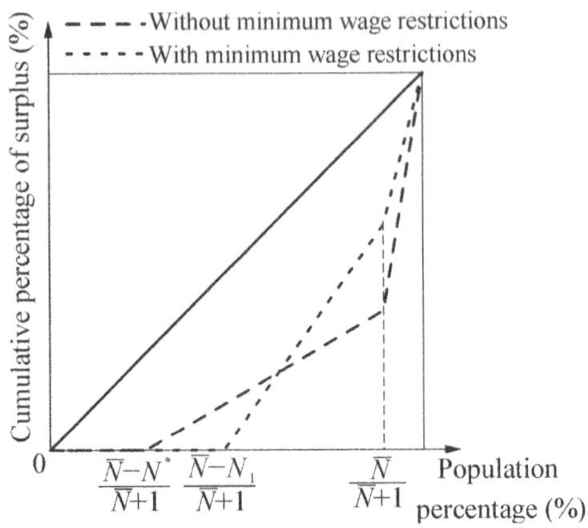

Figure 14.7 The impact of minimum wage restrictions on the Lorenz curve of income distribution in a perfect labor market.

However, Figure 14.7 shows that, if measured by the distribution of social welfare, minimum wage restrictions will surely reduce the inequality of distribution between laborers and capitalists in a society.

Theorem 14.2 also shows that, only when $\underline{w} \leq \frac{1}{2}\left(1-\varepsilon_{DL}\right)B\underline{w}$ is it possible to adopt the minimum wage restrictions to reduce the income inequality between laborers and capitalists. Under the given wage of $\underline{w}$, the smaller the labor demand elasticity, the higher probability that this condition is satisfied. Thus, in industries whose labor demand is less elastic, the implementation of minimum wage restrictions is more likely to reduce the inequality between laborers and capitalists. It is very easy to understand the economic intuition here. In the case of low elasticity of labor demand, the unemployment rate caused by the increase in wages will be low as well. Thus, the effect of minimum wage restrictions on raising wages outweighs its effect on reducing the employment rate so that the income of all laborers will increase and the income ratio between laborers and capitalists will definitely become better. Additionally, in the case of a linear labor demand curve, the interval elasticity of $\varepsilon_{DL} = b\left(w^* + \underline{w}\right)/\left(N_1+N^*\right)$ (where b represents the slope of the demand curve) is directly related to the position of the equilibrium point. Under the given labor demand curve, a flatter labor supply curve indicates a lower equilibrium point and lower elasticity of labor demand near the equilibrium point. Therefore, for the given constant labor demand curve and a flatter labor supply curve, the adoption of minimum supply restrictions are more likely to improve the distribution between laborers and capitalists. So, in those markets with large labor supply, imposing minimum wage restrictions may also reduce the inequality between laborers and capitalists.

According to Figure 14.6, Theorem 14.2, and the above analysis, Property 14.2 regarding the impact of minimum wage restrictions on income distribution can be obtained.

Property 14.2 In an economy with a perfect competitive labor market, relative to an economy without minimum wage restrictions, imposing a minimum wage limit that is not too high will lower the income inequality between laborers and capitalists but will intensify the inequality among laborers. Thus, a minimum wage limit that is not too high may also intensify and reduce income inequality, specifically depending on the original source of inequality in the economy. An excessively high minimum wage limit may aggravate income inequality between laborers and capitalists and within laborers as well.

Section 4 Impact of minimum wage restrictions on inequality in an imperfect competitive labor market

This section discusses the impact of minimum wage restrictions in a perfect competitive labor market on inequality. Just the same as the above section, when there is a minimum wage restriction policy in the economy, the authorities set a minimum wage of $\underline{w}$, as shown in Figure 14.8 (the meanings of other lines and letters in Figure 14.8 are the same as those in the previous two sections). In an economy with a monopolistic labor market, the analysis in Section 1 shows that, in Figure 14.8, the total labor forces employed in the equilibrium state when there is no minimum wage restriction are determined by Nm, the total labor forces employed corresponding to Em and the wage is equal to wm, the wage that corresponds to Nm on the labor supply curve. If minimum wage restrictions are imposed on an economy with a monopolistic labor market, then in Figure 14.8, the labor demand curve for the manufacturers is $\underline{w}E_1D_sC$, their marginal expenditure curve is now $\underline{w}E_1GH$,

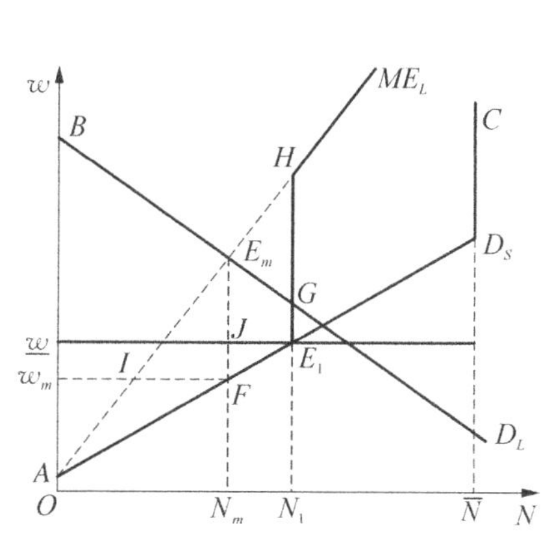

Figure 14.8 The impact of wage regulation on the economy in a perfect competitive labor market of a dual economy.

and the intersection point between the marginal expenditure and marginal labor product value curves is G. So, the equilibrium labor employment level is N1, the employment level that corresponds to point G, and the equilibrium wage is the restricted wage $\underline{w}$. The total output of the society is S_{BGN_1O}; capitalists earn a profit income of $S_{BGE_1\underline{w}}$; all $N1$ laborers employed earn a wage income of $S_{\underline{w}E_1N_1O}$ and they earn a total surplus of $S_{AE_1\underline{w}}$. At this time, a total of $\bar{N} - N_1$ laborers are unemployed and both their wage income and surplus are zero. In the equilibrium state, the $\left(\bar{N} - N_1\right)/(\bar{N}+1)$ of the unemployed people in the society earn the income and total surplus accounting for zero percent of the total output; the $\bar{N}/(\bar{N}+1)$ of the laborers obtain the income accounting for $S_{\underline{w}E_1N_1O}/S_{BGN_1O}$ of the total output and the welfare level accounting for $S_{\underline{w}E_1DA}/S_{BE_1DA}$ of the total surplus.

Compared with the equilibrium of a monopolistic labor market without minimum wage restrictions, the impact of the minimum wage on output and the welfare level is mainly reflected in the following aspects. First, due to wage regulation, the total persons employed increases, the employment level rises from N_m to N_1, the total labor forces increase by N_mN_1, and the output level would rise. The profit of the manufacturer decreases by $S_{\underline{w}JFw_m} - S_{E_mGE_1J}$ and the total surplus of laborers increases by$S_{\underline{w}E_1Fw_m}$. Thus, it is obvious that in a monopolistic labor market, imposing minimum wage restrictions increases the welfare levels of the whole society and laborers but reduces the welfare level for the manufacturer. The impact of minimum wage restrictions on the inequality of income distribution and social welfare distribution will be further discussed below.

Firstly, Theorem 14.3 can be obtained according to Figure 14.8 and the analysis above.

Theorem 14.3 In an economy with a monopolistic labor market, when minimum wage restrictions are imposed, if the legal minimum wage is lower than the marginal productivity of labor at the equilibrium point of monopoly ($\underline{w} < w(N_m)$), then the percentage of the total income earned by laborers over the total output will be larger than that when there is no minimum wage restriction (i.e., $S_{w_mFN_mO}/S_{BE_mN_mO} < S_{\underline{w}E_1N_1O}/S_{BGN_1O}$). The percentage of the total surplus earned by laborers over the total surplus is always larger than that when there is no minimum wage restriction (i.e., $S_{\underline{w}FA}/S_{BE_mFA} < S_{\underline{w}E_1A}/S_{BGE_1A}$).

According to Theorem 14.3, the Lorenz curves of income distribution and surplus distribution with and without minimum wage restrictions in an economy with a monopolistic labor market can be placed in a chart, respectively, as shown in Figure 14.9.

Figure 14.9 shows that, in a monopolistic labor market, whether in terms of inequality in income distribution or in welfare distribution, when minimum wage restrictions are imposed, the degree of inequality is lower than that when there is no minimum wage restriction. Thus, in a monopolistic labor market, imposing minimum wage restrictions is conducive to reducing

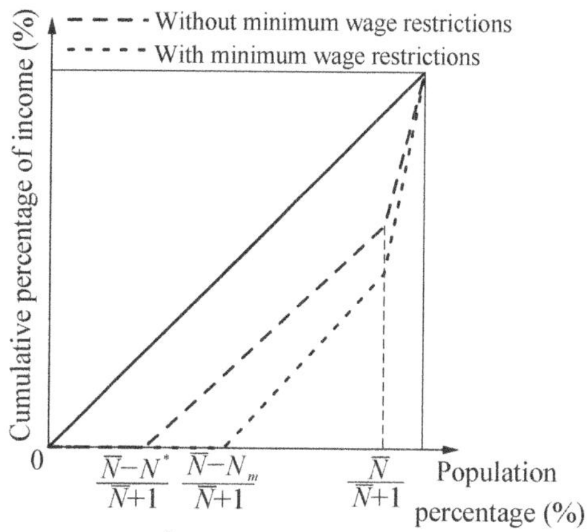

a. Income percentage

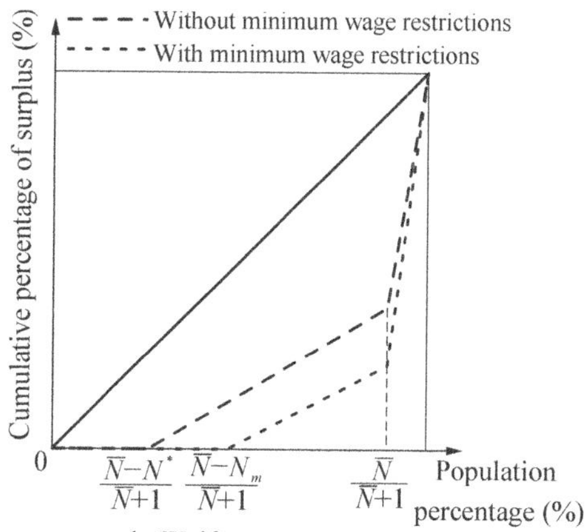

b. Welfare percentage

Figure 14.9 The impact of minimum wage restrictions on the Lorenz curves of income distribution and surplus distribution in a monopolistic labor market.

inequality. The reducing of inequality by the minimum wage restrictions in a monopolistic labor market is mainly reflected in the following two aspects. First, the minimum wage restrictions increase the wages of laborers and the percentage of the total wage income earned by laborers over total output. Thus, the minimum wage restrictions reduce the inequality between laborers and capitalists. Second, due to the fact that the minimum wage restrictions in a monopolistic labor market do not only increase wages but also lift the employment level, such restrictions reduce the inequality between the unemployed and employed laborers as well. For these two reasons, the minimum wage restrictions may greatly reduce the inequality in a monopolistic labor market. Property 14.3 can be obtained according to Figure 14.9 and the above analysis.

Property 14.3 In an economy with a monopolistic labor market, minimum wage restrictions do not only improve the output and employment levels of the whole society but also reduce the inequality of income and welfare distribution of the society.

Notes

1 According to Wang (2002), around 2002, "the total surplus labor forces in China's rural areas were up to about 200 million", and the number of labor forces that could be absorbed by cities at that time was much lower than this number. Therefore, the labor market for migrant workers in the country has been in short supply for long.

2 Regarding the monopolistic pricing of migrant workers by urban manufacturers and enterprises, Lu (2005) provides strong evidence in his research. According to the research of Lu (2005, pp. 257–174), the average monthly wage of migrant workers in Shenzhen in 2001 was 558 yuan (and this figure was lower than the wage level in the 1980s but equivalent to the average wage of village enterprise laborers in the same period), and are often subject to deduction by business owners, while the average monthly wage of employees in Shenzhen during the same period was 2,352 yuan. Even if the low production capacity of migrant workers is taken into account, it would be difficult for us to understand this phenomenon if there is no monopoly and monopolistic pricing over migrant workers by urban manufacturers and enterprises.

3 Logically speaking, in order to make the situation in Figure 14.6a possible, we must also prove that the minimum wage $\underline{w} \leq \frac{1}{2}\left(1-\varepsilon_{DL}\right)B\underline{w}$ that satisfies the conditions has solutions. Strict mathematical proof is a bit complicated. We will only briefly illustrate the possibility of such a minimum wage by setting an example. Assume that the labor demand curve is $L=20-0.1w$ and the labor curve is $L=0.1w$, and the equilibrium wage under perfect competition is $w^*=100$, $L^*=10$. Now assume that the minimum wage is limited to $\underline{w}=100+x$, then $\varepsilon_{DL}=(20+0.1X)/(20-0.1x),=100-x$, then:

$$\frac{1}{2}\left(1-\varepsilon_{DL}\right)B\underline{w} \geq \underline{w} \Leftrightarrow (100-x)(20+0.1x)/(40-0.2x) \geq 100+x \Leftrightarrow x \leq 100, x \geq 200$$

Thus, any wage restriction of higher than 100 at this time satisfies the condition $\underline{w} \leq \frac{1}{2}\left(1-\varepsilon_{DL}\right)B\underline{w}$.

References

[1] Hao, D. H. & Li, L. L., (2006) State Monopoly and Income Inequality in Regional Disparity Reform, *Social Sciences in China*, Issue 2, 110–124.

[2] Lu, X. Y. (2005). Peasant Laborer Problems Need to be Settled Fundamentally. *New View on Current Problems of Chinese Agriculture, Rural Areas and Peasants.* Beijing: Social Sciences Academic Press.

[3] Wang, D. H., & Gong, L. T. (2006). Dynamics of Income and Wealth Distribution in a Neoclassical Growth Model. *China Economic Quarterly*, 5(3).

[4] Wang, G. J. (2002). *Economic Development under the Dual Surplus of Labor and Capital*, Shanghai: Shanghai Sanlian Bookstore Press.

15 Review of China's minimum wage system from the perspective of income distribution and economic development

China promulgated the legislation on minimum wages in 1993. However, for a long time, the country has not seen the full effects of this legislation yet. Although scholars question whether minimum wages can safeguard the interest of the lowest labor income working class, most countries in the world are implementing a minimum wage system. Based on some of the national circumstances in China, this chapter discusses the impact of the minimum wage system on China's income distribution pattern and economic development from a dynamic perspective. The structure of the following parts is as follows. Section 1 briefly discusses the analysis of the minimum wage system of China in the existing literature. Section 2 discusses the potential impact of the minimum wage system on China's economy. And Section 3 analyzes the current situation and implementation of China's minimum wage system.

Section 1 The minimum wage system of China

The impact of the minimum wage system on the economy has always been one of the most controversial issues in economic circles. And the focus of the debate is mainly fairness and efficiency. Although disputes remain in academic circles, the minimum wage system has existed abroad for more than a century. And around the world, almost all developed countries and many developing countries have adopted minimum wage restrictions. China started late in establishing minimum wages. The first time China enacted minimum wage legislation was in1993, and *the Labor law of the People's Republic of China* adopted in 1994 identified the legal status of minimum wages and the minimum wage system started to be formally implemented in China that year. However, this system had always been implemented since then till 2004 when China promulgated the new Minimum Wage Regulations. After 2009, with the easing of the financial crisis and the gradual recovery of China's economy, the issue of minimum wages has become a key focus of the public. Since 2010, minimum wage standards have been continuously improved in all provinces and municipalities of China.

With respect to the advantages and disadvantages of China's implementation of the minimum wage system, there are also many disputes in China's

DOI: 10.4324/9781003261629-19

academic circles. For example, Ping (2005) suggests through theoretical analysis that the implementation of or rise in minimum wages would cause the failure of low-income laborers in finding jobs, rising labor costs in enterprises and capital outflow, etc. So, the government should be cautious about the implementation of the minimum wage system. However, Cai (2010) believes that as China's labor forces shift from surplus to shortage, the government should accept the fact of rising labor costs and improve income distribution by perfecting the minimum wage system. There is no unanimous conclusion in empirical research. For example, Ni et al. (2011) believed in their research that the increase in China's minimum wages from 2000 to 2005 did not produce any significant impact on employment on the whole. The increase in minimum wages of the eastern region significantly reduced employment, but the rise in minimum wages of central and western regions promoted employment instead. Xiao and Xiang (2009), analyzing data from 1995–2006 for six cities including Beijing, Shanghai, and Tianjin, conclude that in terms of wages, there is a spillover effect of minimum wage increases on wages, and the wage gap among employees is reduced; in terms of employment, minimum wage increases significantly increase the total and per capita hours worked by employees, but the effect on total employment is not significant. Mayneris et al. (2014) also believe that the minimum wage system does not produce a significant impact on employment as the increase in employment presented by minimum wages through the improvement of total factor productivity is sufficient to offset the decrease in labor costs due to added labor costs. However, additionally, Luo (2007) and Luo and Cong (2009) found that the rise in minimum wages would lower the employment level of Chinese migrant workers and increase the wages of various industries to a slight extent. Ma et al. (2012) also found that the rise in minimum wages would increase the wages of employees on the whole. For every 10% increase in minimum wages, the average wages of enterprises increase by 0.3% to 0.6%, and the rise in minimum wages also reduces employment. For every 10% increase in minimum wages, the number of employees in enterprises will significantly reduce by around 0.6% and the impact on different industries will vary to a certain extent.

To sum up, inconsistent conclusions about whether minimum wages would affect the employment level are drawn from different research. Due to the space limit, no comment on these controversies will be made here. The following parts of this chapter mainly analyze the potential positive economic effect of the minimum wage system on the Chinese economy from the perspective of income distribution and economic development. The analysis in this chapter argues that an appropriate minimum wage system may have the following three effects in China due to the country's special conditions. First, the minimum wage system has the function of improving China's income distribution pattern and narrowing the income gap. Second, a regionally differentiated minimum wage restriction may promote the transfer of China's industrial structure to the inland and help upgrade

China's industrial structure. Third, minimum wage restrictions may force low human capital laborers to invest in human capital, thereby contributing to the improvement of human capital in China in the long run.

Section 2 Potential economic effect of the minimum wage system

According to the current mainstream viewpoint that opposes minimum wage restrictions, minimum wages would intervene in the mechanism that prices automatically and optimally allocate resources, thereby lowering economic efficiency. However, this view is based on the assumption of a perfect competitive market. China is undergoing a process of dual economic development in its economic system transformation, which is inconsistent with the assumption of a perfect competitive market economy. Thus, just as some of the research suggests, the negative effects that the minimum wage system may intervene in free market pricing may not exist at all in China, and some may be weak if any. Additionally, due to China's special national circumstances, a minimum wage system that is suitable for China's national circumstances, has regional differences, and is strictly enforced may bring some positive economic effects. The following parts of this chapter will discuss the potential positive economic effect of minimum wage restrictions in China from the perspectives of income distribution and economic development.

2.1 Income distribution effect

Since 1978, China's income distribution inequality has been continually worsening. As early as the years before 2000, China's Gini coefficient of income distribution exceeded the internationally recognized warning line of 0.4. In 2008, the country's Gini coefficient almost reached 0.5. Although this figure has dropped since 2009, according to the latest data released by the National Bureau of Statistics of China, China's Gini coefficient was 0.457 in 2017, an increase of 0.0002 over that of 2016. If China's income distribution cannot be improved or continues to worsen, this would not only deviate from the ultimate goal of China's reform but also directly affect the country's social stability and economic development. Thus, for the current China, it is very important to measure the advantages and disadvantages of the minimum wage system and consider its effect on income distribution. So, can the minimum wage system improve income distribution? Chapter 14 in this book demonstrated the following conclusions. Firstly, in a monopsony labor market, the minimum wage system can not only increase the wages of employed laborers but also improve the level of employment. Thus, in this case, the minimum wage system can greatly reduce the inequality of capital and labor income distribution and increase the proportion of labor income. Secondly, even in a perfect competitive labor market, although the

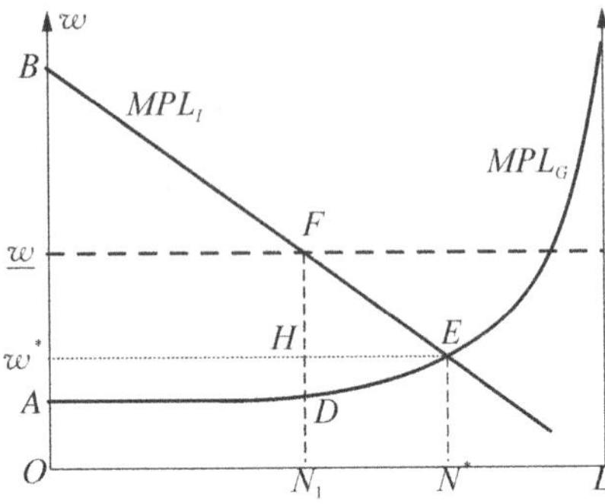

Figure 15.1 The impact of minimum wage restrictions on the capital-labor remunerations ratio in a dual economy.

minimum wage system may reduce employment, it would also reduce the inequality between capital and labor income and increase the proportion of labor income when the labor demand curve is very steep.

More importantly, for a typical dual economy like China, the minimum wage system is more important for improving income distribution. A simple model can be used to analyze the impact of the minimum wage system on income distribution.

Figure 15.1 shows the impact of minimum wage restrictions on income distribution in a dual economy. In this figure, the total labor input of the whole society is OL; the straight line BFE represents the marginal productivity of labor in the industrial sector and also the labor demand curve of the industrial sector, and the curve AEC represents the marginal productivity of labor in the agricultural sector and also the labor supply curve of the industrial sector. If the labor market is perfectly free and competitive, since the wages in the industrial and agricultural sectors must be equal in equilibrium, the wages are Ow*; the total labor input in the agricultural sector is ON*; and the total labor input in the agricultural sector is N*L. The total output of the entire society is SOBFECLO, where the total income earned by laborers is S_{Ow^*HECLO} and the income arising from capital is S_{Bw^*HEB}. If the minimum wage system is adopted, we might as well assume the minimum wage restrictions are $\underline{w}$, when the laborers employed in the industrial sector are ON1 and those in the agricultural sector are N1L; the total output is SOBFDECLO, including the total income earned by laborers $S_{O\underline{w}FDECLO}$ and the income arising from capital $S_{B\underline{w}FB}$. Compared with the absence of the minimum wage, the adoption of the minimum wage reduces the total output of SFDEF, where the net loss of income arising from capital decreases by $S_{w^*\underline{w}FEHw^*}$ and laborers' income increases by $S_{\underline{w}FHw^*} - S_{HDE}$. So, $S_{\underline{w}FHw^*} - S_{HDE}$ must be larger than 0 as long as the rate of change in the marginal productivity of labor in the agricultural sector is smaller than that in the industrial sector or the labor demand curve of the industrial sector is steeper than its supply curve. In this case, the adoption of minimum wage will definitely increase the absolute labor income. Of course, the ratio of capital to labor income will be even better. In particular, in the case of unlimited labor supply in the agricultural sector (i.e., the marginal productivity of labor in the agricultural sector is at a horizontal stage), labor income will definitely increase. Thus, in the presence of a dual economy, the adoption of minimum wage can improve the capital-labor income ratio and reduce the inequality of income distribution.

It follows that, theoretically, minimum wage systems undoubtedly have a significant role to play in improving income distribution. This is perhaps one of the most important reasons minimum wages have existed in various countries for so long. Due to China's special national circumstances, the minimum wage system is more important for improving income distribution. China is a country with a big agricultural population and is in the development stage of a dual economy. Due to the existence of a large surplus population in rural areas, the absolute amount of labor supply has always been in a state of excessive supply.[1] As a result, wages have been maintained at an extremely low level[2] and the share of labor income over GDP has continued to decline. For example, according to Luo and Zhang (2009), the proportion of China's labor income dropped from around 87% in 1987 to about 40% in 2006. Also, according to the data of the *China Statistical Yearbooks*, the proportion of China's labor remunerations over GDP dropped from around 52% in 1987 to about 40% in 2007, slightly increased during the period 2008–2016, and is currently 51%. The proportion of labor renumerations over the total output of the society fell from 60% in 1992 to 52% in 2015 and to 47% in the year with the lowest value, as shown in Figure 15.2. Additionally, due to the restrictions of China's household registration system,

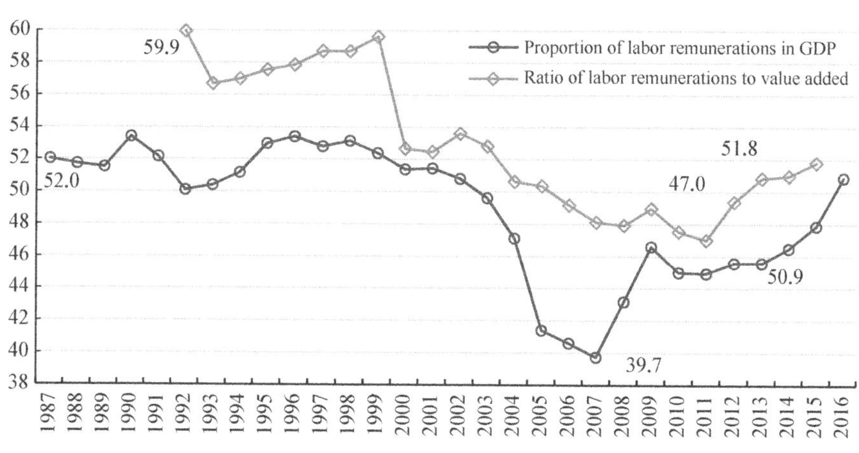

Figure 15.2 Changes in the proportion of China's labor remunerations: 1987–2016.

the segmented market marked by household registration has made the personnel of non-local residents in urban areas receive extremely discriminatory treatment in terms of employment. And for some special groups, they are more likely to be subject to monopolistic wage pricing by the hiring department. Therefore, for the current China, whether from the perspective of increasing the proportion of labor income or breaking the monopoly, it is very useful to implement the minimum wage system for the monopoly of low-wage pricing over migrant workers.

2.2 The industrial structure transfer effect in China and the industrial upgrading effect in coastal areas

The minimum wage system in China can also play another role that may not be available in other countries. That is, the differential minimum wages adopted in each region may enforce China's industrial restructuring and promote industrial upgrading in coastal areas.

According to the historical experience on the economic development of East Asian countries, some labor-intensive industries first obtained rapid development in Japan in the 1950s and 1960s. After the 1960s, labor-intensive industries moved to the Four Asian Tigers and realized the industrialization of these countries and regions. After the 1980s, these industries moved to ASEAN and the coastal areas of China. This theory of industrial transfer has been summarized by Japanese scholars including Kojima Kiyoshi as the "flying-geese model" theory.[3] However, for China, although some capital-intensive and technology-intensive industries have developed in the coastal regions of China to some extent, some labor-intensive industries haven't been transferred from the coastal areas of China to its central region. Why has the industrial structure of the coastal areas of China not transferred to the central and western regions as predicted by the "flying-geese model" theory? The main reason lies in the special labor market structure under China's dual economy structure.

According to the "flying-geese model" theory on industrial development, the main reason the industrial structure can be transferred and upgraded is as follows. On the one hand, with economic development, the technological level of laborers in the original place where the industry is distributed has been continuously improved so that there is a human capital foundation and internal motivation that can enable the development of more higher-end industries. On the other hand, economic development has also led to the continuous increase in laborer's wages and rising labor costs of enterprises. As a result, labor-intensive industries with low added value cannot pay high wage costs, which put the original place of the industry under the external pressure of industrial structure upgrading. However, for a country like China that develops in a dual economy and has huge regional economic development gaps, low-level labor-intensive industries do not undergo the pressure of raising wages in the eastern region as the central and western regions can provide a large amount of low-cost surplus labor for the eastern region. To this end, these enterprises will choose to stay in the original places and wait for the labor forces to flow from the central and western regions to the eastern region, rather than actively move from the eastern region to the central and western regions with some risk. As a result, although some of the industrial structures have been upgraded in some eastern coastal areas, low-level labor-intensive industries have not been transferred out yet. In this case, if China can implement the differential minimum wage restrictions, which make the minimum wages in coastal areas higher than the average wages of inland areas and the minimum wage standards in coastal and inland areas compatible with the productivity level of each region, it will be able to put external pressure on industries to promote some labor-intensive industries to move to the inland, thus achieving both the industrial structure upgrade and promoting the development of the inland economy. Of course, if non-discriminatory minimum wage restrictions are imposed, it may not be possible to achieve this goal of industrial structure transfer and economic development.

3.3 The cumulative effect of long-term human capital

In addition to the two effects above, the minimum wage system may also urge laborers to invest in human capital in the long run, thereby increasing the level of human capital in the entire region and promoting economic development. This is because when a restricted wage system is adopted, there is no way for some laborers with low human capital to be employed by enterprises when the manufacturer employs them at the low prices of marginal productivity due to the fact that their marginal productivity is lower than minimum wages. In the short term, they will lose their jobs as their human capital is unable to be changed. However, in the long run, these laborers can improve human capital through re-education. When the cost of raising human capital is not high enough, unemployed laborers will have incentives to increase human capital and get re-employed. We may explain it by setting a simple example as follows.

Assume that the marginal productivity of a laborer without investing in human capital is A. If he/she makes a human investment at the cost of C, the increase in human capital will make his/her marginal productivity increase to B. In a perfect competitive market, when a manufacturer hires a laborer according to the formula that marginal productivity is equal to the wage, the laborer may get a wage of A without investing in human capital and a wage of B after investing in human capital. Due to the investment cost of C, the net income of the laborer after investing in human capital is B-C. In this case, the laborer's optimal choice is not to invest in human capital as long as $B - C < A$. However, if there are minimum wage restrictions at this time, we might as well assume the minimum wage satisfies $B > \underline{W} > A$. Thus, if the laborer does not invest in human capital, he/her will have no job and his/her marginal productivity will be lower than the minimum wage; he/her will not be employed by the manufacturer and his/her net income will be zero.

If the laborer invests in human capital, the manufacturer is willing to hire the laborer at the wage of the manufacturer's marginal productivity B as the laborer's marginal productivity is higher than the minimum wage, when his/her net income is *B-C*. So, under the minimum wage restrictions, the best choice for individuals is to invest in human capital.

Of course, what needs to be emphasized is that the cumulative effect of the minimum wage system over human capital can only be reflected over a long period of time. It is undeniable that, within a short period of time, the minimum wage system may still cause some groups with low capabilities and some special groups to lose jobs, thus harming the people that should be protected. Therefore, while implementing the minimum wage system, the social security system must be improved at the same time so that the minimum living standards of the unemployed can be guaranteed. Additionally, the cost of reinvesting in human capital may also cause the increase in the cost of the unemployed. Thus, the government should also adopt a free employment retraining program or system. Otherwise, the minimum wage system will greatly weaken the income distribution effect.

Section 3 Status quo of China's minimum wage system

The former Ministry of Labor of China issued the *Regulations on Minimum Wages for Enterprises* in 1993 and started to establish the minimum wage system. It is clearly specified in the Labor Law implemented in 1994 that the minimum wage system shall be adopted so that the system is established in the form of law. In 2004, the Ministry of Labor and Social Security issued the *Minimum Wage Regulations*, promoting the full implementation of the minimum wage system in China. So far, minimum wage standards have been promulgated in all provinces of China. However, there remain the following problems with China's minimum wage system:

Firstly, the minimum wage standards in all provinces of China are relatively low and the more developed these provinces are, the lower their minimum wage standards will be. Figures 15.3 and 15.4 show the ratio of the minimum wage to the average wage of each country in the world, as well as the ratio of the minimum wage to the average wage of each province in China during the years 2018 and 2017. Figure 15.3 shows that the minimum wages in most countries of the world generally account for 40% of their average wages. Figure 15.2 shows that although the minimum wages in China's provinces and municipalities increased from 2008 to 2017, even in 2017, the share of minimum wages over average wages in a majority of China's major provinces was not larger than 35% and some were even smaller than 20%. In the current world, the minimum wages in most countries generally account for 35% of their average wages. Thus, relative to other countries in the world, the ratio of the minimum wage to the average wage in China is currently too low and the minimum wage standard remains to be adjusted. Additionally, with respect to the adjustment of minimum wages,

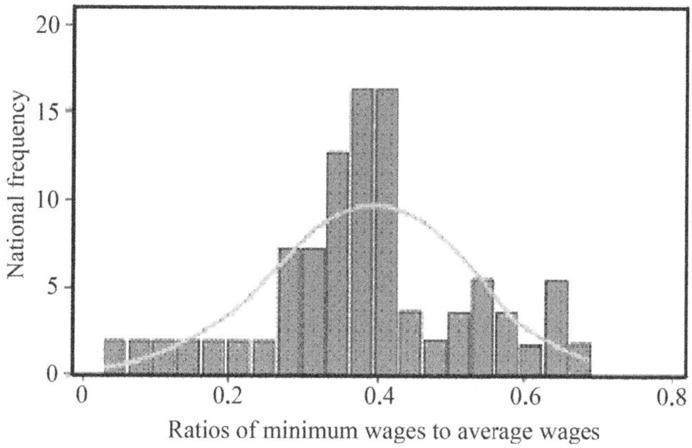

Figure 15.3 Distribution of the ratios of minimum wages to average wages in the countries of the world.

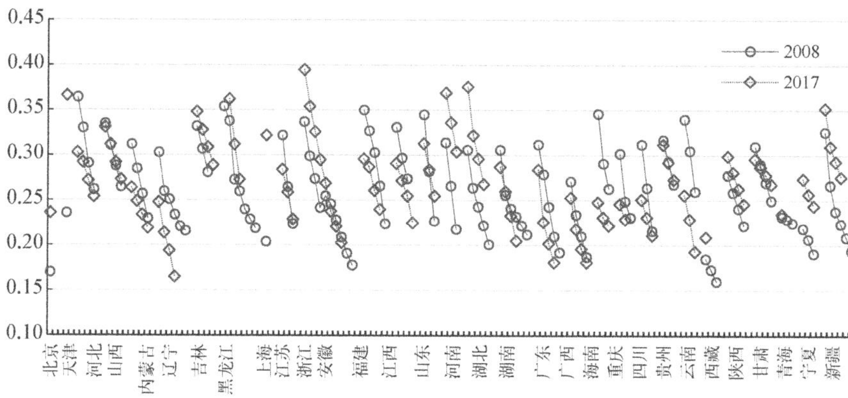

Figure 15.4 Ratios of minimum wages to average wages of China in the years 2008 and 2017.

the ratios of the minimum wages to the average wages in many provinces have even shown a downward trend. For example, the research results of Du and Wang (2008) show that the ratio of the minimum wage to the average wage in 1995 was 0.44 and dropped to 0.28 in 2006. Figure 15.4 shows that the ratios of minimum wages to average wages in Hebei, Liaoning, Jiangsu, Fujian, Jiangxi, Guangxi, Hainan, Sichuan, Chongqing, Yunnan, and other provinces in 2017 were all smaller than those in 2008, and there was partial decline in these ratios in some other provinces.

Of course, the minimum wage standards in China's provinces and municipalities have been adjusted during the past years but remained low relative to China's GDP per capita and average wages. For example, Shanghai further raised the minimum wage standard to 2,420 yuan in March 2018. According to the website of Shanghai Municipal Human Resources and Social Security Bureau, the average monthly wage of employees in the city in 2017 was 7,132 yuan. Thus, the ratio of the minimum wage to the average wage in Shanghai was only 33.9%, far smaller than the internationally accepted standard of 40%. If the fact that the share of China's wage income over GDP is rather low (Luo & Zhang, 2009), the country's minimum wage is even lower.

Secondly, China also has a lot of problems with the implementation of the minimum wage system. Up to now, no institution has been set up yet in China to supervise the implementation of the minimum wage system during the labor employment process of each province. In reality, there are not many companies that can actively follow such a system. In particular, the migrant workers that can be covered by the minimum wage system are even fewer. For example, according to the labor force survey conducted by the Institute of Population and Labor Economics of the Chinese Academy of Social Sciences (CASS) on Shanghai, Wuhan, Shenyang, Fuzhou, and Xi'an in late 2001, at the coverage rate of the hourly minimum wage, the coverage rate of hourly minimum wage for urban labor forces is 79% and that for non-local labor forces is only 48% (Du & Wang, 2008). So, the minimum wage system is not well implemented.

Thirdly, relative to average wages, there is not much difference in the minimum wage standards among provinces, as shown in Table 15.1. Using as examples Beijing and Shanghai, which had the highest average wages in 2008, and Jiangxi and Hubei, which had the lowest average wages that year, the average wages in Beijing and Shanghai were both more than 4,500 yuan while those in Jiangxi and Hubei were both less than 2,000, more than double the average wages. However, the minimum wages in Beijing and Shanghai were 800 yuan and 960 yuan while those in Jiangxi and Hubei were between 480 yuan and 580 yuan. The differences in minimum wages between the former and the latter were obviously smaller than the differences in their average wages. In 2017, the gaps in the minimum wages between provinces and municipalities widened but remained small. Take the minimum wages of Beijing and Shanghai as well as Jiangxi and Hubei as examples. The average wages in Beijing and Shanghai were 8,467 yuan and 7,132 yuan and those in Jiangxi and Hubei were 5,256 yuan and 4,659 yuan, respectively, with a difference in average wages of around 3,000 yuan. And the minimum wages in Beijing and Shanghai were 2,000 yuan and 2,300 yuan and those in Jiangxi and Hubei were 1,530 yuan and 1,750 yuan, with a difference of about 500 to 800 yuan.

Notes

1 According to the research of Cai and Wang (2007), China's total labor forces in 2006 was 764 million, of which rural labor forces amounted to 480 million, accounting for 62.8% of the total labor forces. If the extractive industry is excluded, the employment rate of agriculture is lower than 40%. According to this

percentage, the country's rural surplus labor forces accounts for 20% of the total labor forces, and there are at least 140 million surplus labor forces.

2 According to the study of the Labor and Social Security Task Force (2004), the monthly wages in the Pearl River Delta region have only increased by 68 yuan in the past 12 years. The monthly wages of migrant workers in many enterprises of Foshan have been maintained at 600 to 1,000 yuan.

3 For the "flying-geese model" theory, refer to Wang Bin, *Introduction to the Analysis of International Regional Industrial Structure*, SDX Joint Publishing, Shanghai &Shanghai People's Publishing House, 2001, pp. 28–35.

References

[1] Cai, F. (2010). Demographic Transition, Demographic Dividend, and Lewis Turning Point in China, *Economic Research Journal*, Issue 10, 4–13.

[2] Cai, F., & Wang, M. Y. (2007). *A* New Study on Rural Labor Force Surplus in China and the Relevant Facts. *Chinese Rural Economy*, Issue 10, 4–14.

[3] Du, Y., & Wang, M. Y. (2008). The Implementation of Minimum Wage System and Its Effects in China. *Journal of Graduate School of Chinese Academy of Social Sciences*, Issue 6, 56–62.

[4] Luo, C. Y., & Zhang, J. (2009a). An Economic Explanation of Declined Ratio of Labor Income: Analysis Based on China's Provincial Panel Data. *Management World*, Issue 5, 25–35.

[5] Luo, C. Y., & Zhang, J. (2009b). Labor Income Share and Economic Development: An Empirical Study Based on Chinese Industry-Level Data. *Social Sciences in China*, Issue 4, 65–79.

[6] Luo, X. L. (2007). An Analysis on the Minimum Wage's Employment Effect over the Rural Workers in China, *Journal of Finance and Economics*, Issue 11, 114–123.

[7] Luo, X. L., & Cong, S. H. (2009). Impact of Chinese Minimum Wage on Other Wages Based on the Effect of Catching up with Wage, Statistical Research, Issue 6, 60–65.

[8] Ma, S., Zhang, J. & Zhu, X. (2012). Bilateral Investment Treaties, Institutional Environment and Outward FDI Location Choices of Firms, *Economic Research Journal*, Issue 5, 132–146.

[9] Mayneris, F., Poncet, S. & Zhang, T. (2014) The Cleansing Effect of Minimum Wage: Minimum Wage Rules, Firm Dynamics and Aggregate Productivity in China, CEPII Working Paper, No. 2014-6, CEPII Research Center.

[10] Ni, J., Wang, G. & Yao, X. (2011). Impact of Minimum Wages on Employment: Evidence from China, *Chinese Economy*, 44, 18–38.

[11] Ping, X. Q. (2005). Pay Attention to the Labor-Capital Relations in Private Enterprises, *China Reform*, Issue 4, 50–51.

[12] Xiao, X. & Xiang, B. (2009). The Impact of Minimum Wage Policy on Wages and Employment in China, International Conference on Information Management Innovation Management and Industrial Engineering.

16 Causes and countermeasures of China's widening income gap

This chapter will, based on the research conclusions of the existing literature, discuss the long-term evolution trend of income distribution inequality, analyze the possible factors that affect long-term income inequality, and probe into the causes of China's widening income gap. This chapter is structured as follows: Section 1 discusses the reasons inequality of income distribution takes place, persists, and aggravates; Section 2 analyzes the possible causes and economic mechanisms for the continuous widening of the income gap after China's reform and opening-up; and Section 3 proposes comments and suggestions on how to improve China's income distribution and narrow the country's income gap.

Section 1 Why inequality of income distribution takes place, persists, and aggravates: theoretical study

Regarding dynamic changes in the inequality of income distribution, three issues need to be discussed: first, the causes of income inequality; second, the mechanisms by which the inequality of income distribution affects future income and wealth inequality; and third, long-term changes in inequality, or whether long-term inequality is increasing or tends to stabilize. According to the research conclusions from the existing literature, five causes may lead to persistent inequality, namely the impact of random factors, the difference in personal preference, the differences in ability and age, and the inequality in initial wealth distribution. However, there are many intermediate mechanisms that can make the inequality persist and possibly worsen, as shown in Figure 16.1 (Wang and Gong, 2008a). These factors will be analyzed and discussed one by one below.

1.1 Causes for persistent inequality

The causes for long-term persistent inequality can be summarized as follows:

Firstly, the differences in natural characteristics and socio-economic attributes among individuals are the main causes for persistent inequality. When individuals are inherently different in abilities and/or preferences,

DOI: 10.4324/9781003261629-20

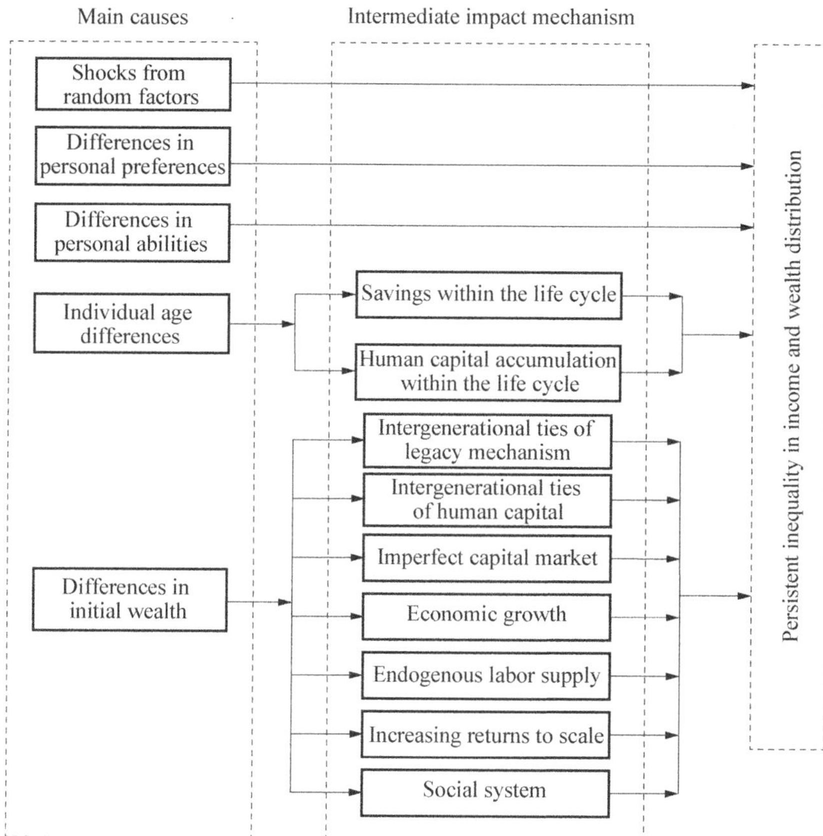

Figure 16.1 Main causes and impacting mechanisms for persistent inequality.

even if the initial level of wealth among individuals is the same, continuous inequality in the distribution of income and wealth will also occur as the economy develops.[1] In the case of distribution by labor or by marginal return on factors, the difference in abilities would lead to a gap in labor income, thus generating income inequality. When the fact that private property ownership and wealth can accumulate with time is admitted, differences in preferences (including preferences to leisure and time) would also cause persistent inequality. The difference in preference to leisure will lead to differences in individuals' working time and labor income, and the difference in preference to time would cause different personal savings and property income. Actually, the differences among individuals, regardless of those in personal inborn characteristics such as abilities and preferences, those in acquired social characteristics, such as identity, status, household registration and class, caused by social politics, system, and ideology, etc.[2]

or those persistent or random, would cause persistent inequality as long as these differences have existed for long. The persistent inequality caused by such differences may be enlarged due to its interaction with other economic mechanisms.

Secondly, the age difference of different groups in society and the inequality of income within the life cycle of individuals are also important causes for persistent inequality. The life cycle theory suggests that, in order to make the consumption within a lifetime smooth, an individual should save money when he/she is young and will dissave when he/she gets old. As a result, individuals have different levels of wealth at different ages and their wealth will change in an inverted "U" shape with age. And people of different ages in society must have different levels of wealth. If income can be earned through interest rates for the wealth level, this will inevitably lead to inequality in the property income of people at different ages (Wang et al., 2011).

Thirdly, professional differentiation and the resulting differences in personal human capital investment are also an important cause for persistent inequality. If different occupations are required to exist at the same time in the economy and require different human capital investment costs or education time, the income inequality among different occupations is bound to exist (Wang and Gong, 2009).

Finally, when private property ownership and property can be inherited and there is always inequality in the distribution of wealth in the previous period, the inequality of income and wealth may be affected. However, whether the impact of the inequality of initial wealth distribution would tend to disappear or become increasingly larger with time is one of the most important issues. That's because redistribution policies and one-time property ownership reform will become crucial if the impact of initial wealth distribution on inequality lasts. Let's discuss this issue below.

1.2 Mechanisms that cause the inequality of initial wealth distribution and produce a lasting effect

In the neoclassical model, if an individual's life was infinite, the inequality of initial wealth would produce a lasting effect. That's because in this model, the equilibrium interest rate is exactly the same as the individual's discount rate on the equilibrium growth path. Thus, everyone will maintain the same consumption level in any period so that their wealth level will remain unchanged. If individuals do not differ in abilities, the inequality of initial wealth distribution will last forever (Rutherford, 1955; Wang and Gong, 2008a). However, in the case of limited lives of individuals, the inequality of initial wealth distribution will not last forever and will tend to disappear in the long run. In the short term, intergenerational wealth ties are the only mechanism that causes wealth distribution in the previous period and affects the wealth of the next period and the inequality of income distribution. Any policies that help to eliminate intergenerational ties can help eliminate the effect of the inequality of initial wealth distribution (Rutherford, 1955; Wang and Gong, 2008b). In reality, the lives of individuals are limited. In the neoclassical model under perfect market economy conditions,[3] the inequality of initial wealth will not cause the existence and aggravation of persistent inequality in the economy. However, in the actual economy, the inequality of initial wealth produces a lasting effect and may even be aggravated with the passage of time due to the effects of many other mechanisms. In brief, the mechanisms that can produce a lasting effect mainly include the following.

1.2.1 Education human capital investment based on intergenerational ties

In an economy where there is education human capital investment, the unequal initial wealth distribution may produce a lasting effect on the economy through education human capital with intergenerational ties most of the time. That's because, in the case of the existence of education human capital, the income level of each generation is related to the human capital investment brought by individuals' education investment. Both high education investment and high human capital would generate high income. If an individual's education human capital investment is affected by the wealth level of a generation through intergenerational ties, the income level of the next generation will be affected by the wealth level of the previous generation. In a general neoclassical model, the impact of wealth in the previous period on the income of the next period is linked through the interest rate level. In the presence of education and human capital investment, the impact of the wealth level of the previous generation on the total income of the next generation will not only be reflected in capital income but also in labor income through human capital investment. This will increase the intergenerational income correlation. In this case, even if education human capital investment does not make the inequality of initial wealth distribution produce a lasting effect, it will prolong the effect of initial wealth inequality on the later inequality. With externalities in education and the segmentation of the education community, education and human capital will inevitably aggravate the inequality of initial wealth (Benabou, 1996a, 1996b; Durlauf, 1996). Of course, education and human capital investments may also work together with other mechanisms (such as imperfect capital lending market) to aggravate the persistent inequality caused by initial wealth.

1.2.2 The structure of capital lending market, its completeness and financial development

The impact of the incompleteness of the capital market on the inequality of income distribution mainly lies in the fact that it makes individuals and all economic activities depend on initial wealth. In an imperfect capital market, by taking advantage of initial wealth, people with high initial wealth obtain the advantage of low lending interest (Aghion and Bolton, 1997; Galor and Zeira, 1993; Piketty, 1997); obtain the opportunity of high-paying independent entrepreneurship (Greenwood and Jovanovic, 1990; Banerjee and Newman, 1993; Matsuyama, 2000, etc.); or receive better education and training opportunities (Loury, 1981; Tamura, 1991; Maoz and Moav, 1999; Mookherjee and Ray, 2002, 2003, etc.). Those people with a low initial wealth level can only stay in low-paying occupations due to the restrictions of their initial wealth on the opportunity of selection in the perfect capital market. So, the rich will obtain a higher rate of return and high income level and leave more wealth by taking advantage of their initial wealth in the next period. Due to the constraints of their initial wealth level, the poor can only get low remunerations and low income, which causes their descendants to have low initial wealth as well. In the next period, the economy will repeat the same story as long as the wealth level still restricts individual choices so that the difference in the initial wealth level will continue. In the long run, as long as the initial wealth level continuously constrains individual choices, the initial inequality will produce a lasting effect on the inequality of income and wealth distribution.

1.2.3 Economic growth and development

Early research believed that there is an inverted U-shaped Kuznets curve between economic growth and inequality. That means the inequality curve of each country generally rises in the initial stage of its economic development and would slowly decline with the further development of its economy. Early empirical studies also supported this conclusion (Anand and Kanbur, 1993).[4] However, some empirical studies conducted after the 1990s have shown that the decline in inequality experienced by developed countries before the 1970s has reversed in the past three decades. Especially since the 1980s, the income inequality of many countries has aggravated significantly (Murphy and Welch, 1992; Juhn et al., 1993; Gottschalk and Smeeding, 2000, etc.). Thus, the inverted U-shaped relationship between inequality and economic development considered by the Kuznets curve is not an inevitable fact during the process of economic growth and development. Theoretically, whether economic growth would cause persistent inequality in income and wealth distribution depends on initial inequality in wealth distribution and also on the relationship between the wealth accumulation rate and the economic growth rate. In a perfect capital market economy, if the wealth accumulation rate is higher than the economic growth rate, the inequality in initial wealth distribution would produce a long-term effect on persistent inequality and the opposite would also be true (Wang and Gong, 2007, 2008b). In the case of diminishing marginal productivity, for an economy with endogenous interest rates, as wealth accumulation will affect the rate of wealth accumulation through interest rates during the economic growth and development, the internal effect of the economy will eventually make the rate of wealth accumulation lower than the economic growth rate. And the effect of initial wealth distribution inequality on persistent inequality will always disappear along with economic development, and faster economic growth means faster disappearance of the effect of initial inequality on future inequality (Wang and Gong, 2007, Wang et al., 2008b). However, even in an economy with endogenous interest rates, the fact that in the presence of initial wealth inequality, economic growth and economic development may continue to increase inequality in the short term cannot be ruled out. Even in this case, the increase in the economic growth rate will weaken the effect of income inequality in the previous period on income inequality in the next period. In an economy with exogenous interest rates, since interest rates and savings rates (depending on personal preferences) are exogenous, the rate of wealth accumulation may be greater or less than the economic growth rate. At this time, the initial wealth distribution inequality may produce a lasting effect on the economy.

In conclusion, as far as individuals are concerned, the cause for the lasting effect of initial wealth inequality is that initial wealth inequality can cause the persistent inequality of personal opportunities through other mechanisms. If this inequality of opportunities is only temporary, economic growth can benefit all individuals and the effect of initial personal wealth will eventually tend to disappear as the economy continues to grow. In this case, developing economy is the best practice to solve the inequality of initial wealth distribution. This practice can be said to be in line with Deng Xiaoping's concept of "we encourage some people to get rich first"; those who get rich first will lead and help those who become rich later and finally move to the vision of "common prosperity" in the socialist construction strategy. However, if other economic mechanisms make the inequality of personal opportunities caused by wealth distribution permanent, the initial wealth inequality will produce a lasting effect on the inequality of individuals' income and wealth in the future. This may make the "development path of common prosperity" impossible. Therefore, removing the restriction of initial wealth over personal opportunities is the key to "common prosperity."

1.3 Mechanisms that aggravate the inequality of wealth and income distribution

What are the causes for the increasing inequality in wealth and income distribution during economic development? This is an issue of vital importance to society and the economy. The continuous widening of wealth and income inequality can be considered from two different perspectives. First, consider a simple situation. Assume that personal preferences and abilities are the same, without being subject to any random shock. But what are the changes in inequality when there is initial wealth inequality? In this case, unless in an economy with exogenous interest rates and growth (Wang and Gong, 2007) or the conditions of non-decreasing returns to scale (Wang, 2009) and perfect market economy are satisfied, the inequality will converge. So, the initial wealth inequality will not aggravate with time (Stiglitz, 1969; Chatterjee, 1994; Caselli and Ventura, 2000; Wang and Gong, 2006). In fact, even in an imperfect capital market economy, inequality cannot always aggravate.[5] It can be said that the market economy itself would not aggravate inequality as a perfect market economy itself does not have an internal mechanism for aggravating inequality. Moreover, in a growth economy with exogenous interest rates or non-decreasing returns to scale of human capital investment, even if there are no random factors in the economy, the inequality of initial wealth distribution may gradually aggravate with time and economic development (Wang and Gong, 2007). In the economy with exogenous interest rates, the cause for the worsening inequality is the excessively high interest rates and the excessively high inheritance rates of individuals for future generations. At this time, if the government can regulate the interest rate level or the inheritance rates, the persistent worsening of inequality can still be eliminated under the conditions of market economy. Additionally, in the case of non-decreasing returns to scale for human capital investment, inequality will aggravate either in a perfect capital market economy or in an economy without a capital market (Wang, 2009, Chapter 9). The root cause of the continuous widening of this inequality lies in the continuous growth of personal wealth level due to the non-decreasing returns to scale in relation to human capital investment. And the individual with a higher wealth level has a faster wealth growth rate. Thus, the continuous widening of inequality is rooted in the conflict between fairness and efficiency. And under this circumstance, the possibility of continued widening of inequality in the market economy is smaller than that in an economy without a capital market. Additionally, the existing literature has also pointed out that some social systems such as regional segmentation, discriminatory concepts, and education systems may also make the effect of initial wealth distribution inequality persist and continue to widen.[6]

Another circumstance where income and wealth inequality continues to widen is in the presence of random shocks, which always exist and include personal abilities, preferences, and other random differences. Obviously, if there are economic forces that can cause the increasing inequality of initial wealth distribution without the effect of random factors, inequality will inevitably continue to aggravate in the economy subject to random shocks. Additionally, in an economy where there is no random shock that affects inequality and would not expand, the inequality may continue to widen if other conditions remain unchanged and there are random shocks, including preferences, abilities, and random income, in each period. The research results of Wang and Gong (2008a) show that if there are random shocks from personal abilities, preferences, and income, there will be an internal mechanism that aggravates inequality in the short term. Therefore, the key to controlling the market mechanism and widening inequality is to control the effect of random shocks on personal income, especially personal non-market random income, such as illegal income, income arising from gambling, and other non-factor income. In the context of personal short-sighted expectations, accelerating economic growth is also an important approach to eliminating rising inequality in the short term as this may increase the proportion of labor income in the total income, thus weakening the impact of random shocks on inequality. However, Wang and Gong (2006) demonstrate that in the case of individuals' limited lives and endogenous interest rates, the shocks from random factors will not lead to the continuous increase in inequality.

Section 2 Why China's income gap continues to widen: discussion based on the literature

Just as the analysis in Chapter 12 shows, the inequality in China's income distribution was not so serious as it is now before the reform and in its early period. It can even be said to be very equal relative to the income distribution of other countries in the world and of the post-reform China. It is even called "egalitarianism" or "egalitarian practice" by scholars. Of course, this type of egalitarian practice has seriously affected the enthusiasm of laborers so that the efficiency of both agricultural productivity in the rural "people's commune" system and state-owned and collective enterprises is very low. After the reform and opening-up, under the socialist market economy reform of "giving priority to efficiency with due consideration to fairness" of China, the distribution by labor and by factors coexisted and distribution was made according to the contribution of the factor market. This has mobilized laborers' enthusiasm for labor and also widened the income gap. However, just as the analysis above showed, the market economy may bring about inequality in income distribution, but there is no mechanism to keep the income widening in place. Therefore, there must be some imperfect market factors and other mechanisms that jointly led to the continuous widening of China's income gap. So, what are the factors and mechanisms that made the income gap of China widen after the reform?

2.1 The market-oriented reform is one of the causes of rising income inequality

Firstly, as people differ in abilities and preferences, there must be uncertainties in life. Unless absolute egalitarianism is adopted, the inequality in income and wealth distribution among individuals would inevitably exist in the presence of private ownership. Even before reform and opening-up, there was still inequality in income and wealth distribution in China. However, due to the implementation of public ownership of the means of production before the reform and opening-up, private enterprises and individual economies accounted for a small share, and residents almost had no property income except for their interest income arising from savings. Secondly, in terms of the policies, the goal pursued then was social justice. And under the guidance of the policy of more savings and less consumption in the early stage of China's socialist construction, the labor income that could be distributed was low and equal then. Finally, the absolute egalitarian system that lacks incentives often led to absolute ineffective egalitarianism and widespread poverty, and the lack of materials would in turn cause even distribution in reality. Thus, the inequality of China's income distribution was mainly reflected in the income gap between laborers and farmers before the reform and opening-up. The substantial inequality mainly reflected the inequality between the actual income of different laborers and their actual abilities and output. However, generally speaking, the inequality of income distribution expressed in the form of labor income is very high.

Since the adoption of the market-oriented reform, the income distribution pattern has shifted from distribution by labor to a combination of distribution by labor and by factors, and then to distribution by the contribution of production factors. The income arising from capital, land, management, knowledge and technology, and other factors accounted for an increasing proportion in personal income. To some extent, the proportion of income earned by individuals in total personal income through these factors even exceeded the income earned by individuals through labor. For example, during the period 1985–2012, family business income accounted for an increasingly smaller proportion in the net income of China's rural residents and the wage income earned by farmers when they went out for work had an increasing proportion in their total income. Among the operating income, the share of income arising from agriculture, forestry, animal husbandry, and fishery was getting smaller and smaller, and that of other commercial operating income increasingly higher, as shown in Figure 16.2. In terms of the ratio of disposable income of urban residents during the period 1990–2016, residents' wage income continued to decline while property income and operating income continued to rise, as shown in Figure 16.3.

Due to the time accumulation effect of individual ownership of factors, the property and land currently owned is equivalent to the labor income accumulated in the previous period. The difference in personal labor capacity will lead to differences in the amount of capital such as long-term property and land. Knowledge and technology are directly determined by an individual's learning ability and educational background and the ownership of knowledge and technology is also related to the individual's ability and even his/her previous wealth. When the income distribution form changes from the simple distribution by labor to that by the contribution of factors, this is actually equivalent to the widening effect of the inequality of personal labor capacity on the income gap, thereby definitely widening the personal income gap. Also, the time accumulation of wealth inequality will also further widen the income gap. For example, according to the research of Zhao

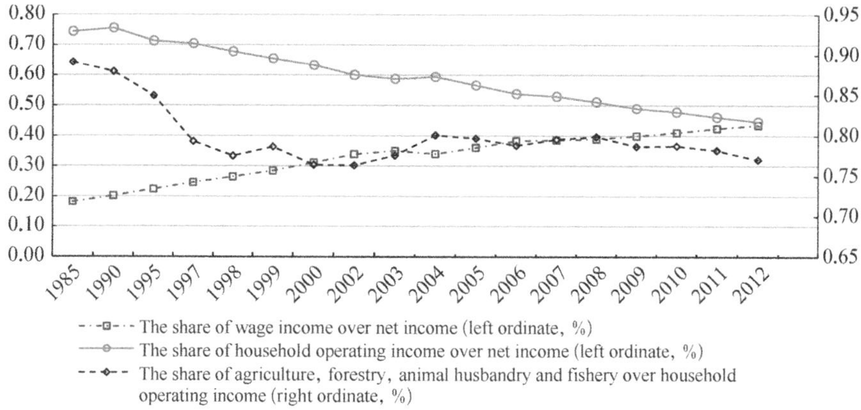

Figure 16.2 Changes in the family income structure of Chinese rural residents: 1985–2012.

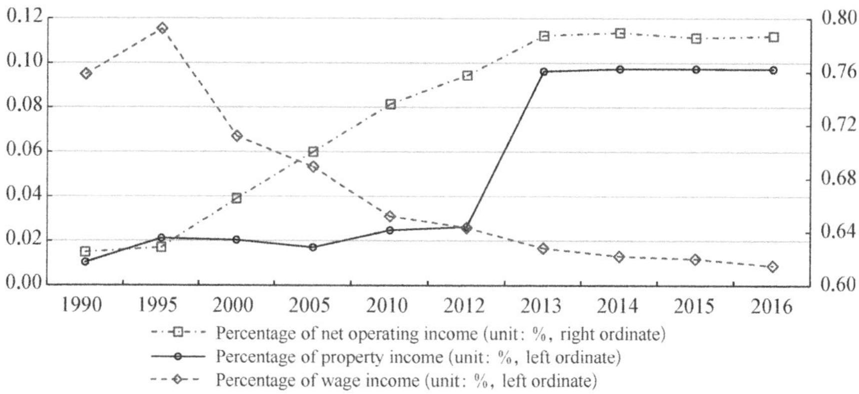

Figure 16.3 Changes in the share of each item in the disposable income of Chinese urban residents: 1990–2016.

and Li (1997), the proportion of urban residents' property income in total personal income rose from 0.49% in 1988 to 1.3% in 1995. If the estimated rent of self-owned houses is also regarded as a type of property income, the property income of urban residents in 1995 reached 11.58%, an increase of 7.19% compared with that of 1988. In addition to the estimated rent of self-owned houses, the current forms of personal property income in China mainly include interest, dividends and rent, etc.

However, whether the natural differences and uncertainties among individuals will eventually lead to the continuous increase in inequality in the income distribution of residents may be related to the socio-economic system and distribution system. Since China's reform and opening-up, the distribution means has changed on the one hand and the private economy is also increasing. These reforms have indeed resulted in the generation and intensification of inequality. And the development of the private economy during the reform process is also one of the reasons for inequality. However, due to the fact that the continuously widening income inequality is not available in the perfect market mechanism itself, it is believed that the reason for China's increasing income inequality is mainly due to China's market economy reform, which is hard to explain in theory at least. Thus, it must due to the incomplete market mechanism reform and other factors that derivate from a perfect market, such as dual economy development, monopolistic power, imperfect capital market, and the urban-rural segmentation and regional segmentation caused by the household registration system that may lead to the persistently intensifying inequality.

2.2 The main causes for the widening urban-rural income gap and the decline in the proportion of labor income in China

Although economic growth would not bring about a sustained increase in income inequality in a monistic economy, it may increase the inequality of income distribution between labor and capital through the dual economy structure. This can be described by a simple model. As shown in Figure 16.4, the total labor input of the whole society is OIOG; the straight lines B1E1 and B2E2 represent the marginal productivity of labor in the industrial sector and also the demand of the industrial sector for labor forces. The curve A E1E2C represents the marginal productivity of labor in the agricultural sector and also the labor supply in the industrial sector. Assume the labor market is perfectly and freely competitive. The marginal productivity curve of the industrial sector at the beginning is B1E1. In the equilibrium state, the wage in the industrial sector is OIwl, the total labor forces employed in the

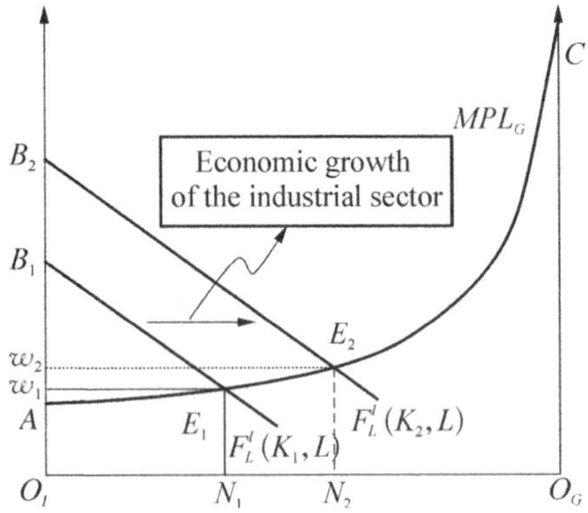

Figure 16.4 The impact of wage regulation on the economy in a perfect competitive labor of dual economy.

agricultural sector is OIN1, and the total labor forces employed in the agricultural sector is OGN1. The total output of the entire society is $S_{O_I B_1 E_1 C O_G O_I}$, in which the total income earned by laborers is $S_{O_I w_1 E_1 N_1 O_I}$ and the income earned through capital is $S_{B_I w_1 E_1 B_I}$. With the increase in the material capital accumulation of the industrial sector or in the technological level of the industrial sector, the industrial sector witnesses economic growth. Thus, the marginal productivity curve of labor in the industrial sector is shifted toward the right, to B2E2. In the equilibrium state, the wage in the industrial sector is OIw2, the total labor forces employed in the agricultural sector is O2N2, and the total labor forces employed in the agricultural sector is OGN2. The total output of the entire society is $S_{O_I B_2 E_2 C O_G O_I}$, in which the total income earned by laborers is $S_{O_I w_2 E_2 N_2 O_I}$ and the income earned through capital is $S_{B_2 w_2 E_2 B_2}$. During this process of economic growth, a large amount of agricultural population moves to the industrial sector. However, due to the large population in the agricultural sector, the marginal productivity of labor in the agricultural sector is extremely low and changes smoothly. Therefore, despite the increase in the population of the industrial sector, the wages witness a minimal increase. Almost all results of economic growth are derived from capital income. During this process, the proportion of labor income in total output decreased, the proportion of capital income in the total output increased, and the income inequality between capital and labor aggravated.

This process explains very well how China's economic growth interacted with the dual economy to increase income distribution inequality in China. The results of this model quite match some phenomena in the process of China's economic growth. Firstly, just as the analysis in Section 1.6 of Chapter 12 showed, the proportion of China's labor income was declining for a long period before the reform. It was probably not until around 2010 that the proportion of labor income rose. During the period 1987–2007, the proportion of labor income in China dropped from 52.0% to 39.7%. Secondly, with the sustained growth of China's economy, the country has witnessed a rapid increase in the number of urban migrant workers. The research of Cai (2007) showed that the income of migrant workers in urban areas increased from 38.9 million yuan in 1997 to 108 million yuan in 2005. According to the estimate of Cai et al. (2007), the income of migrant workers from urban areas grew faster, from 78.49 million in 2000 to 132 million in 2006. Thirdly, the wages of Chinese migrant workers in urban areas have been quite low, roughly equivalent to the wages in the rural market, and their growth has been slow. For example, the average monthly wage of migrant workers in Shenzhen was 588 yuan in 2001, lower than the average level of Shenzhen in the 1980s but almost the same as the average monthly wage of village and township enterprises (Lu, 2005). A survey conducted by the Agricultural Research Team of the National Bureau of Statistics of China also showed that the average monthly wage of Chinese migrant workers was 582 yuan, much lower than the average wage of urban employees (Guo, 2005).

2.3 The root causes for the widening regional income gap

It's generally believed that China's current economic development and rapid economic growth are important reasons for China's widening income gap. While the Kuznets curve suggests there is an inverted U-shaped relationship between inequality and economic development, some scholars believe that China's widening income gap and increasing inequality of income distribution are the inevitable results of the country's current economic development and rapid economic growth. However, just as the previous analysis mentioned, economic growth and development does not necessarily cause the generation and intensification of persistent inequality. On the contrary, in some cases, faster economic growth is also an important factor for eliminating the inequality of initial wealth distribution and accelerating the convergence of inequality. Empirically, the Kuznets curve in economic development is not necessarily valid. As analyzed in Chapter 13 of this book, the unbalanced development of urban and rural areas and regions does not necessarily lead to the widening of urban-rural and regional income gaps. And the unbalanced development under the regional labor market segmentation may also cause the continuous widening of urban-rural and regional income gaps. During the economic development since China's reform, the impact of the interaction among the dual economy model, excessive rural surplus population, and household registration system over the inequality of income distribution is more important than that of economic development itself on income distribution. Many studies believe that the household registration system dividing urban and rural areas and then the economic growth mode of unbalanced development of regional and urban-rural economy may be the most important reasons for the widening income gaps between urban and rural residents and among regions (Cai & Yang, 2000; Cai, 2003; Yao & Lai, 2004; Yan, 2006, etc.).

The unbalanced development of the urban, rural, and regional economy as well as the urban-rural and regional labor market segmentation caused by the household registration system can cause the income gap to continue to widen, which is mainly due to the following reasons. Firstly, the state has implemented preferential supporting policies for urban and rural areas and in different regions during the process of gradual reform, causing the existing unbalanced development between urban and rural areas and among different regions. The household registration system has further limited the possibility that the economic benefits brought about by this unbalanced growth can be shared by all groups. This has led to the continuous widening of the gap between wage compensation and capital compensation between urban and rural areas. Secondly, also more importantly, China's household registration system does not intend to restrict the flow of all people. For those with high educational background, high abilities, and high wealth level, all regions impose no restrictions on them or even encourage them to live in. Therefore, the region with a better economic level will inevitably attract more people with higher abilities to enter under this type of household registration system that does not entirely restrict population flow so that these regions will have more human capital. Also, the inflow of more human capital will also enable these regions to attract more material capital so that the wages of all people in these regions are even higher. This will aggravate the income gap among individuals in different regions, especially the income gap among individuals with low human capital in different regions. The impact of urban-rural segmentation over inequality can be evidenced by the increasing widening urban-rural income gap in China. Thus, the urban-rural segmentation, regional segmentation, and low-ability population flow caused by the household registration system restrict the inequality of regional development, which may be an important factor aggravating China's inequality.

2.4 Important factors for the differentiation of social income classes

The increase in the rate of return on investment in education human capital and the reform of an education system featuring self-funded higher education have also played a significant role in the inequality of China. The previous analysis shows that education and human capital investment produce a big effect on the inequality of personal income and wealth distribution. If personal education is not constrained by initial personal wealth, education will not aggravate income inequality. However, once education is constrained by initial personal wealth, people with low income and at a low wealth level may only receive a low level of education at all times, thus always staying in the low income group. So, education may become an important way to aggravate inequality and may even become the direct cause for polarization. Under China's original publicly funded higher education system, individuals almost do not need to pay for education except with investment in education time. Thus, personal education investment will not be restricted by the initial personal wealth level. However, under the education system featuring self-funded higher education, the cost of higher education is directly borne by individuals and the credit market for China's education investment is not perfect. This means personal education investment directly affected by an individual's current income and wealth level. In particular, education and human capital investments play an increasingly important role in the distribution of personal income and wealth distribution in current China, which will directly widen the personal income gap (Bai, 2004; Guo, 2005; etc.). Thus, the increase in the rate of return on education and human capital investments and the reform of higher education featuring self-funded higher education are the main reasons for the decline in the mobility of China's income distribution and the reduced chance of the poor becoming the rich and also one of the important reasons for the increase in China's labor income. Another adverse effect of the self-funded higher education on income distribution is that the system will restrict the intergenerational mobility in income distribution as it makes personal education investment restrained by the initial personal wealth level. In other words, under the self-funded education system, the possibility of the next generation of the low income group and the intergenerational mobility of the income groups will be greatly reduced. How to eliminate the constraints of the current personal income and wealth income over personal education investment is very important for improving China's inequality.

2.5 The main reasons for the widening income gap among Chinese urban residents

The imperfect capital market is also one of the main reasons for the widening income gap among Chinese residents. In the current financial system of China, due to the imperfect capital market, capital owners can often earn extremely high non-market-based income through the leverage of state-owned resources, which is also the main reason the income of a small number of high-income people is too high. Under the conditions of a market economy, the principle of distribution by the contribution of the factor market has improved the role of capital in capital distribution, which has widened income inequality in terms of the mobility of social class. As the acquisition of capital income causes the income of the previous generation to affect the income of the next generation, the income inequality produces a cumulative effect in terms of time. Nevertheless, if the capital market is perfect, the inequality accumulated through capital income over time will be limited and remain unchanged when it reaches a certain level. However, due to the imperfect capital market in China, capital is a relative scarce factor relative to labor. In order to develop the local economy, local governments attract capital by providing low-cost resources to investors. Capital owners can use capital to control state-owned resources. Once these owners obtain such state-owned monopolistic resources, they can not only obtain capital gains but also monopolistic resource gains. Capital gains earned through the leverage of state-owned resources are much higher than the normal remunerations in the capital market. This greatly increases the income of capital owners and widens the income gap between the high-income class and the lower-middle-income class. This point can be verified by the continuous emergence of rich coal merchants, rich real estate developers, and other resource-oriented rich people in recent years.

2.6 Monopoly, redistribution policies, and "rent-seeking" directly widen the income gap in China

The previous analysis in this chapter shows that, theoretically, in a perfect market economy, if individuals do not experience the impact of abilities, preference differences, and random income, inequality will remain unchanged on the balanced growth route. If economic growth exists, inequality in income distribution may gradually tend to stabilize. However, if the impact of abilities, preference differences, and random income is available in the economy, inequality will continue to increase. Abilities and preferences are generally fixed in the short term. Therefore, random income becomes the main factor related to the distribution system itself and can produce an impact on inequality in the short term. These random factors may be the main reason for the increase in inequality in China during China's market economy reform. Specifically, these random factors[7] include monopoly, income redistribution caused by institutional reform, and other illegal income.

It is quite easy to intuitively understand the impact of monopoly power on inequality in China. Due to the existence of monopoly power, the department with monopoly power can set prices according to the market economy mechanism. In the case of maximum personal interests, the monopoly department will inevitably set a price higher than that under the condition of a perfect competitive market. It is by virtue of this monopoly price that monopolists obtain monopoly income that exceeds market pricing, which will make the income and wealth level higher than that of ordinary people. It can be said that sector monopoly and industry monopoly make a huge contribution to inequality in China. It is not difficult to find this point by comparing the average wages of monopoly sectors and industries with those of non-monopoly ones. For example, wages in sectors such as telecommunications, petroleum, railways, and finance are all higher than the average wages in the market. Existing research has confirmed that the existence of monopoly is one of the main reasons for the continuous widening of the income gap in China's industries (Wang, 2007; Jiang and Yu, 2007; Fu, 2008, etc.). Additionally, if the state exercises price control on monopolistic sectors, these sectors will earn higher illegal income[8] than ordinary people through rent-seeking as the price control would inevitably make the products supplied by these sectors be in short supply. Thus, the existence of monopoly power in the market will inevitably intensify income and wealth inequality. So, breaking various monopolies, including industry monopoly, sector monopoly, and market monopoly, is an indispensable measure to reduce the inequality of income distribution in China.

Secondly, every imperfect system reform by government will cause one-time wealth accumulation and increase income inequality. If the reform is completed at one time, the inequality caused by this one-time reform may gradually disappear as the system gradually stabilizes during the process of economic growth. However, if constant reforms of various new systems emerge and people with wealth advantages can always gain advantages in the wealth redistribution by relying on their wealth advantages in previous system reforms continuous wealth accumulation and increasing income inequality may result. Therefore, with the continuous advancement of reforms, despite the possible perfection of an individual system, the inequality in the entire economy will continue to increase due to the constant emergence of new system reform and wealth redistribution in the economy.[9] Also, the widening of such inequality may interact with market forces and then accumulate. In addition, the preemptive information opportunities and the subsequent benefits in the reform of various systems will also bring about some rent-seeking behaviors. And the resulting corruption, bribery smuggling, and other illegal income channels are also important aspects that intensify the inequality. In this sense, shortening the duration of reform and system instability, improving the transparency of the system, and reducing rent-seeking behaviors are some of the important ways to reduce inequality in China.

Section 3 Bridging income gap by perfecting China's market economy system

Since 1978, the income gap among Chinese residents has been widening. The widening income gap goes against China's reform goal of "common prosperity" and may also lead to a decline in China's domestic consumer demand and affect economic development. So, it has become increasingly important and urgent to narrow the income gap and reduce the inequality in income distribution. Based on the research in this book, China should continuously improve its socialist market mechanism to better the income distribution pattern and narrow the income gap among residents.

3.1 Reforming the household registration system, perfecting the labor market, and narrowing the urban-rural income gap

As is known from the first and second parts, unbalanced urban-rural economic development is the main reason for the income gap between urban and rural areas in China. As far as the overall inequality of China's income distribution is concerned, the unequal income gap among regions is one of the most important reasons. For example, Wang and Xu (2006) found that the continued widening of the urban-rural income gap and regional income gap has the greatest impact on the widening of overall income inequality nationwide, with the widening of urban-rural income being the most important. Similar results have also been obtained from other research (Li & Zhao, 1999). The main reason for the large urban-rural gap in China lies in China's dual economy development and the rapid growth of the urban economy. Due to the excessive population in China's rural areas, the current household registration system also restricts the free transfer of rural permanent residence to urban areas, while the dual economy features backward agricultural production technology and slow growth of agricultural economy. Therefore, the excessive surplus labor forces in rural areas provide sufficient low-cost labor forces for urban economic development so that the urban economy can quickly accumulate capital and develop. However, the wages of the migrant workers who used to be farmers remain at an extremely low level, and the restrictions of household registration do not allow them to be protected by the urban social security system. Many farmers cannot enjoy the fruits of urban economic development and their lives have been shut out of urban economic development. Therefore, changing the economic structure of this dual economic development in urban and rural areas is a fundamental way to narrow the gap between urban and rural areas. To change the urban-rural dual economy structure, the first step is to accelerate the development of the urban economy so that the urban industrial sector and the tertiary sector can absorb the excessive surplus labor forces from the agricultural department. Meanwhile, agriculture can be mechanized and agricultural productivity can be increased only after the excessive surplus agricultural population is transferred to cities in order to achieve the joint development of the agricultural rural economy and urban economy and narrow the gap between the marginal output values of urban and agricultural labor forces, thus eventually narrowing the urban-rural gap. Of course, it is necessary to realize the free transfer of the agricultural population to cities during this process to enable the majority of people to be employed in urban modern economic sectors, reform China's household registration mechanism, eliminate the hierarchical gap and flow restrictions between rural and urban permanent residence, and eliminate discriminatory treatment of rural residents.

3.2 *Balancing economic development of regions promoting the transfer of industrial structure and narrowing the regional gap*

The widening income gap among regions is one of the most important factors leading to the continuous rise in China's inequality. Narrowing the inequality of income distribution among residents is indispensable for reducing inequality in income distribution. The analysis in Chapter 13 showed that, in the case of free flow of labor forces, the inequality of regional economic development does not necessarily lead to the continuous widening of the income gap among regional residents. However, if China's labor market cannot be improved in the short term and the household registration system cannot be cancelled in the short term, promoting regional balanced economic development, and narrowing regional economic gaps has become a necessary approach to narrowing regional income gaps. In terms of China's current economic development pattern, the eastern region generally develops fast and makes great achievements in the development of its secondary and tertiary industries, while the central and western regions are backward in development. In these regions, the primary industry dominates; the secondary industry develops rapidly; and the tertiary industry almost has no development, except in some provincial capitals. Currently, in order to narrow the gap in regional economic development among regions, the first step is to realize the transfer of industrial structure. This requires measures such as industrial policies and taxation policies to support the economic development of the central and western regions, narrow the gap in investment productivity of the central and western regions from the eastern region, promote the transfer of some labor-intensive industries in the eastern region to the central and western regions, and improve the industrial structure of the eastern region itself. Secondly, in order to narrow the economic gap of the eastern region from the central and western regions, it is also necessary to support the central and western regions through fiscal policies, to accelerate the infrastructure and system building in the central and western regions, to improve the working efficiency of governments, to reduce rent-seeking behaviors and non-market transactions in the economy, and to improve the investment environment in the central and western regions (including the soft investment environment in terms of the system and the hard environment in terms of technology). It is also an indispensable factor that allows some labor-intensive industries in the eastern region to transfer to the central and western regions. Thirdly, it is necessary to increase investment in science, technology, and education in the central and western regions, increase the education income per capita in the central and western regions, and popularize compulsory education so as to increase the human capital in the central and western regions.

3.3 Changing the pattern of economic growth, increasing the proportion of labor income, and narrowing the gap between labor and capital

Due to the existence of the dual economic structure and the infinite supply of labor forces in the rural areas of central and western regions, the process of urban economic growth in China has become a process of the decline in labor-capital income ratio, making the inequality between labor income and capital income increasingly intensify. In order to narrow the gap between labor and capital income, it is necessary to change the development model of the eastern region that only relies on the extensive expansion of labor-intensive industries and upgrade the industrial structure of the eastern region so that the industrial structure of the eastern region gradually shifts from the labor-intensive type to the capital- and technology-intensive types and the labor-intensive industry gradually shifts to the central and western regions. So, the upgrading of the industrial structure in the eastern region should occur at the same time with the transfer of labor-intensive industries to the central and western regions, which are two aspects of economic growth mode transformation. Promoting the transfer of labor-intensive industries in the eastern region to the central and western regions while upgrading the economic and industrial structure of the eastern region can increase the proportion of labor income in the eastern region, expand the proportion of the middle class, and narrow the income distribution gap of residents in the eastern region. It can also help the remaining labor forces in the central and western regions find jobs in the local, accelerate the economic development of the central and western regions, narrow the inequality of economic development among regions, and reduce the income inequality among regions. Of course, in order to realize this type of industrial structure transfer, it is necessary to adopt a differentiated industrial policy for the eastern region in addition to the policy support for the economic development of the central and western regions. For capital-intensive and technology-intensive industries in the eastern region, preferential policies should be given to encourage their development. And for labor-intensive industries, preferential policies should be adopted to urge them to exit from the eastern region.

3.4 Deepening the reform of the market economy system, breaking the industry and sector monopoly, establishing anti-monopoly laws and regulations, and narrowing the gap in industry income

Since the reform, the income gap among Chinese industries has been widening and the continuous increase in the income gap among industries has also become one of the important reasons for the inequality of income distribution of Chinese residents and the increase in the Gini coefficient. The most important reason for the widening of the gap in industry income is monopoly (Yue & Wu, 2005; Yang, et al., 2008). Thus, in order to narrow the income gap among industries, improving economic mechanisms and breaking industry monopoly are the sole and necessary measures. Since monopoly may sometimes be a necessary component of market competition, anti-monopoly laws have been formulated in other countries in the world in order to improve the market economy mechanism and break industry or sector monopoly. Most of the current monopolistic industries are sectors and industries monopolized by state-owned enterprises whose markets have not been fully opened, such as banking and insurance in finance, railways, post and telecommunications, water, and electricity. In view of China's national circumstances, in order to fundamentally break industry and sector monopoly and improve the market competition mechanism, the first step is to carry out a thorough economic system reform. Except for those sectors related to the national economy, people's livelihood and national security and with natural monopoly characteristics, other sectors should liberalize administrative monopoly, introduce the market competition mechanism, and allow the market mechanism to lead their development. Only in this way can these monopolized sectors obtain high monopoly profits through monopoly pricing. Of course, formulating anti-monopoly laws to combat monopoly is a common practice for western countries, and enacting and improving anti-monopoly laws should be an important move for China to break monopoly and narrow the income gap in the industry. As far as the current situation is concerned, China's legislation in this respect is quite imperfect. Although the Anti-Unfair Competition Law has been promulgated in China, it is far from being an anti-monopoly law. However, it is designed for enterprises and does not include the government's own monopoly behavior in the scope of anti-monopoly. Although the drafting of the Anti-monopoly Law has been discussed several times in recent years, it has not been promulgated yet. Regulations on various monopolistic industries are also quite incomplete. For example, although the legislation of the telecommunications industry has been under discussion for a long time, only the Ministry of Information Technology has currently promulgated the Telecommunications Regulations and there are only local regulations for tap water, gas, heating, and other industries. For China, most of the monopoly may be derived from the incomplete reform of the planned economy. To this end, we must promptly repeal the laws and regulations that are not conducive to breaking monopoly and realizing free competition, revise and modify related laws such as the Electricity Law, the Aviation Law, and the Railway Law, and accelerate the legislation of the Anti-monopoly Law, the Telecommunications Law, and the Oil and Natural Gas Law so that anti-monopoly has laws to abide by.

3.5 The transmission mechanism for widening the income gap

Another main reason for the widening income gap in China is the inequality of personal education human capital (Yue & Wu, 2005). With the advancement of reforms and the improvement of the market economy system, for the established distribution of education human capital, the income levels of laborers with different amount of education human capital are also different. This is the structure of the market mechanism that allocates resources by marginal productivity. It conforms to the requirements for the market economy mechanism and also the principle that income is distributed by factors in China. However, there are some existing problems in China as follows. First, if the reasonableness of human capital for income distribution is admitted, will the inequality of the distribution of education human capital itself be reasonable? Second, with regard for the established distribution of education human capital, is there any mechanism that allows the income inequality derived from education inequality in China to gradually expand due to the widening gap in the rates of return on different education human capital? Third, is there any mechanism that allows the inequality in the distribution of education human capital to gradually expand? Narrowing the income gap of residents by reducing the inequality of education distribution is an important way to reduce inequality. Existing research shows that the rate of return on education is increasing fast (Huang, 2006), China's rate of return on education tends to increase with the level of education, and the rates of return on education for educators of senior high schools and above are higher than those of junior high schools and below (Zhang, 2006). The gap between the rates of return for different lengths of education is gradually widening and the rate of return on education has shown obvious heterogeneity. The increase in the rate on education in China has led to an increase in wage income inequality (Chen et al., 2004).

3.6 Reforming the fiscal and taxation system and giving play to the role of redistribution means

In the process of market-oriented reform, when the form of income distribution changes from a purely labor-based distribution to a combination of labor-based and factor-based distribution, both the inequality of individual labor capacity and the time-accumulation effect of wealth inequality will affect the income gap in China. In order to avoid the influence of changes in income distribution form on income gap, the government should redistribute national income and adjust the disposable income of individuals through taxation, transfer payment and other policy measures to redistribute national income. To this end, the following reforms are necessary.

First, in terms of fiscal revenue policy, through the reform of the taxation system, taxation can adjust the excessive labor income and capital income generated in the market, and can control some income that is not related to personal capacity and is purely caused by the imperfect system in the market reform. The regulation of excessive capital income and labor income can be conducted through personal income tax. In view of China's current personal income tax collection system issue, the personal income tax has not played a regulating role of "rob the rich to help the poor" for some high income groups but an opposite role instead. Additionally, it is necessary to control the excessive income earned by controlling those state-owned resources during the market reform, such as income arising from the added value of land and its attachments, income arising from minerals due to price marketization, as well as income arising from other resources.

Second, it is necessary to adjust the income distribution gap through fiscal expenditure policies and narrow the income gap of the unemployed and the households in difficulty from other groups by adopting the transfer payment policy on the former.

Third, it is necessary to support the economic development of backward areas and narrow the regional income gap by formulating fiscal policies that treat different regions differently. Specifically, on the one hand, preferential taxation policies should be offered to backward areas to support the economic development of these areas, such as implementing investment tax reduction or exemption or other optimization policies in these areas. On the other hand, it is necessary to transfer payments to economically poor areas to support their economic development by increasing the public infrastructure construction, investment in education and re-education, and urban-rural education human capital.

Fourth, it is also necessary to improve the human capital of backward areas and villages and narrow the urban-rural income gap and regional income gap by increasing education investment in these areas through fiscal expenditure policies.

Notes

1 Individual differences include persistent differences and random differences. The literature on the persistent inequality caused by persistent differences includes Stiglitz (1969), Chatterjee (1994), Caselli and Ventura (2000) and Li et al. (2000). The literature that analyzes random differences can lead to persistent inequality includes Lucas (1992), Wang and Gong (2006; Wang et al., 2008b).
2 Regarding the effect of differences in personal social characteristics on persistent inequality, research literature in this area includes Benabou (1996a, 1996b) and Durlauf (1996), who have studied the effect of community segmentation on persistent inequality, Coate and Loury (1993a, 1993b) and Neal and Johnson (1996), who have studied the effect of statistical discrimination on inequality, and Boudon (1974) and Piketty (1995, 1998), who have studied inequality derived from conceptual self-realization. For review in this respect, see Wang and Gong (2008a).
3 The so-called imperfect market economy here mainly includes the following points: first, personal income only comes from labor income and capital income, that is, income is distributed by factors; second, the capital lending market is perfect, and there is no cross-period lending constraint; third, there is no monopolistic power.
4 The evidence for whether economic growth in underdeveloped countries has led to higher inequality is still unclear. As to whether the Kuznets curve is valid in underdeveloped countries, the research of Adelman and Cynthia (1973) questioned this as early as 30 years ago.
5 Although an imperfect market may cause initial wealth inequality to produce a lasting effect on wealth and income inequality, there is still a stable state of inequality in the economy. Once the economy reaches this state, inequality will no longer change. Thus, inequality cannot increase forever. For literature review in this aspect, see Wang and Gong (2007a, 2008a).
6 The literature that studies the effect of the education system on inequality includes Loury (1981), Benabou (1996a) and Glomm and Ravikumar (1993, 2001). Benabou (1996a, 1996b) and Durlauf (1996) discussed the effect of community segmentation on the dynamic evolution of persistent inequality. The literature that studies the effect of discriminatory ideas on persistent inequality includes Coate and Loury (1993a, 1993b), Neal and Johnson (1996), and so on.
7 The random income mentioned here refers to the random income for individuals in the early of the period. That's because in the period 0, it is not known who can get income beyond the factor income. However, for each specific period of the actual economy, this kind of non-factor income may not be random, as only those who have obtained special status or have special resources can earn income under a certain imperfect market economy system. In this sense, it is not random income.
8 For example, the staff of the railway authorities carried out the act of "scalping tickets" (the case of Liu Zhixiang, deputy director of the China Railway Wuhan Branch as judged by the Wuhan court on March 16, 2006), and the taxation authorities illegally withheld taxes (the "Informant Li Wenjuan" incident broadcast on China Central Television on March 27, 2006), etc.
9 The increase in inequality caused by the initial introduction of various systems in China may be verified by the wealth accumulation phenomenon that has occurred in the reform of the "stock market," the reform of state-owned enterprises, and the reform of the current housing system as every reform will help generate "extremely rich" people and some poor people. Due to the space limit in this chapter, it is impossible to do more in-depth research on this aspect.

References

[1] Adelman, I., & Cynthia, T. M. (1973). *Economic Growth and Social Equity in Developing Countries.* Stanford: StanfordU. Press.

[2] Anand, S., & Ravi Kanbur, S. M. (1993). The Kuznets Process and the Inequality-Development Relationship. *Journal of Development Economics*, 40, 25–52.

[3] Aghion, P., & Bolton, P. (1997). A Theory of Trickle-Down Growth and Development. *Review of Economic Studies*, 64, 151–172.

[4] Bai, X. Z. (2004). Education and Income Inequality: An Empirical Study in China. *Management World*, Issue 6, 53–58.

[5] Banerjee, A., & Newman, A. (1993). Occupational Choice and of Development. *Journal of Political Economy*, 101, 274–298.

[6] Benabou, R. 1996a, Equity and Efficiency in Human Capital Investment: The Local Connection. *Review of Economic Studies*, 63(2), 237–264.

[7] Benabou, R. (1996b). *Heterogeneity, Stratification, and Growth: Macroeconomic Implications of Community Structure and School Finance. American Economic Review*, 86(3), 584–609.

[8] Boudon, R. (1974). *Education, Opportunity and Social Inequality.* New York: Wiley.

[9] Cai, F. (2003). Urban-rural Income Gap and Tipping Point in Institutional Change. *Social Sciences in China*, Issue 6, 16–25.

[10] Cai, F. (2007). Growth and Structural Changes in Employment in Transitional China. *Economic Research Journal*, Issue 7, 4–14.

[11] Cai, F., Du, Y., & Zhao, C. B. (2007). Regional Labour Market Integration since China's World Trade Organization Entry: Evidence from Household-level Data. In *China-Linking Markets for Growth*, edited by G. Ross and Ligang Song. Canberra: Asia Pacific Press.

[12] Cai, F., & Yang, T. (2000). Political Economy of the Income Gap between Urban and Rural Areas. *Social Sciences in China*, Issue 4, 11–22.

[13] Caselli, F., & Ventura, J. (2000). A Representative Consumer Theory of Distribution. *American Economic Review*, 90, 909–926.

[14] Chatterjee, S. (1994). Transitional Dynamics and Distribution of Wealth in a Neoclassical Growth Model. *Journal of Public Economics*, 54, 97–119.

[15] Chen, Y. Y., Wang, Z. G., & Wei, Z. (2004). Income Inequality of Chinese Rural Residents in 1990s and its Changes. *Economic Science*, Issue 6, 16–25.

[16] Coate, S., & Loury, G. (1993a). Antidiscrimination Enforcement and the Problem of Patronization. *American Economic Review*, 83, 92–98.

[17] Coate, S., & Loury, G. (1993b). Will Affirmative-Action Policies Eliminate Negative Stereotypes. *American Economic Review*, 83, 1220–40.

[18] Durlauf, S. (1996). A Theory of Persistent Inequality. *Journal of Economic Growth*, 1, 75–95.

[19] Fu, J. (2008). High Income of Monopolized Industries in China and Its Causes. *The Journal of World Economy,* Issue 7, 67–77.

[20] Galor, O., & Zeira, J. (1993). Income Distribution and Macroeconomics. *Review of Economic Studies*, 60, 35–52.

[21] Glomm, G., & Palumbo, M. (1993). Optimal Intertemporal Consumption Decisions under the Threat of Starvation, *Journal of Development Economics*, 42, 271–291.

[22] Glomm, G., & Ravikumar, B. (2001). Human Capital Accumulation and Endogenous Public Expenditures, *Canadian Journal of Economics*, 34, 807–826

[23] Gottschalk, P.A., & Smeeding, T. M. (2000). Empirical Evidence on Income in Industrialized Countries. In *Handbook of Income Distribution*, Vol. 1, edited by A. B. Atkinson and F. Bourguignon, Printed in The Netherlands, Amsterdam.

[24] Greenwood, J., & Jovanovic, B. (1990). Financial Development, Growth, and the Distribution of Income. *Journal of Political Economy*, 98, 1076–1107.

[25] Guo, J. Q. (2005). A Theory of the Labor Supply of Rural Laborers in China's Urban Secondary Labor Market. *Social Sciences in China,* Issue 5, 16–26.

[26] Guo, J. X. (2005). Human Capital, the Birth Rate and the Narrowing of the Urban-Rural Income Gap. *Social Sciences in China*, Issue 3, 27–37.

[27] Juhn, C., Murphy, K.M., & Pierce, B. (1993). Wage Inequality and the Rise in Returns to Skill. *Journal of Political Economy*, 101, 410–442.

[28] Huang, G. H. (2006). Unobserved Effects and Return to Education. *Journal of Quantitative & Technical Economics*, Issue 4, 70–76.

[29] Jiang, F. X., & Yu. H. (2007). Study on Effect of Statutory Industrial Monopoly in China—Empirical Study from Welfare Loss and Welfare Distribution. *China Industrial Economics*, Issue 10, 71–78.

[30] Li, H., Xie, D., & Zou, H. (2000). Dynamics of Income Distribution. *Canadian Journal of Economics*, 33, 937–961.

[31] Li, S. & Zhao, R. W. (1999). Re-research on Income Distribution of Chinese Residents. *Economic Research Journal*, Issue 4, 3–17.

[32] Loury, G. (1981). Intergenerational Transfers and the Distribution of Earnings. *Econometrica,* 49, 843–867.

[33] Lu, X. Y. (2005). Peasant Laborer Problems Need to be Settled Fundamentally. New View on Current Problems of Chinese Agriculture. *Rural Areas and Peasants.* Beijing: Social Sciences Academic Press.

[34] Lucas, R. (1992). On Efficiency and Distribution. *Economic Journal,* 102, 233–247.

[35] Matsuyama, K. (2000). Endogenous Inequality. *Review of Economics Studies*, 67, 743–759.

[36] Maoz, Y., & Moav, O. (1999). Intergenerational Mobility and the Process of Development. *Economic Journal*, 109, 677–697.

[37] Mookherjee, D., & Ray, D. (2002). Contract and Wealth Accumulation. *American Economic Review*, 92, 818–849.

[38] Mookherjee, D., & Ray, D. (2003). Persistent Inequality. *Review of Economic Studies*, 70, 369–393.

[39] Murphy, K.M., & Welch, F. (1992). The Structure of Wages. *The Quarterly Journal of Economics*, 107(1), 35–78.

[40] Neal, D.A., & Johnson, W. R. (1996). The Role of Premarket Factors in Black-White Wage Differences. *Journal of Political Economy*, 104(5), 869–895.

[41] Piketty, T. (1995). Social Mobility and Redistributive Politics. *Quarterly Journal of Economics*, 110, 551–584.

[42] Piketty, T. (1997). The Dynamics of the Wealth Distribution and the Interest Rate with Credit Rationing. *Review of Economic Studies*, 64, 173–189.

[43] Piketty, T. (1998). Self-fulfilling Beliefs about Social Status. *Journal of Public Economics*, 70, 115–32.

[44] Rutherford, R. S. G. (1955). Income Distributions: A New Model. *Econometrica,* 23(3), 277–294.
[45] Stiglitz, J. (1969). Distribution of Income and Wealth among Individual. *Econometrica,* 37, 382–397.
[46] Tamura, R., 1991, Income Convergence in an Endogenous Growth Model, *Journal of Political Economy*, 99, 522–540.
[47] Wang, D. H. (2009). *Persistent Inequality of Income and Wealth: Dynamic Mothed*, Shanghai: Shanghai Sanlian Bookstore Press.
[48] Wang, D. H., & Gong, L. T. (2006). Dynamics of Income and Wealth Distribution in a Neoclassical Growth Model. *China Economic Quarterly*, 5(3), 777–802.
[49] Wang, D. H., & Gong, L. T. (2007). Consumption and Savings in Economic Growth. *Journal of Financial Research,* Issue 12, 1–16.
[50] Wang, D. H., & Gong, L. T. (2008a). Overview of the Dynamics of Income and Wealth Distribution Inequality. *China Economic Quarterly*, 7(2), 731–773.
[51] Wang, D. H., Gong, L. T., & Li, H. Y. (2008b). Healthy Human Capital, Investment and Economic Growth. *Management World*, Issue 3, 27–39.
[52] Wang, D. H., & Gong, L. T. (2009). Changes in Economic Development, Educational Investment and Wage Inequality. *The Journal of World Economy*, Issue 8, 68–82.
[53] Wang, H. L., & Xu, X. (2006). Interregional and Urban-rural Income Inequality. *Management World*, Issue 11, 41–50.
[54] Wang, R. (2007). Impact of Monopoly on China's Inter-Industry Income Distribution and Corresponding Countermeasures. *On Economic Problems*, Issue 2, 50–52.
[55] Yan, S. P. (2006). Mobility of Urban Labor Market and its Decision Mechanism. *Management World*, Issue 88–17.
[56] Yang, J., Huang, X., & Li, X. Y. (2008). Education Inequality and Income Distribution Disparities in China: An Empirical Analysis. *Management World*, Issue 1, 38–47.
[57] Yao, X.G. and Lai P.Q. (2004). Urban and Rural Huji Differentials in Chinese Labor Relations, *Economic Research Journal*, Issue 7, 82–90.
[58] Yue, C. J., & Wu, S. J. (2005). The Relationship between Externalities of Human Capital and Industrial Income Difference. *Peking University Education Review,* Issue 10, 31–37.
[59] Zhang, C. W. (2006). Changes in Return Rate of Human Capital and Income Disparities: Matthew's Effect and its Policy Implications. *Economic Research Journal*, Issue 12, 59–70.
[60] Zhao, R. W., & Li, S. (1997). The Widening Income Disparities of Chinese Population and the Causes. *Economic Research Journal*, Issue 9, 19–28.

Index

Printed and bound by CPI Group (UK) Ltd, Croydon, CR0 4YY
27/09/2024
01038742-0014